Remote Sensing and Artificial Intelligence in Inland Waters Monitoring

Remote Sensing and Artificial Intelligence in Inland Waters Monitoring

Editors

Miro Govedarica
Flor Álvarez-Taboada
Gordana Jakovljević

Basel • Beijing • Wuhan • Barcelona • Belgrade • Novi Sad • Cluj • Manchester

Editors

Miro Govedarica
University of Novi Sad
Novi Sad
Serbia

Flor Álvarez-Taboada
Universidad de Leon
Ponferrada
Spain

Gordana Jakovljević
University of Banja Luka
Banja Luka
Bosnia and Herzegovina

Editorial Office
MDPI
St. Alban-Anlage 66
4052 Basel, Switzerland

This is a reprint of articles from the Special Issue published online in the open access journal *Remote Sensing* (ISSN 2072-4292) (available at: https://www.mdpi.com/journal/remotesensing/special_issues/V6D07666X5).

For citation purposes, cite each article independently as indicated on the article page online and as indicated below:

Lastname, A.A.; Lastname, B.B. Article Title. *Journal Name* **Year**, *Volume Number*, Page Range.

ISBN 978-3-7258-0573-0 (Hbk)
ISBN 978-3-7258-0574-7 (PDF)
doi.org/10.3390/books978-3-7258-0574-7

Cover image courtesy of Miro Govedarica, Flor Álvarez-Taboada, and Gordana Jakovljević

© 2024 by the authors. Articles in this book are Open Access and distributed under the Creative Commons Attribution (CC BY) license. The book as a whole is distributed by MDPI under the terms and conditions of the Creative Commons Attribution-NonCommercial-NoDerivs (CC BY-NC-ND) license.

Contents

About the Editors vii

Preface ix

Zhengkai Huang, Xin Wu, Haihong Wang, Cheinway Hwang and Xiaoxing He
Monitoring Inland Water Quantity Variations: A Comprehensive Analysis of Multi-Source Satellite Observation Technology Applications
Reprinted from: *Remote Sens.* **2023**, *15*, 3945, doi:10.3390/rs15163945 1

Leonardo F. Arias-Rodriguez, Ulaş Firat Tüzün, Zheng Duan, Jingshui Huang, Ye Tuo and Markus Disse
Global Water Quality of Inland Waters with Harmonized Landsat-8 and Sentinel-2 Using Cloud-Computed Machine Learning
Reprinted from: *Remote Sens.* **2023**, *15*, 1390, doi:10.3390/rs15051390 20

Anna Catherine Cardall, Riley Chad Hales, Kaylee Brooke Tanner, Gustavious Paul Williams and Kel N. Markert
LASSO (L1) Regularization for Development of Sparse Remote-Sensing Models with Applications in Optically Complex Waters Using GEE Tools
Reprinted from: *Remote Sens.* **2023**, *15*, 1670, doi:10.3390/rs15061670 47

Lei Dong, Cailan Gong, Hongyan Huai, Enuo Wu, Zhihua Lu, Yong Hu, et al.
Retrieval of Water Quality Parameters in Dianshan Lake Based on Sentinel-2 MSI Imagery and Machine Learning: Algorithm Evaluation and Spatiotemporal Change Research
Reprinted from: *Remote Sens.* **2023**, *15*, 5001, doi:10.3390/rs15205001 78

Juan Francisco Amieva, Daniele Oxoli and Maria Antonia Brovelli
Machine and Deep Learning Regression of Chlorophyll-a Concentrations in Lakes Using PRISMA Satellite Hyperspectral Imagery
Reprinted from: *Remote Sens.* **2023**, *15*, 5385, doi:10.3390/rs15225385 104

Freddy Hernán Villota-González, Belkis Sulbarán-Rangel, Florentina Zurita-Martínez, Kelly Joel Gurubel-Tun and Virgilio Zúñiga-Grajeda
Assessment of Machine Learning Models for Remote Sensing of Water Quality in Lakes Cajititlán and Zapotlán, Jalisco—Mexico
Reprinted from: *Remote Sens.* **2023**, *15*, 5505, doi:10.3390/rs15235505 126

Gordana Jakovljevic, Flor Álvarez-Taboada and Miro Govedarica
Long-Term Monitoring of Inland Water Quality Parameters Using Landsat Time-Series and Back-Propagated ANN: Assessment and Usability in a Real-Case Scenario
Reprinted from: *Remote Sens.* **2024**, *16*, 68, doi:10.3390/rs16010068 150

Kaire Toming, Hui Liu, Tuuli Soomets, Evelyn Uuemaa, Tiina Nõges and Tiit Kutser
Estimation of the Biogeochemical and Physical Properties of Lakes Based on Remote Sensing and Artificial Intelligence Applications
Reprinted from: *Remote Sens.* **2024**, *16*, 464, doi:10.3390/rs16030464 168

Christine L. Bunyon, Benjamin T. Fraser, Amanda McQuaid and Russell G. Congalton
Using Imagery Collected by an Unmanned Aerial System to Monitor Cyanobacteria in New Hampshire, USA, Lakes
Reprinted from: *Remote Sens.* **2023**, *15*, 2839, doi:10.3390/rs15112839 196

Leonidas Alagialoglou, Ioannis Manakos, Sofia Papadopoulou, Rizos-Theodoros Chadoulis and Afroditi Kita
Mapping Underwater Aquatic Vegetation Using Foundation Models With Air- and Space-Borne Images: The Case of Polyphytos Lake
Reprinted from: *Remote Sens.* **2023**, *15*, 4001, doi:10.3390/rs15164001 . . . . **223**

Hengkai Li, Zikun Xu, Yanbing Zhou, Xiaoxing He and Minghua He
Flood Monitoring Using Sentinel-1 SAR for Agricultural Disaster Assessment in Poyang Lake Region
Reprinted from: *Remote Sens.* **2023**, *15*, 5247, doi:10.3390/rs15215247 . . . . **242**

Pingping Luo, Xiaohui Wang, Lei Zhang, Mohd Remy Rozainy Mohd Arif Zainol, Weili Duan, Maochuan Hu, et al.
Future Land Use and Flood Risk Assessment in the Guanzhong Plain, China: Scenario Analysis and the Impact of Climate Change
Reprinted from: *Remote Sens.* **2023**, *15*, 5778, doi:10.3390/rs15245778 . . . . **259**

About the Editors

Miro Govedarica

Miro Govedarica, Ph.D., is a Full Professor at the Faculty of Technical Sciences, University of Novi Sad, Serbia, head of the Chair of Systems, Signals, and Control Engineering, and head of study programs geodesy and geoinformatics for master's and doctoral studies. His practical and theoretical results pertain to the area of geoinformatics. His domain of interest includes software engineering, geospatial software engineering, geospatial databases, geoservices, the development of service-oriented geoinformation systems, ground-penetrating radar (GPR), photogrammetry, laser scanning, remote sensing, global navigation satellite systems, spatial data infrastructure, spatial big data, GeoAI and the implementation of new geoinformatics trends in education. He is also a member and university representative in many professional bodies including FIG, ISPRS, OGC, UNGGIM, Serbian Commission for Standards I211.

Flor Álvarez-Taboada

Flor Álvarez-Taboada, Ph.D., is an Assistant Professor at the Universidad de León (Spain), Department of Cartographic Engineering, Geodesy and Photogrammetry, in the research field of remote sensing. She has been a visiting scientist at the Pacific Forestry Centre (Canadian Forest Service, Canada), International Training Centre (The Netherlands) and the Technische Universitat Munchen (Germany). Her research is focused on remote sensing and natural resources monitoring, with special attention to forest health. Currently, she studies how to detect and monitor damages in forest ecosystems in near-real time and how to implement early warning systems by using big data and artificial intelligence and sources such as satellite imagery, 3D point clouds, IoT and proximal sensors.

Gordana Jakovljević

Gordana Jakovljevic, Ph.D., is an Assistant Professor at the University of Banja Luka, Bosnia and Herzegovina. Her practical and theoretical research interests lie in the fields of remote sensing, deep learning, and environmental protection, especially in water management. The primary aim of Gordana's research is to develop a standardized, clearly defined methodology for the automated processing of remote sensing data in real or near-real time to increase the usability of remote sensing data in environmental monitoring and decision making. Additionally, her interests include the development of service-oriented GIS, 2D and 3D visualization, and BIM. She is a member of the FIG Task Force "Climate Compass Task Force", FIG Commission 4 and FIG 4.3 working group (mapping plastic).

Preface

Aquatic systems have high natural and economic value. The continuous increase in the human population, urbanization, and dramatic changes in climate impact the structure of the freshwater ecosystem and its chemical and physical characteristics. Due to this, the comprehensive monitoring of water bodies is needed. To address these complex challenges, there is growing interest in using remote sensing technologies and artificial intelligence.

This Special Issues reprint is dedicated to enhancing the leverage of integrating remote sensing data, in situ data, and artificial intelligence in inland water monitoring. It explores the application of cutting-edge technologies such as artificial neural networks and data-driven algorithms to provide information to stakeholders and decision-makers promptly. This Special Issue addresses essential questions in water monitoring, offering the tools and methodologies for a comprehensive understanding of the current status and changes over time as well as identification of the pressures on the local, regional, and global scales. The main goal is to emphasize the potential of integrating remote sensing data and artificial intelligence for sustainable water management, as well as fostering knowledge exchange and innovative research for effective water protection.

Miro Govedarica, Flor Álvarez-Taboada, and Gordana Jakovljević
Editors

Review

Monitoring Inland Water Quantity Variations: A Comprehensive Analysis of Multi-Source Satellite Observation Technology Applications

Zhengkai Huang [1], Xin Wu [1], Haihong Wang [2], Cheinway Hwang [3] and Xiaoxing He [4,*]

[1] School of Transportation Engineering, East China Jiaotong University, Nanchang 330013, China; zhkhuang@whu.edu.cn (Z.H.); 2022138085704007@ectju.edu.cn (X.W.)
[2] School of Geodesy and Geomatics, Wuhan University, Wuhan 430079, China; hhwang@sgg.whu.edu.cn
[3] Department of Civil Engineering, National Yang Ming Chiao Tung University, 1001 Ta Hsueh Road, Hsinchu 300, Taiwan; cheinway@nycu.edu.tw
[4] School of Civil and Surveying & Mapping Engineering, Jiangxi University of Science and Technology, Ganzhou 341000, China
* Correspondence: xxh@jxust.edu.cn

Abstract: The advancement of multi-source Earth observation technology has led to a substantial body of literature on inland water monitoring. This has resulted in the emergence of a distinct interdisciplinary field encompassing the application of multi-source Earth observation techniques in inland water monitoring. Despite this growth, few systematic reviews of this field exist. Therefore, in this paper, we offer a comprehensive analysis based on 30,212 publications spanning the years 1990 to 2022, providing valuable insights. We collected and analyzed fundamental information such as publication year, country, affiliation, journal, and author details. Through co-occurrence analysis, we identified country and author partnerships, while co-citation analysis revealed the influence of journals, authors, and documents. We employed keywords to explore the evolution of hydrological phenomena and study areas, using burst analysis to predict trends and frontiers. We discovered exponential growth in this field with a closer integration of hydrological phenomena and Earth observation techniques. The research focus has shifted from large glaciers to encompass large river basins and the Tibetan Plateau. Long-term research attention has been dedicated to optical properties, sea level, and satellite gravity. The adoption of automatic image recognition and processing, enabled by deep learning and artificial intelligence, has opened new interdisciplinary avenues. The results of the study emphasize the significance of long-term, stable, and accurate global observation and monitoring of inland water, particularly in the context of cloud computing and big data.

Keywords: inland water; multi-source satellite observation technology; scientometrics; CiteSpace

1. Introduction

Inland water refers to water resources including surface water such as ice and snow, rivers, lakes, and groundwater. Changes in inland water reflect the comprehensive impact of natural factors such as regional precipitation, runoff, evapotranspiration, and human activities, as well as important factors affecting the global water cycle [1,2]. In recent years, benefiting from the development of remote sensing technology and improvements in computer and cloud computing capabilities, multi-source satellite Earth observation technology has achieved unprecedented success in inland water monitoring [3]. Extensive regional and global studies have generated valuable insights for understanding water cycle processes and guiding water resource management decisions.

Satellite technology has become widely utilized for monitoring changes in inland water. The Gravity Recovery and Climate Experiment (GRACE) has been applied to studying mass migration and calculating terrestrial water storage [4–7]. Satellite altimetry technology is used for monitoring global sea levels, lake levels, and glacier elevations [8,9]. Remote sensing imagery is employed for extracting information on surface water [10,11]. Some scholars have analyzed the research results of satellite technology in the field of inland water monitoring by reading a large number of studies. This traditional review method often requires a long time to read the literature, and the accuracy of the analysis is highly dependent on the author's experience. Moreover, these articles often only cover a single research direction, which can only provide a macroscopic qualitative description and reveal certain regularities and conclusions. Therefore, traditional literature reviews make it difficult to quantitatively and systematically reveal the development process, and the conclusions lack objectivity [12,13].

The scientific knowledge graph, a method used in scientometrics and information metrics, is capable of uncovering the origin and development patterns of knowledge. It visually represents the structural relationships and evolution of knowledge in related fields [14]. For instance, Yang et al. used scientometric methods to summarize 50 years of satellite altimetry technology research and quantitatively analyze the relationship between technological progress and research trends, offering a clear explanation of the overall development and future directions of satellite altimetry [15]. Similarly, Xu et al. conducted a bibliometric analysis of 998 relevant studies from the Web of Science core collection, constructing a scientific knowledge graph to reveal the future development trends of the normalized difference vegetation index (NDVI) [16]. The knowledge graph they constructed enhances the intuitive and concrete description, benefiting both researchers with limited experience and readers seeking a quick understanding of a specific field.

Therefore, we employed CiteSpace to quantitatively analyze the literature regarding multi-source satellite Earth observation technology in inland water monitoring. The main work of this paper includes (1) statistics and trends of the number of publications based on the dataset; (2) statistics on the quantity of basic information in publications; (3) highly cooperative countries and author groups; (4) highly co-cited journals, authors, and literature; (5) clustering and burst analysis based on keyword co-occurrence; and (6) knowledge extraction based on feature words. In this paper, we summarize the existing literature, systematically reveal the development trends and the law of change in this field, and provide guidance and references for further research.

2. Materials and Methods

2.1. Data Collection

The search topic in the Web of Science core collection was set as TS = (RS OR Remote Sensing OR Satellite Altimetry OR Gravity OR GRACE) AND (River OR Fluvial OR Lake OR Glaciers OR Ice OR Snow OR Wetland OR Groundwater OR Swamp OR Marsh OR Estuary OR Bayou). A total of 30,212 documents published between 1960 and 2022 were refined, including articles and review articles. Table 1 presents the basic information of the dataset, which includes 87,035 authors from 8297 different institutions and 1919 journals in 183 countries and regions. Among the 30,212 articles, the total numbers of citations and quotes at the time of data collection were recorded. On average, each article cited around 50 other articles, and each article was cited by an average of 26–27 articles.

Table 1. Basic information of the Web of Science (WOS) core collection dataset.

Type	Value/Number
Documents	30,212
Authors	87,035
Countries/Regions	183
Institutions	8297
Sources	1919
Average Times Citing per Item	49.62
Average Times Cited per Item	27.31

2.2. Scientometric Analysis

Scientometric analysis of literature is a method of literature analysis that uses bibliometric principles to analyze relevant literature. It involves using mathematical and statistical methods to study the distribution structure, quantitative relationships, and change patterns of the literature. Scientometrics is the study of the quantitative aspects of the process of science as a communication system. It is centrally, but not only, concerned with the analysis of citations in the academic literature. In recent years, it has come to play a major role in the measurement and evaluation of research performance [17].

CiteSpace is one of the common software packages used for scientometric analysis. It is a literature analysis package developed by Professor Chen Chaomei based on Java to conduct statistics, analysis, and mining of the literature on a specific subject. It aims to identify evolutionary trends, development frontiers, and research hotspots within a subject area and generate knowledge network maps based on the analysis results [18,19]. This software has been updated by more than 30 versions. For scientometric analysis, VOSviewer is also a software package that is often used by researchers. VOSviewer was developed by Nees Jan van Eck and Ludo Waltman of the Centre for Science and Technology Studies at Leiden University. Each of these two packages has its own characteristics, and there is a lot of literature that discusses the algorithms and results of both packages. CiteSpace features a time-series-based visualization that can be used to detect trends in subject matter over time and to further predict trends in the subject matter. VOSviewer software mainly uses distance-based visualization methods to draw maps by limiting the relative positions between texts and has strong knowledge graph presentation capabilities [20–22]. In general, the two software packages differ only in their different functions. The purpose of both is the visualization of textual data, so for the analysis in this paper, we used CiteSpace (6.1.R4) and VOSviewer (1.6.18), with CiteSpace as the main package and VOSviewer as a supplement.

2.3. Processing Flow

We first downloaded and formed a dataset of publications that met the requirements of this study. The basic information of this dataset, including year, country, institution, journal, and author, was first counted quantitatively. Next, countries and authors were analyzed using co-occurrence analysis to obtain the cooperative relationship. Co-citation analysis was then used to illustrate the influence of journals and authors, and the resulting co-citation network of literature can reveal the evolution of research themes. To obtain the clustering graph and explore the frontiers of the field, we used co-occurrence analysis and burst analysis on keywords. We detected word frequency based on feature words (title, keywords, and abstract) and obtained the interannual variation in the number of study themes and areas. The flow schematic is shown in Figure 1 below.

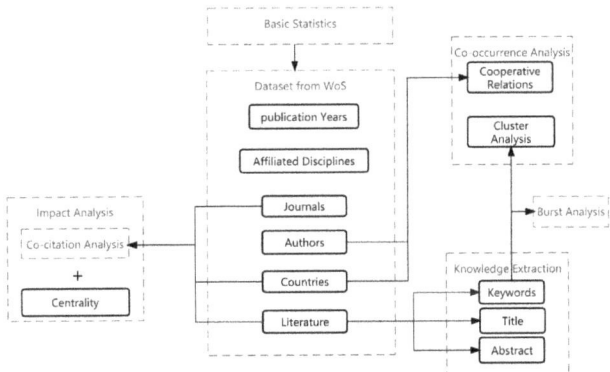

Figure 1. Schematic diagram of scientometric analysis.

3. Results

3.1. Annual Statistics of Publications

We counted 30,212 papers that fit the research theme from 1960 to 2022. In terms of the time series of published papers, it can be roughly divided into three phases, i.e., the start-up, steady growth, and rapid growth phases, as shown in Figure 2. (1) The period 1960–1990 was the start-up stage, when satellite technology was just being developed and was still in the technology verification period. Launched satellites, such as Geosat, Skylab, etc., generally had low accuracy and unstable performance. Therefore, there were no large-scale scientific applications of these satellite data, and thus the number of publications in this period was less than 100. (2) The period 1990–2005 was the steady growth phase. This phase is represented by the T/P family, the ERS family, and Landsat-5. Due to the improvements in satellite orbiting accuracy and sensor accuracy, the stability and accuracy of satellites were greatly improved during this period. As a result, satellite observation technology was gradually used for inland water monitoring, and the number of related studies increased slowly. (3) The third phase, from 2005 to the present, is the rapid growth phase. This phase has involved the development of multiple satellites and accumulated nearly 40 years of continuous observation data. Satellites such as the Interferometric Synthetic Aperture Radar (InSAR) and Global Navigation Satellite System (GNSS) have also been gradually used for inland water monitoring [6]. Therefore, the number of studies has grown rapidly in this phase.

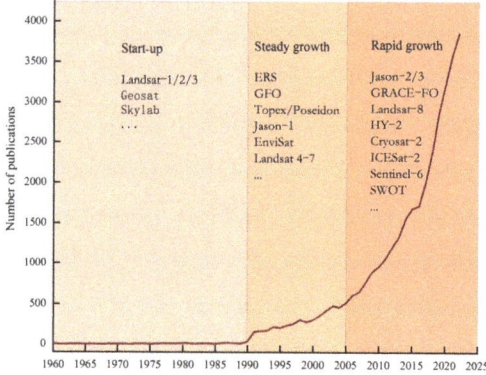

Figure 2. Statistics on the number of publications based on the WOS database.

3.2. Basic Information Statistics

3.2.1. Basic Statistics on the Number of Countries, Institutions, and Authors

According to the analysis, a total of 183 countries published relevant literature. There are 10 countries that have more than 1000 publications: the United States (9424), China (8960), Germany (2508), Canada (2096), the United Kingdom (2056), India (1977), France (1973), Italy (1386), Australia (1374), and the Netherlands (1082). It is estimated that more than 80,000 authors and 8000 affiliations have made contributions to this field. As shown in Figure 3, the Chinese Academy of Sciences (CAS), National Aeronautics and Space Administration (NASA), Centre National de la Recherche Scientifique (CNRS), and Helmholtz Association contributed 34% of the literature, which represents the main portion of the publications. In addition to these institutions, universities such as the University of California, the University of Colorado, the University of the Chinese Academy of Sciences, and Wuhan University in China have also published more than 600 articles. The top 10 authors by the number of publications are also shown in Figure 3 below, including Shum CK (83), Ma RH (79), Li YM (69), Duan HT (68), Hu CM (63), Bresciani M (60), Pradhan B (58), and Song KS (53).

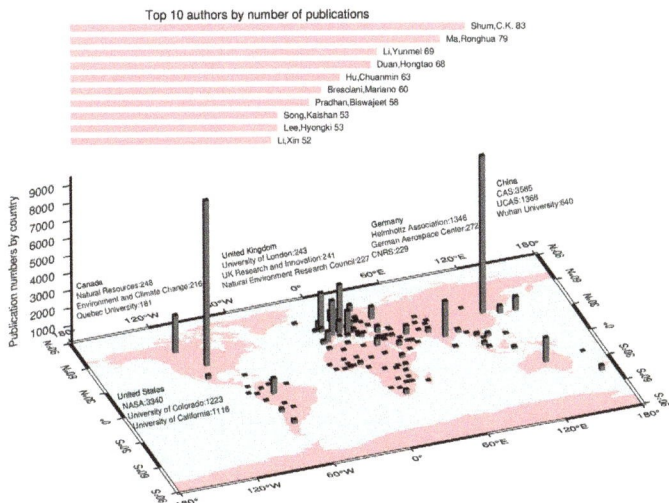

Figure 3. Top 10 authors of publications and geographic distribution of the literature collected by category of affiliation.

3.2.2. Basic Statistics on the Number of Affiliated Disciplines

These publications are divided into 162 disciplines according to the Web of Science categories. The information provided suggests that out of the 30,212 papers analyzed, the majority (over 70%) are distributed among several disciplines. The highest percentage (23.45%) falls into the category of Earth multidisciplinary science. Other significant disciplines include environmental science (19.72%), remote sensing (11.27%), imaging science and technology (9.31%), and water resources (9.04%). The remaining 30% of publications cover a range of disciplines such as geophysics, marine science, atmospheric meteorology, ecology, geology, astrophysics, civil engineering, etc. Figure 4 shows statistics on the main subject groups to which publications belong in different countries. It appears that the focus of research varies across different countries. Publications in the United States, Germany, Canada, the United Kingdom, and France focus mainly on multidisciplinary geosciences, while those in China and India are mostly in the field of environmental sciences. This illustrates the differences in research priorities and academic traditions between countries. This difference is also due to the fact that China and India are populous countries and face greater geographical and water resource management pressures. As a result, these countries are paying more attention to inland water monitoring and environmental protection, which may lead to more research focusing on environmental science.

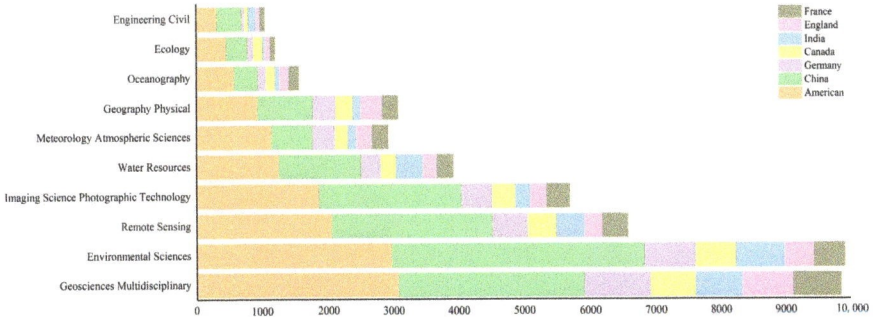

Figure 4. Number of publications by subject category by country.

3.2.3. Basic Statistics on the Number of Journals

The literature was collected from approximately 1919 different journals. Of these journals, two stand out, each with more than 1000 articles. The two journals are Remote Sensing (2373 papers) and Remote Sensing of Environment (1026 papers). Additionally, several other journals have published more than 600 articles each. These include the International Journal of Remote Sensing (718), *Geophysical Research Letters* (631), *Journal of Hydrology* (619), IEEE Transactions on Geoscience and Remote Sensing (614), and Water (547). Figure 5 presents these statistics. Remote Sensing is one of the leading sources of literature on the application of multi-source satellite Earth observation techniques in terrestrial hydrology, with the largest collection of literature. Remote Sensing of Environment focuses on biophysical quantitative methods in respect of terrestrial, oceanic, and atmospheric transport [23,24], with an impact factor of 13.66, making it the most cited journal. The International Journal of Remote Sensing focuses on remote sensing of the atmosphere, biosphere, cryosphere, and Earth, as well as human modifications to the Earth system [25]. The *Journal of Hydrology* publishes original research papers and comprehensive reviews across all subfields of the hydrological sciences. It includes water-based management and policy issues that affect the economy and society. Science and Nature are known for featuring the latest advancements and development trends in various fields. The articles published in these two journals can provide significant references and spark new ideas for scholars. It is important to note that the information provided is based on the specific journals mentioned in the context of the research analysis. There are numerous other journals in different disciplines that contribute to the overall body of literature.

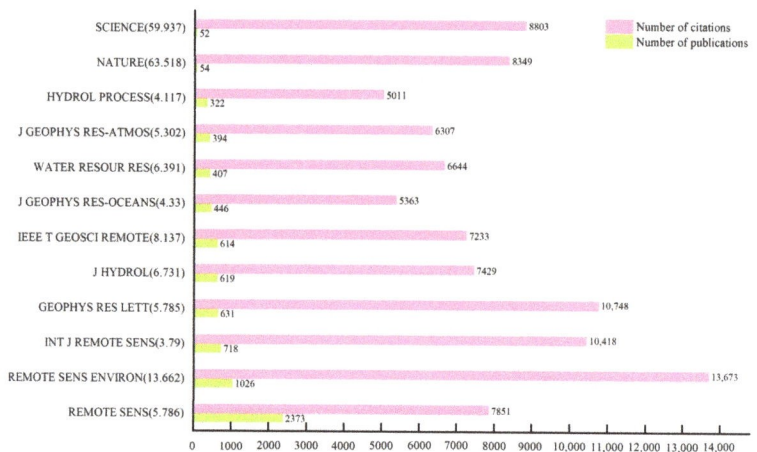

Figure 5. The most published journals and their citations.

3.3. Cooperative Relations

3.3.1. National Cooperative Network

Figure 6 shows the network of cooperation between countries. It is clear from the chart that China and the United States are the two countries with the largest numbers of publications and the highest intensity of cooperation with other countries. China has collaborated with 50 other countries on 3951 articles, of which the United States was the most important collaborator with 1306 links, followed by Germany, Australia, Canada, the Netherlands, and the United Kingdom. The United States, in addition to its close collaboration with China, has established significant partnerships with countries such as the United Kingdom, Germany, France, and Canada. The United States is the most cooperative country, with a total link strength of up to 6646. Indeed, there is a clustering of Denmark, Iceland, Luxembourg, Sweden, and New Zealand into a group, as well as the grouping of Germany, Poland, the Czech Republic, Switzerland, Finland, Hungary, Spain, Italy, and other countries. This phenomenon indicates the influence of regions on the similarity of countries in terms of research collaboration. Geographically close countries in Europe tend to exhibit higher similarities in research collaboration.

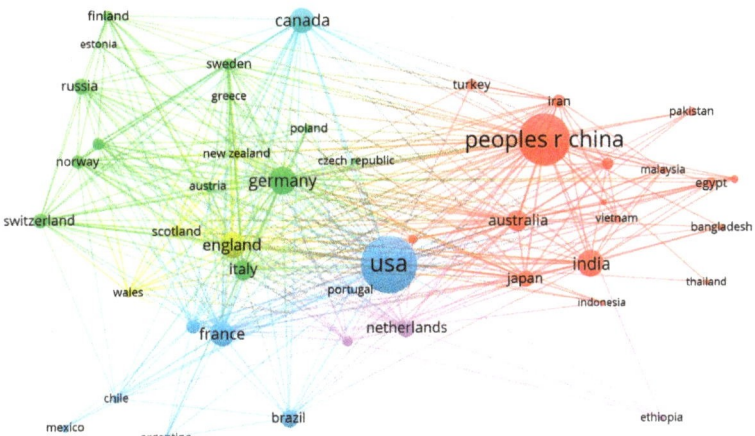

Figure 6. National cooperation networks. A network of 46 countries with more than 100 collaborative papers. The nodes are divided into five groups, each represented by a different color.

3.3.2. Author Cooperative Network

The authors with the highest numbers of collaborative articles are Shum CK (66), Ma RH (63), Hu CM (48), Li YM (47), Bresciani M (44), and Duan HT (43). Figure 7 reflects that there are two core author groups. The core author group formed by Shum CK and Lee H mainly studies the application of satellite altimetry technology and satellite gravity, particularly utilizing GRACE data for regional surface water monitoring and establishing hydrodynamic models [23–26]. The second group consists of Duan HT, Hu CM, Song KS, Li YM, and Ma RH [27–30] and mainly uses visible light remote sensing images to detect inland lakes and interpret corresponding hydrological phenomena. Additionally, authors such as Li X, Chen X, and Wang L act as bridges between these two core author groups, promoting the frequency and close connection between authors.

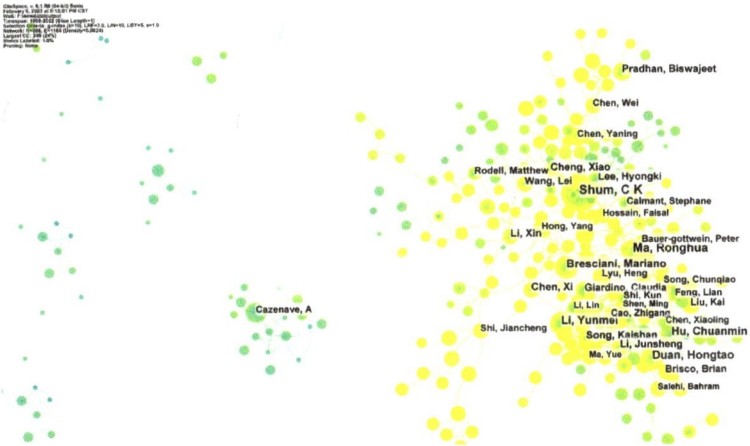

Figure 7. Author collaboration network. This network consists of 998 nodes and 1994 links.

Figure 7 also highlights the presence of smaller author groups. One such small author group consists of Cazenave A, Calmant S, Frappart F, Kouraev AV, and Ramillien G [31,32]. Their research is centered around remote sensing and satellite gravity technology applied to river flow and basin-level calculations. Another group includes authors such as van den Broeke MR, Bamber JL, Rignot E, and Berthier E [32–34]. This group focuses on different monitoring methods to monitor and calculate parameters such as the thickness of polar ice sheets, sea ice, and the mass balance of glaciers. These small author groups tend to have more specialized research interests and themes, despite being smaller in size and less popular than the core author groups. They have created new ideas, innovative methods, and unique perspectives in a specific field. Their small size and specific research direction can make them more flexible in collaborative decision-making.

3.4. Analysis of the Impact

3.4.1. Co-Citation Analysis of Authors and Journals

Centrality is an indicator that compares the activity of an institution or author with that of other institutions, authors, etc. and acts as a bridge between them. Nodes with a centrality of more than 0.1 in CiteSpace are called critical nodes. Figure 8a shows the top 10 most cited journals and their centrality. Remote Sensing of Environment, Geophysical Research Letters, and the International Journal of Remote Sensing are the three journals with the most citations. Different journals have different focuses, and the literature they include is also different. Science of the Total Environment is an international multidisciplinary journal with the widest range of disciplines. Its centrality exceeds 0.1, which is the highest centrality of all the journals.

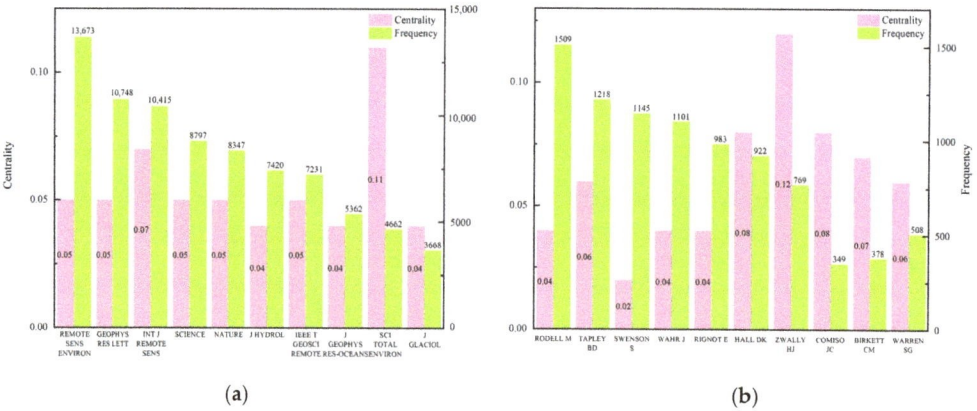

Figure 8. Most influential journals and authors: (**a**) the most frequently cited journals and their centrality; and (**b**) the most frequently cited authors and their centrality.

Figure 8b presents the top 10 authors with the highest citation numbers and centralities in the co-citation author network. Rodell M. primarily focuses on studying large-scale or global temporal and spatial changes in the water cycle. This includes analyzing data from GRACE and GRACE-FO to understand the resulting impacts on climate, drought, and water storage [35–37]. With over 1500 citations, Rodell is considered the most influential author in this research field. Tapley BD and Swenson S are another two prominent authors in the field, with 1218 and 1145 citations, respectively. Zwally HJ is the only author with a centrality of more than 0.1 and plays a role in bridging communication between different authors.

3.4.2. Literature Co-Citation Network

The co-citation network of the literature takes on a static form with a time series. As shown in Figure 9, in this co-citation network, the article written by Gorelick N. et al. on promoting the Google Earth Engine (GEE) in 2017 is the most cited paper [38]. This means that more users can access and take advantage of the data, tools, and functions provided by the platform. This will make data analysis and processing faster and interdisciplinary and cross-border cooperation stronger. GEE also highlights the use of time-series satellite data for large-scale monitoring of land and water dynamics [2,39]. Pekel JF et al. collected millions of Landsat images on GEE and quantified the global changes in surface water between 1984 and 2015, leading to the production of a comprehensive global map of surface water [40]. In an article cited 386 times in the field, the study identified prolonged drought and human activities as significant contributors to global surface water transformation. Moreover, three of the other top five co-cited papers are about GRACE, including the JPL RL05 mascon and CRS RL05 mascon solutions [41,42]. The gravity field model solved using GRACE data has become an important means for large-scale land mass migration changes, such as global sea level transformation, regional surface water monitoring, polar ice sheet and mountain glacier melting, and seismic coseismic change [5,43,44]. At present, the latest GRACE data have been updated to version RL06. The literature in respect of Ice, Cloud, and land Elevation Satellite-2 (ICEsat-2) and Surface Water Ocean Topography (SWOT) has also been co-cited more than 100 times [45,46]. These technologies, along with other relevant datasets such as ECMWF Reanalysis (ERA5), Bedmap, Modern-Era Retrospective Analysis for Research and Applications (MERRA), Global Land Evaporation Amsterdam Model (GLEAM), and Randolf Glacier Inventory (RGI), contribute to the key knowledge of multi-source satellite Earth observation technology in inland water exploration.

Figure 9. Literature co-citation network. The time slice was set to 3 years, and the details display the 33 nodes with the most citations. The literature co-citation network is composed of 904 nodes and 2831 co-citation links.

The co-citation network of literature can not only reflect the citation status but also grasp the development order of the field through basic information such as titles, keywords, and abstracts. From left to right, the theme of evolution in chronological order is represented. As shown in Figure 10, similar literature, such as topics, technologies, or data usage, tends to cluster closely in the network. In the alternation of the observation technology and observation theme, we can see the promotion effect of the advancement of multi-source satellite Earth observation technology on the monitoring of different components of inland water. Initially, satellite altimetry techniques were predominantly employed for glacier monitoring and global mean sea level estimation, where low accuracy requirements were acceptable. Gravity satellites have significantly enhanced the accuracy of global gravity fields while filling the technical gaps in groundwater monitoring. Long-term monitoring of groundwater in California and the North China Plain has been successfully conducted [47–49]. In recent years, researchers have shifted their attention to the extraction and monitoring of surface water, such as rivers and lakes. Mountain glaciers and lakes on the Qinghai–Tibet Plateau became research hotspots during this period. The launch of SWOT will assist researchers in comprehending and tracking the distribution and changes in water worldwide. This mission will be the first comprehensive global survey of Earth's surface water [40]. In addition, with the support of interdisciplinary techniques based on deep convolution, surface water extraction on a global scale has entered a new phase.

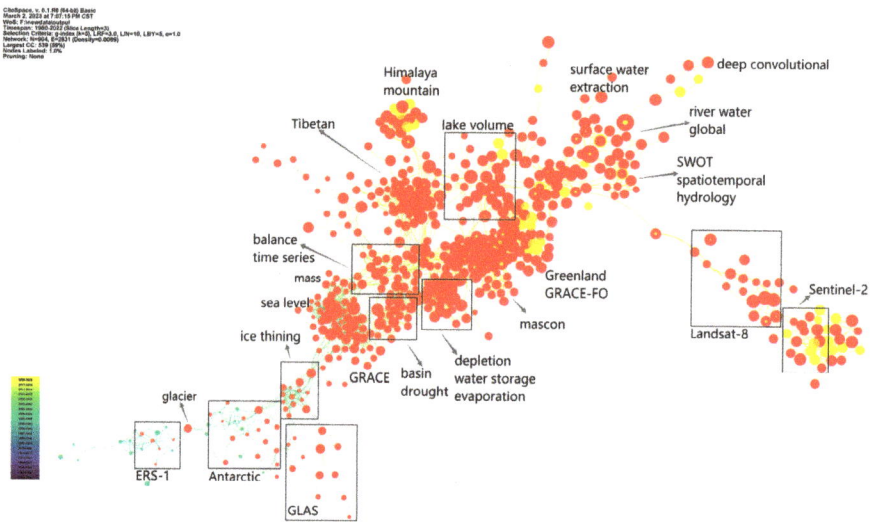

Figure 10. Evolution of research themes over time. Literature with high bursts is shown in red.

3.5. Keyword Co-Occurrence Analysis

Co-occurrence analysis is a commonly used method in text mining and topic modeling. The principle of co-occurrence analysis is to extract keywords and analyze the connections between them based on their co-occurrence frequency. Figure 11 shows the breakdown of the clusters. Cluster 1 is related to remote sensing image and surface water monitoring and consists of the keywords remote sensing, Landsat, lake, river, dynamic, wetland, basin, classification, geographic information system (GIS), etc. Cluster 2 mainly includes keywords such as model, groundwater, climate change, drought, grace, depletion, prediction, etc., which are related to gravity satellite and groundwater monitoring. Cluster 3 relates to MODIS and monitoring the thickness of snow cover. Cluster 4 is associated with the use of satellite altimetry, including radar and laser measurements, for monitoring ice sheets. It involves ice characteristics, mass balance, and hydrological processes, particularly in regions like Greenland. Cluster 5 is significantly far away from the other four clusters; it appears to be relatively independent and less directly related to the other four clusters. This cluster focuses on the application of InSAR and GNSS for observing land subsidence and its dynamic response to changes in inland water storage.

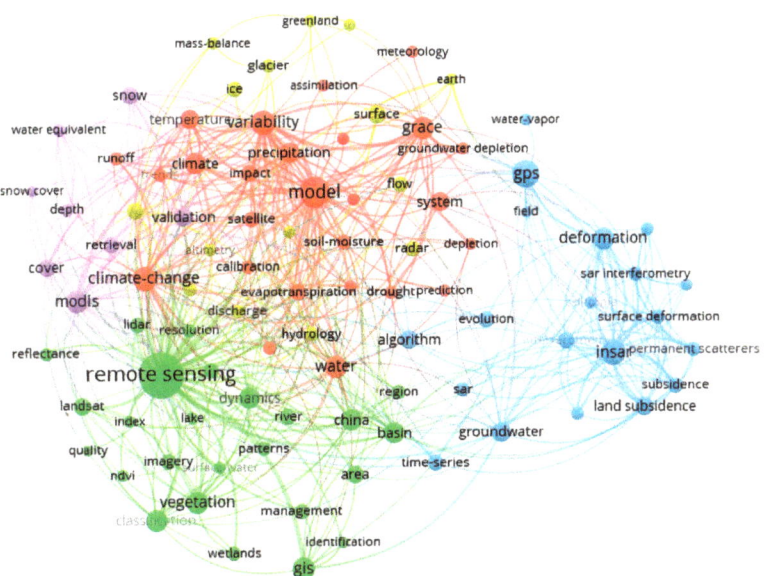

Figure 11. Keyword clustering network. The network only shows keywords that have co-occurred more than 120 times. The network contains 94 nodes and 3839 links. These nodes are clearly divided into five clusters, which are represented by different colors.

3.6. Knowledge Extraction Based on Feature Words (Titles, Keywords, and Abstracts)

To gain insights into the evolution of research topics and identify frontier themes, we also analyzed the frequency of hydrological phenomena and study areas since the 1990s. The search scope encompasses titles, keywords, and abstracts. The analysis tracks the temporal evolution of these topics.

3.6.1. Research Theme

Figure 12 provides insights into the frequency and trends of hydrological phenomena that are of greatest concern to researchers in the field. Overall, the integration of hydrological phenomena and Earth observation is developing exponentially. Studies on precipitation and temperature have accumulated the largest amount of literature, with precipitation appearing 6474 times and temperature appearing 5097 times. Precipitation-related studies have shown an exponential upward trend over the past 30 years. Precipitation and temperature data are often used as meteorological indicators to assist in various hydrological interpretations, such as evapotranspiration calculations, groundwater storage assessments, surface water flow analysis, and drought studies [50–53]. Although a number of studies on snow and ice melt were recorded early on, their growth has been relatively slow, with a total of 2288 records by 2023. This suggests a sustained but modest interest in this phenomenon. Research on surface water exchange started later, with a total of 1296 records. However, the word frequency between 2018 and 2022 reached 732, surpassing 50% of the total from the previous 28 years. This increase is attributed to the emergence of satellite gravity technology, particularly GRACE-FO. Satellite gravity technology provides a means by which to detect groundwater conditions on a large scale, leading to increased interest and studies in this field [54,55]. The phenomenon of runoff and seasonal change returned approximately 2500 records, showing an overall upward trend from 1990 to 2021, with a slight decrease in the period 2021–2022. Evapotranspiration had a relatively lower frequency, with fewer than 1000 occurrences, and showed a modest increase over the past 30 years. Therefore, it appears to be the phenomenon of least concern among the hydrological phenomena studied. There are many challenges to accurately quantifying evapotranspiration. These include the time extension of remote sensing data, the scale transformation of remote sensing information, uncertainty in remote sensing classification, and the universality of remote sensing evapotranspiration models and inversion algorithms [56,57]. In addition, the evaporation paradox is proposed, so accurate quantitative monitoring of evapotranspiration will take a long time to verify.

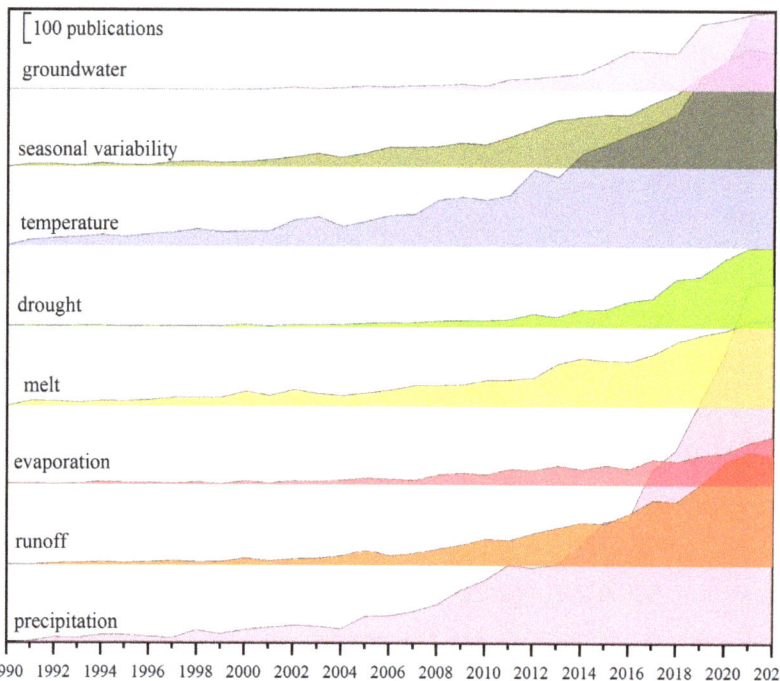

Figure 12. Number of hydrological phenomena researched by year.

3.6.2. Research Area

Figure 13 depicts the 10 study areas with the highest number of occurrences. They are Antarctica (2153), Tibet (2055), the Yangtze River Basin (1799), the Arctic (1342), Greenland (1273), the Alps (1115), the Indian Basin (956), the Amazon Basin (740), the Mississippi Basin (703), and Alaska (682). Compared with other study areas, the study of continental glaciers such as Antarctica and Greenland started early, especially the exploration of Antarctica, accumulating more than 160 publications before the 21st century. According to statistics, the study of polar glaciers has the most overlapping trends, and both locations have seen a decline in numbers in recent years. In the 21st century, there has been a notable increase in quantitative studies focused on regions such as the Indian Basin, Yangtze River Basin, and Qinghai–Tibet Plateau. These areas are heavily influenced by humans and have a wide-ranging impact, making them popular study areas in recent years. These areas are expected to remain hot research topics in the future. Due to the special geographical location and harsh natural environment, the number of hydrological and meteorological stations on the Qinghai–Tibet Plateau is limited. For a long time, research on the climate response mechanism of lake changes on the plateau was mostly restricted to the qualitative description of precipitation, evaporation, temperature, wind speed, cryosphere melting, and other climatic factors. In the past decades, advancements in technology, recognition of the importance of related research, data-sharing initiatives, and interdisciplinary cooperation have resulted in significant progress in the quantitative study of the Qinghai–Tibet Plateau, making it the most popular study area with the fastest growth rate and most increments [58]. In the comparison of the time dimension, the results of this statistic show that the main research area in this field has changed from polar glaciers to the Qinghai–Tibet Plateau and large river basins, such as the Yangtze River Basin and the Indian Basin.

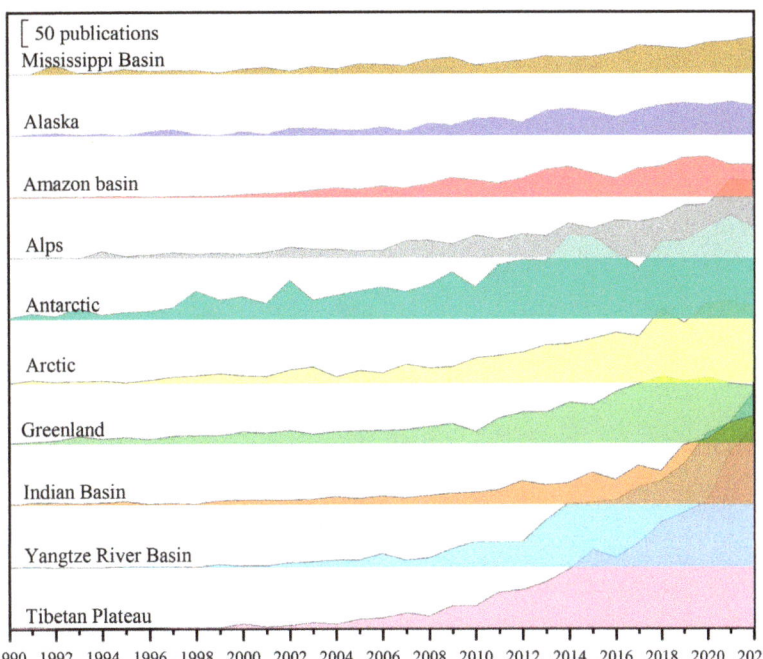

Figure 13. Number of different study areas researched by year.

3.7. Burst Analysis of Keywords

As shown in Figure 14, the results reveal three distinct phases in the evolution of research topics in this field. During the first phase (1990–2000), a significant number of studies utilized technologies such as satellite altimetry for Earth observation. The acquired information was predominantly used for the development of numerical models and general circulation models. The popular study areas during this phase were primarily focused on large glaciers, including Antarctica and Alaska. This phenomenon echoes the conclusions above. In the second phase (2000–2018), researchers increasingly emphasized the application of related technologies to study surface water, glacier mass balance, hydrology, land cover, and other related aspects. This period involved a surge in publications showcasing the practical applications of remote sensing data. In the third phase (2018–present), improvements in the resolution and accuracy of various sensors and a more complete Earth observation series have accumulated massive amounts of data for scientific research. New technologies, such as automatic identification and intelligent batch processing, have emerged. The latest methods for data processing, including random forests, machine learning, and deep learning, have gained prominence. Researchers have turned their attention to a combination of hydrological phenomena and interdisciplinary data-processing algorithms. Intelligent image recognition and data processing based on the above algorithms have become the forefront of development in this field. Throughout the entire timeline, scholars have demonstrated a longstanding interest in studying the optical properties of various sensors, gravity detection, and sea levels. As shown in Figure 14, the timeline of these three keywords is grayed out. This phenomenon indicates their sustained importance in the field of hydrological research.

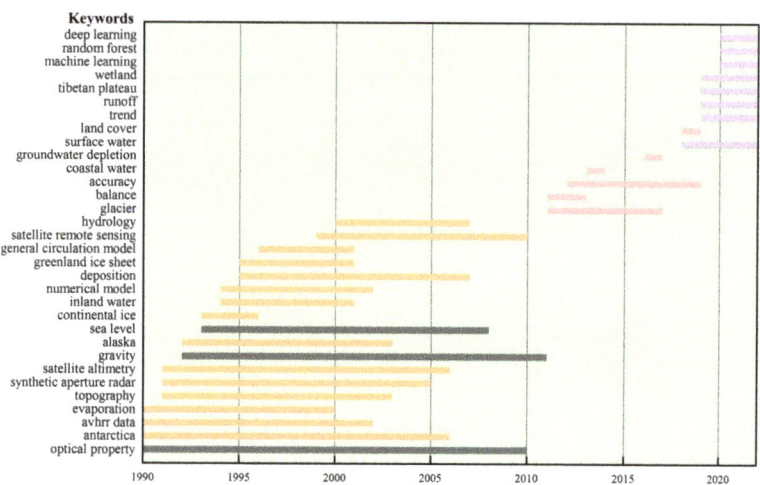

Figure 14. Results of keyword burst analysis. The time slice was set at 3 years. The 32 keywords shown in the graph meet the following requirements: they are in the top 8% of each slice and have the highest bursts.

4. Discussion

4.1. The Role of Time-Varying Quantitative Analysis

One of the contributions of our analysis is the literature on the application of scientometric analysis to the application of multi-source satellite Earth observation techniques to inland waters. This paper is different from the others in that we have added a time-varying quantitative analysis of the research theme and study area, which provides double verification of the evolution of the field and the burst analysis results. This approach enables a more accurate and nuanced quantitative analysis of the evolution and frontiers of the field. Based on the results presented in Sections 3.4.2, 3.6.2 and 3.7, we can determine that the focus in this area has shifted from sea level and polar glaciers to groundwater and surface water. The specific number of changes in relation to different study areas and research topics was quantified. The Tibetan Plateau has been a popular research area in recent years and will continue to be popular in the coming years. Affected by the uneven spatial distribution of freshwater resources in the inflow or outflow basins of the Qinghai–Tibet Plateau caused by climate change, the Yangtze River Basin and the Indian River Basin have become unstable. As the Qinghai–Tibet Plateau is the birthplace of many river basins, the changes in its water environment also have a profound impact on these river basins. Although many scholars have carried out a significant amount of research on climate change and water cycle mechanisms on the Qinghai–Tibet Plateau, there is generally no advanced multi-level coupling model and a lack of ground monitoring [59–61]. Fortunately, the launch of SWOT (https://swot.jpl.nasa.gov/ accessed on 10 July 2023) will effectively improve the monitoring of lake water levels in the region, which will greatly encourage regional and global short-term dynamics and long-term trend monitoring [62,63]. The attention paid to this field will continue to rise in the future.

4.2. Validation of the Accuracy of the Results

In contrast to most reviews with a single research theme, the topics covered in this paper belong to a cross-disciplinary field. In interdisciplinary bibliometric analysis, the primary condition for experimental success is to obtain accurate and complete datasets. In order to obtain the literature that best met the requirements of the research topic, we tested how to identify terms that met the criteria for this paper. From broad search terms to precise feature terms, 100 articles in each dataset were selected, and the number of documents and their accuracy for each search result were determined. The results are shown in Table 2. It can be seen that under more accurate word searches, the number of documents returned is larger and more accurate.

Table 2. Different search terms and the number and accuracy of their returns.

Subject Term of the Retrieval	Number	Accuracy
TS = Satellite AND Inland Water	1262	70%
TS = Satellite AND (River OR Fluvial OR Lake OR Glaciers OR Ice OR Snow OR Wetland OR Groundwater OR Swamp OR Marsh OR Estuary OR Bayou)	29,292	85%
TS = (RS OR Remote Sensing OR Satellite Altimetry OR Gravity OR GRACE) AND Inland Water	1567	82%
TS = (RS OR Remote Sensing OR Satellite Altimetry OR Gravity OR GRACE) AND (River OR Fluvial OR Lake OR Glaciers OR Ice OR Snow OR Wetland OR Groundwater OR Swamp OR Marsh OR Estuary OR Bayou)	30,212	93%

In addition, we used Google Scholar to verify the accuracy of citations in the database (Web of Science) used in this paper. The scope of the Web of Science core collection is limited, mainly to SCI, SSCI, ESCI, and other source journals/conference papers with high authority. Google Scholar includes not only the Web of Science but also EI searches, preprint websites (such as ArXiv, SSRN, etc.), and papers such as university/scholar personal websites. Web of Science and Google Scholar calculate the citations of a paper based on how many papers in their databases cite it. We obtained a total of 100 articles with citations of different orders of magnitude from Google Scholar and compared the data with the Web of Science used in this paper. Figure 15 shows the fitted curve, correlation coefficient, and goodness-of-fit for these 100 samples. The goodness-of-fit degree is greater than 0.9, indicating that the straight line fits the sample values well. The correlation coefficient is 0.9775, and there is a strong correlation between the citations in the two databases. This verifies the reliability of the results of this study to a certain extent.

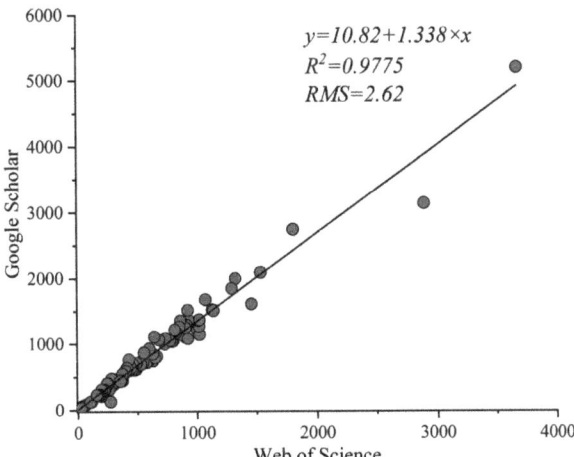

Figure 15. Comparison and correlation of citations in Web of Science and Google Scholar.

4.3. Detailed Setting of the Software

One potential limitation of this study is that different analysis software and different settings will lead to differences in results. However, as far as the current comparative studies are concerned, the two software packages have been verified many times by different researchers, and the results are considered credible. Pan et al., in their comparison of bibliometric software analysis, showed that most researchers using bibliometric software do not provide sufficient usage information, which is not conducive to the reader's reproduction of the processing flow and results [20]. Therefore, in this article, under the condition of ensuring accuracy, we have displayed graphical information based on the principle of clear graphical display and as many nodes as possible. The network set by CiteSpace was sliced over a period of 3 years, and the first 10 nodes of each slice were selected to prepare for display. We adjusted the g-index value to actually control the number of nodes to be displayed; the author cooperation network shows a total of 996 nodes, and the document co-citation network displays a total of 904 nodes. Other relevant settings are reflected in the figure name. A small difference in results is allowed, and differences introduced by different settings do not mean errors. We should also take these differences into account when drawing conclusions.

5. Conclusions

The analysis of publication trends in this field reveals several key findings. The number of publications in this field has exhibited exponential growth, indicating increasing interest and involvement from researchers. Among the top five publications, the United States, China, Germany, Canada, and the United Kingdom produced more than 80% of the publications. The disciplines and degree of cooperation between countries are also geographically linked. In densely populated countries such as China and India, inland water monitoring mainly serves environmental science, while publications in the United States, Britain, France, Germany, and Canada mainly belong to geodisciplinary fields. In terms of cooperation, China and the United States are the two countries with the highest degree of cooperation, but some European countries, such as Germany, Poland, the Czech Republic, Switzerland, Finland, Hungary, Spain, Italy, etc., also have a strong degree of cooperation. The degree of cooperation is related to geographical distance. In addition, a core group of authors, led by Shum CK and Lee H, has emerged as influential contributors in this field. The development of research in this field can be divided into three periods. The period from 1990 to 2000 marked the exploration phase of new detection technologies. The period from 2000 to 2018 involved significant growth in detection technology development. The period after 2018 represents the development phase of cloud computing and intelligent processing applications. The focus of research has shifted from large-scale glaciers to river basins and lakes.

From the review above, key findings emerge: (1) In recent years, there has been a consistent rise in the number of studies focusing on the Tibetan Plateau and its associated basins, including the Indian Basin and the Yangtze River Basin. The maturity of regional-scale research will inevitably give impetus to the short-term and long-term monitoring of inland water on a global scale. After accumulating a large number of regional inland water studies, inland water studies on a global scale will provide a clearer explanation of the inland water cycle and its mechanisms. (2) Inland water monitoring has grown with advancements in multi-source Earth observation technology, driving research in the field. In particular, the launch of SWOT in December 2022 is expected to be a groundbreaking development in global surface water monitoring. SWOT will provide the first comprehensive survey of the Earth's surface water, offering valuable information for understanding and tracking water resources globally. This mission will generate new momentum. (3) Furthermore, the integration of the hydrological field with disciplines such as deep learning and intelligent recognition is opening up new avenues for researchers. The integration of hydrology with various cross-disciplinary fields is expected to facilitate further exploration and research. Researchers can anticipate a growing number of studies that combine knowledge and expertise from hydrology, cloud computing, big data, deep learning, and intelligent recognition. Through the application of these technologies, outcomes will address the challenges and opportunities associated with the long-term and global-scale observation of inland water. Regrettably, our findings do not capture the relationship between study themes, study areas, and the evolution of research methods due to the absence of quantitative statistics on research methods. To address this limitation, future scientific analyses on this topic should aim to quantitatively examine research methods and explore the underlying connections between research themes, regions, and methods. Moreover, existing literature analysis software, such as CiteSpace and VOSviewer, lacks advanced keyword refinement and algorithm integration functions, making it challenging for users to obtain accurate results. However, by ensuring a large and comprehensive sample, the influence of individual incorrect samples can be mitigated. Moving forward, we aspire to further enhance natural language processing by integrating multi-source data and strengthening knowledge graph reasoning capabilities.

Funding: This work was sponsored by the National Natural Science Foundation of China (41974016, 42104023, 42264001), the Major Discipline Academic and Technical Leaders Training Program of Jiangxi Province (20225BCJ23014), Hebei Water Conservancy Research Plan (2022-28).

Conflicts of Interest: The authors declare no conflict of interest.

References

1. Sun, G.; Guo, L.; Chang, C.; Zhao, X.; Li, L. Contrast and analysis of water storage changes in the north slopes and south slopes of the central Tianshan Mountains in Xinjiang. *Arid Land Geogr.* **2016**, *39*, 254–264.
2. Huang, C.; Chen, Y.; Zhang, S.; Wu, J. Detecting, extracting, and monitoring surface water from space using optical sensors: A review. *Rev. Geophys.* **2018**, *56*, 333–360. [CrossRef]
3. Sogno, P.; Klein, I.; Kuenzer, C. Remote Sensing of Surface Water Dynamics in the Context of Global Change—A Review. *Remote Sens.* **2022**, *14*, 2475. [CrossRef]
4. Frappart, F.; Ramillien, G. Monitoring Groundwater Storage Changes Using the Gravity Recovery and Climate Experiment (GRACE) Satellite Mission: A Review. *Remote Sens.* **2018**, *10*, 829. [CrossRef]
5. Tapley, B.D.; Watkins, M.M.; Flechtner, F.; Reigber, C.; Bettadpur, S.; Rodell, M.; Sasgen, I.; Famiglietti, J.S.; Landerer, F.W.; Chambers, D.P.; et al. Contributions of GRACE to understanding climate change. *Nat. Clim. Change* **2019**, *9*, 358–369. [CrossRef]
6. Humphrey, V.; Gudmundsson, L.; Seneviratne, S.I. Assessing Global Water Storage Variability from GRACE: Trends, Seasonal Cycle, Subseasonal Anomalies and Extremes. *Surv. Geophys.* **2016**, *37*, 357–395. [CrossRef]
7. Feng, W.; Shum, C.K.; Zhong, M.; Pan, Y. Groundwater Storage Changes in China from Satellite Gravity: An Overview. *Remote Sens.* **2018**, *10*, 674. [CrossRef]
8. Wouters, B.; van de Wal, R.S.W. Global sea-level budget 1993–present. *Earth Syst. Sci. Data* **2018**, *10*, 1551–1590.
9. Biancamaria, S.; Lettenmaier, D.P.; Pavelsky, T.M. The SWOT Mission and Its Capabilities for Land Hydrology. *Surv. Geophys.* **2016**, *37*, 307–337. [CrossRef]
10. Crétaux, J.-F.; Abarca-del-Río, R.; Berge-Nguyen, M.; Arsen, A.; Drolon, V.; Clos, G.; Maisongrande, P. Lake Volume Monitoring from Space. *Surv. Geophys.* **2016**, *37*, 269–305. [CrossRef]
11. Guo, M.; Li, J.; Sheng, C.; Xu, J.; Wu, L. A Review of Wetland Remote Sensing. *Sensors* **2017**, *17*, 777. [CrossRef]
12. Liu, Z.; Yang, Z.; Chen, M.; Xu, H.; Yang, Y.; Zhang, J.; Wu, Q.; Wang, M.; Song, Z.; Ding, F. Research Hotspots and Frontiers of Mountain Flood Disaster: Bibliometric and Visual Analysis. *Water* **2023**, *15*, 673. [CrossRef]
13. Zhang, J.; Liu, J.; Chen, Y.; Feng, X.; Sun, Z. Knowledge Mapping of Machine Learning Approaches Applied in Agricultural Management—A Scientometric Review with CiteSpace. *Sustainability* **2021**, *13*, 7662. [CrossRef]
14. Chen, C.; Chitose, A.; Kusadokoro, M.; Nie, H.; Xu, W.; Yang, F.; Yang, S. Sustainability and challenges in biodiesel production from waste cooking oil: An advanced bibliometric analysis. *Energy Rep.* **2021**, *7*, 4022–4034. [CrossRef]
15. Yang, L.; Lin, L.; Fan, L.; Liu, N.; Huang, L.; Xu, Y.; Mertikas, S.P.; Jia, Y.; Lin, M. Satellite Altimetry: Achievements and Future Trends by a Scientometrics Analysis. *Remote Sens.* **2022**, *14*, 3332. [CrossRef]
16. Xu, Y.; Yang, Y.; Chen, X.; Liu, Y. Bibliometric Analysis of Global NDVI Research Trends from 1985 to 2021. *Remote Sens.* **2022**, *14*, 3967. [CrossRef]
17. Mingers, J.; Leydesdorff, L. A review of theory and practice in scientometrics. *Eur. J. Oper. Res.* **2015**, *246*, 1–19. [CrossRef]
18. Chen, C. CiteSpace II: Detecting and visualizing emerging trends and transient patterns in scientific literature. *J. Am. Soc. Inf. Sci. Technol.* **2006**, *57*, 359–377. [CrossRef]
19. Chen, C. Science Mapping: A Systematic Review of the Literature. *J. Data Inf. Sci.* **2017**, *2*, 1–40. [CrossRef]
20. Pan, X.; Yan, E.; Cui, M.; Hua, W. Examining the usage, citation, and diffusion patterns of bibliometric mapping software: A comparative study of three tools. *J. Informetr.* **2018**, *12*, 481–493. [CrossRef]
21. Song, X.; Chi, P. Comparative Study of the Data Analysis Results by Vosviewer and Citespace. *Inf. Sci.* **2016**, *108*, 112.
22. van Eck, N.; Waltman, L. Software survey: VOSviewer, a computer program for bibliometric mapping. *Scientometrics* **2010**, *84*, 523–538. [CrossRef] [PubMed]
23. Lee, H.; Beighley, R.E.; Alsdorf, D.; Jung, H.; Shum, C.K.; Duan, J.; Guo, J.; Yamazaki, D.; Andreadis, K. Characterization of terrestrial water dynamics in the Congo Basin using GRACE and satellite radar altimetry. *Remote Sens. Environ.* **2011**, *115*, 3530–3538. [CrossRef]

24. Kim, J.W.; Lu, Z.; Lee, H.; Shum, C.K.; Swarzenski, C.M.; Doyle, T.W.; Baek, S.-H. Integrated analysis of PALSAR/Radarsat-1 InSAR and ENVISAT altimeter data for mapping of absolute water level changes in Louisiana wetlands. *Remote Sens. Environ.* **2009**, *113*, 2356–2365. [CrossRef]
25. Lee, H.; Durand, M.; Jung, H.; Alsdorf, D.; Shum, C.K.; Sheng, Y. Characterization of surface water storage changes in Arctic lakes using simulated SWOT measurements. *Int. J. Remote Sens.* **2010**, *31*, 3931–3953. [CrossRef]
26. Akbor, S.; Hossain, F.; Lee, H.; Shum, C.K. Inter-comparison study of water level estimates derived from hydrodynamic–hydrologic model and satellite altimetry for a complex deltaic environment. *Remote Sens. Environ.* **2011**, *115*, 1522–1531. [CrossRef]
27. Cao, Z.; Duan, H.; Feng, L.; Ma, R.; Xue, K. Climate- and human-induced changes in suspended particulate matter over Lake Hongze on short and long timescales. *Remote Sens. Environ.* **2017**, *192*, 98–113. [CrossRef]
28. Cao, Z.; Ma, R.; Duan, H.; Pahlevan, N.; Melack, J.; Shen, M.; Xue, K. A machine learning approach to estimate chlorophyll-a from Landsat-8 measurements in inland lakes. *Remote Sens. Environ.* **2020**, *248*, 111974. [CrossRef]
29. Wan, W.; Xiao, P.; Feng, X.; Li, H.; Ma, R.; Duan, H.; Zhao, L. Monitoring lake changes of Qinghai-Tibetan Plateau over the past 30. *Chin. Sci. Bull.* **2014**, *59*, 1021–1035. [CrossRef]
30. Sun, F.; Zhao, Y.; Gong, P.; Ma, R.; Dai, Y. Monitoring dynamic changes of global land cover types: Fluctuations of major lakes in China every 8 days during 2000–2010. *Chin. Sci. Bull.* **2014**, *59*, 171–189. [CrossRef]
31. Crétaux, J.-F.; Arsen, A.; Calmant, S.; Kouraev, A.; Vuglinski, V.; Bergé-Nguyen, M.; Gennero, M.-C.; Nino, F.; Del Rio, R.A.; Cazenave, A.; et al. SOLS: A lake database to monitor in the Near Real Time water level and storage variations from remote sensing data. *Adv. Space Res.* **2011**, *47*, 1497–1507. [CrossRef]
32. Schmidt, R.; Schwintzer, P.; Flechtner, F.; Reigber, C.; Güntner, A.; Döll, P.; Ramillien, G.; Cazenave, A.; Petrovic, S.; Jochmann, H.; et al. GRACE observations of changes in continental water storage. *Glob. Planet Chang.* **2006**, *50*, 112–116. [CrossRef]
33. Pfeffer, W.; Arendt, A.; Bliss, A.; Bolch, T.; Cogley, J.; Gardner, A.; Sharp, M. The Randolph Glacier Inventory: A globally complete inventory of glaciers. *J. Glaciol.* **2014**, *60*, 537–552. [CrossRef]
34. Thomas, R.; Rignot, E.; Casassa, G.; Kanagaratnam, P.; Akins, T.; Brecher, H.; Frederick, E.; Gogineni, P.; Krabill, W.; Manizade, S.; et al. Accelerated Sea-Level Rise from West Antarctica. *Science* **2004**, *306*, 255–258. [CrossRef]
35. Rodell, M.; Chen, J.; Kato, H.; Famiglietti, J.S.; Nigro, J.; Wilson, C.R. Estimating groundwater storage changes in the Mississippi River basin (USA) using GRACE. *Hydrogeol. J.* **2007**, *15*, 159–166. [CrossRef]
36. Chen, J.; Famigliett, J.S.; Scanlon, B.R.; Rodell, M. Groundwater Storage Changes: Present Status from GRACE Observations. *Surv. Geophys.* **2016**, *37*, 397–417. [CrossRef]
37. Forman, B.A.; Reichle, R.H.; Rodell, M. Assimilation of terrestrial water storage from GRACE in a snow-dominated basin. *Water Resour. Res.* **2012**, *48*, 01507. [CrossRef]
38. Gorelick, N.; Hancher, M.; Dixon, M.; Ilyushchenko, S.; Thau, D.; Moore, R. Google Earth Engine: Planetary-scale geospatial analysis for everyone. *Remote Sens. Environ.* **2017**, *202*, 18–27. [CrossRef]
39. Hu, B.; Wang, L. Terrestrial water storage change and its attribution: A review and perspective. *Water Resour. Hydropower Eng.* **2021**, *52*, 13–25.
40. Pekel, J.F.; Cottam, A.; Gorelick, N.; Belward, A.S. High-resolution mapping of global surface water and its long-term changes. *Nature* **2016**, *540*, 418–422. [CrossRef]
41. Save, H.; Bettadpur, S.; Tapley, B.D. High-resolution CSR GRACE RL05 mascons. *J. Geophys. Res. Solid Earth* **2016**, *121*, 7547–7569. [CrossRef]
42. Wiese, D.N.; Landerer, F.W.; Watkins, M.M. Quantifying and reducing leakage errors in the JPL RL05M GRACE mascon solution. *Water Resour. Res.* **2016**, *52*, 7490–7502. [CrossRef]
43. Rodell, M.; Famiglietti, J.S.; Wiese, D.N.; Reager, J.T.; Beaudoing, H.K.; Landerer, F.W.; Lo, M.-H. Emerging trends in global freshwater availability. *Nature* **2018**, *557*, 651–659. [CrossRef] [PubMed]
44. Chen, Q.; Shen, Y.; Kusche, J.; Chen, W.; Chen, T.; Zhang, X. High-Resolution GRACE Monthly Spherical Harmonic Solutions. *Solid Earth* **2020**, *126*, B018892. [CrossRef]
45. Markus, T.; Neumann, T.; Martino, A.; Abdalati, W.; Brunt, K.; Csatho, B.; Farrell, S.; Fricker, H.; Gardner, A.; Harding, D.; et al. The Ice, Cloud, and land Elevation Satellite-2 (ICESat-2): Science requirements, concept, and implementation. *Remote Sens. Environ.* **2017**, *190*, 260–273. [CrossRef]
46. Ma, C.; Guo, X.; Zhang, H.; Di, J.; Chen, G. An Investigation of the Influences of SWOT Sampling and Errors on Ocean Eddy Observation. *Remote Sens.* **2020**, *12*, 2682. [CrossRef]
47. Flechtner, F.; Reigber, C.; Rummel, R.; Balmino, G. Satellite Gravimetry: A Review of Its Realization. *Surv. Geophys.* **2021**, *42*, 1029–1074. [CrossRef]
48. Scanlon, B.R.; Longuevergne, L.; Long, D. Ground referencing GRACE satellite estimates of groundwater storage changes in the California Central Valley, USA. *Water Resour. Res.* **2012**, *48*, 4520. [CrossRef]
49. Feng, W.; Zhong, M.; Lemoine, J.M.; Biancale, R.; Hsu, H.-T.; Xia, J. Evaluation of groundwater depletion in North China using the Gravity Recovery and Climate Experiment (GRACE) data and ground-based measurements. *Water Resour. Res.* **2013**, *49*, 2110–2118. [CrossRef]

50. Girotto, M.; Reichle, R.; Rodell, M.; Maggioni, V. Data Assimilation of Terrestrial Water Storage Observations to Estimate Precipitation Fluxes: A Synthetic Experiment. *Remote Sens.* **2021**, *13*, 1223. [CrossRef]
51. Lyu, Y.; Huang, Y.; Bao, A.; Zhong, R.; Yang, H. Temporal/Spatial Variation of Terrestrial Water Storage and Groundwater Storage in Typical Inland River Basins of Central Asia. *Water* **2021**, *13*, 3385. [CrossRef]
52. Abou, Z.N.; Torabi, H.A.; Rossi, P.M.; Tourian, M.J.; Bakhshaee, A.; Kløve, B. Evaluating Impacts of Irrigation and Drought on River, Groundwater and a Terminal Wetland in the Zayanderud Basin. *Water* **2020**, *12*, 1305.
53. Shah, D.; Mishra, V. Strong Influence of Changes in Terrestrial Water Storage on Flood Potential in India. *J. Geophys. Res. Atmos.* **2020**, *126*, D033566. [CrossRef]
54. Rodell, M.; Famiglietti, J.S. The potential for satellite-based monitoring of groundwater storage changes using GRACE: The High Plains aquifer, Central US. *J. Hydrol.* **2002**, *263*, 245–256. [CrossRef]
55. Tu, M.; Liu, Z.; He, C.; Ren, Q.; Lu, W. Research Progress of Groundwater Storage Changes Monitoring in China Based on GRACE Satellite Data. *Adv. Earth Sci.* **2020**, *35*, 643–656.
56. García-Santos, V.; Sánchez, J.M.; Cuxart, J. Evapotranspiration Acquired with Remote Sensing Thermal-Based Algorithms: A State-of-the-Art Review. *Remote Sens.* **2022**, *14*, 3440. [CrossRef]
57. Liou, Y.-A.; Kar, S.K. Evapotranspiration Estimation with Remote Sensing and Various Surface Energy Balance Algorithms—A Review. *Energies* **2014**, *7*, 2821–2849. [CrossRef]
58. Chen, J.; Liu, Y.; Cao, L.; Hu, J.; Liu, S. A review on the research of remote sensing monitoring of lake changes and quantitative estimation of lake water balance in Qinghai-Tibet Plateau. *J. Glaciol. Geocryol.* **2022**, *44*, 1203–1215.
59. Yao, T.; Bolch, T.; Chen, D.; Gao, J.; Immerzeel, W.; Piao, S.; Su, F.; Thompson, L.; Wada, Y.; Wang, L.; et al. The imbalance of the Asian water tower. *Nat. Rev. Earth Environ.* **2022**, *3*, 618–632. [CrossRef]
60. Yao, T.; Thompson, L.G.; Mosbrugger, V.; Zhang, F.; Ma, Y.; Luo, T.; Xu, B.; Yang, X.; Joswiak, D.R.; Wang, W.; et al. Third Pole Environment (TPE). *Environ. Dev.* **2012**, *3*, 52–64. [CrossRef]
61. Yang, K.; Wu, H.; Qin, J.; Lin, C.; Tang, W.; Chen, Y. Recent climate changes over the Tibetan Plateau and their impacts on energy and water cycle: A review. *Glob. Planet. Change* **2014**, *112*, 79–91. [CrossRef]
62. Xiong, J.; Jiang, L.; Qiu, Y.; Wongchuig, S.; Abhishek; Guo, S.; Chen, J. On the capabilities of the SWOT satellite to monitor the lake level change over the Third Pole. *Environ. Res. Lett.* **2023**, *18*, 044008. [CrossRef]
63. Wu, Y.; Yang, F.; Lai, G.; Lin, K. Research progress of knowledge graph learning and reasoning. *J. Chin. Comput. Syst.* **2016**, *37*, 2007–2013.

Disclaimer/Publisher's Note: The statements, opinions and data contained in all publications are solely those of the individual author(s) and contributor(s) and not of MDPI and/or the editor(s). MDPI and/or the editor(s) disclaim responsibility for any injury to people or property resulting from any ideas, methods, instructions or products referred to in the content.

Article

Global Water Quality of Inland Waters with Harmonized Landsat-8 and Sentinel-2 Using Cloud-Computed Machine Learning

Leonardo F. Arias-Rodriguez [1,*], Ulaş Firat Tüzün [1], Zheng Duan [2], Jingshui Huang [1], Ye Tuo [1] and Markus Disse [1]

[1] Hydrology and River Basin Management, TUM School of Engineering and Design, Technical University of Munich, 80333 Munich, Germany
[2] Department of Physical Geography and Ecosystem Science, Lund University, SE-221 00 Lund, Sweden
* Correspondence: leonardo.arias@tum.de

Abstract: Modeling inland water quality by remote sensing has already demonstrated its capacity to make accurate predictions. However, limitations still exist for applicability in diverse regions, as well as to retrieve non-optically active parameters (nOAC). Models are usually trained only with water samples from individual or local groups of waterbodies, which limits their capacity and accuracy in predicting parameters across diverse regions. This study aims to increase data availability to understand the performance of models trained with heterogeneous databases from both remote sensing and field measurement sources to improve machine learning training. This paper seeks to build a dataset with worldwide lake characteristics using data from water monitoring programs around the world paired with harmonized data of Landsat-8 and Sentinel-2. Additional feature engineering is also examined. The dataset is then used for model training and prediction of water quality at the global scale, time series analysis and water quality maps for lakes in different continents. Additionally, the modeling performance of nOACs are also investigated. The results show that trained models achieve moderately high correlations for SDD, TURB and BOD (R^2 = 0.68) but lower performances for TSM and NO3-N (R^2 = 0.43). The extreme learning machine (ELM) and the random forest regression (RFR) demonstrate better performance. The results indicate that ML algorithms can process remote sensing data and additional features to model water quality at the global scale and contribute to address the limitations of transferring and retrieving nOAC. However, significant limitations need to be considered, such as calibrated harmonization of water data and atmospheric correction procedures. Moreover, further understanding of the mechanisms that facilitate nOAC prediction is necessary. We highlight the need for international contributions to global water quality datasets capable of providing extensive water data for the improvement of global water monitoring.

Keywords: remote sensing; water quality; harmonize RS data; machine learning; global modeling

Citation: Arias-Rodriguez, L.F.; Tüzün, U.F.; Duan, Z.; Huang, J.; Tuo, Y.; Disse, M. Global Water Quality of Inland Waters with Harmonized Landsat-8 and Sentinel-2 Using Cloud-Computed Machine Learning. Remote Sens. 2023, 15, 1390. https://doi.org/10.3390/rs15051390

Academic Editors: Flor Alvarez-Taboada, Miro Govedarica and Gordana Jakovljević

Received: 3 January 2023
Revised: 22 February 2023
Accepted: 27 February 2023
Published: 1 March 2023

Copyright: © 2023 by the authors. Licensee MDPI, Basel, Switzerland. This article is an open access article distributed under the terms and conditions of the Creative Commons Attribution (CC BY) license (https://creativecommons.org/licenses/by/4.0/).

1. Introduction

Monitoring water quality of inland waters in different countries is mostly conducted individually by each nation. Global integration of their data is often constrained by a lack of worldwide projects or collaborations [1]. When possible, the countries measure the water quality mainly inside their borders through their monitoring systems and the data are stored locally. Therefore, an important quantity of data that is collected every year is usually not available or is difficult to access for external researchers or international institutions. Currently, there are international projects that aim to homogeneously integrate water quality data from several countries for applications in water resources [2]. However, these programs are in early stages and up to now there no comprehensive and unique sources for global and homogeneous water quality data. At the same time, the global coverage of operational monitoring stations is insufficient or lacks acceptable levels of confidence and precision [1,3,4]. This situation limits considerably the application of current data-driven methods that use big datasets to learn from water quality patterns. Therefore, monitoring water quality remains limited by only conventional analysis such as collection of water samples in the field and laboratory analysis [5,6]. Conventional methods are highly accurate, but also expensive, time demanding and limited in spatial and temporal coverages. Additionally, it is complex to develop a representative understanding of the water quality status in a waterbody from punctual field measurements or limited field campaigns over the course of large periods of time. A solution to increase the scope and capabilities of monitoring water quality is the use of remote sensing data, which contributes to provide data from remote sensors that couple field data and increase the analysis in time and space. International institutions such as the United Nations already encourage the coupling of monitoring systems with remote sensing technologies through its Environment Program [1]. When paired with field data, combined water and remote sensing measurements allow monitoring at a larger scope, since they have the potential to analyze waterbodies at regional or global locations. This is achieved by studying water quality from indicator parameters and dealing with better cost–benefit methods in comparison with the extensive spatial and temporal scales that are analyzed. Several modeling techniques associate remote-sensed signals, mostly in the visible and near-infrared wavelengths (400–900 nm), with the water parameter of interest to derive information of the waterbody. The relationship between optically active constituents (OAC) such as chlorophyll-a (Chl-a), total suspended matter (TSM) and surface radiation arises due to the interaction between the radiation and the OAC through processes such as absorption and scattering [7]. Remote sensing is suited to analyze these relationships because of the high sensitivity in the radiometric resolution of several satellite sensors. As water absorbs within the visible spectrum, low reflectance occurs in the water column in contrast to the high reflectance of land. Therefore, high sensitivity in the spectral sensors is required to detect the slight changes in water reflectance that surpass the absorption of water [8,9]. Currently, sensors such as Landsat-8 OLI and Sentinel-2 MSI are suited to provide remote sensing data for water quality monitoring because of their radiometric and temporal resolutions [10]. While remote-sensing-based models can reproduce the patters and dynamics of key water parameters, it becomes relevant to improve the confidence and accuracy of such methodologies and the data that are provided to calibrate them. From the different approaches developed in the last decades, machine learning algorithms currently offer accurate and precise models for water quality monitoring [11–14]. Machine learning comprises statistical methods which are able to learn from the data they are provided through iterative processes of error adjustment between training and prediction datasets. The process involves providing data to the selected algorithm which is trained with known or predefined features or objects that allows detection, classification or pattern recognition in semi-automated or automated learning. Methodologies combining machine learning with remote sensing data have been used to successfully model water quality [14–21]. Some algorithms are considered standard for machine learning evaluations, such as support vector machines (SVR) and random forest regression (RFR) [22]. Furthermore, deep learning, a subset of machine learning based on neural networks, has demonstrated higher accuracy than other methodologies used to model water quality such as bio-optical or band/ratio models [13,23–26]. Due to its novelty, there are still open challenges in the application of machine learning which require further research [24,27–30].

The availability of paired remote sensing and field water quality data is highly limited because of the independent nature of acquiring both types of data. Monitoring water quality programs in different countries were not designed to take into consideration remote sensing acquisitions or satellite overpasses. Therefore, an important percentage of field data are not feasible to be coupled with remote sensing images [31]. Moreover, remote sensing data originate from multiple instruments with different characteristics. This heterogeneous data, in terms of frequency, spatial and radiometric resolution, demand further data pre-treatment and better machine learning models to reveal meaningful information and may make difficult model transferability. Inherent challenges regarding modeling processes also exist, in particular for deep learning. Yet, a deeper neural network may retrieve more accurate results but at a higher computational cost and with associated risks of overfitting. To determine optimal conditions and parameters of these elements is still a crucial research question [32]. In addition, important water quality parameters such as nutrient concentrations, indicators of oxygen levels or organic compounds are not feasible to be directly retrieved by remote sensing because of their inaction over the spectral response of the water when dissolved, and are therefore known as non-optically active compounds (nOACs). Current research poses the possibilities to determine these parameters on indirect correlations with other optically active components such as chlorophyll-a, turbidity or suspended solids [33]. Finally, due to the nature of machine learning models trained with remote sensing data being inherently empirical, they are expected to be valid mainly in the region from where their training data are originated, and most of these models are applicable only at their specific regions or waterbodies. As these models rely on optical characteristics, which may vary from waterbody to waterbody in complex waters, their transferability is further limited to the origin of their training data. However, a key characteristic of machine learning methodologies is that they learn patterns and behaviors from great amounts of data. Therefore, the existence of a worldwide integrated dataset of water quality and remote sensing data gives the possibility to develop a data-driven approach with the capacity for global estimations of water quality by comprising global lake characteristics in a single dataset. In this study, we aim to create this dataset with the available resources for remote sensing image processing and open-access field water quality measurements. Harmonization of remote sensing data contributes to the increase in data availability by combining remote sensing data from different sensors. A recent example is the harmonization process for Landsat-8 OLI and Sentinel-2 MSI, which have been subject to treatment to homogenize their spectral response and spatial resolution [10,14,34]. This method aims to standardize these differences to produce harmonized datasets that can be used together for various applications such as land cover classification and change detection. This harmonization process represents a significant improvement in multi-temporal and multi-sensor analysis, making it possible to better track changes in the Earth's surface over time. Despite some processes of the harmonization not being specifically designed for inland waters, such as the 6S atmospheric correction, it is already widely used in remote sensing, showing promise for improving the accuracy of water quality retrievals in the future. Similarly, the results of its usage require caution when being interpreted. Ultimately, the adoption of these methodologies enabled the construction of a global dataset for model development and contributed to understanding the potential of machine learning with increased data availability.

To contribute to clarifying the above challenges, this work aims (i) to gather open-access water quality monitoring datasets of the relevant parameters from different regions in the world for their synergistic use with remote sensing; (ii) to maximize the data availability of coupled field and sensor acquisitions by using an image homogenization process for L8 and S2 and produce harmonized images from both satellites, enabling both sensors to be used synergistically and increasing the size available spectral data; (iii) to build a comprehensive dataset created from the coupling of the global dataset and the harmonized remote sensing products; and (iv) to model relevant water quality parameters using machine learning and validate the use of the developed models for global water quality predictions. In addition, we investigate the results using this dataset and machine learning approaches to understand better the optimal balance between computational demand and retrieved accuracy as well as the possibilities of nOAC direct or indirect retrievals.

2. Materials and Methods

2.1. Sources of Global Water Quality Dataset

The main source of field data is the open-access data portals from water and environment national agencies of different countries which make public their archives of field measurements and monitoring activities. A summary of agencies and links of acquisition is provided in Table 1. In its raw form, the dataset contained almost 300,000 total samples. A summary of the number of observations and lakes by region is displayed in Table 2. The global locations of all the stations from the above-mentioned data sources are shown in Figure 1.

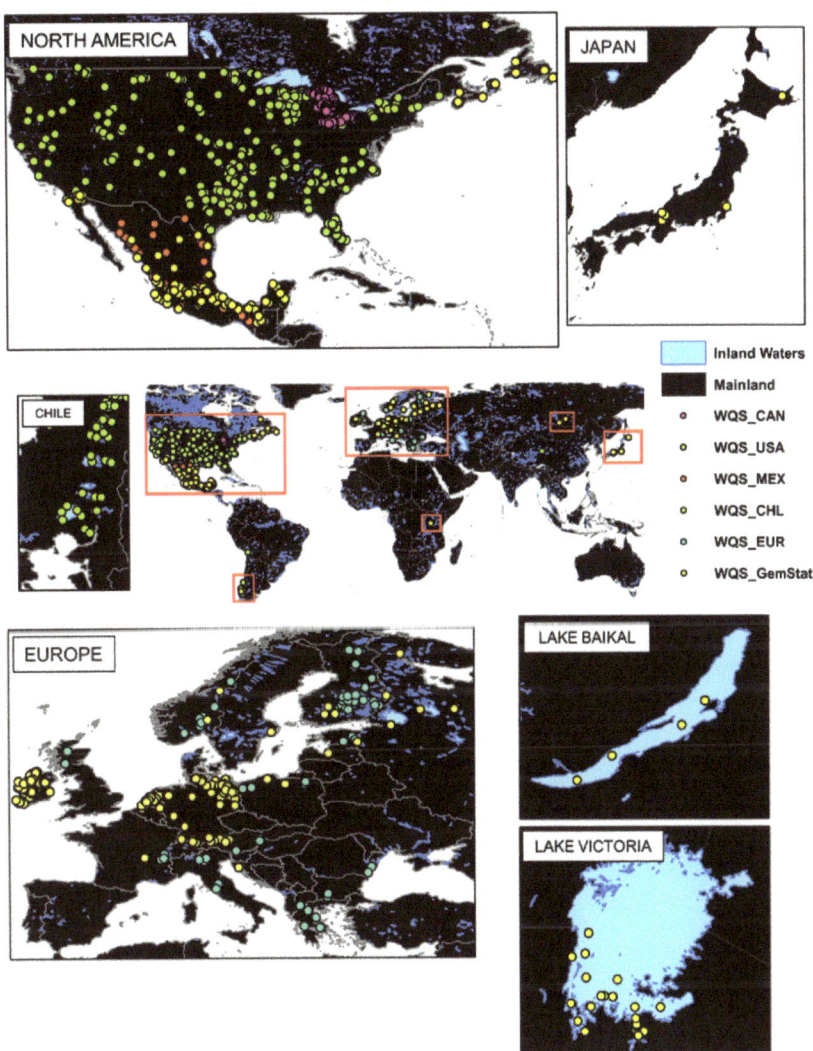

Figure 1. The global location of all the stations from the above-mentioned data sources in raw form.

Table 1. Source of national and international water quality datasets acquired in this study.

Source	Data Location	Region
Water Quality Portal (WQP)	waterqualitydata.us (accessed on 15 January 2022)	United States
European Environment Agency (EEA) Waterbase	eea.europa.eu/data-and-maps/data/waterbase (accessed on 13 January 2022)	Europe
Mexican National Water Monitoring Network	gob.mx/conagua/articulos/calidad-del-agua (accessed on 1 September 2021)	Mexico
Open Government Portal of Canada	open.canada.ca/en/od (accessed on 15 January 2022)	Canada
General Chilean Water Directorade	dga.mop.gob.cl/servicioshidrometeorologicos (accessed on 15 January 2022)	Chile
Global Freshwater Quality Database (GEMStat)	gemstat.org/data (accessed on 7 January 2022)	Global

Table 2. Overview of the number of observations and lakes per region in the raw dataset.

Region	n	Lakes
United States	263,699	43
Europe	17,681	64
Mexico	9086	32
Canada	5412	2
Japan	1292	3
Chile	897	16
Russia	32	1

Recent research of Thorslund and van Vliet [35], indicates that the current state of the global water quality stations monitoring lakes and reservoirs is focused mainly on the U.S. followed by Europe, Mexico and South Africa. Australia has a great number of stations, near 90,000, but most of them are for groundwater, and only 5 are located on lakes or reservoirs. For this study, the gross part of the data components comes from the U.S. and European sources since their data archives are open access and easy to acquire through their respective portals. The U.S. data were acquired from the Water Quality Portal [36] (https://www.waterqualitydata.us/, accessed on 15 January 2022), which is a cooperative service sponsored by the United States Geological Survey (USGS), the Environmental Protection Agency (EPA) and the National Water Quality Monitoring Council (NWQMC) that integrates publicly available water quality data from the USGS National Water Information System (NWIS), the EPA STOrage and RETrieval (STORET) Data Warehouse and the USDA ARS Sustaining The Earth's Watersheds—Agricultural Research Database System (STEWARDS). Data from the European continent were acquired through the European Environment Agency (EEA) Waterbase (https://www.eea.europa.eu/data-and-maps/data/waterbase-water-quality-icm-2, accessed on 13 January 2022), which contains time series of nutrients, organic matter, hazardous substances and other chemicals in rivers, lakes, groundwater and transitional, coastal and marine waters (EEA 2021). Additionally, datasets from the National Water Monitoring Network of Mexico (https://www.gob.mx/conagua/articulos/calidad-del-agua, accessed on 1 September 2021) [37], the Canadian Great Lakes (https://search.open.canada.ca/en/od/, accessed on 15 January 2022) [38], and the Chilean General Water Directory (DGA) lake's database [39] were also acquired (https://dga.mop.gob.cl/servicioshidrometeorologicos/Paginas/default.aspx, accessed on 15 January 2022). Finally, the Global Freshwater Quality Database (GEMStat) (https://gemstat.org/data/, accessed on 7 January 2022), which is a GEMS/Water Program of the United Nations Environment Program (UNEP), was also acquired to account as much as possible for remaining global data around the world. The GEMStat is hosted by the GEMS/Water Data Centre (GWDC) within the International Centre for Water Resources and Global Change (ICWRGC) in Koblenz, Germany [2].

2.2. Field Dataset Compliance by Lake Selection, Satellite Coincidence and Data Curation

For lake selection, the minimum surface area to consider a waterbody was set to 20 km^2. This size ensures the avoidance of adjacency errors in the NIR region from the surrounding land surfaces and bottom reflectance in the sensor acquisitions [40]. At the same time, this area is on the limit to retrieve an adequate number of pixels from the image acquisition based on the spatial resolution per pixel (30 × 30 m) of the intended OLI and MSI sensors to be used as the source of radiometric data.

We used the Level-1 and Level-2 database from the Global Lakes and Wetlands Database (GLWD) developed by the World Wildlife Fund (WWF) and the Center for Environmental Systems Research, University of Kassel, Germany (https://www.worldwildlife.org/pages/global-lakes-and-wetlands-database, accessed on 20 January 2022) [41], to apply lake selection.

The first GLDW product, GLWD-1, comprises 3067 lakes (area > 50 km^2) and 654 reservoirs (storage capacity > 0.5 km^3) worldwide, and includes extensive attribute data. The second GLDW product, GLWD-2, comprises permanent open waterbodies with surface areas larger than 0.1 km^2, from which the minimum area of 20 km^2 was established. Additionally, we applied a rigorous data cleaning process which involved the rejection of samples that (i) predate the launch of Landsat-8 and Sentinel-2, (ii) are not within the ±3 days range of L8 and S2 images, (iii) were taken deeper than 1.0 m, (iv) are duplicate records, (v) are labeled as of poor or suspect data quality, (vi) are below and above the detection limits for every parameter, (vii) have fill values, (viii) are detected as outliers and faulty study parameter measurements or (ix) belong to not-studied parameters. Additionally, it is important to mention that shape of a waterbody, along with its size, is an important factor to consider when accounting for a detailed selection. Narrower waterbodies tend to have a higher adjacency effect due to the reflection of light off the edges of the lake and into the water column. Small waterbodies such as rivers and canals are particularly affected, while larger, more open waterbodies may have a lower adjacency effect.

In its cleaned form the dataset contained almost 7000 total samples. An overview of the number of observations and lakes per region in the cleaned dataset and their respective number of samples per parameter are shown in Tables 3 and 4, respectively. Descriptive statistics of the parameters are provided in Table 5.

Table 3. Overview of the number of observations and lakes per region in the cleaned dataset.

Region	n	Lakes
United States	2032	33
Europe	1540	54
Mexico	2875	32
Canada	16	2
Japan	202	3
Chile	206	14
Russia	13	1

Table 4. Number of cleaned samples per parameter. Type column refers to optically active constituents (OAC) and non-optically active constituents (nOAC).

Parameter	n	Type
Chlorophyll-a (Chl-a: mg/L)	1080	OAC
Turbidity (TURB: NTU)	554	OAC
Total suspended matter (TSM (mg/L)	291	OAC
Secchi disk depth (SDD: m)	694	OAC
Dissolved oxygen (DO: mg/L)	1872	nOAC
Total phosphorus (P_{TOT}: mg/L)	987	nOAC
Nitrate (NO3-N: mg/L)	711	nOAC
Biochemical oxygen demand (BOD: mg/L)	214	nOAC
Chemical oxygen demand (COD: mg/L)	481	nOAC

Table 5. Descriptive statistics of our study parameters. Abbreviations as follows: (St.Dev: Standard Deviation, Perc.: Percentage).

Parameter	Chl-a	TURB	TSM	SDD	DO	P_{TOT}	NO3-N	BOD	COD
Count	1080	711	1872	987	694	291	554	214	481
Mean	26.87	2.89	8.80	0.20	2.73	40.65	24.48	11.25	30.39
St. Dev.	52.53	23.98	2.24	0.39	3.31	54.71	55.11	12.65	27.98
Min	0.00	0.00	1.30	0.00	0.00	1.00	0.10	0.50	2.10
25% Perc.	1.90	0.04	7.60	0.03	0.67	12.00	2.30	3.42	13.00
Median	6.80	0.18	8.90	0.07	1.20	20.00	5.30	5.99	22.00
75% Perc.	22.90	1.41	10.00	0.18	3.20	43.72	18.00	17.00	39.00
Max	561.07	443.00	27.00	5.73	18.00	520.00	578.70	94.00	270.00

2.3. Harmonization of Landsat-8 and Sentinel-2 Data

To increment data availability, harmonization of data from different remote sensors was applied as a feasible solution to increase availability of remote sensing data and, therefore, to increase the possibilities to match up with available water quality measurements. Harmonization is a novel approach, and its implementation has been in development for general applications such as land or crop modeling. Recently, harmonization of Landsat-8 and Sentinel-2 data has been applied for water quality retrievals with promising results [14,33]. However, this process is still challenging and requires several stages of image processing [42], especially when it is intended to be used at a global scale and using entire collections of remote sensors, as in this study. For the purposes of this study, there is the need of an implementation in a cloud platform capable of processing the complete imagery of both Landsat-8 and Sentinel-2. Additionally, atmospheric correction applicable to all images is also necessary to retrieve remote sensing reflectance (Rrs). Google Earth Engine (GEE) is a cloud platform that provides excellent access to complete archives of both Landsat and Sentinel data and allows operations and corrections over the entire imagery. Currently, there are studies that describe and apply this methodology for different cases and study purposes. Particularly, we use the methodology described in [34], which is based on the original methodology by [10]. Following the above-mentioned methodology, the collections of Landsat-8 (L8) top-of-atmosphere (TOA) and Sentinel-2 (S2) Level-1C (L1C) were acquired via Google Earth Engine (GEE) for the studied lakes and dates of measurement. Images were then atmospherically corrected using the Second Simulation of the Satellite Signal in the Solar Spectrum (6S) developed by [43], which uses Radiative Transfer Models (RTMs) to simulate the passage of solar radiation across the atmosphere. The 6S algorithm was adapted to a Python (Py6S) interface [44] and implemented recently for its use with Google Earth Engine [45] via a Python API and Docker container. For cloud detection in L8 images, we applied the CFMask algorithm on GEE based on the implementation of [34]. Cloud detection in S2 images was performed with single-scene pixel-based cloud detector method developed by [46], in which cloud detection is expressed as a machine learning problem that can outperform current threshold-based cloud detection algorithms such as Fmask or Sen2Cor. This detector is already available as the s2cloudless Python package and as a tool of the sentinelhub-py library. Cloud shadow detection was conducted via the Temporal Dark Outlier Mask (TDOM) [34], which is a version adapted from [47]. TDOM applies dark pixel anomaly [48] to predict the position and the extent of a cloud's shadows by using the cloud's shape, height and position of the sun at that time [49]. Co-registration was performed by measuring the misalignment between L8 and S2 images (up to 38 m) [42] and aligning the L8 with its corresponding S2 [50]. Afterwards, reprojection was applied to account for possible differences in band scale and projection [51]. L8 bands from B2 through B7 were reprojected with respect to the red band of S2 (WGS84), and each band's resolution was re-scaled to 30 m using bicubic interpolation [52,53]. The Bidirectional Reflectance Distribution Functions (BRDF) model developed by [47] was applied to reduce the directional effects due to the differences in solar and view angles between L8 and S2 [10]. This correction is based on fixed c-factors provided by [54], where the view angle is set to nadir and the illumination is set based on the center latitude of the tile [10]. The implementation of BRDF correction in GEE is based on results from different studies [54,55]. Topographic correction, which accounts for variations in reflectance due to slope, aspect and elevation, was implemented using the SRTM V3 (30 m SRTM Plus) and GTOPO30 (Global 30 ArcSecond Elevation) products to cover all Earth regions [56]. Adjustment in L8 bands was performed using cross-sensor transformation coefficients from [57] to solve spectral differences with S2 due to independent radiometric and geometric calibration processes. In [57], the absolute difference metrics and major axis linear regression analysis over 10,000 image pairs across the conterminous United States was used to obtain these transformation coefficients. The above process retrieves harmonized Landsat-8 and Sentinel-2 (HLS) images which have corrected surface reflectance with equal spectral and spatial characteristics. A detailed overview of the harmonization process is shown in Figure 2. Pixel extraction of the remote sensing reflectance (Rrs) was performed from the described location (latitude and longitude) of the field stations. We selected the main six bands from the visible, infrared and shortwave infrared, which are relevant for remote sensing of inland waters to reduce processing time.

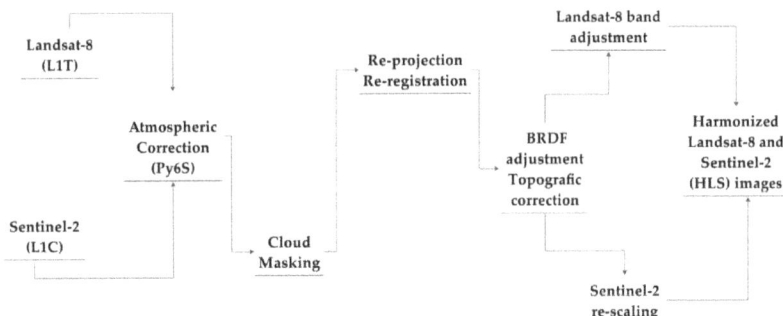

Figure 2. Overview of the HLS processing.

2.4. Feature Engineering and Dataset Arrangement

Additional features were derived from the HLS dataset in search of stronger correlations. Similarly, the effect of adding additional features on the model performance was also evaluated. To this end, different types of datasets were tested. Each dataset contained different engineered features and inherent characteristics of each lake. The main differences were based on the usage of common band ratios applied to remote sensing bands [58–64] and additional non-radiometric features such as time and location characteristics (latitude, longitude, month and year). Data were scaled to account for better performances in the modeling process. Additional feature specifications are shown in Table 6. Four different datasets were evaluated: (i) the harmonized bands (HB) dataset contained purely the HLS bands; (ii) the feature engineering (FE) dataset contained the HLS bands plus the additional band ratios; (iii) the harmonized bands plus region and time (HBRT) dataset which contained the harmonized bands dataset in addition to time and space features, and (iv) the feature engineering plus region and time (FERT) dataset which contained the feature engineering data plus region and time. A summary of each dataset description is provided in Table 7.

Table 6. List of additional features derived from the HLS dataset and lake inherent characteristics.

Feature	Formula	Naming
Ratio of red and green plus near infrared	Red/Green + NIR	SF1
Average of green plus red	(Green + Red)/2	SF2
Ration of green and red	Green/Red	SF3
Ratio of red and green	Red/Green	SF4
Radio of near infrared and green	NIR/Green	SF5
Latitude	-	Lat
Longitude	-	Lon
Month	-	Month
Year	-	Year

Table 7. Summary of the studied datasets.

Dataset	Features	Description
HB (harmonized bands)	HLS bands	Original harmonized Landsat–Sentinel bands
FE (feature engineering)	H-bands, red/green + NIR, (green + red)/2, green/red, red/green, NIR/green	HLS bands and the radiometric band ratios
HBRT (HLS bands and region and time)	HB, latitude, longitude, year and month	HB dataset, region and time
FERT (engineering and region and time)	FE, latitude, longitude, year and month	FE dataset, region and time

2.5. Machine Learning Algorithms

Machine Learning algorithms are data-driven methods, and, therefore, they require enough in situ water quality observations that contribute to the "learning" of the model. In this process, the models establish a relationship between water leaving radiance acquired remotely [65] and the in situ observations [33]. Hence, there is an inherent empirical relationship established between target parameters and predicting features. The learning characteristic of machine learning algorithms is further evaluated in this study by considering additional predicting features that, such as the water leaving reflectance of a specific measuring point, are also intrinsic to each waterbody. This could help to improve retrievals from purely remote sensing features, which often suffer from high correlation and collinearity between them [6]. Recently applied regression models in research of remote sensing of inland waters were used as modeling approaches. Supervised learning algorithms considered were the linear regression (LR) [66–69], support vector regression (SVR) [70–74] and random forest (RF) [22,75–77]. Additionally, we employed deep learning algorithms, which have been less commonly applied in the field, from which we focused on the extreme learning machine (ELM) [13,31,78] and the multilayer perceptron regressor (MLP) [14,79–81].

For every target parameter, each of the above models and hyperparameter optimization with common values in GridSearch was trained and tested. Intensive hyperparameter tuning was not mainly addressed, since the primary goal was to evaluate differences in datasets for machine learning models in similar conditions. The settings of the LR model consider an intercept. Hyperparameters for SVR used a radial basis function (rbf) kernel, regularization parameter of $C = 1.0$ and epsilon = 0.1. We employed RFR with squared error criterion as a function to measure the quality of a split. Different activation functions were tested for ELM depending on the training data (sig, sin, radbas, hardlim, purelin and tansig), with common occurrences of sigmoidal function and hidden nodes ranging from 50–1000 for different parameters. MLP was used having five hidden layers with the ADAM activation function and a learning rate of 0.01, and Bayesian regularized backpropagation was utilized to train the model. The modeling approach was conducted using SciKit Learn (v1.0.2) in Python (v.3.10,3) and the Caret package (v2019.03.27) in R (41.3). Google CoLab was used as the cloud computing platform to perform all calculations.

2.6. Model Evaluation

Cross-validation with k = 5 folds was selected as our main method of model evaluation. The train/test split ratio was 80% training and 20% testing. Random selection of samples in each iteration was performed to ensure representative selection of data in the training and testing stages. The presence of multicollinearity in the predictors was addressed by an initial feature selection with mutual info regression as the scoring function and a second-degree polynomial feature to account for the non-linearity in the data. To ascertain model performance, we used the following quantitative error metrics: the mean absolute error (i), mean squared error (ii), root mean squared error (iii) and R^2 (iv). Additionally, we considered the number of features (v) used as a metric for overall comparison among the models. It was considered that the model with the need for fewer predictors has an advantage in terms of required computing power. The error metrics were calculated for both the training and independent testing dataset. Respectively, each performance metric is defined as

$$R^2(y, \hat{y}) = 1 - \frac{\sum_{i=0}^{n_{samples}-1} (y_i - \hat{y}_i)^2}{\sum_{i=0}^{n_{samples}-1} (y_i - \bar{y}_i)^2} \tag{1}$$

$$RMSE(y, \hat{y}) = \sqrt{\frac{1}{n_{samples}} \sum_{i=0}^{n_{samples}-1} (y_i - \hat{y}_i)^2} \tag{2}$$

$$RMSE(y, \hat{y}) = \frac{1}{n_{samples}} \sum_{i=0}^{n_{samples}-1} (y_i - \hat{y}_i)^2 \tag{3}$$

$$MAE(y, \hat{y}) = 1 - \frac{\sum_{i=0}^{n_{samples}-1} (y_i - \hat{y}_i)^2}{n} \tag{4}$$

where $\hat{y}_i$ is the estimated value, y_i is the observed value and $n_{samples}$ is the number of samples.

3. Results

3.1. Correlation of Water Parameters and Derived Predictors

The correlation between target parameters and predicting features was investigated by the Pearson's coefficient. The range of the coefficient for all features is shown in Figure 3. The bigger thickness in the arrow indicates a higher correlation with specific predictors. Individual plots of nodes and arrows and their correlation matrix are provided in the Supplementary Materials. Overall, the highest positive and negative correlations are in the order of $r \approx 0.50$ and $r \approx -0.48$. The green band is moderately correlated ($\bar{r} \approx 0.38$) with turbidity, SDD, BOD and COD. The red band has a slightly higher correlation ($\bar{r} \approx 0.42$) with TURB, SDD and COD. The NIR band presented the highest correlations on average ($r \approx 0.43$) with TURB, TSM, BOD and COD. The SWIR bands displayed very weak correlations ($0.17 \leq r \leq -0.07$).

From the band ratios, the SF1 and SF2 had a considerable correlation with the targets. SF1 displayed ($\bar{r} \approx 0.39$) with TURB, SDD, BOD and COD. SF4 and SF5 were poorly correlated ($0.20 \leq r \leq -0.20$) with all the parameters, except for an $r = -0.30$ and $r = 0.27$ for TURB. From the SF predictors, SF2 and SF3 showed a higher correlation ($\bar{r} \approx 0.39$ and $\bar{r} \approx 0.36$) with TURB, SDD, BOD and COD. Latitude and longitude were also moderately correlated with SDD, PTOT, BOD and COD, especially latitude ($\bar{r} \approx 0.37$). Year and month were poorly correlated with all analyzed predictors ($0.20 \leq r \leq -0.20$). Overall, the most correlated features were the ones of the visible and near-infrared regions, which showed higher correlation in comparison with the spectral features and the region and time features. Green, red and near-infrared bands showed higher correlations with TURB, SDD and BOD and COD. Short-wave infrared bands 1 and 2 almost completely lacked any significant correlation. Individual correlations are displayed in the supplementary figures (SF1). The NIR band and SDD parameters show the highest correlations for a predictive feature and a target parameter. Similarly, NO3-N and DO show the lower correlations for a feature and target, correspondingly.

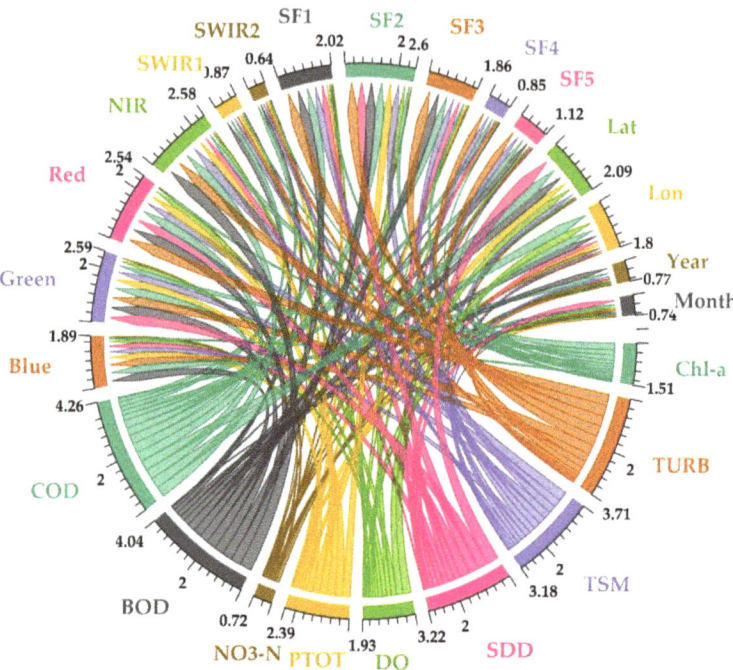

Figure 3. Sum and individual correlations of the water quality parameters with predicting features. The total of each node represents the sum of absolute value of positive and negative correlations between all the parameters with all predictors.

3.2. Model and Dataset Evaluation

Training and test phases were evaluated using the four available datasets (HB, FE, HBRT and FERT) for each algorithm (LR, SVR, RFR, ELM and MLP). The best dataset for each model is then shown in the table alongside the error metrics of better performance. This evaluation was performed for every target parameter. The entire modeling results are summarized in Table 8. In general, LR retrieved low-performance models ($\overline{R^2}$ = 0.33). It performed better on SDD and COD. However, lower performances were shown for TSS and TURB. SVR performed better than LR in most of the parameters, both for the nOACs and OACs, except for COD and Chl-a. Regarding NO3-N, most of the models performed poorly, with only SVR attaining reasonable results by retrieving R^2 = 0.42 using the HBRT dataset. In the beginning of the calibration process, RFR tended to overfit the data, even with a relatively low number of estimators in each random forest (n_estimators = 5000). This was addressed by tuning the maximum depth of each tree and the minimum number of samples required for a split.

Table 8. Summary of the best performing dataset for all models and all parameters in train and test stages. Acronyms and units are as follows: chlorophyll-a (Chl-a: mg/L); turbidity (TURB: NTU); total suspended matter (TSM: mg/L); Secchi disk depth (SDD: m); dissolved oxygen (DO: mg/L); total phosphorus (P_{TOT}: mg/L); nitrate (NO3-N: mg/L); biochemical oxygen demand (BOD: mg/L); chemical oxygen demand (COD: mg/L).

			TRAIN					TEST				
	Model	Dataset	R^2	RMSE	MSE	MAE	# Feat	Dataset	R^2	RMSE	MSE	MAE	# Feat
Chl-a													
	LR	HBRT	0.48	38.42	1475.96	20.58	9	HB	0.43	42.25	1784.68	23.34	6
	SVR	FERT	0.63	33.66	1132.83	13.87	15	FERT	0.42	38.76	1502.37	19.74	15
	RFR	FERT	0.81	23.92	572.21	9.60	10	HBRT	0.53	35.11	1232.70	16.18	9
	ELM	FERT	0.53	36.20	1310.31	19.08	15	FERT	0.53	33.61	1129.74	21.77	15
	MLP	FERT	0.62	60.43	3652.16	25.86	15	FERT	0.37	27.53	758.13	13.53	15
TURB													
	LR	HBRT	0.70	27.53	757.80	13.29	9	HBRT	0.32	45.40	2060.82	21.37	9
	SVR	FERT	0.97	9.21	84.77	1.60	15	FERT	0.41	52.32	2737.40	19.22	15
	RFR	HBRT	0.82	22.01	484.41	7.59	9	HBRT	0.47	50.05	2504.73	16.50	9
	ELM	HBRT	0.43	44.33	1964.97	20.43	10	FERT	0.65	26.97	727.41	16.06	15
	MLP	HBRT	0.60	30.11	906.71	13.46	15	HBRT	0.61	40.44	1635.66	17.40	10
TSM													
	LR	HB	0.51	32.96	1086.33	22.13	6	HB	0.22	40.58	1646.95	26.72	6
	SVR	FERT	0.89	16.02	256.70	4.07	15	HBRT	0.28	54.79	3001.95	25.55	10
	RFR	FERT	0.79	24.18	584.45	15.11	4	HBRT	0.30	52.04	2708.02	28.09	4
	ELM	FERT	0.30	48.57	2358.74	28.39	15	FE	0.43	40.23	1618.31	25.52	11
	MLP	HB	0.28	36.27	1315.51	22.28	6	HB	0.30	48.39	2341.57	26.06	6
SDD													
	LR	HBRT	0.70	1.81	3.28	1.18	9	FERT	0.56	2.26	5.10	1.42	12
	SVR	FERT	0.82	1.39	1.92	0.49	15	HBRT	0.69	2.03	4.14	1.10	7
	RFR	FERT	0.88	1.18	1.40	0.58	14	HBRT	0.72	1.93	3.73	1.02	6
	ELM	FERT	0.70	1.84	3.39	1.20	15	FERT	0.72	1.69	2.84	1.17	15
	MLP	FERT	0.80	2.62	6.87	1.54	15	FERT	0.58	1.65	2.73	0.94	15
DO													
	LR	HBRT	0.40	1.69	2.84	1.17	8	HBRT	0.37	1.75	3.07	1.25	8
	SVR	HBRT	0.44	1.64	2.68	1.06	6	HBRT	0.39	1.76	3.08	1.19	6
	RFR	HBRT	0.83	0.94	0.88	0.58	4	HBRT	0.56	1.55	2.39	0.99	4
	ELM	FERT	0.40	1.72	2.96	1.24	15	FERT	0.32	1.78	3.18	1.32	15
	MLP	HBRT	0.53	1.88	3.53	1.33	10	FERT	0.37	1.69	2.86	1.19	10
P_{TOT}													
	LR	HBRT	0.52	0.25	0.06	0.14	9	HB	0.22	0.43	0.18	0.17	6
	SVR	HBRT	0.79	0.17	0.03	0.05	9	HBRT	0.47	0.26	0.07	0.11	9
	RFR	FERT	0.84	0.15	0.02	0.05	14	FERT	0.56	0.24	0.06	0.09	14
	ELM	FERT	0.57	0.22	0.05	0.13	15	FE	0.41	0.27	0.07	0.16	11
	MLP	FERT	0.58	0.31	0.09	0.14	15	FERT	0.40	0.25	0.06	0.10	15
NO3-N													
	LR	HBRT	0.30	4.66	21.71	0.30	2	FERT	0.03	37.25	1387.90	6.07	1
	SVR	HBRT	0.82	2.48	6.17	0.94	9	FERT	0.42	26.32	692.88	2.96	14
	RFR	HBRT	0.78	2.64	6.98	0.77	2	FERT	-1.52	26.86	721.55	3.19	1
	ELM	FERT	0.42	14.57	212.43	6.58	15	HBRT	0.43	31.31	980.11	6.96	15
	MLP	FE	0.05	4.94	24.40	2.61	11	FE	0.21	25.99	675.47	3.93	11
BOD													
	LR	HB	0.56	7.33	53.80	4.96	5	HB	0.32	10.08	101.54	6.00	5
	SVR	HBRT	0.71	6.01	36.15	2.58	9	FERT	0.41	10.55	111.33	5.68	14
	RFR	HBRT	0.87	4.21	17.72	2.17	7	HBRT	0.56	9.44	89.12	4.74	7
	ELM	FERT	0.42	9.95	98.96	6.16	15	FERT	0.65	7.41	54.96	5.12	15
	MLP	HB	0.57	9.67	93.51	7.09	6	HBRT	0.39	9.19	84.44	5.33	10
COD													
	LR	HBRT	0.52	19.21	368.94	12.45	8	HBRT	0.48	21.11	445.72	13.34	8
	SVR	FERT	0.64	17.86	319.10	8.47	15	HBRT	0.40	20.21	408.63	12.20	6
	RFR	FERT	0.83	11.75	138.15	6.07	8	HBRT	0.54	17.94	321.67	10.56	8
	ELM	FERT	0.38	22.15	490.49	13.92	15	FERT	0.57	16.83	283.16	11.95	15
	MLP	HBRT	0.39	31.23	975.36	15.72	10	HBRT	0.21	20.09	403.41	13.39	10

From this routine, RFR improved greatly and retrieved most of the parameters in acceptable values mostly by using the best on HBRT, and except for NO3-N, RFR performed satisfactorily for DO ($R^2 = 0.56$) and PTOT ($R^2 = 0.56$). Regarding the development of the deep learning models, it was expected to establish a baseline routine of calibrated models with LR and improve it based on the SVR and RFR training methodologies to finally surpass ensemble learning models with neural networks such as ELM and MLP. Overall, ELM performed satisfactorily in most of the analyzed parameters. Specifically, ELM outperformed all algorithms when retrieving Chl-a ($R^2 = 0.53$), TURB ($R^2 = 0.65$), TSM ($R^2 = 0.43$), SDD ($R^2 = 0.72$), BOD ($R^2 = 0.65$) and COD ($R^2 = 0.57$). However, the results we obtained from the MLP were subpar in comparison with ELM or RFR. MLP was trained with relatively high learning rates (1×10^{-2} to 1×10^{-5}), and tests of up to 10 deep layers were used together with the Adam optimizer. Weights were initialized with random normal, as it retrieved better results than Xavier initialization. Except for TURB, MLP results generally have less accuracy than ELM and RFR.

At this point, the main metrics for model performance were R^2, RMSE, MSE, MAE and the number of features utilized to reach optimal error performance in the test phase (# Feat). We compared these metrics in a comprehensive evaluation to determine the best model for each parameter. The five algorithms (LR, SVR, RFR, ELM and MLP) were trained using the best dataset determined in Table 8 to calibrate each model in its best conditions. The results of this evaluation are displayed in radial graphs in Figure 4.

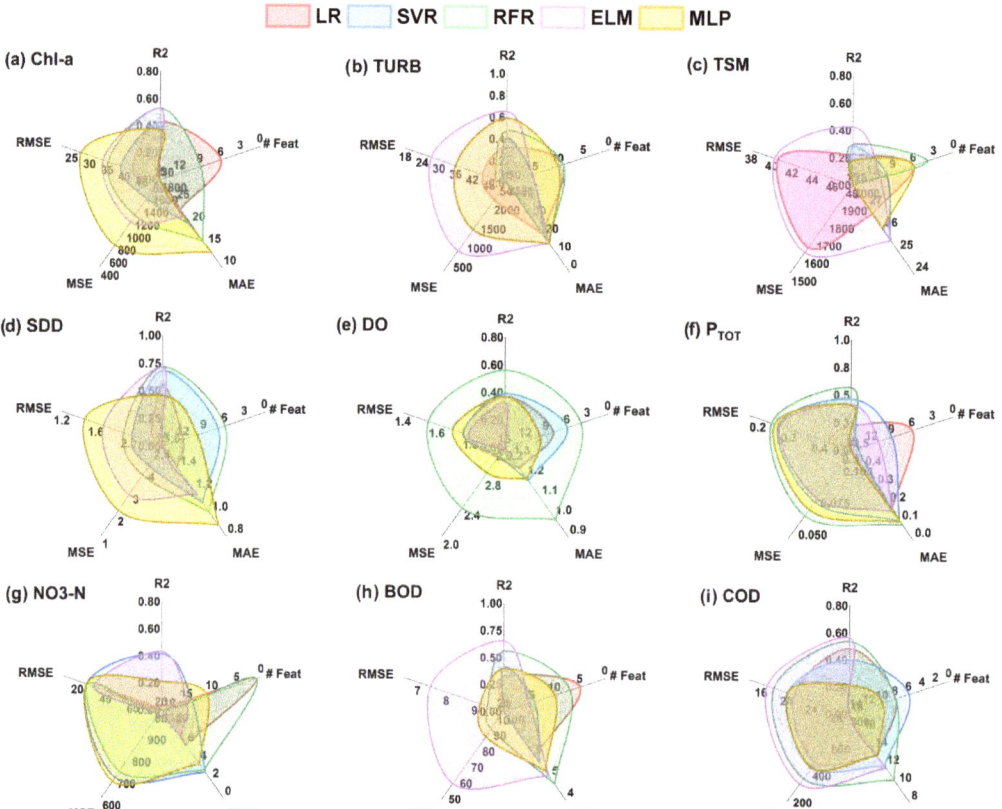

Figure 4. Comprehensive evaluation of tested algorithms based on the relevant error metrics for optimal performance. The algorithms use the best source dataset in all cases.

In general, ELM and RFR resulted in the best models, which outperformed the rest of the machine learning techniques for most of the water parameters (Chl-a, TURB, TSM, SDD, PTOT, BOD and COD) from a comprehensive perspective. SVR performed better for the challenging NO3-N. Scatter plots of target parameters using the models calibrated with the best corresponding dataset are shown in Figure 5 for both train and test datasets. From the scatterplots it is visible that TSM, NO3-N and to a lesser degree TSM were the most challenging parameters to model and that SDD was able to be modeled with high accuracy by the ELM ($R^2 = 0.72$), as seen in the performance in terms of error metrics in Table 8.

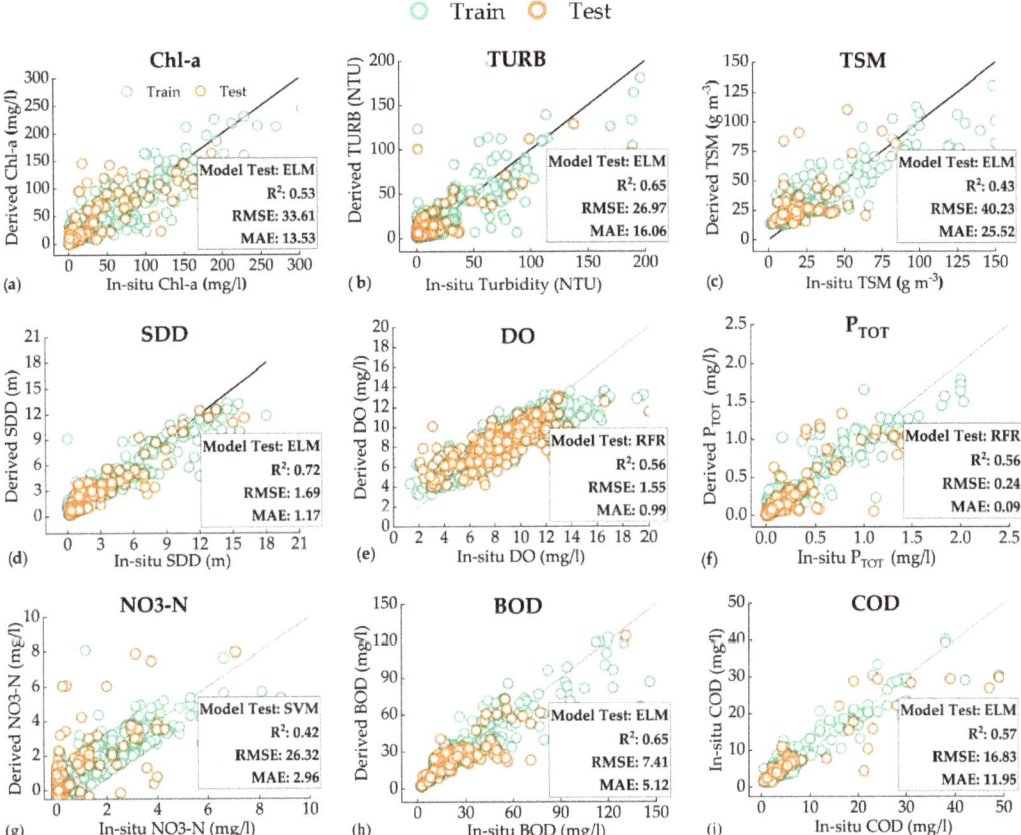

Figure 5. Scatterplots of modeled and measured water quality parameters in the test dataset.

The results also showed that the big majority of the models for all the water parameters performed better when using any of the two datasets aware of region and time (HBRT and FERT). Therefore, a deeper analysis was performed in this direction by comparing the R^2 of each dataset and the performance of each model when trained with different datasets. Figure 6 shows the average R^2 for the complete modeling process, which includes not only the best results summarized in Table 8 but the rest of the models as well. Figure 6a stresses how the performances of both HBRT and FERT are superior to HB and FE for train and test evaluations. Similarly, Figure 6b shows the performance of the algorithms when using different datasets. When trained with HBRT or FERT datasets (Figure 6a, red lines; Figure 6b increased tendency from left to right), all the algorithms reached higher correlations than when trained with HB or FE (Figure 6a, blue lines; Figure 6b decreasing tendency from right to left).

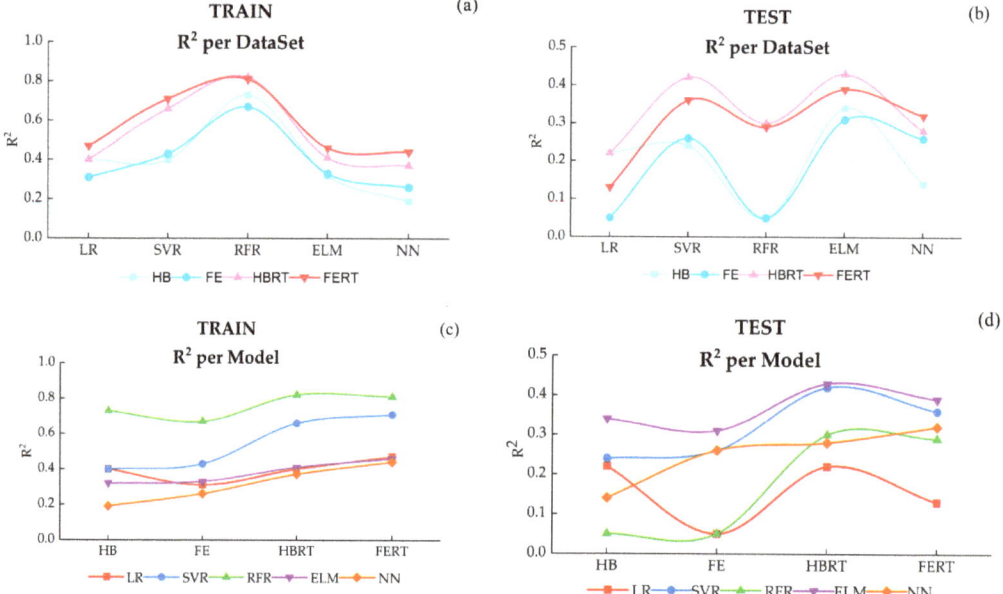

Figure 6. Train and test average R^2 for each algorithm and dataset. In (**a**,**b**) improvement is noticeable when using datasets that have the RT features which are colored in red for both train and test phases. Similarly, the increase in the performance is seen on all the models when using an HBRT or FERT dataset, (**c**,**d**).

3.3. Model Capabilities

To stage model capabilities, we applied the methodology using harmonized products for the period March 2021–March 2022 to estimate time series of specific parameters (Chl-a, DO and SDD) and to model their variations throughout a year. The points marked in the evolution of the targets were used as a suitable date and to map spatial distribution. We selected different lakes around the world to test the transferability of the models. Specifically, Lake Tahoe (U.S.), Lake Trasimeno (Italy) and Lake Vichuquen (Chile) were selected for Chl-a, DO and SDD, respectively, based on field data availability. Time series and parameter maps are shown in Figure 7. Chl-a in Lake Tahoe shows concentrations between 5–10 mg/L for most of the year, but after a breaking point in December 2021, where the concentration reached its highest level above 20 mg/L, it gradually decreased and kept a range between (10–15 mg/L). DO shows low variability during the year, and it is in a range of 8.8–9.5 mg/L in Lake Vichuquen.

The lowest concentration is reached by the end of November 2021, from which it starts a recovery to higher concentrations above 9 mg/L. March, April and mid-May seem to be the months of higher availability of DO in the area. The spatial resolution of 30 m from the harmonized products allows adequate visualization of the distribution of DO even in a relatively small lake as Vichuquen (40 km^2). From the map, it is visible that DO availability is higher in the outlet and inlets, located at north and south, respectively, likely caused by the turbulence and stirring of the incoming and leaving water flows. SDD in Lake Trasimeno ranges on average from 1 to 4 m during the year. The lowest transparency is seen after August 2021 ($\approx$1 m) and remains in this range until its recovery in January 2022 of 2.5 m. The breaking point in August is selected as the date of interest for a spatial visualization (31 August 2021). The surface distribution of SDD reveals a big cluster of lower transparency in the northwest part of the lake. The south part, which is an open bay, remains clearer.

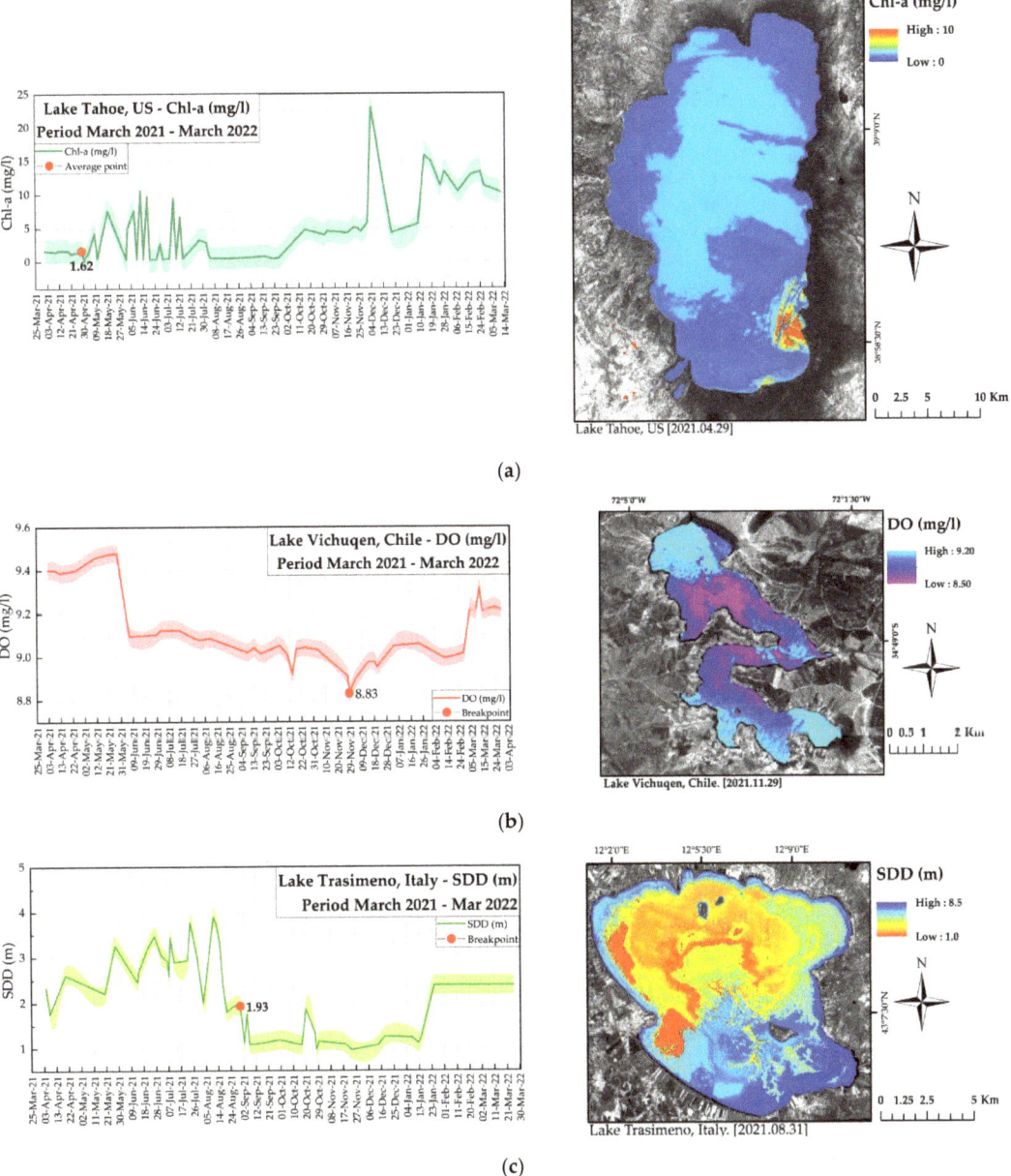

Figure 7. Time series and spatial distribution of (**a**) Chl-a in Lake Tahoe (U.S., 29 November 2021), (**b**) DO in Lake Vichuquen (Chile, 29 November 2021) and (**c**) SDD for Lake Trasimeno (Italy, 31 August 2021). Background image: harmonized red band in greyscale. The plots show the average of the parameter for the whole lake. Spatial variation is visible in the maps.

3.4. Correlation between OAC and nOAC

For the specific case of nOACs (DO, NO3-N, PTOT, BOD and COD), their estimation resulted in a challenging approach, as seen in the results of Table 8 and Figures 4 and 5. For NO3-N only SVR was able to produce reasonable results ($R^2 = 0.42$). To further evaluate the possibility of estimating nOAC using indirect means, a correlation analysis between OAC and nOAC was performed and is displayed in Figure 8. Similar to Figure 3, each node of the Chor diagram shows the sum of absolute values of Pearson's correlation. Separate individual nodes are available in the Supplementary Materials. From the results, no significant correlations between OAC and nOAC were retrieved, as seen in the total absolute value of the nodes in Figure 8, which barely overpass $\bar{r} \approx 0.20$ for TSM (Figure 8a), BOD (Figure 8b) and SDD (Figure 8c). These results stress the difficulty of estimating nOAC from indirect methods which could rely on relevant correlations with OAC that can be computed via remote sensing.

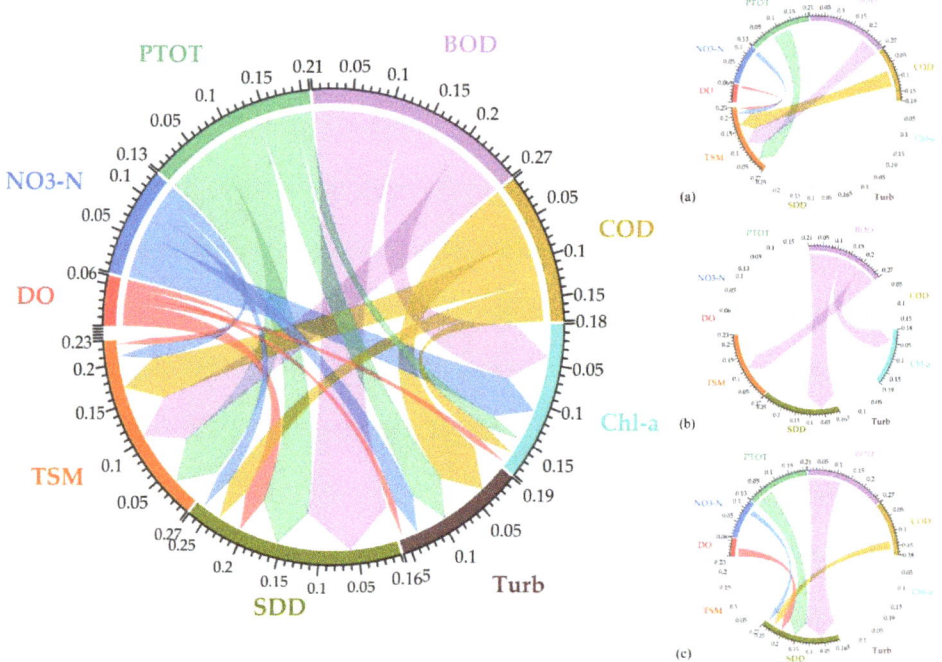

Figure 8. Sum and individual correlations of the OAC with nOAC. Diagrams of (**a**), (**b**) and (**c**) TSM, BOD and SDD, respectively.

4. Discussion

4.1. Global Water Quality Data Availability

The availability of water quality data at a global scale that can be used in synergy with remote sensing data is still very limited. In this study, the raw gathered data were filtered substantially and went from initial 300,000 measurements of all the parameters around the globe to a final dataset of around 7000 samples after data selection. This is still an important amount of data in comparison with the available data in previous years or other studies of water quality in inland waters [12,31,75,82,83]. Regarding the sampling sites and depths in the considered waterbodies, this study considered the location of the sites during the cleaning phase of the data and rejected samples that were adjacent to the shore to avoid the adjacency error. This is a similar approach to a previous study that successfully utilized a wide range of sampling sites in [31]. Although this work focused on the water column and avoided shallow regions close to the coast and bottom of the reservoir, rejection of lakes or reservoirs based on average depth was not performed. Here, it is acknowledged that a more targeted approach to sampling could improve the quality of the results and suggested that future studies consider the location and depth of the sampling sites to minimize potential errors.

However, it cannot be denied that the water availability at a global level is limited by several factors that can be improved based on the inter-cooperation of different instances and technical issues. For example, measuring stations at the global level are limited to certain areas around the world. In this work, we notice a lack of water information for large parts of the planet, particularly in South America, Africa and Asia. As exposed in Section 2, the study of Thorslund and van Vliet [35] indicates that most of the measuring water stations for lakes and reservoirs were located in North America (with big differences) and Europe. This exposes how a very important number of inland waters are not being monitored. Additionally, the integration of global data is constrained by the fact that every nation is responsible for the technical requirements of water monitoring and making data public. Therefore, it is likely that already monitored data from several regions in the world are not yet available to a greater extent due to limitations in this direction, and therefore their usage may be missed for global applications. In worse cases, gathering global data could even be limited by trifling facts as ignorance of foreign languages. Thus, international cooperation is then needed to apply team-work to data availability. In this sense, initiatives such as the Global Freshwater Quality Database (GEMStat) from the UN Environmental Program [1] offer an adequate framework for the previously mentioned challenges.

4.2. Harmonized Remote Sensing Data for Water Quality Estimation

In addition to field data availability, remote sensing also has important limitations in modeling full potential water quality at the global scale. For instance, temporal resolution limits the coupling of spectral and field data. In this study, we addressed this limitation up to a certain degree by harmonizing Landsat-8 and Sentinel-2 data, which increased data availability. This allowed the use of coupled satellite data in a singular dataset, which was one the main objectives of this study.

However, the current harmonization process is not specifically designed for inland waters. Similarly, the atmospheric correction used in [34], the Second Simulation of the Satellite Signal in the Solar Spectrum (6S), is also not designed for waterbodies, as it occurs with other corrections designed for inland waters such as C2RCC. Therefore, the results based on this methodology should be taken with caution, since discrepancies from a harmonization process and an atmospheric correction for different applications than water quality retrievals are likely to exist. The main reason this study applied these methodologies was the existing implementation in the cloud platform used for image processing. There is no current harmonization process or atmospheric correction developed for cloud computing in GEE that is designed to enhance the spectral characteristics of water surfaces, and working with the entire collection of Landsat and Sentinel satellites was not feasible using local computational resources. Developing both a harmonization procedure and an atmospheric correction for the cloud platform was out of the objectives of this research. However, the harmonization procedure is still in development, and it is likely to account for water surface characteristics in the future [84]. Likewise, the 6S atmospheric correction is a common procedure in remote sensing and it has already been implemented in mapping and water quality monitoring [85]. Adopting the above-described methodology allowed the building of a global dataset for model development and contributed to understanding to what extent machine learning can benefit from increased data availability.

Nevertheless, non-coupled satellite acquisitions and dates of water measurements were two of the main filters that avoided the usage of a great portion of the gathered data. The spatial resolution also constrains availability when the resolution is not enough to retrieve enough pixels from very small reservoirs. The pixel size of harmonized data is

30 × 30 m, which allows consideration of a big number of lakes and reservoirs. However, it may not be the best resolution for inland waters below surfaces of 20 km² due to possible errors caused by bottom reflection and adjacency errors caused by land next to shores. Therefore, the revisit time of harmonized data (3 days), even when it may be considered adequate in the field, is probably not good enough to monitor changes in water parameters that could exhibit great variations even during one single day and to account for a great part of the available field data, as seen in this study. Therefore, the tendency to improve temporal and spatial resolutions is highly important, as some ground-based high-frequency sensors already demonstrate [86].

4.3. Machine Learning Models and Cloud Computing

ML models provide research in water quality the possibility to model and estimate different water parameters with a high degree of accuracy based on adequate data availability [21,87,88]. In addition, the variety and distinct nature of available ML algorithms for modeling purposes foster rigorous evaluation of the methodology and contribute to reaching stronger and more developed models [14,33]. In this study, we focused on the "learning" advantage of ML models and tried to provide as much data as possible by means of global measurements and remote sensing data fusion techniques, with the goal of reaching robust models that could retrieve water quality parameters accurately. As in previous research using ML approaches, we could develop models that predict water quality parameters with reasonable results. Furthermore, a key improvement in the direction of modeling at the global scale was achieved, which has been one of the main limitations of modeling water quality of inland waters [6,7] and that was only addressed before by bio-optical models with more complex approaches in terms of development [7,33,89]. The extent of the regionalization modeling is precisely the advantage that ML models offer when providing enough and high-quality data. In this study, we showed how the contribution of enough high-quality input data and adequate calibration of ML models could start pushing existing research barriers. In this sense, the potential for improvement of the ML models is still enormous, particularly with the progressive increment in data availability coming from more frequent field campaigns, better acquisition sensors and disclosure of non-public data. Therefore, modeling global water quality in inland waters should be considered as a continuous area of research and development with the goal to achieve models that improve continuously from constant monitoring. In addition to the above-mentioned limitations, challenges regarding computational power and storage space existed. The large number of models to be tested plus even small calibration techniques resulted in extensive computing periods which could not be covered by our locally available hardware resources. Therefore, a cloud computing platform (Google Colab) was required to address this problem and proceed with model evaluation. Cloud computing allows parallel computing while focusing cloud servers only for computational tasks. This methodology distributes more efficiently available resources and should be considered for similar tasks, especially when dealing with large datasets. Similarly, the usage of Google Earth Engine also allowed working efficiently with the vast quantity of remote sensing data products of the match ups with field measurements, and thanks to previous knowledge of state-of-the-art applications on the harmonizing process [10,14,34,47,54], these limitations were diminished.

The potential for global monitoring was already addressed by [90] with a synthetic dataset of top-of-atmosphere and bottom-of-atmosphere reflectances to comprise optical variability present in inland waters. Regarding field data measured on Earth, and to the extent of the authors' knowledge, this is the first attempt to model water quality on a global scale using remote sensing data based on machine learning algorithms. Therefore, the comparison of the models developed here is complicated because, until the submission of this paper, there are no similar studies that attempt similar modeling scales. However, based on the well-established validation methodology applied, the reasonable performance of the models and its adequate application in time series and water quality maps, we posit that our methodology is on the way to establishing a basis for future development in this research area. With the distances apart and for an exercise of comparison, the results here yielded were compared with novel publications that have successfully developed ML models for inland water quality. For example, error metrics of Chl-a ($R^2 = 0.53$), TURB ($R^2 = 0.65$) and DO $R^2 = 0.56$) from ELM and RFR are comparable with modeling results observed in [33] of Chl-a ($R^2 = 0.48$), TURB ($R^2 = 0.44$) and DO $R^2 = 0.21$. On the other hand, PTOT ($R^2 = 0.56$), NO3-N ($R^2 = 0.42$), BOD ($R^2 = 0.65$) and COD ($R^2 = 0.57$) are comparable with the results of Zhang et al. [88] regarding phosphorus ($R^2 = 0.94$), nitrogen ($R^2 = 0.95$), BOD ($R^2 = 0.91$) and COD ($R^2 = 0.95$), which were retrieved from hyperspectral images. Regarding the poor performance of the MLP, the strategy was to build neural nets deep and wide enough to first overfit the data and then reduce them. However, this operation could not be totally completed due to a lack of dedicated GPUs (even in the cloud server) and time constraints. Even in the best performing parameter (TURB), most of the MLP results were in the underfitting range, and train and test splits showed similar error metrics. These results may provide a clear picture of the behavior of a partially optimized MLP.

4.4. Estimation of OAC and nOAC

The estimation of OAC with remote sensing has been addressed extensively in research for least two decades [12,19,22,60,82,91–99]. Particularly, parameters such as SDD, turbidity or Chl-a and TSM have been studied with great detail, and their estimation has been the target of different modeling approaches, from empirical to semi-analytical models [26,83,95,100–110]. nOAC, however, represented a greater challenge because of its lack of response to absorption or scattering of the electromagnetic light [7].

A direct estimation of nOAC from RS data has been previously investigated. For example, [73] used SVM and SPOT5 data for potassium permanganate index (CODmn), ammonia nitrogen (NH3-N), chemical oxygen demand (COD) and dissolved oxygen (DO) in the Weihe River with better performance than the statistical regression. Recently, [111] used ML models for spatial distributions of the annual and monthly DO variability in Lake Huron from Landsat and MODIS data with consistent values of $R^2 = 0.88$. Similarly, [88] used a Bayesian probabilistic neural network to predict phosphorus, nitrogen, chemical oxygen demand (COD), biochemical oxygen demand (BOD) and chlorophyll-a from hyperspectral images in a river from multispectral images. We compared the average R^2 summary of the OAC (Chl-a, TURB, TSM and SDD) and nOAC (DO, PTOT, NO3-N, BOD and COD) to contrast how the results also show that in general nOAC presents more challenges than OAC (Figure 9). All the models achieved higher results in OAC, but at the same time nOAC results were reasonable and did not show an incapacity to model these parameters. This reinforces the fact that ML models are also suited to deal with parameters with non-linear relationships between remote sensing data or inherent lake characteristics, contributing to the improvement of modeling nOAC.

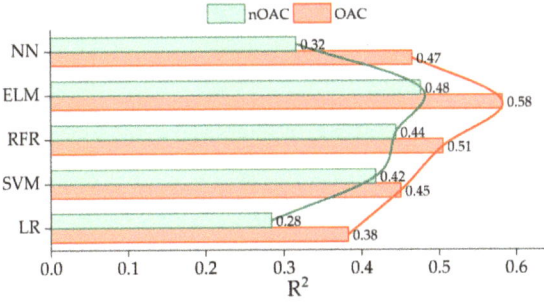

Figure 9. Average R^2 for all the models by the nature of the target parameters. OAC: Chl-a, TURB, TSM and SDD. nOAC: DO, PTOT, NO3-N, BOD and COD.

4.5. Inherent Lakes' Characteristics as Model Improvers

Typically, semi-empirical models in the field of remote sensing of inland waters do rely on the physics knowledge of the optics in the water and the response of water or water constituents to the interaction with the electromagnetic energy. One main objective of this study was to evaluate this conventional approach against more unconventional methodology that could rely more on the learning capability of the ML algorithms. On the basis that these algorithms work better with a higher number of observations and adequate predictors that explain better the behavior of the targets, we selected additional characteristics of each lake to evaluate possible improvements in comparison with purely radiometric remote sensing bands or band ratios already tested in the previous literature. The cautious evaluation of the impact on model performance is that the addition of these characteristics would have led to the creation of four different datasets: HB, FE, HBRT and FERT. Region and time were the selected characteristics added to the original datasets, the product of the remote sensing data. The correlation analysis revealed a moderate correlation with the water parameters for latitude and longitude and very weak correlations for year and month. Figure 10 stresses this situation.

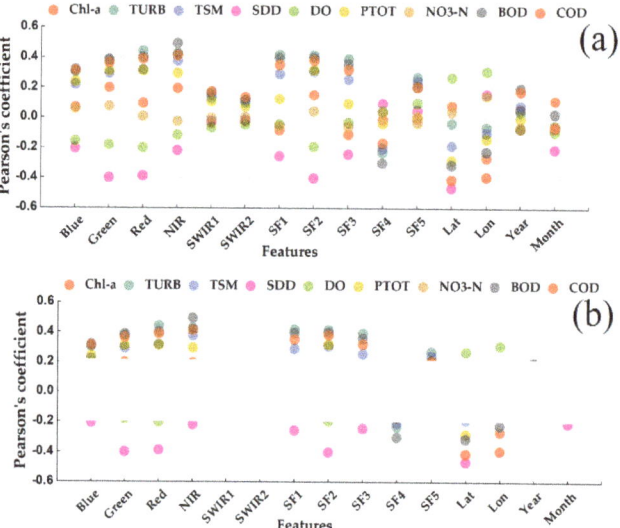

Figure 10. Individual correlation of each predictor with water quality parameters. Features are ranged from −1 to 1 depending on their higher positive or negative correlation. (**a**) displays correlations of predictors and targets. (**b**) fades the areas of very low or zero correlation ($-0.20 \leq r \leq 0.20$).

In Figure 10a it is seen how the visible bands and band ratios show a higher correlation. SWIR bands and year and month are in a very weak range, as displayed in Figure 10b, where the region $-0.20 \leq r \leq 0.20$ is covered to highlight stronger correlations. The occurrence that Lat and Lon are having a stronger correlation than year and month means, therefore, that a greater utility in model development could be due to the fact that year and month are not strictly inherent characteristics of a waterbody. Their inclusion was mainly because of the fact that the time and seasonality have important influences on the behavior of certain water quality, such as the blooming of algae or the arrival of storms that discharge waters with sediment, creating turbidity. Nevertheless, the improvement in error metrics of all the water parameters when ML models used HB and FERT datasets was evident and validated in our methodology (Figure 11). This leads us to the conclusion that this approach resulted in an effective improvement of the modeling of water quality parameters by the addition of inherent lake characteristics that can be useful for ML algorithms.

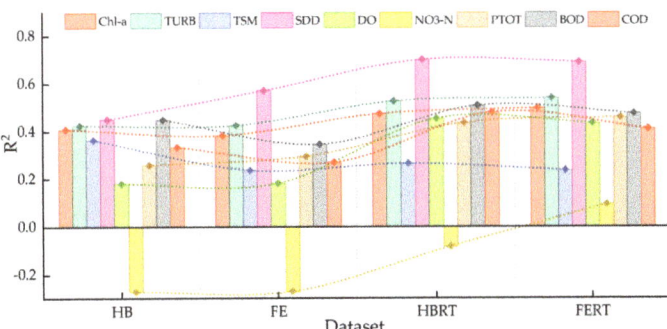

Figure 11. Improvement of temporally and spatially aware models.

Therefore, research in this direction is needed to keep the improvement of the modeling process and to develop more accurate models. There are several inherent characteristics that may be useful for such purposes and that can be found in constant patterns in time, such as trophic state and chemical, biological, physical, limnological or morphological features. Time features can be improved or added as labels for the season of the year, as seen in [111].

5. Conclusions

This work developed machine learning models for water quality retrieval at a global scale using remote homogenized multimodal remote sensing data. This contributed to overcoming the present state of knowledge in which the transferability of models is limited by the origin of field data, and modeling water quality in inland waters at different locations was constrained. These findings directly impact the increment of our ability to analyze lakes and reservoirs globally, particularly for several water parameters of different nature and characteristics, which are key in the overall understanding of water quality in lakes and reservoirs. This work is limited by the amount and origin of the field data gathered and the extent of the remote sensing archives processed. The application of the models developed here was demonstrated at the global scale in different lakes separated by continental distances. However, the usage of these models in regions from where there were no data in the calibration process is likely to be poorly accurate and would lack reliability in results. Therefore, the methodology should be improved by gathering data from more and different sources around the world, particularly from the African, Asian and South American continents. Remote sensing data can be increased by harmonizing data from older satellites, such as the Landsat constellation, and extending the current dataset. Thus, future work should focus on increasing the data availability of both remote sensing and global data in the field and incorporating the advances in remote sensing research such as correction of adjacency errors and improvement of atmospheric correction.

Supplementary Materials: The following supporting information can be downloaded at: https://www.mdpi.com/article/10.3390/rs15051390/s1, Figures: SF1 vidual sum of correlations of each predictor and target in form of Chord diagram.

Author Contributions: L.F.A.-R. conceived this study. U.F.T. conducted main data processing and analysis of the harmonized RS data. U.F.T. and L.F.A.-R. conducted data processing and modeling analysis. L.F.A.-R. wrote the original version of the manuscript. Constructive comments and improvements of the manuscript were provided by Z.D., J.H., Y.T. and M.D. through extensive discussion. All authors have read and agreed to the published version of the manuscript.

Funding: This article was accomplished with the financial support for research of the Mexican National Council for Science and Technology (CONACYT) and the Federal Department of Energy (SENER) through its funding "CONACYT-SENER Sustentabilidad Energética" CVU 678957. In addition, this work was supported by the German Research Foundation (DFG) and the Technical University of Munich (TUM) in the framework of the Open-Access Publishing Program.

Acknowledgments: The authors thank all the national and international agencies and the personnel involved in the acquisition of field water quality data around the world. They would also like to thank the Technical University of Munich (TUM) and its Graduate School (TUM-GS) for the institutional services and facilities necessary to perform this study. The authors also thank the ESA, NASA and USGS agencies for providing the necessary radiometric data and software to process these data. Additionally, they acknowledge Marco Körner from the TUM Chair of Remote Sensing Technology for valuable discussions about the methodology.

Conflicts of Interest: The authors declare no conflict of interest.

References

1. UNEP. *A Snapshot of the World's Water Quality: Towards a Global Assessment*; United Nations Environment Programme: Nairobi, Kenya, 2016; p. 162.
2. UNEP. GEMStat 2020. Website Data Portal. Available online: https://gemstat.bafg.de/applications/public.html?publicuser=PublicUser#gemstat/Stations (accessed on 15 February 2021).
3. Anon. *An Integrated Water-Monitoring Network for Wisconsin*; G.S.U. Water Resources Center, Ed.; University of Wisconsin: Madison, WI, USA, 1998.
4. EPA. *Elements of a State Water Monitoring and Assessment Program*; Environmental Protection Agency, Assessment and Watershed Protection Division, Office of Wetlands, Oceans and Watershed: Washington, DC, USA, 2001.
5. Gholizadeh, M.H.; Melesse, A.M.; Reddi, L. A Comprehensive Review on Water Quality Parameters Estimation Using Remote Sensing Techniques. *Sensors* **2016**, *16*, 1298. [CrossRef]
6. Matthews, M.W. A current review of empirical procedures of remote sensing in inland and near-coastal transitional waters. *Int. J. Remote Sens.* **2011**, *32*, 6855–6899. [CrossRef]
7. Giardino, C.; Brando, V.E.; Gege, P.; Pinnel, N.; Hochberg, E.; Knaeps, E.; Reusen, I.; Doerffer, R.; Bresciani, M.; Braga, F.; et al. Imaging Spectrometry of Inland and Coastal Waters: State of the Art, Achievements and Perspectives. *Surv. Geophys.* **2019**, *40*, 401–429. [CrossRef]
8. Doxaran, D.; Froidefond, J.M.; Lavender, S.; Castaing, P. Spectral signature of highly turbid waters: Application with SPOT data to quantify suspended particulate matter concentrations. *Remote Sens. Environ.* **2002**, *81*, 149–161. [CrossRef]
9. IOCCG. Remote Sensing of Ocean Colour in Coastal, and Other Optically-Complex. In *Waters*; Sathyendranath, S., Ed.; IOCCG: Dartmouth, NS, Canada, 2000.
10. Claverie, M.; Ju, J.; Masek, J.G.; Dungan, J.L.; Vermote, E.F.; Roger, J.-C.; Skakun, S.V.; Justice, C. The Harmonized Landsat and Sentinel-2 surface reflectance data set. *Remote Sens. Environ.* **2018**, *219*, 145–161. [CrossRef]
11. Zhang, Y.; Ma, R.; Duan, H.; Loiselle, S.; Xu, J. A Spectral Decomposition Algorithm for Estimating Chlorophyll-a Concentrations in Lake Taihu, China. *Remote Sens.* **2014**, *6*, 5090–5106. [CrossRef]
12. Bonansea, M.; Rodriguez, M.C.; Pinotti, L.; Ferrero, S. Using multi-temporal Landsat imagery and linear mixed models for assessing water quality parameters in Río Tercero reservoir (Argentina). *Remote Sens. Environ.* **2015**, *158*, 28–41. [CrossRef]
13. Peterson, K.T.; Sagan, V.; Sidike, P.; Cox, A.L.; Martinez, M. Suspended Sediment Concentration Estimation from Landsat Imagery along the Lower Missouri and Middle Mississippi Rivers Using an Extreme Learning Machine. *Remote Sens.* **2018**, *10*, 1503. [CrossRef]
14. Peterson, K.T.; Sagan, V.; Sloan, J.J. Deep learning-based water quality estimation and anomaly detection using Landsat-8/Sentinel-2 virtual constellation and cloud computing. *GISci. Remote Sens.* **2020**, *57*, 510–525. [CrossRef]
15. Pyo, J.; Cho, K.H.; Kim, K.; Baek, S.-S.; Nam, G.; Park, S. Cyanobacteria cell prediction using interpretable deep learning model with observed, numerical, and sensing data assemblage. *Water Res.* **2021**, *203*, 117483. [CrossRef]
16. He, J.; Chen, Y.; Wu, J.; Stow, D.A.; Christakos, G. Space-time chlorophyll-a retrieval in optically complex waters that accounts for remote sensing and modeling uncertainties and improves remote estimation accuracy. *Water Res.* **2020**, *171*, 115403. [CrossRef]
17. Chen, K.; Chen, H.; Zhou, C.; Huang, Y.; Qi, X.; Shen, R.; Liu, F.; Zuo, M.; Zou, X.; Wang, J.; et al. Comparative analysis of surface water quality prediction performance and identification of key water parameters using different machine learning models based on big data. *Water Res.* **2020**, *171*, 115454. [CrossRef]
18. Chen, Y.; Arnold, W.A.; Griffin, C.G.; Olmanson, L.G.; Brezonik, P.L.; Hozalski, R.M. Assessment of the chlorine demand and disinfection byproduct formation potential of surface waters via satellite remote sensing. *Water Res.* **2019**, *165*, 115001. [CrossRef] [PubMed]
19. Li, Y.; Wang, X.; Zhao, Z.; Han, S.; Liu, Z. Lagoon water quality monitoring based on digital image analysis and machine learning estimators. *Water Res.* **2020**, *172*, 115471. [CrossRef] [PubMed]
20. Xu, T.; Coco, G.; Neale, M. A predictive model of recreational water quality based on adaptive synthetic sampling algorithms and machine learning. *Water Res.* **2020**, *177*, 115788. [CrossRef]
21. Zhang, Y.; Wu, L.; Deng, L.; Ouyang, B. Retrieval of water quality parameters from hyperspectral images using a hybrid feedback deep factorization machine model. *Water Res.* **2021**, *204*, 117618. [CrossRef] [PubMed]
22. Arias-Rodriguez, L.F.; Duan, Z.; Sepúlveda, R.; Martinez-Martinez, S.I.; Disse, M. Monitoring Water Quality of Valle de Bravo Reservoir, Mexico, Using Entire Lifespan of MERIS Data and Machine Learning Approaches. *Remote Sens.* **2020**, *12*, 1586. [CrossRef]

23. Hartling, S.; Sagan, V.; Sidike, P.; Maimaitijiang, M.; Carron, J. Urban tree species classification using a WorldView-2/3 and LiDAR data fusion approach and deep learning. *Sensors* **2019**, *19*, 1284. [CrossRef] [PubMed]
24. Sidike, P.; Sagan, V.; Maimaitijiang, M.; Maimaitiyiming, M.; Shakoor, N.; Burken, J.; Mockler, T.; Fritschi, F.B. dPEN: Deep Progressively Expanded Network for mapping heterogeneous agricultural landscape using WorldView-3 satellite imagery. *Remote Sens. Environ.* **2019**, *221*, 756–772. [CrossRef]
25. Maimaitijiang, M.; Sagan, V.; Sidike, P.; Hartling, S.; Esposito, F.; Fritschi, F.B. Soybean yield prediction from UAV using multimodal data fusion and deep learning. *Remote Sens. Environ.* **2020**, *237*, 111599. [CrossRef]
26. Pahlevan, N.; Smith, B.; Schalles, J.; Binding, C.; Cao, Z.; Ma, R.; Alikas, K.; Kangro, K.; Gurlin, D.; Nguyen, H.; et al. Seamless retrievals of chlorophyll-a from Sentinel-2 (MSI) and Sentinel-3 (OLCI) in inland and coastal waters: A machine-learning approach. *Remote Sens. Environ.* **2020**, *240*, 111604. [CrossRef]
27. Zhang, L.; Zhang, L.; Du, B. Deep learning for remote sensing data: A technical tutorial on the state of the art. *IEEE Geosci. Remote Sens. Mag.* **2016**, *4*, 22–40. [CrossRef]
28. Ball, J.E.; Anderson, D.T.; Chan Sr, C.S. Comprehensive survey of deep learning in remote sensing: Theories, tools, and challenges for the community. *J. Appl. Remote Sens.* **2017**, *11*, 042609. [CrossRef]
29. Alom, M.Z.; Taha, T.M.; Yakopcic, C.; Westberg, S.; Sidike, P.; Nasrin, M.S.; Hasan, M.; Van Essen, B.C.; Awwal, A.A.S.; Asari, V.K. A State-of-the-Art Survey on Deep Learning Theory and Architectures. *Electronics* **2019**, *8*, 292. [CrossRef]
30. Ma, L.; Liu, Y.; Zhang, X.; Ye, Y.; Yin, G.; Johnson, B.A. Deep learning in remote sensing applications: A meta-analysis and review. *ISPRS J. Photogramm. Remote Sens.* **2019**, *152*, 166–177. [CrossRef]
31. Arias-Rodriguez, L.F.; Duan, Z.; de Jesús Díaz-Torres, J.; Basilio Hazas, M.; Huang, J.; Kumar, B.U.; Tuo, Y.; Disse, M. Integration of Remote Sensing and Mexican Water Quality Monitoring System Using an Extreme Learning Machine. *Sensors* **2021**, *21*, 4118. [CrossRef]
32. Szegedy, C.; Liu, W.; Jia, Y.; Sermanet, P.; Reed, S.; Anguelov, D.; Erhan, D.; Vanhoucke, V.; Rabinovich, A. Going deeper with convolutions. In Proceedings of the IEEE Conference on Computer Vision and Pattern Recognition, Boston, MA, USA, 7–12 June 2015; pp. 1–9.
33. Sagan, V.; Peterson, K.T.; Maimaitijiang, M.; Sidike, P.; Sloan, J.; Greeling, B.A.; Maalouf, S.; Adams, C. Monitoring inland water quality using remote sensing: Potential and limitations of spectral indices, bio-optical simulations, machine learning, and cloud computing. *Earth-Sci. Rev.* **2020**, *205*, 103187. [CrossRef]
34. Nguyen, M.; Baez-Villanueva, O.; Bui, D.; Nguyen, P.; Ribbe, L. Harmonization of Landsat and Sentinel 2 for Crop Monitoring in Drought Prone Areas: Case Studies of Ninh Thuan (Vietnam) and Bekaa (Lebanon). *Remote Sens.* **2020**, *12*, 281. [CrossRef]
35. Thorslund, J.; van Vliet, M.T. A global dataset of surface water and groundwater salinity measurements from 1980–2019. *Sci. Data* **2020**, *7*, 1–11. [CrossRef] [PubMed]
36. WQP. Water Quality Portal. 2021. Available online: https://www.waterqualitydata.us/wqp_description/ (accessed on 15 January 2022).
37. GobMX. Calidad del agua en México. 2021. Available online: https://www.gob.mx/conagua/articulos/calidad-del-agua (accessed on 15 January 2022).
38. GobCa. Open Government Portal. 2021. Available online: https://search.open.canada.ca/en/od/ (accessed on 15 January 2022).
39. GobChl. Ministerio de Obras Públicas, MOP—Morandé 59, Santiago de Chile. *Direccion General de Aguas*. Available online: https://dga.mop.gob.cl/servicioshidrometeorologicos/Paginas/default.aspx (accessed on 15 January 2022).
40. Bulgarelli, B.; Kiselev, V.; Zibordi, G. Adjacency effects in satellite radiometric products from coastal waters: A theoretical analysis for the northern Adriatic Sea. *Appl. Opt.* **2017**, *53*, 1523–1545. [CrossRef] [PubMed]
41. Lehner, B.; Döll, P. Development and validation of a global database of lakes, reservoirs and wetlands. *J. Hydrol.* **2004**, *296*, 1–22. [CrossRef]
42. Storey, J.; Roy, D.P.; Masek, J.; Gascon, F.; Dwyer, J.; Choate, M. A note on the temporary misregistration of Landsat-8 Operational Land Imager (OLI) and Sentinel-2 Multi Spectral Instrument (MSI) imagery. *Remote Sens. Environ.* **2016**, *186*, 121–122. [CrossRef]
43. Vermote, E.F.; Tanré, D.; Deuze, J.L.; Herman, M.; Morcette, J.-J. Second Simulation of the Satellite Signal in the Solar Spectrum, 6S: An overview. *IEEE Trans. Geosci. Remote Sens.* **1997**, *35*, 675–686. [CrossRef]
44. Wilson, R. Py6S: A Python interface to the 6S radiative transfer model. *Comput. Geosci.* **2012**, *51*, 166–171. Available online: http://rtwilson.com/academic/Wilson_2012_Py6S_Paper.pdf (accessed on 15 January 2022). [CrossRef]
45. Murphy, S. Atmospheric Correction of Sentinel 2 Imagery in Google Earth Engine Using Py6S. 2018. Available online: https://github.com/samsammurphy/gee-atmcorr-S2 (accessed on 7 August 2021).
46. Zupanc, A. Improving Cloud Detection with Machine Learning. 2017. Available online: https://medium.com/sentinel-hub/improving-cloud-detection-with-machine-learning-c09dc5d7cf13 (accessed on 18 August 2021).
47. Poortinga, A.; Tenneson, K.; Shapiro, A.; Nquyen, Q.; San Aung, K.; Chishtie, F.; Saah, D. Mapping Plantations in Myanmar by Fusing Landsat-8, Sentinel-2 and Sentinel-1 Data along with Systematic Error Quantification. *Remote Sens.* **2019**, *11*, 831. [CrossRef]
48. Housman, I.W.; Chastain, R.A.; Finco, M.V. An Evaluation of Forest Health Insect and Disease Survey Data and Satellite-Based Remote Sensing Forest Change Detection Methods: Case Studies in the United States. *Remote Sens.* **2018**, *10*, 1184. [CrossRef]
49. Hollstein, A.; Segl, K.; Guanter, L.; Brell, M.; Enesco, M. Ready-to-Use Methods for the Detection of Clouds, Cirrus, Snow, Shadow, Water and Clear Sky Pixels in Sentinel-2 MSI Images. *Remote Sens.* **2016**, *8*, 666. [CrossRef]
50. GEE. Registering Images. 2021. Available online: https://developers.google.com/earth-engine/guides/register (accessed on 24 August 2021).
51. Masek, J.; Gao, F.; Wolfe, R. Automated registration and orthorectification package for Landsat and Landsat-like data processing. *J. Appl. Remote Sens.* **2009**, *3*, 033515. [CrossRef]

52. Keys, R. Cubic convolution interpolation for digital image processing. *IEEE Trans. Acoust. Speech Signal Process.* **1981**, *29*, 1153–1160. [CrossRef]
53. GEE. Projections. 2021. Available online: https://developers.google.com/earthengine/guides/projections (accessed on 24 August 2021).
54. Roy, D.P.; Zhang, H.K.; Ju, J.; Gomez-Dans, J.L.; Lewis, P.E.; Schaaf, C.B.; Sun, Q.; Li, J.; Huang, H.; Kovalskyy, V. A general method to normalize Landsat reflectance data to nadir BRDF adjusted reflectance. *Remote Sens. Environ.* **2016**, *176*, 255–271. [CrossRef]
55. Roy, D.P.; Li, J.; Zhang, H.K.; Yan, L.; Huang, H.; Li, Z. Examination of Sentinel-2A multi-spectral instrument (MSI) reflectance anisotropy and the suitability of a general method to normalize MSI reflectance to nadir BRDF adjusted reflectance. *Remot. Sens. Environ.* **2017**, *199*, 25–38. [CrossRef]
56. Soenen, S.A.; Peddle, D.R.; Coburn, C.A. SCS+C: A modified Sun-canopy-sensor topographic correction in forested terrain. *IEEE Trans. Geosci. Remote Sens.* **2005**, *43*, 2148–2159. [CrossRef]
57. Chastain, R.; Housman, I.; Goldstein, J.; Finco, M.; Tenneson, K. Empirical cross sensor comparison of Sentinel-2A and 2B MSI, Landsat-8 OLI, and Landsat-7 ETM+ top of atmosphere spectral characteristics over the conterminous United States. *Remote Sens. Environ.* **2019**, *2019*, 274–285. [CrossRef]
58. Dekker, A.; Malthus, T.; Seyhan, E. Quantitative modeling of inland water quality for high-resolution MSS systems. *IEEE Trans. Geosci. Remote Sens.* **1991**, *29*, 89–95. [CrossRef]
59. Doxaran, D.; Froidefond, J.-M.; Castaing, P. Remote-sensing reflectance of turbid sediment-dominated waters. Reduction of sediment type variations and changing illumination conditions effects by use of reflectance ratios. *Appl. Opt.* **2003**, *42*, 2623–2634. [CrossRef] [PubMed]
60. Lathrop, R.G.; Lillesand, T.M. Monitoring water quality and river plume transport in Green Bay, Lake Michigan with SPOT-1 imagery. *Photogramm. Eng. Remote Sens.* **1989**, *55*, 349–354.
61. Odermatt, D.; Gitelson, A.; Brando, V.E.; Schaepman, M. Review of constituent retrieval in optically deep and complex waters from satellite imagery. *Remot. Sens. Environ.* **2012**, *118*, 116–126. [CrossRef]
62. Ritchie, J.C.; Zimba, P.V.; Everitt, J.H. Remote Sensing Techniques to Assess Water Quality. *Photogramm. Eng. Remote Sens.* **2003**, *69*, 695–704. [CrossRef]
63. Sudheer, K.; Chaubey, I.; Garg, V. Lake water quality assessment from landsat thematic mapper data using neural network: An approach to optimal band combination selection. *JAWRA J. Am. Water Resour. Assoc.* **2006**, *42*, 1683–1695. [CrossRef]
64. Svab, E.; Tyler, A.N.; Preston, T.; Présing, M.; Balogh, K.V. Characterizing the spectral reflectance of algae in lake waters with high suspended sediment concentrations. *Int. J. Remote Sens.* **2005**, *26*, 919–928. [CrossRef]
65. Dörnhöfer, K.; Oppelt, N. Remote sensing for lake research and monitoring–Recent advances. *Ecol. Indic.* **2016**, *64*, 105–122. [CrossRef]
66. Bonansea, M.; Ledesma, M.; Rodriguez, M.C.; Pinotti, L. Using new remote sensing satellites for assessing water quality in a reservoir. *Hydrol. Sci. J.* **2019**, *64*, 34–44. [CrossRef]
67. Hicks, B.J.; Stichbury, G.A.; Brabyn, L.K.; Allan, M.G.; Ashraf, S. Hindcasting water clarity from Landsat satellite images of unmonitored shallow lakes in the Waikato region, New Zealand. *Environ. Monit. Assess.* **2013**, *185*, 7245–7261. [CrossRef] [PubMed]
68. Duan, H.; Ma, R.; Zhang, Y.; Zhang, B. Remote-sensing assessment of regional inland lake water clarity in northeast China. *Limnology* **2009**, *10*, 135–141. [CrossRef]
69. Cheng, K.S.; Lei, T.C. Reservoir trophic state evaluation using lanisat tm images 1. *JAWRA J. Am. Water Resour. Assoc.* **2001**, *37*, 1321–1334. [CrossRef]
70. Vapnik, V.; Golowich, S.E.; Smola, A. *Support Vector Method for Function Approximation, Regression Estimation and Signal Processing*; MIT Press: Cambridge, MA, USA, 1997; pp. 281–287.
71. Azamathulla, H.; Wu, F.-C. Support vector machine approach for longitudinal dispersion coefficients in natural streams. *Appl. Soft Comput.* **2011**, *11*, 2902–2905. [CrossRef]
72. Samui, P. Support vector machine applied to settlement of shallow foundations on cohesionless soils. *Comput. Geotech.* **2008**, *35*, 419–427. [CrossRef]
73. Wang, X.; Ma, L.; Wang, X. Apply semi-supervised support vector regression for remote sensing water quality retrieving. In Proceedings of the IEEE International Geoscience and Remote Sensing Symposium, Honolulu, HI, USA, 25–30 July 2010; pp. 2757–2760.
74. Maier, P.M.; Keller, S. Machine learning regression on hyperspectral data to estimate multiple water parameters. In Proceedings of the 9th Workshop on Hyperspectral Image and Signal Processing: Evolution in Remote Sensing (WHISPERS), Amsterdam, The Netherlands, 23–26 September 2018; pp. 1–5.
75. Ruescas, A.B.; Hieronymi, M.; Mateo-Garcia, G.; Koponen, S.; Kallio, K.; Camps-Valls, G. Machine Learning Regression Approaches for Colored Dissolved Organic Matter (CDOM) Retrieval with S2-MSI and S3-OLCI Simulated Data. *Remote Sens.* **2018**, *10*, 786. [CrossRef]
76. Breiman, L. Random forests. *Mach. Learn.* **2001**, *45*, 5–32. [CrossRef]
77. Hastie, T.T. *The Elements of Statistical Learning*; Mathematical Intelligencer, Ed.; Springer: Berlin/Heidelberg, Germany, 2009.
78. Huang, G.-B.; Zhu, Q.-Y.; Siew, C.-K. Extreme learning machine: Theory and applications. *Neurocomputing* **2006**, *70*, 489–501. [CrossRef]
79. Keiner, L.E. Estimating oceanic chlorophyll concentrations with neural networks. *Int. J. Remote Sens.* **1999**, *20*, 189–194. [CrossRef]
80. Giardino, C.; Bresciani, M.; Cazzaniga, I.; Di Nicolantonio, W.; Cacciari, A.; Matta, E.; Rampini, A.; Gianinetto, M.; Ober, G. Combining In Situ and Multi-Sensor Satellite Data to Assess the Impact of Atmospheric Deposition in Lake Garda. In Proceedings of the 2013 European Space Agency Living Planet Symposium, Edinburgh, UK, 9–13 September 2013; pp. 1–5.

81. Panda, S.S.; Garg, V.; Chaubey, I. Artificial neural networks application in lake water quality estimation using satellite imagery. *J. Environ. Inform.* 2004, *4*, 65–74. [CrossRef]
82. Blix, K.; Pálffy, K.; Tóth, V.R.; Eltoft, T. Remote Sensing of Water Quality Parameters over Lake Balaton by Using Sentinel-3 OLCI. *Water* 2018, *10*, 1428. [CrossRef]
83. Delgado, A.L.; Pratolongo, P.D.; Gossn, J.I.; Dogliotti, A.I.; Arena, M.; Villagran, D.; Severini, M.F. Evaluation of derived total suspended matter products from ocean and land colour instrument imagery (OLCI) in the inner and mid-shelf of Buenos Aires Province (Argentina). In Proceedings of the Extended Abstract Submitted to the XXIV Ocean Optics Conference, Dubrovnik, Croatia, 16 October 2018.
84. NASA. A Harmonized Surface Reflectance Product. 2022. Available online: https://hls.gsfc.nasa.gov/ (accessed on 12 September 2022).
85. Kwong, I.H.Y.; Wong, F.K.K.; Fung, T. Automatic Mapping and Monitoring of Marine Water Quality Parameters in Hong Kong Using Sentinel-2 Image Time-Series and Google Earth Engine Cloud Computing. *Front. Mar. Sci.* 2022, *609*, 871470. [CrossRef]
86. Castrillo, M.; García, L. Estimation of high frequency nutrient concentrations from water quality surrogates using machine learning methods. *Water Res.* 2020, *172*, 115490. [CrossRef] [PubMed]
87. Niroumand-Jadidi, M.; Bovolo, F.; Bruzzone, L. Water Quality Retrieval from PRISMA Hyperspectral Images: First Experience in a Turbid Lake and Comparison with Sentinel-2. *Remote Sens.* 2020, *12*, 3984. [CrossRef]
88. Zhang, Y.; Wu, L.; Ren, H.; Deng, L.; Zhang, P. Retrieval of Water Quality Parameters from Hyperspectral Images Using Hybrid Bayesian Probabilistic Neural Network. *Remote Sens.* 2020, *12*, 1567. [CrossRef]
89. Topp, S.N.; Pavelsky, T.M.; Jensen, D.; Simard, M.; Ross, M.R.V. Research Trends in the Use of Remote Sensing for Inland Water Quality Science: Moving Towards Multidisciplinary Applications. *Water* 2020, *12*, 169. [CrossRef]
90. Kravitz, J.; Matthews, M.; Lain, L.; Fawcett, S.; Bernard, S. Potential for High Fidelity Global Mapping of Common Inland Water Quality Products at High Spatial and Temporal Resolutions Based on a Synthetic Data and Machine Learning Approach. *Front. Environ. Sci.* 2021, *9*, 19. [CrossRef]
91. El-Din, M.S.; Gaber, A.; Koch, M.; Ahmed, R.S.; Bahgat, I. Remote sensing application for water quality assessment in lake timsah, suez canal, egypt. *J. Remote Sens. Technol.* 2013, *1*, 61–74. [CrossRef]
92. Gómez, J.A.D.; Alonso, C.A.; García, A.A. Remote sensing as a tool for monitoring water quality parameters for Mediterranean Lakes of European Union water framework directive (WFD) and as a system of surveillance of cyanobacterial harmful algae blooms (SCyanoHABs). *Environ. Monit. Assess.* 2011, *181*, 317–334. [CrossRef] [PubMed]
93. Odermatt, D.; Heege, T.; Nieke, J.; Kneubuhler, M.; Itten, K. Water Quality Monitoring for Lake Constance with a Physically Based Algorithm for MERIS Data. *Sensors* 2008, *8*, 4582–4599. [CrossRef]
94. Wang, F.; Han, L.; Kung, H.-T.; Van Arsdale, R.B. Applications of Landsat-5 TM imagery in assessing and mapping water quality in Reelfoot Lake, Tennessee. *Int. J. Remote Sens.* 2006, *27*, 5269–5283. [CrossRef]
95. Brezonik, P.; Menken, K.D.; Bauer, M. Landsat-based Remote Sensing of Lake Water Quality Characteristics, Including Chlorophyll and Colored Dissolved Organic Matter (CDOM). *Lake Reserv. Manag.* 2005, *21*, 373–382. [CrossRef]
96. Kallio, K.; Kutser, T.; Hannonen, T.; Koponen, S.; Pulliainen, J.; Vepsäläinen, J.; Pyhälahti, T. Retrieval of water quality from airborne imaging spectrometry of various lake types in different seasons. *Sci. Total. Environ.* 2001, *268*, 59–77. [CrossRef]
97. Zilioli, E.; Brivio, P. The satellite derived optical information for the comparative assessment of lacustrine water quality. *Sci. Total. Environ.* 1997, *196*, 229–245. [CrossRef]
98. Pattiaratchi, C.; Lavery, P.; Wyllie, A.; Hick, P. Estimates of water quality in coastal waters using multi-date Landsat Thematic Mapper data. *Int. J. Remote Sens.* 1994, *15*, 1571–1584. [CrossRef]
99. Chacon-Torres, A.; Ross, L.G.; Beveridge, M.; Watson, A.I. The application of SPOT multispectral imagery for the assessment of water quality in Lake Pátzcuaro, Mexico. *Int. J. Remote Sens.* 1992, *13*, 587–603. [CrossRef]
100. Buma, W.; Lee, S.-I. Evaluation of Sentinel-2 and Landsat 8 Images for Estimating Chlorophyll-a Concentrations in Lake Chad, Africa. *Remote Sens.* 2020, *12*, 2437. [CrossRef]
101. Palmer, S.C.J.; Hunter, P.D.; Lankester, T.; Hubbard, S.; Spyrakos, E.; Tyler, A.N.; Présing, M.; Horváth, H.; Lamb, A.; Balzter, H.; et al. Validation of Envisat MERIS algorithms for chlorophyll retrieval in a large, turbid and optically-complex shallow lake. *Remote Sens. Environ.* 2015, *157*, 158–169. [CrossRef]
102. Turner, D. Remote Sensing of Chlorophyll a Concentrations to Support the Deschutes Basin Lake and Reservoirs TMDLs. 2010. Available online: https://www.oregon.gov/deq/FilterDocs/RemoteSensingChlorophylla.pdf (accessed on 12 September 2022).
103. Alikas, K.; Kangro, K.; Reinart, A. Detecting cyanobacterial blooms in large North European lakes using the Maximum Chlorophyll Index. *Oceanologia* 2010, *52*, 237–257. [CrossRef]
104. Han, L.; Jordan, K.J. Estimating and mapping chlorophyll-a concentration in Pensacola Bay, Florida using Landsat ETM+ data. *Int. J. Remote Sens.* 2005, *26*, 5245–5254. [CrossRef]
105. Kallio, K.; Koponen, S.; Pulliainen, J. Feasibility of airborne imaging spectrometry for lake monitoring—A case study of spatial chlorophyll a distribution in two meso-eutrophic lakes. *Int. J. Remote Sens.* 2003, *24*, 3771–3790. [CrossRef]
106. Allee, R.J.; Johnson, J.E. Use of satellite imagery to estimate surface chlorophyll a and Secchi disc depth of Bull Shoals Reservoir, Arkansas, USA. *Int. J. Remote Sens.* 1999, *20*, 1057–1072. [CrossRef]
107. Gower, J.F.R. Observations of in situ fluorescence of chlorophyll-a in Saanich Inlet. *Bound. Layer Meteorol.* 1980, *18*, 235–245. [CrossRef]
108. Bi, S.; Li, Y.; Wang, Q.; Lyu, H.; Liu, G.; Zheng, Z.; Du, C.; Mu, M.; Xu, J.; Lei, S.; et al. Inland Water Atmospheric Correction Based on Turbidity Classification Using OLCI and SLSTR Synergistic Observations. *Remote Sens.* 2018, *10*, 1002. [CrossRef]

109. Pereira, L.S.; Andes, L.C.; Cox, A.L.; Ghulam, A. Measuring Suspended-Sediment Concentration and Turbidity in the Middle Mississippi and Lower Missouri Rivers using Landsat Data. *JAWRA J. Am. Water Resour. Assoc.* **2017**, *54*, 440–450. [CrossRef]
110. Papoutsa, C.R.; Retalis, A.; Toulios, L.; Hadjimitsis, D.G. Defining the Landsat TM/ETM+ and CHRIS/PROBA spectral regions in which turbidity can be retrieved in inland waterbodies using field spectroscopy. *Int. J. Remote Sens.* **2014**, *35*, 1674–1692. [CrossRef]
111. Guo, H.; Huang, J.J.; Zhu, X.; Wang, B.; Tian, S.; Xu, W.; Mai, Y. A generalized machine learning approach for dissolved oxygen estimation at multiple spatiotemporal scales using remote sensing. *Environ. Pollut.* **2021**, *288*, 117734. [CrossRef]

Disclaimer/Publisher's Note: The statements, opinions and data contained in all publications are solely those of the individual author(s) and contributor(s) and not of MDPI and/or the editor(s). MDPI and/or the editor(s) disclaim responsibility for any injury to people or property resulting from any ideas, methods, instructions or products referred to in the content.

Article

LASSO (L1) Regularization for Development of Sparse Remote-Sensing Models with Applications in Optically Complex Waters Using GEE Tools

Anna Catherine Cardall [1], Riley Chad Hales [2], Kaylee Brooke Tanner [2], Gustavious Paul Williams [2,*] and Kel N. Markert [3]

1. Department of Chemical Engineering, Brigham Young University, Provo, UT 84602, USA; cardalla@byu.edu
2. Department of Civil and Construction Engineering, Brigham Young University, Provo, UT 84602, USA; rchales@byu.edu (R.C.H.); k.tanner@byu.edu (K.B.T.)
3. Google LLC, Mountain View, CA 94043, USA; kmarkert@google.com
* Correspondence: gus.williams@byu.edu

Citation: Cardall, A.C.; Hales, R.C.; Tanner, K.B.; Williams, G.P.; Markert, K.N. LASSO (L1) Regularization for Development of Sparse Remote-Sensing Models with Applications in Optically Complex Waters Using GEE Tools. *Remote Sens.* 2023, 15, 1670. https://doi.org/10.3390/rs15061670

Academic Editors: Hatim Sharif, Flor Alvarez-Taboada, Miro Govedarica and Gordana Jakovljević

Received: 26 January 2023
Revised: 14 March 2023
Accepted: 17 March 2023
Published: 20 March 2023

Copyright: © 2023 by the authors. Licensee MDPI, Basel, Switzerland. This article is an open access article distributed under the terms and conditions of the Creative Commons Attribution (CC BY) license (https://creativecommons.org/licenses/by/4.0/).

Abstract: Remote-sensing data are used extensively to monitor water quality parameters such as clarity, temperature, and chlorophyll-a (chl-a) content. This is generally achieved by collecting in situ data coincident with satellite data collections and then creating empirical water quality models using approaches such as multi-linear regression or step-wise linear regression. These approaches, which require modelers to select model parameters, may not be well suited for optically complex waters, where interference from suspended solids, dissolved organic matter, or other constituents may act as "confusers". For these waters, it may be useful to include non-standard terms, which might not be considered when using traditional methods. Recent machine-learning work has demonstrated an ability to explore large feature spaces and generate accurate empirical models that do not require parameter selection. However, these methods, because of the large number of included terms involved, result in models that are not explainable and cannot be analyzed. We explore the use of Least Absolute Shrinkage and Select Operator (LASSO), or L1, regularization to fit linear regression models and produce parsimonious models with limited terms to enable interpretation and explainability. We demonstrate this approach with a case study in which chl-a models are developed for Utah Lake, Utah, USA., an optically complex freshwater body, and compare the resulting model terms to model terms from the literature. We discuss trade-offs between interpretability and model performance while using L1 regularization as a tool. The resulting model terms are both similar to and distinct from those in the literature, thereby suggesting that this approach is useful for the development of models for optically complex water bodies where standard model terms may not be optimal. We investigate the effect of non-coincident data, that is, the length of time between satellite image collection and in situ sampling, on model performance. We find that, for Utah Lake (for which there are extensive data available), three days is the limit, but 12 h provides the best trade-off. This value is site-dependent, and researchers should use site-specific numbers. To document and explain our approach, we provide Colab notebooks for compiling near-coincident data pairs of remote-sensing and in situ data using Google Earth Engine (GEE) and a second notebook implementing L1 model creation using scikitlearn. The second notebook includes data-engineering routines with which to generate band ratios, logs, and other combinations. The notebooks can be easily modified to adapt them to other locations, sensors, or parameters.

Keywords: remote sensing; water quality; model development; linear regression; LASSO regularization; L1; coincident data; Google Earth Engine

1. Introduction
1.1. Remote Sensing of Water Quality

Remote-sensing data are used to monitor water quality [1] by estimating water quality parameters such as clarity, temperature, and chlorophyll-a (chl-a) content [2–4]. Landsat data are often used to estimate chl-a concentrations, which are a common index of water quality [5–10], because their high spatial resolution (approximately 30 m per pixel), high temporal collection rate (every 16 days), large coverage time (~37 years of data), and spectral bands designed for vegetation studies are well suited to the estimation of chl-a concentrations for use in long-term studies [11]. We selected Landsat data as an example dataset for this study because of the long time periods and appropriate spectral information contained in the dataset. These long time periods overlap with more field data, so there are more observations available to create and validate models. Other missions, such as MODIS or Sentinel 1, or multi-spectral images from aircraft or drones could also be used with these methods.

Water quality characterization using earth observation data relies on regression models that estimate the selected water quality parameters based on correlations with measured spectral data. These models are created using spectral data collected coincidentally or near coincidentally with the in situ measurements, so they measure the same conditions. The spectral data are regressed on the in situ measurements, and the resulting regression model is applied to estimate concentrations of interest [12–15]. In addition to regression models, semi-analytical methods are also used and rely on spectral signatures of the parameters of interest, such as chl-a levels, and use equations based on these expected spectral peaks to compute the expected reflectance values from the sensor [16,17]. More recently, studies have reported various machine-learning methods for fitting models, with many of the papers comparing different methods, algorithms, and approaches [18–21]. These methods have proven successful, but the resulting models are complex, and it is not always possible to explain the model terms and their physical meaning. Typically, the regression models used to estimate chl-a and other water quality parameters are created by selecting model parameters based on our understanding of the spectra of the water quality parameter of interest. After the potential model terms are selected, the models are created by either directly fitting the models using multilinear regression methods with a limited set of preselected terms or by pre-selecting a slightly larger number of terms according to the order of the expected correlations and then using step-wise linear regression to limit the number of terms in the final model [15,22,23]. Efron et al. [24] discuss a number of parameter selection methods or automatic parameter selection techniques for multilinear regression models, noting that "good" models are generally categorized based on their prediction accuracy but stressing that parsimony is an important criterion.

Since water quality models are generally developed using in situ data collected co-incidentally with satellite data collections, the resulting models were often only applied to images from the same collection [25,26]. In situ data are rarely collected at the same time as satellite acquisitions, unless they are collected specifically for a remote-sensing study, which limits the applicability of these approaches. Recent research has shown that non-coincident data can be used to develop accurate chl-a models and that these models can be applied to all the historical Landsat images of a given water body [22,23,27]. This significantly increases the number of data available for model development and data analysis, thus supporting the use of remote-sensing data to evaluate long-term trends. This finding potentially supports the use of available in situ data collected through a larger range of conditions for model development, resulting in more robust models. For example, Hansen and Williams [15] used near-coincident data to develop sub-seasonal models that leveraged different spectral signatures based on the seasonal succession of algal species and used these models to analyze conditions over a nearly 40-year period. Tanner et al. [28] applied one of these models developed for Utah Lake to all historic Landsat observations to analyze long-term trends in chl-a concentrations.

1.2. Water Quality Models for Optically Complex Waters

Using remote-sensing data to study water quality in optically complex waters is complicated by factors such as complex optical properties (especially in turbid water bodies such as Utah Lake [25,26,29]), high suspended sediment volumes, shallow depths, and the challenge of differentiating between dense algae blooms and land vegetation in shallow, near-shore areas [8,30]. Multi-linear and step-wise regression result in parsimonious models with only a few terms, where the behavior or correlation of each term can be analyzed. However, the model terms for multi-linear regression, or the model terms and order of the terms for step-wise linear regression, must be selected a priori. Such terms are generally selected based on a spectral understanding of the parameter of interest and may not be optimal for optically complex water.

In this study, we focus on two challenges that impact empirical model development: the first is obtaining sufficient data with which to develop a regression model, and the second is determining the terms to include in the model, especially with regard to optically complex waters where a model may need to account for confounding factors and their resulting spectra. The first challenge can be addressed by using near-coincident data for model development rather than only coincident data and applying the resulting models to historic remote-sensing data. The second can be addressed using machine-learning methods, for which the limitation is that it is difficult to examine and explain individual terms in the model; consequently, the resulting models lack explainability. Our method addresses this latter issue.

Figure 1 shows an image of Utah Lake, our case study area. Utah Lake is optically complex with very high concentrations of suspended sediments, organic matter, and carbonate precipitates (Figure 1). Utah Lake characteristically exhibits the effects these various confusing substances have on the spectral chl-a signal as it has high concentrations of suspended solids, high levels of dissolved organic matter, a significant number of precipitates, and is shallow, thus posing a potential for bottom reflectance, although the water is so turbid the bottom is rarely visible [31].

Recent work demonstrating machine-learning methods has addressed the problem of developing models for optically complex scenarios, as model development can be used to explore a large feature space of non-standard terms. However, because of the large number of parameters and non-linear combinations inherent in most machine-learning methods, it can be difficult to determine the ultimate weight and physical relevance of various parameters and under what circumstances a model might be applicable based on a spectral understanding. Additionally, in most water quality applications, there are a limited number of measured or observed data, and machine-learning methods with a large number of features compared to the number of target data can result in the overfitting of a model, a term used to describe models that fit a training dataset very well but cannot be generalized to other data (even from the same population). This is certainly a concern for water quality applications as in situ water quality datasets are generally small.

Due to the potentially large number of parameters and non-linear combinations inherent in most machine-learning methods, it can be difficult to evaluate a trained machine-learning model to determine the ultimate weight and importance of the various parameters and their physical relevance as well as under what circumstances the model might be applicable based on a spectral understanding.

Our goal is to use machine-learning approaches to develop models with explainable spectral terms for complex waters rather than solely a model with a minimal error metric.

1.3. Approach

In this study, we explore regression models created using Least Absolute Shrinkage and Selection Operator (LASSO) regularization, which is more commonly known as L1 regularization. This results in a familiar multi-term regression model with a limited number of terms that can be evaluated to understand statistical correlations between the spectral terms and in situ data. Using L1 regularization allows us to explore a very large feature space as it does not require the a priori selection of specific model terms or the relatively expected importance or order of those terms. We present a case study wherein the number of features is similar in order or magnitude to the number of measurements used to fit the model. With L1 regularization, the user can trade model accuracy and parsimony using a weighting term. Stine (as summarized in [19]) notes that L1 provides more robust parameter selection than stepwise regression, which is sensitive to user-provided feature selection and order, especially in cases where the number of features is similar to the number of observations.

Figure 1. A Landsat image showing sediment plumes and carbonate precipitation in the northern and southern ends of Utah Lake, with less turbid waters entering the lake through Provo Bay on the right center of the image. Sediment resuspension from boats and other activities can be seen as "tracks", with a boat and its associated tracks evident just west and a little south of Provo Bay.

Ishwaran, in the discussion provided in [24], notes that while we good prediction error performance is desirable, simpler models are also prudent. These goals can be "diametrically" opposed. In theory, lower prediction error should result in more parsimonious models, but in practice, small improvements in prediction often result in larger models [24]. We use L1 regularization to develop a more general model by "shrinking" (i.e., regularizing or constraining) many model coefficients such that they approach zero. This results in models that are less complex and avoid overfitting. For our purposes, this also results in simplified models wherein terms can be examined and explained easily.

There are two related regularization approaches that are commonly used: Ridge (L2) and L1 regularization. Both add a penalty term to the loss function, which is typically the sum of the squared error. The added penalty term is the sum of the coefficients squared for L1 or the sum of the absolute values of the coefficients for L2 regularization. Both approaches minimize the coefficient values in the model as both the number and magnitude of the coefficients increase this term. L2 regularization shrinks the model coefficients such that they approach zero, which results in many terms having small coefficients, but the coefficients do not generally reach zero. Conversely, L1 regularization tends to set coefficient values to zero rather than a small number. L1 regularization can encounter convergent issues because of the step-function that occurs when coefficients are set to zero and, consequently, is used less than L2 regularization. Knight, in the discussion provided in [24], notes that L1 regularization is special in that it usually produces exactly 0 estimates for model coefficients when they are dropped, and that it is robust with respect to the tuning parameter. Loubes and Massart, in the discussion provided in [24], note that parameter selection methods such as L1 allow for the fitting of linear models to noisy data with only a few parameters.

L1 regularization minimizes cost functions, which constitute the prediction error plus the sum of the absolute values of the coefficients, as shown in Equation (1). We implemented a multi-linear regression model with L1 regularization using the *Lasso* model from scikit-learn (sklearn.linear_model.Lasso) [32]. The scikit-learn Lasso model minimizes the cost function, which, in this case, is the L2 norm of the error term squared (i.e., the mean squared error) and the L1 norm of the model coefficients (i.e., the sum of the absolute values of the model coefficients):

$$\min_{2} \frac{1}{2n} \|X \cdot w - y\|_2^2 + \alpha \|w\|_1 \qquad (1)$$

where X denotes the model features, n denotes the number of features; w represents the feature coefficients; y is the target value or measured chl-a concentration; $\|x\|_2^2$ is the squared L2-norm or the square of the sum of x, which, in this case, is the squared error given as $\left(\sqrt{\sum (X \cdot w - y)^2}\right)^2$; X·w are the predicted values (i.e., the dot product of the model coefficients and parameters); and $\|w\|_1$ is the L1-norm or sum of the absolute value of the coefficients $\sum |w|$. This results in a function with a weighted combination of the fitting error and the sum of the absolute value of the model coefficients with alpha (α) as the LASSO weighting parameter.

Minimizing this cost function (Equation (1)) using L1 regularization facilitates the sections of a subset of features for regression analysis. This enhances prediction accuracy by reducing overfitting and facilitates interpretability by limiting the number of resulting model parameters.

L1 regularization can be thought of as an approach used to obtain the best predictive performance with the smallest number of features. However, in some cases, L1 selects parameters based on their interaction with the target value and does not attempt to select the parameters that have the most dominant effect on prediction. L1 does not necessarily approximate a physical model. For example, if multiple features are correlated, L1 tends to choose only one of those features and assigns a weight of 0 to the others. This can cause a model to omit a significant proportion of informative features. Generally, L1 will choose more variables than a traditional model, even with optimal α selection. Due to these issues, a different dataset can cause L1 regularization to select different variables; however, in this study, we found the variable selection process to be very stable. We explore this effect in Section 3.2, where we evaluate a range of α values and datasets using k-fold validations and compute what percentage of the models select various parameters [33,34].

Based on these caveats, we caution other researchers against blindly using models generated via L1 in cases where the number of parameters is of a similar order to the number of training samples, which is typical for most remote-sensing applications where a few hundred samples is considered large. We submit L1 regularization as a means to explore a large parameter space and identify potential model features for optically complex water bodies that would not traditionally be considered.

To demonstrate our approach, we fit a multi-linear regression model using several parameters generated from Landsat band values that were, in turn, generated using feature-engineering options. We then fit a model on the target value (chl-a concentration), using L1 regularization to reduce the number of terms used in the model. We use a very large number of features as we cannot be certain which features might be important for estimating chl-a concentrations in optically complex waters. This approach is a repeatable, quantitative method for the selection of the appropriate features for a given water body, and it allows a model to use terms to address confounding factors present in optically complex waters that may not be obvious.

1.4. Study Area

To demonstrate and explain our approach, we use chl-a data from Utah Lake along with remote-sensing data from the Landsat series; notably, this approach is general and could be applied to other water quality parameters, sensors, or locations. We selected Utah Lake (Figure 1) because it is optically complex with very high concentrations of suspended sediments, organic matter, and carbonate precipitates. Remote-sensing methods are often complicated by the effects of these various confounding factors, including suspended solids and organic matter, dissolved organic matter, precipitates, and bottom reflectance on the expected spectral signal for different water quality parameters [31].

Utah Lake is unique in that it is a very optically complex body of water, has been documented in a number of published remote-sensing and water quality studies, and has been scrutinized through a large dataset of in situ measurements [4,35]. This provides us with a large dataset with which to engage and the ability to compare our models to published models. In this study, we used in situ data from the Utah Ambient Water Quality Monitoring System (AWQMS) database managed by the Utah Department of Water Quality (DWQ).

Utah Lake is a major physical feature in the Utah Valley and a valuable natural resource. It is a shallow, turbid, slightly saline, eutrophic lake in a semi-arid area. It has good pollution degradation and stabilization capacity because of its shallow, well-oxygenated, high-pH waters. It supports and harbors abundant wildlife that forms part of a productive ecosystem. The lake provides and supports a wide range of beneficial applications, including ecological habitats, water storage, and recreation (e.g., boating, sailing, fishing, and hunting). Abundant wildlife and ecological richness are some of its more significant assets [36].

Figure 1 is an example Landsat image of Utah Lake that clearly shows sediment plumes in the south stemming from Goshen Bay, with the "grey" color of much of the lake indicating carbonate precipitation and suspended clays. Optically clearer, less turbid water can be seen entering the lake from Provo Bay on the East side of the lake. Provo Bay receives relatively clear water from Hobble Creek and several smaller tributaries. Examples of sediment resuspension can be seen in boat "tracks"; in Figure 1 a boat and its associated tracks are evident west and a little south of Provo Bay, which is located in the middle of the eastern shoreline. Landsat data have been previously used to evaluate Utah Lake, and this research includes published models for estimating chl-a concentrations [22,27,30].

Table 1 presents data and summary statistics for pertinent Utah Lake parameters. These data were downloaded in August of 2020 from AWQMS based on a search query applied to the period from 1901 through 2019. Utah Lake has Secchi depth measurements of only 0.27 and 0.25 m for its mean and median values, respectively, and a level of total dissolved solids of over 1000 mg/L. These very shallow Secchi depths and the high level of total dissolved solids indicate that Utah Lake is optically complex. Other parameters, which are presented in Table 1, support this conclusion. While the geochemistry of Utah Lake, including its dissolved and suspended solids, is eutrophic, studies have shown that water quality, as measured by chl-a, has been improving over the last 40 years [28].

Table 1. Utah Lake data from the Utah Ambient Water Quality Monitoring System (AWQMS), managed by the Utah Department of Water Quality (DWQ) (downloaded 1 August 2020), for the 2019 period.

Characteristic Name	N	Mean	Median	Max.	Min.	Std. Dev	Skew	Kurt.
Depth, Secchi disk (m)	3083	0.27	0.25	7.00	0.00	0.21	15.29	402.48
Turbidity (NTU)	683	62.30	41.60	790.00	0.10	89.12	5.31	33.68
Total suspended solids (mg/L)	1281	63.26	45.00	900.00	1.00	75.46	5.20	38.85
Total dissolved solids (mg/L)	1061	1016.94	1000.00	2340.00	106.00	281.45	0.26	0.78
Total volatile solids (mg/L)	716	12.30	9.00	110.00	2.00	11.09	3.40	18.40
Specific conductance (µmho/cm)	6614	1758.35	1772.15	20,980.0	0.00	501.40	14.41	539.50
Calcium (mg/L)	1058	62.59	59.00	213.00	24.50	21.93	3.35	13.98
Hardness, Ca, Mg (mg/L)	715	413.27	406.40	898.50	137.20	94.67	1.70	5.04
Carbonate (mg/L)	690	2.89	N/A	123.00	0.00	6.26	10.70	195.91
Chlorophyll a, (µg/L)	821	40.51	21.30	597.50	0.20	58.84	3.92	21.76

Utah Lake, like most water bodies, does not have water sampling data with the spatial and temporal scope required to evaluate long-term trends and spatial patterns; however, it does have more in situ data available than many reservoirs. This reason, combined with its optically complex nature, is why we selected Utah Lake to demonstrate L1 regularization for model selection.

2. Data and Methods

2.1. Overview

We obtained in situ measurements that included the measurement date, sample collection time, measurement location (latitude and longitude), and chl-a concentrations from AQWMS (Table 1). We uploaded these data and used Google Earth Engine (GEE) to acquire all available Landsat pixel data from the in situ data locations along with the time difference between the satellite and field collections. The satellite data included the values for each Landsat band and the image timestamps.

We used a 5-day offset for the initial data extraction process, that is, any data within 5 days of either side of a field collection; however, we performed most computations using a smaller offset and both 30 and 90 m resolution datasets. The 30 m resolution data correspond to a single pixel at the native Landsat resolution, and the 90 m resolution data represent a 3 × 3 grid averaged to mitigate noise and spatial variation. We extracted the band data using GEE, which identified images within the offset window, selected the pixel(s) associated with the in situ measurement location, and computed the 90 m average. These data were exported as a table. The table has one row for each in situ measurement and includes the in situ date/times, locations, offsets to remote-sensing data (in hours), in situ parameter values, and remote-sensing band values. For the Landsat missions, there are 8 additional columns. We generated separate tables for the 30 m and 90 m data. These data can be used to develop models using our approach or any other method. Details and working code used to create this table are provided in a Google Colab Notebook called DataCollectionNotebook (Notebook1).

The remainder of Section 2 outlines the model generation process, providing details and discussion for each step. We use the data generated by Notebook1 in this study (Section 2.2) and select an offset and the features to be considered in model creation, such as bands or band combinations, and generate these features (Section 2.3). We discuss some data issues caused by negative reflectance values (Section 2.4); then, we discuss α value selection (Section 2.5). Subsequently, we present model-fitting and error estimation processes performed (Section 2.6). Details of and working code used to perform model fitting are included in the ModelFitNotebook (Notebook2). We provide a brief description of the two notebooks that contain the example code to perform the feature-engineering and model-fitting steps (Section 2.7). Notebook1 generates the data used to create using the methods provided in Notebook2.

In Section 3, we demonstrate the impacts of resolution, offset, and α selection on model accuracy and discuss best approaches for selecting these parameters. This includes the impacts of the time offset between in situ and remote-sensing data and how the resolution of remote-sensing data impacts model error.

2.2. Study Data

We used AQWMS data collected from 42 Utah Lake locations (Figure 2). We selected "chlorophyll a, uncorrected for pheophytin" surface measurements as the water quality parameter. The data were downloaded in July 2022 and contained 1024 samples from 11 July 1989 through 15 September 2021. We only performed minimal data cleaning and quality assurance with respect to these data. Results presented in later sections indicate that we may have included some outliers, and several duplicate samples, which affected model's results. Since this paper focuses on the model creation methods and not on models' results, we did not expend any additional efforts on data cleaning.

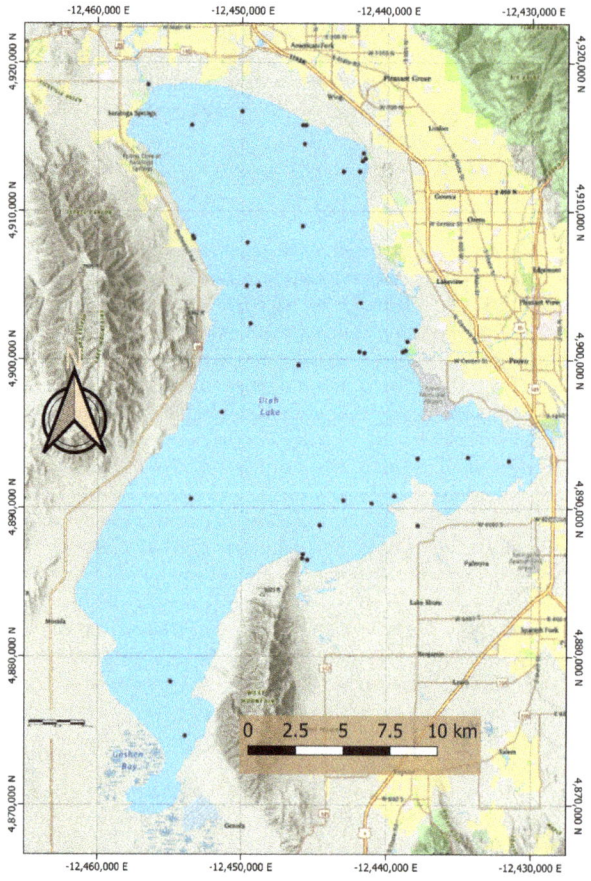

Figure 2. Utah Lake sample locations from the DWQ AQWMS database.

Figure 3 shows that most of these data were collected since 2017. Two outliers with values of 503 and 905 µg/L were excluded in the plot to preserve readability. The 99.5% quantile for these data is 427.63 µg/L. The boxplots (top panel) suggest that the concentration of chl-a is increasing over time, with larger interquartile ranges on the boxplots and large outliers indicating increased variability. However, there is sampling bias in these measurements. Later samples focus on areas prone to algal blooms and higher chl-a concentrations, such as Provo Bay. Recent studies show that chl-a concentrations in the lake, with the exception of small areas of Provo Bay, are decreasing over time [28,30].

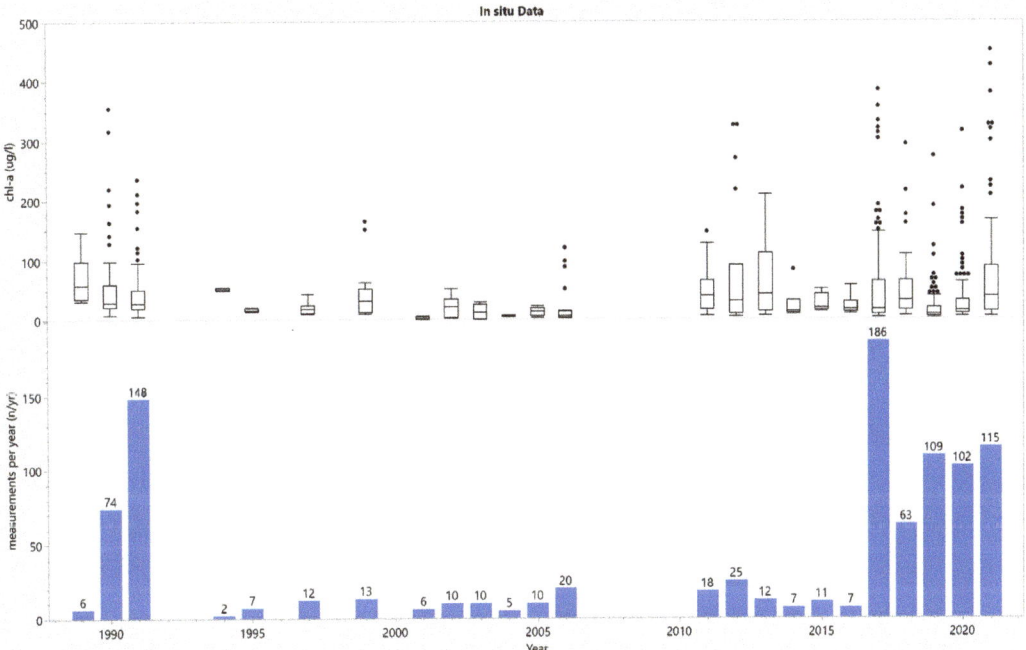

Figure 3. Box plots of chl-a concentrations over time (top panel), with the number of samples collected per year presented in a bar chart (bottom panel). These data were downloaded from the AQWMS database and contain data collected from 11 July 1989 through 15 September 2021, constituting 1024 measurements in total. Outliers in the top plot were clipped to 500 µg/L for visualization purposes.

Figure 4 shows the distribution of chl-a concentrations and statistics for measured values that have near-coincident satellite pixels. These data have a usable Landsat pixel available within the 5-day (120 h) offset (Figure 4). This resulted in a dataset with 531 samples, amounting to about half of the original dataset. These data have a maximum value of 503.3 µg/L and mean and median values of 36.9 and 17.75 µg/L, respectively. The quantile plot and information (Figure 4) show that 99.5% of the data are below 337 µg/L. The data are right-skewed. Most sample concentrations are relatively low, with rare episodic events exhibiting high concentrations (i.e., blooms). The 75th percentile concentration is only 42 µg/L, which is less than 10% of the maximum. The episodic nature of the high concentration data is shown in the relatively large skew and kurtosis values, which match our expectations for algal blooms.

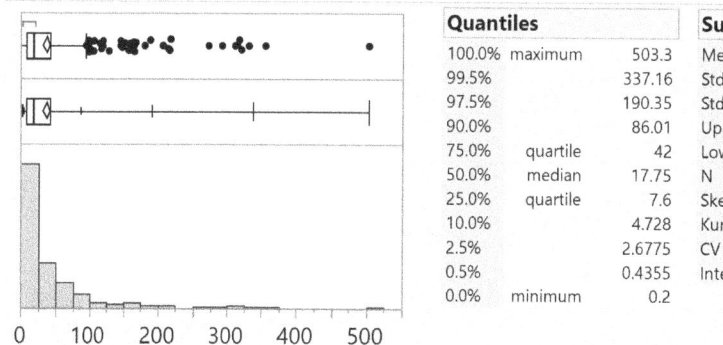

Figure 4. Whisker, quantile, and histogram plots (left) and summary statistics for chl-a values (μg/L) that have a near-coincident Landsat pixel data pair. For these data, we selected a 5-day offset and a 30 m resolution. The quantile values in the second panel match the tick marks in the quantile plot in the left panel (second from the top).

Figure 5 depicts the in situ measurements plotted against the absolute value of the offset (in hours) between the in situ measurements and their nearest Landsat image. The absolute offset value includes in situ data collected either before or after the satellite passed over. The dividing lines occur at 12 h increments until 72 h (3 days); then, they occur at 24 h increments to 120 h (5 days). In between each line is a number indicating the number of pairs that occurred in that interval. Figure 5 highlights the relationship between Landsat collections and field work. Landsat collections occurred at 10:30 am local time. The plots show that field data are often collected in the mornings, with data clustered around 24 h (1-day) offsets. This plot shows that our in situ data were generally collected within a few hours of 10:30 local solar time. The clusters show that the data from the "morning" sampling trips were collected about two and a half hours before and after the satellite's overpass, or from about 8:00 am to about 1:00 pm, a pattern we followed in our own water-sampling campaigns. This morning sampling pattern is clearly presented in Figure 5 with sample clusters at 24, 48, and 72 h, wherein the dividing line represents the time splitting the data clusters. While in this study we maintained multiples of 12 for our offset, we recommend that each researcher should carefully examine examine their data, and potentially use offsets other than 12 h intervals. For example, the 30 h window includes data within a cluster of samples that would otherwise be excluded by 24 h window (Figure 5). These samples were only a few hours beyond the 24 h mark, and the inclusion of these samples significantly increased the size of the available data. In other words, in Figure 5, a cutoff of 30 h keeps the entire cluster of pairs around the 24 h mark rather than only the pairs to the left of it. In subsequent computations, we limited data to an offset of 3 days, or 72 h, for model development; however, we also present models with smaller offsets.

Table 2 provides the number of pairs in an offset period and the mean, median, and standard deviation of the values in the period. It also provides the cumulative number of data pairs that were used for model development, along with the cumulative statistics. The last line presents the statistics for all the data, which is a subset of the information provided in Figure 4. The cumulative mean matches the mean of all the data, while the cumulative standard deviation is slightly different due to rounding errors. The data in the different time slices along with the cumulative datasets show variation, wherein mean, median, and standard deviation values clustered around the values for the entire dataset. We compared the data in each 6 h offset bin using both a Student's T test and the Tukey–Kramer test for unequal size groups. The resulting comparison shows that there was no significant difference among any of the bins at an α level of 0.01.

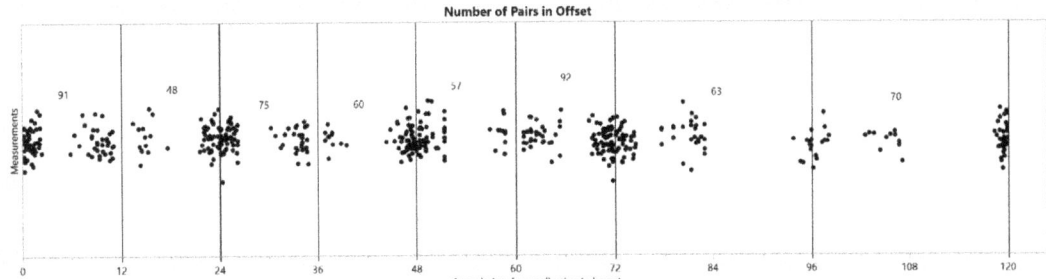

Figure 5. Satellite collection and in situ data pairs shown as the absolute offset in hours from the satellite collection.

Table 2. Number of in situ/satellite image pairs for different outsets, with descriptive statistics provided for the in situ chl-a data.

Offset (Hours)	N	Mean	Median	Std Dev	Cumulative N	Cum. Mean	Cum. Std Dev
0–12	91	32.84	16.6	60.37	91	32.84	60.37
12–24	48	31.06	11.35	73.12	139	32.23	65.03
24–36	75	32.94	15.16	46.42	214	32.48	59.17
36–48	60	44.24	31.75	48.33	274	35.05	56.98
48–60	57	28.87	11.5	37.21	331	33.99	54.10
60–72	92	33.62	23.35	35.28	423	33.91	50.59
72–96	63	44.74	21.30	57.57	486	35.31	51.55
96–120	70	48.00	21.62	69.72	556	36.91	54.17
All	556	36.91	17.75	54.25	N/A	36.91	54.25

We acquired the near-coincident remote-sensing data used in this study using GEE [37] from the Landsat 5, 7, 8, and 9 missions included in the Collection 2 data generated by the USGS. These datasets have the following GEE image collection identifiers: LANDSAT/LT05/C02/T1_L2, L2LANDSAT/LE07/C02/T1_L2, LANDSAT/LC08/C02/T1_L2, and LANDSAT/LC09/C02/T1_L2, respectively. The collection identifiers include the overall mission (LANDSAT), the satellite (LT05–LC09), the collection (C02), and the processing level (T1_L2). While Landsat 5 and Landsat 7 have the same band designations [11], Landsat 8 has different band designations (Table 3). We mapped the bands to a common set of names (Table 3) and combined the Landsat datasets into a single image collection using GEE.

Table 3. Mapping of band names to satellite bands for the three Landsat missions used in this paper.

Band Name	Satellite Bands		
	Landsat 8	Landsat 7	Landsat 5
Blue	SR_B2	SR_B1	SR_B1
green	SR_B3	SR_B2	SR_B2
red	SR_B4	SR_B3	SR_B3
NIR [1]	SR_B5	SR_B4	SR_B4
SWIR1 [2]	SR_B6	SR_B5	SR_B5
SWIR2 [2]	SR_B7	SR_B7	SR_B7
SurfTempK [3]	ST_B10	ST_B6	ST_B6

[1] Near-infrared (NIR); [2] shortwave infrared (SWIR); [3] surface temperature (Kelvin).

We used the calibrated surface reflectance data from the USGS Level 2 Collection 2 Tier 1 data [38,39], thereby eliminating the need to perform atmospheric corrections. The USGS produces three data tiers; for this dataset, tier 1 (T1) meets geometric and radiometric quality standards, and Level 2 data correspond to data that are calibrated and ready for analysis.

Using GEE, we generated an image collection from all the images from Landsat missions 5, 7, 8, and 9 that included Utah Lake. However, since the coverage period of our in situ data ended in September 2021, we did not use any Landsat 9 images in this study. Data in the GEE image collections were stored as integers; we converted the integers to surface reflectance floating-point values using the USGS-supplied multipliers before analysis.

We used the quality assessment (QA) band to eliminate pixels that were clouded, had cloud shadows, or were otherwise contaminated and to identify water pixels [38]. For 30 m data, the pixels that contained the in situ measurement points needed to pass the quality-screening test. For the 90 m data, either all 9 or any of the 9 pixels in the 3 × 3 group nearest the in situ point needed to pass the quality-screening procedure to be selected. This method is similar to those described by Cardall, Tanner, and Williams [37].

The result of this process was a dataset containing the in situ measurement value, the offset in hours between the measurement and the pixel value, and the band values of the corresponding Landsat image pixels. We recommend collecting data at a large offset and filtering the data at the model-fitting stage to avoid incrementally collecting more data for larger time offsets.

We have provided Notebook1, which contains working code, to better describe and demonstrate the method. Notebook1 accepts a CSV file with date, location (in latitude and longitude), and a measurement value of any in situ data as input. It outputs a CSV file that echoes this input and adds columns with the offset information and the reflectance value for each of the satellite bands. Notebook1 is designed to select Landsat data but could be modified for other sensors.

2.3. Model Parameters

We used 6 Landsat bands (Table 3) corresponding to the blue, green, red, near-infrared (NIR), shortwave infrared-1 (SWIR1), and shortwave infrared-2 (SWIR2) regions. We did not use the surface temperature band as a potential model feature. Since we expected high chl-a values to be strongly correlated with warm temperatures, we excluded temperature from the model to avoid an overfit and poor model performance in non-summer months. Surface temperature may be an appropriate feature for some models, such as a seasonal model trained for summer months.

We generated potential features for the linear regression model that include: the Landsat bands (6), the inverse of the natural log of each band ($1/\ln x$) (6), the natural logs of each band ($\ln x$) (6), the inverse of each band ($1/x$) (6), the square of each band (x^2) (6), band ratios (x_1/x_2) (30), normalized band differences ($[x_1 - x_2]/[x_1 + x_2]$) (15), and band pair multiplications ($x_1 * x_2$) (15). We included the inverse and squared terms for the bands so that we could consider non-linear model relationships in a LASSO multi-linear regression. The inclusion of the 6 bands and all the engineered features resulted in 90 different potential features in the model. The use of other sensors, such as MODIS or Sentinel II, would result in a different number bands, band spectral range, and features.

Initially, we generated all the features for SWIR1 and SWIR2 bands. The resulting models preferably selected the inverse of these two bands as features. However, while the number of errors was relatively low, these bands are noisy and correlated with water temperature, which we intentionally did not include as a potential feature; therefore, these features will likely be excluded in models designed to achieve maximum performance. In the work reported below, we retained the SWIR1 and SWIR2 band features but did not include any engineered features using these bands, e.g., band inverses, band ratios, squares, or other features. We retained SWIR1 because some of the published Utah Lake models use SWIR1.

2.4. Negative and Small Reflectance Values

The USGS calibration process for surface reflectance data can result in the acquirement of negative values for the blue and SWIR bands over water, as water has low reflectance in these wavelengths. These negative values are not physically possible but are artifacts of data processing. In the coincident data pairs, with a coincidence window of 5 days, there were 16, 2, 37, 40, and 40 negative values for the blue, red, NIR, SWIR1, and SWIR2 bands, respectively. The values, while negative, have small absolute values. This occurs because water is highly light-absorbent in the SWIR range. Due to the high concentrations of suspended solids in Utah Lake, it is possible that light in the SWIR range can scatter back from suspended material if the scatterers are shallow enough, thereby providing the small values observed in the data. For instance, at 1640 nm (~SWIR1), the absorption coefficient for water is 6.35/cm [40]; thus, if light scatters back from 1 cm depth, only $e^{-12.70}$ ~3×10^{-6} of the light that reaches that far will be reflected from the surface. Likewise, the SWIR2 band has an absorption coefficient of about 20/cm, which is generally higher throughout the bandpass [40]. Due to this high level of light absorption, the SWIR bands are very sensitive to any unremoved glint (from skylight or sunlight). Landsat level 2 reflectance data are highly optimized for land and are not corrected for glint from water surfaces.

Most physically based models (i.e., based on response of chlorophyll and accounting for other constituents in the water) use visible and near-infrared wavelengths (see, for example, [41]). For Utah Lake, suspended calcium carbonate and sediments are currently present in the upper portion of the water column, and these allow for the return of light; additionally, as noted, we retained the SWIR1 band because published Utah Lake models used this band.

We found that if we fit a model with these small, negative values (with bands set to a minimal positive value before computing inverses or logs), a few predicted chl-a values (fewer than 10 of the approximately 500-member dataset) consequently corresponded to large, negative values. We used an ad hoc approach to evaluate different methods to address this issue. For this study, we replaced extremely small or negative values reflectance for the blue, red, NIR, and SWIR1 bands with values of 0.01, 0.01, 0.001, and 0.001, respectively. Offset methods may be more appropriate in order to maintain original, small band values distinct from these changes. Data-cleaning operations are required and are specific to any given dataset. We recommend more advanced methods, such as an offset approach, but did not evaluate other methods for this study.

2.5. Alpha

The degree to which L1 reduces the number of model parameters is tuned using the α parameter, which computes the penalty function with a weighted combination of the fitting error and the sum of the absolute value of the model coefficients (Equation (1)). A larger α value increases the weight of the coefficient sum and results in fewer parameters in the final model, while a lower α value results in more terms as it favors a small error with less weight assigned to the number of features. At the extremes, an α value of zero retains all the potential model parameters, while a large α value results in a linear model that is a single constant, i.e., all coefficients are set to zero and the model is just a constant. In the latter case, the model error, which is the first term in the loss function (Equation (1)), constitutes the variance of the data (square of the standard deviation). This extremely large α value results in a model of the form of $\hat{y} = c$ or causes the prediction to be a constant that is equal to the mean of the dataset.

We explore α selection in detail in the case study provided in Section 3.1. We suggest that practitioners compute the variance of their dataset and evaluate their coefficients' magnitude for a full model (i.e., α = 0). This will provide some insight into the expected range of the α value. Conversely, using the scikit-learn library, one can quickly select different values of α and evaluate the results, thus enabling the simple identification of the range of α values that provides a model with the preferred number of terms.

This approach facilitates the exploration of a wide feature space. For example, a priori, we do not know if the best model is linear or non-linear. By including band inverses, logs of bands, and squared band values, we can use linear regression methods to fit non-linear models and allow the algorithm to determine which is the best method to model the data. We allow L1 regression to determine whether linear, non-linear, or a combination of both types of terms provides higher predictive capabilities while providing a parsimonious model where parameter contributions can be explored and explained. However, L1 regularization will generally discard correlated features, while the most informative model may include these correlated features. This is discussed in Section 4.

2.6. Model Training, Error Estimation, and Evaluation

For the case study, we used the default values to fit the scikit-learn Lasso model (with the exception of α, which we adjusted). We explicitly set the maximum interactions to 1000; this is also the default value. The Lasso model uses coordinate descent to minimize the cost function and fit the model [32]. We used k-fold cross-validation to determine model's performance. Unless otherwise stated, we used 10 folds and 20 repeats. For each fold, 10% of the data were reserved as the test set, and the model was fit to the remaining 90% of the data; then, the accuracy was computed using the test data. This was repeated 20 times, with the data stochastically sampled for each fold. This resulted in 200 model realizations that were used to estimate the error for any given model. While it is common to use train–test–validate splits to develop and evaluate models, in this case, since the number of parameters and number of samples are similar, we used the k-fold approach as there was not a sufficient number of data to render the train–test–validate approach viable. For example, for a time offset of 12 h, there are 91 data pairs, which almost matches the number of potential features (90). In this case, 90% of the dataset equates to approximately 80 values, that is, the number in each fold, which is less than the number of total potential parameters.

We computed several error metrics, including the root-mean-squared error (RMSE), which we will generally use for reporting in subsequent sections. After evaluating model accuracy using k-fold cross validation, we generated the final model using the full dataset with no data reserved. We used k-fold analysis to select the model parameters and estimate error; then, we used the resulting parameters with all the data to develop an accurate but parsimonious model that could be used and explained.

We evaluated feature selection over a range of α values to determine if the features selected by the L1 algorithm were robust or if the selected features changed significantly with different α values or over the duration of the stochastic realizations. We evaluated feature stability by counting how many times each feature was selected for a model with a given number of parameters, wherein any of the models had at least 200 realizations. We present details of this analysis in Section 3.

After selecting the appropriate model parameters, such as α, and estimating the error, we then used the model, trained with respect to all the data, to evaluate the impact of coincidence time offsets on model accuracy. This analysis, presented in Sections 3.3 and 3.4, provides practitioners with guidelines and methods for evaluating the trade-offs between data quantity and variation with time.

2.7. Code and Notebooks

We have provided example code in two separate Google Colab notebooks to help communicate the details of the methods we developed and provide readers with a starting point if they should choose to evaluate these techniques.

Notebook1 takes a CSV file of in situ measurements, including the measurement date, latitude, longitude, measured value, and maximum offset window, as an input. It outputs a CSV file that includes the original data, the measured satellite band values (currently, the Landsat series), and the offset time from the in situ sample to the satellite collection.

Notebook1 uses the complete Landsat image collection (Landsat 5, 7, 8, and 9) with data from the early 1980s to the present. Notebook1 can be easily modified to obtain data from other collections such as MODIS or Sentinel 2.

Notebook2 reads in the data file generated by Notebook1, performs minimal data cleaning, and conducts feature engineering; then, it uses L1 regularization to generate a multi-linear regression model in either normal or log-space. The level of data cleaning is minimal, consisting of the removal of blank rows or rows where there are NaN values. Notebook2 performs a feature-engineering task that generates additional model features. The features are selectable by checkboxes, and choices include the following bands: log(band), inverse log(band), inverse bands, band ratios, normalized band differences, square of bands, and band products. Notebook2 can save a CSV file with all the measurements and features to allow a practitioner to use their own software or methods for model fitting. For accurate model development, we recommend a more in-depth data-cleaning step that is data-specific and not algorithmic.

Notebook2 generates a multi-linear regression model by regressing the features on the measured in situ data using L1 regularization. Both the offset amount (i.e., time window for coincident samples) and the L1 α value are selectable. Notebook2 also allows the features to be normalized or scaled using either min–max scaling or normal (z-score) scaling. We did not scale data or evaluate data scaling for this study.

Notebook2 provides some simple visualizations to aid model fitting and estimates model error using repeated k-fold validation with 10 folds and 20 repeats, which is easily changeable. It outputs a CSV file with the selected offset, pixel scaling (i.e., 3×3 or 9×9), number of data points used in the model, list of all the features used in fitting, parameter coefficients, and error estimates.

3. Case Study and Results

3.1. Impact of Alpha Selection

Figure 6 presents the parameter coefficients for the models created with α values (displayed on the x-axis) ranging from 1000 to 1 and from 100 to 1×10^{-2} for the chl-a model (top panel) and log(chl-a) model (bottom panel), respectively. In Figure 6, each line represents the value of a coefficient for a model feature that has been selected by the algorithm. At large α values, most coefficients are zero, with the number and size of the parameter coefficients increasing with decreasing α values. Small α values weight error higher than feature count, resulting in more of the features being included in the model. These plots were made with 90 potential features and a 72 h (3 day) time window, thereby providing 402 measurements.

At large α values, which are displayed on the left side of both the top and bottom panels (Figure 6, top), most of the parameter coefficients are zero or low, as expected. As the α value decreases, both the number and value of the parameter coefficients increase.

The parameter coefficients for 1/NIR and 1/blue bands are the first parameters selected and do not reach zero until they are near larger α values. None of the other features are selected (i.e., the parameter coefficients become non-zero) until an α value below about 0.8 or 1 for the chl-a model or log(chl-a) model, respectively, when the coefficient for the 1/red and blue/NIR feature becomes non-zero for the chl-a model and log(chl-a) model, respectively. Additional features are added to the selections (i.e., the parameters are assigned non-zero coefficients) as the α value continues to decrease.

Figure 6 does not reach extreme α values allowing it to show models with all 90 features; this occurs at α values near 1×10^{-8}, and such models are not realistic for a dataset of only 400 measurements. In this region, some of the features have large positive and negative offsetting coefficients, which are also unreasonable.

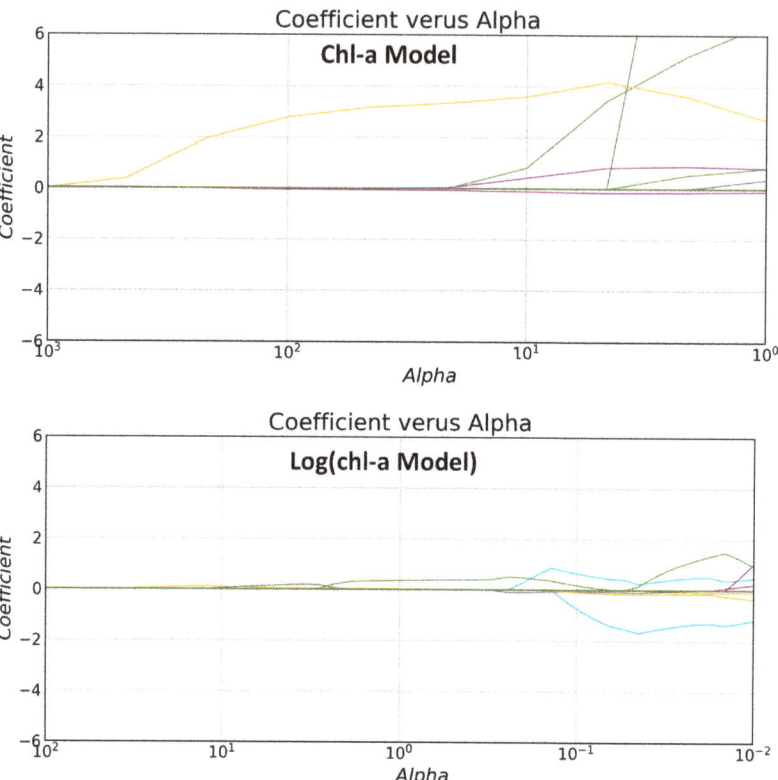

Figure 6. The model coefficient values with a 72 h (3 day) time window for the chl-a (**top**) and log(chl-a) (**bottom**) models whose α values vary from 1000 to 1 and 100 to 1×10^{-2}, respectively (x-axis is log scale) plotted on a log scale. This plot shows the number and size of the parameter coefficients, where each line represents the coefficient for a model feature. The number of coefficients (parameters) increases with decreasing α values (i.e., more lines), with absolute coefficient values also increasing (i.e., line magnitude).

The bottom panel of Figure 6 shows the behavior of L1 regularization for a model that predicts the log of chl-a (log(chl-a)) content rather than chl-a content directly. Figure 6 shows that various features are added to the model at significantly lower α values compared to the direct chl-a model. This is in part because the absolute value of the error is lower in the L1 algorithm because the log of the values is significantly smaller than the values themselves.

We evaluated the accuracy of the models with different α values and used k-fold validation to estimate errors (Figure 7). For this analysis, we used data with an offset or time window of 12 h. We used ten folds with 20 repeats to compute error metrics for different values of α, which are shown as points on the graph; thus, the error estimates for each α value, or graph point, are based on 200 realizations. We evaluated both the direct chl-a model and the log(chl-a) model, which are presented in the top and bottom panels of Figure 7, respectively.

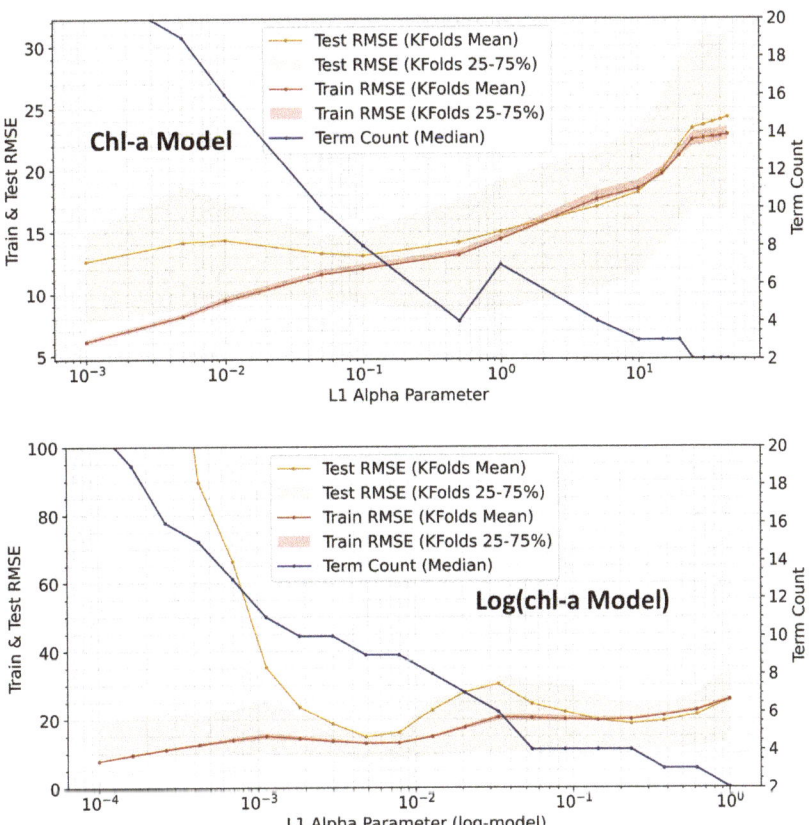

Figure 7. Test and training error versus α value computed using 200 k-fold realizations for each α value, where number of model coefficients for the chl-a and log(chl-a) models is depicted in the top and bottom panels, respectively. These plots used data with a 12 h (1 day) time window. The blue line shows the number of terms in the model versus α or the L1 regularization weight.

Figure 7 graphically presents the results and trade-offs of different α values for the chl-a and log(chl-a) models in the top and bottom panels, respectively. These figures show the mean RMSE of the training and test datasets and the mode of the number of model terms vs. α. The standard model uses α values from 0.001 to 50, while the log(chl-a) model uses α values from 0.0001 to 1. There are 200 stochastic realizations for each data point. The shaded area in the plot represents the 25th and 75th quartiles and shows the variability of the test error metric over the 200 realizations. For small α values, the mean of the error is well outside the 75th percentile. This is because a few of the 200 realizations have very large errors and skew the dataset. Both models behave as expected, where the test data error is initially very high—indicating overfitting—and then reduces to a value similar to the training error (Figure 7). The training error has significantly less variation for all the realizations compared to the test error, as shown by the width of the shaded area.

For both models, chl-a and log(chl-a), the variance in the test error increases with an increasing α. A great deal of this behavior can be attributed to the small size of our dataset. For a time offset of 12 h, there are only 82 measurements. With 10 folds, that means that the test dataset has only 7 or 8 values, leaving the training datasets with about 70 values. These data have a mean of about 30 and a standard deviation of about 60 (Table 2); therefore, there was significant variation in the test data for any given realization. These plots show general trends, but the variation in the test error for any given realization is large, with the shaded portion, itself large, containing only half (~100) of the 200 realizations for each data point on the graph. However, the variation in the error computed for the training data is relatively small, indicating little variation over the 200 realizations.

The chl-a model plot indicates overfitting until about the middle of the plots; then, both the training and test errors become similar and increase with decreasing α values. Figure 7 shows that as α increases, the number of retained features (blue line) decreases, as the former places a higher penalty on the sum of the coefficients. The model with the fewest terms has the highest RMSE as the model moves towards predicting a constant.

For the chl-a model, the difference between training and testing also decreases until an α value of about 1.0, at which point they become similar, and there are four to six terms retained for the model. At this point the errors are similar and increase with increasing α values as the model essentially only predicts the mean of the test or training dataset.

The bottom panel of Figure 7 shows the results of the log(chl-a) model, which has similar trends but presents a larger gap between the testing and training datasets at low α values. For this dataset, the log(chl-a)-model indicates clear overfitting at small α values, with less overfitting as α increases. One interesting aspect of this plot is that at low α values, the mean RMSE is well outside the 75th percentile (even more so than in the top panel). This occurs because the dataset includes three large values; if these three values all appear in the testing data, the resulting model can be severely overfit with respect to the low values. The 200 realizations produced a few models with very large, unrealistic values for these few cases, which resulted in a very large mean value, though only for a few realizations; over 50 % of the realizations (between the 25th and 75th percentiles) are close to the test dataset error.

Table 4 summarizes the impact of α values on the number of terms in the model. This table was generated using all the data with a 72 h offset rather than the 12 h offset used in the plots. The RMSE was also computed using all the data (i.e., the training data). The number of terms in the model drops to five when α is equal to twelve and does not drop to four until α is five for the chl-a model. While not shown in Figure 7, the variation in the number of coefficients is small.

Table 4. The number of terms included in calibrated chl-a and log(chl-a) models and the corresponding range of α values with a 72 h (3-day) time window using all the data.

Chl-a Model	Chl-a Model	Chl-a Model	Log(chl-a) Model	Log(chl-a) Model	Log(chl-a) Model
Alpha (α)	Number of Terms	RMSE	Alpha (α)	Number of Terms	RMSE
0.005	22	25.46	0.0001	23	36.89
0.01	20	25.82	0.0002	20	36.35
0.05	16	26.69	0.0005	19	35.69
0.1	12	27.24	0.0010	14	35.96
0.5	8	27.52	0.0022	11	35.81
1	8	27.89	0.0046	10	35.73
5	4	31.10	0.0100	10	37.31
10	3	31.32	0.0215	9	42.32
25	3	31.94	0.0464	8	53.91
50	2	32.61	0.1000	7	64.34

We have not provided a suggested range or value for α because the correct value depends on the variation in the target data, the range of the parameters, and the number of parameters in the final model. However, the mean value of the dataset can provide insight into the ranges to explore for determining the value of α. Evaluating the dataset's mean and variation through Equation (1) can provide some guidance. For example, if the dataset variation is in the 10s of units, e.g., 50 μg/L, and the expected features have coefficient values in the range of 0–1 and we want five parameters in the model, then the sum of the five coefficients needs to be in the same order of magnitude as the variation in the dataset. In this case, an α of 1 would assign approximately equal weight to the prediction error and the coefficients, while an α value of 500 would probably result in a model with only a single constant. However, depending on the range of feature values, coefficient values are frequently less than 1, which would require a larger α value to generate a model with five features. For this example, you could use an iterative approach with α values in the range of 1 to 100 to determine which α values result in a five-term model.

3.2. Model Terms and Stability

We evaluated the stability of the terms selected by L1 regularization. Specifically, we were interested in whether the realizations generated for the stochastic k-fold analysis would select the same equation terms with different coefficients or if each realization would select different terms. We found that the features selected by L1 regularization remained relatively constant with very little variation, for which old features were retained and new terms were selected as α decreased.

Figure 8 presents heatmaps for the chl-a (top panel) and log(chl-a) models (bottom panel), displaying the number of model terms selected (y-axis) versus the selected features (x-axis). We used k-fold realizations to generate this plot, for which there were 200 realizations per α value. The values for any given feature number are based on several hundred to a few thousand realizations, as a range of α values may result in the same number of features. The features in each panel are ordered by the percentage of time, or probability, that the feature was selected in any model, with the most-selected features depicted on the left. The color and number in the box reflect the probability that a feature was selected in the realizations. For each realization, we determined the number of features in the resulting model and which features were selected. We then computed, for any given feature count, the probability that a given feature was selected. The number of features is somewhat variable for a given α, and a range of α values can result in models with the same number of terms, which means that for any given feature count, there were at least 400, usually significantly more, realizations. Figure 8 shows that while there is some variability in the terms that were selected, in general, once a term was selected at a low feature count, it was retained in models with higher feature counts. For a given feature count, the selected terms remained consistent.

In the first row of the heatmap for the chl-a model (with a median feature count of 25), 25 of the most probable features (columns) were selected 100% of the time. For the next row, consisting of 24 features, 17 features were selected over 90% of the time, while 7 other features were selected over 80% of the time. As the number of terms in the model decreases (increasing α), so does the number of features, and the features that are selected are selected over 90 to 100% of the time, while other features are rarely chosen.

Figure 8 shows that the first two features, $\frac{1}{\rho_{NIR}}$ and $\frac{1}{\rho_{blue}}$, for either model are selected over 80% and 90% of the time in any model for the chl-a and log(chl-a) models, respectively, with either feature being selected 100% of the time for most feature counts. Other features are similar, with the next two features for either model being selected 100% of the time for the log(chl-a) model, while there is slightly more variation for the chl-a model.

For actual model development, this type of analysis should be performed, and modelers should consider which parameters should be included in the final model.

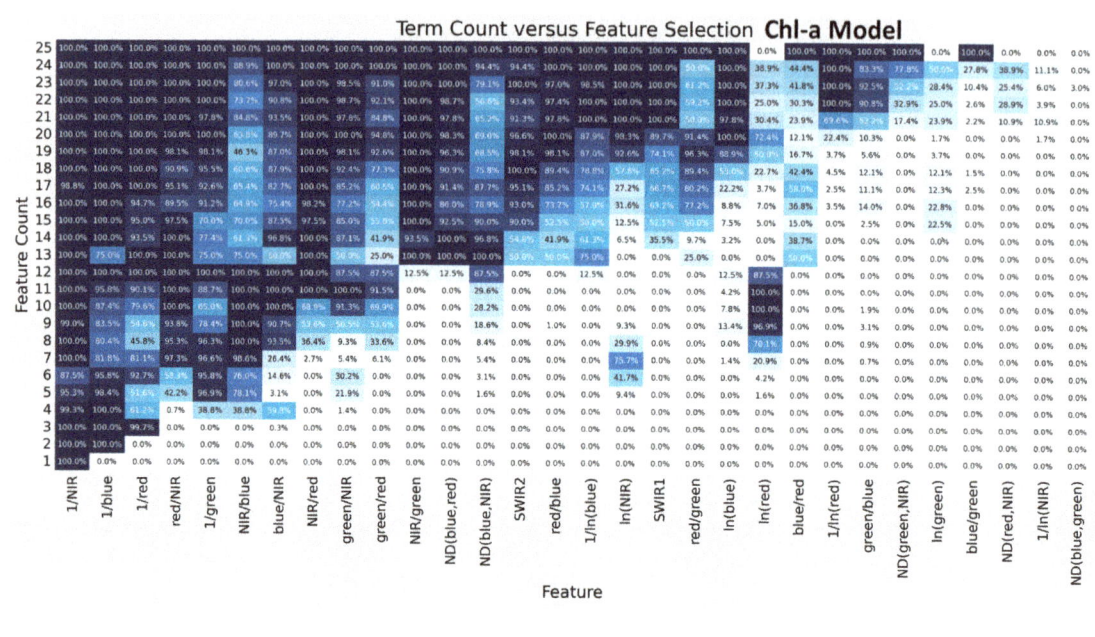

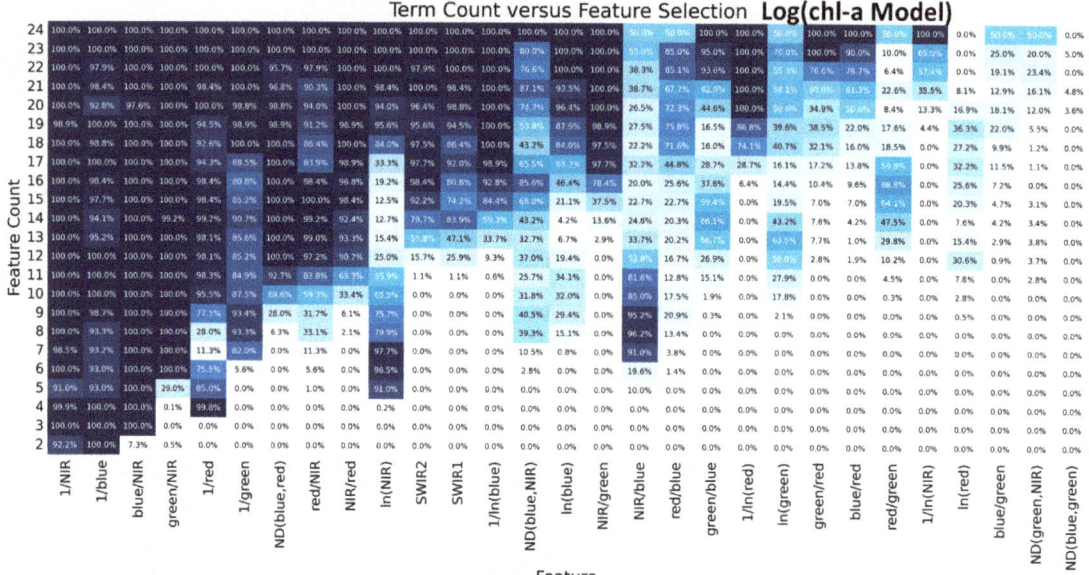

Figure 8. Heatmap of feature selection probability in the trained L1 model vs. feature names for the chl-a model (**top** panel) and the log(chl-a) model (**bottom** panel), respectively. This shows that for a given feature count, the selected features are consistent over hundreds of realizations. The standard model uses α values from 0.001 to 50, while the log(chl-a) model uses α values from 0.0001 to 1.

3.3. Impact of Time Coincidence

We used both the chl-a and log(chl-a) models with α values of 0.5 and 0.04, respectively, to analyze the impact of coincidence measurements or the offset between when satellite and in situ data were collected. We used k-fold validation with 10 splits and 20 repeats to compute the RMSE error (Table 5). A time offset impacts a model in two different ways. For samples taken later in time, it is likely that conditions have changed, which generally tends to decrease the accuracy of the models, but with an increasing time window there are more in situ–satellite measurement pairs, which generally increases model accuracy, and the tradeoffs between these two processes are not obvious. Accordingly, it is often unclear which offset should be used to develop the best model; is it better to have more representative data (i.e., small offset) or more data (i.e., large offset)? We present the results of different offsets to provide insight into how our dataset behaved. Care should be taken when interpreting these results, as different datasets will behave differently from our example.

Table 5. Impact of the time window size for near-coincident measures on the median RMSE for models with an α of 0.5 (chl-a) and 0.04 (log(chl-a)).

Window Size (Hours)	# of Data Pairs	RMSE (chla)	RMSE (log(chla))
6	55	11.67	11.09
12	85	10.78	16.99
18	99	12.12	16.52
24	123	15.80	20.54
30	168	17.44	23.12
36	193	19.55	22.98
42	202	20.98	25.24
48	249	26.04	33.53
54	290	26.07	33.37
60	300	26.22	33.63
66	328	28.38	35.87
72	388	27.40	34.45

We obtained an extensive dataset that contains over 500 in situ measurements. Table 5 shows that as the window size decreases, the number of data pairs also decreases, changing from 388 to 55 data pairs for time windows of 72 to 6 h, respectively. Even with a short window of 6 h, we have 55 data points, which is more than many published studies.

For our data, the RMSE decreases from about 28 to about 12 and about 35 to about 11 for the chl-a and log(chl-a) models, respectively, as the time window decreases from 72 to 6 h, i.e., 388 to 55 data pairs. The largest time window, 72 h, has an RMSE larger than the RMSE of the smallest offset, 6 h, by factor of about 2 to 3 for the chl-a and log(chl-a) models, respectively.

Table 5 has implications for model developers. It shows that the tradeoffs between the data collected coincidentally or near-coincidentally and the number of data points available for model fitting can significantly affect the error. In our case study, we have a very large number of available in situ measurements, over 500, which means that we have sufficient data for the models (even with small time offsets). For many locations, this may not be the case. Many published studies use 10 measurements or fewer for model development but generally have measurements taken within a few hours of the satellite collection.

Our results imply that the use of a 12 h offset for our dataset resulted in the best model. This model is slightly better than the model created with data pairs from a 6 h offset. In addition, since we used a k-fold validation with 10 folds, we computed errors using models trained on only 90% of the available data. Utah Lake is large and subject to wind disturbance, which can rapidly change algae distribution, so a shorter window may be more important for Utah Lake than for other locations. For lakes that are more protected or smaller, a larger time window might be appropriate, especially if data are limited, and a larger offset allows more data. Rather than making a recommendation on an appropriate time window, we see this work as a guide that practitioners can use to conduct similar evaluations.

3.4. Pixel Resolution

We evaluated the impact of satellite data resolution on the development of a model used to examine Utah Lake. In prior sections, we used data with 30 m resolution, which is the default resolution of Landsat data. However, when evaluating non-coincident data, others [15] used 90 m pixels computed by the spatial averaging of the Landsat data to reduce variation or noise. They reasoned that since the data were not acquired coincidentally with satellite collection, using spatially averaged data may help reduce the impact of local variations. To evaluate the impact of 90 m data, we averaged a 3×3 Landsat pixel array around each in situ measurement location. Our algorithm provides averages even if all the pixels were unusable because they were occluded by clouds, cloud shadows, or other data quality issues. For example, some computed averages may consist of fewer than nine measurements. In general, this 90 m dataset presented a small increase in the number of data pairs for any given time window, as some of the in situ measurements had low quality pixels at the measurement location but usable pixels within the 90 m area.

Table 6 shows the impact of using averaged data for the chl-a models developed with offsets from 6 to 72 h and an α value of 0.50. We used k-fold validation with 10 folds and 20 repeats to compute RMSE from the testing data. For most offsets, there are a few more data pairs in the 90 m dataset. For most time windows, the 90 m dataset produces a slightly smaller error, although this is not the case for all of them. In general, the errors are essentially the same, except for time windows greater than 42 h, where the error for the 90 m dataset is slightly larger.

Table 6. Impact of pixel resolution with near-coincident measures on the median RMSE for models with an α of 0.5 (chl-a).

Window Size (Hours)	30 m # Data Pairs	30 m Test RMSE	90 m # Data Pairs	90 m Test RMSE
6	55	11.67	55	12.45
12	85	10.78	86	15.82
18	99	12.12	99	15.76
24	123	15.80	126	20.23
30	168	17.44	173	25.46
36	193	19.55	198	21.94
42	202	20.98	209	24.23
48	249	26.04	258	32.71
54	290	26.07	304	32.58
60	300	26.22	318	33.33
66	328	28.38	349	36.56
72	388	27.40	411	35.14

Tables 7 and 8 show the impact of the α values on the number of terms and RMSE values for the 30 m and 90 m datasets, respectively. We did not use k-fold validation on these data but computed the error for the entire dataset. This resulted in slightly different values than those shown in Table 6. The 90 m data consistently resulted in models with fewer terms than the 30 m models, for which slightly different RMSE values, both higher and lower, were obtained for the chl-a and log(chl-a) models, respectively. While the number of terms may be significant, the difference in RMSE is within the expected variation of the data.

The use of the 90 m data rather than the 30 m data resulted in slightly better models, for which there were fewer terms for a given α value and similar RMSE values. We attribute this finding to the fact that in situ measurements are point values that may differ from the average value over a pixel measured by a satellite. In addition, due to winds and currents, algal blooms can move between the time the sample was taken and that of the satellite overpass. In both cases, the 90 m data capture a greater degree of variation, though with less precision. Hansen and Williams [15] suggested using 90 m data; while our results agree with this suggestion, they also show that users need to evaluate their data to determine the impact of using average pixel values versus single pixel values for model development.

Table 7. A comparison of 30 m and 90 m versus α in calibrated chl-a models with a 12 h (3-day) time window and using all the data.

Alpha Values (α)	30 m Chl-a Number of Terms	30 m Chl-a RMSE	90 m Chl-a Number of Terms	90 m Chl-a RMSE
0.005	20	8.45	17	9.44
0.01	18	9.73	15	10.90
0.05	11	11.72	10	12.25
0.1	8	12.15	8	12.53
0.5	4	13.15	6	13.54
1	7	14.61	5	13.74
5	4	17.68	4	15.21
10	3	18.50	3	16.44
25	2	22.54	3	21.39
50	2	23.01	2	22.74

Table 8. A comparison of 30 m and 90 m data versus α in calibrated log(chl-a) models with a 12 h (3-day) time window and using all the data.

Alpha (α) Values	30 m Log(chl-a) Number of Terms	30 m Log(chl-a) RMSE	90 m Log(chl-a) Number of Terms	90 m Log(chl-a) RMSE
0.0001	22	55.76	20	53.47
0.0002	18	54.96	18	52.83
0.0005	15	54.39	14	51.88
0.0010	10	54.52	11	51.17
0.0022	10	54.18	7	50.87
0.0046	10	54.73	8	51.58
0.0100	9	56.04	7	52.86
0.0215	7	59.74	5	55.55
0.0464	4	59.87	4	60.24
0.1000	4	57.41	4	56.61

3.5. Model Comparisons

For this analysis, we generated both chl-a (Equation (2)) and log(chl-a) (Equation (3)) models using a time window of 12 h, which provided 24 h of data. These models were generated using all the data, with no data reserved for error analysis. Errors were computed for all the data (i.e., training data). We used α values of 0.5 and 0.04 for the chl-a and log(chl-a) models, respectively, which yielded four or five model terms plus the intercepts for the chl-a and log(chl-a) models, respectively. For all these models, chl-a concentrations are provided in μg/L. As these are regression equations, the coefficients for each term in the model have the correct units with which to be converted to μg/L; however, for conciseness, we did not assign units to the model coefficients.

The chl-a model that uses an α value of 0.5 and the data within 12 h of the satellite collection is defined as follows:

$$chla = 3.03 + 2.10 \frac{1}{\rho_{blue}} - 3.731 \frac{1}{\rho_{green}} - 0.0139 \frac{1}{\rho_{NIR}} + 0.016 \frac{\rho_{blue}}{\rho_{NIR}} \quad (2)$$

where *chla* is the chl-a concentration in μg/L and ρ_x represents the mean Landsat Level 2 reflectance from band *x*.

The log(chl-a) model generated using an α value of 0.04 and incorporating the data within 12 h of the satellite collection is defined as follows:

$$\ln(chla) = 3.66 + 0.84\ln(\rho_{NIR}) + 0.052\frac{1}{\rho_{blue}} - 0.0438\frac{1}{\rho_{red}} + 0.005\frac{1}{\rho_{NIR}} - 0.257\frac{\rho_{blue}}{\rho_{NIR}} \quad (3)$$

where *chla* is the chl-a concentration in μg/L and ρ_x represents the mean Landsat Level 2 reflectance from band x.

The models have three shared terms that appear in both models. The three shared terms include two band inverse values, $\frac{1}{\rho_{blue}}$ and $\frac{1}{\rho_{NIR}}$, and a band ratio, $\frac{\rho_{blue}}{\rho_{NIR}}$. The chl-a and log(chl-a) models have unique band inverse terms of $\frac{1}{\rho_{green}}$ and $\frac{1}{\rho_{red}}$, respectively, while the log(chl-a) model also has an $\ln(\rho_{NIR})$ term.

Matthews [42] conducted an exhaustive literature search of water quality models. The models he selected were not explicitly developed for optically complex waters, though a few might have been. He reported 18 different models for estimating chl-a concentrations and these models included 14 different terms, with half of the terms (7) being used only by a single model and not by any of the other models. The most common terms, which were used in more than one model, were blue, green, red, and NIR bands, which were used in nine, six, four, and three models, respectively. The SWIR1 and SWIR2 bands, along with the ratio of the blue and red bands ($\frac{\rho_{blue}}{\rho_{red}}$), were used in two different models. Matthews [42] only specified if a band, band ratio, or a log of a band or band ratio was included in the models. Therefore, the reported bands could have been band inverses (i.e., 1/band). If this is the case, then the band ratio terms and the $\frac{\rho_{blue}}{\rho_{NIR}}$ terms from our models match the reported bands, with only the $\ln(\rho_{NIR})$ term not reported in this study.

Hansen and Williams [15] published three seasonal models specifically for Utah Lake. These models were developed either using all available data or data from specific seasons. The investigated hypothesis was that phytoplankton populations change with seasons and present different spectral signatures. These models consisted of a whole-season (Equation (4)), an early-season (Equation (5)), and a late-season (Equation (6)) model. All three models estimated ln(chl-a):

$$\ln(chl) = -1.53 + 2.55\frac{\rho_{NIR}}{\rho_{blue}} - 1.15\ln(\rho_{blue}) \quad (4)$$

$$\ln(chl) = -14.23 + 9.33\frac{\rho_{green}}{\rho_{blue}} + 0.003 \cdot \rho_{blue} - 0.004 \cdot \rho_{SWIR1} \quad (5)$$

$$\ln(chl) = 7.33 - 0.004 \cdot \rho_{blue} - 0.05\frac{\rho_{green}}{\rho_{SWIR2}} + 0.01\frac{\rho_{red}}{\rho_{SWIR1}} \quad (6)$$

where *chla* is the chl-a concentration in μg/L and ρ_x represents the mean Landsat Level 2 reflectance from band x.

In these three models there are nine unique terms, with only the blue band shared between all three models; none of the other terms are shared. The $\frac{\rho_{NIR}}{\rho_{blue}}$ ratio term is in both our models and in the whole season model [15]. Our models both include a $\frac{1}{\rho_{blue}}$ term, while their models include ρ_{blue} or $\ln(\rho_{blue})$ terms, which are similar. These Utah Lake models share the blue and SWIR bands with those reported by [42] but share none of the other terms.

These comparisons show that the terms selected by L1 regularization are commonly used in published chl-a models. However, our approach allows the model to select terms that are generally not considered for model development, such as the log of band values.

Figure 9 compares the errors of our L1-created models and the models developed by Hansen and Williams [15]. Figure 9 shows the results from the L1 models that were trained using the data with a 12 h offset and α values of 0.5 and 0.04 for the chl-a and log(chl-a) models, respectively. We applied the L1-created Hansen and Williams [15] models to data with a time offset of 6 to 72 h. For the L1 models, this means that any data with time offsets of greater than 12 h had not been used in training and constitute a test set.

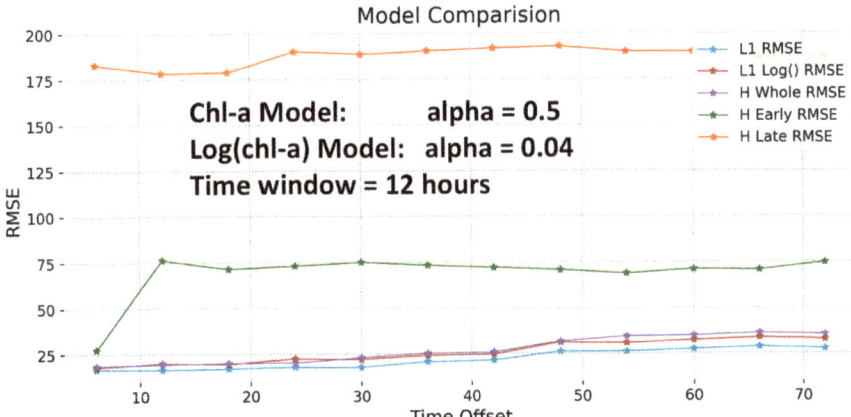

Figure 9. A comparison of errors for the L1 and Hansen models. The errors were computed using the entire dataset. The L1 models were fitted with the data with a time offset of 12 h.

Figure 9 shows that both the L1 and L1-log models closely match, and are slightly superior to, Hansen and Williams' [15] whole-season model and are better than the seasonal models. We did not fit L1 seasonal models for this paper nor did we compute errors for the Hansen models only concerning seasonal data, but we expect that the results would be similar. Hansen and Williams [15] showed that the seasonal models adequately corresponded to the seasonal data and outperformed the models generated on all the data; however, seasonal models are limited by the fact that there are often only very limited datasets for any given season. The L1 models trained on any given dataset generally perform worse than the whole-lake model on data from larger time offsets, though not always. As shown in Figure 9, if the L1 models are trained on the same data, they perform essentially the same as the whole-season model.

3.6. Optically Complex Water and SWIR1

Our goal in exploring the use of L1 regularization for the creation of remote-sensing models was to determine if this approach would be useful for optically complex waters where non-standard bands may be useful. Specifically, we sought to determine whether it would choose bands or other features that would not be selected based on the expected physics of the problem. Figure 10 demonstrates an example of where this might occur. For the following discussion, we have no ground truth, but the image supports our hypothesis.

Water has very high absorbance in the SWIR wavelength; therefore, its atmospherically corrected surface reflectance values are low. For example, at a wavelength of 1640 nanometers, which is about equal to that of the SWIR1 band for Landsat images, the absorption coefficient is 6.35/cm; thus, only about 0.01 (1%) of the light is reflected from a depth of ~0.36 cm below the water surface [40]. SWIR2 is similar but with a higher level of absorbance. This means that SWIR1 or SWIR2 can only interrogate a few millimeters of the top of a body of water. For this reason, these bands are not included in remote-sensing models for the chl-a concentrations in water. While our final model did not include either SWIR1 or SWIR2 bands, Figure 8 shows that the SWIR1 band is selected as the 17th and 12th most common parameter for all models for the chl-a and log(chl-a) models, respectively. The SWIR2 band is selected as the 14th and 11th most common parameter for all models for the chl-a and log(chl-a) models, respectively.

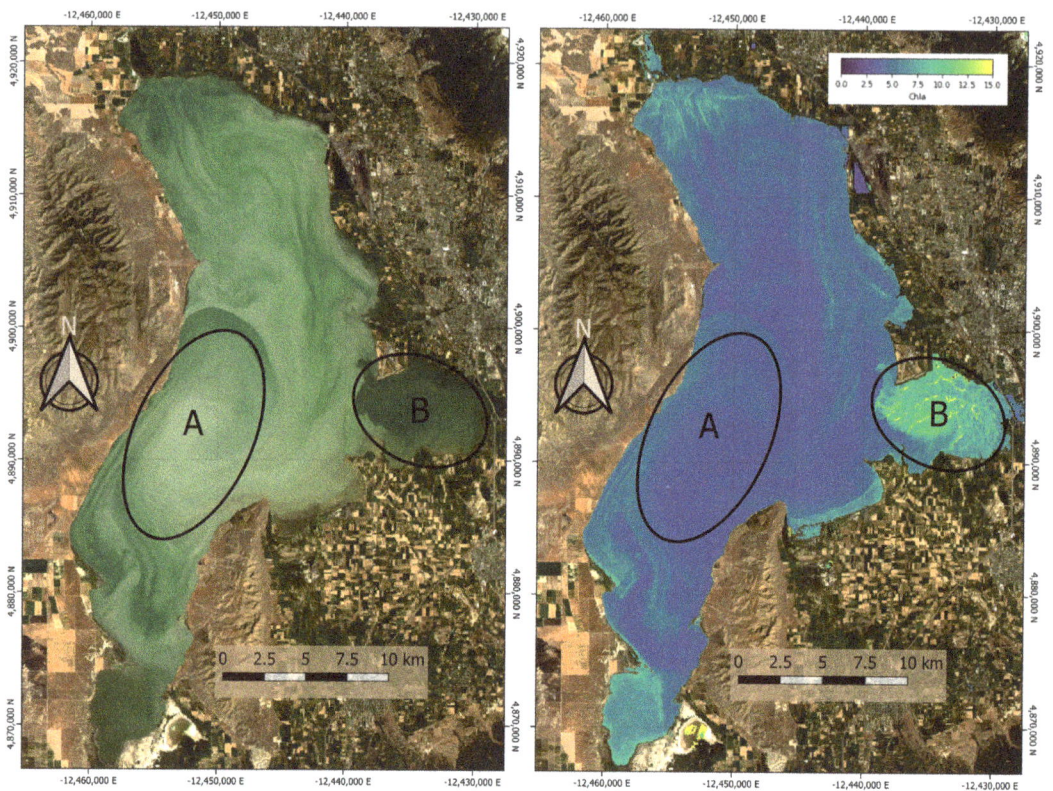

Figure 10. A Landsat image from 17 July 1986, with visual imagery from the RBG Landsat bands and estimated chl-a concentration maps on the right and left panels, respectively. Water from Hobble Creek flows into area B, resulting in relatively clear water in Provo Bay, which is shown in the ellipse labeled "B"; the remainder of the lake exhibits significant amounts of sediment from a recent storm, especially the area in the ellipse labeled "A". The clear water in "B" has a significant estimated chl-a concentration, while the water in "A" has a very low, ~0, chl-a concentration.

Figure 10 is an image based on the RGB Landsat bands from July 17, 1989, that demonstrates why a model created with L1 regularization might include the SWIR1 or SWIR2 bands. The left panel is a real-color image of Utah Lake. Area A contains a large silt plume precipitated by a recent storm. Utah Lake is shallow, with depths less than 3 m, and has a long fetch and reach on the order of 40 and 15 km, respectively. Accordingly, wind generates very large waves that suspend significant amounts of sediment (Area A). Area B is where Hobble Creek, a larger tributary, flows into Provo Bay. The water in Area B is relatively clear, as indicated by the darker color, as light is reflecting from the bottom of the bay. The right panel of Figure 10 shows the estimated chl-a concentration on the same date using the model given in Equation (3). This panel shows that Area A has a chl-a concentration of approximately 0, while Area B has a relatively high concentration, up to 15 µg/L. While we have no ground truth, the sediment concentration in Area A is high enough to reflect light in the SWIR1 and SWIR2 bands, while the relatively clear water in Area B does not reflect light in these bands. We have obtained field data with Secchi disc readings of less than 10 cm that support this idea that suspended sediments significantly affect the refection and absorption normally associated with water.

The model generated using L1 regularization may have selected SWIR1 and SWIR2 to differentiate between sediment plumes and algae plumes. In the left panel, Area A does have a "green" color that could be an algal bloom; however, the model clearly shows that there are no algae present in this area. In contrast, Area B appears to have relatively clear water in the image, but the model shows that its chl-a concentrations are significantly higher than those in the lake. This is an example of why models created with L1 regularization might select either the SWIR1 or SWIR2 bands, though we know that reflectance from water in these bands should essentially be zero.

Due to the high absorption of water in the SWIR1 and SWIR2 bands, it is easy to use this image as an example. We have surmised that similar issues are involved in the feature selection process for models with only a few parameters. As discussed above, the features selected by the L1 algorithm are similar to, but not the same as, most published chl-a models. We have surmised that this is because of the very optically complex nature of Utah Lake, where water does not look like water, as demonstrated in the left panel of Figure 10.

As an aside, Tanner, Cardall, and Williams [28] hypothesize that algal growth in Utah Lake is light-limited and that blooms do not start in the turbid mid-lake waters. Rather, they postulate that blooms generally start in the bays, where water is clearer and warmer, and then move out into the lake.

4. Discussion
4.1. L1 Regularization

Our goal was to evaluate L1 regularization to determine if it is an appropriate method for use in the exploration of a large parameter space. This is especially important in cases where the number of features or predictors (p) is similar to, or larger than, the number of observations (n). In many remote-sensing applications, there are a limited number of in situ observations, and features or predictors are typically chosen using prior understanding of the spectral behavior of the target features, such as chl-a concentrations. Other constituents in optically complex water can interfere with the spectral signatures of chl-a, so non-traditional terms might be useful for predictions.

Prior to performing this research, it was not clear if L1 regularization could be used for models wherein the number of potential features and the number of measurements were of similar magnitudes. Our model runs showed that an L1 model converges to the same set of features, even over a large number of realizations. This allows the model to explore the entire feature space. This is different than step-wise regression, where the order in which the terms are presented to the algorithm is important and the modeler is required to determine the order of importance of the selected terms.

L1 regularization evaluated model terms not commonly found in published models, though most of the selected terms were similar. In the beginning of our study, we noted that our initial search space included various engineered terms corresponding to the SWIR1 and SWIR2 bands. We found that despite these models' low error metrics, they demonstrated significant noise when they were applied to the lake. Subsequently, we re-explored the parameter space without these features and generated better models. Based on this experience, we recommend L1 regularization for exploring large parameter spaces, followed by the performance of an additional exploration of the selected features. One of the strengths and weaknesses of L1 is that it selects features that are informative and excludes other correlated features that may be useful in a model. In this study, L1 selected the smallest number of features to achieve the highest predictive performance. This can result in an acceptable model but may also result in a less robust or efficient model. In general, L1 can be thought of as selecting features based on their interaction and main effects on the target variable. This can occur because the main effects are not as informative as the interactions. This can result in L1's failure to select some useful variables. We evaluated our L1 models on multiple samples from the same dataset using the k-fold method and found that the sets of predictor variables that were returned were stable.

4.2. Significance of Temporal Coincidence and Spatial Resolution

We explored the impact of time coincidence and pixel resolution on model development using L1 regularization. Accuracy decreased and variability increased with increasing time offsets. We attribute this to the fact that the in situ data and the satellite collection data were measured at slightly different times, as conditions can rapidly change over a three-day period. We performed an evaluation using the average of a 3×3 (9) pixel grid to help mitigate issues associated with both spatial and temporal variances in algal distribution. We found that the 3×3 grid slightly increased accuracy but to an extent well within the variation computed using 200 k-fold realizations. For much of this paper, we used the closest single pixel and varying offsets. For modelers using this approach, both time offset and pixel average methods should be explored. Especially with regard to a time offset, there are direct tradeoffs with respect to the number of data pairs available for model development.

4.3. Data Engineering and Feature Selection

The L1 models selected features that have been reported in the published literature and performed very well, even with respect to the optically complex water of Utah Lake. For actual model development, the normalization of some or all of the engineered features may result in a more robust model. We minimally explored normalization with min–max and z-scores (both of which are available in the notebook), but we did not examine this in-depth because our research goal was to demonstrate the use of L1 regularization to explore large feature spaces for optically complex models and not to generate the best model for Utah Lake. Evaluating different normalization methods and determining which variables to normalize would have added significant complexity to this paper without adding any useful information, as most model builders are familiar with normalization and each application would be data- and site-specific. Another potential approach, which we did not explore, would be the use of offsets rather than minimum values for negative band values. This would retain relative quantities, while setting these low values to a minimum would not. We did not evaluate methods for addressing negative band values; as discussed in Section 2.4, we simply replaced the negative values of the blue, red, NIR, and SWIR1 bands with values of 0.01, 0.01, 0.001, and 0.001, respectively. This probably affected the models' accuracy for low concentrations. Aside from normalization, another approach that modelers should consider is the offsetting of all the values by a amount. This would result in all positive values but have little impact on values above the median. This would also allow the L1 models to include features in these bands to help address complexity caused by the high concentrations of suspended solids, clays, calcite, and silts present in Utah Lake (Figure 10).

4.4. Model Creation

We have shown that L1 regularization can be used for remote-sensing models and to explore a feature space with a size similar to the data space, that is, where the number of features and number of observations are similar. It is an efficient model development approach, which is capable of generating hundreds of models on a desktop machine in just a few minutes. This facilitates approaches such as the use/development of seasonal models [15,43] and site-specific models that consider changing or complex optical characteristics. However, we believe that modelers should be careful when accepting the first model generated by the L1 methods. They should carefully evaluate input data and features. Techniques such as normalization or other data-cleaning methods may aid model development. After an performing an initial model evaluation in a very large feature space, it may prove beneficial to explore a smaller feature space. For example, one could eliminate the top features and determine if the model selects existing model features and a correlated feature that had previously been excluded. A single model can be generated almost immediately, so this type of exploration should be considered.

L1 regularization with data that have correlated informative features tends to select one feature and push the others toward 0. This results in a model that can omit significant informative features. L1 regularization will often choose more features than are required because of this issue. This can be gleaned by comparing the L1 model to the published models. Our L1 models have four or five features, while the published models have only two or three features.

5. Conclusions

The goal of this numerical experiment was to evaluate the ability of using L1 regularization to generate remote-sensing models using a large feature space. This is important because for most remote-sensing models, the availability of in situ observations is limited, often amounting to only a few tens of measurements. We also briefly explored the impact of non-coincident measurements and pixel resolution on model accuracy. We found that L1 regularization is a useful technique and can be used to explore large feature spaces. L1 selects features based on which features have significant interaction effects, and generally will not select two features that are highly correlated. This means that features that are directly correlated with the target variable may not be selected. The evaluation of this behavior is beyond the scope of this article, but it has been given an in-depth treatment in [44].

In addition to demonstrating the application of L1 regularization to feature selection, we provided an in-depth example of which types of analysis, visualizations, and other approaches modelers should use if they adopt this method.

In addition to the manuscript, we have provided two Google Earth Engine Colab notebooks. The first (Notebook1) demonstrates and provides tools for obtaining non-coincident remote-sensing data, provided that a list of sample dates, values, and locations is available. It provides computations for feature engineering, generating 90 features from the 6 Landsat bands we used. Currently, the notebook retrieves Landsat data, but it can be easily modified to operate with other sensors. The second notebook (Notebook2) applies L1 regularization and generates a model that can be used to estimate target measurements.

Our explorations showed that L1 regularization is useful for exploring large feature spaces and identifying features not traditionally used. This is especially useful for optically complex waters. However, while L1 regularization is useful, the final model may not be the best model that can be developed. We recommend evaluating the features L1 selects along with traditional features and performing an analysis to create a final model.

Colab notebooks that implement and describe this approach are available on GitHub at https://github.com/BYU-Hydroinformatics/ee-wq-lasso (5 March 2023). Occasionally, these notebooks may be updated.

Author Contributions: Conceptualization, G.P.W. and A.C.C.; methodology, A.C.C., R.C.H., K.N.M. and G.P.W.; software, A.C.C., R.C.H., K.N.M. and G.P.W.; writing—original draft preparation, G.P.W., A.C.C., R.C.H. and K.B.T.; writing—review and editing, R.C.H., K.N.M., G.P.W., K.B.T. and A.C.C.; supervision, G.P.W.; project administration, G.P.W.; funding acquisition, A.C.C., K.B.T. and G.P.W. All authors have read and agreed to the published version of the manuscript.

Funding: This research received no external funding. Students were supported in their studies by the Utah NASA Space Grant Consortium student fellowship program.

Data Availability Statement: We used Google Earth Engine (GEE) to access and process the data. Within GEE, we used Landsat 5, 7, 8, and 9 missions Collection 2 data generated by the USGS. These datasets have the following GEE image collection identifiers: LANDSAT/LT05/C02/T1_L2, L2LANDSAT/LE07/C02/T1_L2, LANDSAT/LC08/C02/T1_L2, and LANDSAT/LC09/C02/T1_L2, respectively. We provide Google Colab notebook at https://github.com/BYU-Hydroinformatics/ee-wq-lasso (5 March 2023) to grant access to the tools we used to acquire and process these data. The observed water quality data originated from the Utah AQWMS database. Access was granted through the State of Utah.

Acknowledgments: We would like to acknowledge the BYU College of Engineering, the BYU Department of Civil and Construction Engineering, and the NASA Utah Space Grant program for their support.

Conflicts of Interest: The authors declare no conflict of interest.

References

1. Sellner, K.G.; Doucette, G.J.; Kirkpatrick, G.J. Harmful algal blooms: Causes, impacts and detection. *J. Ind. Microbiol. Biotechnol.* **2003**, *30*, 383–406. [CrossRef]
2. Kloiber, S.M.; Brezonik, P.L.; Olmanson, L.G.; Bauer, M.E. A procedure for regional lake water clarity assessment using Landsat multispectral data. *Remote Sens. Environ.* **2002**, *82*, 38–47. [CrossRef]
3. Fuller, L.M.; Aichele, S.S.; Minnerick, R.J. *Predicting Water Quality by Relating Secchi-Disk Transparency and CHLORophyll a Measurements to Satellite Imagery for Michigan Inland Lakes, August 2002*; U.S. Geological Survey: Reston, VA, USA, 2004; pp. 2004–5086.
4. Olmanson, L.G.; Bauer, M.E.; Brezonik, P.L. A 20-year Landsat water clarity census of Minnesota's 10,000 lakes. *Remote Sens. Environ.* **2008**, *112*, 4086–4097. [CrossRef]
5. Allan, M.G.; Hamilton, D.P.; Hicks, B.; Brabyn, L. Empirical and semi-analytical chlorophyll a algorithms for multi-temporal monitoring of New Zealand lakes using Landsat. *Environ. Monit. Assess.* **2015**, *187*, 1–24. [CrossRef]
6. Brezonik, P.; Menken, K.D.; Bauer, M. Landsat-Based Remote Sensing of Lake Water Quality Characteristics, Including Chlorophyll and Colored Dissolved Organic Matter (CDOM). *Lake Reserv. Manag.* **2005**, *21*, 373–382. [CrossRef]
7. Brivio, P.A.; Giardino, C.; Zilioli, E. Determination of chlorophyll concentration changes in Lake Garda using an image-based radiative transfer code for Landsat TM images. *Int. J. Remote Sens.* **2001**, *22*, 487–502. [CrossRef]
8. Kutser, T. Quantitative detection of chlorophyll in cyanobacterial blooms by satellite remote sensing. *Limnol. Oceanogr.* **2004**, *49*, 2179–2189. [CrossRef]
9. Mayo, M.; Gitelson, A.; Yacobi, Y.; Ben-Avraham, Z. Chlorophyll distribution in lake Kinneret determined from Landsat Thematic Mapper data. *Remote Sens.* **1995**, *16*, 175–182. [CrossRef]
10. Yip, H.; Johansson, J.; Hudson, J. A 29-year assessment of the water clarity and chlorophyll-a concentration of a large reservoir: Investigating spatial and temporal changes using Landsat imagery. *J. Great Lakes Res.* **2015**, *41*, 34–44. [CrossRef]
11. NASA. *Landsat—Earth Observation Satellites*; 2015–3081; National Aeronautics and Space Administration: Reston, VA, USA, 2016; p. 4.
12. Potes, M.; Rodrigues, G.; Penha, A.M.; Novais, M.H.; Costa, M.J.; Salgado, R.; Morais, M.M. Use of Sentinel 2–MSI for water quality monitoring at Alqueva reservoir, Portugal. *Proc. IAHS* **2018**, *380*, 73–79. [CrossRef]
13. Vargas-Lopez, I.A.; Rivera-Monroy, V.H.; Day, J.W.; Whitbeck, J.; Maiti, K.; Madden, C.J.; Trasviña-Castro, A. Assessing chlorophyll a spatiotemporal patterns combining in situ continuous fluorometry measurements and Landsat 8/OLI data across the Barataria Basin (Louisiana, USA). *Water* **2021**, *13*, 512. [CrossRef]
14. Hansen, C.H.; Burian, S.J.; Dennison, P.E.; Williams, G.P. Spatiotemporal variability of lake water quality in the context of remote sensing models. *Remote Sens.* **2017**, *9*, 409. [CrossRef]
15. Hansen, C.H.; Williams, G.P. Evaluating remote sensing model specification methods for estimating water quality in optically diverse lakes throughout the growing season. *Hydrology* **2018**, *5*, 62. [CrossRef]
16. Carder, K.L.; Chen, F.; Lee, Z.; Hawes, S.; Kamykowski, D. Semianalytic Moderate-Resolution Imaging Spectrometer algorithms for chlorophyll a and absorption with bio-optical domains based on nitrate-depletion temperatures. *J. Geophys. Res. Ocean.* **1999**, *104*, 5403–5421. [CrossRef]
17. Garver, S.A.; Siegel, D.A. Inherent optical property inversion of ocean color spectra and its biogeochemical interpretation: 1. Time series from the Sargasso Sea. *J. Geophys. Res. Ocean.* **1997**, *102*, 18607–18625. [CrossRef]
18. Peterson, K.T.; Sagan, V.; Sloan, J.J. Deep learning-based water quality estimation and anomaly detection using Landsat-8/Sentinel-2 virtual constellation and cloud computing. *GIScience Remote Sens.* **2020**, *57*, 510–525. [CrossRef]
19. Sagan, V.; Peterson, K.T.; Maimaitijiang, M.; Sidike, P.; Sloan, J.; Greeling, B.A.; Maalouf, S.; Adams, C. Monitoring inland water quality using remote sensing: Potential and limitations of spectral indices, bio-optical simulations, machine learning, and cloud computing. *Earth-Sci. Rev.* **2020**, *205*, 103187. [CrossRef]
20. Hafeez, S.; Wong, M.S.; Ho, H.C.; Nazeer, M.; Nichol, J.; Abbas, S.; Tang, D.; Lee, K.H.; Pun, L. Comparison of machine learning algorithms for retrieval of water quality indicators in case-II waters: A case study of Hong Kong. *Remote Sens.* **2019**, *11*, 617. [CrossRef]
21. Cao, Z.; Ma, R.; Duan, H.; Pahlevan, N.; Melack, J.; Shen, M.; Xue, K. A machine learning approach to estimate chlorophyll-a from Landsat-8 measurements in inland lakes. *Remote Sens. Environ.* **2020**, *248*, 111974. [CrossRef]
22. Hansen, C.H.; Burian, S.J.; Dennison, P.E.; Williams, G.P. Evaluating historical trends and influences of meteorological and seasonal climate conditions on lake chlorophyll a using remote sensing. *Lake Reserv. Manag.* **2019**, *36*, 45–63. [CrossRef]
23. Hansen, C.H.; Williams, G.P.; Adjei, Z.; Barlow, A.; Nelson, E.J.; Miller, A.W. Reservoir water quality monitoring using remote sensing with seasonal models: Case study of five central-Utah reservoirs. *Lake Reserv. Manag.* **2015**, *31*, 225–240. [CrossRef]
24. Efron, B.; Hastie, T.; Johnstone, I.; Tibshirani, R. Least angle regression. *Ann. Stat.* **2004**, *32*, 407–499. [CrossRef]

25. Le, C.; Li, Y.; Zha, Y.; Wang, Q.; Zhang, H.; Yin, B. Remote sensing of phycocyanin pigment in highly turbid inland waters in Lake Taihu, China. *Int. J. Remote Sens.* **2011**, *32*, 8253–8269. [CrossRef]
26. Gons, H.J. Optical Teledetection of Chlorophyll*a* in Turbid Inland Waters. *Environ. Sci. Technol.* **1999**, *33*, 1127–1132. [CrossRef]
27. Hansen, C.H.; Williams, G.P.; Adjei, Z. Long-Term Application of Remote Sensing Chlorophyll Detection Models: Jordanelle Reservoir Case Study. *Nat. Resour.* **2015**, *06*, 123–129. [CrossRef]
28. Tanner, K.B.; Cardall, A.C.; Williams, G.P. A Spatial Long-Term Trend Analysis of Estimated Chlorophyll-a Concentrations in Utah Lake Using Earth Observation Data. *Remote Sens.* **2022**, *14*, 3664. [CrossRef]
29. Bertani, I.; Steger, C.E.; Obenour, D.R.; Fahnenstiel, G.L.; Bridgeman, T.B.; Johengen, T.H.; Sayers, M.J.; Shuchman, R.A.; Scavia, D. Tracking cyanobacteria blooms: Do different monitoring approaches tell the same story? *Sci. Total Environ.* **2017**, *575*, 294–308. [CrossRef]
30. Tate, R.S. Landsat Collections Reveal Long-Term Algal Bloom Hot Spots of Utah Lake. Master's Thesis, Brigham Young University, Provo, UT, USA, 2019.
31. Pettersson, L.H.; Pozdnyakov, D. Potential of remote sensing for identification, delineation, and monitoring of harmful algal blooms. In *Monitoring of Harmful Algal Blooms*; Springer: New York, NY, USA, 2013; pp. 49–111.
32. Buitinck, L.; Louppe, G.; Blondel, M.; Pedregosa, F.; Mueller, A.; Grisel, O.; Niculae, V.; Prettenhofer, P.; Gramfort, A.; Grobler, J. API design for machine learning software: Experiences from the scikit-learn project. *arXiv* **2013**, arXiv:1309.0238.
33. Meinshausen, N.; Bühlmann, P. Stability selection. *J. R. Stat. Soc. Ser. B Stat. Methodol.* **2010**, *72*, 417–473. [CrossRef]
34. Bühlmann, P.; Van De Geer, S. *Statistics for High-Dimensional Data: Methods, Theory and Applications*; Springer Science & Business Media: New York, NY, USA, 2011.
35. Nelson, S.A.C.; Soranno, P.A.; Cheruvelil, K.S.; Batzli, S.A.; Skole, D.L. Regional assessment of lake water clarity using satellite remote sensing. *J. Limnol.* **2003**, *62*, 27. [CrossRef]
36. Merritt, L.B.; Miller, A.W. *Interim Report on Nutrient Loadings to Utah Lake: 2016*; Jordan River, Farmington Bay & Utah Lake Water Quality Council: Provo, UT, USA, 2016.
37. Cardall, A.; Tanner, K.B.; Williams, G.P. Google Earth Engine Tools for Long-Term Spatiotemporal Monitoring of Chlorophyll-a Concentrations. *Open Water J.* **2021**, *7*, 4.
38. Masek, J.G.; Vermote, E.F.; Saleous, N.E.; Wolfe, R.; Hall, F.G.; Huemmrich, K.F.; Feng, G.; Kutler, J.; Teng-Kui, L. A Landsat surface reflectance dataset for North America, 1990–2000. *IEEE Geosci. Remote Sens. Lett.* **2006**, *3*, 68–72. [CrossRef]
39. Vermote, E.; Justice, C.; Claverie, M.; Franch, B. Preliminary analysis of the performance of the Landsat 8/OLI land surface reflectance product. *Remote Sens. Environ.* **2016**, *185*, 46–56. [CrossRef] [PubMed]
40. Kou, L.; Labrie, D.; Chylek, P. Refractive indices of water and ice in the 0.65-to 2.5-µm spectral range. *Appl. Opt.* **1993**, *32*, 3531–3540. [CrossRef] [PubMed]
41. Smith, B.; Pahlevan, N.; Schalles, J.; Ruberg, S.; Errera, R.; Ma, R.; Giardino, C.; Bresciani, M.; Barbosa, C.; Moore, T.; et al. A Chlorophyll-a Algorithm for Landsat-8 Based on Mixture Density Networks. *Front. Remote Sens.* **2021**, *1*, 623678. [CrossRef]
42. Matthews, M.W. A current review of empirical procedures of remote sensing in inland and near-coastal transitional waters. *Int. J. Remote Sens.* **2011**, *32*, 6855–6899. [CrossRef]
43. Hansen, C.; Swain, N.; Munson, K.; Adjei, Z.; Williams, G.P.; Miller, W. Development of sub-seasonal remote sensing chlorophyll-a detection models. *Am. J. Plant Sci.* **2013**, *4*, 21–26. [CrossRef]
44. Hastie, T.; Tibshirani, R.; Wainwright, M. *Statistical Learning with Sparsity*; CRC Press; Taylor and Francis Group: Boca Raton, FL, USA, 2015; Volume 143.

Disclaimer/Publisher's Note: The statements, opinions and data contained in all publications are solely those of the individual author(s) and contributor(s) and not of MDPI and/or the editor(s). MDPI and/or the editor(s) disclaim responsibility for any injury to people or property resulting from any ideas, methods, instructions or products referred to in the content.

Article

Retrieval of Water Quality Parameters in Dianshan Lake Based on Sentinel-2 MSI Imagery and Machine Learning: Algorithm Evaluation and Spatiotemporal Change Research

Lei Dong [1,2], Cailan Gong [1,*], Hongyan Huai [3], Enuo Wu [4], Zhihua Lu [3], Yong Hu [1], Lan Li [1] and Zhe Yang [1,2]

1 Key Laboratory of Infrared System Detection and Imaging Technologies, Shanghai Institute of Technical Physics, Chinese Academy of Sciences, Shanghai 200083, China; fcdl@mail.ustc.edu.cn (L.D.); lilan@mail.sitp.ac.cn (L.L.)
2 University of Chinese Academy of Sciences, Beijing 100049, China
3 Shanghai Environment Monitoring Center, Shanghai 200235, China; huaihy@sheemc.cn (H.H.); luzh@saes.sh.cn (Z.L.)
4 Shanghai Academy of Environmental Sciences, Shanghai 200233, China; wuan@sheemc.cn
* Correspondence: gcl@mail.sitp.ac.cn

Citation: Dong, L.; Gong, C.; Huai, H.; Wu, E.; Lu, Z.; Hu, Y.; Li, L.; Yang, Z. Retrieval of Water Quality Parameters in Dianshan Lake Based on Sentinel-2 MSI Imagery and Machine Learning: Algorithm Evaluation and Spatiotemporal Change Research. *Remote Sens.* 2023, 15, 5001. https://doi.org/10.3390/rs15205001

Academic Editors: Miro Govedarica, Flor Alvarez-Taboada and Gordana Jakovljević

Received: 5 September 2023
Revised: 12 October 2023
Accepted: 13 October 2023
Published: 18 October 2023

Copyright: © 2023 by the authors. Licensee MDPI, Basel, Switzerland. This article is an open access article distributed under the terms and conditions of the Creative Commons Attribution (CC BY) license (https:// creativecommons.org/licenses/by/ 4.0/).

Abstract: According to current research, machine learning algorithms have been proven to be effective in detecting both optical and non-optical parameters of water quality. The use of satellite remote sensing is a valuable method for monitoring long-term changes in the quality of lake water. In this study, Sentinel-2 MSI images and in situ data from the Dianshan Lake area from 2017 to 2023 were used. Four machine learning methods were tested, and optimal detection models were determined for each water quality parameter. It was ultimately determined that these models could be applied to long-term images to analyze the spatiotemporal variations and distribution patterns of water quality in Dianshan Lake. Based on the research findings, integrated learning algorithms, especially CatBoost, have achieved good results in the retrieval of all water quality parameters. Spatiotemporal analysis reveals that the overall distribution of water quality parameters is uneven, with significant spatial variations. Permanganate index (COD_{Mn}), Total Nitrogen (TN), and Total Phosphorus (TP) show relatively small interannual differences, generally exhibiting a decreasing trend in concentrations. In contrast, chlorophyll-a (Chl-a), dissolved oxygen (DO), and Secchi Disk Depth (SDD) exhibit significant interannual and inter-year differences. Chl-a reached its peak in 2020, followed by a decrease, while DO and SDD showed the opposite trend. Further analysis indicated that the distribution of water quality parameters is significantly influenced by climatic factors and human activities such as agricultural expansion. Overall, there has been an improvement in the water quality of Dianshan Lake. The study demonstrates the feasibility of accurately monitoring water quality even without measured spectral data, using machine learning methods and satellite reflectance data. The research results presented in this paper can provide new insights into water quality monitoring and water resource management in Dianshan Lake.

Keywords: machine learning; water quality parameters; spatiotemporal distribution; Dianshan Lake; Sentinel-2

1. Introduction

The effective provision of water resources is closely intertwined with the progress of cities, ecological equilibrium, and economic prosperity [1,2]. Inland water bodies such as lakes are vital in maintaining ecological balance, supporting industrial production, and ensuring human well-being [3,4]. However, in recent years, the compounded impacts of human activities and climate change have posed severe threats to the ecological equilibrium of water bodies, resulting in intensified global freshwater eutrophication and deterioration of water quality [2,5]. Against this backdrop, the effective assessment of lake water quality is paramount in maintaining ecosystem stability. This evaluation relies on key nutrient indicators, namely, Chl-a, TP, TN, SDD, and COD_{Mn} [6–8]. Chl-a, a primary pigment in phytoplankton, functions as a biomarker for phytoplankton biomass, thereby significantly influencing the overall health of the ecosystem [9]. SDD, quantified using the Secchi disk transparency method, provides insights into the nutrient status of the lake and assumes a critical role in monitoring water quality [3,10,11]. Elevated levels of TN and TP serve as indicators of potential eutrophication concerns [12,13]. The measurement of DO, which is closely correlated with Chl-a, plays a pivotal role in evaluating water quality and its impact on aquatic life [14,15]. The proper management and interpretation of these key indicators are imperative for ensuring sustainable water resource management and safeguarding the delicate balance of lake ecosystems [16].

Traditional water quality monitoring involves manual in situ sampling and lab analysis, providing accurate data but with limited spatial coverage and efficiency. Unlike time-consuming conventional techniques, satellites offer high-frequency, wide-ranging, and long-term water quality data, thus overcoming limitations [4,17–21]. Specialized watercolor satellites have been developed for aquatic environments and are widely used [22,23]. However, lakes smaller than 100 sq. km constitute 63% of the total lake area [24]. Due to watercolor satellites' relatively low spatial resolution, smaller lakes may not be fully monitored. In contrast, Landsat and Sentinel satellite data have higher spatial resolution and are more suitable for monitoring small inland water bodies [18,25,26]. Some studies have effectively employed Sentinel-2 and Landsat imagery for coastal and inland lake water quality monitoring [27–30].

Methods for evaluating water quality parameters using satellite remote sensing data can be categorized into two types: empirical modeling and bio-optical modeling [14]. In recent years, bio-optical modeling has made some progress; however, it is severely constrained by data limitations and challenges in atmospheric correction accuracy [18], because atmospheric correction is a factor that must be considered in aquatic remote sensing [31–35]. A subset of researchers has initiated exploration into direct modeling methods utilizing satellite reflectance data. Their goal is to mitigate errors and uncertainties arising from atmospheric correction to the greatest extent possible. In recent years, with the development of the field of artificial intelligence, the application of machine learning algorithms in water quality assessment has been increasing gradually [14]. Machine learning models can uncover underlying complex nonlinear relationships, thus providing a general and optimized approach for water quality parameter detection [36–38]. Its application in water quality modeling and detection shows a continuous growth trend [39–42]. Common machine learning methods used for water quality assessment include Support Vector Machine Regression (SVR) and Random Forest Regression (RF). In recent years, XGBoost Regression (XGBoost) and CatBoost Regression (CatBoost) have also gained increasing popularity.

Current research utilizing machine learning combined with satellite data for the retrieval of water quality parameters has been successfully applied in multiple cases [14,18,24,25,29,42]. However, there are significant differences in the water quality parameters used, and the spatial and radiometric resolution of sensors in different regions, leading to variations in retrieval algorithms [43]. Dianshan Lake, which receives water from Taihu Lake and is influenced by agricultural activities and residential wastewater discharge in the surrounding areas, has experienced several water pollution incidents over the past two decades. Water quality monitoring has been a focal point for government water authorities and the research community [44]. Presently, there is limited research on the spatiotemporal characteristics of water quality evolution and driving factors in Dianshan Lake using remote sensing algorithms, making it challenging to provide targeted recommendations for environmental protection, management, and control measures. Therefore, the central objective of this study is to directly utilize satellite reflectance data to develop and validate models for retrieving water quality parameters. The specific objectives are as follows: (1) Utilize four machine learning methods (RF, XGBoost, CatBoost, and SVR) to establish optimal retrieval models for various water quality parameters (Chl-a,

COD_{Mn}, DO, SDD, TN, TP). (2) Employ Sentinel-2 satellite remote sensing imagery from 2017 to 2023 to retrieve various water quality parameters for spatiotemporal change analysis. The study aims to provide a scientific basis for lake management and environmental protection efforts.

2. Materials and Methods

2.1. Study Area

Dianshan Lake (31°04′–31°12′N, 120°54′–121°01′E) is situated on the border of Qingpu District in Shanghai and Kunshan City in Jiangsu Province, China. Its location in China is shown in Figure 1a. With an area of approximately 62 square kilometers and an average depth of 2.5 m, the lake plays a pivotal role in various social and ecological functions. It serves as the receiving end of water from the Wujiang area of Taihu Lake and functions as the headwaters of the Huangpu River.

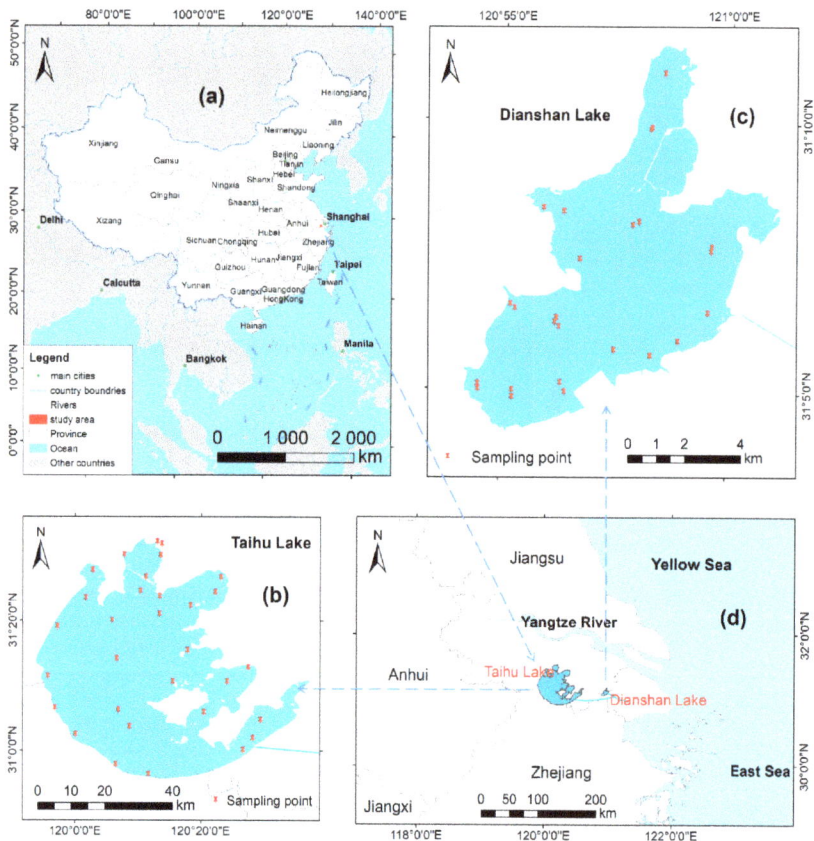

Figure 1. (**a**) Location schematic diagram of the study area, (**b**) Distribution of sampling points in Taihu Lake, (**c**) Distribution of sampling points in Dianshan Lake, (**d**) Schematic diagram of the relative positions of Taihu Lake and Dianshan Lake.

2.2. Dataset

This study employed three types of datasets: (1) Sentinel-2 MSI satellite imagery data spanning the period from 2017 to 2023, utilized to retrieve water quality parameters; (2) Concentration data of Chl-a, COD_{Mn}, DO, SDD, TN, and TP acquired through sampling in Dianshan Lake. These data were employed for the development and evaluation of machine learning methods; (3) Measured Chl-a, COD_{Mn}, DO, SDD, TN, and TP concentration data from Taihu Lake were utilized to further validate the model's applicability.

2.2.1. Satellite Data

Both Sentinel-2 MSI and Landsat offer high-resolution remote sensing image data for Earth observation and environmental monitoring. Considering Sentinel-2 MSI's distinct advantages over Landsat, which include shorter revisit periods, a greater number of spectral bands, higher spatial resolution, and an open data policy, this study harnessed the capabilities of Sentinel-2 MSI. Specifically, we utilized a dataset of 100 Sentinel-2 MSI images acquired from the Copernicus Open Access Hub (https://scihub.copernicus.eu/, accessed on 15 June 2023) spanning the period from 2017 to April 2023. The selection of these downloaded images adhered to strict criteria, ensuring cloud-free conditions above the lake and minimal sun glint on the lake surface. The distribution of data according to the quantity of time is shown in Figure 2.

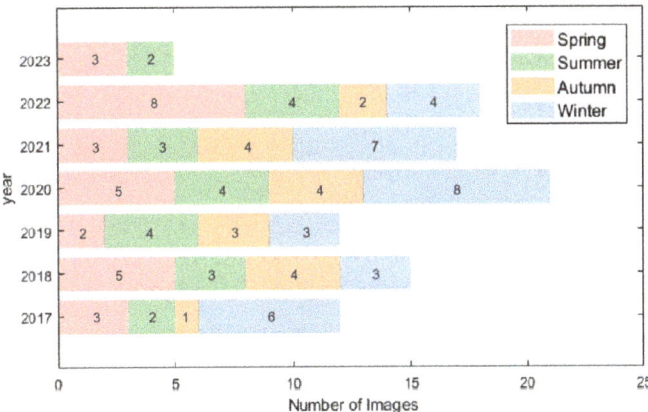

Figure 2. Temporal and Quantitative Distribution of Sentinel-2 MSI Images Used in This Study.

The radiation received by sensors at the top of the atmosphere (TOA) can be primarily attributed to Rayleigh scattering and aerosol scattering [45]. Atmospheric correction is a process aimed at mitigating the impacts of Rayleigh scattering, Mie scattering, atmospheric absorption, and aerosol influence on remote sensing images. Some researchers have proposed that using uncorrected TOA images can yield superior results compared to images that have undergone atmospheric correction [46]. In this study, we employed the SNAP software for Rayleigh correction of the images, resulting in dimensionless Rayleigh-corrected reflectance. Following this, the image resolution was resampled to 20 m, and the Normalized Difference Water Index (NDWI) [47] was utilized to delineate water regions. Before performing water quality modeling, and to mitigate uncertainties stemming from aerosols and other factors, an enhanced MD09 method [48,49] was implemented for aerosol correction. This method involves a straightforward Rayleigh reflectance correction technique that entails subtracting the minimum value from the shortwave infrared band (Band 11 in MSI images) within the visible and near-infrared bands. The resulting value is then divided by π.

2.2.2. Field Data

From 2017 to 2022, a monthly routine water sampling campaign was conducted in Dianshan Lake to collect data on water quality parameters. The study specifically selected data points falling within a ±5-day range of the satellite overpass time as the focal dataset, resulting in a total of 398 datasets. The statistical description of the data is shown in Table 1. The precise locations of the sampling sites within Dianshan Lake are illustrated in Figure 1c.

Table 1. Statistical description of measured water quality parameters in Dianshan Lake.

Water Quality Parameter	Range	Mean ± Std	Median	CV	N
Chl-a (mg/m^3)	1.34–51	15.04 ± 10.35	12.80	0.69	398
COD$_{Mn}$ (mg/L)	2.10–7.00	3.96 ± 0.80	3.80	0.20	398
DO (mg/L)	3.90–13.84	8.73 ± 1.97	8.60	0.23	398
TN (mg/L)	0.33–5.23	2.04 ± 1.00	1.87	0.49	398
TP (mg/L)	0.03–0.26	0.10 ± 0.05	0.090	0.45	398
SDD (m)	0.1–1.1	0.42 ± 0.4	0.17	0.41	398

The water samples collected during in situ experiments were transported to the laboratory for analysis of water quality parameters. The laboratory analysis methods adhered to the water quality parameter determination procedures outlined in the Chinese National Standard GB3838-2002. Table A1 presents a compilation of the names of different water quality parameters, alongside their corresponding determination methods.

To assess the transferability of the optimal model to different geographical regions, additional data were collected from 2018 to 2022 at 32 monitoring stations situated around Taihu Lake. Due to the high level of eutrophication in Taihu Lake, surface blooms of cyanobacteria are frequent. To ensure water body consistency as much as possible, we utilized a visual interpretation method to identify sampling points unaffected by cyanobacterial blooms in satellite true-color images as supplementary data. There were a total of 161 validation points in Taihu Lake. The statistical description of the data is shown in Table 2 and the sampling site locations in the Taihu Lake region are visually depicted in Figure 1b.

Table 2. Statistical description of measured water quality parameters in Taihu Lake.

Water Quality Parameter	Arrange	Mean ± Std	Median	CV	N
Chl-a (mg/m^3)	6.34–63.38	21.41–9.63	19.62	0.45	130
COD$_{Mn}$ (mg/L)	3.37–5.15	4.24–0.42	4.30	0.10	130
DO (mg/L)	6.10–11.55	7.98–1.20	7.70	0.15	130
TN (mg/L)	0.24–0.53	0.36–0.07	0.34	0.19	130
TP (mg/L)	0.83–3.51	1.73–0.54	1.60	0.31	130
SDD (m)	0.066–0.329	0.112–0.029	0.111	0.26	130

2.3. Modeling

Based on the latitude and longitude coordinates of the actual measurement sites, the corresponding image reflectance for the respective dates is extracted. To ensure data consistency, a 3 × 3 pixel window surrounding each site is considered. The average reflectance within this window is then computed and utilized as the matched data.

In the investigation of the six water quality parameters, our study explored four distinct machine learning methods, namely: (1) Random Forest Regression (RF), (2) XGBoost Regression (XGB), (3) CatBoost Regression (CatBoost), and (4) SVR. The selection of these methods was grounded in their performance and characteristics across various data scenarios. Moreover, these techniques have been demonstrated as successful applications in estimating water quality parameters in several inland lakes previously [18,24,29,38,50–54].

These methods possess distinct characteristics. In the landscape of ensemble learning techniques, Random Forest Regression (RF) has garnered substantial interest due to its commendable performance and robust characteristics. By constructing multiple decision trees and aggregating their predictions, RF not only mitigates the risk of overfitting but also accommodates a diverse range of data types, including both continuous and categorical features. In contrast, XGBoost Regression (XGB) distinguishes itself through its efficient gradient boosting algorithm, which facilitates exceptional performance on large-scale datasets. XGB incorporates regularization techniques to control model complexity and exhibits considerable proficiency in handling missing values and feature engineering. Conversely, CatBoost Regression (CatBoost) specializes in the treatment of categorical features, autonomously affecting feature transformations without necessitating additional preprocessing steps. This confers it with advantages in certain domains. Support Vector Regression (SVR) is one of the most frequently used methods in recent years. SVR excels in regression with high dimensions, noise, and nonlinearity. Its adaptable kernels and robustness with small datasets contribute to its significance in ensemble learning.

For each model, an identical set of input features was chosen to assess the ultimate outcomes. In this study, we utilized the Pearson correlation coefficient to ascertain the relationships between various water quality parameters and some widely employed spectral band combinations.

Prior researchers have demonstrated the robustness of band ratio algorithm ($R_{rs}(\lambda1) - R_{rs}(\lambda2)$) and band difference algorithm ($\frac{R_{rs}(\lambda1)}{R_{rs}(\lambda2)}$) when applied to the retrieval of water quality in optical complex inland lakes [38]. In this study, we also incorporated the Normalized Difference Band Calculation algorithm ($\frac{R_{rs}(\lambda2)-R_{rs}(\lambda1)}{R_{rs}(\lambda2)+R_{rs}(\lambda1)}$) [40] and the three-band combination form ($R_{rs}(\lambda3) \times \left(\frac{1}{R_{rs}(\lambda2)} - \frac{1}{R_{rs}(\lambda1)}\right)$) [39] to assess their correlations with water quality parameters. The objective was to identify the optimal inputs for the machine learning models. In the process of constructing retrieval models for each water quality parameter, a comprehensive set of 13 input features was employed. Among these input variables, the combination of these 13 variables exhibited the most optimal performance. These encompassed the initial 9 visible and near-infrared bands from the MSI image, alongside the band combinations from each method that exhibited the highest correlation with the concentration of water quality parameters. Please refer to Table 3 for the most relevant band combinations for each water quality parameter.

Table 3. Input features for various water quality parameters (only wavelength combinations listed).

Band Combination Form	Chl-a	COD_{Mn}	DO	SDD	TN	TP
$R_{rs}(\lambda1) - R_{rs}(\lambda2)$	B7 [1] B9	B7 B2	B6 B7	B5 B2	B2 B3	B7 B6
$\frac{R_{rs}(\lambda1)}{R_{rs}(\lambda2)}$	B4 B5	B6 B7	B6 B7	B2 B5	B6 B7	B7 B6
$\frac{R_{rs}(\lambda2)-R_{rs}(\lambda1)}{R_{rs}(\lambda2)+R_{rs}(\lambda1)}$	B4 B5	B6 B7	B6 B7	B5 B2	B7 B6	B6 B7
$R_{rs}(\lambda3) \times \left(\frac{1}{R_{rs}(\lambda2)} - \frac{1}{R_{rs}(\lambda1)}\right)$	B5 B4 B2	B7 B6 B5	B6 B7 B1	B3 B5 B6	B6 B7 B1	B7 B6 B2

[1] The wavelengths of Sentinel-2 MSI image bands.

It is noteworthy that the selection of hyperparameters in machine learning substantially influences the model's performance and generalization capability. This process directly impacts the model's robustness and governs its complexity to mitigate overfitting. In our study, the Python programming language was employed to conduct a grid search technique for determining the model's hyperparameters. Each training session incorporated a fivefold cross-validation strategy to comprehensively evaluate the model's performance.

In SVR, the C parameter controls the degree of regularization, the kernel parameter defines the type of kernel function, and the gamma parameter influences the range of the kernel function's impact. By judiciously adjusting these parameters, a balance between model complexity and regularization can be achieved to enhance performance. Optimizing the performance of the XGBoost model depends on the selection of several key hyperparameters. Smaller learning rates and larger gamma values contribute to improved generalization performance, while parameters like min child weight, max depth, and reg alpha help stabilize the model, preventing overfitting. Random Forest (RF) can effectively control the number and depth of trees in the forest by tuning parameters such as n estimators, max depth, min samples split, min samples leaf, and max features, thereby enhancing model performance. CatBoost can optimize model complexity and regularization by adjusting parameters like iterations, learning rate, depth, and l2 leaf reg, resulting in improved performance.

The grid search strategies for each model are summarized in Table 4, and the optimal parameters chosen for different water quality parameters in each model are presented in Table A2.

Table 4. Hyperparameter grid search table for each model.

Model	Hyperparameters	Options
RF	n_estimators	np.arange [1] (10, 600, 10)
	max_depth	np.arange (10, 50, 5)
	min_samples_split	np.arange (1, 50, 1)
	min_samples_leaf	np.arange (1, 12, 1)
SVR	C	np.arange (1, 10, 0.01)
	kernel	['linear', 'rbf', 'sigmoid']
	gamma	np.arange (1, 100, 0.001)
XGBoost	learning_rate	np.arange (0.15, 0.2, 0.005)
	gamma	np.arange (0.001, 0.005, 0.001)
	min_child_weight	np.arange (5, 10, 1)
	max_depth	np.arange (2, 10, 1)
	sub_sample	[0.8, 1]
	reg_alpha	[0.001, 0.01, 0.1, 1]
CatBoost	iterations	np.arange (50, 500, 10)
	learning_rate	np.arange (0.01, 0.05, 0.01)
	depth	np.arange (2,10,1)
	l2_leaf_reg	np.arange (1,10,1)

[1] 'np.arange(10, 600, 10)' generates a sequence of numbers, starting at 10 and increasing by 10 at each step, until it is just below 600.

2.4. Accuracy Evaluation

The metrics chosen for assessing the models' performance encompassed the coefficient of determination (R^2), mean absolute percentage error ($MAPE$), root mean squared error ($RMSE$), and bias.

$$R^2(y, \hat{y}) = 1 - \frac{\sum_{i=1}^{N}(y_i - \hat{y}_i)^2}{\sum_{i=1}^{N}(y_i - \overline{y})^2} \tag{1}$$

$$MAPE = \frac{1}{N}\sum_{i=1}^{N}\left|\frac{y_i - \hat{y}_i}{y_i}\right| \times 100\% \tag{2}$$

$$RMSE(y, \hat{y}) = \sqrt{\frac{\sum_{i=1}^{N}(y_i - \hat{y}_i)^2}{N}} \tag{3}$$

$$bias = \frac{1}{N}\sum_{i=1}^{N}(y_i - \overline{y}) \tag{4}$$

where N represents the sample size, y_i is the value of the i-th observed data point, $\hat{y}_i$ is the value of the i-th predicted data point, and $\overline{y}$ is the mean value of N observed data points.

3. Results and Analysis

3.1. Model Calibration and Validation

Out of the entire synchronized dataset, 80% of the data (N = 318) was randomly allocated for constructing the models, whereas the remaining 20% of the data (N = 80) was employed to assess the models' performance. It is essential to emphasize that a consistent training dataset was utilized across all experiments for training and validation.

Regarding Chl-a estimation (Figure 3), it was observed that all models tended to underestimate high-concentration values, possibly due to the limited availability of data points for such values. Nevertheless, the CatBoost, RF, and XGBoost models exhibited significantly improved performance in accurately predicting true values across both the training and test datasets when compared to the SVR models. In particular, the CatBoost model showcased a well-distributed scatter around the 1:1 line for both the training set ($RMSE = 3.26$ mg/m^2, $MAPE = 15.18\%$) and the test set ($RMSE = 11.11$ mg/m^2, $MAPE = 28.12\%$). This signifies a higher level of accuracy. Consequently, the CatBoost model emerges as the optimal choice for Chl-a retrieval.

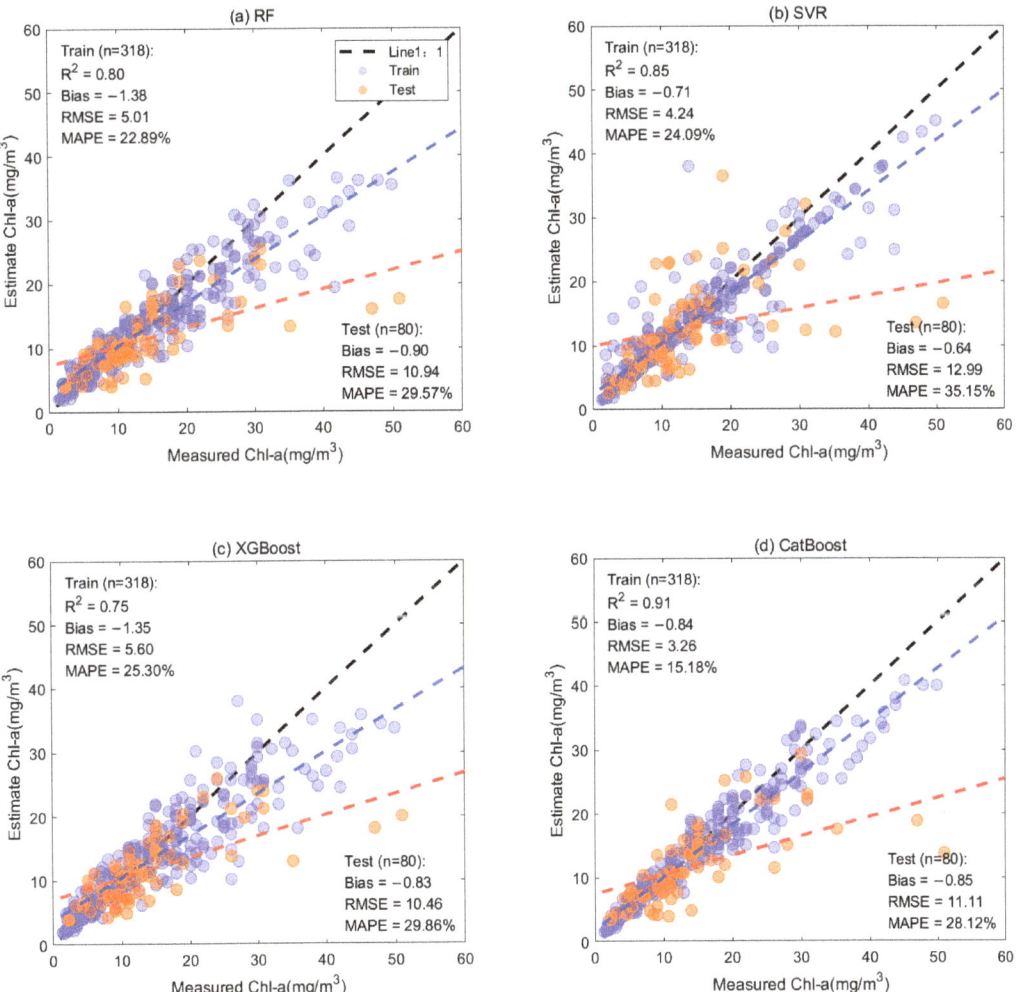

Figure 3. For the training set (n = 318) and test set (n = 80) in Dianshan Lake, scatter plots of the results of (**a**) RF, (**b**) SVR, (**c**) XGBoost, and (**d**) CatBoost for Chl-a retrieval are presented. The black, blue, and red lines represent the 1:1 line and regression lines between measured and estimated values on the training and test datasets, respectively. The blue dots and red dots represent the training set and test set, respectively.

Regarding the COD$_{Mn}$ index (Figure 4), all models exhibited an overestimation of values with COD$_{Mn}$ < 4.5 mg/L and an underestimation of values with COD$_{Mn}$ > 4.5 mg/L. This phenomenon was particularly prominent in the SVR model. Although the *MAPE* values for all models remained below 15%, the performance of CatBoost stood out as notably superior to that of XGBoost, RF, and SVR. Among these models, CatBoost yielded the most favorable results for COD_{Mn} estimation (training set: $RMSE$ = 0.33 mg/L, $MAPE$ = 6.85%; test set: $RMSE$ = 0.55 mg/L, $MAPE$ = 10.55%). Thus, the RF model emerges as a preferred choice for COD_{Mn} estimation.

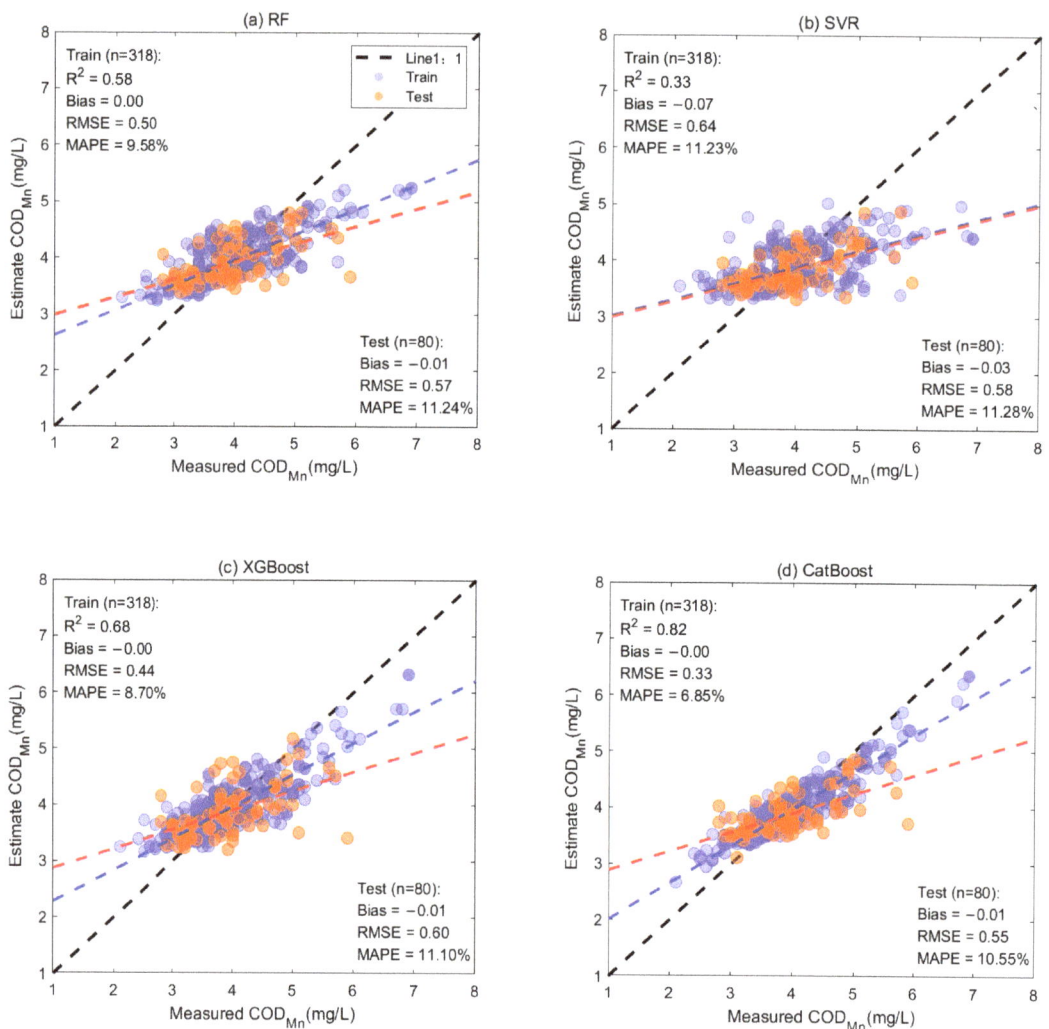

Figure 4. For the training set (n = 318) and test set (n = 80) in Dianshan Lake, scatter plots of the results of (**a**) RF, (**b**) SVR, (**c**) XGBoost, and (**d**) CatBoost for COD_{Mn} retrieval are presented. The black, blue, and red lines represent the 1:1 line and regression lines between measured and estimated values on the training and test datasets, respectively. The blue dots and red dots represent the training set and test set, respectively.

Concerning the DO index (Figure 5), all models consistently displayed a slight overestimation of low-concentration values and an underestimation of high-concentration values. It is important to highlight that all models exhibited a high degree of accuracy in estimating DO concentrations on both the training and test sets ($RMSE$ < 1.5 mg/L, $MAPE$ < 15%). In terms of various error metrics, it is obvious that the SVR model yields the poorest performance. Although the training set results are similar for CatBoost and XGBoost, XGBoost performs slightly better than CatBoost on the test set. As a result, the XGBoost model (training set: $RMSE$ = 1.01 mg/L, $MAPE$ = 9.78%; test set: $RMSE$ = 1.2 mg/L, $MAPE$ = 12.11%) is considered the optimal choice for DO retrieval.

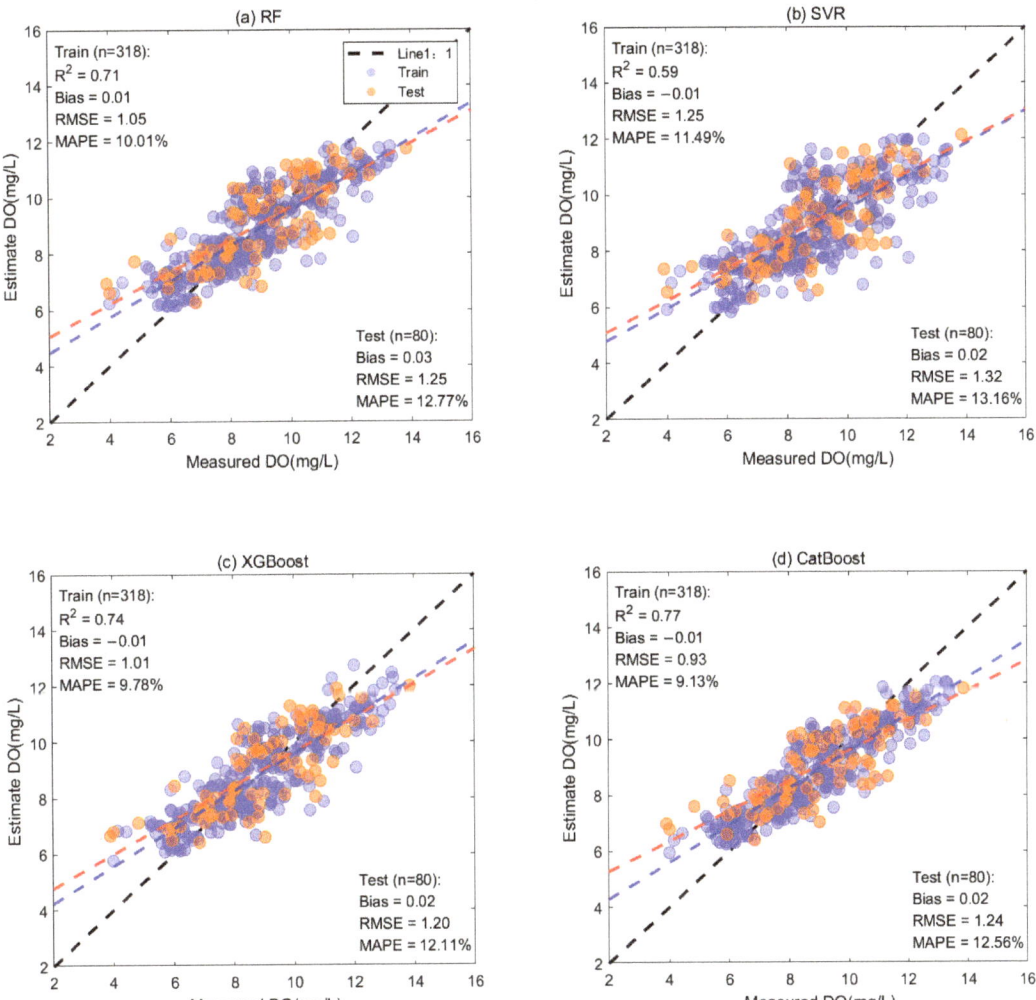

Figure 5. For the training set (n = 318) and test set (n = 80) in Dianshan Lake, scatter plots of the results of (**a**) RF, (**b**) SVR, (**c**) XGBoost, and (**d**) CatBoost models for DO retrieval are presented. The black, blue, and red lines represent the 1:1 line and regression lines between measured and estimated values on the training and test datasets, respectively. The blue dots and red dots represent the training set and test set, respectively.

In the case of the transparency index (Figure 6), the XGBoost, RF, and CatBoost models exhibited favorable results in the training set. Notably, all four models tended to overestimate SDD values when SDD < 0.4 m and underestimate values when SDD > 0.6 m. In summary, the XGBoost model showcased the best performance across both the training and test sets (training set: $RMSE$ = 0.07 m, $MAPE$ = 15.12%; test set: $RMSE$ = 0.155 m, $MAPE$ = 34.14%). Consequently, it is deemed the optimal choice for SDD retrieval.

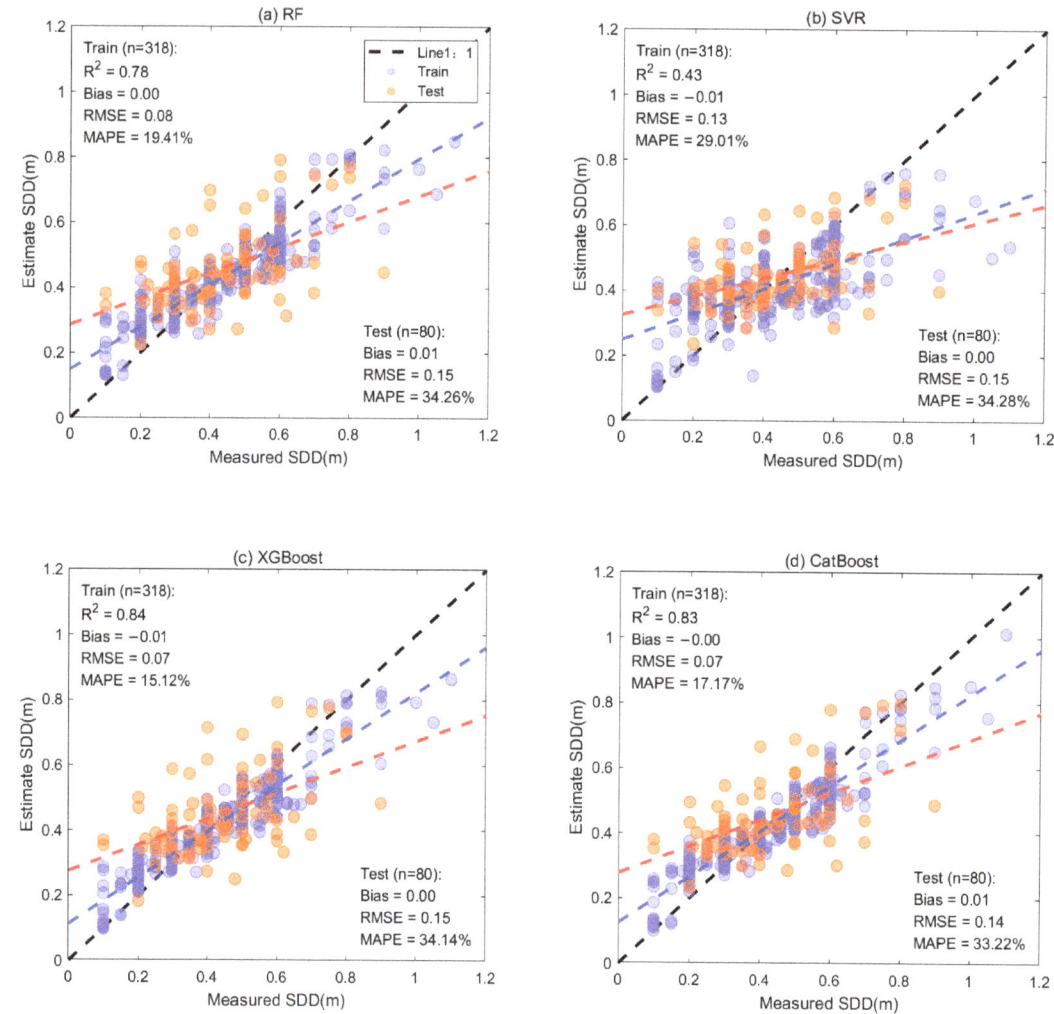

Figure 6. For the training set (n = 318) and test set (n = 80) in Dianshan Lake, scatter plots of the results of (**a**) RF, (**b**) SVR, (**c**) XGBoost, and (**d**) CatBoost models for SDD retrieval are presented. The black, blue, and red lines represent the 1:1 line and regression lines between measured and estimated values on the training and test datasets, respectively. The blue dots and red dots represent the training set and test set, respectively.

In terms of the TN index (Figure 7), the results retrieved by the four models exhibit a notable similarity. Concerning the training dataset, both the Random Forest (RF) and XGBoost models show superior performance. Their *MAPE* is below 20%. Analyzing the bias, RF outperforms all other models. Specifically, for the training set, RF demonstrates an *RMSE* of 0.45 mg/L, a *MAPE* of 19.45%, and a bias of 0. For the test set, the metrics are an *RMSE* of 0.54 mg/L, a *MAPE* of 21.83%, and a bias of −0.01. These outcomes underscore RF's heightened accuracy and stability in predictions, compared to the alternative models.

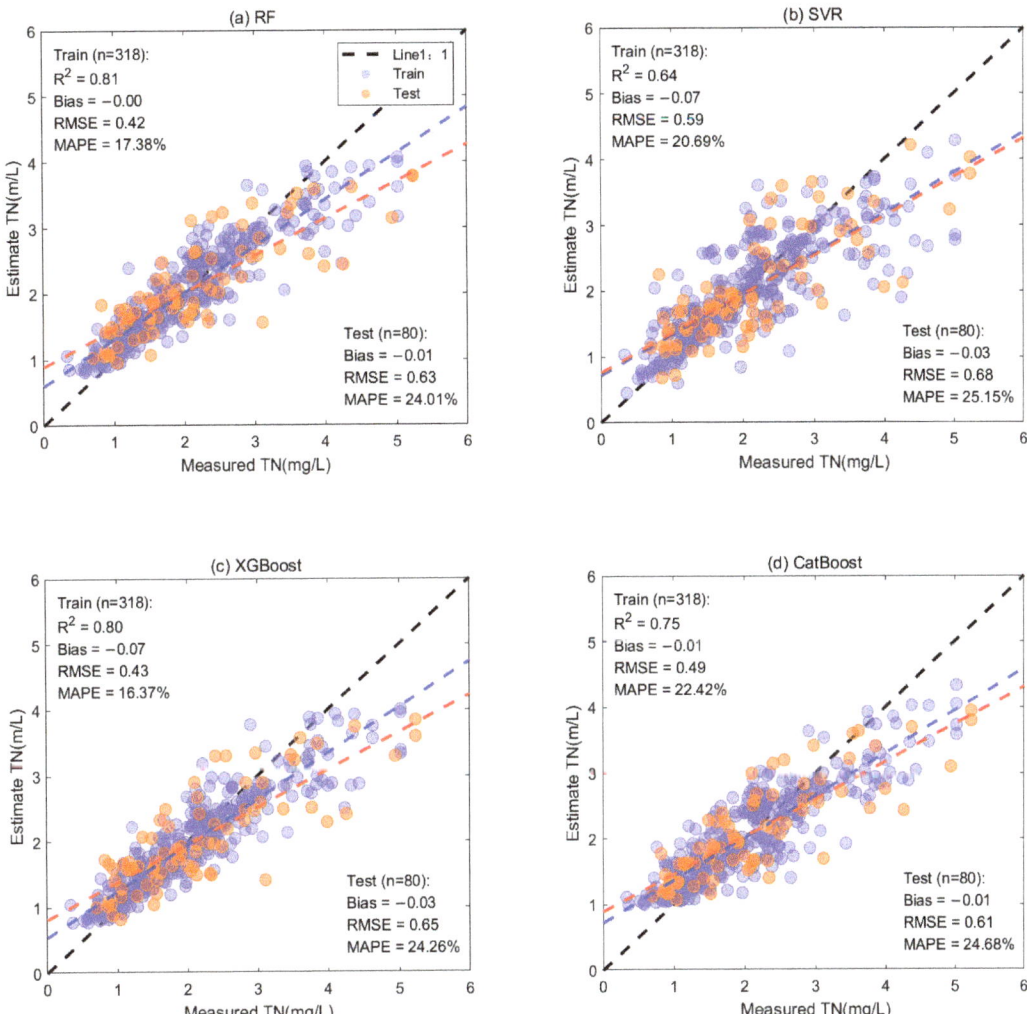

Figure 7. For the training set (n = 318) and test set (n = 80) in Dianshan Lake, scatter plots of the results of (**a**) RF, (**b**) SVR, (**c**) XGBoost, and (**d**) CatBoost models for TN retrieval are presented. The black, blue, and red lines represent the 1:1 line and regression lines between measured and estimated values on the training and test datasets, respectively. The blue dots and red dots represent the training set and test set, respectively.

Regarding the TP index (Figure 8), CatBoost notably outperformed the other models, exhibiting the best outcomes (training set: $RMSE = 0.02$ mg/L, $MAPE = 19.2\%$; test set: $RMSE = 0.036$ mg/L, $MAPE = 29.34\%$). Notably, the R2 values for both the training and test sets surpassed 0.75, and the $MAPE$ values remained below 30%. Conversely, SVR showcased less favorable results, yielding $MAPE$ values exceeding 65% across the training and test sets.

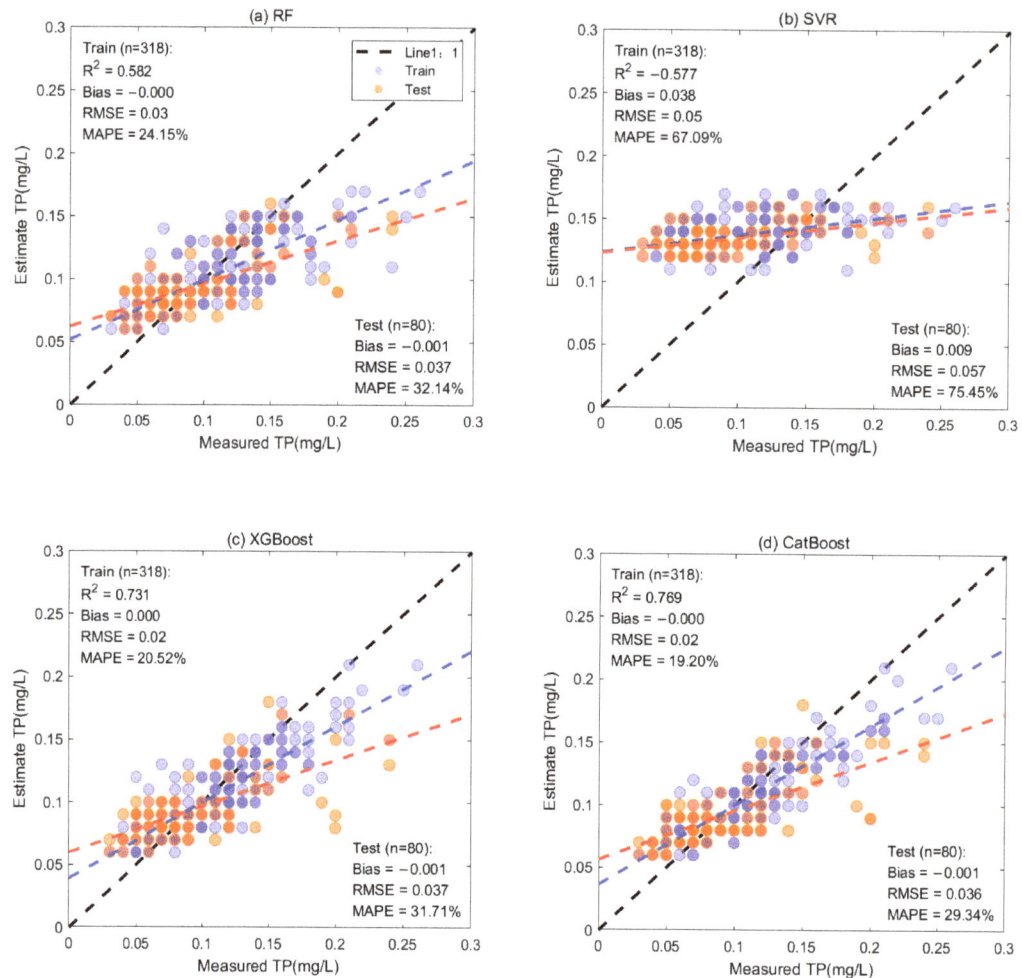

Figure 8. For the training set (n = 318) and test set (n = 80) in Dianshan Lake, scatter plots of the results of (**a**) RF, (**b**) SVR, (**c**) XGBoost, and (**d**) CatBoost models for TP retrieval are presented. The black, blue, and red lines represent the 1:1 line and regression lines between measured and estimated values on the training and test datasets, respectively.

Distinct characteristics are observed among various machine learning algorithms when predicting water quality parameters. By ranking the assessment results of the six water quality parameters, it is evident that CatBoost consistently achieves the most favorable outcomes across all four instances. XGBoost ranks within the top two positions in five out of six cases, whereas SVR consistently yields relatively inferior results across all six water quality parameters. Overall, in the evaluation of retrieval results for the six water quality parameters, CatBoost performs the best, followed by XGBoost in second place, RF in third, and SVR in the last position.

3.2. Spatiotemporal Patterns of Diandao Lake Water Quality Based on Sentinel-2

3.2.1. Temporal Variation

According to Section 3.1, it can be observed that the best models for Chl-a, CODMn, DO, SDD, TN, and TP are CatBoost, CatBoost, XGBoost, XGBoost, RF, and CatBoost, respectively. For ease of understanding and readability, we shall refer to them as BM-Chl-a, BM-CODMn, BM-DO, BM-SDD, BM-TN, and BM-TP. In this section, the best models were employed to estimate the concentrations of Chl-a, DO, CODMn, SDD, TN, and TP. Yearly average images (Figure 9) for these water quality parameters were calculated from 2017 to 2022 (data for 2023 were available only for the first four months and were excluded from this analysis). In addition, we also plotted the overall monthly average image (Figure 10) from 2017 to 2023. To gain a more intuitive understanding of the temporal changes in various water quality parameters, we have compiled their quarterly averages for each year (Figure 11).

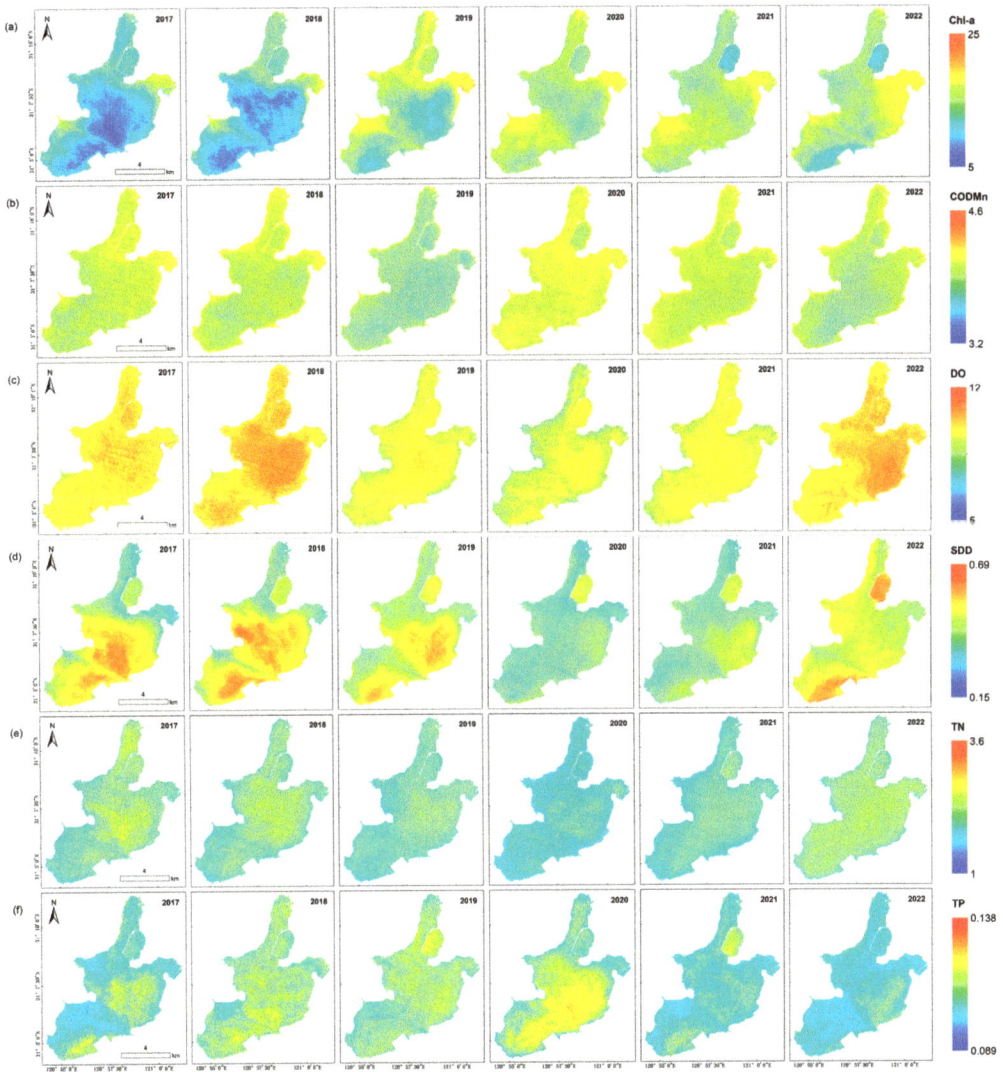

Figure 9. Images depicting the annual average concentrations of (**a**) Chl-a, (**b**) COD$_{Mn}$, (**c**) DO, (**d**) SDD, (**e**) TN, and (**f**) TP in Dianshan Lake, retrieved using Sentinel-2 MSI imagery, for the years 2017 to 2022.

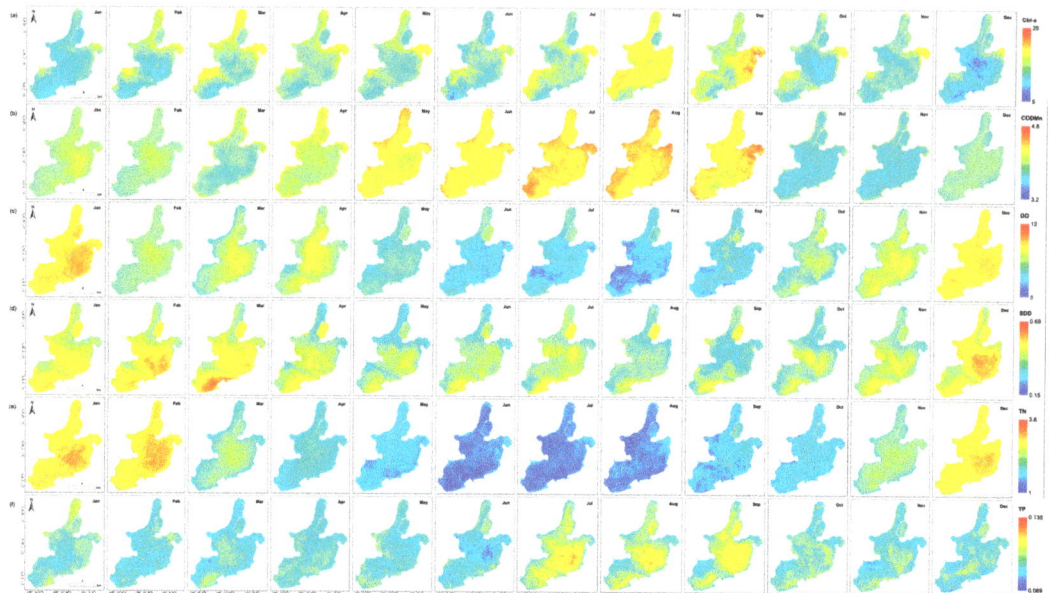

Figure 10. Images depicting the monthly average concentrations of (**a**) Chl-a, (**b**) COD$_{Mn}$, (**c**) DO, (**d**) SDD, (**e**) TN, and (**f**) TP in Dianshan Lake, retrieved using Sentinel-2 MSI imagery, for the years 2017 to 2023.

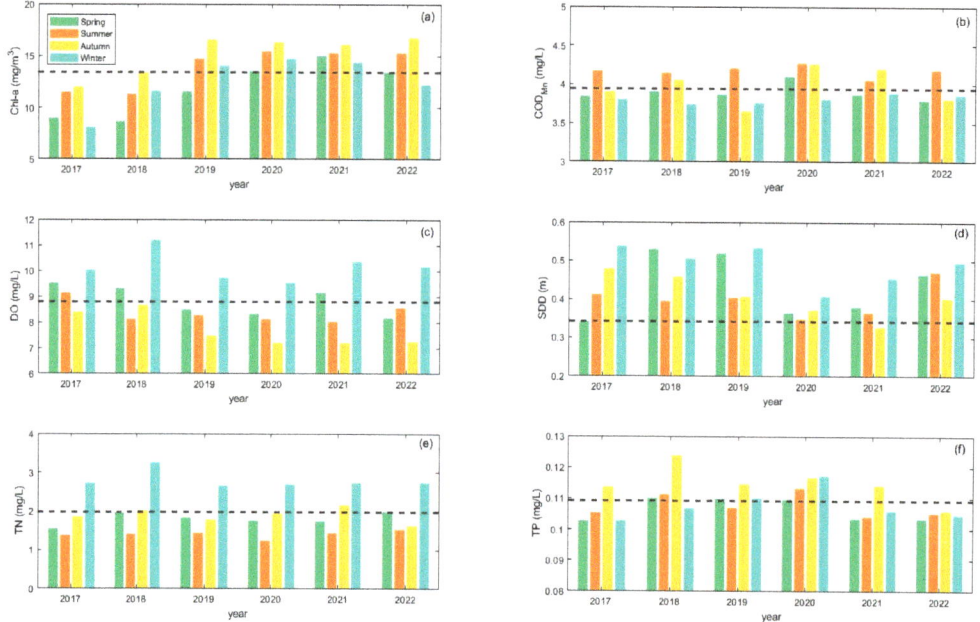

Figure 11. Bar charts illustrating the seasonally average concentration distribution of (**a**) Chl-a, (**b**) COD$_{Mn}$, (**c**) DO, (**d**) SDD, (**e**) TN, and (**f**) TP in Dianshan Lake from 2017 to 2023. The black dashed line represents the average value of water quality parameters calculated using six years of data from 2017 to 2022.

Upon analysis, the average Chl-a concentration over the six years was found to be 13.53 ± 2 mg/m^3. The lowest recorded value occurred in 2017 at 10.86 mg/m^3, while the highest was observed in 2020 at 15.03 mg/m^3. There was a continuous upward trend in Chl-a concentration from 2017 to 2020, with relatively minor interannual differences between 2020 and 2022. However, during the summer, autumn, and winter seasons, the concentrations showed a decreasing trend compared to 2020 (Figure 11a). The average COD_{Mn} concentration was determined to be 3.94 ± 0.4 mg/L. COD_{Mn} exhibited overall small fluctuations, with seasonal averages ranging between 3.5 and 4.5 mg/L across the years (Figure 11b). The lowest value was observed in 2019 at 3.9 mg/L, while the highest was recorded in 2020 at 4.04 mg/L. The average DO concentration amounted to 9.89 ± 0.42 mg/L. The lowest concentration was observed in 2020 at 9.37 mg/L, while the highest concentration was noted in 2018 at 10.38 mg/L. DO also showed a declining trend from 2017 to 2020, with an increase in concentration observed in the spring and winter of 2021, followed by another decrease in 2022 (Figure 11c). For SDD, the average value was 0.44 ± 0.04 m. SDD did not exhibit a clear pattern of change, but overall, it showed a trend of initially decreasing and then increasing. SDD values were higher in 2017–2019, lower in 2020 and 2021, and increased again in 2022 (Figure 11d). The average TN concentration was calculated to be 2.08 ± 0.1 mg/L. The lowest concentration occurred in 2019 at 1.91 mg/L, and the highest was observed in 2021 at 2.21 mg/L. TN displayed relatively small interannual differences, indicating stable changes over the years (Figure 11e). Lastly, the average TP concentration was measured at 0.109 ± 0.003 mg/L. The lowest value was registered in 2022 at 0.105 mg/L, whereas the highest value was recorded in 2020 at 0.111 mg/L.

The seasonal variations in water quality parameters mirror their monthly fluctuations. Chl-a, COD_{Mn}, and TN concentrations exhibit higher levels in the summer and autumn, while they demonstrate lower levels in the spring and winter. Conversely, other water quality parameters display the opposite trend (Figures 10 and 11).

3.2.2. Spatial Variation

To explore the spatial variations of various water quality parameters within Dianshan Lake, we conducted a comprehensive analysis by computing the mean values based on data collected from 100 images. The annual average values obtained for Dianshan Lake were 13.73 mg/m^3 for Chl-a, 3.94 mg/L for COD_{Mn}, 8.92 mg/L for DO, 0.44 m for SDD, 2.09 mg/L for TN, and 0.11 mg/L for TP, respectively. The corresponding standard deviations were recorded as 4.4 mg/m^3, 0.29 mg/L, 1.47 mg/L, 0.11 m, 0.74 mg/L, and 0.013 mg/L.

The mean images of each water quality parameter reveal distinct spatial patterns within Dianshan Lake. There is a clear negative correlation between Chl-a and SDD distributions, wherein areas with higher Chl-a concentrations tend to exhibit lower transparency (Figure 12a,d). Within the lake area, the northern and southwestern regions demonstrate elevated Chl-a concentrations, particularly near the entrances of Jishuigang Harbor in the northeast and the western region, where Chl-a concentrations reach their peaks. In contrast, the central open areas of the lake and the southeastern region exhibit lower Chl-a concentrations.

Similar to Chl-a, the spatial distribution of COD_{Mn} and TN also displays a correlation (Figure 12b,e). COD_{Mn} exhibits a discernible distribution pattern throughout the lake, with higher concentrations observed along the lake's edges and lower concentrations in the open areas within the lake. DO concentrations are lowest near the entrance of Jishuigang Harbor in the southwestern region, while the central open areas and northern regions of the lake demonstrate higher DO concentrations (Figure 12c).

Regarding nitrogen content, TN concentrations are lower in the lake's edge regions and higher in the open areas within the lake (Figure 12e). Similarly, the spatial distribution trend of TP resembles that of TN (Figure 12f). The southwestern and northeastern regions of the lake exhibit lower TP concentrations, while the eastern areas and central open regions display higher TP concentrations.

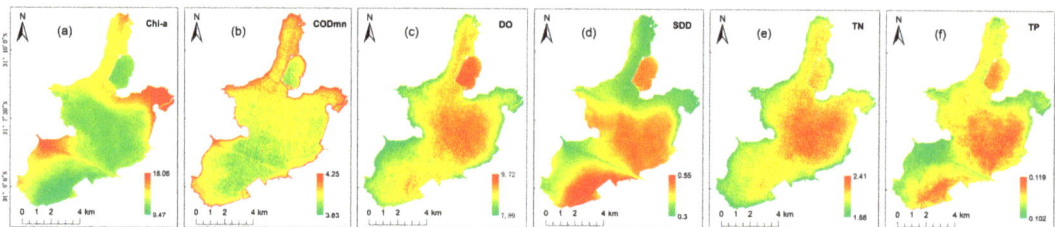

Figure 12. Average concentration maps of (**a**) Chl-a, (**b**) COD$_{Mn}$, (**c**) DO, (**d**) SDD, (**e**) TN, and (**f**) TP in Dianshan Lake from 2017 to 2022.

To investigate the spatial variations of Dianshan Lake more comprehensively, we calculated the coefficient of variation map for the entire lake area (Figure 13). It can be observed that regions with higher concentrations of DO, TN, and TP tend to exhibit larger variability. Similarly, SDD follows a similar pattern, with regions showing higher values appearing in red hues, indicating greater coefficients of variation. In contrast, the standard deviation of COD$_{Mn}$ remains relatively consistent across the entirety of the lake, suggesting an overall lower variability, which is in line with its temporal variation image. The situation for Chl-a is slightly different, whereby regions with lower average concentrations across the lake display relatively unstable conditions, implying significant variability.

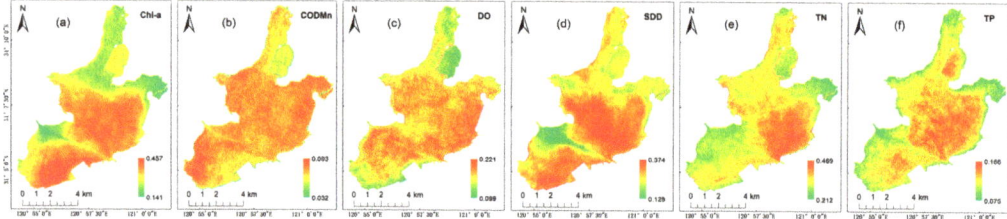

Figure 13. Coefficient of variation maps of (**a**) Chl-a, (**b**) COD$_{Mn}$, (**c**) DO, (**d**) SDD, (**e**) TN, and (**f**) TP concentrations in Dianshan Lake from 2017 to 2022.

4. Discussion

4.1. Applicability of the Models

In the practical application of Dianshan Lake, promising outcomes have been achieved through the construction of models utilizing both actual measurement data from Dianshan Lake and satellite reflectance data, enabling the prediction of various water quality parameters. To comprehensively assess the applicability of the established best models for various water quality parameters, further in-depth research was conducted. Considering Dianshan Lake as a representative small lake with poor-to-low nutrient levels, we extended our investigation to Taihu Lake—a larger lake characterized by higher nutrient levels. The primary objective was to validate the generality and stability of BM-Chl-a, BM-CODMn, BM-DO, BM-SDD, BM-TN, and BM-TP across diverse environmental contexts. The performance of the best model for each parameter in the Taihu Lake dataset is shown in Table 5.

Based on the outcomes, noteworthy shifts were observed in the prediction performance of Chl-a. The *RMSE* of Chl-a escalated to 19.88 mg/m^2, while the *MAPE* surged to 45%, nearly doubling the previous values. Consequently, BM-Chl-a exhibited substantial errors in predicting Chl-a, signifying a diminished predictive capacity for this parameter. The prediction errors of BM-CODMn and BM-DO also displayed some increase. The *RMSE* values (0.74 mg/L and 1.69 mg/L) and *MAPE* values (15% and 15%) both grew by approximately half. Although the prediction outcomes remained within a certain range, in comparison to the prior test data, these two models exhibited heightened uncertainty in predicting COD_{Mn} and DO. Regarding BM-SDD, the model's predictive performance showed improvement, as reflected by diminished $RMSE$ (0.07 m) and $MAPE$ (16%) values, indicating enhanced accuracy in forecasting water transparency concentrations. However, in the instances of BM-TN and BM-TP, the models' performance faltered. The predictive errors for these two indicators markedly increased when contrasted with the test data from Dianshan Lake, particularly the $MAPE$ values (55% and 68%), which tripled. Consequently, BM-TN and BM-TP demonstrated marked limitations, with their forecasts significantly diverging from actual conditions.

Table 5. Performance of the best model of each parameter on Taihu Lake.

Water Quality Parameter	RMSE	MAPE	Bias
Chl-a	19.88 mg/m^3	44.88%	−12.14 mg/m^3
COD_{Mn}	0.74 mg/L	14.61%	0.08 mg/L
DO	1.69 mg/L	14.88%	−1.25 mg/L
SDD	0.07 m	15.7%	−0.013 m
TN	1.5 mg/L	54.78%	10.45 mg/L
TP	0.05 mg/L	67.56%	0.034 mg/L

In light of the models' predictive outcomes compared to the authentic test data from Taihu Lake, it can be deduced that the predictive performance of parameters such as Chl-a, COD_{Mn}, DO, TN, and TP exhibited varying degrees of decline or fluctuation. Only the predictive performance for SSD maintained a relatively favorable state. In essence, the best models for Dianshan Lake displayed specific restrictions and inadequacies in predicting water quality parameters for Taihu Lake. Further enhancement and optimization are imperative through the incorporation of localized data to augment its predictive prowess.

4.2. Performance and Evaluation of Machine Learning Algorithms

4.2.1. Analysis of Error Sources Affecting Model Performance

In the realm of machine learning, the quality of the dataset has a direct bearing on the performance of the model. Additionally, the congruence between field estimations and satellite-derived estimations stands as a crucial criterion for evaluating the efficacy of the proposed Chl-a algorithm. Given the foundation of our study in employing satellite reflectance and measurement data to construct retrieval models, the quality of satellite reflectance data becomes particularly salient.

First and foremost, atmospheric correction presents itself as a principal source of error. Particularly, in comparison to expansive oceanic regions, atmospheric correction for inland water body imagery proves to be a more intricate endeavor due to intricate interactions with neighboring land pixels. Rectifying atmospheric effects over water surfaces is particularly demanding, often requiring a higher degree of precision compared to correction procedures applied over terrestrial areas. In this study, a specialized atmospheric correction method tailored for inland water bodies [48,49] was employed. Following Rayleigh correction, the "dark pixel method" was transferred to the shortwave near-infrared band [32,45,50,55] to mitigate aerosol effects. This approach ensures a maximum level of correction accuracy, even in the presence of unavoidable errors.

Furthermore, the alignment of time windows [56] and pixel window [57] sizes for on-site estimations and satellite data introduces error sources within the retrieval model. While Sentinel-2 MSI imagery follows a five-day orbital cycle, practical limitations arising from adverse weather conditions considerably restrict the number of images that effectively align with measured data. According to statistics from pertinent water management authorities in Shanghai, Dianshan Lake has an approximate water turnover cycle of seven days. Accordingly, we extended the time window to five days to secure a more substantial dataset alignment. Apart from Chl-a, the correlation between other water quality parameters and single-band reflectance remains relatively low (Figure 14). Encouragingly, correlations involving combinations of bands display improved trends. Looking ahead, enhancing the frequency of in situ measurements to shorten the time window and acquire more aligned data warrants consideration.

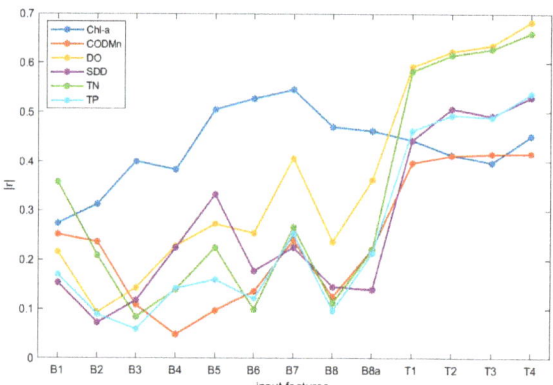

Figure 14. Machine learning input features and correlation coefficients of each water quality parameter. B1~B8a represent the corresponding bands of the Sentinel-2 MSI image, and T1~T4 represent the band combination with the greatest correlation with each water quality parameter ($R_{rs}(\lambda 1) - R_{rs}(\lambda 2)$, $\frac{R_{rs}(\lambda 1)}{R_{rs}(\lambda 2)}$, $\frac{R_{rs}(\lambda 2) - R_{rs}(\lambda 1)}{R_{rs}(\lambda 2) + R_{rs}(\lambda 1)}$, $R_{rs}(\lambda 3) \times (\frac{1}{R_{rs}(\lambda 2)} - \frac{1}{R_{rs}(\lambda 1)})$).

Moreover, to demonstrate the effectiveness of satellite reflectance pixel windows, different window sizes were employed in constructing retrieval models, including single-pixel windows, 3 × 3 pixel window averages, and 5 × 5 pixel window averages.

RMSE and *MAPE* are employed as performance metrics. As illustrated in Table 6, for both *RMSE* and *MAPE*, the 3 × 3 pixel window consistently yields the lowest error across various water quality parameter retrievals. This aligns with our predicted outcomes. The single-pixel window exhibits higher variability, potentially stemming from greater noise. The 5 × 5 pixel window, with a ground resolution of 100 m × 100 m, might excessively "smooth" the data, thus diminishing spectral features. In contrast, the 3 × 3 pixel window effectively eliminates noise while retaining significant water feature information in the region, thereby maximizing water quality uniformity.

Table 6. Accuracy display of water quality parameters using different pixel windows and different methods to build models.

Parameters	Methods	1 × 1		3 × 3		5 × 5	
		RMSE	*MAPE* (%)	*RMSE*	*MAPE* (%)	*RMSE*	*MAPE* (%)
Chl-a (mg/m³)	CatBoost	11.19	29.12	11.11	28.12	11.21	29.12
	RF	10.94	29.87	10.94	29.57	10.99	31.57
	SVR	13.99	38.15	12.99	35.15	13.99	39.15
	XGBoost	10.46	29.86	10.46	30.86	10.96	31.86
CODMn (mg/L)	CatBoost	0.58	11.29	0.57	11.24	0.59	11.87
	RF	0.60	11.33	0.58	11.28	0.62	12.19
	SVR	0.61	11.63	0.60	11.10	0.61	12.11
	XGBoost	0.57	10.60	0.55	10.55	0.57	11.32
DO (mg/L)	CatBoost	1.27	12.89	1.25	12.77	1.31	13.16
	RF	1.32	13.24	1.32	13.16	1.35	13.68
	SVR	1.24	12.29	1.20	12.11	1.24	12.29
	XGBoost	1.34	13.14	1.24	12.56	1.28	12.97

Table 6. Cont.

Parameters	Methods	1 × 1		3 × 3		5 × 5	
		RMSE	MAPE (%)	RMSE	MAPE (%)	RMSE	MAPE (%)
SDD (m)	CatBoost	14.44	34.38	14.73	34.26	14.65	34.63
	RF	14.69	34.44	14.77	34.28	14.75	34.90
	SVR	14.80	34.14	14.74	34.14	14.81	34.57
	XGBoost	14.38	34.03	14.15	33.22	14.35	34.31
TN (mg/L)	CatBoost	0.72	25.83	0.63	24.01	0.68	26.14
	RF	0.82	26.08	0.68	25.15	0.65	26.33
	SVR	0.73	24.80	0.65	24.26	0.62	25.07
	XGBoost	0.69	25.81	0.61	24.68	0.61	24.76
TP (mg/L)	CatBoost	0.04	33.13	0.04	32.14	0.04	32.91
	RF	0.06	78.09	0.06	75.45	0.06	74.07
	SVR	0.04	32.47	0.04	31.71	0.04	32.02
	XGBoost	0.04	30.20	0.04	29.34	0.04	31.88

4.2.2. Evaluation of the Models

Based on the previous analysis, it is evident that CatBoost has the greatest potential for application in inland water quality assessment. It demonstrated superior performance in predicting Chl-a, COD$_{Mn}$, SDD, and TP. The convincing results are particularly evident in Table 6, where changes in pixel window size did not affect the accuracy trend. The main challenge of machine learning modeling is the need for extensive samples. CatBoost excels with small datasets, effectively curbing overfitting and providing valuable insights into feature importance, aiding in understanding model performance and predictions [58].

Among the models, SVR exhibited the weakest performance. It notably erred significantly in predicting TP (Figure 8). SVR's performance might excel with high-quality data [38], which could explain its unsatisfactory performance when modeling satellite reflectance data due to atmospheric correction errors. XGBoost and RF also show promise, as prior studies highlight their utility in inland lake water quality assessment [24,38].

4.3. Spatiotemporal Change Analysis

After analysis, it was found that there were minimal overall differences in the temporal variations of COD$_{Mn}$, TN, and TP, which may be related to the nutrient status of Dianshan Lake. The lake's overall eutrophication is not severe, with occasional occurrences of algae blooms in late summer and early autumn. Except for TN, almost all other parameters indicate better water quality during the winter and spring seasons compared to the summer and autumn seasons. TN, in particular, exhibits a pronounced seasonal variation trend over six years, with notably high values during the winter. This phenomenon may result from the combined influence of multiple factors.

Environmental and meteorological factors such as water temperature, air temperature, and precipitation can affect water quality [59]. We compiled monthly average values of environmental factors (water temperature, pH, conductivity) and meteorological factors (air temperature, precipitation, wind speed) for Dianshan Lake and examined their relationships with water quality parameters through correlation analysis (Table 7). Water temperature, air temperature, and precipitation showed strong correlations with various water quality parameters, while pH and conductivity were significantly correlated only with Chl-a and TP, and wind speed exhibited weak correlations with all parameters. Due to climate-related factors, both air and water temperatures reach their lowest points in winter (December, January, February) and peak in late summer and early autumn (August, September). Similarly, precipitation is very high in summer and very low in winter. These factors can influence the intensity of chemical reactions in the water, as well as the variation of nutrients and chemicals released from sediments, leading to changes in water chemistry and characteristics. Precipitation also drives the input of nutrients from the lake's surroundings, which can promote algal growth and increase concentrations of Chl-a, thus improving water quality in spring and winter compared to summer and autumn.

Table 7. Pearson correlation coefficient of water quality parameters and environmental factors.

Index	Chl-a	COD_{Mn}	DO	SDD	TN	TP
Water temperature	0.38	0.71 *	−0.94 *	−0.86 *	−0.32	−0.1
PH	0.73 *	0.46	−0.35	−0.19	−0.24	−0.25
Conductivity	−0.4	−0.12	0.43	0.56	0.38	0.39
Air temperature	0.41	0.82 *	−0.97 *	−0.82 *	−0.35	−0.13
Precipitation	0.78 *	0.45	−0.72 *	−0.42	−0.67 *	−0.37
Wind speed	0.15	0.43	−0.42	−0.21	−0.49	−0.33

* Represents significant correlation, Pearson correlation coefficient > 0.6.

Agricultural nonpoint source pollution is widely recognized as one of the most important nutrient sources contributing to water quality deterioration [60]. Therefore, changes in land use, especially in the area of farmland, can also impact water quality parameters [43]. Dianshan Lake is designated as a protected area for drinking water resources, with restrictions on industrial development and a ban on livestock farming. Previous research has indicated that agriculture is the primary source of pollution leading to deteriorating water quality in this region [61]. One of the primary reasons for agricultural pollution of water quality is the widespread use of agricultural chemicals such as fertilizers and pesticides. These chemicals are washed into lakes by rainwater, leading to an increase in the concentrations of TN and TP in the water, thereby triggering eutrophication issues. As TN and TP levels rise, the content of Chl-a also increases, resulting in the overgrowth of algae in the water body. This leads to a decline in water quality, characterized by severe eutrophication, and a potential decrease in the concentration of DO, adversely affecting aquatic organisms. Additionally, due to soil erosion and wastewater discharges, there may be an increase in suspended solids in the water, leading to increased water turbidity and reduced water transparency. These changes in the range of water quality parameters can be attributed to the adverse impact of agricultural activities on the water body. Data obtained from the Statistical Yearbook website (http://www.tjnjw.com/, accessed on 4 September 2023) show that the farmland area in Qingpu District decreased from 25,466 hectares in 2017 to 20,581 hectares in 2019 and then increased to 25,400 hectares in 2021. The farmland area decreased initially and then increased, with the smallest area recorded in 2019, coinciding with the year when various parameters reached extreme values over the six years (as observed in Section 3.2.1). This suggests a strong correlation between the area of farmland around Dianshan Lake and water quality: when the farmland area decreases, water quality improves, and when the farmland area increases, water quality deteriorates.

As indicated in Section 3.2.2, water quality parameters exhibit noticeable spatial differences, which could be related to the uneven distribution of water flow, sediment, and nutrient inputs. It is noteworthy that there are significant differences between the water quality parameters at the inlet and outlet of Dianshan Lake. The inlet is typically a critical area for water quality changes, as it is directly influenced by the surrounding environment, while the outlet may be influenced by internal lake ecosystems and processes. Based on the mean values of water quality parameters (Figure 12), at the inlet of Dianshan Lake, the Chl-a concentration and COD_{Mn} concentration are higher, while DO and SDD concentrations are lower. Conversely, at the outlet, the opposite trend is observed. Jishui Port takes the shipping channel as the main water function, and the traffic discharge enters the lake area along with the entrance. The influx of water from tributaries introduces a large amount of suspended sediment and organic matter, increasing the concentrations of Chl-a and COD_{Mn}. The water near the inlet of the lake is much turbid compared to the open areas within the lake, resulting in lower transparency.

4.4. Strengths and Limitations of the Study

This study possesses significant strengths across various dimensions. Firstly, our study adopts a direct model built upon image reflectance data. This strategy mitigates the influence of atmospheric correction on research outcomes to a certain extent, effectively curtailing error propagation from modeled measured data to satellite image application. Consequently, this approach bolsters the stability of the proposed model. Secondly, our study transcends the limitations of assessing algorithm performance solely based on individual water quality parameters. Instead, we amalgamate multiple pivotal water quality parameters and gauge the efficacy of six distinct machine learning methods. In comparison to appraising methods solely on a singular water quality parameter, our all-encompassing evaluation strategy is more holistic and precise. This curtails uncertainty in evaluation findings and enhances the trustworthiness of research conclusions. Lastly, our study ventures beyond the exploration of modeling techniques. It encompasses a spatiotemporal analysis of diverse water quality parameters within Dianshan Lake. This examination of spatiotemporal distribution furnishes invaluable insights into water quality retrieval within small lakes. Moreover, our study deepens the comprehension of small lake ecosystems, delivering substantial groundwork for informed decisions regarding lake water quality management and preservation. The analytical results furnish novel viewpoints and avenues for research and practical applications in related spheres.

While this study has made commendable advancements, it is important to address a few noteworthy considerations. Firstly, regarding the distribution of the dataset, we acknowledge that there are certain limitations in terms of data samples within high- and low-concentration ranges. In our application of the model to the Taihu Lake region, we observed that predictions only for SDD (water transparency) were notably accurate. Therefore, there might be room for improvement in predicting other water quality parameters. This disparity could potentially arise from the distinct characteristics of Dianshan Lake and Taihu Lake, but it has not impeded the model's practical applicability across different regions. Secondly, when machine learning is used for prediction, the precision of measured parameter concentrations can significantly impact the model's performance, as evident in the prediction of TP and SDD. Since TP concentrations are typically quite low, often below 0.1 mg/L, and our actual measurements are controlled only up to 0.001 mg/L, this results in multiple identical TP concentration values in the measured data. This accuracy issue leads to a situation where a specific TP concentration may correspond to multiple different reflectance spectral data, increasing the difficulty for the model to distinguish similar values and, consequently, resulting in poorer model performance. The same holds true for SDD. Future work could consider improving measurement precision based on the concentration distribution of measured water quality parameters to enhance model performance. Finally, we employed a time window of five days to synchronize the measured and satellite data. It is acknowledged that changes within the water body could transpire during this period, and future research could contemplate the integration of additional observational data to expand the dataset's scope.

5. Conclusions

This study utilized satellite data and in situ measurements to determine the optimal models for Chl-a, COD_{Mn}, DO, SDD, TN, and TP from four machine learning models (RF, SVR, XGBoost, and CatBoost), which were identified as CatBoost, CatBoost, XGBoost, XGBoost, RF, and CatBoost, respectively. The applicability of these models was validated using data from Taihu Lake. These models were then applied to Sentinel-2 imagery from 2017 to 2023 to obtain the spatiotemporal distribution of water quality parameters in Dianshan Lake. Image inversion results indicated that the overall distribution of water quality parameters in the study area was uneven, with significant spatial variation, relatively minor interannual differences, and significant seasonal patterns. Further analysis revealed that the spatiotemporal variation of water quality parameters was influenced by climatic factors such as temperature and precipitation, as well as human activities including agriculture and industry. The results of this study indicate that constructing models using multispectral satellite image reflectance and in situ water quality parameter sampling data is effective. Furthermore, in the future, model enhancement can be further achieved by improving the precision of in situ data, reducing the data time window, such as utilizing multisource satellite data, and implementing other methods. In conclusion, our study demonstrates advantages in methodology, data processing, and practical implementation. It provides valuable practical experience for the accurate monitoring of water quality parameters in small water bodies using satellite data and offers essential data support for local water resource management and environmental protection.

Author Contributions: Conceptualization, C.G. and L.D.; methodology, L.D.; validation, L.L., Z.Y. and C.G.; resources, H.H., E.W. and Z.L.; data curation, C.G.; writing—original draft preparation, L.D.; writing—review and editing, L.D.; supervision, Z.Y.; project administration, Y.H.; funding acquisition, E.W. All authors have read and agreed to the published version of the manuscript.

Funding: This research was funded by the Shanghai 2021 "Science and Technology Innovation Action Plan" Social Development Science and Technology Research Project (21DZ1202500), the Jiangsu Provincial Water Conservancy Science and Technology Research Project (No. 2020068), and the Science and Technology Project of the Shanghai Municipal Water Bureau (Shanghai Branch 2021-10, Shanghai Branch 2018-07).

Data Availability Statement: Not applicable.

Acknowledgments: We are also thankful to all anonymous reviewers for their constructive comments provided on the study.

Conflicts of Interest: The authors declare no conflict of interest.

Appendix A

Table A1. Methods for Determining Some Water Quality Parameters in Chinese National Standard GB3838-2002.

Water Quality Parameter	Determination Method
Chl-a	Nitrite Reduction Method and Continuous-Flow Analysis
COD_{Mn}	High-Temperature Oxidation Method and Continuous-Flow Analysis
DO	Electrode Method and Continuous-Flow Analysis
SDD	Potassium Permanganate Spectrophotometric Method and Continuous-Flow Analysis
TN	Ether Extraction–Spectrophotometric Method
TP	Transparency Meter Measurement

Table A2. The best hyperparameters found by grid optimization of the models.

Model	Hyperparameters	Chl-a	COD_{Mn}	DO	SDD	TN	TP
RF	n_estimators	450	500	360	390	490	300
	max_depth	40	25	10	45	20	20
	min_samples_split	5	4	5	11	7	3
	min_samples_leaf	3	5	7	2	3	7
SVR	C	4.91	2	8.67	9.82	7.52	2.94
	kernel	'rbf'	'rbf'	'rbf'	'rbf'	'rbf'	'linear'
	gamma	88.109	58.907	29.329	80.078	66.251	16.369
XGBoost	learning_rate	0.16	0.015	0.085	0.04	0.035	0.155
	gamma	0.001	0.003	0.003	0.001	0.001	0.003
	min_child_weight	9	5	8	8	9	6
	max_depth	2	2	10	6	6	8
	sub_sample	1	1	0.8	1	0.8	1
	reg_alpha	0.1	1	1	0.01	1	0.01
CatBoost	iterations	200	170	370	430	230	450
	learning_rate	0.03	0.03	0.01	0.04	0.02	0.01
	depth	6	9	8	8	6	9
	l2_leaf_reg	2	1	2	9	2	2

References

1. Ho, J.C.; Michalak, A.M.; Pahlevan, N. Widespread global increase in intense lake phytoplankton blooms since the 1980s. *Nature* **2019**, *574*, 667–670. [CrossRef]
2. Yang, Z.; Gong, C.; Ji, T.; Hu, Y.; Li, L. Water Quality Retrieval from ZY1-02D Hyperspectral Imagery in Urban Water Bodies and Comparison with Sentinel-2. *Remote Sens.* **2022**, *14*, 5029. [CrossRef]
3. Pi, X.; Feng, L.; Li, W.; Zhao, D.; Kuang, X.; Li, J. Water clarity changes in 64 large alpine lakes on the Tibetan Plateau and the potential responses to lake expansion. *ISPRS-J. Photogramm. Remote Sens.* **2020**, *170*, 192–204. [CrossRef]
4. Ma, Y.; Song, K.; Wen, Z.; Liu, G.; Shang, Y.; Lyu, L.; Du, J.; Yang, Q.; Li, S.; Tao, H.; et al. Remote Sensing of Turbidity for Lakes in Northeast China Using Sentinel-2 Images with Machine Learning Algorithms. *IEEE J. Sel. Top. Appl. Earth Observ. Remote Sens.* **2021**, *14*, 9132–9146. [CrossRef]
5. Cao, Z.; Ma, R.; Melack, J.M.; Duan, H.; Liu, M.; Kutser, T.; Xue, K.; Shen, M.; Qi, T.; Yuan, H. Landsat observations of chlorophyll-a variations in Lake Taihu from 1984 to 2019. *Int. J. Appl. Earth Obs. Geoinf.* **2022**, *106*, 102642. [CrossRef]
6. Chen, J.; Lyu, Y.; Zhao, Z.; Liu, H.; Zhao, H.; Li, Z. Using the multidimensional synthesis methods with non-parameter test, multiple time scales analysis to assess water quality trend and its characteristics over the past 25 years in the Fuxian Lake, China. *Sci. Total Environ.* **2019**, *655*, 242–254. [CrossRef]
7. Wang, J.; Fu, Z.; Qiao, H.; Liu, F. Assessment of eutrophication and water quality in the estuarine area of Lake Wuli, Lake Taihu, China. *Sci. Total Environ.* **2019**, *650*, 1392–1402. [CrossRef]
8. Wang, Y.; Guo, Y.; Zhao, Y.; Wang, L.; Chen, Y.; Yang, L. Spatiotemporal heterogeneities and driving factors of water quality and trophic state of a typical urban shallow lake (Taihu, China). *Environ. Sci. Pollut. Res.* **2022**, *29*, 53831–53843. [CrossRef]
9. Pahlevan, N.; Smith, B.; Alikas, K.; Anstee, J.; Barbosa, C.; Binding, C.; Bresciani, M.; Cremella, B.; Giardino, C.; Gurlin, D.; et al. Simultaneous retrieval of selected optical water quality indicators from Landsat-8, Sentinel-2, and Sentinel-3. *Remote Sens. Environ.* **2022**, *270*, 112860. [CrossRef]
10. Shi, K.; Zhang, Y.; Zhu, G.; Qin, B.; Pan, D. Deteriorating water clarity in shallow waters: Evidence from long-term MODIS and in-situ observations. *Int. J. Appl. Earth Obs. Geoinf.* **2018**, *68*, 287–297. [CrossRef]
11. Lee, Z.; Shang, S.; Hu, C.; Du, K.; Weidemann, A.; Hou, W.; Lin, J.; Lin, G. Secchi disk depth: A new theory and mechanistic model for underwater visibility. *Remote Sens. Environ.* **2015**, *169*, 139–149. [CrossRef]
12. Sun, D.; Qiu, Z.; Li, Y.; Shi, K.; Gong, S. Detection of Total Phosphorus Concentrations of Turbid Inland Waters Using a Remote Sensing Method. *Water Air Soil Pollut.* **2014**, *225*, 1953. [CrossRef]
13. Xu, W.; Duan, L.; Wen, X.; Li, H.; Li, D.; Zhang, Y.; Zhang, H. Effects of Seasonal Variation on Water Quality Parameters and Eutrophication in Lake Yangzong. *Water* **2022**, *14*, 2732. [CrossRef]
14. Sagan, V.; Peterson, K.T.; Maimaitijiang, M.; Sidike, P.; Sloan, J.; Greeling, B.A.; Maalouf, S.; Adams, C. Monitoring inland water quality using remote sensing: Potential and limitations of spectral indices, bio-optical simulations, machine learning, and cloud computing. *Earth-Sci. Rev.* **2020**, *205*, 103187. [CrossRef]
15. Chen, K.; Duan, L.; Liu, Q.; Zhang, Y.; Zhang, X.; Liu, F.; Zhang, H. Spatiotemporal Changes in Water Quality Parameters and the Eutrophication in Lake Erhai of Southwest China. *Water* **2022**, *14*, 3398. [CrossRef]
16. Tian, S.; Guo, H.; Xu, W.; Zhu, X.; Wang, B.; Zeng, Q.; Mai, Y.; Huang, J.J. Remote sensing retrieval of inland water quality parameters using Sentinel-2 and multiple machine learning algorithms. *Environ. Sci. Pollut. Res.* **2023**, *30*, 18617–18630. [CrossRef] [PubMed]
17. Duan, W.; Takara, K.; He, B.; Luo, P.; Nover, D.; Yamashiki, Y. Spatial, and temporal trends in estimates of nutrient and suspended sediment loads in the Ishikari River, Japan, 1985 to 2010. *Sci. Total Environ.* **2013**, *461–462*, 499–508. [CrossRef]
18. Li, S.; Song, K.; Wang, S.; Liu, G.; Wen, Z.; Shang, Y.; Lyu, L.; Chen, F.; Xu, S.; Tao, H.; et al. Quantification of chlorophyll-a in typical lakes across China using Sentinel-2 MSI imagery with machine learning algorithm. *Sci. Total Environ.* **2021**, *778*, 146271. [CrossRef]
19. Peterson, K.T.; Sagan, V.; Sloan, J.J. Deep learning-based water quality estimation and anomaly detection using Landsat-8/Sentinel-2 virtual constellation and cloud computing. *GISci. Remote Sens.* **2020**, *57*, 510–525. [CrossRef]
20. Li, L.; Gu, M.; Gong, C.; Hu, Y.; Wang, X.; Yang, Z.; He, Z. An advanced remote sensing retrieval method for urban non-optically active water quality parameters: An example from Shanghai. *Sci. Total Environ.* **2023**, *880*, 163370. [CrossRef]
21. Yang, H.; Kong, J.; Hu, H.; Du, Y.; Gao, M.; Chen, F. A Review of Remote Sensing for Water Quality Retrieval: Progress and Challenges. *Remote Sens.* **2022**, *14*, 1770. [CrossRef]
22. Palmer, S.C.J.; Kutser, T.; Hunter, P.D. Remote sensing of inland waters: Challenges, progress and future directions. *Remote Sens. Environ.* **2015**, *157*, 1–8. [CrossRef]
23. Topp, S.N.; Pavelsky, T.M.; Jensen, D.; Simard, M.; Ross, M.R.V. Research Trends in the Use of Remote Sensing for Inland Water Quality Science: Moving Towards Multidisciplinary Applications. *Water* **2020**, *12*, 169. [CrossRef]
24. Cao, Z.; Ma, R.; Duan, H.; Pahlevan, N.; Melack, J.; Shen, M.; Xue, K. A machine learning approach to estimate chlorophyll-a from Landsat-8 measurements in inland lakes. *Remote Sens. Environ.* **2020**, *248*, 111974. [CrossRef]
25. Swain, R.; Sahoo, B. Improving river water quality monitoring using satellite data products and a genetic algorithm processing approach. *Sustain. Water Qual. Ecol.* **2017**, *9–10*, 88–114. [CrossRef]
26. Xu, S.; Li, S.; Tao, Z.; Song, K.; Wen, Z.; Li, Y.; Chen, F. Remote Sensing of Chlorophyll-a in Xinkai Lake Using Machine Learning and GF-6 WFV Images. *Remote Sens.* **2022**, *14*, 5136. [CrossRef]

27. Bramich, J.; Bolch, C.J.S.; Fischer, A. Improved red-edge chlorophyll-a detection for Sentinel 2. *Ecol. Indic.* **2021**, *120*, 106876. [CrossRef]
28. Shi, X.; Gu, L.; Jiang, T.; Jiang, M.; Butler, J.J.; Xiong, X.J.; Gu, X. Retrieval of chlorophyll-a concentration based on Sentinel-2 images in inland lakes. In Proceedings of the Earth Observing Systems XXVII, San Diego, CA, USA, 23–25 August 2022; Volume 12232.
29. Shi, X.; Gu, L.; Jiang, T.; Zheng, X.; Dong, W.; Tao, Z. Retrieval of Chlorophyll-a Concentrations Using Sentinel-2 MSI Imagery in Lake Chagan Based on Assessments with Machine Learning Models. *Remote Sens.* **2022**, *14*, 4924. [CrossRef]
30. Yang, F.; He, B.; Zhou, Y.; Li, W.; Zhang, X.; Feng, Q. Trophic status observations for Honghu Lake in China from 2000 to 2021 using Landsat Satellites. *Ecol. Indic.* **2023**, *146*, 109898. [CrossRef]
31. Gordon, H.R.; Clark, D.K.; Brown, J.W.; Brown, O.B.; Evans, R.H.; Broenkow, W.W. Phytoplankton pigment concentrations in the Middle Atlantic Bight: Comparison of ship determinations and CZCS estimates. *Appl. Opt.* **1983**, *22*, 20–36. [CrossRef]
32. Schroeder, T.; Schaale, M.; Lovell, J.; Blondeau-Patissier, D. An ensemble neural network atmospheric correction for Sentinel-3 OLCI over coastal waters providing inherent model uncertainty estimation and sensor noise propagation. *Remote Sens. Environ.* **2022**, *270*, 112848. [CrossRef]
33. Mouw, C.B.; Greb, S.; Aurin, D.; DiGiacomo, P.M.; Lee, Z.; Twardowski, M.; Binding, C.; Hu, C.; Ma, R.; Moore, T.; et al. Aquatic color radiometry remote sensing of coastal and inland waters: Challenges and recommendations for future satellite missions. *Remote Sens. Environ.* **2015**, *160*, 15–30. [CrossRef]
34. Mobley, C.; Werdell, J.; Franz, B.A.; Ahmad, Z.; Bailey, S. *Atmospheric Correction for Satellite Ocean Color Radiometry*; NASA: Washington, DC, USA, 2016.
35. Kuhn, C.; de Matos Valerio, A.; Ward, N.; Loken, L.; Sawakuchi, H.O.; Kampel, M.; Richey, J.; Stadler, P.; Crawford, J.; Striegl, R.; et al. Performance of Landsat-8 and Sentinel-2 surface reflectance products for river remote sensing retrievals of chlorophyll-a and turbidity. *Remote Sens. Environ.* **2019**, *224*, 104–118. [CrossRef]
36. Niroumand-Jadidi, M.; Bovolo, F.; Bresciani, M.; Gege, P.; Giardino, C. Water Quality Retrieval from Landsat-9 (OLI-2) Imagery and Comparison to Sentinel-2. *Remote Sens.* **2022**, *14*, 4596. [CrossRef]
37. He, Y.; Gong, Z.; Zheng, Y.; Zhang, Y. Inland Reservoir Water Quality Inversion and Eutrophication Evaluation Using BP Neural Network and Remote Sensing Imagery: A Case Study of Dashahe Reservoir. *Water* **2021**, *13*, 2844. [CrossRef]
38. Shen, M.; Luo, J.; Cao, Z.; Xue, K.; Qi, T.; Ma, J.; Liu, D.; Song, K.; Feng, L.; Duan, H. Random forest: An optimal chlorophyll-a algorithm for optically complex inland water suffering atmospheric correction uncertainties. *J. Hydrol.* **2022**, *615*, 128685. [CrossRef]
39. Ioannou, I.; Gilerson, A.; Gross, B.; Moshary, F.; Ahmed, S. Deriving ocean color products using neural networks. *Remote Sens. Environ.* **2013**, *134*, 78–91. [CrossRef]
40. Chang, N.; Xuan, Z.; Yang, Y.J. Exploring spatiotemporal patterns of phosphorus concentrations in a coastal bay with MODIS images and machine learning models. *Remote Sens. Environ.* **2013**, *134*, 100–110. [CrossRef]
41. Chang, N.; Vannah, B.W.; Yang, Y.J.; Elovitz, M. Integrated data fusion and mining techniques for monitoring total organic carbon concentrations in a lake. *Int. J. Remote Sens.* **2014**, *35*, 1064–1093. [CrossRef]
42. Arias-Rodriguez, L.F.; Duan, Z.; Sepúlveda, R.; Martinez-Martinez, S.I.; Disse, M. Monitoring Water Quality of Valle de Bravo Reservoir, Mexico, Using Entire Lifespan of MERIS Data and Machine Learning Approaches. *Remote Sens.* **2020**, *12*, 1586. [CrossRef]
43. Yuan, X.; Wang, S.; Fan, F.; Dong, Y.; Li, Y.; Lin, W.; Zhou, C. Spatiotemporal dynamics and anthropologically dominated drivers of chlorophyll-a, TN and TP concentrations in the Pearl River Estuary based on retrieval algorithm and random forest regression. *Environ. Res.* **2022**, *215*, 114380. [CrossRef] [PubMed]
44. Xiong, G.; Wang, G.; Wang, D.; Yang, W.; Chen, Y.; Chen, Z. Spatio-Temporal Distribution of Total Nitrogen and Phosphorus in Dianshan Lake, China: The External Loading and Self-Purification Capability. *Sustainability* **2017**, *9*, 500. [CrossRef]
45. Feng, L.; Hou, X.; Li, J.; Zheng, Y. Exploring the potential of Rayleigh-corrected reflectance in coastal and inland water applications: A simple aerosol correction method and its merits. *ISPRS-J. Photogramm. Remote Sens.* **2018**, *146*, 52–64. [CrossRef]
46. Olmanson, L.G.; Brezonik, P.L.; Bauer, M.E. Evaluation of medium to low resolution satellite imagery for regional lake water quality assessments. *Water Resour. Res.* **2011**, *47*. [CrossRef]
47. McFEETERS, S.K. The use of the Normalized Difference Water Index (NDWI) in the delineation of open water features. *Int. J. Remote Sens.* **1996**, *17*, 1425–1432. [CrossRef]
48. Werther, M.; Odermatt, D.; Simis, S.G.H.; Gurlin, D.; Jorge, D.S.F.; Loisel, H.; Hunter, P.D.; Tyler, A.N.; Spyrakos, E. Characterising retrieval uncertainty of chlorophyll-a algorithms in oligotrophic and mesotrophic lakes and reservoirs. *ISPRS-J. Photogramm. Remote Sens.* **2022**, *190*, 279–300. [CrossRef]
49. Wang, X.; Gong, C.; Ji, T.; Hu, Y.; Li, L. Inland water quality parameters retrieval based on the VIP-SPCA by hyperspectral remote sensing. *J. Appl. Remote Sens.* **2021**, *15*, 42609. [CrossRef]
50. Lo, Y.; Fu, L.; Lu, T.; Huang, H.; Kong, L.; Xu, Y.; Zhang, C. Medium-Sized Lake Water Quality Parameters Retrieval Using Multispectral UAV Image and Machine Learning Algorithms: A Case Study of the Yuandang Lake, China. *Drones* **2023**, *7*, 244. [CrossRef]
51. Guan, Q.; Feng, L.; Hou, X.; Schurgers, G.; Zheng, Y.; Tang, J. Eutrophication changes in fifty large lakes on the Yangtze Plain of China derived from MERIS and OLCI observations. *Remote Sens. Environ.* **2020**, *246*, 111890. [CrossRef]

52. He, J.; Chen, Y.; Wu, J.; Stow, D.A.; Christakos, G. Space-time chlorophyll-a retrieval in optically complex waters that accounts for remote sensing and modeling uncertainties and improves remote estimation accuracy. *Water Res.* **2020**, *171*, 115403. [CrossRef]
53. Mountrakis, G.; Im, J.; Ogole, C. Support vector machines in remote sensing: A review. *ISPRS-J. Photogramm. Remote Sens.* **2011**, *66*, 247–259. [CrossRef]
54. Haghiabi, A.H.; Nasrolahi, A.H.; Parsaie, A. Water quality prediction using machine learning methods. *Water Qual. Res. J.* **2018**, *53*, 3–13. [CrossRef]
55. Shenglei, W.; Junsheng, L.; Bing, Z.; Qian, S.; Fangfang, Z.; Zhaoyi, L. A simple correction method for the MODIS surface reflectance product over typical inland waters in China. *Int. J. Remote Sens.* **2016**, *37*, 6076–6096. [CrossRef]
56. Zhang, Y.; Shi, K.; Cao, Z.; Lai, L.; Geng, J.; Yu, K.; Zhan, P.; Liu, Z. Effects of satellite temporal resolutions on the remote derivation of trends in phytoplankton blooms in inland waters. *ISPRS-J. Photogramm. Remote Sens.* **2022**, *191*, 188–202. [CrossRef]
57. Li, J.; Gao, M.; Feng, L.; Zhao, H.; Shen, Q.; Zhang, F.; Wang, S.; Zhang, B. Estimation of Chlorophyll-a Concentrations in a Highly Turbid Eutrophic Lake Using a Classification-Based MODIS Land-Band Algorithm. *IEEE J. Sel. Top. Appl. Earth Observ. Remote Sens.* **2019**, *12*, 3769–3783. [CrossRef]
58. Bentéjac, C.; Csörgő, A.; Martínez-Muñoz, G. A comparative analysis of gradient boosting algorithms. *Artif. Intell. Rev.* **2021**, *54*, 1937–1967. [CrossRef]
59. Chen, Z.; An, C.; Tan, Q.; Tian, X.; Li, G.; Zhou, Y. Spatiotemporal analysis of land use pattern and stream water quality in southern Alberta, Canada. *J. Contam. Hydrol.* **2021**, *242*, 103852. [CrossRef] [PubMed]
60. Huang, J.; Zhang, Y.; Bing, H.; Peng, J.; Dong, F.; Gao, J.; Arhonditsis, G.B. Characterizing the river water quality in China: Recent progress and on-going challenges. *Water Res.* **2021**, *201*, 117309. [CrossRef] [PubMed]
61. Wang, S.; Ma, X.; Fan, Z.; Zhang, W.; Qian, X. Impact of nutrient losses from agricultural lands on nutrient stocks in Dianshan Lake in Shanghai, China. *Water Sci. Eng.* **2014**, *7*, 373–383.

Disclaimer/Publisher's Note: The statements, opinions and data contained in all publications are solely those of the individual author(s) and contributor(s) and not of MDPI and/or the editor(s). MDPI and/or the editor(s) disclaim responsibility for any injury to people or property resulting from any ideas, methods, instructions or products referred to in the content.

Article

Machine and Deep Learning Regression of Chlorophyll-a Concentrations in Lakes Using PRISMA Satellite Hyperspectral Imagery

Juan Francisco Amieva *, Daniele Oxoli and Maria Antonia Brovelli

Department of Civil and Environmental Engineering, Politecnico di Milano, 20133 Milan, Italy; daniele.oxoli@polimi.it (D.O.); maria.brovelli@polimi.it (M.A.B.)
* Correspondence: juanfrancisco.amieva@mail.polimi.it

Abstract: The estimation of Chlorophyll-a concentration is crucial for monitoring freshwater ecosystem health, particularly in lakes, as it is closely linked to eutrophication processes. Satellite imagery enables synoptic and frequent evaluations of Chlorophyll-a in water bodies, providing essential insights into spatiotemporal eutrophication dynamics. Frontier applications in water remote sensing support the utilization of machine and deep learning models applied to hyperspectral satellite imagery. This paper presents a comparative analysis of conventional machine and deep learning models—namely, Random Forest Regressor, Support Vector Regressor, Long Short-Term Memory, and Gated Recurrent Unit networks—for estimating Chlorophyll-a concentrations. The analysis is based on data from the PRecursore IperSpettrale della Missione Applicativa (PRISMA) hyperspectral mission, complemented by low-resolution Chlorophyll-a concentration maps. The analysis focuses on three sub-alpine lakes, spanning Northern Italy and Switzerland as testing areas. Through a series of modelling experiments, best-performing model configurations are pinpointed for both Chlorophyll-a concentration estimations and the improvement of spatial resolution in predictions. Support Vector Regressor demonstrated a superior performance in Chlorophyll-a concentration estimations, while Random Forest Regressor emerged as the most effective solution for refining the spatial resolution of predictions.

Keywords: machine learning; deep learning; hyperspectral imagery; PRISMA satellite; Chlorophyll-a; water quality; lakes eutrophication

Citation: Amieva, J.F.; Oxoli, D.; Brovelli, M.A. Machine and Deep Learning Regression of Chlorophyll-a Concentrations in Lakes Using PRISMA Satellite Hyperspectral Imagery. *Remote Sens.* **2023**, *15*, 5385. https://doi.org/10.3390/rs15225385

Academic Editors: Miro Govedarica, Flor Alvarez-Taboada and Gordana Jakovljević

Received: 13 October 2023
Revised: 7 November 2023
Accepted: 14 November 2023
Published: 16 November 2023

Copyright: © 2023 by the authors. Licensee MDPI, Basel, Switzerland. This article is an open access article distributed under the terms and conditions of the Creative Commons Attribution (CC BY) license (https://creativecommons.org/licenses/by/4.0/).

1. Introduction

Eutrophication is predominantly an anthropogenic process characterized by an excessive accumulation of nutrients, primarily nitrogen and phosphorus, in surface freshwater ecosystems such as lakes. This nutrient excess promotes the rapid growth of algae and aquatic plants which can increase both water turbidity and, as algae die and decompose, water oxygen depletion, leading to negative impacts on aquatic life and lake ecosystems [1]. Human disturbances to the water cycle, such as agricultural runoff, urban development, and wastewater discharge, mostly contribute to eutrophication [2]. Therefore, controlling and mitigating lake eutrophication is essential to protect both freshwater ecosystems and human well-being by maintaining the ecological and economic value of lakes [3]. The need to preserve freshwater ecosystems is further enforced by their direct connection with the United Nations Sustainable Development Goal 6 (SDG 6: Ensure availability and sustainable management of water and sanitation for all) [4]. Accordingly, effective control and mitigation actions towards freshwater ecosystem protection are imperative and require both space- and time-resolved monitoring and quantification of eutrophication levels in surface water bodies [5].

A significant indicator of eutrophication is the concentration of Chlorophyll in water, which is a major component of algae pigments and cyanobacteria and allows for the estimation of algal biomass in water bodies [6]. Specifically, Chlorophyll-a (Chl-a) is mostly used as a proxy for total algal biomass [7]. Chl-a concentration is relatively easy to measure using various techniques, including imaging spectroscopy [8], and both in-situ and remote sensing methods are often applied in the practice [9]. In-situ monitoring generally suffers from limitations in terms of space–time coverage of measurements [10]. Conversely, remote sensing methods, such as satellite multispectral and hyperspectral imagery, allow for the synoptic assessment of Chl-a concentration over the whole water body's surface and provide repeated measurements over time, which are critical to capturing eutrophication space–time dynamics [11]. Imaging spectroscopy exploits characteristic Chl-a sunlight absorption and reflection patterns at specific wavelengths including green, blue, red, and near-infrared bands [12] to determine its concentration in water. Airborne and spaceborne imagery has been employed since the 1980s for monitoring Chl-a concentration, proving to be more successful in ocean and seawater applications rather than inland waters due mainly to the limited spatial and spectral resolution of data available at that time [10]. Moreover, the optical complexity of inland waters, primarily caused by a high presence of suspended particles, reduces the reliability of both atmospheric corrections and estimation models initially designed for land and ocean applications [12]. Nonetheless, the detailed and frequent retrieval of inland water biochemical parameters, including Chl-a, has become possible thanks to the latest generation of medium to high spatial resolution multispectral spaceborne sensors, such as those onboard Landsat-8/9, Sentinel-2, and Sentinel-3 satellites [13].

Frontier applications of inland water quality remote monitoring involve hyperspectral satellite imagery, on which bio-optical algorithms demonstrated improved performances compared with multispectral imagery [14,15]. These applications are also favoured by new advancements in global hyperspectral remote sensing, proven by the recent or upcoming launches of hyperspectral satellites [16]. An early example of the above is the Hyperion imager, launched by the United States (US) National Aeronautics and Space Administration (NASA) in 2000 and operational until 2017 [17]. Relevant examples of the most recent missions that provide publicly available imagery are as follows: the German Aerospace Center Earth Sensing Imaging Spectrometer (DESIS) [18] and the hyperspectral imager aboard the Environmental Mapping and Analysis Program (EnMAP) satellite mission [19], the Chinese Advanced Hyperspectral Imager (AHSI) aboard the GaoFeng-5 satellite [20], followed by the launch of the PRecursore IperSpettrale della Missione Applicative (PRISMA) sensor by the Italian Space Agency (ASI) [21], and HyperScout instruments launched on nanosatellites by the European Space Agency (ESA) [22]. These imaging systems offer data cubes where each pixel is composed of several spectral bands enabling space, time and spectral resolved detection of water biochemical constituents [23].

As the resolution and coverage of satellite hyperspectral images continue to improve, cutting-edge data technologies, particularly the implementation of machine and deep learning algorithms [24], are playing a pivotal role in advancing the diffusion and enhancing the capabilities of Chl-a estimation models. Alongside traditional spectral indices and physics-based models [25], machine and deep learning approaches have been frequently exploited in the literature within hyperspectral imaging for Chl-a and other biochemical constituents estimation in water bodies [26]. Recent and pertinent examples are as follows. In [27], Partial Least Squares (PLS) is utilized to determine Chl-a and Total Suspended Matter (TSM). Ref. [28] models in-situ measurements using linear models and Support Vector Machines (SVM) to predict Chl-a concentrations in Lake Taihu (China). Ref. [29] estimates water quality parameters, including Chl-a, for the Elbe River using ten different machine-learning regression models. Ref. [30] evaluates Random Forest (RF), SVM, and Artificial Neural Networks (ANN) for predicting Chl-a concentrations in various inland water bodies, also exploring the inclusion of spectral derivatives as input data. Ref. [31] developed a PLS-ANN model for Chl-a prediction in Lake Erie. Additionally, Ref. [32] utilizes simulated hyperspectral satellite data to predict Chl-a concentrations in lakes, employing an array of models including RF, SVM, Multivariate Adaptive Regression Spline (MARS), and CNN. Ref. [33] generates synthetic EnMAP hyperspectral imagery using EnMAP end-to-end simulator software (EeteS) [34] for Chl-a prediction in Czech Republic water reservoirs using Principal Component Regression, PLS Regression, and RF models. Finally, Refs. [35,36] utilize hyperspectral data from the Hyperspectral Imager for the Coastal Ocean (HICO) [37] and the PRISMA satellite, respectively, to predict Chl-a concentrations using Mixture Density Network (MDN) models.

Despite the availability of machine and deep learning algorithms, there are persistent challenges in implementing them for operational monitoring tasks, often due to a lack of the space–time resolved reference data necessary to train and validate such models [25,38]. With this in mind, the present study aims to employ a variety of machine and deep learning regression models and subsequently conduct a comparative assessment across diverse experimental setups, with the goal of predicting Chl-a concentration maps from medium-resolution hyperspectral satellite imagery through the training and evaluation of these models with reference data characterized by lower spatial resolution, heightened acquisition frequency up to 2 days, and a wide swath width. The objective of the analysis is twofold. Firstly, it aims to verify that the use of the rich spectral information of hyperspectral imagery, coupled with machine and deep learning models, is suitable for reconstructing Chl-a concentration maps using pre-existing and widely accessible reference data. Secondly, it aims to assess the potential for enhancing the spatial resolution of pre-existing Chl-a concentration maps by aligning it with the hyperspectral imagery employed as the regressor in model implementation.

The selected study area includes three sub-alpine lakes between Northern Italy and Switzerland, specifically Lake Como, Lake Maggiore, and Lake Lugano (see Figure 1). These lakes were chosen because they align with the selection made by the "Informative System for the Integrated Monitoring of Insubric Lakes and their Ecosystems" (SIMILE) project, within which this research is conducted. The SIMILE project is funded by the Interreg program of the European Union, which primarily focuses on enhancing coordinated management and stakeholder involvement in monitoring the water quality of sub-alpine lakes between Northern Italy and Switzerland [39,40]. It exploits a combination of in-situ measurements and remote sensing techniques to fulfil its objectives. Within the realm of satellite remote sensing, the project computes three key indicators for assessing lake water quality: Lake Water Surface Temperature derived from Landsat 8 imagery, Total Suspended Matter, and Chl-a concentrations [41] derived from the Sentinel-3 A/B Ocean and Land Colour Instrument (OLCI) imagery at 300 m resolution, which provides a revisit time of less than 2 days. Each of these indicators is monitored by generating time-series of raster maps [42].

In this study, hyperspectral images obtained from the PRISMA mission are used. PRISMA imagery features 239 bands spanning the Visible and Near-Infrared (VNIR) and Short-Wave Infrared (SWIR) regions of the electromagnetic spectrum (400–2500 nm) [21]. PRISMA images have a spatial resolution of 30 m, a Spectral Sampling Interval (SSI) of 12 nm, and a revisit time of 29 days [21]. For model training and testing, time-series maps of Chl-a concentration generated by the SIMILE project team from Sentinel-3 data are employed as low-resolution reference data. Quality assessment for these maps was provided by [40] through comparisons with in-situ measurements, supporting their use as reference Chl-a concentration data in this work. The study considers both machine learning models, such as RF Regressor and SVR, as well as deep learning models such as Long Short-Term Memory (LSTM) networks [43,44] and Gated Recurrent Unit (GRU) networks [45]. The choice of these models is based on empirical evidence from the literature and is primarily guided by two key characteristics, as suggested by [24] and summarized as follows. First, when considering RF Regressor and SVR models, their effectiveness in handling non-linear dependencies within the input data is a primary factor. Moreover, when integrated with dimensionality reduction techniques, these models excel in reducing redundant spectral information. Second, LSTM and GRU models are preferred for their suitability in dealing with hyperspectral imagery. This preference is rooted in the sequential nature of the hyperspectral data, enabling them to capture both long and short-range dependencies of the contiguous bands in the spectral dimension.

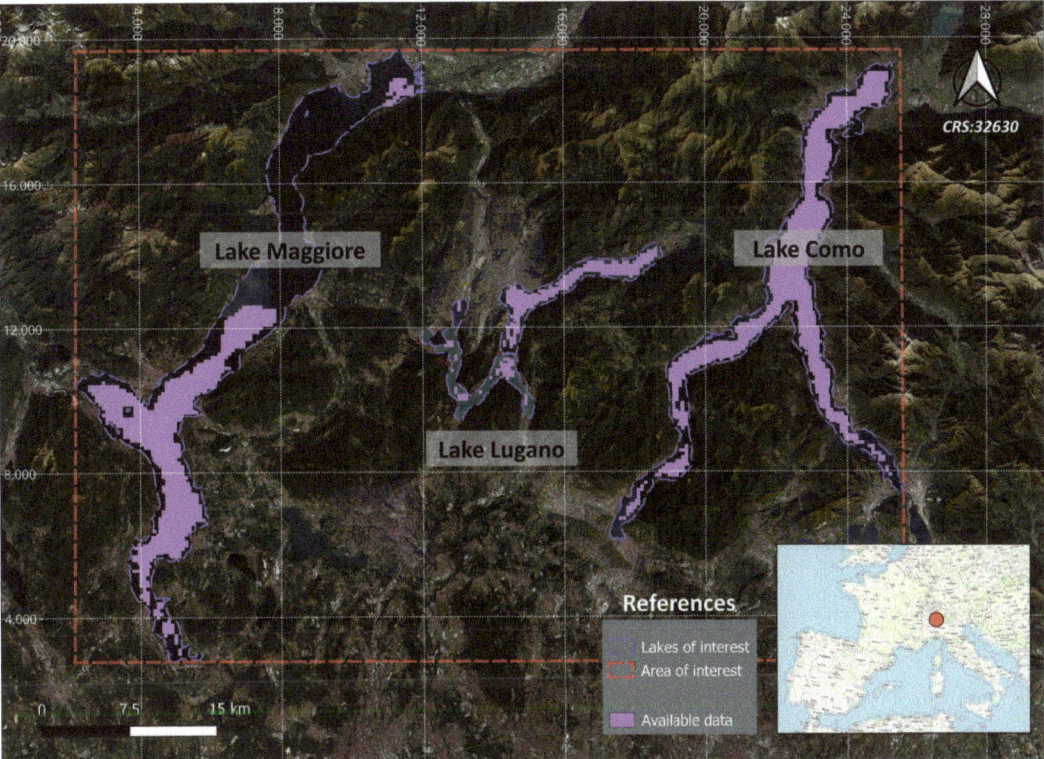

Figure 1. Summary of available data (pixels with information of Chl-a maps and PRISMA acquisitions) within the study's AOI. In the reference map is highlighted the approximate location of the AOI within Europe (red dot).

The models are employed to (i) reconstruct reference Chl-a concentrations maps computed from Sentinel-3 data, and (ii) augment the spatial resolution of such maps from 300 m to 30 m, thereby aligning them with the resolution of PRISMA imagery. The ultimate goal of such applications is to evaluate the performance of different models in reconstructing the reference Chl-a maps exploiting PRISMA images. Several experiments involving different configurations of model hyperparameters and resolutions for the training/testing datasets were conducted. The resulting accuracies were analyzed statistically to delineate and recommend the most effective models and experimental settings. The SVR model performed best for reconstructing reference Chl-a maps at 300 m spatial resolution, while the RF Regressor model proved to be the most effective for predicting Chl-a maps at 30 m spatial resolution.

The remainder of the paper is as follows. Section 2 describes the data utilized in the study, detailing the criteria for dataset selection, outlining data preparation techniques, and introducing the models considered along with their respective hyperparameter settings. Section 3 presents the outcomes of the modelling experiments, offering a discussion of the significant findings compared with the experimental settings adopted. Finally, Section 4 includes conclusions and future directions of the work.

2. Data and Methods

2.1. Data Procurement and Preprocessing

This study examined two input datasets, namely reference Chl-a concentration raster maps (generated by the SIMILE project at a spatial resolution of 300 m and co-registered on a common grid) and PRISMA hyperspectral imagery with a resolution of 30 m. PRISMA Level L2D geocoded and bottom-of-atmosphere reflectance data [46] were employed in the analysis. The complete time series of reference Chl-a concentration maps encompasses a total of 389 layers, each providing complete coverage of the designated Area of Interest (AOI) within this study (see Figure 1). This time series spans from 15 January 2019 to 5 November 2022. Through the examination of the accessible hyperspectral PRISMA images catalogued in the official missions data portal (http://prisma.asi.it/js-cat-client-prisma-src (accessed on 22 May 2023)), 27 acquisitions that intersected with the AOI in the timeframe of the reference Chl-a maps time series were identified. All bands of each considered PRISMA image were manipulated in the preprocessing operations. Following an initial manual screening process based on the extent of intersection with the reference Chl-a maps, cloud coverage within each PRISMA acquisition, and sun glint disturbance, a total of 12 PRISMA images were deemed suitable. The chosen PRISMA image tiles provided only partial coverage of the AOI, as illustrated in Figure 1. Notably, part of Lake Maggiore is excluded from the analysis due to the unavailability of PRISMA tiles in the catalogue covering that area.

Table 1 provides an overview of the dataset utilized in this study. While the acquisition dates of the reference Chl-a maps and the corresponding PRISMA images do not coincide, the maximum temporal discrepancy is limited to 2 days. The table also includes information about the lakes covered by each PRISMA acquisition.

Figure 1 additionally provides a synopsis of the regions containing accessible data, defined as pixels incorporating information on each pair of Chl-a concentration maps and corresponding PRISMA acquisitions across the entirety of the dataset. This pertains to the three lakes within the AOI.

Table 1. Selected pairs of Chl-a maps and PRISMA images with acquisition dates and lakes' coverage. ID acquisitions are sorted by dates and refer to the original 27 PRISMA acquisitions available in the official mission data portal. Missing IDs correspond to acquisitions excluded after the manual screening.

ID Acquisition	PRISMA Acquisition Date	Lake Como	Lake Maggiore	Lake Lugano	Reference Chl-a Map Date
1	24 April 2020	YES	NO	YES	23 April 2020
2	24 April 2020	YES	NO	NO	23 April 2020
4	25 April 2020	NO	YES	NO	23 April 2020
6	3 July 2020	NO	YES	NO	5 July 2020
10	9 July 2021	YES	NO	YES	9 July 2021
13	31 August 2021	YES	NO	NO	31 August 2021
17	16 October 2021	NO	YES	NO	16 October 2021
18	22 October 2021	YES	NO	NO	22 October 2021
19	22 October 2021	YES	NO	YES	22 October 2021
21	26 November 2021	NO	NO	YES	24 November 2021
23	9 February 2022	NO	YES	NO	9 February 2022
24	27 March 2022	YES	NO	NO	25 March 2022

Following the acquisition of PRISMA images, an array of preprocessing operations was executed. This included co-registration, intersection with their reference Chl-a maps, and the removal of null values and anomalous pixels possibly affected by disturbances in water surface spectral signature. The schematic representation of these pre-processing steps is depicted in Figure 2.

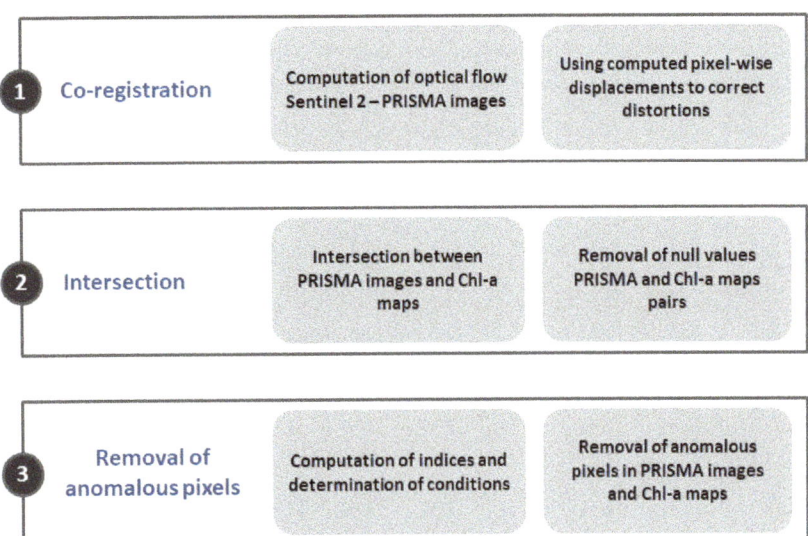

Figure 2. Schematic of pre-processing operations on the input data.

While the L2D PRISMA imagery used in this study is already geocoded, an extra step of co-registration was necessary to rectify both local and global distortions. For this purpose, the Python library Gefolki [47] was employed. The co-registration process was critical to ensure accurate alignment of the PRISMA images with the reference data.

The co-registration algorithm implemented in Gefolki computes pixel-wise displacements (optical flow) between pairs of images. A reference grid from the Sentinel-2 mission was considered because of its higher spatial resolution (10 m) and positional accuracy than the original PRISMA grid. To accomplish this, a mosaic using Sentinel-2 images from the period of 11 September 2022 to 18 September 2022 covering the entire AOI was employed. The full AOI coverage could not be achieved with a single Sentinel-2 image tile. Each PRISMA image was resampled to 10 m spatial resolution to perform the co-registration with the Sentinel-2 reference image. The Sentinel-2 mosaic was cropped to the intersected area with the associated PRISMA image, and the displacements between the pixels of the PRISMA image and the reference image were estimated and used to correct the original distortions. Finally, the PRISMA images were resampled to their original resolution (30 m). This procedure is used to co-register all the PRISMA images on a common grid in the final dataset.

After completing the co-registration of the PRISMA images, the next step involved intersecting the co-registered images with their corresponding Chl-a maps. This process aimed to preserve the overlapping regions shared by each acquisition pair. During this operation, pixels with no data in the PRISMA image were set to null in the corresponding Chl-a map, and conversely, for all the acquisition pairs.

The final pre-processing step involved removing anomalous pixels which contained values in the spectral signature inconsistent with the Chl-a concentration recorded in the Chl-a concentration maps, or pixels possibly associated with disturbances on the water surface, such as scum or foam. Anomalous pixels were removed from both the PRISMA images and the corresponding Chl-a maps. To detect the anomalous pixels, the procedure adopted in this study consisted of determining different spectral indices by using the reflectance values of the Sentinel 3 A/B OLCI images that generated the Chl-a maps. These indices are based on bands algebra and were retrieved from the literature with no name associated. The indices were then used to verify the following conditions and identify the anomalous pixel values as shown in Figure 3.

The first condition implies assessing whether, for each pixel, its corresponding value of the Index 1 [48], which is computed using Equation (1), is less than one while the associated Chl-a value exceeds 10 µg/L. Under these circumstances, the pixel is considered anomalous. This is attributed to the expectation that pixels with an index less than one are more likely associated with very low Chl-a concentrations, and conversely.

$$\text{Index 1} = \frac{\text{Band 11 (708 nm)}}{\text{Band 8 (665 nm)}}. \quad (1)$$

It is important to specify that in Equation (1), band 11 of Sentinel-3 A/B OLCI corresponds to the red edge transition of the Chlorophyll fluorescence baseline, while band 8 is linked to the second peak of Chlorophyll absorption [49]. A second condition is used instead to check whether the subsequent ratio [50], computed using Equation (2) and referred to in this work as Index 2, is higher than one for a specific pixel. If so, that pixel should be removed as it may indicate an anomaly on the water surface, likely associated with noise, scum, or foam.

$$\text{Index 2} = \frac{\text{Band 12 (753 nm)}}{\text{Band 11 (708 nm)}}. \quad (2)$$

In Equation (2), band 12 of Sentinel-3 A/B OLCI is used because of its connection to the absorption of oxygen, as well as the presence of clouds and vegetation [49]. The last condition is verified by comparing two indices which are computed using Equations (3) and (4), and referred to in this work respectively as Index 3a and Index 3b. Where one of them is above 1 but the other is not, the pixel is considered anomalous [51]. If both indices are below one, this means that the pixel refers to an area of deep blue water and if the two indices are above one, it is likely that the pixel is related to the presence of phytoplankton.

$$\text{Index 3a} = \frac{\text{Band 6 (560 nm)}}{\text{Band 3 (442.5 nm)}} \quad (3)$$

$$\text{Index 3b} = \frac{\text{Band 6 (560 nm)}}{\text{Band 4 (490 nm)}}. \quad (4)$$

In Equations (3) and (4), band 3 of Sentinel-3 A/B OLCI corresponds to the point where Chlorophyll absorption is at its highest, while band 4 indicates areas with high Chlorophyll concentration. Band 6 serves instead as a reference indicator for the lowest Chlorophyll concentration in the image [49].

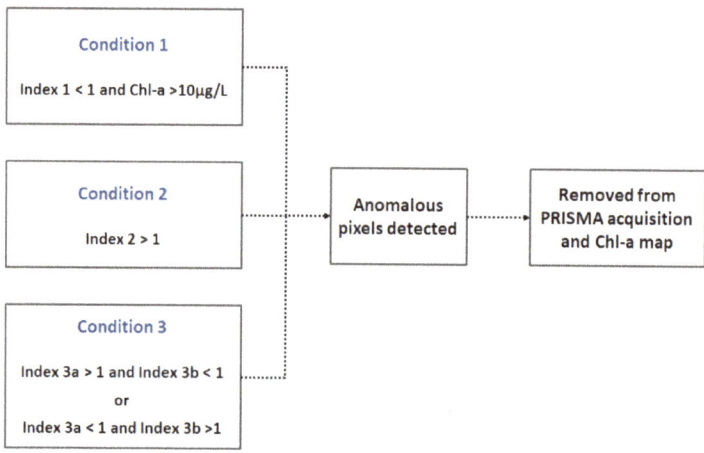

Figure 3. Schematic of the anomalous pixels removal procedure.

2.2. Training and Test Datasets Preparation

Following the pre-processing of reference Chl-a maps, it became necessary to devise a data-splitting strategy for the three primary phases involved in the implementation of machine and deep learning models: training (train set), validation (validation set), and evaluation (test set). To accomplish this, an iterative methodology was adopted to uphold consistent distributions between the test set and the combined training and validation set. By allocating pairs of acquisitions to one of the two alternate groups, the distribution of Chl-a values for each group was assessed. The aim was to achieve the most accurate fit to the identity function. To this end, a Quantile-Quantile plot (QQ-plot) was employed (see Figure 4), yielding an R^2 of 0.876, thus indicating a robust alignment with the target function. As a result of this process, acquisitions 4, 23, and 24 (see Table 1) were assigned to the test set while the remaining ones were preserved for the training and validation set. Subsequently, the training-validation set was partitioned using a fixed ratio of 80% for training and 20% for validation. Considering the distribution of Chl-a concentrations in the whole dataset, the acquisitions in the test set embed a broad range of Chl-a concentrations. Specifically, acquisition 4 is associated with relatively low-to-medium Chl-a concentrations (mean equal to 3.07 µg/L and a maximum equal to 4.49 µg/L). Acquisitions 23 and 24 depict medium to high Chl-a concentrations, with respective mean concentrations of 5.21 µg/L and 5.21 µg/L, and maximum concentrations of 8.92 µg/L and 7.06 µg/L. This choice was adopted to mitigate possible model over-fitting due to the low number of acquisitions for the study area in the considered time period and to evaluate models on the widest available array of Chl-a concentration episodes. Because of data availability, very high or low Chl-a concentrations could not be included in the test set.

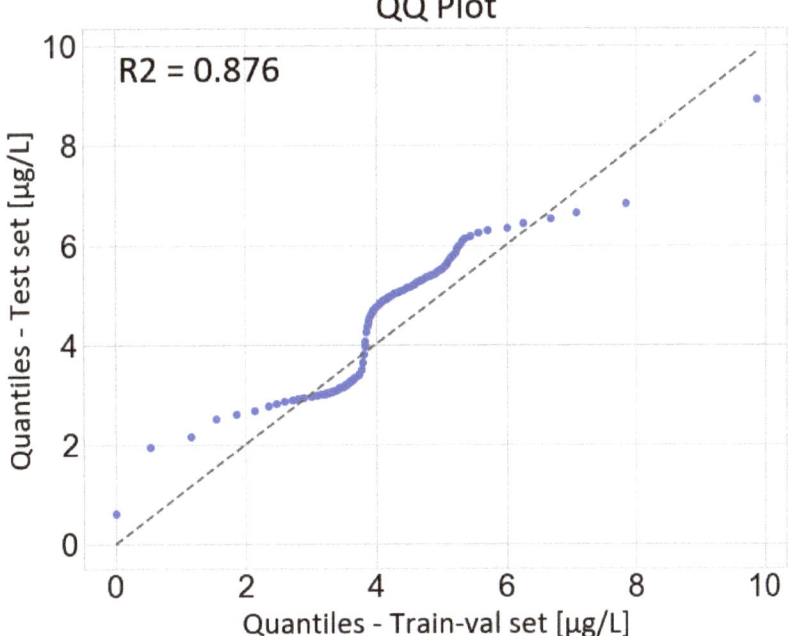

Figure 4. QQ-plot of training and test sets. Blue dots represent quantiles of pixel values distribution from reference Chl-a maps in the training set (X-axis) and test set (Y-axis).

2.3. PRISMA Images Normalization and Dimensionality Reduction

Further operations were conducted on PRISMA images, including normalization and dimensionality reduction. The PRISMA images were initially transformed from their original Digital Number (DN) units to reflectance values, employing the standard formula (see Equation (5)) outlined in the PRISMA data manual [52].

$$x_{scaled} = L2scaleXX_{min} + x_{DN}\frac{(L2scaleXX_{max} - L2scaleXX_{min})}{65.535}. \quad (5)$$

The term "XX" in Equation (5) denotes a particular region within the input spectrum, either "VNIR" or "SWIR". L2scale min and max represent the minimum and maximum scaling factors provided in the metadata for each PRISMA image. The normalization value of 65.535 is derived from the computation of $2^{16} - 1$, which accounts for the 16-bit coding used to store pixel information. Then, these reflectance values were scaled to a range of $[0-2^{16}]$ to store them as unsigned integers (uint16). Starting with this information, three alternative approaches for normalizing the PRISMA images were considered: (i) Min-max scaling, (ii) standard scaling, and (iii) normalization to float reflectance units within the range [0–1], i.e., dividing by the fixed factor of 2^{16}. Another assessed aspect was the dimensionality reduction of the hyperspectral images. For this purpose, the Principal Component Analysis (PCA) technique was exploited to reduce the spectral dimension to 30 Principal Components (PCs). Finally, the benefits of reducing the spatial dimension were explored by lowering the resolution of the PRISMA images to match that of the associated Chl-a maps, i.e., from 30 m to 300 m. For this case study, the use of 30 PCs explained more than 99% of the variance for all the acquisitions. This was considered sufficient for testing purposes and used as a sample case in the modelling experiments. Different normalization and dimensionality reduction approaches were tested within different modelling experiments, as explained in the following section.

2.4. Machine and Deep Learning Regression Models for Chl-a Concentration

Performances of two machine learning (RF Regressor and SVR) and two deep learning (LSTM and GRU) models in estimating Chl-a concentrations maps by combining Sentinel-3 derived data and PRISMA hyperspectral imagery were explored. The evaluation encompasses a range of hyperparameter settings to identify the most effective combination. Several experiments were designed for each model by intervening in one or more settings. Details are provided in Section 3. The general settings used to define the modelling experiments are outlined below.

1. Normalization approach: A set of experiments was conducted to determine the best normalization approach among the ones discussed in Section 2.3.
2. Spectral dimensionality reduction: An experiment was conducted to investigate whether the PCA technique contributes or not to the model performances.
3. Data augmentation: For the machine learning models, additional bands extracted using image filters were included in the processing. The considered filters were the Sobel X and Sobel Y filters [53], and the Mean filter [54].
4. Model hyperparameters: Different hyperparameter settings were investigated for each model following a grid search strategy. The considered hyperparameters are listed in Tables 2–4.
5. Tests on best input spatial resolution: First, all experiments used 300 m spatial resolution inputs and then, considering the best experiment for each model typology, it was repeated using inputs at 30 m resolution to determine which of the two approaches performed better. This approach was followed because, despite the different spatial resolution, the data derives from the same original distribution, ensuring that the model selection step remains unaffected.

The machine learning models considered in this study were the RF Regressor [55] and the SVR [56]. In some of the experiments, where the spatial downsampling of the PRISMA images to the spatial resolution of the associated Chl-a maps was applied, data augmentation approaches were implemented. These approaches involved extracting additional bands from the input images using the Sobel X and Sobel Y filters, and the Mean filter. The extracted bands were stacked into the input data to augment the dataset size, compensating for the reduction induced by spatial downsampling.

For the implementation of the RF Regressor model, the Scikit-learn Python library was used [57]. Model hyperparameters considered for tuning are described in Table 2.

Table 2. RF Regressor hyperparameters [58].

Parameter	Description
Number of estimators	It is the number of decision trees built. Higher values are expected to improve performance while increasing computational time.
Minimum number of samples per leaf	It sets the minimum samples required for a leaf node, reducing over-fitting with higher values.
Maximum depth of each decision tree	It controls model complexity; large values can lead to over-fitting.

Table 3. SVR hyperparameters [59].

Parameter	Description
Gamma	Kernel coefficient for the RBF. It governs the shape of the decision boundary. A high value leads to an extended or complex decision boundary, which, if not carefully controlled, may result in over-fitting.
C	It influences the width of the margin and the tolerance for misclassified data points. It is a regularization hyperparameter which enables to balance between training and testing errors.

For the implementation of the SVR model, the Radial Basis Function (RBF) kernel, computed using the Scikit-learn Python library, was used to conduct trials for the empirical definition of the best hyperparameter values, as detailed in Table 3.

Regarding deep learning models, two architectures were considered, namely LSTM [43,44] and GRU [45] networks. Both are recurrent architectures well suited for the sequential structure of the hyperspectral data. The Tsai Python package [60] was used for their implementation. The hyperparameters considered for the definition of the experiments are explained in Table 4 and these are common for both architectures.

Table 4. LSTM and GRU hyperparameters.

Parameter	Description
Number of layers	The number of LSTM or GRU cells stacked on top of each other.
Dropout in the recurrent neural network cells	Effective regularization method that contrast over-fitting by randomly deactivating a portion of neurons [61]. When dealing with recurrent neurons, dropout is specifically applied to the connections between consecutive recurrent hidden cells.

Table 4. *Cont.*

Parameter	Description
Dropout in the fully connected layer	Proportion of dropout applied to the fully connected layers' outputs.
Directionality	Both unidirectional and bidirectional networks were investigated. The difference is that bidirectional networks calculate the hidden state at each time step using information from both past and future inputs, whereas unidirectional networks utilize only past inputs in their calculations.
Hidden size	The number of features in the hidden state.

3. Results and Discussion

This section reports the results of the modelling experiments described in Section 2.4. The predictive performances of the different models under different settings are reported and compared using well-known metrics, such as the Mean Absolute Error (MAE) and the Root Mean Square Error (RMSE). The evaluation is based on the acquisitions from the test set, specifically acquisitions 4, 23, and 24 (see Section 2.2).

3.1. RF Regressor

A total of 12 experiments with different settings were performed using the RF Regressor model. Experimental settings and results are reported in Table 5.

Considering the PRISMA image normalization approaches introduced in Section 2.3, three experiments were carried out (RF-1 to RF-3) to establish the best option. The results achieved by the three experiments are identical in terms of predictive performances, suggesting a negligible effect of the normalization approach on the output.

The fourth experiment (RF-4) was used to evaluate the benefits of applying the PCA technique to reduce the spectral dimension to 30 PCs. As observed in Table 5, this experiment yielded a worse performance in comparison with the previous three cases. This may be attributed to the ensemble nature of RF which utilizes decision trees, known to be robust against multicollinearity. Consequently, in this particular context, PCA may not yield substantial advantages, given that the algorithm inherently handles a multitude of features and their complex interactions.

In the fifth experiment (RF-5), it was investigated whether including additional bands would benefit the performance of the model. The same normalization approach of Experiment RF-2 (standard scaling) and no dimensionality reduction were applied. For each pixel, the Mean and the Sobel x and Sobel y filters were applied. According to the result, the addition of these new features was not helpful in terms of predictive performance.

In order to determine the optimal configuration for the model's hyperparameters, five experiments were undertaken, denoted as RF-6 through RF-11. These experiments assessed various combinations of hyperparameters to ascertain which yielded the most favourable outcomes. Experiment RF-10 emerged as the top-performing RF Regressor model configuration.

The final experiment (RF-12) aimed to assess whether utilizing input data at a 30-m spatial resolution could lead to improved performance compared to the previously identified best-performing model configuration (i.e., RF-10). To achieve this, Chl-a maps needed to be upsampled to match the spatial resolution of the PRISMA images. The Nearest Neighbour method was employed for this purpose. It is important to note that, due to computational limitations, the number of trees was reduced to 1000 in this experiment compared to RF-10. Under these specified conditions, the results of Experiment RF-12 demonstrate a higher level of error compared to RF-10.

Table 5. Settings and results of RF Regressor model experiments. MAE and RMSE represent the average score of the metrics from the application of the experiments to each of the acquisitions in the test set.

Exp. ID	Exp. Setting	Res [m]	PCA	Norm.	Data Augm.	N Trees	Min. Leaf	Max. Depth	MAE [µg/L]	RMSE [µg/L]
RF-1	Norm.	300	No	Minmax	No	1000	3	10	0.931	1.112
RF-2	Norm.	300	No	Std.	No	1000	3	10	0.931	1.112
RF-3	Norm.	300	No	Reflect.	No	1000	3	10	0.931	1.112
RF-4	Spec. red.	300	30 PCs	Std.	No	1000	3	10	1.020	1.245
RF-5	Data augm.	300	No	Std.	Yes	1000	3	10	1.106	1.296
RF-6	Model hyperp.	300	No	Std.	No	1000	3	5	1.032	1.192
RF-7	Model hyperp.	300	No	Std.	No	1000	3	20	0.930	1.113
RF-8	Model hyperp.	300	No	Std.	No	100	3	20	0.947	1.128
RF-9	Model hyperp.	300	No	Std.	No	10,000	3	20	0.924	1.107
RF-10	Model hyperp.	300	No	Std.	No	10,000	2	20	**0.915**	**1.099**
RF-11	Model hyperp.	300	No	Std.	No	10,000	10	20	0.934	1.114
RF-12	Spatial res.	30	No	Std.	No	1000	2	20	0.986	1.181

Table abbreviations: Experiment ID (Exp. ID), Experiment setting (Exp. Setting), Input resolution (Res), Normalization (Norm.), Data augmentation (Data augm.), Numbers of estimators (N trees), Minimum number of samples per leaf (Min. leaf), Maximum depth of each decision tree (Max. depth), Spectral dimensionality reduction (Spec. red.), Min-max scaling (Minmax), standard scaling (Std.), normalization to float reflectance units within the range [0, 1] (Reflect.), Model hyperparameters (Model hyperp.).

3.2. SVR

A total of 10 experiments with different settings were performed using the SVR model. The experimental settings and results are reported in Table 6.

The effect of PRISMA image normalization approaches was analysed through three experiments (SVR-1 to SVR-3). The standard scaling resulted in the most effective approach in terms of prediction performances. The effect of PCA application for reducing the spectral dimension of the PRISMA images was evaluated in Experiment SVR-4. In this case, prediction performance resulted to be significantly improved with the use of 30 PCs instead of the original PRISMA bands. This result may be explained by the fact that the SVR model is based on an RBF kernel, which incorporates feature distances and may be sensitive to multicollinearity, thereby possibly resulting in over-fitting. Experiment SVR-5 investigated the advantages of employing data augmentation on the input data. This did not lead to an improvement in the model's performance, achieving a less favourable outcome compared to SVR-4. Different setups for the SVR model hyperparameters, C and gamma, were assessed in experiments SVR-6 to SVR-9. Despite the evaluations, it was found that Experiment SVR-4 consistently yielded the most favourable outcomes. Therefore, SVR-4 was identified as the best-performing model configuration. The final experiment (SVR-10) assessed the impact of employing a 30-m spatial resolution for the input data, which included the original PRISMA images and the Chl-a maps upsampled via the Nearest Neighbor technique. Unfortunately, the results from SVR-10 were not satisfactory, with both MAE and RMSE metrics surpassing those attained by the previously identified top-performing model configuration, SVR-4.

Table 6. Settings and results of SVR model experiments. MAE and RMSE represent the average score of the metrics from the application of the experiments to each of the acquisitions in the test set.

Exp. ID	Exp. Setting	Res [m]	PCA	Norm.	Data Augm.	Gamma	C	MAE [µg/L]	RMSE [µg/L]
SVR-1	Norm.	300	No	Minmax	No	0.001	15	1.285	1.431
SVR-2	Norm.	300	No	Std.	No	0.001	15	0.699	0.898
SVR-3	Norm.	300	No	Reflect.	No	0.001	15	1.253	1.394
SVR-4	Spec. red.	300	30 PCs	Std.	No	0.001	15	**0.687**	**0.895**
SVR-5	Data augm.	300	30 PCs	Std.	Yes	0.001	15	0.909	1.126
SVR-6	Model hyperp.	300	30 PCs	Std.	No	0.0001	15	0.752	0.993
SVR-7	Model hyperp.	300	30 PCs	Std.	No	0.01	15	0.956	1.152
SVR-8	Model hyperp.	300	30 PCs	Std.	No	0.001	1.5	0.756	0.955
SVR-9	Model hyperp.	300	30 PCs	Std.	No	0.001	150	1.106	1.307
SVR-10	Spatial res.	30	30 PCs	Std.	No	0.001	15	1.260	1.555

Table abbreviations: Experiment ID (Exp. ID), Experiment setting (Exp. Setting), Input resolution (Res), Normalization (Norm.), Data augmentation (Data augm.), Spectral dimensionality reduction (Spec. red.), Min-max scaling (Minmax), standard scaling (Std.), normalization to float reflectance units within the range [0, 1] (Reflect.), Model hyperparameters (Model hyperp.), Spatial resolution (Spatial res.).

3.3. LSTM Network

A total of 14 experiments with different settings were performed using the LSTM network. Experimental settings and results are reported in Table 7.

The first three experiments (LSTM-1 to LSTM-3) explored the best normalization approach. The best performance was achieved with the experiment LSTM-2 which corresponds to the standard scaling method. Experiment LSTM-4 explored the spectral dimensionality reduction, and determined that this technique was useful for improving the performance as it achieved a lower level of error. From Experiment LSTM-5 to Experiment LSTM-12, all the hyperparameters of this model architecture were systematically adjusted. Among these experiments, the best-performing configuration was the Experiment LSTM-10. Furthermore, Experiment LSTM-13 used the same hyperparameter settings as LSTM-10 but incorporated bidirectional flow. Notably, this modification improved the performance compared to LSTM-10. The utilization of 30-m resolution inputs was examined in Experiment LSTM-14. The model hyperparameters and input normalization were kept identical to those in Experiment LSTM-13. However, the outcome did not show any improvement over the performance metrics of the best-performing model configuration, LSTM-13.

Table 7. Settings and results of LSTM model experiments. MAE and RMSE represent the average score of the metrics from the application of the experiments to each of the acquisitions in the test set.

Exp. ID	Exp. Setting	Res [m]	PCA	Norm.	Hidden Size	N Layers	Drop. RNN	Drop. FCN	Bidir.	MAE [µg/L]	RMSE [µg/L]
LSTM-1	Norm.	300	No	Minmax	10	2	0.6	0.4	No	1.443	1.584
LSTM-2	Norm.	300	No	Std.	10	2	0.6	0.4	No	1.303	1.431
LSTM-3	Norm.	300	No	Reflect.	10	2	0.6	0.4	No	1.897	2.012
LSTM-4	Spec. red.	300	30 PCs	Std.	10	2	0.6	0.4	No	1.298	1.428
LSTM-5	Model hyperp.	300	30 PCs	Std.	5	2	0.6	0.4	No	1.386	1.522
LSTM-6	Model hyperp.	300	30 PCs	Std.	15	2	0.6	0.4	No	1.323	1.452
LSTM-7	Model hyperp.	300	30 PCs	Std.	10	4	0.6	0.4	No	1.494	1.635
LSTM-8	Model hyperp.	300	30 PCs	Std.	10	1	0.6	0.4	No	1.334	1.490
LSTM-9	Model hyperp.	300	30 PCs	Std.	10	2	0.2	0.4	No	1.342	1.475
LSTM-10	Model hyperp.	300	30 PCs	Std.	10	2	0.8	0.4	No	1.278	1.407
LSTM-11	Model hyperp.	300	30 PCs	Std.	10	2	0.8	0.6	No	1.366	1.498
LSTM-12	Model hyperp.	300	30 PCs	Std.	10	2	0.8	0.2	No	1.305	1.434
LSTM-13	Dir. flow	300	30 PCs	Std.	10	2	0.8	0.4	Yes	**1.211**	**1.345**
LSTM-14	Spatial res.	30	30 PCs	Std.	10	2	0.8	0.4	Yes	1.278	1.455

Table abbreviations: Experiment ID (Exp. ID), Experiment setting (Exp. Setting), Input resolution (Res), Normalization (Norm.), Data augmentation (Data augm.), Spectral dimensionality reduction (Spec. red.), Min-max scaling (Minmax), standard scaling (Std.), normalization to float reflectance units within the range [0, 1] (Reflect.), Model hyperparameters (Model hyperp.), Spatial resolution (Spatial res.), Number of layers (N layers), Dropout in the recurrent neural network cells (Drop. RNN), Dropout in the fully connected layer (Drop. FCN), Directionality (Bdir.).

3.4. GRU Network

A total of 17 experiments with different settings were performed using the GRU network. Experimental settings and results are reported in Table 8.

The first three experiments (GRU-1 to GRU-3) focused on investigating the effect of normalization approaches. The standard scaling method (GRU-2) emerged once again as the most effective approach. The results obtained from Experiment GRU-4 indicate that employing the PCA method for this model did not yield any significant benefit. Hyperparameter tuning was carried out by experiments GRU-5 to GRU-15, with Experiment GRU-8 resulting as the best-performing model configuration. Experiment GRU-16 was used to determine whether configuring the GRU-8 network with bidirectional flow would enhance its performance. The results indicate a decrease in performance. Finally, Experiment GRU-17 maintained an identical configuration to Experiment GRU-8, except for the utilization of 30-m input data. However, this adjustment did not yield any improvements in the model's performance. As a result, the best-performing model configuration was identified as that of Experiment GRU-8.

Table 8. Settings and results of GRU model experiments. MAE and RMSE represent the average score of the metrics from the application of the experiments to each of the acquisitions in the test set.

Exp. ID	Exp. Setting	Res [m]	PCA	Norm.	Hidden Size	N Layers	Drop. RNN	Drop. FCN	Bidir.	MAE [µg/L]	RMSE [µg/L]
GRU-1	Norm.	300	No	Minmax	10	2	0.6	0.4	No	1.367	1.499
GRU-2	Norm.	300	No	Std.	10	2	0.6	0.4	No	1.287	1.416
GRU-3	Norm.	300	No	Reflect.	10	2	0.6	0.4	No	1.559	1.698
GRU-4	Spec. red.	300	30 PCs	Std.	10	2	0.6	0.4	No	1.305	1.433
GRU-5	Model hyperp.	300	No	Std.	5	2	0.6	0.4	No	1.435	1.575
GRU-6	Model hyperp.	300	No	Std.	20	2	0.6	0.4	No	1.235	1.366
GRU-7	Model hyperp.	300	No	Std.	40	2	0.6	0.4	No	1.221	1.352
GRU-8	Model hyperp.	300	No	Std.	60	2	0.6	0.4	No	**1.186**	**1.321**
GRU-9	Model hyperp.	300	No	Std.	100	2	0.6	0.4	No	1.271	1.408
GRU-10	Model hyperp.	300	No	Std.	60	1	0.6	0.4	No	1.236	1.373
GRU-11	Model hyperp.	300	No	Std.	60	10	0.6	0.4	No	1.231	1.362
GRU-12	Model hyperp.	300	No	Std.	60	2	0.2	0.4	No	1.272	1.419
GRU-13	Model hyperp.	300	No	Std.	60	2	0.8	0.4	No	1.194	1.340
GRU-14	Model hyperp.	300	No	Std.	60	2	0.6	0.2	No	1.202	1.355
GRU-15	Model hyperp.	300	No	Std.	60	2	0.6	0.8	No	1.260	1.399
GRU-16	Dir. flow	300	No	Std.	60	2	0.6	0.4	Yes	1.213	1.363
GRU-17	Spatial res.	30	No	Std.	60	2	0.6	0.4	No	1.203	1.382

Table abbreviations: Experiment ID (Exp. ID), Experiment setting (Exp. Setting), Input resolution (Res), Normalization (Norm.), Data augmentation (Data augm.), Spectral dimensionality reduction (Spec. red.), Min-max scaling (Minmax), standard scaling (Std.), normalization to float reflectance units within the range [0, 1] (Reflect.), Model hyperparameters (Model hyperp.), Spatial resolution (Spatial res.), Number of layers (N layers), Dropout in the recurrent neural network cells (Drop. RNN), Dropout in the fully connected layer (Drop. FCN), Directionality (Bidir.).

3.5. Summary of Best Models and Inference on 30 m

Drawing from the aforementioned experiments, it is evident that the best performances were attained when training and assessing the models with 300-m input datasets. The details of the best-performing configurations for each model are consolidated in Table 9, with SVR (Experiment SVR-4) emerging as the top-performing model overall.

Figure 5 presents the visual results for Experiment SVR-4 with its model setting applied to the test acquisitions (ID 4, 23 and 24; see Table 1) and Figure 6 shows the distribution of the errors for each of the acquisitions in the test set.

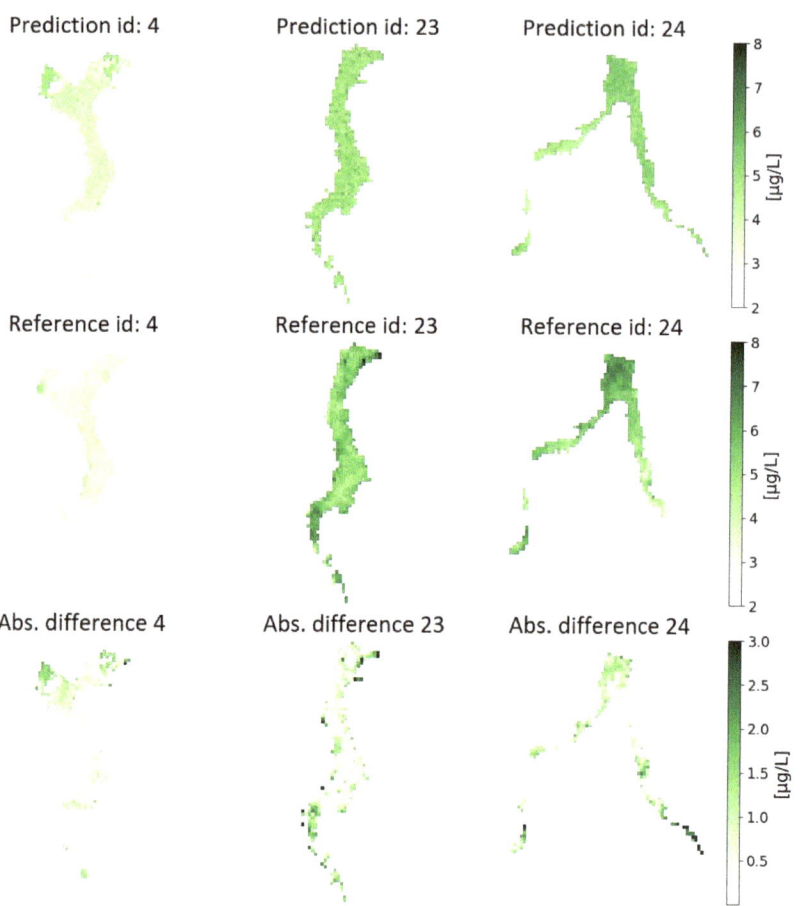

Figure 5. Predictions and reference Chl-a map and their absolute difference (Abs. difference) computed from Experiment SVR-4 applied to each of the acquisitions in the test set.

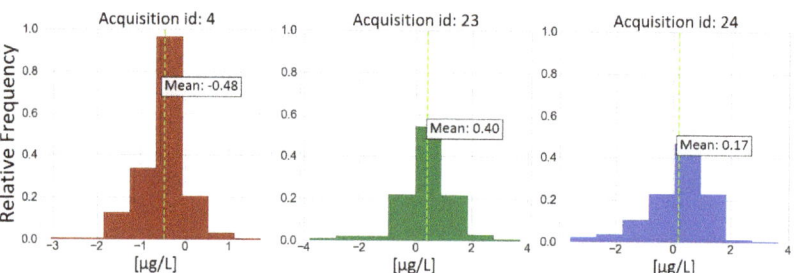

Figure 6. Distribution of the errors of Experiment SVR-4 applied to each of the acquisitions in the test set.

Table 9. Comparison of metrics for the best-performing configuration for each model applied to each of the acquisitions in the test set. Overall MAE and RMSE represent the average score of the metrics from the application of the experiments on the test set acquisitions. Values are reported in [µg/L].

Exp. ID	Model	MAE Overall	RMSE Overall	MAE-4	RMSE-4	MAE-23	RMSE-23	MAE-24	RMSE-24
SVR-4	SVR	**0.687**	**0.895**	0.544	0.688	0.712	0.961	0.806	1.036
RF-10	RF	0.915	1.099	0.464	0.622	0.903	1.106	1.378	1.570
GRU-8	GRU	1.186	1.321	0.929	0.997	1.262	1.420	1.365	1.544
LSTM-13	LSTM	1.211	1.345	0.992	1.053	1.288	1.442	1.355	1.538

Until this moment, the output spatial resolution of 300 m was overlooked, and only the resulting performance was analyzed. However, recognizing that output with a finer spatial resolution of 30 m could yield more valuable results, efforts were directed towards determining the optimal approach to achieve predictions at this higher resolution.

For this purpose, two alternative approaches were identified. The first, which has already been investigated, consisted of using 30-m data for model training, validation, and evaluation (testing). The second approach involved the use of the best-performing configurations of each considered model, which were trained with 300 m data (a summary of the results is included in Table 9), and to perform an inference on 30-m data for their evaluation. Figure 7 provides a schematic of these two alternative approaches.

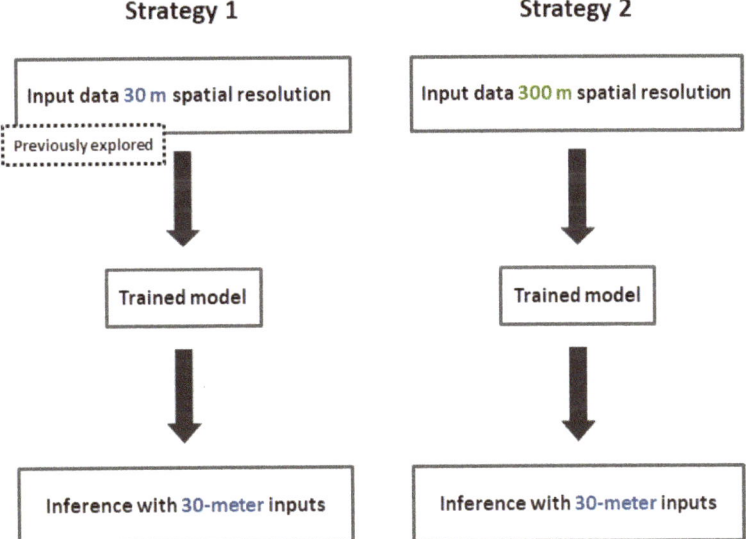

Figure 7. Schematic of the inference procedures on 30 m spatial resolution output.

After evaluating both approaches with the best-performing configurations of the four model typologies, the RF Regressor (Experiment RF-12) both trained and evaluated with 30-m data, emerged as the best alternative for achieving a prediction with 30 m of spatial resolution. The summary of these results is reported in Table 10.

Table 10. Comparison of metrics for the best-performing configuration for each model using 30 m spatial resolution data, applied for each of the acquisitions in the test set. Training set (Train res.) and evaluation set (Eval. res) spatial resolutions are reported in dedicated columns. Overall MAE and RMSE represent the average scores for the metrics obtained from applying the experiments to each of the acquisitions in the test set. Values are reported in [µg/L].

Exp. ID	Model	Train. Res. [m]	Eval. Res. [m]	MAE Overall	RMSE Overall	MAE-4	RMSE-4	MAE-23	RMSE-23	MAE-24	RMSE-24
RF-10	RF	300	30	1.076	1.241	0.988	1.071	0.836	1.068	1.405	1.585
RF-12	**RF**	**30**	**30**	**0.986**	**1.181**	0.815	0.921	0.707	0.987	1.435	1.635
SVR-4	SVR	300	30	1.107	1.266	1.578	1.620	0.778	1.017	0.964	1.161
SVR-10	SVR	30	30	1.260	1.555	1.052	1.571	1.043	1.235	1.686	1.859
LSTM-13	LSTM	300	30	1.234	1.369	0.826	0.905	1.413	1.556	1.462	1.648
LSTM-14	LSTM	30	30	1.278	1.455	1.004	1.112	1.004	1.214	1.826	2.039
GRU-8	GRU	300	30	1.248	1.393	0.643	0.746	1.294	1.448	1.808	1.986
GRU-17	GRU	30	30	1.203	1.382	0.598	0.727	1.518	1.732	1.493	1.686

Figure 8 presents the visual results of Experiment RF-12, trained and evaluated at 30-m spatial resolution data and applied to each of the acquisitions in the test set. The associated errors' distributions are shown in Figure 9.

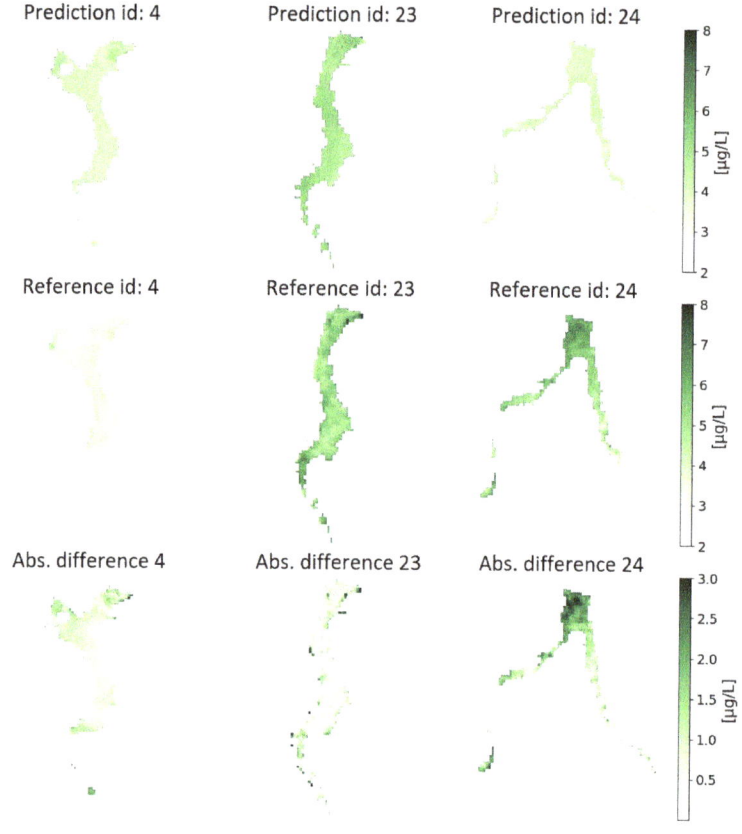

Figure 8. Predictions and reference Chl-a map and their absolute difference (Abs. difference) computed from Experiment RF-12 trained and evaluated at 30-m spatial resolution data and applied to each of the acquisitions in the test set.

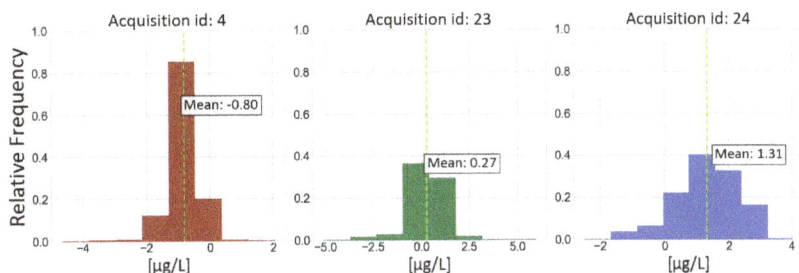

Figure 9. Distribution of the errors of Experiment RF-12 trained and evaluated at 30-m spatial resolution data and applied to each of the acquisitions in the test set.

A final observation drawn from the presented results is the tendency of the considered machine learning models to underestimate Chl-a values in high local concentration spots. Further considerations on the above are reported in the following section.

4. Conclusions and Outlook

This study addressed the implementation aspects related to the generation of Chl-a concentration maps utilizing PRISMA hyperspectral imagery, with low-resolution training data derived from Sentinel-3 imagery. The complete workflow for preparing input data for a range of machine and deep learning models was outlined. Performances of the models under various hyperparameter configurations were compared to offer empirical insights into the best-performing solutions for estimating multi-resolution Chl-a concentrations in lakes using hyperspectral imagery and pre-existing Chl-a concentration maps at lower spatial but higher temporal resolution.

By conducting several modelling experiments, the optimal configurations for each of the four analyzed models were determined. Specifically, the most favourable performances were attained when employing 300 m spatial resolution inputs for all experiments. The best results were achieved with the SVR model. Supplementary experiments were conducted to evaluate model performances in enhancing the spatial resolution of Chl-a concentration predictions from the original 300 m reference data (i.e., Sentinel-3 derived Chl-a concentration maps) to 30 m resolution such as the one of PRISMA hyperspectral imagery. The RF Regressor proved to deliver the best performance for this last objective.

While the obtained performances are relevant for all model typologies, it is worth noting that these results could be potentially improved with the availability of additional PRISMA acquisitions. As discernible from the presented results, the selected machine learning models demonstrated a tendency to underestimate regions characterized by high Chl-a concentrations. The inclusion of supplementary PRISMA acquisitions linked to high Chl-a concentration spots in the input dataset (which were limited in the dataset used for this study) is expected to mitigate this discrepancy and represents a critical improvement for future developments of this work.

Given the limitations to the accessibility of ground truth data for training and evaluating machine and deep learning models, the approach outlined in this study is promising for preliminary large-scale estimates of Chl-a concentrations in freshwater bodies. This is because it suggests strategies for the use of low-resolution and widely accessible training and testing datasets by leading to a final product with a significantly higher spatial resolution than the reference data while maintaining an acceptable margin of error. This enhancement is achieved by leveraging both spectral and spatial characteristics of the emerging hyperspectral satellite imagery. It is worth remarking that operations such as resampling low-resolution reference data for model evaluation on 30 m resolution outputs were tested for purely experimental purposes. The use of high-resolution reference data is envisaged to improve both the quality and reliability of the proposed procedure, especially of local gradients of Chl-a concentrations in each single water body.

The outcomes of the suggested method have the potential to function as supportive resources for the monitoring and administration of the lakes under investigation. The use of global coverage and freely available data, coupled with open modelling tools, additionally strengthens this groundwork for enhancements and replications in different geographic regions.

Author Contributions: Conceptualization, J.F.A., M.A.B. and D.O.; methodology, J.F.A. and M.A.B.; software, J.F.A.; validation, J.F.A.; formal analysis, J.F.A.; investigation, J.F.A. and M.A.B.; resources, M.A.B.; data curation, J.F.A.; writing—original draft preparation, J.F.A. and D.O.; writing—review and editing, J.F.A. and D.O.; visualization, J.F.A.; supervision, M.A.B. and D.O.; project administration, M.A.B. All authors have read and agreed to the published version of the manuscript.

Funding: This research has been partially funded by the project "SIMILE" within the Interreg Co-operation Programme 2014–2020 (ID 523544).

Data Availability Statement: PRISMA satellite images are accessible from the mission official website https://prisma.asi.it (accessed on 7 November 2023) upon approval of a formal data request to the Italian Space Agency. Reference Chl-a concentration maps were obtained from the SIMILE project and they are openly accessible from the project geoportal https://www.geonode.eo.simile.polimi.it (accessed on 7 November 2023).

Conflicts of Interest: The authors declare no conflict of interest.

Abbreviations

The following abbreviations are used in this manuscript:

AHSI	Advanced Hyperspectral Imager
ANN	Artificial Neural Networks
AOI	Area of Interest
ASI	Italian Space Agency
Chl-a	Chlorophyll-a
CNN	Convolutional Neural Network
DESIS	German Aerospace Center Earth Sensing Imaging Spectrometer
DN	Digital Number
EeTeS	EnMAP end-to-end Simulator Software
EnMAP	Environmental Mapping and Analysis Program
ESA	European Space Agency
FCN	Fully-connected Network
GRU	Gated Recurrent Unit
HICO	Hyperspectral Imager for the Coastal Ocean
LSTM	Long-short Term Memory
MAE	Mean Absolute Error
MARS	Multivariate Adaptive Regression Spline
MDN	Mixture Density Network
NASA	National Aeronautics and Space Administration
OLCI	Ocean and Land Colour Instrument
PCA	Principal Component Analysis
PCs	Principal Components
PLS	Partial Least Squares
PRISMA	PRecursore IperSpettrale della Missione Applicativa
QQ-plot	Quantile-Quantile plot
RBF	Radial Basis Function
RF	Random Forest
RMSE	Root Mean Square Error
RNN	Recurrent Neural Network
SIMILE	Informative System for the Integrated Monitoring of Insubric Lakes and their Ecosystems
SSI	Spectral Sampling Interval
SVM	Support Vector Machines
SVR	Support Vector Regressor

SWIR	Short-Wave Infrared
TSM	Total Suspended Matter
US	United States
VNIR	Visible and Near-infrared

References

1. Vollenweider, R.; Kerekes, J. *Eutrophication of Waters: Monitoring, Assessment and Control*; OECD: Wiley, Hoboken, NJ, USA, 1982.
2. Bhagowati, B.; Ahamad, K.U. A review on lake eutrophication dynamics and recent developments in lake modeling. *Ecohydrol. Hydrobiol.* **2019**, *19*, 155–166. [CrossRef]
3. Grizzetti, B.; Liquete, C.; Pistocchi, A.; Vigiak, O.; Zulian, G.; Bouraoui, F.; De Roo, A.; Cardoso, A. Relationship between ecological condition and ecosystem services in European rivers, lakes and coastal waters. *Sci. Total Environ.* **2019**, *671*, 452–465. [CrossRef] [PubMed]
4. United Nations. Transforming our world: The 2030 Agenda for Sustainable Development. 2015. Available online: https://sdgs.un.org/2030agenda (accessed on 7 November 2023).
5. Schindler, D.W.; Carpenter, S.R.; Chapra, S.C.; Hecky, R.E.; Orihel, D.M. Reducing phosphorus to curb lake eutrophication is a success. *Environ. Sci. Technol.* **2016**, *50*, 8923–8929. [CrossRef]
6. Wetzel, R.G.; Likens, G. *Limnological Analyses*; Springer Science & Business Media: Berlin/Heidelberg, Germany, 2000.
7. Kahlert, M.; McKie, B.G. Comparing new and conventional methods to estimate benthic algal biomass and composition in freshwaters. *Environ. Sci. Process. Impacts* **2014**, *16*, 2627–2634. [CrossRef]
8. Guyot, G.; Baret, F.; Jacquemoud, S. *Imaging Spectroscopy for Vegetation Studies*; Kluwer Academic Publishers: Norwell, MA, USA, 1992; Volume 2.
9. Gohin, F.; Van der Zande, D.; Tilstone, G.; Eleveld, M.A.; Lefebvre, A.; Andrieux-Loyer, F.; Blauw, A.N.; Bryère, P.; Devreker, D.; Garnesson, P.; et al. Twenty years of satellite and in situ observations of surface chlorophyll-a from the northern Bay of Biscay to the eastern English Channel. Is the water quality improving? *Remote Sens. Environ.* **2019**, *233*, 111343. [CrossRef]
10. Maier, P.M.; Keller, S. Estimating chlorophyll a concentrations of several inland waters with hyperspectral data and machine learning models. *arXiv* **2019**, arXiv:1904.02052.
11. Lioumbas, J.; Christodoulou, A.; Katsiapi, M.; Xanthopoulou, N.; Stournara, P.; Spahos, T.; Seretoudi, G.; Mentes, A.; Theodoridou, N. Satellite remote sensing to improve source water quality monitoring: A water utility's perspective. *Remote Sens. Appl. Soc. Environ.* **2023**, *32*, 101042. [CrossRef]
12. Giardino, C.; Brando, V.; Gege, P.; Pinnel, N.; Hochberg, E.; Knaeps, E.; Reusen, I.; Doerffer, R.; Bresciani, M.; Braga, F.; et al. Imaging spectrometry of inland and coastal waters: State of the art, achievements and perspectives. *Surv. Geophys.* **2019**, *40*, 401–429. [CrossRef]
13. Hafeez, S.; Wong, M.S.; Abbas, S.; Asim, M. Evaluating landsat-8 and sentinel-2 data consistency for high spatiotemporal inland and coastal water quality monitoring. *Remote Sens.* **2022**, *14*, 3155. [CrossRef]
14. Hestir, E.L.; Brando, V.E.; Bresciani, M.; Giardino, C.; Matta, E.; Villa, P.; Dekker, A.G. Measuring freshwater aquatic ecosystems: The need for a hyperspectral global mapping satellite mission. *Remote Sens. Environ.* **2015**, *167*, 181–195. [CrossRef]
15. Ma, T.; Zhang, D.; Li, X.; Huang, Y.; Zhang, L.; Zhu, Z.; Sun, X.; Lan, Z.; Guo, W. Hyperspectral remote sensing technology for water quality monitoring: Knowledge graph analysis and Frontier trend. *Front. Environ. Sci.* **2023**, *11*. [CrossRef]
16. Dierssen, H.M.; Ackleson, S.G.; Joyce, K.E.; Hestir, E.L.; Castagna, A.; Lavender, S.; McManus, M.A. Living up to the hype of hyperspectral aquatic remote sensing: Science, resources and outlook. *Front. Environ. Sci.* **2021**, *9*. [CrossRef]
17. Folkman, M.A.; Pearlman, J.; Liao, L.B.; Jarecke, P.J. EO-1/Hyperion hyperspectral imager design, development, characterization, and calibration. *Hyperspectral Remote Sens. Land Atmos.* **2001**, *4151*, 40–51.
18. Alonso, K.; Bachmann, M.; Burch, K.; Carmona, E.; Cerra, D.; De los Reyes, R.; Dietrich, D.; Heiden, U.; Hölderlin, A.; Ickes, J.; et al. Data products, quality and validation of the DLR earth sensing imaging spectrometer (DESIS). *Sensors* **2019**, *19*, 4471. [PubMed]
19. Guanter, L.; Kaufmann, H.; Segl, K.; Foerster, S.; Rogass, C.; Chabrillat, S.; Kuester, T.; Hollstein, A.; Rossner, G.; Chlebek, C.; et al. The EnMAP spaceborne imaging spectroscopy mission for earth observation. *Remote Sens.* **2015**, *7*, 8830–8857.
20. Liu, Y.N.; Sun, D.X.; Hu, X.N.; Ye, X.; Li, Y.D.; Liu, S.F.; Cao, K.Q.; Chai, M.Y.; Zhang, J.; Zhang, Y.; et al. The advanced hyperspectral imager: Aboard China's gaoFen-5 satellite. *IEEE Geosci. Remote Sens. Mag.* **2019**, *7*, 23–32.
21. Cogliati, S.; Sarti, F.; Chiarantini, L.; Cosi, M.; Lorusso, R.; Lopinto, E.; Miglietta, F.; Genesio, L.; Guanter, L.; Damm, A.; et al. The PRISMA imaging spectroscopy mission: Overview and first performance analysis. *Remote Sens. Environ.* **2021**, *262*, 112499.
22. Esposito, M.; Marchi, A.Z. In-orbit demonstration of the first hyperspectral imager for nanosatellites. In Proceedings of the International Conference on Space Optics—ICSO, Chania, Greece, 9-12 October 2018; Volume 11180, pp. 760–770. [CrossRef]
23. Qian, S.E. Hyperspectral satellites, evolution, and development history. *IEEE J. Sel. Top. Appl. Earth Obs. Remote Sens.* **2021**, *14*, 7032–7056.
24. Audebert, N.; Le Saux, B.; Lefèvre, S. Deep learning for classification of hyperspectral data: A comparative review. *IEEE Geosci. Remote Sens. Mag.* **2019**, *7*, 159–173.
25. Shi, K.; Zhang, Y.; Qin, B.; Zhou, B. Remote sensing of cyanobacterial blooms in inland waters: Present knowledge and future challenges. *Sci. Bull.* **2019**, *64*, 1540–1556.

26. Gholizadeh, M.H.; Melesse, A.M.; Reddi, L. A comprehensive review on water quality parameters estimation using remote sensing techniques. *Sensors* **2016**, *16*, 1298. [PubMed]
27. Ali, K.A.; Ortiz, J.D. Multivariate approach for chlorophyll-a and suspended matter retrievals in Case II type waters using hyperspectral data. *Hydrol. Sci. J.* **2016**, *61*, 200–213. [CrossRef]
28. Sun, D.; Li, Y.; Wang, Q. A unified model for remotely estimating chlorophyll a in Lake Taihu, China, based on SVM and in situ hyperspectral data. *IEEE Trans. Geosci. Remote Sens.* **2009**, *47*, 2957–2965.
29. Keller, S.; Maier, P.M.; Riese, F.M.; Norra, S.; Holbach, A.; Börsig, N.; Wilhelms, A.; Moldaenke, C.; Zaake, A.; Hinz, S. Hyperspectral data and machine learning for estimating CDOM, chlorophyll a, diatoms, green algae and turbidity. *Int. J. Environ. Res. Public Health* **2018**, *15*, 1881. [CrossRef] [PubMed]
30. Maier, P.M.; Keller, S. Application of different simulated spectral data and machine learning to estimate the chlorophyll a concentration of several inland waters. In Proceedings of the 2019 10th Workshop on Hyperspectral Imaging and Signal Processing: Evolution in Remote Sensing (WHISPERS), Amsterdam, The Netherlands, 24–26 September 2019; IEEE: Piscataway, NJ, USA, 2019; pp. 1–5.
31. Ali, K.A.; Moses, W.J. Application of a PLS-augmented ANN model for retrieving chlorophyll-a from hyperspectral data in case 2 waters of the western basin of Lake Erie. *Remote Sens.* **2022**, *14*, 3729. [CrossRef]
32. Maier, P.M.; Keller, S.; Hinz, S. Deep learning with WASI simulation data for estimating chlorophyll a concentration of inland water bodies. *Remote Sens.* **2021**, *13*, 718. [CrossRef]
33. Saberioon, M.; Khosravi, V.; Brom, J.; Gholizadeh, A.; Segl, K. Examining the sensitivity of simulated EnMAP data for estimating chlorophyll-a and total suspended solids in inland waters. *Ecol. Inform.* **2023**, *75*, 102058.
34. Segl, K.; Guanter, L.; Rogass, C.; Kuester, T.; Roessner, S.; Kaufmann, H.; Sang, B.; Mogulsky, V.; Hofer, S. EeteS—The EnMAP End-to-End Simulation Tool. *IEEE J. Sel. Top. Appl. Earth Obs. Remote Sens.* **2012**, *5*, 522–530. [CrossRef]
35. Pahlevan, N.; Smith, B.; Binding, C.; Gurlin, D.; Li, L.; Bresciani, M.; Giardino, C. Hyperspectral retrievals of phytoplankton absorption and chlorophyll-a in inland and nearshore coastal waters. *Remote Sens. Environ.* **2021**, *253*, 112200. [CrossRef]
36. Lima, T.M.A.d.; Giardino, C.; Bresciani, M.; Barbosa, C.C.F.; Fabbretto, A.; Pellegrino, A.; Begliomini, F.N. Assessment of Estimated Phycocyanin and Chlorophyll-a Concentration from PRISMA and OLCI in Brazilian Inland Waters: A Comparison between Semi-Analytical and Machine Learning Algorithms. *Remote Sens.* **2023**, *15*, 1299. [CrossRef]
37. Mosher, T.; Mitchell, M. Hyperspectral imager for the coastal ocean (HICO). In Proceedings of the 2004 IEEE Aerospace Conference Proceedings (IEEE Cat. No. 04TH8720), Biloxi, MS, USA, 26–29 October 2009; IEEE: Piscataway, NJ, USA, 2004; Volume 1.
38. Yuan, Q.; Shen, H.; Li, T.; Li, Z.; Li, S.; Jiang, Y.; Xu, H.; Tan, W.; Yang, Q.; Wang, J.; et al. Deep learning in environmental remote sensing: Achievements and challenges. *Remote Sens. Environ.* **2020**, *241*, 111716.
39. Brovelli, M.; Cannata, M.; Rogora, M. Simile, a geospatial enabler of the monitoring of sustainable development goal 6 (ensure availability and sustainability of water for all). *Int. Arch. Photogramm. Remote Sens. Spat. Inf. Sci.* **2019**, *42*, 3–10. [CrossRef]
40. Luciani, G.; Bresciani, M.; Biraghi, C.A.; Ghirardi, N.; Carrion, D.; Rogora, M.; Brovelli, M.A. Satellite Monitoring system of Subalpine lakes with open source software: The case of SIMILE Project. *Balt. J. Mod. Comput.* **2021**, *9*, 135–144. [CrossRef]
41. Amieva, J.; Austoni, A.; Bresciani, M.; Brovelli, M. Analysis of the Remotely Sensed Water Quality Parameters of the Insubric Lakes: Methods and Results of the Interreg Simile Project. *Int. Arch. Photogramm. Remote Sens. Spat. Inf. Sci.* **2023**, *48*, 9–16. [CrossRef]
42. Toro Herrera, J.; Carrion, D.; Bresciani, M.; Bratić, G. Semi-automated production and filtering of satellite derived water quality parameters. *Int. Arch. Photogramm. Remote Sens. Spat. Inf. Sci.* **2022**, *43*, 1019–1026. [CrossRef]
43. Hochreiter, S.; Schmidhuber, J. Long short-term memory. *Neural Comput.* **1997**, *9*, 1735–1780. [CrossRef] [PubMed]
44. Gers, F.A.; Schmidhuber, J.; Cummins, F. Learning to forget: Continual prediction with LSTM. *Neural Comput.* **2000**, *12*, 2451–2471. [CrossRef]
45. Cho, K.; van Merriënboer, B.; Gulcehre, C.; Bahdanau, D.; Bougares, F.; Schwenk, H.; Bengio, Y. Learning phrase representations using RNN encoder-decoder for statistical machine translation. In Proceedings of the 2014 Conference on Empirical Methods in Natural Language Processing (EMNLP), Doha, Qatar, 25–29 October 2014; Association for Computational Linguistics: Stroudsburg, PA, USA, 2014; pp. 1724–1734.
46. Agency, I.S. *PRISMA Products Specification Document—Issue 2.3*; Italian Space Agency: Rome, Italy, 2020.
47. Plyer, A.; Colin-Koeniguer, E.; Weissgerber, F. A new coregistration algorithm for recent applications on urban SAR images. *IEEE Geosci. Remote Sens. Lett.* **2015**, *12*, 2198–2202. [CrossRef]
48. Gilerson, A.; Gitelson, A.; Zhou, J.G.D.; Moses, W.; Ioannou, I.; Ahmed, S. Algorithms for remote estimation of chlorophyll-a in coastal and inland waters using red and near infrared bands. *Opt. Express* **2010**, *8*, 24109–24125. [CrossRef] [PubMed]
49. ESA. Radiometric Resolution—21 bands in VIS/SWIR. 2023. Available online: https://sentinels.copernicus.eu/web/sentinel/user-guides/sentinel-3-olci/resolutions/radiometric (accessed on 7 November 2023).
50. Bresciani, M.; Adamo, M.; De Carolis, G.; Matta, E.; Pasquariello, G.; Vaičiūtė, D.; Giardino, C. Monitoring blooms and surface accumulation of cyanobacteria in the Curonian Lagoon by combining MERIS and ASAR data. *Remote Sens. Environ.* **2014**, *146*, 124–135. [CrossRef]
51. Mobley, C.D. *Light and Water: Radiative Transfer in Natural Waters*; JSTOR: New York, NY, USA, 1994.

52. Agenzia Spaziale Italiana (ASI). PRISMA Product Specification. 2020. Available online: https://prisma.asi.it/missionselect/docs/PRISMA%20Product%20Specifications_Is2_3.pdf (accessed on 22 May 2023).
53. Sobel, I. An isotropic 3 × 3 image gradient operator. In Proceedings of the 5th Annual Symposium on Theory of Computing, Austin, TX, USA, 30 April–2 May 1973; ACM: New York, NY, USA, 1973; pp. 271–272.
54. Gonzalez, R.C.; Woods, R.E. *Digital Image Processing*, 4th ed.; Pearson: London, UK, 2018.
55. Breiman, L. Random forests. *Mach. Learn.* **2001**, *45*, 5–32. [CrossRef]
56. Drucker, H.; Wu, D.; Vapnik, V.N. Support vector regression machines. *Adv. Neural Inf. Process. Syst.* **1997**, *9*, 155–161.
57. Pedregosa, F.; Varoquaux, G.; Gramfort, A.; Michel, V.; Thirion, B.; Grisel, O.; Blondel, M.; Prettenhofer, P.; Weiss, R.; Dubourg, V.; et al. Scikit-learn: Machine Learning in Python. *J. Mach. Learn. Res.* **2011**, *12*, 2825–2830.
58. Scikit-Learn. Random Forest Regressor. 2023. Available online: https://scikit-learn.org/stable/modules/generated/sklearn.ensemble.RandomForestRegressor.html (accessed on 22 May 2023).
59. Scikit-Learn. Support Vector Machines. 2023. Available online: https://scikit-learn.org/stable/modules/svm.html (accessed on 22 May 2023).
60. Oguiza, I. tsai—A State-of-the-Art Deep Learning Library for Time Series and Sequential Data. 2022. Available online: https://github.com/timeseriesAI/tsai (accessed on 22 May 2023).
61. Srivastava, N.; Hinton, G.; Krizhevsky, A.; Sutskever, I.; Salakhutdinov, R. Dropout: A simple way to prevent neural networks from overfitting. *J. Mach. Learn. Res.* **2014**, *15*, 1929–1958.

Disclaimer/Publisher's Note: The statements, opinions and data contained in all publications are solely those of the individual author(s) and contributor(s) and not of MDPI and/or the editor(s). MDPI and/or the editor(s) disclaim responsibility for any injury to people or property resulting from any ideas, methods, instructions or products referred to in the content.

Article

Assessment of Machine Learning Models for Remote Sensing of Water Quality in Lakes Cajititlán and Zapotlán, Jalisco—Mexico

Freddy Hernán Villota-González [1], Belkis Sulbarán-Rangel [1], Florentina Zurita-Martínez [2], Kelly Joel Gurubel-Tun [1] and Virgilio Zúñiga-Grajeda [3,*]

1. Department of Water and Energy, University of Guadalajara, Campus Tonalá, Tonalá 45425, Mexico; freddyvillota@gmail.com (F.H.V.-G.); belkis.sulbaran@academicos.udg.mx (B.S.-R.); joel.gurubel@academicos.udg.mx (K.J.G.-T.)
2. Environmental Quality Research Center, University of Guadalajara, Campus Ciénega, Ocotlán 47810, Mexico; florentina.zurita@academicos.udg.mx
3. Information Sciences and Technological Development, University of Guadalajara, Campus Tonalá, Tonalá 45425, Mexico
* Correspondence: virgilio.zuniga@academicos.udg.mx

Citation: Villota-González, F.H.; Sulbarán-Rangel, B.; Zurita-Martínez, F.; Gurubel-Tun, K.J.; Zúñiga-Grajeda, V. Assessment of Machine Learning Models for Remote Sensing of Water Quality in Lakes Cajititlán and Zapotlán, Jalisco—Mexico. *Remote Sens.* **2023**, *15*, 5505. https://doi.org/10.3390/rs15235505

Academic Editors: Miro Govedarica, Flor Alvarez-Taboada and Gordana Jakovljević

Received: 1 October 2023
Revised: 9 November 2023
Accepted: 21 November 2023
Published: 26 November 2023

Copyright: © 2023 by the authors. Licensee MDPI, Basel, Switzerland. This article is an open access article distributed under the terms and conditions of the Creative Commons Attribution (CC BY) license (https://creativecommons.org/licenses/by/4.0/).

Abstract: Remote sensing has emerged as a promising tool for monitoring water quality (WQ) in aquatic ecosystems. This study evaluates the effectiveness of remote sensing in assessing WQ parameters in Cajititlán and Zapotlán lakes in the state of Jalisco, Mexico. Over time, these lakes have witnessed a significant decline in WQ, necessitating the adoption of advanced monitoring techniques. In this research, satellite-based remote sensing data were combined with ground-based measurements from the National Water Quality Monitoring Network of Mexico (RNMCA). These data sources were harnessed to train and evaluate the performance of six distinct categories of machine learning (ML) algorithms aimed at estimating WQ parameters with active spectral signals, including chlorophyll-a (Chl-a), turbidity, and total suspended solids (TSS). Various limitations were encountered during the study, primarily due to atmospheric conditions and cloud cover. These challenges affected both the quality and quantity of the data. However, these limitations were overcome through rigorous data preprocessing, the application of ML techniques designed for data-scarce scenarios, and extensive hyperparameter tuning. The superlearner algorithm (SLA), which leverages a combination of individual algorithms, and the multilayer perceptron (MLP), capable of handling complex and non-linear problems, outperformed others in terms of predictive accuracy. Notably, in Lake Cajititlán, these models provided the most accurate predictions for turbidity (r^2 = 0.82, RMSE = 9.93 NTU, MAE = 7.69 NTU), Chl-a (r^2 = 0.60, RMSE = 48.06 mg/m^3, MAE = 37.98 mg/m^3), and TSS (r^2 = 0.68, RMSE = 13.42 mg/L, MAE = 10.36 mg/L) when using radiometric data from Landsat-8. In Lake Zapotlán, better predictive performance was observed for turbidity (r^2 = 0.75, RMSE = 2.05 NTU, MAE = 1.10 NTU) and Chl-a (r^2 = 0.71, RMSE = 6.16 mg/m^3, MAE = 4.97 mg/m^3) with Landsat-8 radiometric data, while TSS (r^2 = 0.72, RMSE = 2.71 mg/L, MAE = 2.12 mg/L) improved when Sentinel-2 data were employed. While r^2 values indicate that the models do not exhibit a perfect fit, those approaching unity suggest that the predictor variables offer valuable insights into the corresponding responses. Moreover, the model's robustness could be enhanced by increasing the quantity and quality of input variables. Consequently, remote sensing emerges as a valuable tool to support the objectives of WQ monitoring systems.

Keywords: machine learning algorithms; in situ water quality data; lakes; Landsat-8; Sentinel-2

1. Introduction

Water resources provide ecosystem services of high natural and economic value for the population in general. Consequently, more than 40% of human settlements are located near coastal regions and on the shores of lotic and lentic resources [1,2]. Unfortunately, this makes these bodies of water more susceptible to pollution and overexploitation. In this way, WQ monitoring has become the most suitable strategy to evaluate sustainability in water management practices [3,4]. In recent years, there has been an increase in continuous monitoring campaigns for WQ parameters in various Latin American countries [5]. These initiatives aim to comprehend and proactively address WQ degradation by analyzing data collected during monitoring campaigns.

Conventional monitoring determines the WQ parameters by collecting samples in the field and their subsequent analysis in the laboratory. This is why it becomes a highly precise technique, but its complexity increases when working in large bodies of water. Consequently, the work is laborious and time-consuming, which results in an increase in costs that governments in many poor or developing countries cannot afford [6]. In addition, the sampling points may be limited due to restricted access in sectors with irregular topographies. Therefore, the accuracy and precision of the data may be compromised, including by in situ sampling error or laboratory analysis error. Hence, conventional methods cannot easily identify temporal and spatial variations of WQ parameters. Consequently, it is not possible to represent the complete state of the water surface and thus an obstacle prevents the monitoring and management of the quality of water masses [1,5–7].

On the other hand, advances in space science, cloud computing and ML contribute to the development of new techniques to work with natural resource management. For instance, satellites have built-in optical and thermal sensors that measure reflected electromagnetic radiation. This information is used to evaluate WQ with high spectral and spatial resolution [2,8]. Remote sensing as a technique to monitor WQ has been used since the 1970s, so that, since that decade, studies with methodological approaches have been developed to take advantage of the advantages offered by satellites [9]. The satellite radiometers used up to now are designed for the observation of the ocean and the terrestrial surface; therefore, they are not suitable for observing continental waters [10,11]. However, the fine spatial resolution of terrestrial sensors enables the acquisition of acceptable results for monitoring WQ parameters [4,12].

The literature review underscores the increasing utilization of Landsat-8 and Sentinel-2 sensors, highlighting their remarkable advantages in terms of fine spatial and temporal resolution [13,14]. Landsat-8, for instance, provides data at 16-day intervals, roughly equivalent to 22 annual images, depending on the location, while Sentinel-2 captures images every 5 days, resulting in approximately 73 images annually. These attributes have played a pivotal role in yielding highly promising results in the remote detection of WQ parameters within continental water bodies [15–18].

Nevertheless, a significant challenge for these studies has been the limitation in accessing sufficient training data for ML models [2,19]. The acquisition of satellite images is constrained by adverse climatic factors, such as persistent cloud cover or precipitation, which hinder the capture of surface water reflectance values [20]. The pressing need for an adequate quantity of training data materializes as a substantial challenge in this research domain. To address this data limitation, several studies employ the k-Fold-Cross-Validation technique to maximize the use of limited data and build robust models [18]. It is heartening to note that the relationship between the reflected light from specific parameters and their field-measured concentrations has proven to be an effective avenue for generating promising results in predictive models [21].

Furthermore, to overcome the shortage of training data for ML models, several studies opt to incorporate in situ data from monitoring activities available through open-access portals of national water and environmental agencies across diverse nations [19]. For instance, Papenfus et al. [22] employed data from the United States Environmental Protection Agency's Water Quality Portal to facilitate remote sensing of Chl-a in lakes and reservoirs within the United States. Similarly, other data sources include the European Environment Agency (EEA) Waterbase portal in Europe, the Global Freshwater Quality Database (GEMStat) at a global scale, and Canada's Open Government Portal [19].

In Latin America, studies such as that by Rodríguez López et al. [23] used in situ data from Dirección General de Aguas de Chile to estimate Chl-a concentration using Landsat-8 and obtained r^2 values ranging from 0.64 to 0.93 when testing various neural networks. In Brazil, Bettencourt et al. [24] estimated turbidity and Chl-a through in situ data from the National Agency of Waters (ANA-Hidroweb). In Argentina, Germán et al. [25] estimated Chl-a levels using Sentinel-2 satellite data in conjunction with in situ measurements obtained from a monitoring program conducted by the Ministry of Water, Environment, and Public Services of the province of Córdoba. Their findings revealed an r^2 of 0.77. In Mexico, Otto et al. [26] used data from the RNMCA together with Landsat radiometric data as input variables to develop empirical models and estimate turbidity in Lake Chapala; the authors obtained an r^2 of 0.7. Similarly, Torres Vera [27], based on data from the RNMCA, developed an ML model to estimate TSS in Lake Chapala using Landsat images; the r^2 obtained was 0.81. Another significant work was conducted by Arias Rodríguez et al. [5], where the authors evaluated an extreme learning machine (ELM), a support vector regression, and a linear regression to estimate Chl-a, turbidity, TSS, and Secchi disk depth in the lakes of the Mexican territory (Chapala, Cuitzeo, Patzcuaro, Yuriria, and Catemaco). They integrated in situ measurements of the RNMCA with data from Landsat-8, Sentinel-3, and Sentinel-2, and reported that the atmospherically corrected Sentinel-3 data and ELM models performed better, particularly for turbidity ($r^2 = 0.7$). This illustrates the remarkable evolution in the application of remote sensing technologies for WQ monitoring in Latin American countries while emphasizing the innovative strategies employed to address the challenges in this research field.

Despite the vast scientific literature dedicated to WQ monitoring through remote sensing techniques, the global environment remains a complex and evolving system, as emphasized by Sagan et al. [8]. In light of this understanding, dependence solely on existing research becomes inadequate and occasionally unfeasible. To tackle this challenge, it is essential to engage in continuous research and monitoring of water bodies that have not undergone comprehensive analysis.

This situation is exemplified in the case of lakes Cajititlán and Zapotlán, distinguished by their unique geography, hydrology, surrounding land use, and environmental conditions, rendering them particularly pertinent to this study. Each water body constitutes a distinct system, and solutions effective in one may not be directly applicable in the other. The diversity and distinctiveness of these ecosystems underscore the necessity of data collection and the generation of specific contextual information for future water research and management projects [14]. Furthermore, both lakes hold ecological and touristic significance within the country, as their waters are employed for agricultural irrigation and recreational purposes [28,29].

In the perspective of developing countries like Mexico, budget constraints often limit the resources allocated for water management [30]. Accessing advanced equipment, such as hyperspectral sensors or drones equipped with high-resolution multispectral cameras, can pose a significant challenge due to financial restrictions [31,32]. In this context, the study's primary objective is to introduce an innovative and cost-effective solution for monitoring WQ in Lakes Cajititlán and Zapotlán. By breaking new ground, the aim is to contribute to filling the critical gap in the field of remote sensing studies, where these particular bodies of water have remained largely unexplored. To achieve this goal, a wide range of ML algorithms were systematically evaluated, distinguishing the best performing ones to ensure the effectiveness and robustness of the method. By addressing this research gap, this work advances the understanding and management of WQ, thereby establishing a valuable precedent for future studies in similar ecological contexts.

Utilizing the data made available by the National Water Commission (CONAGUA) and delivering a pragmatic management tool for these bodies of water, a valuable resource was provided that serves the interests of both the scientific community and the local population. In the present day, society assumes a pivotal role in the decision-making processes related to water resource management [33]. There is a growing demand for robust tools that streamline the acquisition of pertinent information concerning WQ in these natural resources. Such information is indispensable for preempting environmental challenges, including water pollution, and proactively mitigating these issues [34].

This study involved correlating radiometric data from Landsat-8 and Sentinel-2 with WQ parameters characterized by an active spectral signal. While existing methods from the literature were employed, the uniqueness of this research is corroborated by the examination of water bodies that had not previously been monitored by remote sensing. Furthermore, the advantage lies in the availability of RNMCA data from 2009 to the present, which effectively increases the volume of input data for training ML algorithms.

The effectiveness of eight state-of-the-art ML algorithms spanning various categories was evaluated, introducing a broader range compared to previous studies using RNMCA data. The scope of hyperparameter adjustment was expanded through grid search techniques to enhance the model performance. The first category of algorithms encompasses ensemble methods, where the Gradient Boosting Regressor was considered for its capacity to amalgamate the predictive prowess of multiple decision trees. This attribute renders it particularly adept at capturing the intricate and interrelated dynamics inherent in WQ parameters [35]. Concomitantly, the Random Forest Regressor, a model that harnesses an ensemble of decision trees, was engaged to deliver precise predictions [36]. Furthermore, the SLA was leveraged to enhance predictive performance. The SLA operates by stacking the outputs of individual estimators and utilizing a regressor to compute the final prediction, harnessing the collective strength of each constituent estimator [37]. The second category encompasses neural networks, where the MLP assumes a pivotal role. The MLP, renowned for its proficiency in apprehending intricate relationships, excels at modeling non-linear dependencies between WQ input and output variables more effectively than conventional linear regression models [21,38]. Within the third category, regularization techniques were incorporated, with particular emphasis on the Ridge regression algorithm. Ridge regression, through the introduction of a penalty term, effectively mitigates the risk of overfitting in linear regression models [36]. The fourth category, consisting of instance-based methods, introduced the K-Neighbors Regressor. This algorithm relies on the similarity between data points to make predictions, rendering it well-suited for the estimation of WQ parameters [35]. In the fifth category, decision trees were comprehensively explored for their inherent interpretability and effectiveness [21]. Finally, the sixth category extended the evaluation to encompass other algorithms, such as Support Vector Machines, renowned for their distinctive capabilities in modeling intricate and non-linear relationships [36].

The thorough investigation of these diverse ML algorithms underlines the primary objective of the study: to identify the most effective approach for addressing the intricate and nonlinear characteristics inherent to WQ parameters [21]. Additionally, the strategic adjustment of hyperparameters, encompassing broad ranges, played a pivotal role in enhancing the predictive model's performance. This comprehensive analysis ensures that the results are not only robust but also capable of meeting the complex challenges posed by WQ parameter estimation.

2. Materials and Methods

2.1. Description of the Study Area

Lake Cajititlán is located in the municipality of Tlajomulco de Zúñiga in the state of Jalisco, Mexico at the geographic coordinates: 20.41543° in latitude and −103.335317° in longitude. It has a length of 7.5 km, a width of 2.0 km and a depth of 2.5 m [39]. Lake Zapotlán is located in the south of the State of Jalisco at the geographic coordinates: 19.755395° in latitude and −103.483733° in longitude. It has an approximate area of 16.73 km^2 and an average depth of 4.5 m. Figure 1 shows the location of the lakes with their respective monitoring points managed by the RNMCA.

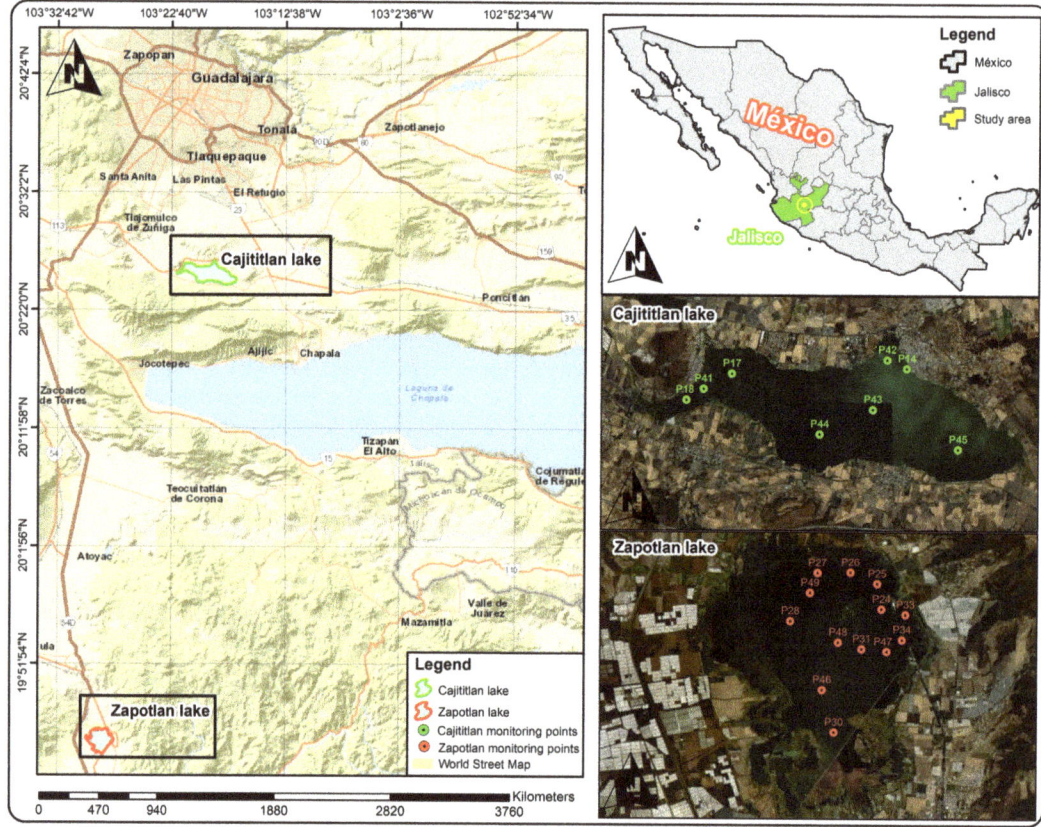

Figure 1. Location map of the Cajititlán and Zapotlán lakes with the water quality sampling points administered by the RNMCA.

2.2. Lake Water Quality Data

The in situ data were acquired from the platform of the Jalisco State Water Commission through the open data service of the WQ system of the RNMCA [40]. Three optically active parameters (Chl-a, turbidity and TSS) were selected, which interact with light and change the energy spectrum of the radiation reflected from water bodies, so that they can be measured with remote sensors. The RNMCA uses the 10200-H extraction method described in the American Public Health Association to measure Chl-a [41]. Turbidity is measured by the nephelometry method referred to in NMX-AA-038-SCFI-2001 [42]. The TSS are determined by the procedures of the Mexican standard NMX-AA-034-SCFI-2015 [43].

2.3. Satellite Data

The reflectance values of the Landsat-8 and Sentinel-2 images of the pixels where the fixed monitoring points are established were extracted (Figure 1). Matching satellite products were identified within a tolerance of ±3 days based on in situ monitoring dates [5,44]. The RNMCA has in situ data spanning from 2009 to the present. Consequently, data filtering was performed based on satellite image availability. Landsat-8 data, consisting of L2 surface reflectance level images, are available from April 2013 to the present date. In parallel, the Sentinel-2 images used in this study belonged to surface reflectance level 2A and have been accessible since March 2017. For Cajititlán, 33 Landsat-8 and 36 Sentinel-2 images were matched, and for Zapotlán 19 Landsat-8 and 32 Sentinel-2 images.

The Landsat-8 and Sentinel-2 images were obtained and processed on the Google Earth Engine (GEE) platform, which is powered by Google's cloud infrastructure and uses a JavaScript programming language, as well as on the platform from Google Colaboratory using the Earth Engine Python API using the geemap library [45]. Numerous images showed cloud cover over the monitoring points, posing a significant challenge in acquiring accurate lake surface reflectance values. To mitigate this issue, specialized functions that operate in the BQA bands for Landsat-8 and the QA60 band for Sentinel-2 were employed. These functions, as suggested by studies conducted by Braaten et al. [46,47], Kochenour et al. [47], and Vanhellemont et al. [48], provided instrumental in the identification and removal of pixels affected by shadows and clouds within the images. This meticulous process aimed to eliminate values that do not correspond to the true surface reflectance of the lake water mirror, ensuring the generation of a dataset without serious alteration and suitable for training ML algorithms. [46–48]. Detailed descriptions of the Landsat-8 and Sentiel-2 satellite products can be reviewed in Tables A1 and A2 of Appendix A.

2.4. Machine Learning Models

Eight regression algorithms from six different categories were evaluated to develop the predictive models (Table 1). The open-source Python resources available in the Scikit-learn library were used and executed in the Google Colaboratory environment that uses Google cloud servers [35].

Table 1. Categories of the regression algorithms used in the study.

Category	Algorithm	Abbr.
Ensemble	Gradient Boosting Regressor	GBR
Ensemble	Random Forest Regressor	RFR
Ensemble	Super Learner Algorithm	SLA
Neural networks	Multilayer Perceptron	MLP
Regularization	Ridge Regressor	Ridge
Instance based	K-Neighbors Regressor	KNR
Decision Tree	Decision Tree Regressor	DTR
Others	Support Vector Regressor	SVR

The algorithms have been grouped into categories based on their approaches and applications, making it easier to understand the different techniques used in data analysis.

In the study, the use of the MLP feedforward was prioritized due to its ability to model non-linear and complex phenomena. This supervised learning algorithm learns a function $f(.) = R^o \rightarrow R^o$ by training on a data set, where m is the number of dimensions for the input and o is the number of dimensions for the output. Given a set of features $X = x_1, x_2, \ldots x_m$ and an objective y it can learn a nonlinear function approximator for classification or regression [35,49].

2.4.1. Data Processing and Algorithm Training

The process was developed by running code in the Python programming language. It began with the identification of the numerical variables that correspond to the satellite reflectance and the concentration values of the WQ parameter to be predicted. Non-numeric values were removed, and a data distribution analysis was performed using the method of Shapiro and Wilk [50] with a 95% confidence interval. Outliers were identified and eliminated using the pandas library boxplot graph and the interquartile range method (IQR) [51]. A correlation analysis matrix was also constructed using Pandas in Python, employing the Pearson correlation coefficient (R) to assess the spectral bands of the sensors that exhibited the strongest correlation with the WQ parameters. This analysis enabled to pinpoint the specific wavelengths where the parameters demonstrated their highest peak of reflected energy [5].

A Pipeline was created that includes three phases. In the first phase, the data are divided randomly, identifying the predictor variables and the response variable. In this way, 80% of the data was selected for training and 20% for validation. For each of the ML algorithms, in the second phase, the training data were scaled and in the third phase, by implementing the Exhaustive Feature Selector class from the mlxtend library, the spectral bands of Landsat-8 and Sentinel-2 were selected as most relevant input variables. All possible combinations were sampled and evaluated with a cross-validation of 8 folds for Landsat-8 and 12 folds for Sentinel-2, matching numbers according to the number of bands analyzed [52].

With the processed data, the hyperparameter adjustment was performed, so the optimal values were identified by testing different possibilities through an exhaustive search with the grid search method. In this way, the models were trained, and their respective errors were estimated using the Repeated k-Fold-Cross-Validation validation method. In the end, the new model was fitted with all of the training data and with the best hyperparameters found.

To illustrate the flow of the methodology on data processing and algorithm training, a diagram is provided in Figure 2.

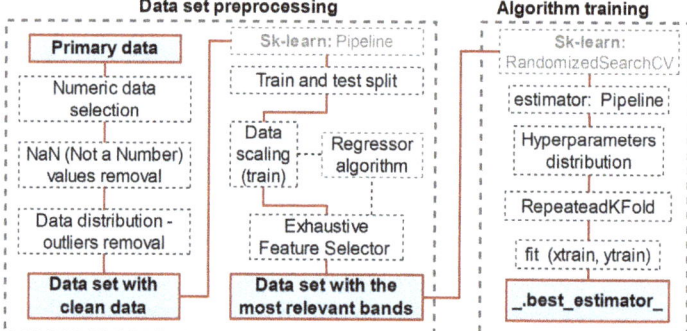

Figure 2. Workflow for data processing and training of ML algorithms.

2.4.2. Model Validation

The Repeated k-Fold-Cross-Validation method divided the training observations into n folds (sets) of the same size, repeating the cross-validation procedure with different randomization. The metrics used were: the Root Mean Square Error (RMSE), the Mean Absolute Error (MAE), and the coefficient of determination (r^2) that corresponds to the proportion of the total variance. They can be defined as follows [35]:

$$\text{RMSE}(y, \hat{y}) = \sqrt{\frac{\sum_{i=0}^{N-1}(y_i - \hat{y}_i)^2}{N}} CrossRef] \quad (1)$$

$$\text{MAE}(y, \hat{y}) = \frac{\sum_{i=0}^{N-1}|y_i - \hat{y}_i|}{N}. \quad (2)$$

$$r^2(y, \hat{y}) = 1 - \frac{\sum_{i=1}^{N}(y_i - \hat{y}_i)^2}{\sum_{i=1}^{N}(y_i - \bar{y})^2}. \quad (3)$$

where ($\hat{y}_i$) is the estimated value, (y_i) is the observed value and (N) is the number of samples.

3. Results

3.1. Data Preprocessing and Evaluation

The presence of cloudiness in the satellite images considerably reduced the number of coincident records between the radiometric data and the in situ data. A total of 34 low-quality satellite products affected by the presence of clouds in the total surface of the lakes were identified, therefore, they do not contain water reflectance information and were discarded for the study. Of these 34 images, 8 Landsat-8 and 16 Sentinel-2 images were identified for Lake Cajititlán, while for Lake Zapotlán there were 6 Landsat-8 and 4 Sentinel-2 images. On the other hand, there were images that presented cloudiness, only in some sampling points; therefore, they were corrected by means of masks that eliminated the pixels of clouds and shadows, keeping only the pixels with reflectance values of the surface of the lake water. In the final dataset, a total of 128 records were retained for the CA parameters in Cajitilán when using Landsat-8, while 98 records remained when Sentinel-2 was employed. For Zapotlán, 78 records were obtained for both Landsat-8 and Sentinel-2. It is worth noting that these records represent the data that aligned with the in situ monitoring. From these records, some extreme outliers of certain parameters were removed, so the number of records used to train the algorithms is variable. A comprehensive breakdown of the specific record counts employed for algorithm training is provided in Supplementary Table S1.

Figure 3 shows an example of cloud mask application for the Landsat-8 image of Lake Cajititlán, working with the combination of true color bands L8-b4 - L8-b3 - L8-b2 to identify clouds and bodies of water.

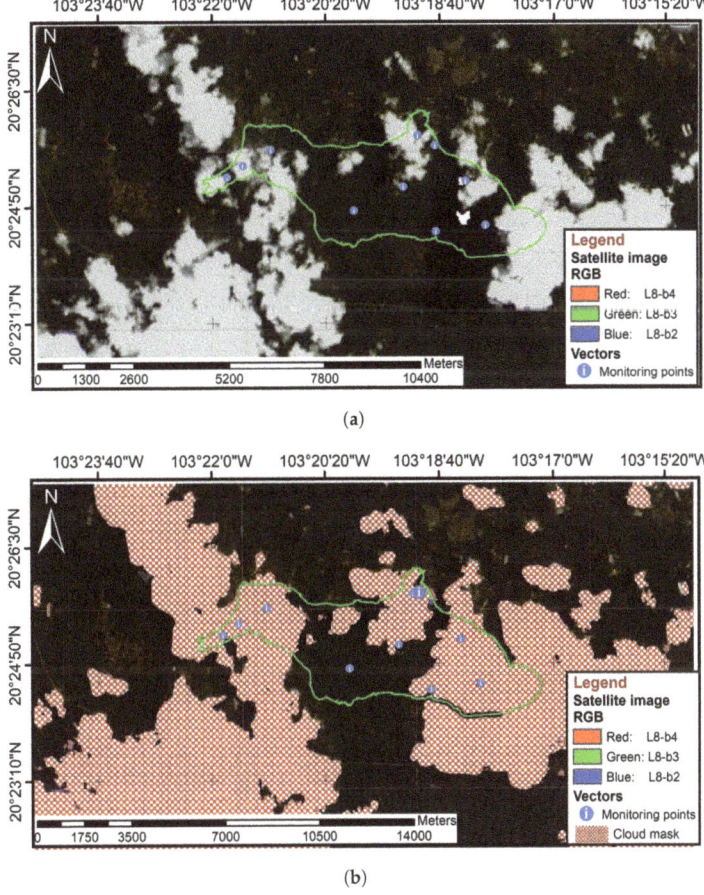

Figure 3. Application of cloud masks to Landsat-8 images of Lake Cajititlán. (**a**) Original image with cloudiness. (**b**) Image with cloud mask.

Radiometric data from Landsat-8 and Sentinel-2 were matched with data from the RNMCA creating a separate dataset for each lake. The normality test of Shapiro and Wilk [50] with a confidence interval of 95% reported that the data of the WQ parameters and the radiometric data of the Landsat-8 and Sentinel-2 images do not follow a normal distribution. The statistical results can be reviewed in Tables A3–A5 of the Appendix A. For Lake Cajititlán, a broader distribution of the Chl-a data was evidenced, varying from a minimum value of 0.34 mg/m^3 and to a maximum value of 1387.59 mg/m^3. In the case of turbidity, the range was between 9 NTU and 140 NTU, and for TSS, between 10 mg/L and 170 mg/L. On the other hand, for Lake Zapotlán, the distribution of the data for the parameters was found in a lower range than in Cajititlán. Thus, the ranges were: Chl-a between 0.30 mg/m^3 and 81 mg/m^3, TSS between 7 mg/L and 64 mg/L, and turbidity between 3.70 NTU and 100 NTU. For a more complete analysis, the distribution of the variables was graphically represented in a boxplot, as shown in Figure 4. Consequently, extreme outliers that were far from the mean were identified, mainly in the Chl-a data sets in Lake Cajititlán (Figure 4a) and turbidity in Lake Zapotlán (Figure 4b).

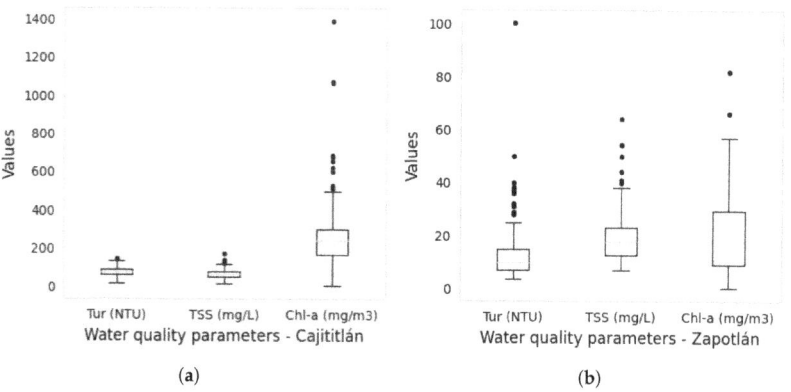

Figure 4. Distribution of the data set of water quality parameters for (**a**) Cajititlán, and (**b**) Zapotlán.

Figure 5 shows the analysis of the distribution of the Landsat-8 and Sentinel-2 radiometric data for the Cajititlán and Zapotlán lakes. The Landsat-8 images were generated by OLI sensors that measure the visible (VIS), near-infrared (NIR), and short-wavelength infrared (SWIR) regions of the spectrum. For its part, the Sentinel-2 images were generated by a multispectral instrument, which samples 13 VIS and NIR spectral bands at 10 m, red edge and SWIR at 20 m, and atmospheric bands at 60 m of spatial resolution in a wide strip with a global review frequency of 5 days. Thus, a larger interquartile range was reported for Sentinel-2, thus demonstrating a wider range in the distribution of this data set. Additionally, positive asymmetric biases are recorded for all the Landsat-8 and Sentinel-2 spectral bands, demonstrating that there are high reflectance values that move away from the majority concentration of the data. On the other hand, a greater number of outliers are recorded in the Landsat-8 (Figure 5a) and Sentinel-2 (Figure 5c) radiometric data for Lake Cajititlán, which are far from each other. Likewise, for Lake Zapotlán, there were fewer outliers in the Sentinel-2 (Figure 5d) and Landsat-8 radiometric data (Figure 5b), so that the range of dispersion of values is more adjusted except for L8-b5.

Figure 6 shows the heat map of the correlation matrix between the RNMCA values with the radiometric data of the Landsat-8 and Sentinel-2 spectral bands for the Cajititlán and Zapotlán lakes. According to this exploratory analysis, in Lake Cajititlán better correlations are reported between the in situ values of the RNMCA and the radiometric data of L8-b3 (green), L8-b4 (red) from the VIS and L8-b5 from the NIR. TSS registered the highest correlation coefficients, R = 0.68 in L8-b5, R = 0.55 in L8-b3 and R = 0.52 in L8-b4. Sentinel-2 showed slightly better correlations between RNMCA and S2-b5 (Red Edge 1), S2-b6 (Red

Edge 2), S2-b7 (Red Edge 3) and S2-b8 (NIR1), where Chl- a presented the best record with coefficients of R = 0.33 in S2-b6 and S2-b7, R = 0.31 in S2-b8 and R = 0.30 in S2-b5. On the other hand, for Lake Zapotlán, the best correlation records between the RNMCA and the Landsat-8 radiometric data occurred in L8-b3 and L8-b4 of the VIS. Turbidity was the parameter with the highest correlation values, R = 0.69 in L8-b3 and R = 0.57 in L8-b4. Likewise, the correlation between the RNMCA and the radiometric data from Sentinel-2 reported slightly better results in S2-b1 (aerosol), S2-b2 (blue), S2-b3 (green), S2-b4 (red) and S2-b5 (NIR). Turbidity was the parameter with the highest correlation values R = 0.36 in S2-b1, S2-b3 and S2-b5; R = 0.33 in S2-b2; and R = 0.31 in S2-b4. Consequently, the best correlations of the RNMCA data with the spectral bands in the spectral range of the VIS and NIR are evident. However, there are other wavelengths that maintain weaker correlations but can be identified by ML models and find patterns to improve predictive performance [4,21,38]. The combinations of spectral bands selected as predictors for each ML algorithm are presented in Table S1 of the Supplementary Material.

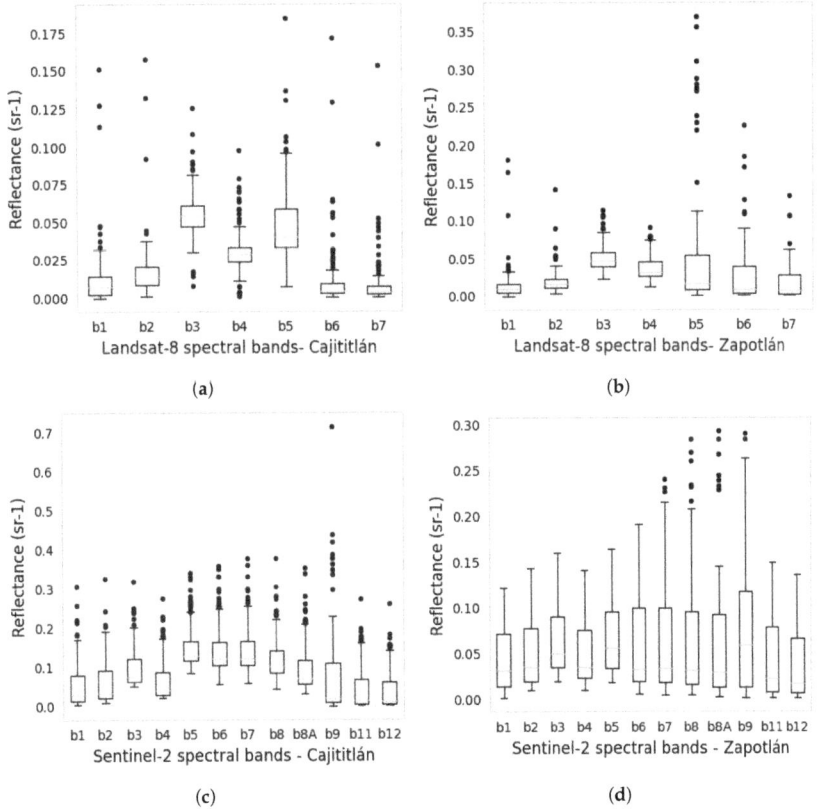

Figure 5. Distribution of radiometric data (**a**) Landsat-8 Cajititlán, and (**b**) Landsat-8 Zapotlán, (**c**) Sentinel-2 Cajititlán and (**d**) Sentinel-2 Zapotlán.

Figure 6. Heat map of the correlation matrix between the RNMCA values with the Landsat-8 and Sentinel-2 spectral bands for the Cajititlán and Zapotlán lakes.

3.2. Performance of Machine Learning Models

The best performances for the modeling were identified by comparing the r^2 values. In each of the lakes, the best results for the prediction of TSS, turbidity and Chl-a were found based on the ML algorithms and radiometric data evaluated. Figure 7a shows the results for Lake Cajititlán. It is observed that the Landsat-8 radiometric data were the most appropriate input variables to develop the ML predictive models. For example, for turbidity r^2 values between 0.64 and 0.82 were obtained, for TSS r^2 were between 0.42 and 0.68, and for Chl-a r^2 were between 0.34 and 0.60. Likewise, the models that presented the best performance were the MLP with r^2 between 0.58 and 0.78 and SLA with r^2 between 0.60 and 0.82, while the lowest performance was reported by the DTR with r^2 between 0.36 and 0.70. In the case of the models developed with Sentinel-2 radiometric data for turbidity, r^2 values between 0.14 and 0.57 were obtained, for TSS they reached a range of r^2 between 0.15 and 0.61, and for Chl-a the r^2 comprised results between 0.10 and 0.45. For this case, the most acceptable performances were achieved with the Ridge models with r^2 between 0.47 and 0.54, SLA with r^2 between 0.14 and 0.61, and MLP with r^2 between 0.24 and 0.55.

On the other hand, Figure 7b shows the results for the WQ prediction of Lake Zapotlán. It is observed that the results were more varied, not identifying a strong trend for any of the satellite products evaluated. Although, if a general average is analyzed for all ML models, r^2 = 0.44 is reported for Landsat-8 data models and r^2 = 0.49 for Sentiel-2 data models. These averages for each of the lakes, in fusion of the ML models, WQ parameters and satellite products can be seen in Tables A6 and A7 of the Appendix A. In Lake Zapotlán, the predictive capacity for turbidity with the Landsat-8 models reached r^2 values between 0.22 and 0.75, while the Sentinel-2 models registered r^2 between 0.27 and 0.69, lower values compared to those found in the lake Cajitlán. The same trend is observed for TSS with Landsat-8, this is, the r^2 vary between 0.18 and 0.58 while for Sentinel-2 the r^2 values are between 0.45 and 0.72. Finally, it is also observed that for Chl-a the values of r^2 are between 0.17 and 0.71 for Landsat-8 models, and r^2 between 0.22 and 0.57 for Sentinel-2 models. Another difference with what was found in Lake Cajititlán is that the MLP and SLA models were the best predictors for the Landsat-8 models, while the lowest performance was for DTR (r^2 between 0.17 and 0.23). In the case of the Sentinel-2 models, the MLP (r^2 between 0.57 and 0.70) and SLA (r^2 between 0.55 and 0.72) reached the best predictive capacity, and the DTR (r^2 between 0.26 and 0.45) reported the lowest performance. The difference found with the Sentinel-2 and Landsat-8 data is evident since the modeled algorithms varied in each of the lakes according to the approach, the hyperparameters, and the size of the training sample.

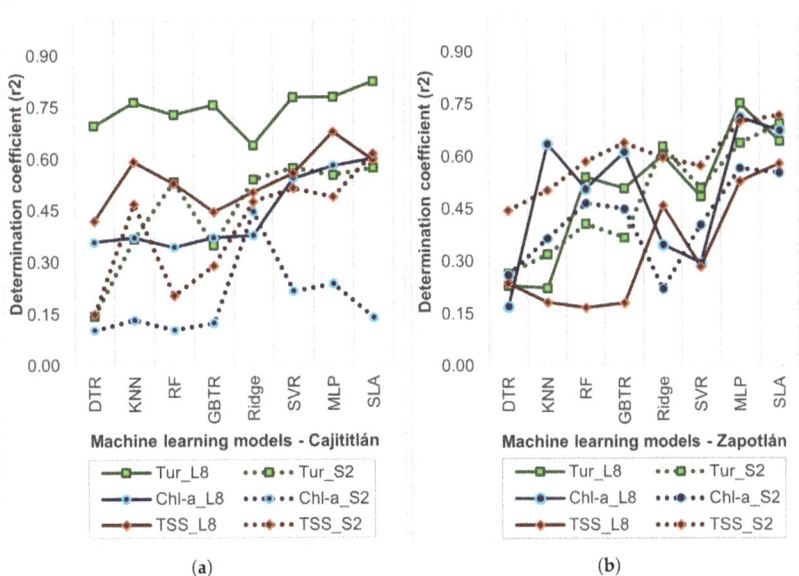

Figure 7. Assessment of the predictive capabilities of ML models for (**a**) Lake Cajititlán and (**b**) Lake Zapotlán. The models are identified by distinct symbols and colors, with green denoting turbidity, red representing TSS, and blue signifying Chl-a. Furthermore, solid lines correspond to models developed using Landsat 8 data (L8), while dashed lines correspond to models utilizing Sentinel-2 data (S2).

The r^2 in general does not present a perfect adjustment; however, the values close to the unit explain that the predictive variables have the tendency to provide valuable information about the response. Full validation of the ML models showing the error metrics, r^2, best algorithm, predictor spectral bands, and WQ parameters for each lake are shown in Table S1 of the Supplementary Material.

According to the results of the Repeated k-Fold-Cross-Validation, the best predictive models for TSS, Chl-a, and turbidity in each of the lakes were selected. In this way, Figure 8 presents the scatter diagrams of the residuals (in situ values vs. predicted values) for the in situ data of the WQ parameters that result from the best selected models. In the context of Lake Cajititlán, the SLA models developed using Landsat-8 radiometric data displayed superior performance for predicting turbidity, with $r^2 = 0.82$, RMSE = 9.93 NTU, and MAE = 7.69 NTU (Figure 8a). For Chl-a, $r^2 = 0.60$, RMSE = 48.06 mg/m^3 and MAE = 37.98 mg/m^3 were observed (Figure 8c). The MLP model, trained with Landsat-8 radiometric data, delivered the best results for TSS prediction, yielding $r^2 = 0.68$, RMSE = 13.42 mg/L and MAE = 10.36 mg/L (Figure 8e). Conversely, Lake Zapotlán exhibited distinct results, with the MLP models trained with Landsat-8 radiometric data outperforming other models. Turbidity prediction achieved $r^2 = 0.75$, RMSE = 2.05 NTU, and MAE = 1.10 NTU (Figure 8b) while Chl-a prediction displayed an $r^2 = 0.71$, RMSE = 6.16 mg/m^3 and MAE = 4.97 mg/m^3 (Figure 8d). In the case of TSS, the SLA model, trained with Sentinel-2 radiometric data, produced the best results, with an $r^2 = 0.72$, RMSE = 2.71 mg/L and MAE = 2.12 mg/L (Figure 8f).

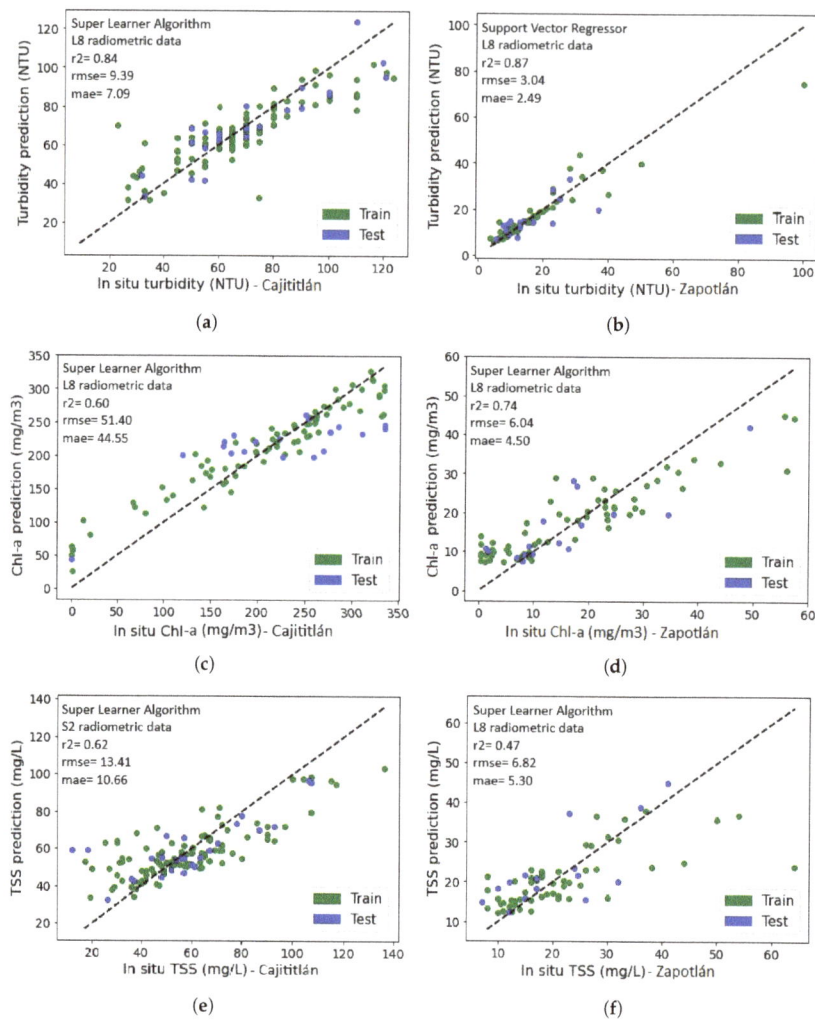

Figure 8. Distribution of the residuals for the ML models with the best performance in the prediction of the WQ parameters: (**a**) Turbidity in Cajititlán, (**b**) Turbidity in Zapotlán, (**c**) Chl-a in Cajititlán, (**d**) Chl-a in Zapotlán, (**e**) TSS in Cajititlán. (**f**) TSS in Zapotlán.

3.3. Water Quality Parameter Predictions

The best-performing ML models were used to predict the WQ parameters. The input data for the model were obtained from the Landsat-8 image of collection 2 and level 2 dated 10 November 2022. This image was not part of the training of the algorithms and was the most current available on the Earth Engine Data Catalog. Figure 9a,c show the qualitative analysis of the Landsat-8 image in natural color (combination: L8-b4, L8-b3, L8-b2), where a greenish coloration is observed for the two Lakes, being more intense in Lake Cajititlán. In addition, it is possible to perceive color variations in the water mirror of each lake, so that the variation in the spatial distribution of the WQ parameters is evident. Likewise, the spectral signatures of the sampling points of Lake Cajititlán showed high peaks at L8-b3 and L8-b5 (Figure 9b). This indicates a predominance of green color and energy in the NIR region, as shown in Figure 9a. For Lake Zapotlán, it is observed that the highest values of reflected energy are in the green region (L8-b3) as seen in Figure 9d. In general, when comparing the reflectance between the lakes, it is observed that the highest values are found in Lake Cajititlán and this is in accordance with the values of the WQ parameters in situ, where it is evident that there is a higher concentration of Chl-a, TSS, and turbidity in this lake.

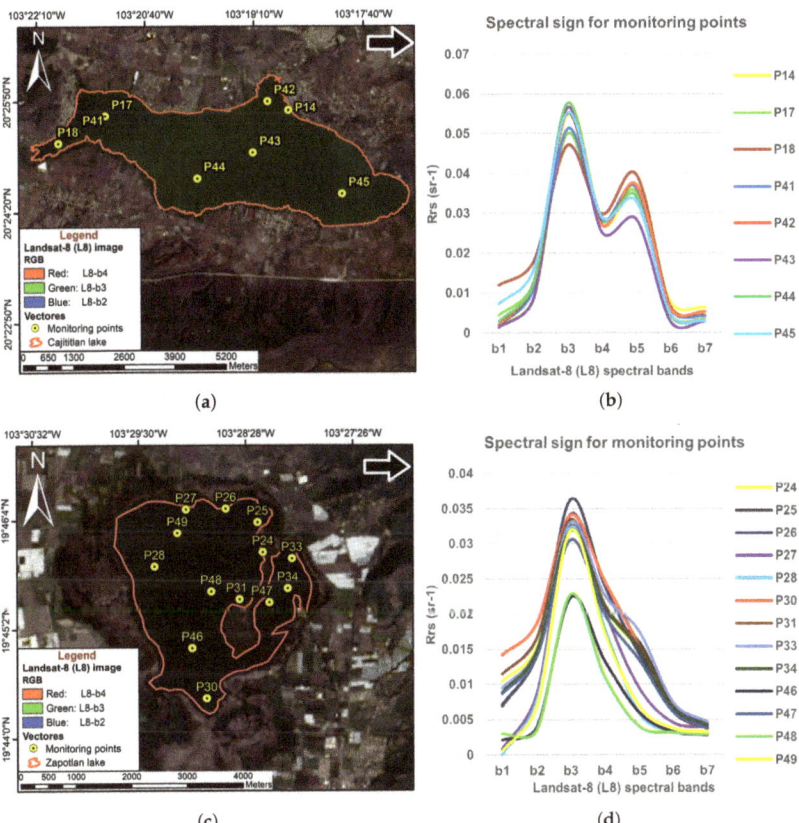

Figure 9. Landsat-8 image in natural color for lakes (**a**) Cajititlán and (**c**) Zapotlán. Spectral signal for the monitoring points managed by the RNMC for (**b**) Cajititlán and (**d**) Zapotlán.

The morphology of the lakes varies over time depending on several factors. Therefore, for the results of the predictions of the WQ parameters, the water mirror was delimited according to the optical information of the selected Landsat-8 image. For this, the combination of bands was used: L8-b6, L8-b5, and L8-b4 of vegetation analysis. Consequently, the pixels of the lake that represent vegetation on the shores of the two lakes and floating aquatic plants were eliminated, as is the case of Zapotlán, which has a considerable area of the water mirror covered by *Eichhornia crassipes* and *Typha latifolia* L. In this way, the input data for the prediction of WQ parameters were only pixels of the water surface, eliminating pixels of vegetation.

Figure 10 depicts the spatial distribution of Chl-a, SST, and turbidity on the water surface based on predictions generated by the best-performing ML models evaluated. It was evident that the concentrations of water quality parameters in Lake Cajititlán (Figure 10a) exceeded those observed in Lake Zapotlán (Figure 10b), indicating higher contamination levels in Cajititlán. In this context, lake Cajititlán was classified as a lake in a hypereutrophic state, according to the Carlson and Simpson [53] Trophic Status Index for Chl-a ($TSIChl - a = 9.81 * ln(Chl - a) + 30.6$). The spatial distribution of Chl-a oscillates between 90 mg/m^3 and 302 mg/m^3, and the largest surface area of the water mirror is above 200 mg/m^3. TSS levels range between 45.7 mg/L and 71 mg/L and according to the standards by CONAGUA [54] in the RNMCA, these values correspond to surface waters with low TSS content, that means generally natural conditions that favor the conservation of aquatic communities and unrestricted agricultural irrigation. Turbidity registers values in a range of 48 mg/L and 84 mg/L, these values are derived from the presence of high levels of suspended particles and algae according to the values recorded in the previous parameters. On the other hand, the spatial distribution of Chl-a in Lake Zapotlán classified the lake as mesotrophic where the concentrations were lower with values between 8 mg/m^3 and 25 mg/m^3. Likewise, in the highest concentrations, with values ranging between 25 mg/m^3 and 40 mg/m^3, the lake is classified as eutrophic. TSS levels were recorded between 11 mg/L and 17.5/L and according to CONAGUA [54] standards, these are excellent waters with particularly good quality. The turbidity of the lake presented low values that oscillate between 1.76 NTU and 12.46 NTU.

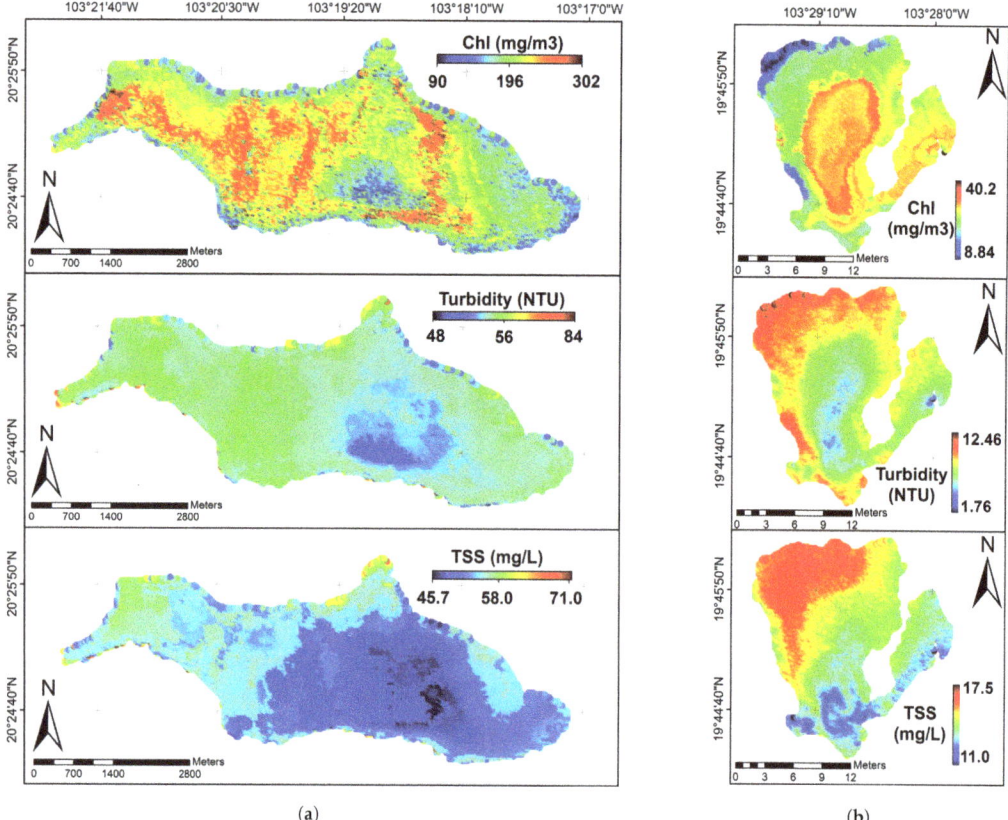

Figure 10. Spatial distribution maps for the estimation of Chl-a, TSS and turbidity with radiometric data from Landsat-8 10 November 2022). Results for Lake Cajititlán in the left column (**a**) and Zapotlán in the right column (**b**).

4. Discussion

4.1. Data Processing

Limited access to training data for ML algorithms was a notable challenge in this study. While the study had access to a substantial database from the RNMCA, aligning it with the acquisition data of satellite images proved to be a complex task. As a result, Landsat-8 and Sentinel-2 imagery was chosen, as these sensors offered lower temporal resolution compared to others and were suitable for capturing data from the relatively small continental water bodies under study. This choice aligns with common practices in the field, as documented in the literature review by Chen et al. [38], Yang et al. [14], Sagan et al. [8] and Topp et al. [4].

Subsequent to data acquisition, thorough data processing played a pivotal role. On one hand, the in situ data analysis revealed that the observed values did not conform to a normal distribution. Furthermore, the identification and removal of extreme outliers became essential to prevent their negative influence on the performance of ML algorithms. Outliers, as noted by Najah et al. [21], possess the potential to distort descriptive statistics such as mean and standard deviation, consequently leading to inaccurate predictions by the models. On the other hand, satellite data introduced limitations, primarily attributed to atmospheric conditions. The presence of clouds acted as a barrier, obstructing the retrieval of reflectance values from the water's surface [20]. Accurate predictive model development and validation depends on the availability of WQ data that aligns with uncontaminated reflectance data. When cloud cover affects reflectance data, it complicates the process of model calibration and validation, as noted by Gulati and Sharma [55] and Gholizadeh et al. [1]. Consequently, this study opted to eliminate pixels corresponding to cloud or shadow values. This was achieved by employing masking functions to identify and exclude such pixels, in line with recommendations from previous studies, such as Kochenour [56]. However, alternative methods, such as image reconstruction, warrant further exploration to potentially recover information and thereby increase the dataset available for training the predictive models [57,58].

The disparities in the correlations of WQ parameters between lakes Cajititlán and Zapotlán may be attributed to variations in factors such as the physical and chemical composition of the water in each lake. Parameters like Chl-a concentration, turbidity, and TSS have a direct impact on how light is reflected on the water's surface [4]. Additionally, rapid changes in water conditions could be influenced by factors like water flow, seasonality, and nearby pollution sources [14]. The geographical and topographical features of the surrounding region also play a significant role. Factors like vegetation, latitude, and altitude can affect the interaction of light with the water [1]. Moreover, disparities were observed in parameter-sensor correlations, with Landsat-8 exhibiting a more suitable spectral range for certain parameters. These findings underscore the necessity of accounting for the heterogeneity of water bodies and sensor characteristics when interpreting correlations in WQ studies utilizing satellite data. It highlights the complexity of WQ monitoring and the importance of evaluating the specific conditions of each lake to obtain accurate results [59].

4.2. ML Models Performance

The atmospheric effects and optical complexities observed in Lakes Cajititlán and Zapotlán had a noticeable impact on the quality of the input data used for the ML models. These limitations affected the scale and robustness of the models and are consistent with findings from other studies [1,8,14]. The optical complexities of these lakes were evident in the concentration values of WQ parameters, with Lake Cajititlán showing higher contamination levels compared to Lake Zapotlán. The quality of the radiometric data was also affected during cloud masking, where some shadow pixels remained unremoved, leading to alterations in the reflectance values of the water surface, as reported in other studies [4,20,57,58].

To address these challenges, the authors recommend developing models tailored to each specific body of water and adjusting hyperparameters based on the quality of the input data obtained during processing [2,38]. Choosing the right ML algorithms can be challenging due to the wide array of options available. Key considerations for selection include the quantity and quality of the available data. This is particularly relevant in fields like medicine, ecology, or geoscience, where data collection can be resource-intensive and may have ethical constraints [35,36]. To overcome limited datasets, researchers often turn to ML techniques specifically designed for such scenarios. These techniques aim to optimize ML models to deliver the best possible performance with the available data [21]. In this study, k-Fold-Cross-Validation was used to evaluate and enhance model performance, a technique previously employed by researchers such as Blix et al. [60], even with smaller training datasets. For extremely limited data, some researchers like Arias et al. [7] opt for leave-one-out cross-validation (LOOCV), although this approach demands substantial computational resources.

While some investigations [1,14] focus on using only visible (VIS) and near-infrared (NIR) spectral regions due to their empirical and semi-analytical modeling capabilities, this study initially leveraged all the spectral bands from Landsat-8 and Sentinel-2 satellites. This approach enabled access to information across a wide range of wavelengths, offering a more comprehensive view of the water surface and its characteristics [4,5]. Subsequently, the exhaustive feature selector was employed for feature selection to identify the most representative predictor bands [52]. This process aimed to assess the contributions of different spectral regions to the model, leading to the use of optimal spectral band combinations. Conclusively, the study did not definitively establish the most suitable spectral bands to use, as various models employing different combinations depending on the lake and the parameter being estimated. This ongoing challenge highlights the complexity of applying remote sensing in WQ detection. For instance, in the case of Chl-a, Zhang and Han [61] reported a strong correlation between Landsat-8 bands 1 and 4 and their combinations, while Kim et al. [62] used Landsat-8 bands 1 and 2, in addition to a ratio of band 2 to band 4. A more recent study by Arias et al. [5] used data from the RNMCA and used all Landsat-8 bands. On the other hand, for TSS and turbidity, several studies have been found that report a good correlation between the first five Landsat bands [1,12]. Lim and Choi [63] built multiple regression models to recover TSS from b2 and b5 of Landsat-8. In this way, the alternatives that can be used to define the input data for ML models are evidenced. What could be determined is that ML algorithms can produce models that capture complex and non-linear relationships between remotely sensed reflectance and WQ parameters [38].

To ensure the robustness of the models, a critical aspect involves randomizing the selection of training data and subsequently fine-tuning the hyperparameters of the ML algorithms, as recommended in prior research [64,65]. It is worth noting that hyperparameter tuning requires meticulous analysis and incurs a significant computational cost due to the multitude of alternatives that must be tested using GridSearch. Furthermore, the evaluation through cross-validation is imperative [66,67]. Among the ML models assessed, Support SVR and Ridge linear models demand calibration of fewer hyperparameters compared to their counterparts. The models that exhibited the highest performance were the SLA and the MLP. The MLP, being an artificial neural network model, uses backpropagation to adjust the weights between neurons, resulting in enhancing prediction accuracy. Its ability to handle complex and non-linear datasets provides it with a distinct advantage over other ML models [35,36]. In the case of the SLA, its superior performance can be attributed to its strategy of combining predictions from multiple models that individually demonstrated the best performance. Notably, the MLP and Ridge models were frequently selected due to their capacity to contribute to a diverse ensemble that can enhance individual predictions. This diversity is vital because if all combined models are too similar to one another, they may not effectively complement each other [64].

In summary, the prediction outcomes of this study are consistent with previous research conducted by Otto et al. [26], Torres [27], and Arias et al. [5], who investigated different water bodies. However, this study's distinct contribution lies in the evaluation of eight ML algorithms, introducing greater variability and overall performance improvement. The increased data overlap and performance enhancements achieved in this study highlighted the potential of remote sensing supported by ML techniques in the domain of WQ monitoring.

4.3. Prediction of WQ Parameters and Practical Application

This study presents a significant contribution in the field of WQ monitoring in aquatic bodies, specifically in the Cajititlán and Zapotlán lakes in the state of Jalisco, Mexico. One of the main distinguishing features of this work is that these lakes, which until now had remained largely unexplored in terms of remote sensing WQ monitoring, have been the subject of extensive analysis. This approach is essential in the current context, since, despite the extensive scientific literature dedicated to remote sensing techniques, our planet continues to be a dynamic and complex system in constant evolution [68]. Therefore, exclusive reliance on existing studies has proven insufficient and impractical [4]. Assessment of these lakes, which face continued deterioration in WQ over time, becomes an essential task.

The predictive ML models developed in this study open the door to new possibilities. The MLP and SLA algorithms, which were noted for their high performance, presented a promising approach for WQ monitoring in these lakes. These results have significant practical implications. First of all, the study highlights the importance of the integration of these techniques in the RNMCA. Since there are water bodies that have been excluded from monitoring campaigns due to certain limitations [5], the application of remote sensing supported by ML can expand the scope of analysis and contribute to the advancement of environmental monitoring efforts [2]. This integration would not only be beneficial in improving monitoring coverage but can also serve as an important precedent for early decision making. By enabling remote analysis of contamination, these techniques provide valuable information before physical site visits are made, which can be essential in proactive decision making [14]. In a broader social context, these techniques have direct relevance to society. By involving the community in assessing WQ and monitoring water bodies, citizen participation is encouraged, and greater awareness is promoted about the importance of conserving these resources. This collaboration between the community and researchers can empower society by providing them with the tools and knowledge necessary to actively participate in activities related to WQ preservation [2].

5. Conclusions

Working with historical data from the RNMCA, which conducts long-term monitoring campaigns spanning from 2009 to the present, has facilitated the development of a useful database for the study. Despite facing limitations stemming from atmospheric factors and occasional satellite data mismatches, this dataset has proven to be helpful for the development of ML models. To address these challenges, extensive hyperparameter tuning was performed and the widely used k-Fold-Cross-Validation technique was applied in data-limited scenarios. As a result, the ML models exhibited varying predictive capacities, with the MLP and SLA algorithms demonstrating superior performance, yielding valuable insights into the spatial distribution of Chl-a, SST, and turbidity in Lakes Cajititlán and Zapotlán.

Underscoring the significance of remote sensing, the study revealed that only through a qualitative analysis of spectral signatures within satellite images was it possible to identify heightened light reflection in the green and near-infrared wavelengths, a telltale sign of the greenish coloration characteristic of eutrophic waters in Lake Cajititlán.

Within this context, the study meticulously developed models that showcase the highest predictive capabilities. Importantly, these models were fine-tuned to accommodate the unique characteristics of each lake. The inability to generalize findings arises from the differences in water composition, topography, and various other environmental factors that distinguish the two lakes. This research has, therefore, generated invaluable data for the comprehensive analysis of these lakes, hitherto untouched in the realm of WQ monitoring through remote sensing. Consequently, this study lays the groundwork for future research endeavors in a rapidly growing field that has garnered the attention of both researchers and water management authorities.

The outcomes of the study also underscore the immense potential of integrating remote sensing techniques into the monitoring campaigns conducted by the RNMCA. This expansion offers the possibility of including more water bodies in monitoring efforts that were previously excluded due to a range of limitations. Furthermore, it sets a promising precedent for advancing environmental monitoring practices, ultimately facilitating more informed and timely decision making in water resource management.

Supplementary Materials: The following supporting information can be downloaded at: https://www.mdpi.com/article/10.3390/rs15235505/s1, Table S1: Validation Metrics for ML Models: Lake-Specific Results, Satellite Data, Hyperparameters, and Best Band Predictors.

Author Contributions: Conceptualization, V.Z.-G. and B.S.-R.; methodology F.H.V.-G.; formal analysis, K.J.G.-T., F.Z.-M. and B.S.-R.; investigation, F.H.V.-G. and K.J.G.-T.; writing—original draft preparation, F.H.V.-G.; writing—review and editing V.Z.-G., B.S.-R. and F.Z.-M. All authors have read and agreed to the published version of the manuscript.

Funding: This research was partially funded by a student scholarship awarded by the National Council of Humanities, Sciences and Technologies (CONAHCYT)—Mexico.

Data Availability Statement: The data presented in this study are available on request from the corresponding author. The data are not publicly available due to privacy restrictions.

Acknowledgments: We thank the United Stated Geological Service (USGS) and the European Space Agency (ESA) for providing the necessary Landsat-8 and Sentinel-2 images for the spectral data adquisition for this study. We are further grateful to the Comision Estatal del Agua (CONAGUA) for providing the field water quality measurements through the National Water Quality Monitoring Network (RNMCA). Finally, we would like to thank the Consejo Nacional de Ciencia y Tecnología (CONAHCYT) for the support through the student maintenance scholarship.

Conflicts of Interest: The authors declare no conflict of interest.

Abbreviations

The following abbreviations are used in this manuscript:

WQ	Water Quality
ML	Machine Learning
RNMCA	National Water Quality Monitoring Network
TSS	Total Suspended Solids
Chl-a	Chlorophyll-a
MLP	Multilayer Perceptron
SLA	Super Learner Algorithm
GEE	Google Earth Engine
MRSE	Mean Square Error
MAE	Mean Absolute Error
r^2	Coefficient of Determination
L8	Landsat-8
S2	Sentinel-2
VIS	Visible
NIR	Near Infrared
SWIR	Short Wavelength Infrared

Appendix A

Table A1. Characteristics of Landsat-8 satellite products.

Band	Sensor	Wavelength (μm)	Spatial Resolution (m)	Radiometric Resolution
1—Ultra blue (Coastal Aerosol)	OLI	0.43–0.45	30	16 bits
2—Blue	OLI	0.45–0.51	30	16 bits
3—Green	OLI	0.53–0.59	30	16 bits
4—Red	OLI	0.64–0.67	30	16 bits
5—Near infrared (NIR)	OLI	0.85–0.88	30	16 bits
6—Shortwave infrared (SWIR1)	OLI	1.57–1.65	30	16 bits
7—Shortwave infrared (SWIR2)	OLI	2.11–2.29	30	16 bits
8—Panchromatic	OLI	0.52–0.90	15	16 bits
9—Cirrus	OLI	1.36–1.38	30	16 bits
10—Thermal infrared 1	TIRS	10.60–11.19	100	16 bits
11—Thermal infrared 2	TIRS	11.50–12.51	100	16 bits

Table A2. Characteristics of Sentinel-2 satellite products.

Band	S2A Central Wavelength (nm)	S2A Band Width (nm)	S2B Central Wavelength (nm)	S2B Band Width (nm)	Spatial Resolution (m)
1—Coastal aerosol	443.9	27	442.3	45	60
2—Blue	496.6	98	492.1	98	10
3—Green	560.0	45	559	46	10
4—Red	664.5	38	665	39	10
5—Vegetation red edge	703.9	19	703.8	20	20
6—Vegetation red edge	740.2	18	739.1	18	20
7—Vegetation red edge	782.5	28	779.7	28	20
8—NIR	835.1	145	833	133	10
8a—Vegetation red edge	864.8	33	864	32	20
9—Water vapor	945.0	26	943.2	27	60
10—SWIR - cirrus	1373.5	75	1376.9	76	60
11—SWIR	1610.4	141	1613.7	143	20
12—SWIR	2185.7	238	2202.4	242	20

Table A3. Water Quality Parameters—Descriptive Statistics and Shapiro-Wilk Test.

Lake	Parameter	Count	Mean	Std	Min	25%	50%	75%	Max	Statistic	p-Value (95%)
Cajititlán	TSS	252.00	63.71	24.28	10.00	48.00	62.50	76.00	170.00	0.98	1.64×10^{-3}
	Tur	252.00	71.71	24.23	9.00	55.00	70.00	88.13	140.00	0.98	1.38×10^{-3}
	Chl-a	252.00	241.46	154.87	0.34	166.25	239.18	299.89	1387.59	0.76	6.36×10^{-19}
Zapotlán	TSS	153.00	19.58	9.67	7.00	13.00	18.00	23.00	64.00	0.86	5.74×10^{-11}
	Tur	153.00	12.99	10.54	3.70	7.30	10.00	15.00	100.00	0.63	5.15×10^{-18}
	Chl-a	153.00	21.20	14.82	0.30	10.11	19.43	28.44	81.78	0.94	7.17×10^{-6}

Table A4. Landsat-8 radiometric data set—Descriptive Statistics and Shapiro-Wilk Test.

Lake	Parameter	Count	Mean	Std	Min	25%	50%	75%	Max	Statistic	p-Value (95%)
Cajititlán	L8-b1	129	0.0130	0.0210	0.00004	0.0020	0.0076	0.0144	0.15	0.53	1.36×10^{-18}
	L8-b2	129	0.0183	0.0197	0.0010	0.0087	0.0137	0.0205	0.16	0.54	2.40×10^{-18}
	L8-b3	129	0.0554	0.0164	0.0081	0.0471	0.0543	0.0611	0.13	0.93	4.13×10^{-6}
	L8-b4	129	0.0309	0.0154	0.0012	0.0235	0.0287	0.0335	0.10	0.89	1.65×10^{-8}
	L8-b5	129	0.0477	0.0269	0.0075	0.0331	0.0400	0.0583	0.18	0.86	1.52×10^{-9}
	L8-b6	129	0.0113	0.0217	0.0003	0.0030	0.0044	0.0093	0.17	0.45	6.42×10^{-20}
	L8-b7	129	0.0092	0.0181	0.0005	0.0025	0.0034	0.0076	0.15	0.42	2.02×10^{-20}

Table A4. Cont.

Lake	Parameter	Count	Mean	Std	Min	25%	50%	75%	Max	Statistic	p-Value (95%)
	L8-b10	129	23.87	3.94	11.15	21.36	24.18	26.77	31.16	0.97	4.13×10^{-3}
	L8-b1	78	0.0174	0.0296	0.0001	0.0049	0.0095	0.0162	0.18	0.49	5.78×10^{-15}
	L8-b2	78	0.0219	0.0203	0.0034	0.0105	0.0162	0.0229	0.14	0.67	5.66×10^{-12}
	L8-b3	78	0.0521	0.0208	0.0224	0.0383	0.0468	0.0579	0.11	0.88	1.62×10^{-6}
Zapotlán	L8-b4	78	0.0374	0.0195	0.0119	0.0259	0.0307	0.0454	0.09	0.88	1.68×10^{-6}
	L8-b5	78	0.0596	0.0923	0.0007	0.0088	0.0158	0.0546	0.37	0.63	8.57×10^{-13}
	L8-b6	78	0.0303	0.0446	0.0008	0.0029	0.0083	0.0390	0.23	0.68	1.06×10^{-11}
	L8-b7	78	0.0193	0.0262	0.0007	0.0024	0.0071	0.0272	0.13	0.71	4.00×10^{-11}
	L8-b10	78	23.27	4.03	8.63	20.89	24.34	26.47	29.13	0.90	2.10×10^{-5}

Table A5. Sentinel-2 radiometric data set—Descriptive statistics and Shapiro-Wilk Test.

Lake	Parameter	Count	Mean	Std	Min	25%	50%	75%	Max	Statistic	p-Value (95%)
	S2-b1	128	0.0572	0.0613	0.0035	0.0127	0.0284	0.0790	0.31	0.79	2.76×10^{-12}
	S2-b2	128	0.0634	0.0600	0.0091	0.0203	0.0341	0.0928	0.33	0.79	3.75×10^{-12}
	S2-b3	128	0.1017	0.0558	0.0508	0.0624	0.0739	0.1206	0.32	0.80	5.55×10^{-12}
	S2-b4	128	0.0694	0.0586	0.0209	0.0279	0.0402	0.0878	0.27	0.77	6.13×10^{-13}
Cajititlán	S2-b5	128	0.1547	0.0575	0.0856	0.1162	0.1289	0.1658	0.34	0.80	4.55×10^{-12}
	S2-b6	128	0.1449	0.0648	0.0554	0.1048	0.1205	0.1628	0.36	0.85	3.23×10^{-10}
	S2-b7	128	0.1461	0.0674	0.0575	0.1036	0.1216	0.1640	0.38	0.85	4.28×10^{-10}
	S2-b8	128	0.1242	0.0639	0.0419	0.0851	0.1005	0.1401	0.38	0.84	1.24×10^{-10}
	S2-b8A	128	0.1004	0.0690	0.0313	0.0555	0.0690	0.1172	0.35	0.80	8.03×10^{-12}
	S2-b9	128	0.0738	0.1126	0.0003	0.0091	0.0192	0.1100	0.71	0.66	6.99×10^{-16}
	S2-b11	128	0.0471	0.0604	0.0015	0.0050	0.0136	0.0676	0.27	0.74	1.16×10^{-13}
	S2-b12	128	0.0423	0.0553	0.0009	0.0043	0.0118	0.0600	0.26	0.74	8.44×10^{-14}
	S2-b1	79	0.0421	0.0330	0.0007	0.0129	0.0314	0.0709	0.12	0.88	3.30×10^{-6}
	S2-b2	79	0.0476	0.0344	0.0090	0.0188	0.0342	0.0768	0.14	0.88	2.42×10^{-6}
	S2-b3	79	0.0633	0.0362	0.0180	0.0344	0.0491	0.0890	0.16	0.89	3.42×10^{-6}
	S2-b4	79	0.0501	0.0361	0.0091	0.0222	0.0345	0.0745	0.14	0.87	7.48×10^{-7}
Zapotlán	S2-b5	79	0.0660	0.0399	0.0178	0.0326	0.0553	0.0947	0.16	0.91	5.45×10^{-5}
	S2-b6	79	0.0613	0.0537	0.0049	0.0182	0.0324	0.0982	0.19	0.86	5.85×10^{-7}
	S2-b7	79	0.0656	0.0629	0.0042	0.0175	0.0333	0.0984	0.24	0.83	4.25×10^{-8}
	S2-b8	79	0.0637	0.0683	0.0034	0.0152	0.0312	0.0943	0.28	0.79	2.84×10^{-9}
	S2-b8A	79	0.0645	0.0725	0.0017	0.0121	0.0293	0.0917	0.29	0.78	2.01×10^{-9}
	S2-b9	79	0.0781	0.0802	0.0005	0.0125	0.0584	0.1164	0.29	0.85	1.60×10^{-7}
	S2-b11	79	0.0439	0.0430	0.0007	0.0071	0.0214	0.0773	0.15	0.85	2.54×10^{-7}
	S2-b12	79	0.0353	0.0346	0.0012	0.0060	0.0163	0.0652	0.13	0.85	2.01×10^{-7}

Table A6. Means of the coefficient of determination (r^2) for the modeling results for Lake Cajititlán, as a function of CA parameters, ML models and satellite products.

ML Models	Tur-L8	Chl-a-L8	TSS-L8	Mean for Models	Tur-S2	Chl-a-S2	TSS-S2	Mean for Models
DTR	0.70	0.36	0.42	0.49	0.14	0.10	0.15	0.13
KNN	0.76	0.37	0.59	0.58	0.37	0.13	0.47	0.32
RF	0.73	0.34	0.53	0.53	0.53	0.10	0.20	0.28
GBTR	0.76	0.37	0.44	0.52	0.35	0.12	0.29	0.25
Ridge	0.64	0.38	0.50	0.51	0.54	0.45	0.47	0.49
SVR	0.78	0.54	0.56	0.63	0.57	0.22	0.51	0.43
MLP	0.78	0.58	0.68	0.68	0.55	0.24	0.49	0.43
SLA	0.82	0.60	0.60	0.67	0.57	0.14	0.61	0.44
Mean for WQ parameters	0.75	0.44	0.54	-	0.45	0.19	0.40	0.35
General mean		0.58				0.35		

The table displays the horizontal averages for the ML models and the vertical averages for the CA parameters. The overall average corresponds to the average of all ML models for each set of satellite data (Landsat-8 and Sentinel-2).

Table A7. Means of the coefficient of determination (r2) for the modeling results for Lake Zapotlán, as a function of CA parameters, ML models and satellite products.

ML Models	Tur-L8	Chl-a-L8	TSS-L8	Mean for Models	Tur-S2	Chl-a-S2	TSS-S2	Mean for Models
DTR	0.23	0.17	0.24	0.21	0.27	0.26	0.45	0.32
KNN	0.22	0.64	0.18	0.35	0.32	0.37	0.50	0.40
RF	0.54	0.51	0.17	0.41	0.41	0.47	0.59	0.49
GBTR	0.51	0.61	0.18	0.43	0.37	0.45	0.64	0.49
Ridge	0.60	0.35	0.46	0.47	0.63	0.22	0.60	0.48
SVR	0.48	0.29	0.28	0.35	0.51	0.40	0.57	0.50
MLP	0.75	0.71	0.53	0.66	0.64	0.57	0.70	0.63
SLA	0.64	0.67	0.58	0.63	0.69	0.55	0.72	0.65
Mean for WQ parameters	0.50	0.49	0.33	-	0.48	0.41	0.59	0.49
General mean		0.44				0.49		

The table displays the horizontal averages for the ML models and the vertical averages for the CA parameters. The overall average corresponds to the average of all ML models for each set of satellite data (Landsat-8 and Sentinel-2).

References

1. Gholizadeh, M.H.; Melesse, A.M.; Reddi, L. A Comprehensive Review on Water Quality Parameters Estimation Using Remote Sensing Techniques. *Sensors* **2016**, *16*, 1298. [CrossRef]
2. Giardino, C.; Brando, V.E.; Gege, P.; Pinnel, N.; Hochberg, E.; Knaeps, E.; Reusen, I.; Doerffer, R.; Bresciani, M.; Braga, F.; et al. Imaging Spectrometry of Inland and Coastal Waters: State of the Art, Achievements and Perspectives. *Surv. Geophys.* **2019**, *40*, 401–429. [CrossRef]
3. Spyrakos, E.; O'Donnell, R.; Hunter, P.D.; Miller, C.; Scott, M.; Simis, S.G.; Neil, C.; Barbosa, C.C.; Binding, C.E.; Bradt, S.; et al. Optical types of inland and coastal waters. *Limnol. Oceanogr.* **2018**, *63*, 846–870. [CrossRef]
4. Topp, S.N.; Pavelsky, T.M.; Jensen, D.; Simard, M.; Ross, M.R.V. Research Trends in the Use of Remote Sensing for Inland Water Quality Science: Moving Towards Multidisciplinary Applications. *Water* **2020**, *12*, 169. [CrossRef]
5. Rodríguez, L.F.A.; Duan, Z.; Torres, J.D.D.; Hazas, M.B.; Huang, J.; Kumar, B.U.; Tuo, Y.; Disse, M. Integration of Remote Sensing and Mexican Water Quality Monitoring System Using an Extreme Learning Machine. *Sensors* **2021**, *21*, 4118. [CrossRef]
6. Ritchie, J.; Zimba, P.; Everitt, J. Remote sensing techniques to assess water quality. *Photogramm. Eng. Remote Sens.* **2003**, *69*, 695 704.
7. Rodríguez, L.F.A.; Duan, Z.; Sepúlveda, R.; Martinez, S.I.M.; Disse, M. Monitoring Water Quality of Valle de Bravo Reservoir, Mexico, Using Entire Lifespan of MERIS Data and Machine Learning Approaches. *Remote Sens.* **2020**, *12*, 1586. [CrossRef]
8. Sagan, V.; Peterson, K.T.; Maimaitijiang, M.; Sidike, P.; Sloan, J.; Greeling, B.A.; Maalouf, S.; Adams, C. Monitoring inland water quality using remote sensing: Potential and limitations of spectral indices, bio-optical simulations, machine learning, and cloud computing. *Earth-Sci. Rev.* **2020**, *205*, 103187. [CrossRef]
9. Ritchie, J.C.; Schiebe, F.R.; McHenry, R.J. Remote sensing of suspended sediments in surface waters. *Photogramm Eng. Remote Sens.* **1976**, *42*, 1539–1545.
10. Papa, F.; Frappart, F. Surface Water Storage in Rivers and Wetlands Derived from Satellite Observations: A Review of Current Advances and Future Opportunities for Hydrological Sciences. *Remote Sens.* **2021**, *13*, 4162. [CrossRef]
11. Cretaux, J.F.; Calmant, S.; Papa, F.; Frappart, F.; Paris, A.; Berge-Nguyen, M. Inland surface waters quantity monitored from remote sensing. *Surv. Geophys.* **2023**, *44*, 1519–1552.
12. Wang, H.; Wang, J.; Cui, Y.; Yan, S. Consistency of Suspended Particulate Matter Concentration in Turbid Water Retrieved from Sentinel-2 MSI and Landsat-8 OLI Sensors. *Sensors* **2021**, *21*, 1662.
13. Chawla, I.; Karthikeyan, L.; Mishra, A.K. A review of remote sensing applications for water security: Quantity, quality, and extremes. *J. Hydrol.* **2020**, *585*, 124826. [CrossRef]
14. Yang, H.; Kong, J.; Hu, H.; Du, Y.; Gao, M.; Chen, F. A Review of Remote Sensing for Water Quality Retrieval: Progress and Challenges. *Remote Sens.* **2022**, *14*, 1770. [CrossRef]
15. Abdelal, Q.; Assaf, M.N.; Al-Rawabdeh, A.; Arabasi, S.; Rawashdeh, N.A. Assessment of Sentinel-2 and Landsat-8 OLI for Small-Scale Inland Water Quality Modeling and Monitoring Based on Handheld Hyperspectral Ground Truthing. *J. Sensors* **2022**, *2022*, 4643924. [CrossRef]
16. Caballero, I.; Roca, M.; Santos Echeandía, J.; Bernárdez, P.; Navarro, G. Use of the Sentinel-2 and Landsat-8 Satellites for Water Quality Monitoring: An Early Warning Tool in the Mar Menor Coastal Lagoon. *Remote Sens.* **2022**, *14*, 2744. [CrossRef]
17. Hafeez, S.; Wong, M.S.; Abbas, S.; Asim, M. Evaluating Landsat-8 and Sentinel-2 Data Consistency for High Spatiotemporal Inland and Coastal Water Quality Monitoring. *Remote Sens.* **2022**, *14*, 3155. [CrossRef]
18. Leggesse, E.S.; Zimale, F.A.; Sultan, D.; Enku, T.; Srinivasan, R.; Tilahun, S.A. Predicting Optical Water Quality Indicators from Remote Sensing Using Machine Learning Algorithms in Tropical Highlands of Ethiopia. *Hydrology* **2023**, *10*, 110. [CrossRef]
19. Rodríguez, L.F.A.; Tüzün, U.F.; Duan, Z.; Huang, J.; Tuo, Y.; Disse, M. Global Water Quality of Inland Waters with Harmonized Landsat-8 and Sentinel-2 Using Cloud-Computed Machine Learning. *Remote Sens.* **2023**, *15*, 1390. [CrossRef]

20. Skakun, S.; Wevers, J.; Brockmann, C.; Doxani, G.; Aleksandrov, M.; Batič, M.; Frantz, D.; Gascon, F.; Gómez-Chova, L.; Hagolle, O.; et al. Cloud Mask Intercomparison eXercise (CMIX): An evaluation of cloud masking algorithms for Landsat 8 and Sentinel-2. *Remote Sens. Environ.* **2022**, *274*, 112990. [CrossRef]
21. Ahmed, A.N.; Othman, F.B.; Afan, H.A.; Ibrahim, R.K.; Fai, C.M.; Hossain, M.S.; Ehteram, M.; Elshafie, A. Machine learning methods for better water quality prediction. *J. Hydrol.* **2019**, *578*, 124084. [CrossRef]
22. Papenfus, M.; Schaeffer, B.; Pollard, A.I.; Loftin, K. Exploring the potential value of satellite remote sensing to monitor chlorophyll-a for US lakes and reservoirs. *Environ. Monit. Assess.* **2020**, *192*. [CrossRef]
23. Rodríguez López, L.; Usta, D.B.; Duran Llacer, I.; Alvarez, L.B.; Yépez, S.; Bourrel, L.; Frappart, F.; Urrutia, R. Estimation of Water Quality Parameters through a Combination of Deep Learning and Remote Sensing Techniques in a Lake in Southern Chile. *Remote Sens.* **2023**, *15*, 4157. [CrossRef]
24. Bettencourt, P.; Wasserman, J.C.; Ferreira Dias, F.; Alves, P.R.; Bernardino Bezerra, D.; Américo Santos, C.; Perez Zotes, L.; Barros, S.R. Remote Sensing Applied to the Evaluation of Spatial and Temporal Variation of Water Quality in a Coastal Environment, Southeast Brazil. *J. Geogr. Inf. Syst.* **2019**, *11*, 500–521. [CrossRef]
25. Germán, A.; Shimoni, M.; Beltramone, G.; Rodríguez, M.I.; Muchiut, J.; Bonansea, M.; Scavuzzo, C.M.; Ferral, A. Space-time monitoring of water quality in an eutrophic reservoir using SENTINEL-2 data - A case study of San Roque, Argentina. *Remote Sens. Appl. Soc. Environ.* **2021**, *24*, 100614. [CrossRef]
26. Otto, P.; Rodríguez, R.V.; Keesstra, S.; Becerril, E.L.; de Anda, J.; Mena, L.H.; del Real Olvera, J.; de Jesús Díaz Torres, J. Time Delay Evaluation on the Water-Leaving Irradiance Retrieved from Empirical Models and Satellite Imagery. *Remote Sens.* **2019**, *12*, 87. [CrossRef]
27. Vera, M.A.T. Mapping of total suspended solids using Landsat imagery and machine learning. *Int. J. Environ. Sci. Technol.* **2023**, *20*, 11877–11890. [CrossRef]
28. CONAGUA. *Actualización de la Disponibilidad Media Anual de Agua en el Acuífero Cajititlán (1403), Estado de Jalisco*; Subdirección General Técnica Gerencia de Aguas Subterráneas: Ciudad de México, Mexico, 2020.
29. Instituto Nacional de Estadística y Geografía (INEGI). Cuenca hidrológica Laguna de Zapotlán. *Humedales* **2019**, *8*, 32.
30. Morán-Valencia, M.; Flegl, M.; Güemes-Castorena, D. A state-level analysis of the water system management efficiency in Mexico: Two-stage DEA approach. *Water Resour. Ind.* **2023**, *29*, 100200.
31. Niroumand-Jadidi, M.; Bovolo, F.; Bruzzone, L. Water quality retrieval from PRISMA hyperspectral images: First experience in a turbid lake and comparison with sentinel-2. *Remote Sens.* **2020**, *12*, 3984.
32. Mbongowo, M. Use of Hyperspectral Remote Sensing to Estimate Water Quality. In *Processing and Analysis of Hyperspectral Data*; Chen, J., Song, Y., Li, H., Eds.; IntechOpen: Rijeka, Croatia, 2019; Chapter 6. [CrossRef]
33. Anderson, E.P.; Jackson, S.; Tharme, R.E.; Douglas, M.; Flotemersch, J.E.; Zwarteveen, M.; Lokgariwar, C.; Montoya, M.; Wali, A.; Tipa, G.T.; et al. Understanding rivers and their social relations: A critical step to advance environmental water management. *Wiley Interdiscip. Rev. Water* **2019**, *6*, e1381.
34. Caro Borrero, A.; Carmona Jiménez, J.; Figueroa, F. Water resources conservation and rural livelihoods in protected areas of central Mexico. *J. Rural Stud.* **2020**, *78*, 12–24.
35. Pedregosa, F.; Varoquaux, G.; Gramfort, A.; Michel, V.; Thirion, B.; Grisel, O.; Blondel, M.; Prettenhofer, P.; Weiss, R.; Dubourg, V.; et al. Scikit-learn: Machine Learning in Python. *J. Mach. Learn. Res.* **2011**, *12*, 2825–2830.
36. Botón, C.C.; Pérez, D.C.; CasanovaMateo, C.; Ghimire, S.; Prada, E.C.; Gutierrez, P.A.; Deo, R.C.; Sanz, S.S. Machine learning regression and classification methods for fog events prediction. *Atmos. Res.* **2022**, *272*, 106157. [CrossRef]
37. Lemaitre, G. sklearn.ensemble.StackingRegressor, 2023. Available online: https://scikit-learn.org/stable/modules/generated/sklearn.ensemble.StackingRegressor.html (accessed on 21 April 2023).
38. Chen, Y.; Song, L.; Liu, Y.; Yang, L.; Li, D. A Review of the Artificial Neural Network Models for Water Quality Prediction. *Appl. Sci.* **2020**, *10*, 5776. [CrossRef]
39. Caro Becerra, J.L.; Vizcaíno Rodríguez, L.A.; Michel Parra, J.G.; Mayoral Ruiz, P.A.; Reyes Barragán, J.L. The Importance of Informative Data Base of the Wetlands in the Lake Cajititlán, Previous Step for the Proposal as a Ramsar Site. In *Water Availability and Management in Mexico*; Otazo Sánchez, E.M., Navarro Frómeta, A.E., Singh, V.P., Eds.; Springer International Publishing: Cham, Switzerland, 2020; pp. 233–245. [CrossRef]
40. CEA-Jalisco. Datos Abiertos del Sistema de Calidad del Agua, 2022. Available online: https://www.ceajalisco.gob.mx/contenido/datos_abiertos/ (accessed on 16 March 2022).
41. APHA. *Standard Methods for the Examination of Water and Wastewater*; Water Environmental Federation: Alexandria, VA, USA, 1985.
42. Secretaría de Economía. NMX-AA-038-SCFI-2001. Análisis de agua—Determinación de turbiedad en aguas naturales, residuales y residuales tratadas—Método de prueba (Cancela a la NMX-AA038-1981). *Official Gazette of the Federation*, 1 August 2001. p. 15
43. Secretaría de Economía. NMX-AA-034-SCFI-2015. Análisis de agua—Medición de sólidos y sales disueltas en aguas naturales, residuales y residuales tratadas—Método de prueba (Cancela a la NMX-AA-034-SCFI-2001). *Official Gazette of the Federation*, 16 October 2015; p. 16
44. Kutser, T.; Paavel, B.; Verpoorter, C.; Ligi, M.; Soomets, T.; Toming, K.; Casal, G.; Zhang, Y.; Giardino, C.; Li, L.; et al. Remote Sensing of Black Lakes and Using 810 nm Reflectance Peak for Retrieving Water Quality Parameters of Optically Complex Waters. *Remote Sens.* **2016**, *8*, 497. [CrossRef]

45. Attard, G. An Intro to the Earth Engine Python API. 2023. Available online: https://developers.google.com/earth-engine/tutorials/community/intro-to-python-api (accessed on 13 February 2023).
46. Braaten, J. Sentinel-2 Cloud Masking with s2cloudless. 2023. Available online: https://developers.google.com/earth-engine/tutorials/community/sentinel-2-s2cloudless (accessed on 25 February 2023).
47. Kochenour, C. Remote Sensing with Google Earth Engine. 2020. Available online: https://calekochenour.github.io/remote-sensing-textbook/03-beginner/chapter12-cloud-masking.html (accessed on 17 April 2022).
48. Vanhellemont, Q.; Ruddick, K. Atmospheric correction of metre-scale optical satellite data for inland and coastal water applications. *Remote Sens. Environ.* **2018**, *216*, 586–597. [CrossRef]
49. Nair, J.P.; Vijaya, M. River water quality prediction and index classification using machine learning. *J. Phys. Conf. Ser.* **2022**, *2325*, 012011.
50. Shapiro, S.S.; Wilk, M.B. An analysis of variance test for normality (complete samples). *Biometrika* **1965**, *52*, 591–611.
51. Vinutha, H.P.; Poornima, B.; Sagar, B.M. Detection of outliers using interquartile range technique from intrusion dataset. *Adv. Intell. Syst. Comput.* **2018**, *701*, 511–518. [CrossRef]
52. Raschka, S. MLxtend: Providing machine learning and data science utilities and extensions to Python's scientific computing stack. *J. Open Source Softw.* **2018**, *3*, 638. [CrossRef]
53. Carlson, R.E.; Simpson, J. A coordinator's guide to volunteer lake monitoring methods. *N. Am. Lake Manag. Soc.* **1996**, *96*, 305.
54. CONAGUA. Red Nacional de Monitoreo de la Calidad del Agua. 2020. Available online: http://dgeiawf.semarnat.gob.mx:8080/ibi_apps/WFServlet?IBIF_ex=D3_R_AGUA05_03&IBIC_user=dgeia_mce&IBIC_pass=dgeia_mce (accessed on 19 October 2021).
55. Gulati, S.; Sharma, S. Challenges and Responses Towards Sustainable Future Through Machine Learning and Deep Learning. In *Data Visualization and Knowledge Engineering: Spotting Data Points with Artificial Intelligence*; Hemanth, J., Bhatia, M., Geman, O., Eds.; Springer International Publishing: Cham, Switzerland, 2020; pp. 151–169. [CrossRef]
56. Kachroud, M.; Trolard, F.; Kefi, M.; Jebari, S.; Bourrié, G. Water quality indices: Challenges and application limits in the literature. *Water* **2019**, *11*, 361.
57. Ravishankar, S.; Ye, J.C.; Fessler, J.A. Image Reconstruction: From Sparsity to Data-Adaptive Methods and Machine Learning. *Proc. IEEE* **2020**, *108*, 86–109. [CrossRef]
58. Wang, G.; Ye, J.C.; Mueller, K.; Fessler, J.A. Image Reconstruction is a New Frontier of Machine Learning. *IEEE Trans. Med. Imaging* **2018**, *37*, 1289–1296. [CrossRef]
59. Wagle, N.; Acharya, T.D.; Lee, D.H. Comprehensive Review on Application of Machine Learning Algorithms for Water Quality Parameter Estimation Using Remote Sensing Data. *Sensors Mater.* **2020**, *32*, 3879–3892. [CrossRef]
60. Blix, K.; Pálffy, K.; Tóth, V.R.; Eltoft, T. Remote Sensing of Water Quality Parameters over Lake Balaton by Using Sentinel-3 OLCI. *Water* **2018**, *10*, 1428. [CrossRef]
61. Zhang, C.; Han, M.I.N. Mapping chlorophyll-a concentration in Laizhou Bay using Landsat 8 OLI data. In Proceedings of the 36th IAHR World Congress, The Hague, The Netherlands, 28 June–3 July 2015.
62. Kim, S.I.; Kim, H.C.; Hyun, C.U. High Resolution Ocean Color Products Estimation in Fjord of Svalbard, Arctic Sea using Landsat-8 OLI. *Korean J. Remote Sens.* **2014**, *30*, 809–816. [CrossRef]
63. Lim, J.; Choi, M. Assessment of water quality based on Landsat 8 operational land imager associated with human activities in Korea. *Environ. Monit. Assess.* **2015**, *187*, 384. [CrossRef]
64. Rodrigo, J.A. Machine Learning con Python y Scikitlearn, 2023. Available online: https://cienciadedatos.net/documentos/py06_machine_learning_python_scikitlearn (accessed on 18 April 2023).
65. Zhang, X. Chapter Machine Learning. In *A Matrix Algebra Approach to Artificial Intelligence*; Springer: Berlin/Heidelberg, Germany, 2020; pp. 223–440.
66. Tougui, I.; Jilbab, A.; El Mhamdi, J. Impact of the choice of cross-validation techniques on the results of machine learning-based diagnostic applications. *Healthc. Inform. Res.* **2021**, *27*, 189–199.
67. Louargant, M.; Jones, G.; Faroux, R.; Paoli, J.N.; Maillot, T.; Gée, C.; Villette, S. Unsupervised Classification Algorithm for Early Weed Detection in Row-Crops by Combining Spatial and Spectral Information. *Remote Sens.* **2018**, *10*, 761. [CrossRef]
68. Muller Karger, F.E.; Hestir, E.; Ade, C.; Turpie, K.; Roberts, D.A.; Siegel, D.; Miller, R.J.; Humm, D.; Izenberg, N.; Keller, M.; et al. Satellite sensor requirements for monitoring essential biodiversity variables of coastal ecosystems. *Ecol. Appl.* **2018**, *28*, 749–760. [CrossRef]

Disclaimer/Publisher's Note: The statements, opinions and data contained in all publications are solely those of the individual author(s) and contributor(s) and not of MDPI and/or the editor(s). MDPI and/or the editor(s) disclaim responsibility for any injury to people or property resulting from any ideas, methods, instructions or products referred to in the content.

Article

Long-Term Monitoring of Inland Water Quality Parameters Using Landsat Time-Series and Back-Propagated ANN: Assessment and Usability in a Real-Case Scenario

Gordana Jakovljevic [1], Flor Álvarez-Taboada [2,*] and Miro Govedarica [3]

[1] Faculty of Architecture, Civil Engineering and Geodesy, University of Banja Luka, 78000 Banja Luka, Bosnia and Herzegovina; gordana.jakovljevic@aggf.unibl.org
[2] Department of Mining Engineering, School of Agrarian and Forest Engineering, Ponferrada Campus, Universidad de León, 24404 Ponferrada, Spain
[3] Faculty of Technical Science, University of Novi Sad, 2100 Novi Sad, Serbia; miro@uns.ac.rs
* Correspondence: flor.alvarez@unileon.es

Citation: Jakovljevic, G.; Álvarez-Taboada, F.; Govedarica, M. Long-Term Monitoring of Inland Water Quality Parameters Using Landsat Time-Series and Back-Propagated ANN: Assessment and Usability in a Real-Case Scenario. *Remote Sens.* **2024**, *16*, 68. https://doi.org/10.3390/rs16010068

Academic Editor: Mhd. Suhyb Salama

Received: 26 November 2023
Revised: 20 December 2023
Accepted: 21 December 2023
Published: 23 December 2023

Copyright: © 2023 by the authors. Licensee MDPI, Basel, Switzerland. This article is an open access article distributed under the terms and conditions of the Creative Commons Attribution (CC BY) license (https://creativecommons.org/licenses/by/4.0/).

Abstract: Water scarcity and quality deterioration, driven by rapid population growth, urbanization, and intensive industrial and agricultural activities, emphasize the urgency for effective water management. This study aims to develop a model to comprehensively monitor various water quality parameters (WQP) and evaluate the feasibility of implementing this model in real-world scenarios, addressing the limitations of conventional in-situ sampling. Thus, a comprehensive model for monitoring WQP was developed using a 38-year dataset of Landsat imagery and in-situ data from the Water Information System of Europe (WISE), employing Back-Propagated Artificial Neural Networks (ANN). Correlation analyses revealed strong associations between remote sensing data and various WQPs, including Total Suspended Solids (TSS), chlorophyll-a (chl-a), Dissolved Oxygen (DO), Total Nitrogen (TN), and Total Phosphorus (TP). Optimal band combinations for each parameter were identified, enhancing the accuracy of the WQP estimation. The ANN-based model exhibited very high accuracy, particularly for chl-a and TSS ($R^2 > 0.90$, NRMSE < 0.79%), surpassing previous studies. The independent validation showcased accurate classification for TSS and TN, while DO estimation faced challenges during high variation periods, highlighting the complexity of DO dynamics. The usability of the developed model was successfully tested in a real-case scenario, proving to be an operational tool for water management. Future research avenues include exploring additional data sources for improved model accuracy, potentially enhancing predictions and expanding the model's utility in diverse environmental contexts.

Keywords: water quality monitoring; Artificial Neural Network (ANN); artificial intelligence; WISE; sustainable water management

1. Introduction

Water is vital for the life of humans, animals, plants, and ecosystems. Human health, food security, economic growth, energy production, and ecosystems are all water-dependent. Growing population and urbanization, intensive industrial development, agriculture, increasing demand, and misuse of water have increased water stress, making water a scarce and expensive resource, especially in undeveloped countries.

This growing issue has been recognized and several policies have been adopted in order to provide sustainable management and prevent further decreases in water quality and quantity. The 2030 Agenda for Sustainable Development [1], adopted by United Nations Member states, within Sustainable Development Goals (SDG) 6 [2] emphasizes the water-related issue. SDG 6 has eight targets including water quality. In Europe, the Water Framework Directive (WFD) [3] defines a framework for the protection of the aquatic environment (rivers, lakes, transitional waters, groundwaters, and coastal waters.).

The primary aim of WFD is to achieve at least a good status in all water bodies. To assess the status of the water bodies, monitoring of biological, hydromorphological, and physicochemical water quality parameters (WQP) as defined within Annex V and Annex X [4] needs to be conducted.

The WFD implies that rivers with catchment areas greater than 10 km^2 and lakes greater than 0.5 km^2 in surface area and all of the water bodies into which priority substances are discharged need to be included within the water status assessment and monitoring. WQP is traditionally determined by the collection of in-situ samples and then analyzing them in the laboratory [3]. Although this method provides high accuracy, it is labor, time, and cost-intensive. Therefore, monitoring all water bodies as defined by WFD would require major financial investments. Moreover, the conventional methodology determines the WQP concentration at the sampling point. The water quality within water bodies is rarely constant due to unpredictable events such as storms, accidental spillages, or leakages. and it is highly influenced by hydrodynamic characteristics such as flow direction and discharge. Due to that the monitoring of spatial and temporal variations and trends in large water bodies by conventional methods is challenging.

To overcome those limits, remote sensing technologies, which have the advantage of large spatial coverage and high temporal resolution, have been used to identify and monitor water bodies more effectively and efficiently [5–7]. The remote sensing monitoring of WQP is based on establishing the correlation between in-situ monitoring data and corresponding surface reflection. The spectral characteristics of water are functions of the hydrological, biological, and chemical characteristics of water [8]. Therefore, the amount of radiation at various wavelengths reflected from the water surface can be used directly or indirectly to detect WQP.

The clear water reflects light with wavelengths < 600 nm, resulting in high reflectance in the blue-green while absorbing radiation at the Near-Infra Red (NIR) portion of the spectrum and beyond. The increase of chlorophyll-a (chl-a) concentration increases absorption in Red (R) and strongly absorbs Blue (B) light while the reflection peak is located at the green (G) part of the spectrum [9]. Water clarity is the function of Total Suspended Solids (TSS) concentration. TSS is the measure of the weight of inorganic particulates suspended in the water column and it is responsible for most of the scattering [10]. By influencing the scattering of light, TSS directly controls the transparency and oxygen content of the water body [11]. The increased concentration of TSS causes the peak to shift from G toward the R region and increases water reflectance in the NIR region.

Thus, many studies have used band combinations and spectral indices to develop empirical algorithms for the estimation of optical active WQP and achieved good results [12,13]. Various spectral bands have been used to quantify the chl-a and TSS (Table 1).

Table 1. Remote sensing data used for monitoring of WQP.

Author	Platform	WQP	Spectral Bands	Algorithm	Accuracy
[14]	Landsat 8	chl-a	R, G		
[15]	Landsat 8	chl-a	B, G, R, NIR, NIR/R	MLR	$R^2 = 0.77$
		TSS	G, NIR, NIR/R		$R^2 = 0.78$
		TN	G, R, NIR		$R^2 = 0.55$
		TP	B, G, R, NIR		$R^2 = 0.57$
[6]	Landsat 5	chl-a	NIR, NIR/B	LR	$R^2 = 0.6$
		TSS	R		$R^2 = 0.67$
[16]	Ikonos 2	chl-a	B, G		
		TSS	G, R		
[17]	Landsat 8	chl-a	B, G, R, NIR, SWIR1, SWIR2		
[18]	Landsat 5	TSS	R/G, NIR, R	RF	
[19]	Landsat 8	TN	(B + R)/G, Coastal/NIR, G/NIR	MLR	$R^2 = 0.75$

Table 1. Cont.

Author	Platform	WQP	Spectral Bands	Algorithm	Accuracy
[20]	Landsat 5, 7, 8	chl-a	B, G, R, NIR, R/B^2, NIR/B^2	ANN	$R^2 = 0.89$
		SS	B, G, R, NIR, R^2, R/B, B*R, G*R		$R^2 = 0.93$
[21]	Landsat 8	TN	R/(G + NIR)	LR	$R^2 = 0.71$
		TP	(Coastal + G + R)/NIR		$R^2 = 0.66$
[22]	Landsat 8	TN	R, G/B	ANN	$R^2 = 0.86$
		TP	G, G/B		$R^2 = 0.64$

However, inland waters are seriously affected by human activities, due to optical properties being complex and highly variable. Therefore, each band is not only sensitive to one but also to other WQP which can lead to significant uncertainty in the results produced.

In addition, WQPs such as Total Nitrogen (TN), Total Phosphorus (TP), and Dissolved Oxygen (DO) are important information for understanding water body dynamics. Increased levels of nutrients can lead to algal blooms and oxygen depletion.

However, since the relationship between surface reflectance and concentration of those parameters is indirect and non-linear, the estimation of their concentration represents a great challenge if they are based on traditional empirical algorithms. In recent years, with the increase in processing power and the development of artificial intelligence, machine learning (ML) algorithms have been increasingly used for WQP monitoring. The most common ML models for water quality parameters are Random Forest (RF), Supported Vector Machine (SVM) and Artificial Neural Network (ANN).

Guo et al. [23] used the Landsat and MODIS reflection and SVM for monitoring of DO in Lake Huron. Results show good robustness with average $R^2 = 0.91$. Qian et al. [24] tested Multiple Linear Regression (MLR), SVM, RF and ANN for monitoring of three non-optical (pH, DO, Electrical Conductivity (EC)) and one optical parameter (Turbidity) at Qingcaosha Reservoir based on Sentinel 2 images. The results indicated that ANN showed more robust performance for all WQP (RMSE: 0.33; 0.49; 0.38; 0.26 for pH, DO, EC, and Turbidity, respectively) compared to traditional ML algorithms. Guo et al. [25] monitored the TP, TN, and Chemical Oxygen Demand (COD) by using Sentinel 2 imagery and NN, RF, and SVM algorithms. Their results showed that ML can significantly improve the estimation accuracy of non-optical parameters with Normalized Root Mean Square Error (NRMSE) of TP: 16.8%; TN: 29.64% and COD 18.75. Similarly, Ref. [26] tested the performance of MLR, SVM, and ANN for monitoring of chl-a, DO, Turbidity, blue-green algae (BGA), and fluorescent dissolved organic matter (fDOM) from Sentinel 2 and Landsat 8 images. The DNN outperformed the ML algorithms resulting in Root Mean Square Error (RMSE) of 0.86, 7.56, 1.81, 14.50, and 5.19 for BGA, chl-a, DO, fDOM, and Turbidity, respectively. Hafeez et al. [20] estimated the concentration of TSS, chl-a and Turbidity with several ML algorithms including ANN, RF, and SVM by using Landsat (5, 7, 8) imagery. ANN outperformed RMSE chl-a:1.4; TSS: 2; Turbidity: 3.10) followed by SVM. Leggesse et al. [27] compared the six ML algorithms integrated with Landsat 8 imagery for the prediction of three optically active WQP (chl-a, Turbidity and Total Dissolved solids (TDS)). The results indicated that XGBoost regression performed best for chl-a (RMSE: 9.47) while RF performed best for the rest of the parameters (RMSE TDS: 12.3; Turbidity: 7.82) while ANN and SVM provided lower accuracy. Gomez et al. [28] tested the performance of RF, SVM and ANN on a balanced dataset for the monitoring of chl-a based on Sentinel 2 images. The results showed that RF performed better compared to others (RMSE: RF 0.82; SVM 1.45; ANN 1.75).

It has been shown that ANN and SVM have provided excellent performance in monitoring both optically active and non-active WQP [20,26,28,29]. ANN, as a nonlinear approximation method, is more flexible for WQP monitoring. However, the resulting accuracy of ML is generally a function of the selected model and the quality and size of the training data. The development of an ANN model requires large training datasets and extensive experience in order to determine the optimal NN architecture. Using too many layers can result in overfitting, which involves the fitting of noise in training data and lower generalization to new data [30]. On the other hand, a low number of layers can lead to underfitting when the model cannot represent the complexity of data adequately. Due to that, SVM and RF can have a higher generalization ability than ANN. Govedarica et al. [7] tested the performance of ANN and SVM for monitoring Turbidity, TSS, TN, and TP. The results showed that SVM outperformed ANN for Landsat 8 data while ANN produced better results for Sentinel 2 data. The reason for the higher performance of SVM can be due to being less sensitive to small data samples and mixed pixels [30,31] and it avoids the occurrence of overtraining and optimization of fewer parameters [32,33]. However, an increase in the number of training data can make SVM difficult to implement.

On the other hand [27,28] show that RF had better generalization ability and was less affected by overfitting compared with ANN and SVM. It was noticed that there was an increase in RF performance with an increase in the number of features used in the prediction [28] while it can be decreased for small training datasets [34,35]. The RF algorithm is characterized by the considerable time expenditures for training the trees in the ensemble when the datasets are large [36]. Compared to SVM, RF can take up to four times longer to train and optimize [37].

In addition to ML, deep learning algorithms (DL) have been widely applied in remote sensing image classification. Convolution Neural Networks (CNN) are capable of extracting intrinsic features and have provided state-of-the-art accuracy. Pu et al. [38] used CNN to classify the water quality of a lake based on Landsat 8 images. The results showed that CNN outperformed SVM and RF (OA: CNN 97.12%; SVM 96.89%; RF 86.15%). Cui et al. [39] used CNN and a combination of Landsat 8 and Sentinel 2 images for monitoring water transparency reaching an R^2 of 0.85. Similarly, Ref. [40] demonstrated chl-a retrieved from Sentinel-2 images using CNN regression resulting in an R^2 of 0.92. Although CNN has demonstrated increased accuracy and robustness, most of the research that is based on moderate-resolution satellite images deals with large water bodies such as lakes, and transitional or coastal waters. This is mostly due to the fact that CNN uses convolution filters of varying sizes (3×3, 5×5, or 7×7 pixels) to extract meaningful higher-level abstract features and increase accuracy. However, taking into account spatial resolution and the width of rivers these patches can represent heterogeneous classes limiting the accuracy of the model [40].

The main aims of this paper are (a) to develop a comprehensive ANN-based model for monitoring water body status, and (b) to test the usability of the developed model in real-case scenarios.

2. Materials and Methods

2.1. Study Area

The study area (Figure 1) for this research focused on water quality monitoring based on remote sensing data for the main water bodies within the Republic of Serbia. The Republic of Serbia is located in southeast Europe between $41°53'$N and $46°11'$N latitude and $18°51'$E and $23°01'$E longitude. The North part represents the Pannonian Plain with dominant flat terrain while the central and south parts represent hilly regions. Most of the rivers belong to the Black Sea basin. The longest river is the Danube. In addition to the Danube, there are three navigable rivers: Sava, Tisa and part of the Great Morava.

On the territory of the Republic of Serbia, there are 498 surface water bodies, 99% of these are represented by streams and 1% are lakes. According to the classification of WFD, these streams are classified as rivers (69%), heavily modified water bodies (28%) and artificial water bodies (3%) [41]. The monitoring program for surface water bodies in the 2017–2019 period includes 137 monitoring stations (123 profiles on streams and 14 locations on accumulations) located on 121 water bodies. In that period, 76% of the water bodies were not included in the monitoring program. The assessment of the ecological potential was performed on 24% of the water bodies from which 2% had a good, 8% moderate, 9% poor, and 5% bad ecological status [42].

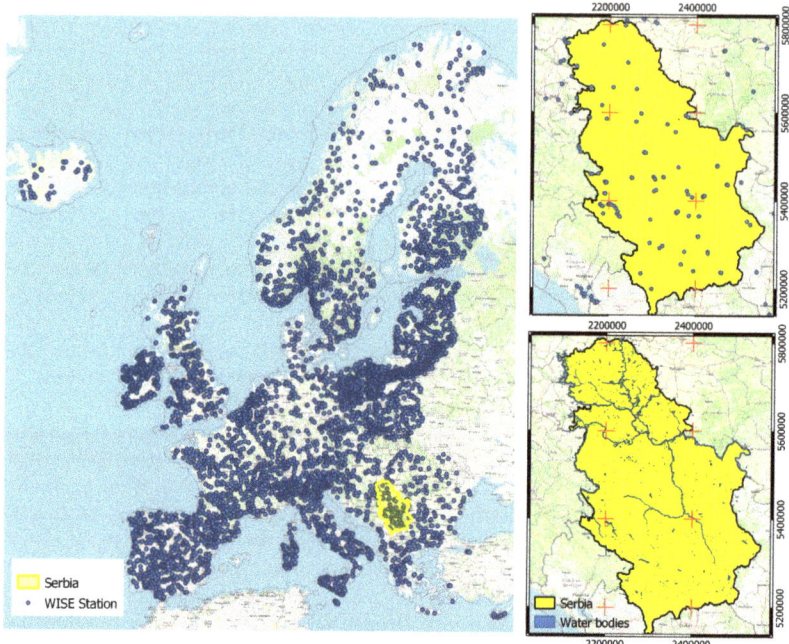

Figure 1. Study area. (**Left**): location of the Water Information System of Europe (WISE) monitoring stations in Europe. (**Upper Right**): Location of monitoring stations in the Republic of Serbia. (**Lower Right**): Location of main water bodies in Serbia.

2.2. Data

Optical remote sensing monitoring of WQP is based on the correlation between the in-situ measurement and the corresponding surface reflectance.

In this paper, the in-situ data were provided by the Water Information System of Europe (WISE). WISE was launched in 2007, as a joint initiative from European Commission and European Environmental Agency, providing a web portal for water-related information ranging from inland to marine [43]. WISE represents the formal reporting tool for EU water legislation enabling the sharing of water-related information at a European level. The WISE-WFD database contains data reported by EU Member States, Norway and the United Kingdom according to article 13 of the WFD. The database includes aggregated and disaggregated information as well as spatial references about ground and surface water bodies. The disaggregated database represents raw in-situ observed values of WQP [44] reported on an annual basis. Currently, there are more than 60,000,000 in-situ observations and more than 70,000 spatial object identifiers. Data were collected in the period from 1984 to 2022. The sampling location for in-situ water quality monitoring, used in this research, was located along the main inland water bodies (river, lake, and transitional) in Europe to obtain a range of hydrological and atmospheric conditions across a continental scale (Figure 1).

Landsat 5, Landsat 7, and Landsat 8 surface reflectance products from 1984 to 2022 over Europe were used. In total, 213,117 images were analyzed to create a long time series and train the model for WQP monitoring. The date ranges and number of images per sensor are provided in Table 2.

Table 2. Time frame and number of images per sensor.

Sensor	Start Date	End Date	Number of Images
Landsat 5 TM	19 March 1984.	29 September 2015.	99,319
Landsat 7 ETM+	30 June 1999.	31 December 2021.	76,224
Landsat 8 OLI	21 March 2013.	31 December 2021.	37,574

Landsat Surface reflectance imagery is atmospherically corrected, containing six (B, G, R, NIR, SWIR, SWIR 2) bands processed to orthorectified surface reflectance using LEDAPS [45]. The Landsat mission is to achieve global coverage once every 16 days with a spatial resolution of 30 m for the multispectral bands. The Google Earth Engine API integrated into Google Colab was used as an access point to the images.

The consistency and standardization of Landsat data across its various missions (Landsat 5, 7 and 8, in this case) is crucial for enabling comparability and consistent analysis over different time periods using time series and to ensure a seamless multi-sensor data record where observed satellite changes can be ascribed to surface changes and not to instrument changes. This consistency is maintained through several factors [46]: (i) rigorous calibration procedures to ensure that sensor characteristics, such as spectral response and radiometric accuracy, remain consistent across the different platforms, to minimize variations between sensors, enabling data continuity [47] (ii) standardized data processing algorithms employed consistently across different Landsat missions, which are corrected for atmospheric effects, geometric distortions, and other artifacts, ensuring that data from different satellites can be combined and compared accurately [48], and (iii) metadata and data format, which documents sensor characteristics, acquisition parameters and processing methods. Although the complete normalization of these factors within the USGS Landsat processing framework remains pending [46], the efforts made to produce consistent and analysis-ready Landsat data across different missions have made possible its broad use for water quality assessment and monitoring [49].

2.3. Methodology

Figure 2 summarizes the approach followed in this paper. It consists of three main steps: preprocessing, processing, and prediction.

Preprocessing: The Sentinel 2 Level 2A satellite images were used to detect water bodies. Level 2A was atmospherically corrected by using Sentinel 2 Atmospherically Correction, which is based on [50,51]. The Level 2A images also contain the Scene Classification Layer (SCL), which provides a pixel classification map with four different classes for clouds and six different classes for shadows, cloud shadows, vegetation, soil, water, and snow [52]. Visual inspection showed that water pixels are mostly classified as water or dark pixels. Waterbody masks were created by using the region grow algorithm where water pixels are used as seeds, and neighboring pixels that were classified as dark pixels and had reflectance values lower than 800 in the SWIR 2 band were added to the region. Corresponding water masks were created for each Landsat image used for the prediction of WQP concentration in 2020 in the study area.

The coordinates of the monitoring station were reprojected from WGS84 to WGS84/UTM 34 N projection to match the Landsat imagery coordinate system. Since WQP monitoring is based on remote sensing, the monitoring stations located on small inland water bodies and groundwaters were excluded from the dataset. Additionally, the location of each station was checked against detected water bodies in order to make sure that the extracted value represented water reflectance.

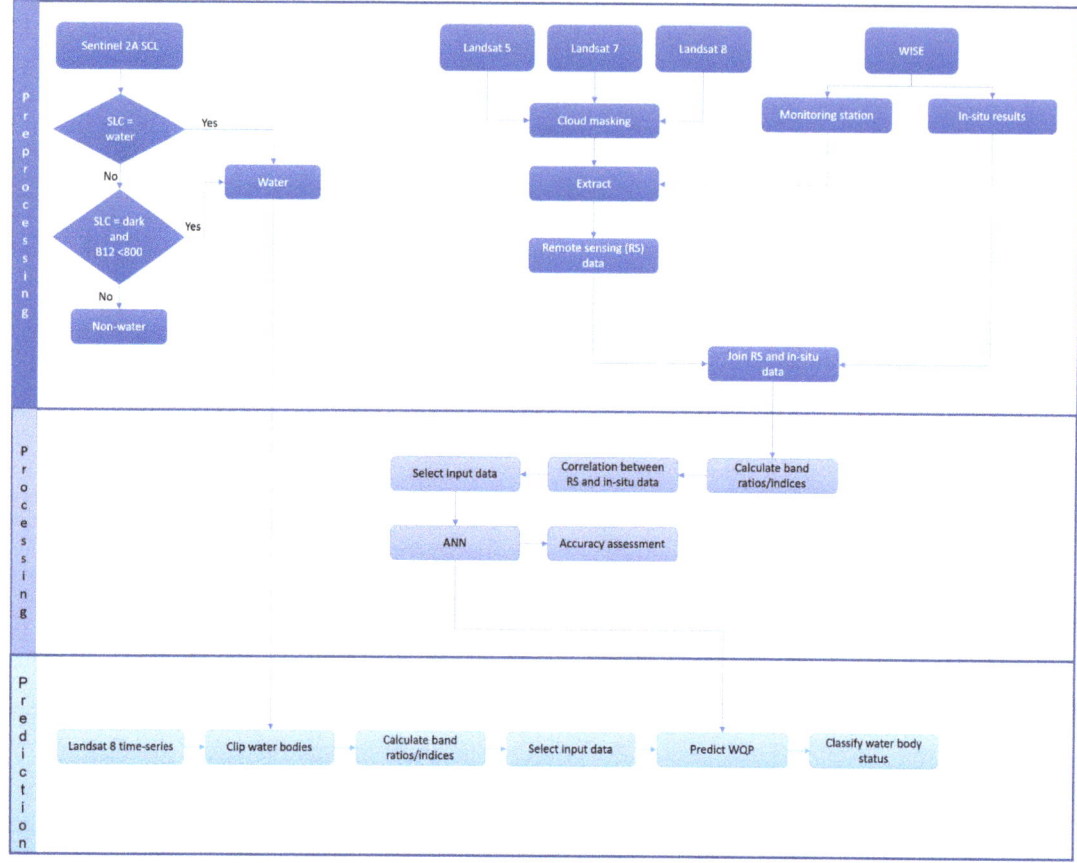

Figure 2. Workflow.

For each point, the values of surface reflectance were extracted from available Landsat 5, Landsat 7, and Landsat 8 Surface Reflectance Level 2A images. The cloud and shadow masking were performed in order to provide clean water pixels. The resulting table contained the identifier of monitoring stations, the corresponding value of surface reflectance, and the sensing date. The surface reflectance was filtered by date to match the in-situ data. The maximum time gap between the in-situ sampling and satellite overpass was 3 days. Final training data contained the surface reflectance of B, G, R, NIR, SWIR1, SWIR 2 band, band ratios NIR/R, G/R, G/B, B/R, R/G, R/B^2, NIR/B^2, G/SWIR2, spectral indices NDVI, NDWI and NDTU, as well as B*R, G*R, (B + R + NIR)/G and NIR/(R + SWIR) and the corresponding concentration of WQP. The Pearson correlation analysis was used to investigate the association between remote sensing and in-situ data with a correlation coefficient (r). Based on the correlation the input data set for each WQP was defined. The data were standardized to fit a normal distribution with a mean value of 0 and standard deviation of 1 and split into training and test sets (80% and 20%, correspondingly).

Processing: The relationship between the WQP concentration and surface reflectance was modeled by using ANN. ANNs are pattern-recognition algorithms that consist of an interconnected group of artificial neurons, and they process information using a connection approach to computation [53] In this study, a fully connected back-propagation neural network was applied. The network had three layers: input, hidden, and output (Figure 3). The input layer represents predictor or independent variables (in this case radiance measurement of different wavelengths). Hidden layers contain a varying number of neurons. The number of nodes in the hidden layer depends on the complexity of the approximated function and sample numbers. If the network is too small, the self-learning ability and precision of the network will decrease, causing under-fitting. Meanwhile, if the network is too large, training time will increase, and the generalization capability of the network will decrease, producing over-fitting [54]. There is no theoretical formula that can be used for the selection of optimum NN architecture. The architecture was fixed by using a trial-and-error approach. The output values of the hidden layer were the input values of the output layer, which also performs the summation and activation functions. The output of this layer was the target of water quality parameters. To derive the correct output, the network learned by training on the subsets of in-situ data. In the back-propagated network, the outputs were then compared with actual values from the training data set, the error was calculated, and the results were transferred to the output layer. As the data passed through the network many times, weights were adjusted and errors were reduced (Figure 3).

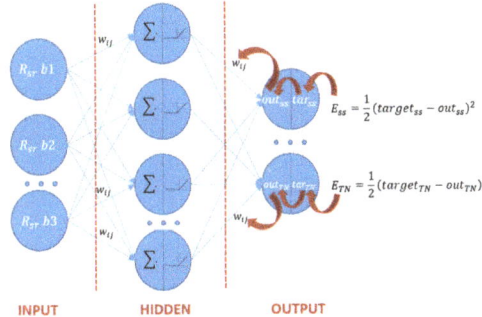

Figure 3. ANN architecture.

Accuracy assessment: The performance of the developed ANN model was evaluated based on common statistical measures: coefficient of determination (R^2) (Equation (1)), RMSE (Equation (2)), normalized RMSE (NRMSE) (Equation (3)), Mean Square Error (MSE) (Equation (4)), Mean Absolute Error (MAE) (Equation (5)). A RMSE measures the quality of the model fit; 0 indicates a perfect fit for the data, while large values are obtained if the estimated concentration of WQP and true concentration differ substantially. NRMSE is used to compare results between models with different scales.

$$R^2 = 1 - \frac{\sum_{i=1}^{n}(y_i - \hat{y}_i)^2}{\sum_{i=1}^{n}(\hat{y}_i - \overline{y})^2} \tag{1}$$

$$RMSE = \sqrt{\frac{1}{n}\sum_{i=1}^{n}(y_i - \hat{y}_i)^2} \tag{2}$$

$$NRMSE = \frac{RMSE}{y_{max} - y_{min}} \tag{3}$$

$$MAE = \frac{1}{n}\sum_{i=1}^{n}|y_i - \hat{y}_i| \tag{4}$$

$$MSE = \frac{1}{n}\sum_{i=1}^{n}(y_i - \hat{y}_i)^2 \tag{5}$$

where y_i is actual value, $\hat{y}_i$ is the predicted value, n sample size, $\overline{y}$ mean of the n actual values, y_{max} is the maximum of n actual values and y_{min} is the minimal of n actual values. A model with a high R^2 and low *RMSE* and *NRMSE* would be suitable for WQP monitoring.

The R^2 factor is essential for the evaluation of the developed prediction model with the following classification: excellent prediction $R^2 > 0.9$, good prediction $0.82 \leq R^2 < 0.90$, approximate quantitative prediction $0.66 \leq R^2 \leq 0.81$, a prediction that can possibly distinguish between high and low values $0.50 \leq R^2 \leq 0.65$, and unsuccessful prediction $R^2 < 0.5$ [55,56].

Prediction: The trained ANN models were used to monitor the WQP concentration based on Landsat 8 Level 2A images for the year 2020 in the study area. Before making the prediction, the images needed to be masked using a water mask (created in the preprocessing phase) in order to ensure that all the pixels represent the water and do not contain surrounding classes. After the prediction of the WQP concentration water quality was classified into classes based on values presented in Table 3. Those values were defined to be in line with those as defined by the legal documents in the field for the Republic of Serbia [57–59].

Table 3. Limit values of WQP concentration for classification of water body status [57–59].

Class/Parameter	chl-a	DO	TSS	TN	TP
I (High)	0–25	8.5>	0–25	<1	0–0.05
II (Good)	25–50	7–8.5	25-	1–2	0.05–0.30
III (Moderate)	50–100	5–7	-	2–8	0.30–0.40
IV (Poor)	100–250	4–5	-	8–15	0.40–1
V (Bad)	>250	<4	-	>15	>1

In order to gain a deeper insight into the performance of the developed models and assess their practical application, validation was performed. To validate the developed models in the Republic of Serbia, we compared the satellite-derived results and field measurements for the year 2020 for the Zemun monitoring station in the Danube River (which was not included in the training data). Since the in-situ sampling was not regular, there were no matches between the exact dates of satellite-derived results and field sampling, and therefore, the classical statistical measures (R^2, RMSE, NRMSE) were not calculated.

2.4. Implementation

The developed workflow was implemented in the Python programming language. The workflow consisted of three modules for the creation of training data, prediction, and monitoring of WQP, and it is fully automated. Manual input is only used for the selection of optimal NN architecture. The remote sensing data were accessed and preprocessed by using GEE Python API. The data set and NN architecture were defined for each WQP. The proposed architecture consisted of input, hidden, and output layers with an activation function (Table 4). The number of the input neurons was selected to be equal to the selected input bands that had a strong correlation with WQPs, and the number of output neurons was selected to be one. The trial-and-error approach was used for the selection of a proper number of hidden neurons. All of the data sets were split at 80% for training and 20% for validation. The learning rate and decay rate were determined through grid search (Learning rate: [0.0001, 0.001, 0.01, 0.1]; Weight decay: [0.000001, 0.00001, 0.0001]). To avoid overfitting, early stopping was used. Early stopping is a commonly used form of regularization that interrupts the training process when there is no improvement of validation loss for a predefined number of epochs. Each time the validation loss improves, the copy of model parameters is stored. After training the algorithm terminates, and those parameters are used instead of the last parameters.

Table 4. Parameters used to train the model for water quality monitoring.

Parameter	Dataset Size	ANN Architecture	Input	Epoch	Optimizer	Loss	Min	Max
chl-a	3450	9-20-15-20-6-1	B, G, G/B, R/B^2, G/SWIR	438	RMSprop	MSE	0	45
DO	11,585	128-32-8-1	SWIR2, NDWI, NDTU, GSWIR, NIR/R, R/G, R/(B + NIR), R-NIR, B-NIR	684	Adam	MSE	0.2	23.8
TSS	11,078	128-32-16-8-1	B, G, R, NDTU, G/SWIR, G/R, R/G, I2, R-NIR, B*R, G*R	1500	Adam	MSE	0.1	260
TN	12,307	128-32-8-1	B, G, NIR, SWIR, B/R, G/SWIR, G/R, R/G, (NIR + R)/G, (B + NIR)/G, R-NIR, R + NIR, B-NIR	1043	Adam	MSE	0.0008	8.96
TP	12,164	128-32-8-1	NIR, G/SWIR, R-NIR	310	Adam	MSE	0.0008	3.0

The training of the networks was conducted using the publicly available cloud platform Collaboratory (Google Colab), which is based on Jupyter Notebooks. The parameters used in the model training are presented in Table 4.

3. Results

The selection of optimal band combination for each WQP was performed (Table 4) allowing for the development of the high-accuracy model. The back-propagated ANN algorithms were proven to be very efficient in monitoring and estimating concentrations of different WQP, for both optically and non-optically active parameters, with highly acceptable results. In general, very positive results were obtained for all WQP and, as shown in Figure 4, coefficients of determination (R^2) vary between 0.91 and 0.99 at the validation phase. Since the $R^2 > 0.9$, the developed models provided an excellent prediction for all WQPs.

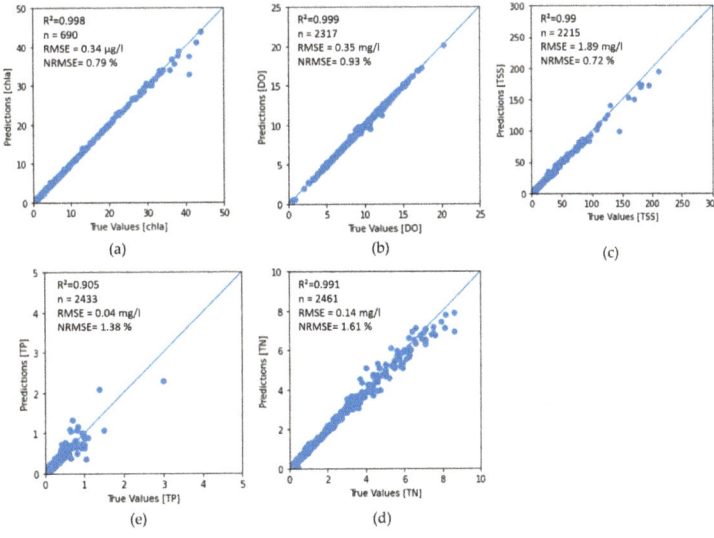

Figure 4. Graphical fit of predicted results in validation phase (a) chl-a, (b) DO, (c) TSS, (d) TN and (e) TP.

The results of the accuracy assessment are presented in Table 5. As expected, the highest accuracy and lowest NRMSE were obtained for the optically active WQP, i.e., chl-a and TSS (0.79% and 0.72%, respectively).

Table 5. Accuracy assessment of WQP monitoring using back-propagated ANN algorithms.

Parameter	Training		Validation		RMSE	NRMSE [%]
	MAE	MSE	MAE	MSE		
chl-a [µg/L]	0.065	0.023	0.083	0.070	0.34	0.79
DO [mg/L]	0.040	0.008	0.052	0.024	0.35	0.93
TSS [mg/L]	0.951	6.566	1.049	13.749	1.89	0.72
TN [mg/L]	0.084	0.040	0.065	0.020	0.14	1.61
TP [mg/L]	0.015	0.003	0.015	0.0024	0.04	1.38

The results of the independent validation of the developed model are presented in Table 6, which showed that the models developed for TSS and TN provided accurate classification for all months, while DO reached the lowest values (the water body status matched only in 37.5% of the cases).

Table 6. Comparison between estimated and measured concentrations of TSS, DO, TN for the Zemun monitoring station in 2020 where M—results of in-situ measurement, P—results of prediction, (C)—water body status based on Table 3. The data for January, February, November and December have been omitted since there were no RS data collected for that period. I–IV are water body status classes.

Month	Date	TSS		DO		TN		TP	
		M (C)	P (C)	M (C)	P (C)	M (C)	P (C)	M (C)	P (C)
March	8		4.4 (I)	7.5 (II)		1.9 (II)			0.051 (II)
	18	6 (I)		11.4 (I)		1.5 (II)		0.111 (II)	
April	15	17 (I)		10.8 (I)		1.5 (II)		0.057 (II)	
	25		17.6 (I)	15 (I)		1.6 (II)			0.046 (I)
May	11		18.8 (I)	14.6 (I)		1.8 (II)			0.038 (I)
	20	9 (I)		9.6 (I)		1.1 (II)		0.031 (I)	
June	3		15.8 (I)	8.6 (I)		1.9 (II)			0.092 (II)
	12		18.9 (I)	8.9 (I)		1.1 (II)			0.290 (II)
	17	20 (I)			7.7 (II)	1 (II)		0.246 (II)	
	19		21 (I)	12 (I)		1.3 (II)			0.300 (II)
	28		17.9 (I)	13.8 (I)		1.1 (II)			0.310 (III)
July	14		5.6 (I)	7.9 (II)		1.8 (II)			0.320 (III)
	15	4 (I)			6.5 (III)	1.5 (II)		0.235 (II)	
	31		3.57 (I)	9.8 (I)		1.9 (II)			0.279 (II)
August	15		17.5 (I)	7.3 (II)		1.9 (II)			0.450 (IV)
	19	7 (I)			6.2 (III)	1.5 (II)		0.456 (IV)	
	22		11.8 (I)	9.5 (I)		1.6 (II)			0.500 (IV)
September	9		14.4 (I)	13.2 (I)		1.6 (II)			0.076 (II)
	16	8 (I)			7.7 (II)	1.2 (II)		0.18 (II)	
October	3		15.1 (I)	16.9 (I)		1.9 (II)			0.064 (II)
	21	16 (I)		9.5 (I)		1.4 (II)		0.166 (II)	
	25		15.5 (I)	15.1 (I)		1.4 (II)			0.054 (II)

4. Discussion

4.1. Proposed Model for WQP Monitoring

Aquatic environments have been impacted by various pressures that affect their status and increase water stress. To move towards a more sustainable use of water resources, an appropriate water quality monitoring program needs to be established. In this study, a 38-year long time-series of Landsat and in-situ data were used for the monitoring of WQP based on back-propagated ANN.

As expected, the results of the correlation analysis showed that the highest correlation between remote sensing data and WQP was obtained for TSS. TSS had a significant positive correlation with visible bands and G*R, B*R, and R + NIR while a negative correlation was noticed for G/SWIR. The strong correlation between TSS and visible bands and G*B and B*R was also reported in [20] since higher concentrations of TSS increase water leaving radiance across the whole visible spectrum. Additionally, Refs. [10,60], and others have demonstrated that the R band is suitable for monitoring TSS. Similarly, the highest positive correlation was obtained between chl-a and the green band and the G/B ratio, while the G/SWIR ratio showed a strong negative correlation. The high correlation between chl-a and G bands is consistent with previous studies since water with an increased chl-a concentration reflects a high amount of G radiation [9,61]. DO had a positive correlation with SWIR2, NIR/R and R-NIR while a significant negative correlation was noticed for G/SWIR, R/(B + NIR), and NDWI. The TN and TP had a positive correlation with G, NIR and the R + NIR and NIR band, respectively, while a negative correlation was noticed between TN and NDWI and G/SWIR for TP. The highest correlation between TN and TP and NIR and G band was also reported by [25,62].

According to the results, the highest accuracy (R^2, NRMSE [%]) was obtained for chl-a and TSS (Table 5). This is expected since those are optically active water parameters. For chl-a, the accuracy attained in this paper (R^2: 0.99, NRMSE: 0.79%) was higher than the ones reported in previous studies. Barraza-Moraga et al. [62] achieved an NRMSE of 3.6% (R^2: 0.97, RMSE: 2.58) using Sentinel 2 images to develop an MLE model for chl-a monitoring, while [63] used UAV images and MLR resulting in a R^2 of 0.91 and RMSE of 0.07. Along the same lines, Ref. [64] used UAV images to build a CNN model and obtained an R^2 of 0.79 (RMSE: 8.76), while [65] used Sentinel 2 images and Ada boost regression resulting in a R^2 of 0.90 (RMSE: 1.48). Hafeez et al. [20] used ANN achieving an NRMSE of 5.1% (R^2: 0.87, RMSE: 1.4) while [66] reached an R^2 of 0.88 using CNN and Sentinel 2 and Geo-Fan 2.

Also, the model developed for monitoring the TSS achieved a high accuracy (R^2: 0.99, RMSE: 1.89, NRMSE: 0.72%), larger than the values reported by [65] using Sentinel-2 and RF (R^2: 0.6, RMSE: 2.97), and more accurate than the models developed by [20] and [17] using Landsat images and NN, which yielded an R^2 of 0.89 (RMSE: 2, NRMSE: 6.2%) and a R^2 of 0.93 (RMSE: 0.99, NRMSE: 2.2%), respectively.

Similar results were also obtained for DO, TN and TP (Table 5), with higher accuracies than the ones obtained by [20] to monitor TN using Landsat 8 and a stepwise regression function (R^2: 0.61), The same author, when using the RF algorithm, increased the accuracy of R^2 to 0.88 [64] and of R^2 to 0.94 when using NN [25]. Refs. [22,67] used NN, reaching accuracies of R^2 of 0.95 and 0.86, respectively. Lower accuracies were achieved by [22] by using NN to model TN (R^2: 0.64, RMSE: 0.04), similar to [56], who used partial least square regression on Landsat 8 and Sentinel 2 data achieving an R^2 of 0.63 and 0.77, respectively.

For DO, the accuracies obtained in this study were also higher than the ones obtained by [17,24,68] using NN, or [65], who obtained an R^2 of 0.74 by using an Ada boost regression and Sentinel 2 images.

The results in Table 5 showed that NN, as a nonlinear approximation method, provided more accurate results for WQP monitoring. However, the training of NN models requires a large training dataset, otherwise, they may lead to overfitting or underfitting, which greatly limits the extraction of general rules and the generalization ability of the model [69]. Taking into account that most of the previously analyzed papers used small training data sets, such as 125 [22], 60 [25], 155 [64], and 92 [66] samples, it was expected that the proposed method would have a higher accuracy. In addition, the selection of optimal input data as well as the usage of the large time series covering a wide variety of conditions and an early stopping function [70] to avoid overfitting probably had an impact on the increase in the model accuracy.

Regarding the independent validation of the developed model which is shown in (Table 6), although there is no exact coincidence between the date of measurement and estimated concentration, the lowest accuracy was obtained for DO since the water body status matched only in 37.5% of the cases. This can be explained by the high variation of the DO concentration especially in summer months. The results show that the DO concentration can decrease from class I to III within one day [71]. The waterbody status for TP was accurately classified at 75%. However, it was noticed that the developed model tended to overestimate TP during increased concentration. The models developed for TSS and TN provided an accurate classification for all the months. It should be taken into account that the exclusion of monitoring stations located on small inland water bodies and groundwater due to remote sensing-based monitoring limitations might limit the comprehensive coverage of water quality assessments. This exclusion could introduce potential biases in the model's training dataset, affecting its adaptability to diverse water body sizes and types.

4.2. Usability of the Developed Model in a Real-Case Scenario: Dobrodol Water Reservoir

The developed models and satellite imagery pixel values for larger water bodies in the Republic of Serbia were used to estimate the WQP concentration., since for water management, the classification of water status is necessary. Based on the estimated WQP concentrations and water quality standards for surface water classify each water-quality parameter into five classes indicating water status from "Excellent" to "Bad".

The change in water body status during 2020 for the Dobrodol water reservoir is presented in Figure 5. It shows that areas close to shorelines with point and diffuse pollution arising from human activity have relatively poor water quality compared to the deeper areas. Generally, the water status of the Dobrodol water body during 2020 could be classified as good, mostly due to the higher concentration of TN. This was expected due to nutrient-rich agriculture discharging from the surrounding land [69]. The visual inspection shows that the chl-a concentration was the highest at the banks and that it decreased when you moved toward the center of the water reservoir, which is in line with either the physical process of sedimentation or algae encroachment [70]. The higher concentration of chl-a was noted during summer. The increase in the growth of algae accelerated the escape of oxygen from the water column, which resulted in an increase of chl-a and a reduction in DO content and the ecological health and balance in the aquatic environment [71,72].

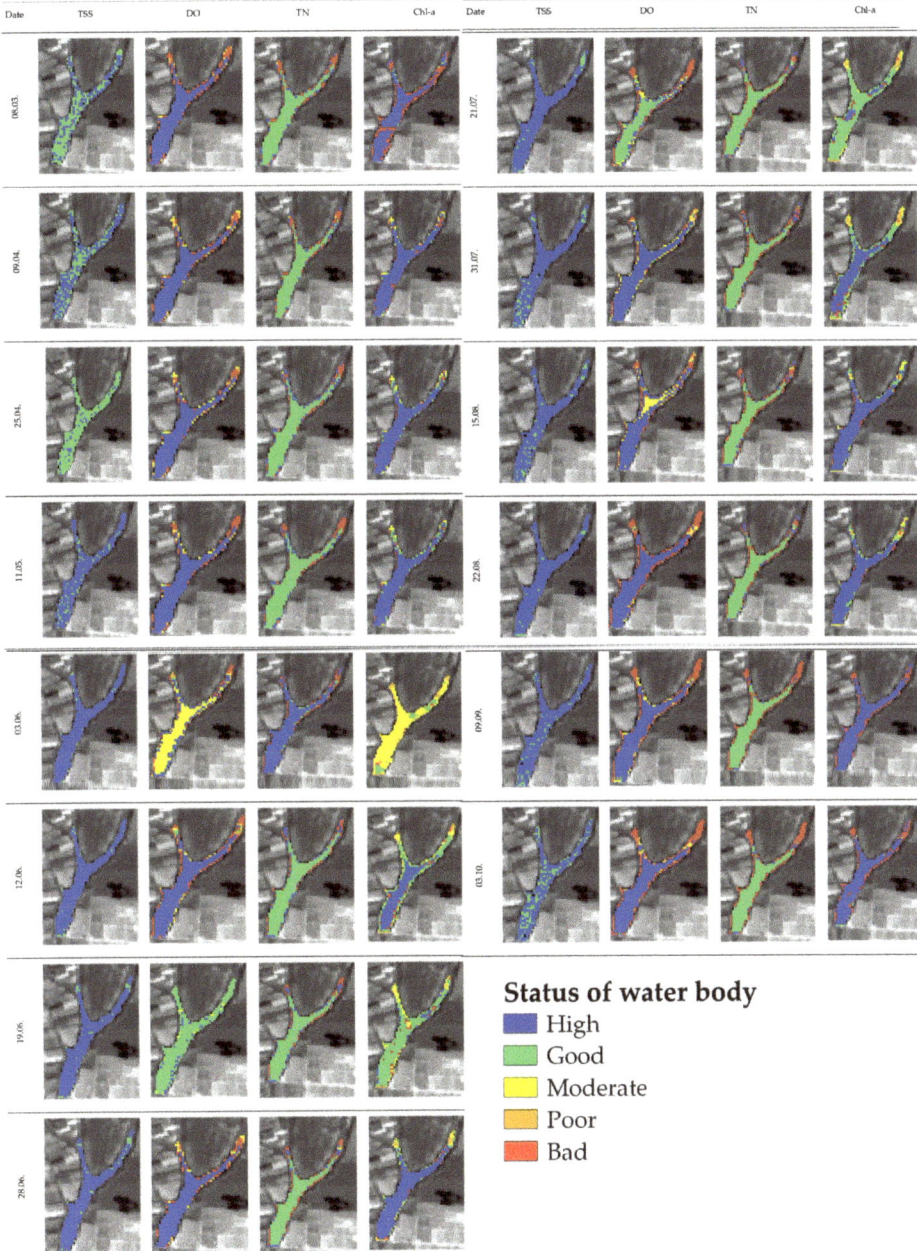

Figure 5. Water body status classification and spatial variation of WQP for the Dobrodol water body.

5. Conclusions

The study successfully established a robust water quality monitoring program using a 38-year time series of Landsat and in-situ data, coupled with a back-propagated Artificial Neural Network (ANN) model. This model demonstrated high accuracy in monitoring various water quality parameters (WQP), showcasing its potential for sustainable water resource management.

The correlation analysis revealed strong associations between remote sensing data and specific WQPs, such as Total Suspended Solids (TSS), chlorophyll-a (chl-a), Dissolved Oxygen (DO), Total Nitrogen (TN), and Total Phosphorus (TP). Optimal band combinations for each parameter were identified, providing valuable insights into the spectral relationships aiding accurate WQP estimation.

The ANN-based model exhibited exceptional accuracy, particularly for optically active parameters like chl-a and TSS, surpassing results from previous studies that used different remote sensing techniques. This underscores the superiority of the developed model in achieving high precision in WQP estimations, surpassing various existing methods and algorithms.

The study highlighted the efficacy of Neural Networks as a nonlinear approximation method for WQP monitoring. It outperformed other techniques but emphasized the necessity for substantial training datasets to avoid overfitting or underfitting. Optimal input data selection and the use of extensive time series data contributed significantly to model accuracy enhancement.

The independent validation of the developed model revealed a strong ability to classify WQP concentrations accurately. Notably, while the models for TSS and TN provided consistent and accurate classifications, DO estimation faced challenges, especially during high variation periods. This underscores the complexity of DO dynamics in water bodies, particularly during seasonal shifts.

Regarding further research, exploring the integration of additional data sources, such as high-resolution imagery or meteorological data, could further refine the model's accuracy. Incorporating these data could potentially improve predictions by capturing more intricate environmental parameters that contribute to water quality dynamics. This would contribute to advancing the understanding of the model's robustness and applicability in different environmental contexts, potentially improving its performance and expanding its utility for broader water quality monitoring and management objectives. Aligning when the sampling data are obtained with satellite overpasses would also be recommended in order to increase the accuracy of the models.

Addressing these weaknesses could potentially strengthen the paper's findings by providing a more comprehensive assessment of the model's performance in real scenarios and expanding its applicability across various water body sizes and types.

Author Contributions: Conceptualization, G.J., M.G. and F.Á.-T.; methodology, G.J. and M.G.; software, G.J.; validation, G.J.; formal analysis, G.J., M.G. and F.Á.-T.; investigation, G.J.; writing—original draft preparation, G.J. and M.G.; writing—review and editing, G.J., M.G. and F.Á.-T.; visualization, G.J.; supervision M.G. and F.Á.-T. All authors have read and agreed to the published version of the manuscript.

Funding: This research received no external funding.

Data Availability Statement: The used data are available at https://github.com/jakovljevicg/WQP (accessed on 20 December 2023).

Acknowledgments: The authors would like to thank the anonymous reviewers who helped improve the manuscript with their comments and suggestions.

Conflicts of Interest: The authors declare no conflict of interest.

References

1. UN General Assembly. Transforming Our World: The 2030 Agenda for Sustainable Development. 21 October 2015. Available online: https://www.refworld.org/docid/57b6e3e44.html (accessed on 5 December 2022).
2. United Nations. *Goal 6: Ensure Access to Water and Sanitation for All*; UN: New York, NY, USA, 2018.
3. European Parliament. *Directive 2000/60/EC—Framework for Community Action in the Field of Water Policy*; European Parliament: Bruxelles, Belgium, 2003.

4. European Communities. *Guidance Document n.o 7 Monitoring under the Water Framework Directive*; Office for Official Publica-tions of the European Communities: Luxembourg, 2003.
5. He, J.; Chen, Y.; Wu, J.; Stow, D.A.; Christakos, G. Space-Time Chlorophyll-a Retrieval in Optically Complex Waters that Accounts for Remote Sensing and Modeling Uncertainties and Improves Remote Estimation Accuracy. *Water Res.* **2019**, *171*, 115403. [CrossRef]
6. Nas, B.; Ekercin, S.; Karabörk, H.; Berktay, A.; Mulla, D.J. An Application of Landsat-5TM Image Data for Water Quality Mapping in Lake Beysehir, Turkey. *Water Air Soil Pollut.* **2010**, *212*, 183–197. [CrossRef]
7. Govedarica, M.; Jakovljevic, G. Monitoring spatial and temporal variation of water quality parameters using time series of open multispectral data. In Proceedings of the SPIE 11174 Seventh International Conference on Remote Sensing and Geoinformation of the Environment, Paphos, Cyprus, 18–21 March 2019.
8. Wu, C.; Wu, J.; Qi, J.; Zhang, L.; Huang, H.; Lou, L.; Chen, Y. Empirical estimation of total phosphorus concentration in the mainstream of the Qiantang River in China using Landsat TM data. *Int. J. Remote Sens.* **2010**, *31*, 2309–2324. [CrossRef]
9. Ha, N.; Koike, K.; Nhuan, M. Improved Accuracy of Chlorophyll-a Concentration Estimates from MODIS Imagery Using a Two-Band Ratio Algorithm and Geostatistics: As Applied to the Monitoring of Eutrophication Processes over Tien Yen Bay (Norther Vietnam). *Remote Sens.* **2013**, *6*, 421–442. [CrossRef]
10. Nechad, B.; Ruddick, K.; Park, Y. Calibration and validation of a generic multisensor algorithm for mapping of total suspended matter in turbid waters. *Remote Sens. Environ.* **2010**, *114*, 854–866. [CrossRef]
11. Zhang, Y.; Wu, Z.; Liu, M.; He, J.; Shi, K.; Wang, M.; Yu, Z. Thermal structure and response to long-term climatic changes in Lake Qiandaohu, a deep subtropical reservoir in China. *Limnol. Oceanogr.* **2014**, *59*, 1193–1202. [CrossRef]
12. Brezonik, P.L.; Olmanson, L.G.; Finlay, J.C.; Bauer, M.E. Factors Affecting the Measurement of CDOM by Remote Sensing of Optically Complex Inland Waters. *Remote Sens. Environ.* **2015**, *157*, 199–215. [CrossRef]
13. Shahzad, M.I.; Meraj, M.; Nazeer, M.; Zia, I.; Inam, A.; Mehmood, K.; Zafar, H. Empirical Estimation of Suspended Solids Concentration in the Indus Delta Region Using Landsat-7 ETM+ Imagery. *J. Environ. Manag.* **2018**, *209*, 254–261. [CrossRef]
14. Bonansea, M.; Rodriguez, M.C.; Pinotti, L.; Ferrero, S. Using multitemporal Landsat imagery and linear mixed models for assessing water quality parameters in Río Tercero reservoir (Argentina). *Remote Sens. Environ.* **2015**, *158*, 28–41. [CrossRef]
15. Lim, J.; Choi, M. Assessment of water quality based on Landsat 8 operational land imager associated with human activities in Korea. *Environ. Monit. Assess.* **2015**, *187*, 1–7. [CrossRef]
16. Ekercin, S. Water Quality Retrievals from High Resolution Ikonos Multispectral Imagery: A Case Study in Istanbul, Turkey. *Water Air Soil Pollut.* **2007**, *183*, 239–251. [CrossRef]
17. Din, E.S.E.; Zhang, Y.; Suliman, A. Mapping concentrations of surface water quality parameters using a novel remote sensing and artificial intelligence framework. *Int. J. Remote Sens.* **2017**, *38*, 1023–1042. [CrossRef]
18. Umar, M.; Rhoads, B.L.; Greenberg, J.A. Use of multispectral satellite remote sensing to assess mixing of suspended sediment downstream of large river confluences. *J. Hydrol.* **2018**, *556*, 325–338. [CrossRef]
19. Guo, Y.; Deng, R.; Li, J.; Hua, Z.; Wang, J.; Zhang, R.; Liang, Y.; Tang, Y. Remote Sensing Retrieval of Total Nitrogen in the Pearl River Delta Based on Landsat8. *Water* **2022**, *14*, 3710. [CrossRef]
20. Hafeez, S.; Wong, M.S.; Ho, H.C.; Nazeer, M.; Nichol, J.E.; Abbas, S.; Tang, D.; Lee, K.-H.; Pun, L. Comparison of Machine Learning Algorithms for Retrieval of Water Quality Indicators in Case-II Waters: A Case Study of Hong Kong. *Remote Sens.* **2019**, *11*, 617. [CrossRef]
21. Li, Y.; Zhang, Y.; Shi, K.; Zhu, G.; Zhuo, Y.; Zhang, Y.; Guo, Y. Monitoring spatiotemporal variations in nutrients in a large drinking water reservoir and their relationships with hydrological and meteorological conditions based on Landsat 8 imagery. *Sci. Total. Environ.* **2017**, *599*, 1705–1717. [CrossRef]
22. Vakili, T.; Amanollahi, J. Determination of optically inactive water quality variables using Landsat 8 data: A case study in Geshlagh reservoir affected by agricultural land use. *J. Clean. Prod.* **2019**, *247*, 119134. [CrossRef]
23. Guo, H.; Huang, J.J.; Zhu, X.; Wang, B.; Tian, S.; Xu, W.; Mai, Y. A generalized machine learning approach for dissolved oxygen estimation at multiple spatiotemporal scales using remote sensing. *Environ. Pollut.* **2021**, *288*, 117734. [CrossRef] [PubMed]
24. Qian, J.; Liu, H.; Qian, L.; Bauer, J.; Xue, X.; Yu, G.; He, Q.; Zhou, Q.; Bi, Y.; Norra, S. Water quality monitoring and assessment based on cruise monitoring, remote sensing, and deep learning: A case study of Qingcaosha Reservoir. *Front. Environ. Sci.* **2022**, *10*, 979133. [CrossRef]
25. Guo, H.; Huang, J.J.; Chen, B.; Guo, X.; Singh, V.P. A machine learning-based strategy for estimating non-optically active water quality parameters using Sentinel-2 imagery. *Int. J. Remote Sens.* **2020**, *42*, 1841–1866. [CrossRef]
26. Peterson, K.T.; Sagan, V.; Sloan, J.J. Deep learning-based water quality estimation and anomaly detection using Land-sat-8/Sentinel-2 virtual constellation and cloud computing. *Giscience Remote Sens.* **2020**, *57*, 510–525. [CrossRef]
27. Leggesse, E.S.; Zimale, F.A.; Sultan, D.; Enku, T.; Srinivasan, R.; Tilahun, S.A. Predicting Optical Water Quality Indicators from Remote Sensing Using Machine Learning Algorithms in Tropical Highlands of Ethiopia. *Hydrology* **2023**, *10*, 110. [CrossRef]
28. Gómez, D.; Salvador, P.; Sanz, J.; Casanova, J.L. A new approach to monitor water quality in the Menor sea (Spain) using satellite data and machine learning methods. *Environ. Pollut.* **2021**, *286*, 117489. [CrossRef] [PubMed]
29. Balabin, R.M.; Lomakina, E.I. Support vector machine regression (SVR/LS-SVM)—An alternative to neural networks (ANN) for analytical chemistry? Comparison of nonlinear methods on near infrared (NIR) spectroscopy data. *Analyst* **2011**, *136*, 1703–1710. [CrossRef] [PubMed]

30. Jakovljevic, G.; Govedarica, M.; Alvarez-Taboada, F. Water body mapping: A comparison of remotely sensed and GIS open data sources. *Int. J. Remote Sens.* **2018**, *40*, 2936–2964. [CrossRef]
31. Nolan, B.T.; Fienen, M.N.; Lorenz, D.L. A statistical learning framework for groundwater nitrate models of the Central Valley, California, USA. *J. Hydrol.* **2015**, *531*, 902–911. [CrossRef]
32. Singh, K.P.; Basant, N.; Gupta, S. Support vector machines in water quality management. *Anal. Chim. Acta* **2011**, *703*, 152–162. [CrossRef] [PubMed]
33. Liu, M.; Lu, J. Support vector machine—An alternative to artificial neuron network for water quality forecasting in an agricultural nonpoint source polluted river? *Environ. Sci. Pollut. Res.* **2014**, *21*, 11036–11053. [CrossRef]
34. Kim, Y.H.; Im, J.; Ha, H.K.; Choi, J.-K.; Ha, S. Machine learning approaches to coastal water quality monitoring using GOCI satellite data. *GIScience Remote Sens.* **2014**, *51*, 158–174. [CrossRef]
35. Li, M.; Im, J.; Beier, C. Machine learning approaches for forest classification and change analysis using multitemporal Landsat TM images over Huntington Wildlife Forest. *GIScience Remote Sens.* **2013**, *50*, 361–384. [CrossRef]
36. Ramezan, C.A.; Warner, T.A.; Maxwell, A.E.; Price, B.S. Effects of Training Set Size on Supervised Machine-Learning Land-Cover Classification of Large-Area High-Resolution Remotely Sensed Data. *Remote Sens.* **2021**, *13*, 368. [CrossRef]
37. Zeng, W.; Xu, K.; Cheng, S.; Zhao, L.; Yang, K. Regional Remote Sensing od Lake Water Transparency Based on Google Earth Engine: Preformance of Empircal Algorithm and Machine Learning. *Appl. Sci.* **2023**, *13*, 4007. [CrossRef]
38. Pu, F.; Ding, C.; Chao, Z.; Yu, Y.; Xu, X. Water-Quality Classification of Inland Lakes Using Landsat8 Images by Convolutional Neural Networks. *Remote Sens.* **2019**, *11*, 1674. [CrossRef]
39. Cui, Y.; Yan, Z.; Wang, J.; Hao, S.; Liu, Y. Deep learning–based remote sensing estimation of water transparency in shallow lakes by combining Landsat 8 and Sentinel 2 images. *Environ. Sci. Pollut. Res.* **2021**, *29*, 4401–4413. [CrossRef] [PubMed]
40. Aptoula, E.; Ariman, S. Chlorophyll-a Retrieval from Sentinel-2 Images Using Convolutional Neural Network Regression. *IEEE Geosci. Remote Sens. Lett.* **2021**, *19*, 1–5. [CrossRef]
41. Sl Glasnik RS br 96/2010. *Pravilnik o Utvrđivanju Vodnih tela Površinskih i Podzemnih Voda*; Sl glasnik RS: Beograd, Serbia, 2010.
42. Agencija za zastitu zivotne sredine. *Ministarstvo za Zaštitu Životne Sredine Status Površinskih voda Srbije u Periodu od 2017–2019*; Agencija za zastitu zivotne sredine: Beograd, Serbia, 2021.
43. European Environment Agency. WISE. Available online: https://water.europa.eu/#:~:text=The%20Water%20Information%20System%20for,from%20inland%20waters%20to%20marine (accessed on 1 December 2022).
44. European Environment Agency. Eionet. Available online: https://dd.eionet.europa.eu/tables/11122 (accessed on 1 December 2022).
45. USGS. Landsat 4-7 Collection 1 Surface Reflectance Code LEDAPS Product Guide. Available online: https://d9-wret.s3.us-west-2.amazonaws.com/assets/palladium/production/s3fs-public/atoms/files/LSDS-1370_L4-7_C1-SurfaceReflectance-LEDAPS_ProductGuide-v3.pdf (accessed on 25 November 2022).
46. Wulder, M.A.; Roy, D.P.; Radeloff, V.C.; Loveland, T.R.; Anderson, M.C.; Johnson, D.M.; Healey, S.; Zhu, Z.; Scambos, T.A.; Pahlevan, N.; et al. Fifty years of Landsat science and impacts. *Remote Sens. Environ.* **2022**, *280*. [CrossRef]
47. Mishra, N.; Haque, M.O.; Leigh, L.; Aaron, D.; Helder, D.; Markham, B. Radiometric Cross Calibration of Landsat 8 Operational Land Imager (OLI) and Landsat 7 Enhanced Thematic Mapper Plus (ETM+). *Remote Sens.* **2014**, *6*, 12619–12638. [CrossRef]
48. Mishra, N.; Helder, D.; Barsi, J.; Markham, B. Continuous calibration improvement in solar reflective bands: Landsat 5 through Landsat 8. *Remote Sens. Environ.* **2016**, *185*, 7–15. [CrossRef]
49. Yang, H.; Kong, J.; Hu, H.; Du, Y.; Gao, M.; Chen, F. A Review of Remote Sensing for Water Quality Retrieval: Progress and Challenges. *Remote Sens.* **2022**, *14*, 1770. [CrossRef]
50. Richter, R.; Schläpfer, D. *Atmospheric/Topographic Correction for Satellite Imagery: ATCOR-2/3 UserGuide*; DLR: Wessling, Germany, 2011.
51. Mayer, B.; Kylling, A. Technical note: The libRadtran software package for radiative transfer calculations—description and examples of use. *Atmos. Chem. Phys.* **2005**, *5*, 1855–1877. [CrossRef]
52. ESA. Level-2A Algorithm Overview. Available online: https://earth.esa.int/web/sentinel/technical-guides/sentinel-2-msi/level-2a/algorithm (accessed on 15 August 2020).
53. Fausset, L.V. *Fundamentals of Neural Networks: Architectures, Algorithms and Applications*; Pearson: New York, NY, USA, 1993.
54. Krasnopolsky, V.; Gemmill, W.; Breaker, L. A neural network multipara meter algorithm for SSM/I ocean retrievals: Comparisons and validations. *Remote Sens. Environ.* **2000**, *72*, 133–142. [CrossRef]
55. Vohland, M.; Besold, J.; Hill, J.; Fründ, H.-C. Comparing different multivariate calibration methods for the determination of soil organic carbon pools with visible to near infrared spectroscopy. *Geoderma* **2011**, *166*, 198–205. [CrossRef]
56. Liang, Y.; Yin, F.; Xie, D.; Liu, L.; Zhang, Y.; Ashraf, T. Inversion and Monitoring of the TP Concentration in Taihu Lake Using the Landsat-8 and Sentinel-2 Images. *Remote Sens.* **2022**, *14*, 6284. [CrossRef]
57. S. R. b. 74/2011. *Uredba o klasifikaciji Voda*; Sluzbeni glasnik RS: Beograd, Serbia, 1968.
58. S. R. b. 50/2012. *Uredba o Graničnim Vrednostima Zagađujućih Materija u Površinskim i Podzemnim Vodama i Sedimentu i Rokovima za Njihovo Dostizanje*; Sluzbeni Glasnik: Beograd, Serbia, 2012.
59. S. R. b. 74/2011. *Pravilnik o Parametrima Ekološkog i Hemijskog Statusa Površinskih Voda i Parametrima Hemijskog i Kvantitativnog Statusa Podzemnih Voda*; Sluzbeni Glasnik: Beograd, Serbia, 2011.
60. Miller, R.L.; McKeen, B.A. Using MODIS Terra 250 m Imagery to Map Concentrations of Total Suspended Matter in Coastal Waters. *Remote Sens. Environ.* **2004**, *93*, 259–266. [CrossRef]

61. Sadeghi, A.; Dinter, T.; Vountas, M.; Taylor, B.B.; Altenburg-Soppa, M.; Peeken, I.; Bracher, A. Improvement to the PhytoDOAS method for identification of coccolithophores using hyperspectral satellite data. *Ocean Sci.* **2012**, *8*, 1055–1070. [CrossRef]
62. Barraza-Moraga, F.; Alcayaga, H.; Pizarro, A.; Félez-Bernal, J.; Urrutia, R. Estimation of Chlorophyll-a Concentrations in Lanalhue Lake Using Sentinel-2 MSI Satellite Images. *Remote Sens.* **2022**, *14*, 5647. [CrossRef]
63. Roman, A.; Tovar-Sanchez, A.; Gauci, A.; Deidun, A.; Cabellero, I.; Colica, E.; D'Amivo, S.; Navarro, G. Water-Quality Moni-toring with a UAV-Mounted Multispectral Camera in Coastal Waters. *Remote Sens.* **2023**, *15*, 237. [CrossRef]
64. Zhao, X.; Li, Y.; Chen, Y.; Qiao, X.; Qian, W. Water Chlorophyll a Estimation Using UAV-Based Multispectral Data and Machine Learning. *Drones* **2023**, *7*, 2. [CrossRef]
65. Quang, N.H.; Dinh, N.T.; Dien, N.R.; Son, L.T. Calibration of Sentinel-2 Surface Reflectance for Water Quality Modelling in Binh Dinh's Coastal Zone of Vietnam. *Sustainability* **2023**, *15*, 1410. [CrossRef]
66. Yang, H.; Du, Y.; Zhao, H.; Chen, F. Water Quality Chl-a Inversion Based on Spatio-Temporal Fusion and Convolutional Neural Network. *Remote Sens.* **2022**, *14*, 1267. [CrossRef]
67. Chebud, Y.A.; Naja, G.M.; Rivero, R.G.; Melessa, A.M. Water Quality Monitoring Using Remote Sensing and an Artificial Neural Network. *Water Air Soil Pollut.* **2012**, *223*, 4875–4887. [CrossRef]
68. Ahmed, M.; Mumtaz, R.; Anwar, Z.; Shaukat, A.; Arif, O.; Shafait, F. A Multi–Step Approach for Optically Active and Inactive Water Quality Parameter Estimation Using Deep Learning and Remote Sensing. *Water* **2022**, *14*, 2112. [CrossRef]
69. Schmidhuber, J. Deep Learning in Neural Networks: An Overview. *arXiv* **2014**, arXiv:1404.7828v4. [CrossRef] [PubMed]
70. Prechelt, L. Early Stopping—But When. In *Neural Networks: Tricks of the Trade*; Springer: Berlin, Germany, 2012; pp. 53–67.
71. SEPA. Stanje Kvaliteta Vode Vodotoka. Agencija za Životnu Sredinu. Available online: http://77.46.150.213:8080/apex/f?p=406: 2:::::: (accessed on 15 October 2023).
72. Seyhan, E.; Dekker, A. Application of remote sensing techniques for water quality monitoring. *Aquat. Ecol.* **1986**, *20*, 41–50. [CrossRef]

Disclaimer/Publisher's Note: The statements, opinions and data contained in all publications are solely those of the individual author(s) and contributor(s) and not of MDPI and/or the editor(s). MDPI and/or the editor(s) disclaim responsibility for any injury to people or property resulting from any ideas, methods, instructions or products referred to in the content.

Article

Estimation of the Biogeochemical and Physical Properties of Lakes Based on Remote Sensing and Artificial Intelligence Applications

Kaire Toming [1,2,*], Hui Liu [3], Tuuli Soomets [1], Evelyn Uuemaa [4], Tiina Nõges [2] and Tiit Kutser [1]

1 Estonian Marine Institute, University of Tartu, Mäealuse 14, EE-12618 Tallinn, Estonia
2 Chair of Hydrobiology and Fishery, Institute of Agricultural and Environmental Sciences, Estonian University of Life Sciences, Kreutzwaldi 5, EE-51006 Tartu, Estonia
3 Department of Forestry, Mississippi State University, Starkville, MS 39762, USA
4 Institute of Ecology and Earth Sciences, University of Tartu, Vanemuise 46, EE-51014 Tartu, Estonia
* Correspondence: kaire.toming.001@ut.ee

Citation: Toming, K.; Liu, H.; Soomets, T.; Uuemaa, E.; Nõges, T.; Kutser, T. Estimation of the Biogeochemical and Physical Properties of Lakes Based on Remote Sensing and Artificial Intelligence Applications. *Remote Sens.* **2024**, *16*, 464. https://doi.org/10.3390/rs16030464

Academic Editors: Flor Alvarez-Taboada, Miro Govedarica and Gordana Jakovljević

Received: 17 December 2023
Revised: 19 January 2024
Accepted: 19 January 2024
Published: 25 January 2024

Copyright: © 2024 by the authors. Licensee MDPI, Basel, Switzerland. This article is an open access article distributed under the terms and conditions of the Creative Commons Attribution (CC BY) license (https://creativecommons.org/licenses/by/4.0/).

Abstract: Lakes play a crucial role in the global biogeochemical cycles through the transport, storage, and transformation of different biogeochemical compounds. Their regulatory service appears to be disproportionately important relative to their small areal extent, necessitating continuous monitoring. This study leverages the potential of optical remote sensing sensors, specifically Sentinel-2 Multispectral Imagery (MSI), to monitor and predict water quality parameters in lakes. Optically active parameters, such as chlorophyll a (CHL), total suspended matter (TSM), and colored dissolved matter (CDOM), can be directly detected using optical remote sensing sensors. However, the challenge lies in detecting non-optically active substances, which lack direct spectral characteristics. The capabilities of artificial intelligence applications can be used in the identification of optically non-active compounds from remote sensing data. This study aims to employ a machine learning approach (combining the Genetic Algorithm (GA) and Extreme Gradient Boost (XGBoost)) and in situ and Sentinel-2 Multispectral Imagery data to construct inversion models for 16 physical and biogeochemical water quality parameters including CHL, CDOM, TSM, total nitrogen (TN), total phosphorus (TP), phosphate (PO_4), sulphate, ammonium nitrogen, 5-day biochemical oxygen demand (BOD_5), chemical oxygen demand (COD), and the biomasses of phytoplankton and cyanobacteria, pH, dissolved oxygen (O_2), water temperature (WT) and transparency (SD). GA_XGBoost exhibited strong predictive capabilities and it was able to accurately predict 10 biogeochemical and 2 physical water quality parameters. Additionally, this study provides a practical demonstration of the developed inversion models, illustrating their applicability in estimating various water quality parameters simultaneously across multiple lakes on five different dates. The study highlights the need for ongoing research and refinement of machine learning methodologies in environmental monitoring, particularly in remote sensing applications for water quality assessment. Results emphasize the need for broader temporal scopes, longer-term datasets, and enhanced model selection strategies to improve the robustness and generalizability of these models. In general, the outcomes of this study provide the basis for a better understanding of the role of lakes in the biogeochemical cycle and will allow the formulation of reliable recommendations for various applications used in the studies of ecology, water quality, the climate, and the carbon cycle.

Keywords: water quality; lakes; remote sensing; Sentinel-2; artificial intelligence; machine learning; genetic algorithm; Extreme Gradient Boosting (XGBoost); water monitoring

1. Introduction

There are more than 117 million lakes (>0.002 km^2) on Earth [1]. They comprise only 4% of the Earth's land surface but contain 85% of the global freshwater resource upon which society relies for drinking, agriculture, fisheries, energy, transport, recreation, and tourism [2]. Moreover, lakes offer diverse habitats, support high levels of biodiversity, provide ecosystem services [3], and play a crucial role in the global biogeochemical cycles through the transport, storage, and transformation of biogeochemical compounds [4–6]. They contribute to climate regulation and are recognized as valuable sentinels of global environmental change [7].

The wide ecological, environmental, and socio-economic importance of lakes demands continuous monitoring of the water quality of lakes. Therefore, the need for improved and innovative approaches and techniques to obtain the required high-quality information on biogeochemical and physical water quality parameters is continuously growing. However, traditional in situ data collection and analysis methods are labor-intensive and often expensive, leading to only a small fraction of lakes being regularly observed, typically at a single point, and providing only a snapshot in time [8,9]. It is difficult to detect spatial or temporal variations in water quality [10]. Remote sensing offers an alternative to these limitations, but it presents challenges due to the optical complexity of lake water, the lack of in situ data needed for validation, and the absence of satellite sensors specifically designed for remote sensing of lakes [11]. The available spatial, temporal, spectral, and radiometric resolutions of ocean and land surface remote sensors are often not sufficient for remote sensing of lake water quality [12–17]. The technical issues have been partly improved by the European Space Agency (ESA) with the launch of Multispectral Instruments (MSI) on board of Sentinel-2A and of Sentinel-2B. Although it was originally designed for land monitoring, Sentinel-2 MSI has proven suitable for estimating lake water quality [16,18–21]. Sentinel-2 MSI has a revisit time of two to five days and an acceptable radiometric resolution, and it allows data acquisition at 10 m, 20 m, and 60 m spatial resolutions. These capabilities enable the assessment of an unprecedented number of lakes on a global scale.

Water quality can be estimated based on different biogeochemical and physical parameters of the water. The optically active parameters of water, such as colored dissolved organic matter (CDOM), total suspended matter (TSM), and chlorophyll-a (CHL), can be directly detected using the optical remote sensing sensors, making them the most commonly used parameters in remote sensing studies and monitoring programs [22–28]. There are also some physical parameters of water, such as transparency (e.g., Secchi disk depth, SD) and water surface temperature (WT), that can be estimated directly from remote sensing data and have been widely used in inland water quality studies [29–31].

Estimating non-optically active biogeochemical and physical water quality parameters, such as dissolved organic carbon (DOC), total nitrogen (TN), total phosphorus (TP), ammonia nitrogen (NH_3-N), ortho-phosphate (PO_4), biochemical oxygen demand (BOD), chemical oxygen demand (COD), dissolved oxygen (O_2), etc., that have no direct spectral characteristics, is much more challenging with optical remote sensing. However, the relationships between optically non-active and optically active lake water quality parameters allow the optical determination of non-active substances indirectly from remote sensing data [16,32–61]. While the estimation of optically non-active parameters in water, which lack direct optical signatures and spectral characteristics, has been limited historically, pioneering studies trace back to the 1990s [14,62]. However, advancements in space science and increased computing capacity have fueled a notable and rapidly growing trend in estimating optically non-active water quality parameters through remote sensing [55,58,63,64].

Remote sensing-based water quality retrieval methods can be categorized into empirical, semi-empirical, analytical (physical), and semi-analytical methods [65–68]. Empirical techniques focus on statistical relationships between spectral bands or band combinations and observed water parameters, without considering the spectral characteristics of the water components or providing a physical justification for the association [69]. Semi-empirical approaches generate algorithms based on physical and spectral information, which are connected to the optical properties of the observed components [65,66,68]. Analytical methods use inherent and apparent optical properties to predict the reflectance of surface water and calculate the concentrations of water constituents, while semi-analytical methods employ simplified analytical models [70].

Empirical and semi-empirical approaches are usually restricted to a given location and time of calibration and they often have poor inversion precision and weak generalization in retrieving water quality parameters in optically complex waters with nonlinear relationships between the concentrations and optical signatures [71,72]. Machine learning, an application of artificial intelligence, can detect both linear and nonlinear interactions and improves the identification of complex relationships between independent and dependent variables through the model itself [72,73]. Different types of machine learning approaches, such as supervised (e.g., Decision Tree, Random Forest, Support Vector Machines, Extreme Gradient Boosting), unsupervised (e.g., K-Means Clustering), and reinforcement learning (e.g., Principal Component Analysis), have been used in previous studies of water quality remote sensing [55,72,74–76]. While machine learning does pose challenges, such as complex model parameters, broad generalizability, overfitting, and difficulty finding the best parameter combination through self-regulation [72,77], it is worth noting the positive aspects. For example, Extreme Gradient Boosting (XGBoost), which is known for its ensemble learning capabilities, offers distinct advantages such as the effective handling of complex relationships within the data, robustness against overfitting, and optimal performance even with limited samples [72,78]. The decision to utilize XGBoost is underpinned by its track record as one of the most successful machine learning techniques across various domains in recent years [79–84]. Notably, while widely acknowledged in broader applications, its potential in limnology, specifically in the realm of remote sensing of lakes, has been underexplored. The numerous tuning parameters in XGBoost significantly impact the model accuracy and performance, posing a challenge in manually tuning global parameters to achieve optimal results [72]. In addressing this, the Genetic Algorithm (GA), a search-based optimization method, has demonstrated success in optimizing parameter settings for machine learning models in various studies [72,85,86]. Together, XGBoost and GA form a synergistic pairing, well-suited to meet the challenges related to the remote sensing applications in lakes.

Considering all the above, this study aims to (1) use the GA_XGBoost machine learning algorithm along with in situ and Sentinel-2 MSI data to construct inversion models of 14 biogeochemical (TN, TP, PO_4, sulfate (SO_4), ammonium nitrogen (NH_4N), 5 days BOD (BOD_5), COD, CHL, CDOM, TSM, biomass of phytoplankton (FPBM), biomass of cyanobacteria (CYBM), pH, O_2) and two physical (WT, SD) lake water quality parameters; and (2) provide a practical demonstration of the developed inversion models, illustrating their applicability in estimating various water quality parameters simultaneously across multiple lakes on five different dates. The results of this study will provide the basis for a better understanding of the role of lakes in the biogeochemical cycle and will facilitate reliable recommendations for various applications in the studies of ecology, water quality, the climate, and the carbon cycle. Additionally, the results will lead to the possibility to improve the cost-efficiency of lake monitoring and facilitate making detailed recommendations for decision-makers.

2. Materials and Methods

2.1. Study Sites

Biogeochemical and physical water quality parameters used as input data for the GA_XGBoost model in the current study were collected from the surface layer (0.5 m) of 45 Estonian lakes (Figure 1) from April to September in the years 2015 to 2020.

The surface areas of the in situ studied lakes are between 0.07 km^2 to 27.4 km^2 and the mean and the maximum depths vary from 0.3 m to 12 m, and from 1 m to 38 m, accordingly. These 45 lakes represent five different lake classes [87]: oligotrophic (3 lakes), mesotrophic (10 lakes), eutrophic/hypertrophic (25 lakes), semidystrophic/dystrophic (6 lakes), and acidotrophic (1 lake). Both soft-water and hard-water lakes were represented (see detailed information and sampling dates in Appendix A, Table A1). All lakes are included in the state monitoring program of Estonia and were sampled one to ten times during the study period. Data were collected by the Institute of Environmental and Agricultural Sciences of the Estonian University of Life Sciences and provided by the Environmental Monitoring Database (KESE) of the Estonian Environment Agency.

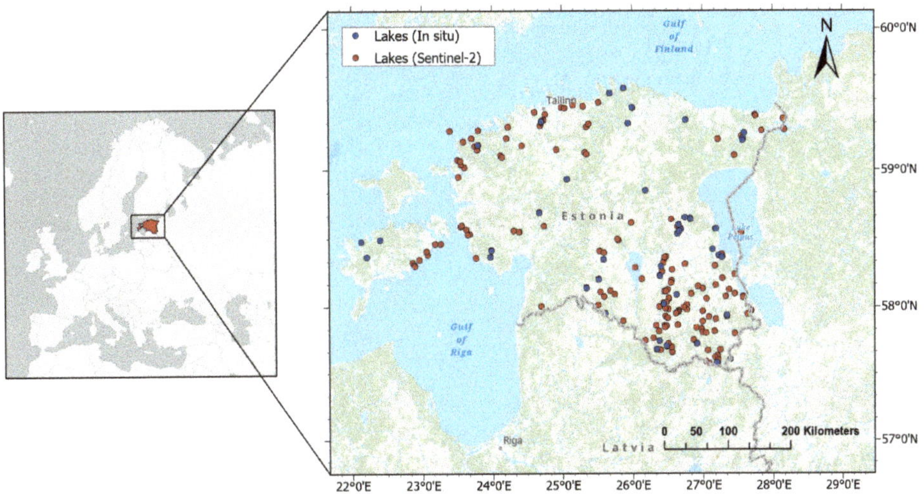

Figure 1. Study area, 45 lakes of the input data for the GA_XGBoost model (Lakes (In situ), blue dots); and 180 Estonian lakes (>0.1 km^2), whose biogeochemical and physical water quality parameters were retrieved using the GA_XGBoost models and Sentinel-2 data (Lakes (Sentinel-2), red dots).

Based on the validated GA_XGBoost models, the biogeochemical and physical water quality parameters of 180 Estonian lakes with size >0.1 km^2 (Figure 1) were retrieved from Sentinel-2 images on five different dates (19 April 2021; 10 May 2018; 18 June 2021; 18 July 2020; 17 August 2020) to demonstrate the implementation of the developed models. Although there are 354 lakes in Estonia that are larger than 0.1 km^2, only 180 of them were cloudless on all five dates. An Analysis of Variance (ANOVA) test was used to analyze the differences among means of water quality parameters on different dates. Additionally, the Tukey's Honest Significant Difference test (Tukey's HSD), a post-hoc test based on the studentized range distribution, was employed to assess whether the biogeochemical and physical parameters on five different dates exhibited significant differences from each other.

2.2. Biogeochemical and Physical Water Quality Parameters

Most of the biogeochemical and physical parameters covered by the current study are optically non-active (13 parameters), while 3 parameters are optically active (Table 1).

The statistical information of the biogeochemical and physical water quality parameters of study lakes is summarized in the Table 2. Since the lakes with different trophic levels and different alkalinity from six different months were included in the study, a large variability of in situ data was expected. TP, PO$_4$, NH$_4$N, CHL, and CDOM showed the highest variability. Nevertheless, the skewness (showing the asymmetry of distribution) and kurtosis (showing whether the data are heavy-tailed or light-tailed relative to a normal distribution) values of in situ datasets remained mostly in the acceptable range (skewness was between −2 and 2 and kurtosis was between −7 and 7). However, some studied parameters were highly skewed, for example, TP, which followed log-normal distribution. In general, machine learning models (e.g., XGBoost) do not assume any normality and they also work well with non-normally distributed data. Despite this, log-transformed data were used in the case of highly skewed TP. In addition, CHL is known to be log-normally distributed, so log-transformed values are often used. Therefore, log-transformed data were also used for CHL in the current study.

Table 1. Biogeochemical and physical parameters covered by the current study, their abbreviations, measurement units, and reference to measurement methodologies. Optically active parameters are underlined.

Parameter	Abbreviation	Unit	Reference/Standard
Total nitrogen	TN	mgN/L	ISO, 2003 [88]
Total phosphorus	TP	mgP/L	ISO, 2018 [89]
Phosphate	PO$_4$	mg/L	ISO, 2004 [90]
Sulfate	SO$_4$	mg/L	ISO, 2007 [91]
Ammonium nitrogen	NH$_4$N	mg/L	ISO, 1984 [92]
5-day biochemical oxygen demand	BOD$_5$	mgO$_2$/L	ISO, 2019 [93]
Dichromatic chemical oxygen demand	COD	mgO$_2$/L	ISO, 2004 [94]
Biomass of phytoplankton	FPBM	mg/L	ISO, 1992 [95]
Biomass of cyanobacteria	CYBM	mg/L	ISO, 1992 [95]
pH	pH		ISO, 2012a [96]
Dissolved oxygen	O$_2$	mg/L	ISO, 2012b [97]
Water temperature	WT	°C	[98]
Secchi disk depth	SD	m	[99]
Chlorophyll a	CHL	μg/L	ISO, 1992 [95]
Colored dissolved organic matter	CDOM	mg/L	[98]
Total suspended matter	TSM	mg/L	[98]

Table 2. Means (mean), standard deviations (std), minimum (min) and maximum (max) values, 25th percentile, 50th percentile, 75th percentile, Kurtosis, and Skewness of biogeochemical and physical water quality parameters of study lakes (2015–2020). The names and units of the parameters are available in Table 1. Count shows the number of samples as well as the matchups with Sentinel-2 MSI data.

	Count	Mean	Std	Min	25%	50%	75%	Max	Skewness	Kurtosis
TN	102	0.90	0.61	0.15	0.51	0.73	1.10	3.90	2.23	6.77
TP	102	0.06	0.19	0.01	0.02	0.03	0.05	1.60	7.02	50.4
PO$_4$	99	0.008	0.007	0.002	0.003	0.006	0.01	0.05	2.90	10.4
SO$_4$	100	7.70	7.28	0.10	1.70	4.65	12.0	31.0	1.13	0.58
NH$_4$N	102	0.023	0.021	0.01	0.01	0.02	0.024	0.14	3.57	15.9
BOD$_5$	102	2.15	1.39	0.70	1.30	1.70	2.68	7.50	1.77	3.45
COD	87	42.1	29.2	15.0	23.0	36.0	48.0	160	1.99	4.20
CHL	102	13.6	14.9	1.00	3.45	8.30	17.5	100	2.60	10.4
CDOM	102	10.9	15.9	0.85	3.10	5.55	10.8	81.0	3.22	10.7
TSM	38	156	95.9	8.23	99.1	154	223	371	0.24	−0.6
FPBM	80	4.73	5.40	0.16	0.76	2.60	6.78	21.7	1.36	0.82
CYBM	58	1.81	3.24	0.00	0.03	0.33	2.05	13.0	2.22	4.29
PH	83	7.98	1.07	3.65	7.85	8.21	8.53	9.40	−2.16	5.05
O$_2$	84	8.62	2.42	2.63	7.21	8.80	10.1	15.6	−0.06	0.41
WT	85	17.1	5.08	5.20	13.7	18.0	20.6	26.9	−0.40	−0.35
SD	98	1.88	1.24	0.25	0.70	1.75	2.60	5.00	0.67	−0.37

2.3. Satellite Data

Copernicus Sentinel-2A and -2B MSI data were used to retrieve the biogeochemical and physical water quality parameters of lakes. The Sentinel-2 MSI is available in 13 spectral bands with different spatial resolutions. Band 1 to Band 8a were used in the current study. The spatial resolution of Band 2 (B2; central wavelength, CWL = 492.1 nm), Band 3 (B3; CWL = 559 nm), and Band 4 (B4; CWL = 665 nm) is 10 m. The spatial resolution of Band 5 (B5; CWL = 703.8 nm), Band 6 (B6; CWL = 739.1 nm), Band 7 (B7; CWL = 779.7 nm), and Band 8A (B8A; CWL = 864.80 nm) is 20 m. The spatial resolution of Band 1 (B1; CWL = 442.30 nm) is 60 m. Prior to the processing, all the Sentinel-2 images were resampled to 20 m spatial resolution. Sentinel-2 Level-1 data were processed using the ESTHub Processing Platform—Portal for Earth observation data processing (EstHub) provided by

Land Board of Estonia and the Sentinel Application Platform (SNAP 8.0) and developed by Brockmann Consult (Hamburg, Germany), SkyWatch (Kitchener, UK), and C-S, Le Plessis Robinson (France). For atmospheric correction, Case 2 Regional CoastColour processor with C2X (v1.5.) neuronal nets [100] for S2 MSI (C2X) and the multisensor pixel identification tool (IdePix) were used. C2X was deliberately chosen for atmospheric correction due to its demonstrated effectiveness in previous studies, particularly in lakes with diverse optical properties within the same geographical region as in the present study [21,101]. To remove low quality or invalid pixels, following flags were used: IDEPIX_CLOUD, IDEPIX_CLOUD_AMBIGUOUS, IDEPIX_CLOUD_SURE, IDEPIX_CLOUD_BUFFER, IDEPIX_CLOUD_SHADOW, IDEPIX_COASTLINE, IDEPIX_LAND, IDEPIX_CIRRUS_SURE, IDEPIX_CIRRUS_AMBIGUOUS, IDEPIX_POTENTIAL_SHADOW, and IDEPIX_CLUSTERED_CLOUD_SHADOW.

The match-ups were extracted as the means of 3 × 3 pixels centered in the in situ sampling point. If the in situ sampling point was located too close to shoreline, the pixels of the center of the lake were extracted to minimize the adjacency effect. Match-ups were selected with up to 2 days difference between the Sentinel-2 image acquisition and the in situ measurement date. In this study, we obtained one (19 lakes), two (11 lakes), three (6 lakes), four (2 lakes), or 5–10 (6 lakes) matchups with Sentinel-2 data from April to September 2015–2020 (Appendix A, Table A1). The exact number of match-ups for each biogeochemical and physical water quality parameter is seen in Table 2.

2.4. Retrieval of Biogeochemical and Physical Water Quality Parameters

Fifteen different formulae based on 2- or 3-band or band ratios were used (Table 3). Every formula was tested with different band combinations.

Table 3. The basic formulae used in this study. B notes the atmospherically corrected angular dependent water-leaving reflectance and index a, b, or c denotes different Sentinel-2 bands (8 bands in different options).

Formula
1. $B_a + B_b$
2. $B_a - B_b$
3. B_a / B_b
4. $B_a * B_b$
5. $B_a + B_b + B_c$
6. $B_a + B_b * B_c$
7. $(B_a + B_b) * B_c$
8. $(B_a - B_b) * B_c$
9. $(B_a + B_b) / B_c$
10. $B_a * B_b / B_c$
11. $(B_a - B_b) / (B_a + B_b)$
12. $(B_a / B_b) * (B_a / B_b)$
13. $B_a / B_b - B_a / B_c$
14. $B_a - (B_b + B_c)/2$
15. $B_a / (B_b + B_c)$

A total of 3034 unique band combinations was generated. For each biogeochemical and physical water quality parameter, we initially employed all the input variables (single bands and band combinations), and then selected the best top ten inputs, and ultimately determined the optimal input combination within the top ten inputs range using a filter-based feature selection method. Subsequently, these selected combinations were employed in the GA_XGBoost model, and the best combinations for each parameter were determined based on model performance.

2.5. Extreme Gradient Boosting Model and Genetic Algorithm

The XGBoost modelling procedure starts with continuous iteration, when the tree will be added in each iteration to fit the residuals from the last fit, finally forming a robust estimator that integrates many tree models, thereby improving the model effect [72]. The predicted value in the gradient lifting regression tree is the weighted sum of the prediction results for all weak classifiers [72]. For XGBoost, each leaf node of a tree has a prediction score, i.e., the leaf weight, which is the regression value of all samples on that leaf node in that tree, and the sum of the leaf weights on all weak classifiers is the predicted value [72]. A more detailed description of XGBoost model can be found in [78].

GA was added to the XGBoost to optimize the tuning parameter selection process of the model (the model is continuously iterated until the optimal solution is reached). The GA_XGBoost algorithm successfully combines the advantages of small sample regression of XGBoost, controlling model complexity, and reducing model overfitting [72].

The parameter tuning of GA_XGBoost included the following (XGBoost Tutorials—xgboost 1.0.0-SNAPSHOT documentation [102]):

(1) General parameters selection: Related to which booster to use for boosting. Gbtree booster that uses a tree-based model was selected;
(2) Booster parameters:
- Step size shrinkage used in the update to avoid overfitting (learning_rate). Range 0–1.
- Maximum depth of a tree (max_depth). The higher the value the more complex the model and the probability of overfitting is higher. Range 0–∞.
- Minimum sum of instance weight (hessian) required in a child (min_child_weight). The larger min_child_weight is, the more conservative the algorithm. Range 0–∞.
- Subsample ratio of training instances (subsample). Setting it to 0.5 means that XGBoost will randomly sample half of the training data before trees grow, preventing overfitting. Subsampling occurs once in each boosting iteration. Range 0–1.
- The subsample ratio of columns when building each tree (colsample_bytree). Subsampling is performed once for each tree constructed. Range 0–1.
(3) Learning task parameters: specify the learning task and the consistent learning objective. Objective reg:squarederror (regression with squared loss) was applied.

Train/test/validation split was made prior to implementing the GA_XGBoost using 60% of the data for training, 20% of the data for validation, and 20% of the data for testing. The number of samples in each split varied by parameter because the initial set of samples was not the same per parameter. The training dataset was used for training the GA_XGBoost algorithm, while the test dataset was used for helping to adjust GA_XGBoost parameters to control the precision. The validation dataset was completely independent from the one that was used for testing the performance of the developed GA_XGBoost algorithm. The training, testing, and validation processes of the GA_XGBoost model were applied using the Scikit-learn Python modules and XGBoost Python package in Python 3.9.

2.6. Accuracy Evaluation

The ranking system based on different statistical metrics was used to find the best model for retrieval of the biogeochemical and physical water quality parameters from satellite data. A statistical metric, the coefficient of determination (R^2), was scaled from 0 (minimum value) to 1 (maximum value) and a p-value < 0.001 was given 1, a p-value between 0.001 and 0.05 was given 0.5, and a p-value >0.05 was given 0. The root-mean-squared error (RMSE) and mean absolute percentage error (MAPE) were scaled from 0 (maximum value) to 1 (minimum value). Finally, all four values were summed and the model with the highest score was nominated as the best model for retrieval. Scikit-learn metrics module (sklearn.metrics, [103]) in Python 3.9 was used to calculate R^2, RMSE, and MAPE. R^2 denotes the squared correlation between the measured and predicted values.

With R^2, a p-value was calculated. RMSE denotes the mean difference between the measured and predicted values. RMSE is calculated using Equation (1).

$$\text{RMSE} = \sqrt{\frac{1}{n}\sum_{i=1}^{n}(\hat{y}_i - y_i)^2} \tag{1}$$

where $\hat{y}_i$ is the predicted value, y_i is the measured value, and n is the number of measurements. MAPE denotes the mean absolute percentage error from the measured value and the predicted values divided by the measured value. MAPE is calculated using Equation (2).

$$\text{MAPE} = \frac{100\%}{n}\sum_{i=1}^{n}\left|\frac{y_i - \hat{y}_i}{y_i}\right| \qquad (2)$$

where $\hat{y}_i$ is the predicted value, y_i is the measured value, and n is the number of measurements.

3. Results

3.1. Correlations between Optically Active and Optically Non-Active Parameters

Almost all the optically non-active parameters covered by the current study showed a statistically significant correlation (p-value < 0.05) with at least one of the optically active parameters (Figure 2). There were statistically significant positive correlations between CHL and TN, TP, BOD_5, COD, FPBM, and CYBM. The same optically non-active water quality parameters gave negative correlations with SD. CDOM was positively correlated with TN, TP, PO_4, NH_4N, and COD, and was negatively correlated with pH. TSM showed positive correlations with SO_4 and pH, and negative correlations with TP, PO_4, and COD. O_2 was the only parameter that did not show a statistically significant correlation with any optically active parameters. However, O_2 was correlated with pH and BOD_5, which correlated strongly with CDOM and CHL, respectively (Figure 2).

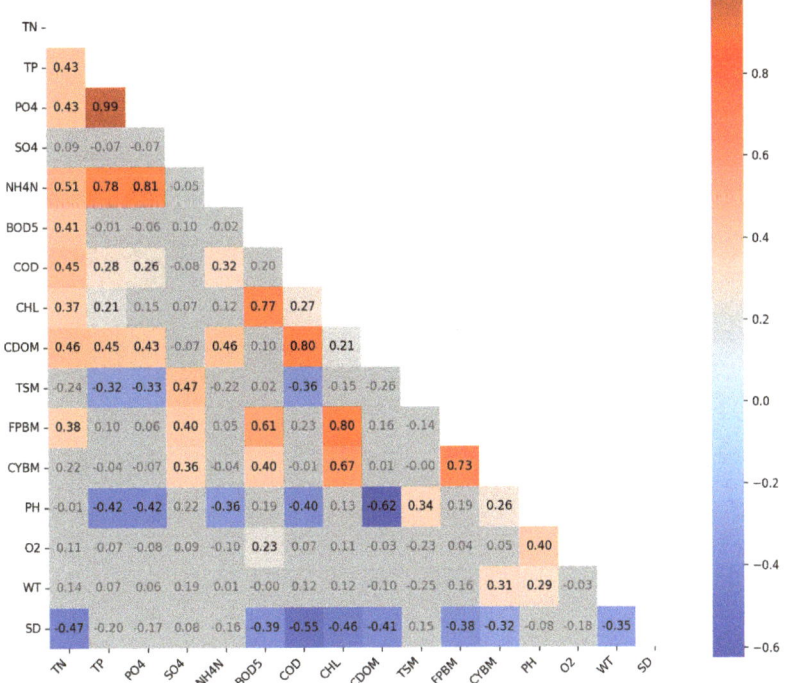

Figure 2. Heatmap of Pearson correlations between biogeochemical and physical water quality parameters. Statistically significant correlations (p-value < 0.05) are colored either red (positive) or blue (negative), while correlations that were not significant (p > 0.05) are marked as grey.

Given that various optically active substances exert an influence on different segments of the reflectance spectrum, the approach to non-optical substances involves seeking connections with the spectral regions affected by the correlated optical substances. Simultaneously, non-active substances are often associated with multiple optically active parameters. Therefore, our approach involved a thorough examination across various spectral bands to elucidate the rationale behind retrieving non-optically active parameter values through remote sensing methods.

3.2. Reflectance Spectra of Sentinel-2 MSI

The spectral characteristics of optically active substances varied among lakes with different trophic statuses, reflecting differences in their concentration and composition (Figure 3). Commonly, the mean reflectance spectra of oligotrophic lakes showed high values at shorter wavelengths and low values in the red part of the spectra. The mean reflectance spectra of mesotrophic and eutrophic lakes with turbid and productive waters showed typical peaks around 560 and 700–710 nm. The peak near 700–710 nm indicated a very high biomass in the water. Acidotrophic and dystrophic lakes were brown in color and were found mainly in forest and peatland areas. Their typical reflectance spectra were very similar and are combined into one class in Figure 3. In lakes with brown water, the water-leaving signal is usually very low in most parts of the spectrum due to a very high concentration of CDOM. However, the reflectance increased towards red wavelengths as CDOM absorption decreased exponentially with the increasing wavelength. As mentioned above, C2X was intentionally selected for atmospheric correction based on its established efficacy in prior studies, specifically in lakes exhibiting diverse optical properties within the identical geographical region as the current study [21,101], and the consistency of the reflectance spectra with the expected shapes reaffirms the reliability and robust performance of C2X, substantiating its effective application in waters characterized by diverse optical properties.

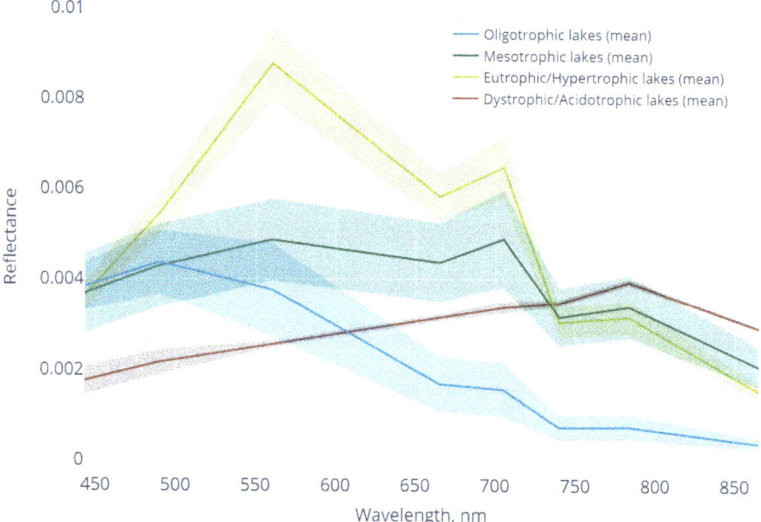

Figure 3. The mean Sentinel-2 MSI atmospherically corrected reflectance spectra sorted by the trophic state of study lakes. Sentinel-2 data are derived from each match-up point. Thick lines show the mean value, and the semitransparent area shows the standard error ($\pm$) of the mean.

3.3. GA_XGBoost Model Performance and Evaluation

The best combinations of the two- or three-band or band ratio algorithms that outperformed other combinations from a total of 3034 algorithms were used in the GA_XGBoost model as an input variable (x) to predict one of the water quality parameters (y) (Table 4). Band 4 (665 nm) was used most frequently in the two or three bands or band ratio algorithms of the best models, followed by bands 2 (490 nm), 3 (560 nm), 5 (705 nm), and 6 (740 nm). Bands 1 (443 nm), 7 (783 nm) and 8a (865 nm) appeared somewhat less frequently. This was not surprising as the water leaving signal in the blue band (B1) was often negligible in our lakes due to the high concentration of CDOM and phytoplankton, both of which absorb blue light strongly. The water-leaving signal in NIR (Bands 7 and 8a) is usually negligible in aquatic environments due to the very high absorption of light by water molecules at those wavelengths. However, a very high biomass of phytoplankton (bloom) or a very high concentration of mineral particles results in non-negligible water reflectance in NIR [104–106]. The studied lakes usually did not have very high concentrations of mineral particles, while the high biomass was seen also in the 705 nm (B5) peak in the reflectance spectra of many lakes.

Table 4. The two- or three-band or band ratio algorithms (selected using filter-based feature selection method) for deriving biogeochemical and physical water quality parameters (y) from Sentinel-2 MSI data that were used as input data (x) in the GA_XGBoost model. The full names and units of the parameters are available in Table 1 and the accuracy indices of the best models are shown in Table 5.

Water Quality Parameter (y)	x
TP	'B2 * B6', '(B1 − B5) * B3', '(B7/B3)*(B7/B3)', 'B4/B2-B4/B7', '(B7 + B2)/B3', '(B2 − B4)*B6', '(B3 + B5) * B1'
TN	'B5 − (B4 + B3)/2', 'B7/(B2 + B4)', 'B7 − (B4 + B8A)/2', '(B4 + B1)/B3', 'B1 − (B7 + B5)/2', '(B1 + B8A)/B3'
PO$_4$	'B2 * B6/B1', 'B3 * B6/B2', 'B7 * B3/B2', 'B2/(B7 + B6)', 'B2 − (B6 + B4)/2', 'B5 − (B2 + B3)/2', '(B2 − B7) * B4', '(B2 − B6)/(B2 − B6)', '(B2/B6) * (B2/B6)'
NH$_4$	'B2 − (B3 + B4)/2', 'B3 − (B6 + B1)/2', '(B6 − B8A) * B5', 'B2/B4 − B2/B6', 'B2/B6 − B2/B4', 'B4/B8A − B4/B1'
SO$_4$	'B3 * B8A/B4', 'B4 * B1/B7', 'B4/B2 − B4/B1', 'B1/(B7 + B2)', '(B3 + B5)/B1', '(B7 + B2)/B1', 'B1 − (B7 + B6)/2', '(B1 − B3) * B5', '(B8A − B7) * B6'
O$_2$	'B5 * B2/B3', '(B4 + B8A) * B3', 'B5 − (B4 + B8A)/2', '(B1 − B8A) * B6'
pH	'B2 − B1', '(B6 + B8A)/B7', 'B2 − (B1 + B3)/2', 'B4 − (B3 + B5)/2', '(B4 − B5) * B3', 'B4/B2 − B4/B1'
WT	'(B1 − B3) * B6', '(B1 − B4) * B6', '(B2 − B3) * B4'
COD	'B8A * B6/B1', 'B7 + B4 * B5', 'B7 + B5 * B4', 'B4 − (B5 + B8A)/2', '(B5 − B6)/(B5 − B6)', 'B1/B3 − B1/B4', 'B1/B4 − B1/B3'
BOD$_5$	'B4/B5', '(B5 + B6)/B4', 'B6 − (B1 + B8A)/2', '(B5/B4) * (B5/B4)'
SD	'B6 * B5/B4', '(B1 − B2) * B6', '(B2 − B1) * B6', '(B2 − B5) * B6'
FPBM	'B6 * B2/B1', 'B7 + B3 * B2', '(B7 + B6) * B8A', '(B8A + B4) * B6'
CYBM	'B4 + B3 * B7', '(B5 + B4) * B8A', '(B8A + B4) * B7'
CHL	'(B2 + B4) * B8A', '(B2/B6) * (B2/B6)', 'B4/B1 − B4/B5'
CDOM	'B2/B5 − B2/B6', 'B2/B6 − B2/B4', 'B4/B6 − B4/B5', 'B6/B7 − B6/B5', 'B7/B6 − B7/B5'
TSM	'B6-B2', 'B2-(B6 + B7)/2', '(B3 − B4) * B1', '(B4 − B3) * B1', '(B5 − B4) * B8A', '(B6 − B8A) * B7'

The scatter plots of training, test, and validation datasets produced using the best GA_XGBoost_model for deriving biogeochemical and physical water quality parameters from Sentinel-2 are shown in Figure 4. The performance metrics of the best GA_XGBoost models of different water quality parameters (Table 5) showed that the MAPE and RMSE increased and R^2 decreased from the training stage to the testing stage (e.g., TN, SO$_4$, O$_2$, WT, COD, and SD). The change was generally smaller and rather minor when moving from the testing phase to the validation phase, with some exceptions (TP, TN, PO$_4$, NH$_4$, and SO$_4$). Overall, GA_XGBoost models for optically active substances and parameters highly correlated with them (BOD$_5$, FPBM, CYBM) performed significantly better than other models and showed high accuracy (R^2 between 0.79 and 0.92). However, the MAPE exceeded the acceptable range (>50%) in the case of FPBM, CYBM, SO$_4$, and NH$_4$N. This was in contrast to TP, TN, PO$_4$, O$_2$, pH, WT, COD and SD, for which models had a somewhat lower R^2, but MAPE remained <50%. The MAPE values for FPBM, CYBM, SO$_4$, and NH$_4$N surpassed the acceptable range, rendering it challenging to achieve accurate retrievals of the corresponding water quality parameters using these models. Thus, GA_XGBoost was able to predict 12 biogeochemical and physical water quality parameters with acceptable accuracy (TN, TP, PO$_4$, BOD$_5$, COD, CHL, CDOM, TSM, pH, O$_2$, WT, SD). These 12 GA_XGBoost models were used to retrieve the biogeochemical and physical water quality parameters of 180 Estonian lakes >0.1 km^2 from Sentinel-2 images simultaneously on five different dates (19 April 2021; 10 May 2018; 18 June 2021; 18 July 2020; 17 August 2020) to provide a practical demonstration of the developed inversion models.

Table 5. The performance metrics of the best GA_XGBoost model for deriving biogeochemical and physical water quality parameters from Sentinel-2 data. n shows the number of match-ups between in situ and Sentinel-2 data; R^2-is the coefficient of determination; MAPE is mean absolute percentage error (%); and RMSE is the root-mean-square error. Accuracy indices (R^2, MAPE, RMSE) of the training, testing and validating phases are shown.

Water Quality Parameter	Total n	Training				Testing				Validation		
		n	R^2	MAPE(%)	RMSE	n	R^2	MAPE(%)	RMSE	n	R^2	MAPE(%)	RMSE
TP	102	60	0.99	0.16	0.00	21	0.90	36.5	0.02	21	0.60	34.4	0.02
TN	102	60	0.99	0.21	0.00	21	0.68	36.0	0.24	21	0.46	32.0	0.32
PO$_4$	99	59	0.99	7.24	0.0005	20	0.87	43.9	0.003	20	0.45	43.8	0.004
NH$_4$	102	60	0.99	3.39	0.0008	21	0.79	75.5	0.02	21	0.68	161	0.19
SO$_4$	100	60	0.99	0.89	0.03	20	0.69	168	3.26	20	0.58	123	5.20
O$_2$	84	50	0.99	1.98	0.21	17	0.62	15.2	1.31	17	0.62	46.1	4.54
pH	83	49	0.99	0.59	0.05	17	0.72	7.02	0.64	17	0.71	7.27	0.67
WT	85	51	0.99	1.37	0.78	17	0.63	14.1	3.08	17	0.58	17.3	3.96
COD	87	51	0.99	0.27	0.17	18	0.49	29.6	12.9	18	0.42	43.9	17.9
BOD$_5$	102	60	0.99	0.03	0.0005	21	0.90	17.8	0.56	21	0.85	30.1	0.66
SD	98	58	0.99	7.70	0.12	20	0.58	37.9	0.86	20	0.57	38.7	0.81
FPBM	80	48	0.99	1.32	0.01	16	0.79	169	2.01	16	0.79	109	2.19
CYBM	58	34	0.99	4.94	0.0008	12	0.85	684	1.64	12	0.88	532	1.81
CHL	102	60	0.96	17.3	3.41	21	0.80	71.5	9.87	21	0.82	48.8	4.78
CDOM	102	60	0.99	0.01	0.001	21	0.94	41.5	3.77	21	0.92	40.7	6.72
TSM	38	22	0.99	0.0007	0.001	8	0.94	20.3	22.3	8	0.83	43.8	32.1

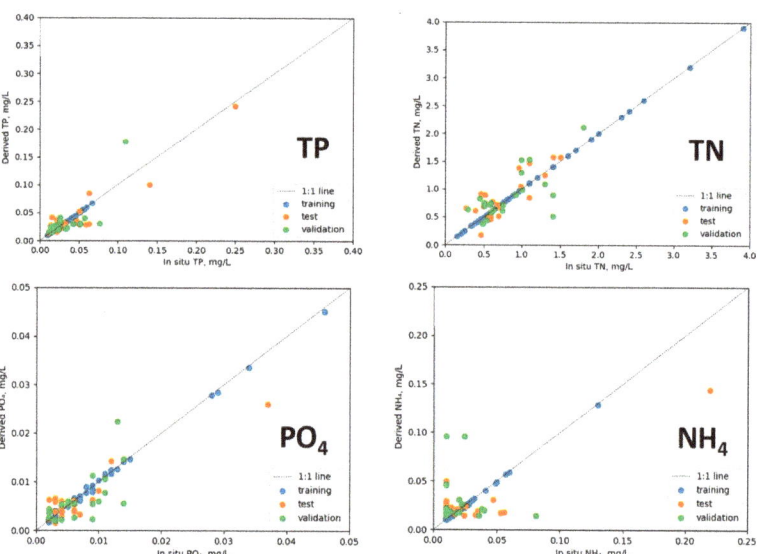

Figure 4. Cont.

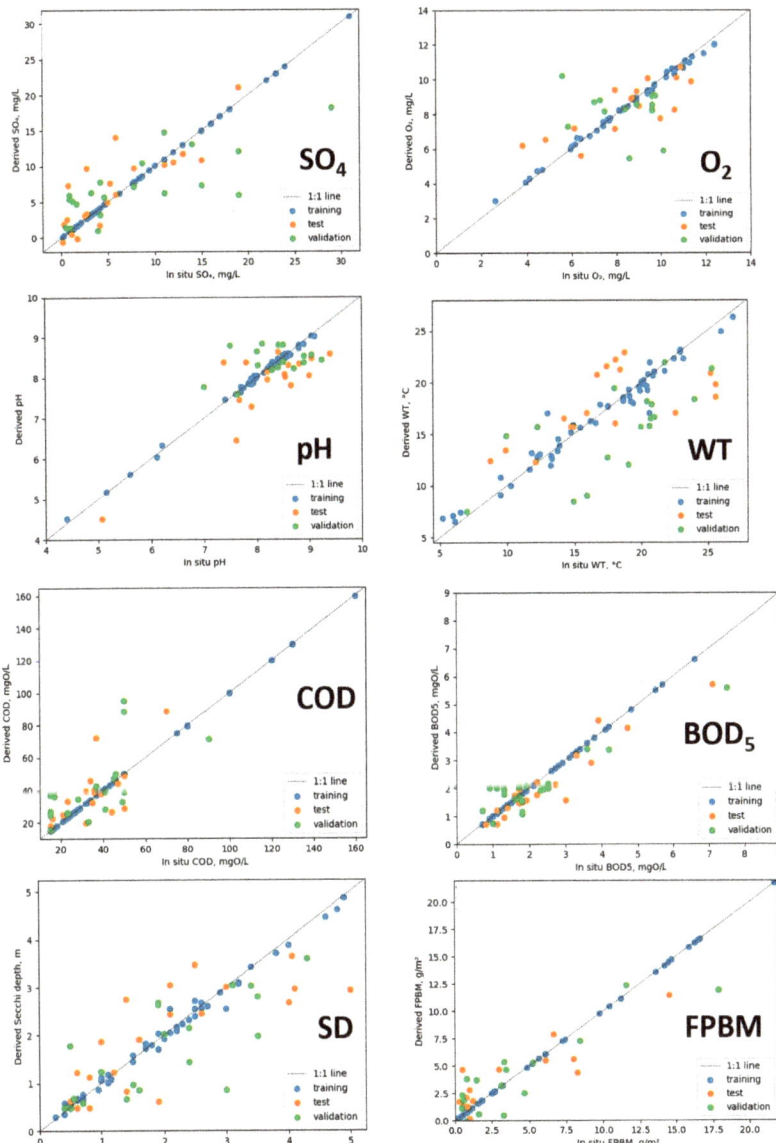

Figure 4. *Cont.*

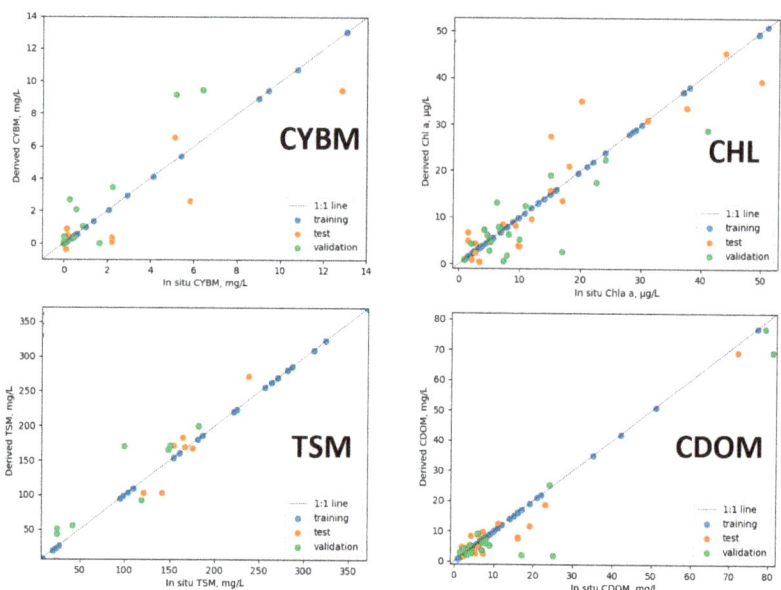

Figure 4. Scatter plots of training, test, and validation datasets produced using the best GA_XGB_model for deriving biogeochemical and physical water quality parameters from Sentinel-2 data along with the ideal model (1:1 line). The figure starts on the previous page.

3.4. A Practical Demonstration of the Developed Inversion Models

To demonstrate the practical utility of the developed models, the GA_XGBoost algorithms were employed to map biogeochemical and physical water quality parameters across 180 lakes on five distinct dates. We considered it important to choose dates when as many lakes as possible were cloud-free. Therefore, dates from different years are presented (Figure 5). However, we tried to ensure that all months from April to August were represented, regardless of the specific year. Furthermore, the aim was not to examine all 180 lakes in depth, but rather to provide a general demonstration of the developed models' practical applicability.

In general, statistically significant differences were found between the mean values of biogeochemical and physical water quality parameters at different dates (ANOVA, p-value < 0.05). TP, TN, PO_4, CHL, and CDOM were the highest on 19 April 2021 (0.05 mg/L, 0.98 mg/L, 0.011 mg/L, 12.9 µg/L, and 12.4 mg/L, respectively), and decreased in other months (Figure 5). The mean PO_4 was significantly different from other dates on 19 April 2021 (Tukey's HSD, p-value < 0.05), and the mean values of CDOM on 19 April 2021 and 10 May 2018 were significantly different from 18 July 2020 and 17 August 2020 (Tukey's HSD, p-value < 0.05). The mean concentrations of TP, TN, TSM, and CHL differed most significantly on all five dates (Tukey's HSD, p-value < 0.05). CHL reached its lowest values on 18 June 2021 (mean, 5.97 µg/L), TN and CDOM reached their lowest values on 18 July 2020 (the mean values were 0.76 mg/L and 8.74 mg/L, respectively), and TP and PO_4 reached their lowest values on 17 August 2020 (the mean values were 0.02 mg/L and 0.007 mg/L, respectively). The concentrations of TSM were very variable in different lakes and the mean values showed no significant trend throughout the season. The average TN:TP ratio varied from 25 to 56 on different dates, having the highest mean values and being statistically distinct from the other dates in August 2020 (Tukey's HSD, p-value < 0.05), indicating a high phosphorus limitation at that time of year at most of the lakes. The concentrations of BOD_5 and COD decreased from April to July and increased slightly in August, similarly to CHL, with the mean values significantly different from others dates on 19 April 2021 (Tukey's HSD,

p-value < 0.05). Overall, the average BOD$_5$ values were around 2 mg O$_2$/L on all five dates and did not exceed 6 mg O$_2$/L in any of the 180 lakes referring to clear or moderately polluted lakes. The mean value of COD ranged from 33.1 to 36.9 mg O$_2$/L. The mean concentration of O$_2$ was highest (8.53 mg/L) and the mean value of WT was lowest (17.4 °C) on 19 April 2021. The mean value of SD was also significantly lower (1.20 m) on 19 April 2021 compared to other dates (Tukey's HSD, p-value < 0.05). Similarly to the mean concentration of CHL, the mean values of pH were somewhat higher on 19 April 2021 (8.09) and on 17 August 2020 (7.95).

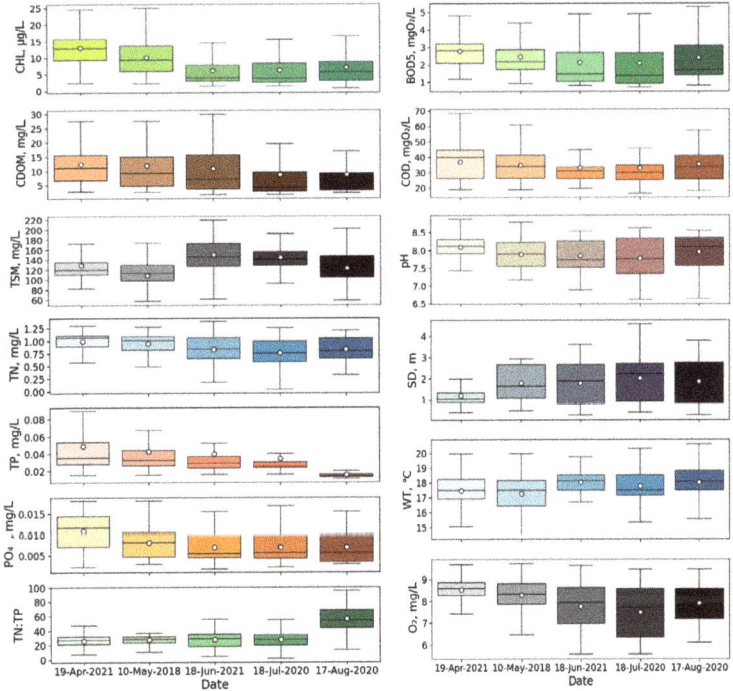

Figure 5. The boxplots of the mean values of chlorophyll a (CHL, µg/L), colored dissolved organic matter (CDOM, mg/L), total suspended matter (TSM, mg/L), total nitrogen (TN, mg/L), total phosphorus (TP, mg/L), PO$_4$ (mg/L), TN:TP ratio, BOD$_5$ (mg O$_2$/L), COD (mg O$_2$/L), pH, Secchi depth (SD, m), water temperature (WT, C°), and O$_2$ (mg/L) in 180 Estonian lakes > 0.1 km^2 on five different dates using Sentinel-2 data. On the plots the line indicates the median, the circle is the mean, the box shows the interquartile range, and the upper and lower whiskers are the maximum and minimum, respectively.

4. Discussion

The correlation with optically active substances serves as a valuable consideration for the assessment of non-optically active water quality parameters using remote sensing. Furthermore, the goal is not merely to establish correlations but, more importantly, to determine causative relationships. This distinction underscores the significance of understanding the underlying mechanisms and interactions between optical and non-optical parameters for accurate remote sensing assessments of water quality. In our research, the statistical correlations between optically active substances and non-optically active water quality parameters can be considered causative. For example, TN, TP, BOD$_5$, COD, FPBM, and CYBM were statistically significantly correlated with CHL. Nutrients influence CHL concentrations by inducing phytoplankton productivity and biomass growth [107]. Additionally, BOD$_5$ shows the amount of the oxygen consumed by organisms and the readily decomposable organic matter in the water. The strong correlations between CHL and BOD_5 revealed that phytoplankton and other aquatic plants are the primary sources of rapidly decaying organics [108], indicating an autochthonous carbon dominance in our study lakes. COD is a measure of oxygen used up during chemical oxidation. COD also refers to the amount of organic matter in water, but it also involves the refractory to decomposition allochthonous carbon, which is not reflected by BOD. Indeed, in our study, COD had a stronger correlation with CDOM than with CHL. CDOM also correlated well with nutrients, indicating their similar terrestrial origin [109]. The acidity of surface waters is affected by CDOM [110], which accounted for the significant negative correlation between pH and CDOM in our study. TSM and phosphorus in water have been demonstrated to be correlated [111–114], and were also correlated in this study. The particle size distribution, geographical variance, and percentage of phosphorous attached to particles all have an impact on the correlation between TP and TSM [114]. Moreover, in accordance with TSM concentrations, it may either absorb or desorb nutrients. Generally, 20% of the nutrients are present in particulate form in waters at TSM concentrations of 10 mg/L, 60% at TSM concentrations of 100 mg/L, and 80% at TSM concentrations of 1000 mg/L [114]. Recognizing the causative nature of these correlations improves remote sensing's efficacy in assessing water quality, emphasizing the importance of taking into account both optical and non-optical parameters for a thorough understanding of environmental conditions in lakes.

As most optically non-active water quality parameters were impacted by several optical substances, no specific bands or band combinations were chosen, but rather as many various combinations as possible were tested to identify the most sensitive ones. The best results were obtained by combining different band combinations as GA XGBoost feature inputs. Similarly to us, Chen et al. [72] also obtained the best results for predicting CHL, TP, TN, NH_3-N, and turbidity by combining multiple two- or three-band or band ratio algorithms in the GA_XGBoost model. Sentinel-2 MSI Band 4 (665 nm) was discovered to be the most applied band in the models. Band 4 or the bands near 665 nm of other sensors have previously been used as representative bands across the CHL, CDOM, and TSM two- or three-band or band ratio algorithms [16,18,115–118]. Utilizing diverse band combinations improves the robustness of predictive models, aligning with the broader trend of optimizing satellite-derived data for water quality assessment.

This study used the GA_XGBoost machine learning algorithm along with in situ and Sentinel-2 MSI data to construct the inversion models of 14 biogeochemical (TN, TP, PO_4, SO_4, NH_4N, BOD_5, COD, CHL, CDOM, TSM, FPBM, CYBM, pH, O_2) and two physical (WT, SD) lake water quality parameters. XGBoost is a scalable end-to-end tree-boosting algorithm proposed by Chen et al. [78]. It has gained increasing attention in recent years due to its high efficiency and prediction accuracy. The most significant feature behind the effectiveness of XGBoost is its scalability in all setups due to several important systems and algorithmic optimizations [78]. XGBoost can be described as a novel tree-learning algorithm to handle sparse data and a theoretically based weighted quantile sketch method that enables the handling of instance weights in approximate tree learning [78]. Additionally, it has parallel and distributed computing and out-of-core computation accelerated learning, which enables faster model exploration and achieves a balance between model performance and computing speed inherent to XGBoost [78]. Adding regularization elements to the objective function controls the complexity of the model and supports feature sampling, which can prevent the overfitting of the model [78]. In our study, GA_XGBoost was able to predict ten biogeochemical (TN, TP, PO_4, BOD_5, COD, CHL, CDOM, TSM, pH, O_2) and two physical water quality parameters (WT, SD). We have introduced performance scores to ensure the algorithm performs optimally across all three datasets (testing, training, validation). Upon examining the performance metrics in Table 5, it is noteworthy that there was an observed increase in MAPE and RMSE, accompanied by a decrease in R^2 during the transition from the training to testing stages. Unfortunately, this pattern underscores the potential concern for overfitting, especially for certain parameters. The shift from testing to validation phases indicated a relatively smaller and more moderate change. However, it is advisable to employ a more effective approach for model selection, adjustments, and tuning in future studies to clearly avoid potential overfitting concerns. Additionally, the observed low accuracy in Table 5, particularly in the statistics for certain water quality parameters such as SO_4, NH_4N, FPBM, CYBM, and COD underline specific challenges faced by the GA_XGBoost machine learning algorithm. While our study achieved overall success, it is crucial to delve into the difficulties encountered, shedding light on the limitations of machine learning methods in environmental modelling using remote sensing. For example, COD, as an optically non-active parameter, presents inherent challenges due to the complexity of its determination. Unlike optically active substances, COD lacks direct spectral characteristics, making its estimation dependent on complicated relationships with other parameters. The difficulty lies in discerning these complex interactions accurately, contributing to variations in predictive performance. The complexities associated with the relationships between these substances and optically active parameters pose challenges that may not be fully addressed by machine learning algorithms alone. This challenge extends to other optically non-active parameters, such as SO_4, NH_4N, FPBM, and CYBM, as reflected in elevated performance metrics.

Moreover, the dataset size is an important aspect that might significantly influence the performance and generalizability of machine learning models. Unfortunately, the limitations in dataset size are inherent in remote sensing studies, particularly when dealing with match-ups between in situ measurements and satellite data. Given the constraints posed by the nature of remote sensing data and the relatively short study period, the choice of the XGBoost machine learning approach was deliberate. The XGBoost algorithm's ability to handle smaller datasets efficiently played a crucial role in addressing the challenges set by the available data. This aligns with the established literature, including works by Chen et al. [72], which acknowledges the suitability of XGBoost for smaller datasets.

Furthermore, the dynamic nature of the biogeochemical and physical properties of lakes presents a challenge in ensuring the reliability of results produced using machine learning methods. Table 2 shows a diverse range of measured values for each water quality parameter, providing a snapshot of the variability in water quality conditions within the study area. While the dataset may not cover every conceivable scenario, it captures substantial variation that allowed the models to discern patterns and relationships. Additionally, our study incorporated data from different seasons to capture the temporal variability in these properties. However, it is essential to acknowledge that the dynamic nature of lakes introduces complexities that may impact the predictive accuracy of machine learning models. While we aimed to represent diverse seasonal conditions, the variability over time could present limitations, especially when attempting to generalize the models to broader contexts. Future studies could benefit from expanding the temporal scope and considering longer-term datasets to enhance the robustness of machine learning models in capturing the dynamic nature of lakes.

Even in light of these challenges, our results were in good consistency in terms of accuracy with the research of other authors who concentrated on individual lakes and only one or two parameters. In previous studies, XGBoost has been used to retrieve mostly CHL, TN, and TP, but also COD, electrical conductivity (EC), NH_3-N, O_2, pH, SD, SiO_2, TSM, turbidity, and WT from mainly individual Chinese rivers, lakes, and reservoirs, primarily using Sentinel-2 MSI, Landsat 8 OLI, or an unmanned aerial vehicle (UAV) [72,74,119–123]. In these studies, XGBoost models demonstrated high accuracy in retrieving various water quality parameters in inland waters, outperforming other machine learning models such as Random Forest (RF), Support Vector Regressor (SVR), Deep Neural Network (DNN), Lasso, etc., as well as linear, quadratic polynomial, logarithmic, power, and exponential regression models (Appendix B, Table A2). While the developed machine learning models consistently yield reliable results in localized studies, it is important to acknowledge their potential limitations when applied to broader contexts. For instance, in large-scale water quality assessments, variations in geographical and environmental factors may necessitate adjustments, such as new band selection and parameter tuning, as highlighted by Guo et al. [46].

In general, the mean values and the variability of the estimated water quality parameters allowed us to demonstrate that it is possible to obtain reliable results for multiple lakes at the same time using the developed GA_XGBoost model and Sentinel-2 MSI data. Nutrient concentrations, and thus CHL, were greater in April and May. In spring, more light becomes available, the surface water gets warmer, the water column stratifies, and due to the inhibition of vertical mixing, phytoplankton and nutrients are compressed in the euphotic zone. As a result, an environment with relatively high nutrient and light levels is created, promoting fast phytoplankton development [124]. The mean concentrations of CHL were lower in June and July due to the decreasing nutrients in water. Nutrient depletion and increased zooplankton grazing often promote spring bloom collapse and maintain low phytoplankton biomass over summer [124]. A slight increase in CHL and TN concentrations in August revealed the presence of cyanobacteria in at least some lakes at that time as diazotrophic cyanobacteria may fix atmospheric nitrogen to meet their nitrogen needs [125]. The pH showed a similar seasonal trend as CHL, whose seasonal course is driven by primary production, which fixes inorganic carbon and therefore raises the pH during periods of intense growth [126]. In April and May, when the largest river discharge typically takes place [127], the mean concentration of CDOM was at its maximum. Water transparency (given as SD) was the lowest in April, which is typical of the spring months, confirming that CHL and CDOM concentrations have a strong impact on water clarity [128,129]. The mean water temperature was highest in June 2021, the same month that Estonia experienced the warmest June ever [130]. In April and May, the mean oxygen concentration was at its maximum. Firstly, oxygen dissolves better in cold water, and secondly, this is the peak period for primary production that produces oxygen as a by-product [131]. The high amount of CDOM in spring and the oxygen used in its decomposition may be the reason that the mean oxygen concentration did not reach saturation levels even in April [132]. The application of the GA_XGBoost model, combined with satellite data, indeed represents a powerful approach for remote sensing in the assessment of water quality across a diverse range of lakes. This method not only validates the efficiency of remote sensing, but also highlights its potential to provide comprehensive insights into spatiotemporal variations of numerous water quality parameters simultaneously across a large number of lakes.

5. Conclusions

This study aimed to use the GA_XGBoost machine learning algorithm along with in situ and Sentinel-2 MSI data to monitor and predict water quality parameters in lakes. We constructed inversion models of 16 physical and biogeochemical water quality parameters (TN, TP, PO_4, SO_4, NH_4N, BOD_5, COD, CHL, CDOM, TSM, FPBM, CYBM, pH, O_2, WT, and SD) and provided a practical demonstration of the developed inversion models, illustrating their applicability in estimating various water quality parameters simultaneously across multiple lakes on five different dates.

- GA_XGBoost exhibited strong predictive capabilities and it was able to accurately predict ten biogeochemical and two physical water quality parameters (TN, TP, PO_4, BOD_5, COD, CHL, CDOM, TSM, pH, O_2, WT, and SD), showcasing its effectiveness in water quality and remote sensing applications.
- The observed increase in MAPE and RMSE, accompanied by a decrease in R^2 during the transition from training to testing stages, highlighted the potential concern for overfitting, especially for specific parameters. This emphasizes the need for careful model selection, adjustments, and tuning in future studies.
- Despite the dynamic nature of lakes, our results demonstrated reliable estimates for multiple lakes simultaneously, considering the seasonal variations in water quality parameters.

While our findings contribute to the growing body of knowledge on remote sensing applications for water quality assessment, it is crucial to acknowledge certain limitations. Challenges linked to optically non-active parameters, the potential for overfitting, and the limitations of remote sensing datasets highlight the necessity for ongoing research and refinement of machine learning methodologies in environmental monitoring. Future investigations should delve into broader temporal scopes, incorporate longer-term datasets, and employ enhanced model selection strategies. These efforts are crucial for advancing the robustness and generalizability of remote sensing-based water quality models.

Author Contributions: T.K.: conceptualization, methodology, formal analysis, visualization, writing—original draft, writing—review and editing, funding acquisition. H.L.: methodology, formal analysis, writing—review and editing. T.S.: methodology, writing—review and editing. E.U.: formal analysis, writing—review and editing. K.T.: funding acquisition, writing—review and editing. T.N.: funding acquisition, writing—review and editing. All authors have read and agreed to the published version of the manuscript.

Funding: This research was funded by the Estonian Research Council (under grants PRG302, PRG709, and PRG1764), the European Regional Developing Fund, and the program Mobilitas Pluss (grant number MOBTP106).

Data Availability Statement: Publicly available datasets were analyzed in this study. This data can be found here: https://kese.envir.ee/ and https://dataspace.copernicus.eu/.

Acknowledgments: Estonian Environment Agency is acknowledged for providing biogeochemical and physical water quality parameters. The European Space Agency (ESA) and the European Union's Earth observation program Copernicus are acknowledged for providing Sentinel-2 MSI data. The Estonian National Satellite Data Centre ESTHub is acknowledged for the possibility to search, download, and process the Copernicus program data. The three anonymous reviewers are acknowledged for their insightful comments and constructive feedback which significantly contributed to the improvement of this manuscript.

Conflicts of Interest: The authors declare that they have no known competing financial interests or personal relationships that could have appeared to influence the work reported in this paper.

Appendix A

Table A1. Names, coordinates, maximum and mean depth, catchment area, and lake area of 45 Estonian lakes by sampling dates where in situ data of the current study were collected.

Lake Name	Lat (N)	Lon (E)	Max Depth, m	Mean Depth, m	Catch. Area, km²	Area, km²	Trophic State	Sampling Date
Aheru järv/Kandsi järv	57.68844	26.35283	7.4	3.4	52.4	2.34	Eutrophic (hard water)	12 September 2016
Elistvere järv	58.57139	26.70728	3.5	2	171	1.29	Eutrophic (macrophyte)	9 May 2016
Elistvere järv	58.57139	26.70728	3.5	2	171	1.29	Eutrophic (macrophyte)	15 September 2016
Endla järv	58.85357	26.19651	2.4	1.5	433	2.84	Mixotrophic (hard water)	16 May 2018
Ermistu järv	58.36923	23.98146	2.9	1.3	32.3	4.49	Eutrophic (macrophyte)	30 May 2017
Hino järv	57.58357	27.20177	10.4	3.1	2.12	1.99	Oligotrophic	6 May 2020
Hino järv	57.58357	27.20177	10.4	3.1	2.12	1.99	Oligotrophic	12 August 2020
Hino järv	57.58357	27.20177	10.4	3.1	2.12	1.99	Oligotrophic	7 September 2020
Jõemõisa järv	58.65372	26.82892	3.2	2.6	216	0.72	Mixotrophic (hard water)	5 August 2015
Järise järv	58.49416	22.41262	1.4	0.7	11.1	0.96	Eutrophic (macrophyte)	22 August 2018
Kaiavere järv	58.60383	26.67486	5	2.8	92.2	2.47	Eutrophic (hard water)	9 May 2016
Kaiavere järv	58.60383	26.67486	5	2.8	92.2	2.47	Eutrophic (hard water)	20 July 2016
Kaiavere järv	58.60383	26.67486	5	2.8	92.2	2.47	Eutrophic (hard water)	15 September 2016
Kaisma järv	58.69312	24.68132	2.1	1.25	16	1.4	Mixotrophic (hard water)	20 May 2019
Kaisma järv	58.69312	24.68132	2.1	1.25	16	1.4	Mixotrophic (hard water)	18 July 2019
Kaiu järv	58.64201	26.8389	3	2.6	216	1.34	Mixotrophic (hard water)	5 August 2015
Kalli järv	58.37695	27.23623	1.4	1.1	82.8	1.99	Eutrophic (macrophyte)	9 May 2020
Karijärv	58.29831	26.41993	14.5	5.7	11.1	0.82	Eutrophic (hard water)	14 September 2015
Karijärv	58.29831	26.41993	14.5	5.7	11.1	0.82	Eutrophic (hard water)	3 July 2019

Table A1. Cont.

Lake Name	Lat (N)	Lon (E)	Max Depth, m	Mean Depth, m	Catch. Area, km²	Area, km²	Trophic State	Sampling Date
Karijärv	58.29831	26.41993	14.5	5.7	11.1	0.82	Eutrophic (hard water)	4 September 2019
Kariste järv	58.14161	25.3484	7.2	3.3	128	0.61	Eutrophic (hard water)	30 May 2017
Kariste järv	58.14161	25.3484	7.2	3.3	128	0.61	Eutrophic (hard water)	25 September 2017
Karujärv	58.37102	22.2161	6	1.6	16.1	3.46	Eutrophic (hard water)	28 May 2018
Karujärv	58.37102	22.2161	6	1.6	16.1	3.46	Eutrophic (hard water)	22 August 2018
Konsu järv	59.22656	27.58052	10.2	5.8	27	1.39	Mixotrophic (hard water)	25 June 2019
Konsu järv	59.22656	27.58052	10.2	5.8	27	1.39	Mixotrophic (hard water)	22 April 2020
Kooru järv	58.48363	22.13946	1.2	0.3	38.7	0.85	Eutrophic (halotrophic)	16 August 2015
Kooru järv	58.48363	22.13946	1.2	0.3	38.7	0.85	Eutrophic (halotrophic)	27 September 2015
Kooru järv	58.48363	22.13946	1.2	0.3	38.7	0.85	Eutrophic (halotrophic)	28 September 2015
Kooru järv	58.48363	22.13946	1.2	0.3	38.7	0.85	Eutrophic (halotrophic)	29 May 2017
Kooru järv	58.48363	22.13946	1.2	0.3	38.7	0.85	Eutrophic (halotrophic)	28 May 2018
Kooru järv	58.48363	22.13946	1.2	0.3	38.7	0.85	Eutrophic (halotrophic)	28 July 2019
Kooru järv	58.48363	22.13946	1.2	0.3	38.7	0.85	Eutrophic (halotrophic)	29 August 2020
Koosa järv	58.4257	27.14411	1.9	1.2	75.9	2.83	Mixotrophic (macrophyte)	20 July 2020
Käsmu järv	59.58175	25.88399	3.3	2.2	16.5	0.49	Mixotrophic (soft water)	12 August 2015
Käsmu järv	59.58175	25.88399	3.3	2.2	16.5	0.49	Mixotrophic (soft water)	12 August 2020
Köstrijärv	57.75009	26.39461	4.4	3.3	1.8	0.12	Eutrophic (macrophyte)	7 May 2018
Lahepera järv	58.57375	27.19274	4.2	2.4	28.9	0.1	Eutrophic (macrophyte)	11 May 2020
Lahepera järv	58.57375	27.19274	4.2	2.4	28.9	0.1	Eutrophic (macrophyte)	20 July 2020
Leegu järv	58.36587	27.27614	1	0.6	5.6	0.86	Eutrophic (macrophyte)	20 July 2020
Lohja järv	59.54821	25.69092	3.7	2.2	12.3	0.56	Mixotrophic (soft water)	12 August 2015
Lohja järv	59.54821	25.69092	3.7	2.2	12.3	0.56	Mixotrophic (soft water)	8 July 2020
Lohja järv	59.54821	25.69092	3.7	2.2	12.3	0.56	Mixotrophic (soft water)	12 August 2020
Loosalu järv	58.93337	25.0777	5	3.7	1.6	0.35	Dystrophic	20 May 2018
Mustjärv (Nohipalo Mustjärv)	57.93201	27.34217	8.9	3.9	9.7	0.22	Acidotrophic	2 May 2016
Mustjärv (Nohipalo Mustjärv)	57.93201	27.34217	8.9	3.9	9.7	0.22	Acidotrophic	2 May 2017
Mustjärv (Nohipalo Mustjärv)	57.93201	27.34217	8.9	3.9	9.7	0.22	Acidotrophic	7 May 2020
Männiku järv	59.34583	24.71239	9	5	13	0.1	Eutrophic (hard water)	25 August 2015
Ohepalu järv	59.33395	25.95198	2.5	0.5	7.5	0.68	Dystrophic	23 July 2015
Ohepalu järv	59.33395	25.95198	2.5	0.5	7.5	0.68	Dystrophic	12 August 2020
Pabra järv	57.60901	27.39527	3.6	2.4	36.5	0.76	Semidystrophic	16 August 2017
Peenjärv	59.21377	27.57548	-	-	-	0.08	Mixotrophic (hard water)	25 June 2019
Pikkjärv (Viitna Pikkjärv)	59.4465	26.01005	6.2	3	1.1	0.16	Oligotrophic	14 August 2017
Pikkjärv (Viitna Pikkjärv)	59.4465	26.01005	6.2	3	1.1	0.16	Oligotrophic	15 May 2018
Pikkjärv (Viitna Pikkjärv)	59.4465	26.01005	6.2	3	1.1	0.16	Oligotrophic	19 May 2020
Pikkjärv (Viitna Pikkjärv)	59.4465	26.01005	6.2	3	1.1	0.16	Oligotrophic	17 August 2020
Pühajärv	58.02409	26.45667	8.5	4.3	44	2.98	Eutrophic (hard water)	2 May 2016
Pühajärv	58.02409	26.45667	8.5	4.3	44	2.98	Eutrophic (hard water)	2 May 2017
Pühajärv	58.02409	26.45667	8.5	4.3	44	2.98	Eutrophic (hard water)	2 May 2018
Pühajärv	58.02409	26.45667	8.5	4.3	44	2.98	Eutrophic (hard water)	7 August 2018
Pühajärv	58.02409	26.45667	8.5	4.3	44	2.98	Eutrophic (hard water)	1 July 2019
Pühajärv	58.02409	26.45667	8.5	4.3	44	2.98	Eutrophic (hard water)	2 September 2019
Pühajärv	58.02409	26.45667	8.5	4.3	44	2.98	Eutrophic (hard water)	4 May 2020
Pühajärv	58.02409	26.45667	8.5	4.3	44	2.98	Eutrophic (hard water)	7 May 2020
Saadjärv	58.53688	26.65778	25	8	31.9	7.23	Eutrophic (hard water)	9 May 2016
Saadjärv	58.53688	26.65778	25	8	31.9	7.23	Eutrophic (hard water)	14 July 2016
Saare järv	58.65489	26.7627	5.6	4.2	8.5	27.4	Eutrophic (hard water)	5 August 2015
Soitsjärv	58.55667	26.68168	8	1.2	15.2	1.58	Mixotrophic (macrophyte)	9 May 2016
Suurjärv (Rouge Suurjärv)	57.7275	26.92278	38	12	25.8	0.135	Eutrophic (hard water)	4 August 2015
Suurjärv (Rouge Suurjärv)	57.7275	26.92278	38	12	25.8	0.135	Eutrophic (hard water)	4 May 2017
Suurjärv (Rouge Suurjärv)	57.7275	26.92278	38	12	25.8	0.135	Eutrophic (hard water)	4 September 2019
Suurjärv (Rouge Suurjärv)	57.7275	26.92278	38	12	25.8	0.135	Eutrophic (hard water)	5 May 2020
Suurjärv (Rouge Suurjärv)	57.7275	26.92278	38	12	25.8	0.135	Eutrophic (hard water)	6 May 2020
Suurjärv (Rouge Suurjärv)	57.7275	26.92278	38	12	25.8	0.135	Eutrophic (hard water)	7 September 2020
Tõhela järv	58.41785	23.99619	1.5	1.3	21.7	4.07	Eutrophic (macrophyte)	30 May 2017
Tõhela järv	58.41785	23.99619	1.5	1.3	21.7	4.07	Eutrophic (macrophyte)	25 July 2017
Tõhela järv	58.41785	23.99619	1.5	1.3	21.7	4.07	Eutrophic (macrophyte)	21 July 2020
Tänavjärv	59.17897	23.80563	2.5	1.8	4.7	1.39	Semidystrophic	17 August 2015

Table A1. Cont.

Lake Name	Lat (N)	Lon (E)	Max Depth, m	Mean Depth, m	Catch. Area, km²	Area, km²	Trophic State	Sampling Date
Tänavjärv	59.17897	23.80563	2.5	1.8	4.7	1.39	Semidystrophic	29 May 2016
Tänavjärv	59.17897	23.80563	2.5	1.8	4.7	1.39	Semidystrophic	30 August 2016
Tänavjärv	59.17897	23.80563	2.5	1.8	4.7	1.39	Semidystrophic	26 September 2016
Tänavjärv	59.17897	23.80563	2.5	1.8	4.7	1.39	Semidystrophic	27 September 2016
Tänavjärv	59.17897	23.80563	2.5	1.8	4.7	1.39	Semidystrophic	20 May 2019
Tänavjärv	59.17897	23.80563	2.5	1.8	4.7	1.39	Semidystrophic	24 May 2020
Tänavjärv	59.17897	23.80563	2.5	1.8	4.7	1.39	Semidystrophic	18 July 2020
Tänavjärv	59.17897	23.80563	2.5	1.8	4.7	1.39	Semidystrophic	16 August 2020
Tündre järv	57.95075	25.61889	10.6	4.9	7.1	0.716	Eutrophic (hard water)	11 May 2016
Uljaste järv	59.3594	26.77396	6.4	2.2	1.1	0.63	Semidystrophic	14 August 2017
Uljaste järv	59.3594	26.77396	6.4	2.2	1.1	0.63	Semidystrophic	25 September 2017
Uljaste järv	59.3594	26.77396	6.4	2.2	1.1	0.63	Semidystrophic	15 May 2019
Uljaste järv	59.3594	26.77396	6.4	2.2	1.1	0.63	Semidystrophic	17 August 2020
Valgejärv (Kurtna Valgejärv)	59.26342	27.59712	10.5	4.2	1	0.08	Semidystrophic	15 May 2019
Valgjärv	58.08903	26.64033	5.5	3.2	4.9	0.65	Eutrophic (hard water)	4 May 2017
Valgjärv	58.08903	26.64033	5.5	3.2	4.9	0.65	Eutrophic (hard water)	5 July 2017
Valgojärv (Nohipalo Valgojärv)	57.9412	27.34662	12.5	6.2	2.2	0.07	Oligotrophic	2 May 2017
Valgojärv (Nohipalo Valgojärv)	57.9412	27.34662	12.5	6.2	2.2	0.07	Oligotrophic	1 August 2017
Valgojärv (Nohipalo Valgojärv)	57.9412	27.34662	12.5	6.2	2.2	0.07	Oligotrophic	2 September 2019
Valgojärv (Nohipalo Valgojärv)	57.9412	27.34662	12.5	6.2	2.2	0.07	Oligotrophic	7 May 2020
Verevi järv	58.23074	26.40464	11	3.6	1.1	0.12	Hypertrophic	8 August 2017
Verevi järv	58.23074	26.40464	11	3.6	1.1	0.12	Hypertrophic	6 May 2020
Viljandi järv	58.35027	25.59324	11	5.6	66.8	1.58	Eutrophic (hard water)	6 May 2020
Õisu järv	58.20532	25.52078	4.3	2.8	199	1.93	Eutrophic (hard water)	8 July 2019
Ähijärv	57.71297	26.49654	5.5	3.8	14.7	1.81	Eutrophic (hard water)	4 August 2015
Ähijärv	57.71297	26.49654	5.5	3.8	14.7	1.81	Eutrophic (hard water)	11 May 2016
Ähijärv	57.71297	26.49654	5.5	3.8	14.7	1.81	Eutrophic (hard water)	3 August 2016
Ähijärv	57.71297	26.49654	5.5	3.8	14.7	1.81	Eutrophic (hard water)	12 September 2016
Ähijärv	57.71297	26.49654	5.5	3.8	14.7	1.81	Eutrophic (hard water)	4 May 2017
Ähijärv	57.71297	26.49654	5.5	3.8	14.7	1.81	Eutrophic (hard water)	7 May 2018
Ähijärv	57.71297	26.49654	5.5	3.8	14.7	1.81	Eutrophic (hard water)	3 July 2019
Ähijärv	57.71297	26.49654	5.5	3.8	14.7	1.81	Eutrophic (hard water)	4 September 2019
Ähijärv	57.71297	26.49654	5.5	3.8	14.7	1.81	Eutrophic (hard water)	6 May 2020
Ähijärv	57.71297	26.49654	5.5	3.8	14.7	1.81	Eutrophic (hard water)	16 September 2020

Appendix B

Table A2. The performance metrics of different models for deriving biogeochemical and physical water quality parameters from remote sensing data. R^2, R-squared; MAPE, mean absolute percentage error (%); RMSE, root-mean-square error; N, number of data.

Water Quality Parameter	Model	R^2	MAE	RMSE	MAPE	Remote Sensing Platform/Sensor	Spatial Resolution	Waterbody	N	Reference
CHL	GA_XGBoost	0.86	0.02	0.05	-	UAV	0.1	Nanfei River	67	[72]
CHL	XGBoost	0.82	0.03	0.05	-	UAV	0.1	Nanfei River	67	[72]
CHL	XGBoost	-	11.50	14.70	30.2	Landsat 5 TM	30 m	Lake Taihu	163	[119]
CHL	XGBoost	-	7.20	12.90	34.8	Landsat 7 ETM+	30 m	Lake Taihu	163	[119]
CHL	XGBoost	-	11.60	15.70	35.2	Landsat 8 OLI	30 m	Lake Taihu	163	[119]
CHL	XGBoost	0.42	1.52	2.07	-	UAV	1600 × 1300 pixels	The Zhanghe River	45	[119]
CHL	XGBoost	0.73	-	0.26	7.59	Sentinel-2 MSI	20 m	Q reservoir	96	[74]
CHL	XGBoost	0.84	-	6.65	-	Zhuhai-No.1, CMOS	30 m	Dushan Lake, Weishan Lake	99	[123]
CHL	GA_RF	0.80	0.03	0.05	-	UAV	0.1	Nanfei River	67	[72]
CHL	RF	0.74	0.04	0.06	-	UAV	0.1	Nanfei River	67	[72]
CHL	RF	-	8.90	14.40	18.3	Landsat 5 TM	30 m	Lake Taihu	163	[119]
CHL	RF	-	7.70	13.80	44.1	Landsat 7 ETM+	30 m	Lake Taihu	163	[119]
CHL	RF	-	10.70	14.90	33.8	Landsat 8 OLI	30 m	Lake Taihu	163	[119]
CHL	RF	0.32	1.51	1.94	-	UAV	1600 × 1300 pixels	The Zhanghe River	45	[119]
CHL	RF	0.67	-	0.30	13.13	Sentinel-2 MSI	20 m	Q reservoir	96	[74]
CHL	AdaBoost	0.78	0.03	0.06	-	UAV	0.1	Nanfei River	67	[72]
CHL	GA_AdaBoost	0.83	0.03	0.05	-	UAV	0.1	Nanfei River	67	[72]
CHL	SVR	-	13.40	17.60	46.5	Landsat 5 TM	30 m	Lake Taihu	163	[119]

Table A2. Cont.

Water Quality Parameter	Model	R^2	MAE	RMSE	MAPE	Remote Sensing Platform/Sensor	Spatial Resolution	Waterbody	N	Reference
CHL	SVR	-	8.40	18.70	37.7	Landsat 7 ETM+	30 m	Lake Taihu	163	[119]
CHL	SVR	-	13.10	15.60	32.2	Landsat 8 OLI	30 m	Lake Taihu	163	[119]
CHL	SVR	0.46	-	0.36	14.3	Sentinel-2 MSI	20 m	Q reservoir	96	[74]
CHL	ANN	0.15	-	0.45	17.94	Sentinel-2 MSI	20 m	Q reservoir	96	[74]
CHL	DNN	0.81	0.03	0.05	-	UAV	0.1	Nanfei River	67	[72]
CHL	BP	0.12	1.57	2.21	-	UAV	1600 × 1300 pixels	The Zhanghe River	45	[119]
CHL	Lasso	0.20	1.54	2.08	-	UAV	1600 × 1300 pixels	The Zhanghe River	45	[119]
CHL	MLR	0.10	1.60	2.24	-	UAV	1600 × 1300 pixels	The Zhanghe River	45	[119]
CODMn	XGBoost	0.11	0.79	0.86	-	UAV	1600 × 1300 pixels	The Zhanghe River	45	[119]
CODMn	RF	0.20	0.71	0.80	-	UAV	1600 × 1300 pixels	The Zhanghe River	45	[119]
CODMn	BP	0.22	0.69	0.80	-	UAV	1600 × 1300 pixels	The Zhanghe River	45	[119]
CODMn	Lasso	0.07	0.70	0.83	-	UAV	1600 × 1300 pixels	The Zhanghe River	45	[119]
CODMn	MLR	0.06	0.71	0.83	-	UAV	1600 × 1300 pixels	The Zhanghe River	45	[119]
CODMn	ML-MLR	0.19	0.72	0.82	-	UAV	1600 × 1300 pixels	The Zhanghe River	45	[119]
EC	XGBoost	0.27	-	1.23	-	Landsat 8 OLI	30	The Ganga River Basin, Cluster 0	159	[133]
EC	XGBoost	0.33	-	2.57	-	Landsat 8 OLI	30	The Ganga River Basin, Cluster 1	159	[133]
EC	XGBoost	0.21	-	2.85	-	Landsat 8 OLI	30	The Ganga River Basin, Cluster 2	159	[133]
EC	XGBoost	0.32	-	2.58	-	Landsat 8 OLI	30	The Ganga River Basin, Cluster 3	159	[133]
NH_3-N	GA_XGBoost	0.69	0.14	0.16	-	UAV	0.1	Nanfei River	67	[72]
NH_3-N	XGBoost	0.65	0.15	0.17	-	UAV	0.1	Nanfei River	67	[72]
NH_3-N	XGBoost	0.82	-	0.14	28.6	Sentinel-2 MSI	20 m	Q reservoir	96	[74]
NH_3-N	GA_RF	0.62	0.15	0.17	-	UAV	0.1	Nanfei River	67	[72]
NH_3-N	RF	0.60	0.15	0.19	-	UAV	0.1	Nanfei River	67	[72]
NH_3-N	RF	0.12	-	0.22	73.53	Sentinel-2 MSI	20 m	Q reservoir	96	[74]
NH_3-N	AdaBoost	0.55	0.15	0.20	-	UAV	0.1	Nanfei River	67	[72]
NH_3-N	GA_AdaBoost	0.67	0.15	0.17	-	UAV	0.1	Nanfei River	67	[72]
NH_3-N	SVR	0.49	-	0.15	118.45	Sentinel-2 MSI	20 m	Q reservoir	96	[74]
NH_3-N	ANN	0.25	-	0.17	107.43	Sentinel-2 MSI	20 m	Q reservoir	96	[74]
NH_3-N	DNN	0.63	0.15	0.18	-	UAV	0.1	Nanfei River	67	[72]
O_2	XGBoost	0.97	-	0.01	-	Landsat 8 OLI	30	The Ganga River Basin, Cluster 0	159	[133]
O_2	XGBoost	0.93	-	0.01	-	Landsat 8 OLI	30	The Ganga River Basin, Cluster 1	159	[133]
O_2	XGBoost	0.90	-	0.01	-	Landsat 8 OLI	30	The Ganga River Basin, Cluster 2	159	[133]
O_2	XGBoost	0.96	-	0.01	-	Landsat 8 OLI	30	The Ganga River Basin, Cluster 3	159	[133]
O_2	XGBoost	0.90	-	0.14	0.07	Sentinel-2 MSI	20 m	Q reservoir	96	[74]
O_2	RF	0.77	-	0.34	3.43	Sentinel-2 MSI	20 m	Q reservoir	96	[74]
O_2	SVR	0.85	-	0.17	1.38	Sentinel-2 MSI	20 m	Q reservoir	96	[74]
O_2	ANN	0.79	-	0.20	2.04	Sentinel-2 MSI	20 m	Q reservoir	96	[74]
pH	XGBoost	0.78	-	0.08	-	Landsat 8 OLI	30	The Ganga River Basin, Cluster 0	159	[133]
pH	XGBoost	0.74	-	0.19	-	Landsat 8 OLI	30	The Ganga River Basin, Cluster 1	159	[133]
pH	XGBoost	0.74	-	0.26	-	Landsat 8 OLI	30	The Ganga River Basin, Cluster 2	159	[133]
pH	XGBoost	0.76	-	0.09	-	Landsat 8 OLI	30	The Ganga River Basin, Cluster 3	159	[133]
SD	XGBoost	0.84	0.64	1.14	-	Landsat 5 TM	30	Different lake datasets from Europe, China, and America	4099	[123]
SD	XGBoost	0.76	0.89	1.87	-	Landsat 7 ETM+	30	Different lake datasets from Europe, China, and America	2420	[123]
SD	XGBoost	0.88	0.50	0.80	-	Landsat 8 OLI	30	Different lake datasets from Europe, China, and America	1249	[123]

Table A2. Cont.

Water Quality Parameter	Model	R²	MAE	RMSE	MAPE	Remote Sensing Platform/Sensor	Spatial Resolution	Waterbody	N	Reference
SD	XGBoost	0.98	2.01	2.52	-	UAV	0.185 m	The Shahu Port channel, The Xunsi River	72	[120]
SD	RF	0.97	1.98	2.81	-	UAV	0.185 m	The Shahu Port channel, The Xunsi River	72	[120]
SD	RF	0.82	0.62	1.13	-	Landsat 5 TM	30	Different lake datasets from Europe, China, and America	4099	[123]
SD	RF	0.78	0.84	1.84	-	Landsat 7 ETM+	30 m	Different lake datasets from Europe, China, and America	2420	[123]
SD	RF	0.85	0.47	0.74	-	Landsat 8 OLI	30 m	Different lake datasets from Europe, China, and America	1249	[123]
SD	AdaBoost	0.98	2.00	2.55	-	UAV	0.185 m	The Shahu Port channel, The Xunsi River	72	[120]
SD	GBDT	0.91	3.62	4.75	-	UAV	0.185 m	The Shahu Port channel, The Xunsi River	72	[120]
SD	Exponential function	0.45	-	12.48	-	UAV	0.185 m	The Shahu Port channel, The Xunsi River	72	[120]
SD	Linear function	0.80	-	7.59	-	UAV	0.185 m	The Shahu Port channel, The Xunsi River	72	[120]
SD	Logarithmic function	0.80	-	7.58	-	UAV	0.185 m	The Shahu Port channel, The Xunsi River	72	[120]
SD	Power function	0.68	-	9.44	-	UAV	0.185 m	The Shahu Port channel, The Xunsi River	72	[120]
SD	Quadratic polynomial	0.80	-	7.65	-	UAV	0.185 m	The Shahu Port channel, The Xunsi River	72	[120]
SiO_2	XGBoost	0.98	-	0.01	-	Landsat 8 OLI	30	The Ganga River Basin, Cluster 0	159	[133]
SiO_2	XGBoost	0.96	-	0.01	-	Landsat 8 OLI	30	The Ganga River Basin, Cluster 1	159	[133]
SiO_2	XGBoost	0.97	-	0.00	-	Landsat 8 OLI	30	The Ganga River Basin, Cluster 2	159	[133]
SiO_2	XGBoost	0.97	-	0.00	-	Landsat 8 OLI	30	The Ganga River Basin, Cluster 3	159	[133]
TN	GA_XGBoost	0.79	0.74	1.09	-	UAV	0.1	Nanfei River	67	[72]
TN	XGBoost	0.70	0.81	1.28	-	UAV	0.1	Nanfei River	67	[72]
TN	XGBoost	0.71	1.03	1.33	-	UAV	1600 × 1300 pixels	The Zhanghe River	45	[119]
TN	GA_RF	0.67	0.91	1.35	-	UAV	0.1	Nanfei River	67	[72]
TN	RF	0.67	0.90	1.36	-	UAV	0.1	Nanfei River	67	[72]
TN	RF	0.70	1.13	1.50	-	UAV	1600 × 1300 pixels	The Zhanghe River	45	[119]
TN	AdaBoost	0.61	1.22	1.55	-	UAV	0.1	Nanfei River	67	[72]
TN	GA_AdaBoost	0.67	0.89	1.36	-	UAV	0.1	Nanfei River	67	[72]
TN	DNN	0.77	0.84	1.14	-	UAV	0.1	Nanfei River	67	[72]
TN	BP	0.82	0.84	1.27	-	UAV	1600 × 1300 pixels	The Zhanghe River	45	[119]
TN	Lasso	0.64	1.28	1.45	-	UAV	1600 × 1300 pixels	The Zhanghe River	45	[119]
TN	MLR	0.64	1.27	1.46	-	UAV	1600 × 1300 pixels	The Zhanghe River	45	[119]
TN	ML-MLR	0.82	0.87	1.28	-	UAV	1600 × 1300 pixels	The Zhanghe River	45	[119]
TP	GA_XGBoost	0.70	0.03	0.03	-	UAV	0.1	Nanfei River	67	[72]
TP	XGBoost	0.61	0.03	0.04	-	UAV	0.1	Nanfei River	67	[72]
TP	XGBoost	0.28	0.05	0.07	-	UAV	1600 × 1300 pixels	The Zhanghe River	45	[119]
TP	GA_RF	0.55	0.03	0.04	-	UAV	0.1	Nanfei River	67	[72]
TP	RF	0.46	0.03	0.05	-	UAV	0.1	Nanfei River	67	[72]
TP	RF	0.35	0.04	0.06	-	UAV	1600 × 1300 pixels	The Zhanghe River	45	[119]
TP	AdaBoost	0.61	0.03	0.04	-	UAV	0.1	Nanfei River	67	[72]
TP	GA_AdaBoost	0.64	0.03	0.04	-	UAV	0.1	Nanfei River	67	[72]

Table A2. Cont.

Water Quality Parameter	Model	R²	MAE	RMSE	MAPE	Remote Sensing Platform/Sensor	Spatial Resolution	Waterbody	N	Reference
TP	DNN	0.56	0.03	0.04	-	UAV	0.1	Nanfei River	67	[72]
TP	BP	0.43	0.05	0.05	-	UAV	1600 × 1300 pixels	The Zhanghe River	45	[119]
TP	Lasso	0.38	0.05	0.06	-	UAV	1600 × 1300 pixels	The Zhanghe River	45	[119]
TP	MLR	0.38	0.05	0.06	-	UAV	1600 × 1300 pixels	The Zhanghe River	45	[119]
TP	ML-MLR	0.27	0.04	0.07	-	UAV	1600 × 1300 pixels	The Zhanghe River	45	[119]
TSM	XGBoost	0.18	641.20	751.90	-	Landsat 8 OLI	30 m	Ebinur Lake, China	102	[121]
TSM	XGBoost	0.24	798.85	884.85	-	Sentinel-2 MSI	20 m	Ebinur Lake, China	102	[121]
TSM	RF	0.68	215.88	256.92	-	Landsat 8 OLI	30 m	Ebinur Lake, China	102	[121]
TSM	RF	0.73	220.27	222.69	-	Sentinel-2 MSI	20 m	Ebinur Lake, China	102	[121]
TUB	GA_XGBoost	0.60	9.82	10.13	-	UAV	0.1	Nanfei River	67	[72]
TUB	XGBoost	0.52	9.97	11.47	-	UAV	0.1	Nanfei River	67	[72]
TUB	GA_RF	0.45	10.27	12.16	-	UAV	0.1	Nanfei River	67	[72]
TUB	RF	0.37	10.56	13.20	-	UAV	0.1	Nanfei River	67	[72]
TUB	AdaBoost	0.39	10.36	12.67	-	UAV	0.1	Nanfei River	67	[72]
TUB	GA_AdaBoost	0.45	10.28	12.26	-	UAV	0.1	Nanfei River	67	[72]
TUB	DNN	0.54	9.92	11.03	-	UAV	0.1	Nanfei River	67	[72]
WT	XGBoost	0.73	-	0.15	-	Landsat 8 OLI	30	The Ganga River Basin, Cluster 0	159	[133]
WT	XGBoost	0.89	-	0.10	-	Landsat 8 OLI	30	The Ganga River Basin, Cluster 1	159	[133]
WT	XGBoost	0.89	-	0.08	-	Landsat 8 OLI	30	The Ganga River Basin, Cluster 2	159	[133]
WT	XGBoost	0.90	-	0.01	-	Landsat 8 OLI	30	The Ganga River Basin, Cluster 3	159	[133]

References

1. Verpoorter, C.; Kutser, T.; Seekell, D.A.; Tranvik, L.J. A Global Inventory of Lakes Based on High-Resolution Satellite Imagery. *Geophys. Res. Lett.* **2014**, *41*, 6396–6402. [CrossRef]
2. Postel, S.L. Entering an Era of Water Scarcity: The Challeenges Ahead. *Ecol. Appl.* **2000**, *10*, 941–948. [CrossRef]
3. Brönmark, C.; Hansson, L.A. Environmental Issues in Lakes and Ponds: Current State and Perspectives. *Environ. Conserv.* **2002**, *29*, 290–307. [CrossRef]
4. Bastviken, D.; Tranvik, L.J.; Downing, J.A.; Crill, P.M.; Enrich-Prast, A. Freshwater Methane Emissions Offset the Continental Carbon Sink. *Science* **2011**, *331*, 50. [CrossRef]
5. Tranvik, L.J.; Downing, J.A.; Cotner, J.B.; Loiselle, S.A.; Striegl, R.G.; Ballatore, T.J.; Dillon, P.; Finlay, K.; Fortino, K.; Knoll, L.B.; et al. Lakes and Reservoirs as Regulators of Carbon Cycling and Climate. *Limnol. Ocean.* **2009**, *54*, 2298–2314. [CrossRef]
6. Tranvik, L.J.; Cole, J.J.; Prairie, Y.T. The Study of Carbon in Inland Waters-from Isolated Ecosystems to Players in the Global Carbon Cycle. *Limnol. Ocean. Lett.* **2018**, *3*, 41–48. [CrossRef]
7. Adrian, R.; O'Reilly, C.M.; Zagarese, H.; Baines, S.B.; Hessen, D.O.; Keller, W.; Livingstone, D.M.; Sommaruga, R.; Straile, D.; van Donk, E.; et al. Lakes as Sentinels of Climate Change. *Limnol. Ocean.* **2009**, *54*, 2283–2297. [CrossRef]
8. Papenfus, M.; Schaeffer, B.; Pollard, A.I.; Loftin, K. Exploring the Potential Value of Satellite Remote Sensing to Monitor Chlorophyll-a for US Lakes and Reservoirs. *Environ. Monit. Assess.* **2020**, *192*, 808. [CrossRef] [PubMed]
9. Mumby, P.J.; Green, E.P.; Edwards, A.J.; Clark, C.D. The Cost-Effectiveness of Remote Sensing for Tropical Coastal Resources Assessment and Management. *J. Environ. Manag.* **1999**, *55*, 157–166. [CrossRef]
10. Marcé, R.; George, G.; Buscarinu, P.; Deidda, M.; Dunalska, J.; de Eyto, E.; Flaim, G.; Grossart, H.P.; Istvanovics, V.; Lenhardt, M.; et al. Automatic High Frequency Monitoring for Improved Lake and Reservoir Management. *Environ. Sci. Technol.* **2016**, *50*, 10780–10794. [CrossRef] [PubMed]
11. Palmer, S.C.J.; Kutser, T.; Hunter, P.D. Remote Sensing of Inland Waters: Challenges, Progress and Future Directions. *Remote Sens. Environ.* **2015**, *157*, 1–8. [CrossRef]
12. Palmer, S.C.J.; Odermatt, D.; Hunter, P.D.; Brockmann, C.; Présing, M.; Balzter, H.; Tóth, V.R. Satellite Remote Sensing of Phytoplankton Phenology in Lake Balaton Using 10 years of MERIS Observations. *Remote Sens. Environ.* **2015**, *158*, 441–452. [CrossRef]
13. Bresciani, M.; Vascellari, M.; Giardino, C.; Matta, E. Remote Sensing Supports the Definition of the Water Quality Status of Lake Omodeo (Italy). *Eur. J. Remote Sens.* **2012**, *45*, 349–360. [CrossRef]
14. Dekker, A.G.; Peters, S.W.M. The Use of the Thematic Mapper for the Analysis of Eutrophic Lakes: A Case Study in the Netherlands. *Int. J. Remote Sens.* **1993**, *14*, 799–821. [CrossRef]

15. Lee, Z.; Shang, S.; Qi, L.; Yan, J.; Lin, G. A Semi-Analytical Scheme to Estimate Secchi-Disk Depth from Landsat-8 Measurements. *Remote Sens. Environ.* **2016**, *177*, 101–106. [CrossRef]
16. Toming, K.; Kutser, T.; Laas, A.; Sepp, M.; Paavel, B.; Nõges, T. First Experiences in Mapping Lakewater Quality Parameters with Sentinel-2 MSI Imagery. *Remote Sens.* **2016**, *8*, 640. [CrossRef]
17. Kutser, T.; Paavel, B.; Verpoorter, C.; Ligi, M.; Soomets, T.; Toming, K.; Casal, G. Remote Sensing of Black Lakes and Using 810 Nm Reflectance Peak for Retrieving Water Quality Parameters of Optically Complex Waters. *Remote Sens.* **2016**, *8*, 497. [CrossRef]
18. Chen, J.; Zhu, W.; Tian, Y.Q.; Yu, Q.; Zheng, Y.; Huang, L. Remote Estimation of Colored Dissolved Organic Matter and Chlorophyll-a in Lake Huron Using Sentinel-2 Measurements. *J. Appl. Remote Sens.* **2017**, *11*, 036007. [CrossRef]
19. Liu, H.; Li, Q.; Shi, T.; Hu, S.; Wu, G.; Zhou, Q. Application of Sentinel 2 MSI Images to Retrieve Suspended Particulate Matter Concentrations in Poyang Lake. *Remote Sens.* **2017**, *9*, 761. [CrossRef]
20. Ogashawara, I.; Kiel, C.; Jechow, A.; Kohnert, K.; Ruhtz, T.; Grossart, H.-P.; Hölker, F.; Nejstgaard, J.C.; Berger, S.A.; Wollrab, S. The Use of Sentinel-2 for Chlorophyll-a Spatial Dynamics Assessment: A Comparative Study on Different Lakes in Northern Germany. *Remote Sens.* **2021**, *13*, 1542. [CrossRef]
21. Soomets, T.; Uudeberg, K.; Jakovels, D.; Brauns, A.; Zagars, M.; Kutser, T. Validation and Comparison of Water Quality Products in Baltic Lakes Using Sentinel-2 MSI and Sentinel-3 OLCI Data. *Sensors* **2020**, *20*, 742. [CrossRef]
22. Ekstrand, S. Landsat TM Based Quantification of Chlorophyll-a during Algae Blooms in Coastal Waters. *Int. J. Remote Sens.* **1992**, *13*, 1913–1926. [CrossRef]
23. Bresciani, M.; Stroppiana, D.; Odermatt, D.; Morabito, G.; Giardino, C. Assessing Remotely Sensed Chlorophyll-a for the Implementation of the Water Framework Directive in European Perialpine Lakes. *Sci. Total Environ.* **2011**, *409*, 3083–3091. [CrossRef] [PubMed]
24. Chen, X.Y.; Zhang, J.; Tong, C.; Liu, R.J.; Mu, B.; Ding, J. Retrieval Algorithm of Chlorophyll-a Concentration in Turbid Waters from Satellite HY-1C Coastal Zone Imager Data. *J. Coast. Res.* **2019**, *90*, 146–155. [CrossRef]
25. Kutser, T. Monitoring Long Time Trends in Lake Cdom Using Landsat Image Archive. In Proceedings of the 2010 IEEE International Geoscience and Remote Sensing Symposium, Honolulu, HI, USA, 25–30 July 2010; pp. 389–392.
26. Kutser, T.; Tranvik, L.; Pierson, D.C. Variations in Colored Dissolved Organic Matter between Boreal Lakes Studied by Satellite Remote Sensing. *J. Appl. Remote Sens.* **2009**, *3*, 033538. [CrossRef]
27. Kutser, T.; Pierson, D.C.; Tranvik, L.; Reinart, A.; Sobek, S.; Kallio, K. Using Satellite Remote Sensing to Estimate the Colored Dissolved Organic Matter Absorption Coefficient in Lakes. *Ecosystems* **2005**, *8*, 709–720. [CrossRef]
28. Knaeps, E.; Ruddick, K.G.; Doxaran, D.; Dogliotti, A.I.; Nechad, B.; Raymaekers, D.; Sterckx, S. A SWIR Based Algorithm to Retrieve Total Suspended Matter in Extremely Turbid Waters. *Remote Sens. Environ.* **2015**, *168*, 66–79. [CrossRef]
29. Giardino, C.; Pepe, M.; Brivio, P.A.; Ghezzi, P.; Zilioli, E. Detecting Chlorophyll, Secchi Disk Depth and Surface Temperature in a Sub-Alpine Lake Using Landsat Imagery. *Sci. Total Environ.* **2001**, *268*, 19–29. [CrossRef] [PubMed]
30. Wang, S.; Li, J.; Zhang, B.; Lee, Z.; Spyrakos, E.; Feng, L.; Liu, C.; Zhao, H.; Wu, Y.; Zhu, L.; et al. Changes of Water Clarity in Large Lakes and Reservoirs across China Observed from Long-Term MODIS. *Remote Sens. Environ.* **2020**, *247*, 111949. [CrossRef]
31. Harrington, J.A.; Schiebe, F.R.; Nix, J.F. Remote Sensing of Lake Chicot, Arkansas: Monitoring Suspended Sediments, Turbidity, and Secchi Depth with Landsat MSS Data. *Remote Sens. Environ.* **1992**, *39*, 15–27. [CrossRef]
32. Huang, C.; Yunmei, L.; Liu, G.; Guo, Y.; Yang, H.; Zhu, A.; Song, T.; Huang, T.; Zhang, M.; Shi, K. Tracing High Time-Resolution Fluctuations in Dissolved Organic Carbon Using Satellite and Buoy Observations: Case Study in Lake Taihu, China. *Int. J. Appl. Earth Obs. Geoinf.* **2017**, *62*, 174–182. [CrossRef]
33. Li, S.; Toming, K.; Nõges, T.; Kutser, T. Integrating Remote Sensing of Hydrological Processes and Dissolved Organic Carbon Fluxes in Long-Term Lake Studies. *J. Hydrol.* **2022**, *605*, 127331. [CrossRef]
34. Chen, J.; Zhu, W.; Tian, Y.Q.; Yu, Q. Monitoring Dissolved Organic Carbon by Combining Landsat-8 and Sentinel-2 Satellites: Case Study in Saginaw River Estuary, Lake Huron. *Sci. Total Environ.* **2020**, *718*, 137374. [CrossRef]
35. Cao, F.; Tzortziou, M. Capturing Dissolved Organic Carbon Dynamics with Landsat-8 and Sentinel-2 in Tidally Influenced Wetland–Estuarine Systems. *Sci. Total Environ.* **2021**, *777*, 145910. [CrossRef]
36. Arenz, R.F.; Lewis, W.M.; Saunders, J.F. Determination of Chlorophyll and Dissolved Organic Carbon from Reflectance Data for Colorado Reservoirs. *Int. J. Remote Sens.* **1996**, *17*, 1547–1565. [CrossRef]
37. Shuchman, R.A.; Leshkevich, G.; Sayers, M.J.; Johengen, T.H.; Brooks, C.N.; Pozdnyakov, D. An Algorithm to Retrieve Chlorophyll, Dissolved Organic Carbon, and Suspended Minerals from Great Lakes Satellite Data. *J. Great Lakes Res.* **2013**, *39*, 14–33. [CrossRef]
38. Winn, N.; Williamson, C.E.; Abbitt, R.; Rose, K.; Renwick, W.; Henry, M.; Saros, J. Modeling Dissolved Organic Carbon in Subalpine and Alpine Lakes with GIS and Remote Sensing. *Landsc. Ecol.* **2009**, *24*, 807–816. [CrossRef]
39. Alcântara, E.; Bernardo, N.; Rodrigues, T.; Watanabe, F. Modeling the Spatio-Temporal Dissolved Organic Carbon Concentration in Barra Bonita Reservoir Using OLI/Landsat-8 Images. *Model. Earth Syst. Environ.* **2017**, *3*, 11. [CrossRef]
40. Hirtle, H.; Rencz, A. The Relation between Spectral Reflectance and Dissolved Organic Carbon in Lake Water: Kejimkujik National Park, Nova Scotia, Canada. *Int. J. Remote Sens.* **2003**, *24*, 953–967. [CrossRef]
41. Liu, D.; Yu, S.; Xiao, Q.; Qi, T.; Duan, H. Satellite Estimation of Dissolved Organic Carbon in Eutrophic Lake Taihu, China. *Remote Sens. Environ.* **2021**, *264*, 112572. [CrossRef]
42. Jiang, G.; Ma, R.; Loiselle, S.A.; Duan, H. Optical Approaches to Examining the Dynamics of Dissolved Organic Carbon in Optically Complex Inland Waters. *Environ. Res. Lett.* **2012**, *7*, 034014. [CrossRef]

43. Cai, X.; Li, Y.; Lei, S.; Zeng, S.; Zhao, Z.; Lyu, H.; Dong, X.; Li, J.; Wang, H.; Xu, J.; et al. A Hybrid Remote Sensing Approach for Estimating Chemical Oxygen Demand Concentration in Optically Complex Waters: A Case Study in Inland Lake Waters in Eastern China. *Sci. Total Environ.* **2023**, *856*, 158869. [CrossRef]
44. Luo, J.; Pu, R.; Ma, R.; Wang, X.; Lai, X.; Mao, Z.; Zhang, L.; Peng, Z.; Sun, Z. Mapping Long-Term Spatiotemporal Dynamics of Pen Aquaculture in a Shallow Lake: Less Aquaculture Coming along Better Water Quality. *Remote Sens.* **2020**, *12*, 1866. [CrossRef]
45. Cai, J.; Meng, L.; Liu, H.; Chen, J.; Xing, Q. Estimating Chemical Oxygen Demand in Estuarine Urban Rivers Using Unmanned Aerial Vehicle Hyperspectral Images. *Ecol. Indic.* **2022**, *139*, 108936. [CrossRef]
46. Guo, H.; Huang, J.J.; Zhu, X.; Wang, B.; Tian, S.; Xu, W.; Mai, Y. A Generalized Machine Learning Approach for Dissolved Oxygen Estimation at Multiple Spatiotemporal Scales Using Remote Sensing. *Environ. Pollut.* **2021**, *288*, 117734. [CrossRef]
47. Sharaf El Din, E.; Zhang, Y. Estimation of Both Optical and Nonoptical Surface Water Quality Parameters Using Landsat 8 OLI Imagery and Statistical Techniques. *J. Appl. Remote Sens.* **2017**, *11*, 1. [CrossRef]
48. Elsayed, S.; Ibrahim, H.; Hussein, H.; Elsherbiny, O.; Elmetwalli, A.H.; Moghanm, F.S.; Ghoneim, A.M.; Danish, S.; Datta, R.; Gad, M. Assessment of Water Quality in Lake Qaroun Using Ground-Based Remote Sensing Data and Artificial Neural Networks. *Water* **2021**, *13*, 3094. [CrossRef]
49. Ha, N.-T.; Nguyen, H.Q.; Truong, N.C.Q.; Le, T.L.; Thai, V.N.; Pham, T.L. Estimation of Nitrogen and Phosphorus Concentrations from Water Quality Surrogates Using Machine Learning in the Tri and Reservoir, Vietnam. *Environ. Monit. Assess.* **2020**, *192*, 789. [CrossRef] [PubMed]
50. Dong, G.; Hu, Z.; Liu, X.; Fu, Y.; Zhang, W. Spatio-Temporal Variation of Total Nitrogen and Ammonia Nitrogen in the Water Source of the Middle Route of the South-To-North Water Diversion Project. *Water* **2020**, *12*, 2615. [CrossRef]
51. Zhang, T.; Hu, H.; Ma, X.; Zhang, Y. Long-Term Spatiotemporal Variation and Environmental Driving Forces Analyses of Algal Blooms in Taihu Lake Based on Multi-Source Satellite and Land Observations. *Water* **2020**, *12*, 1035. [CrossRef]
52. Yu, X.; Yi, H.; Liu, X.; Wang, Y.; Liu, X.; Zhang, H. Remote-Sensing Estimation of Dissolved Inorganic Nitrogen Concentration in the Bohai Sea Using Band Combinations Derived from MODIS Data. *Int. J. Remote Sens.* **2016**, *37*, 327–340. [CrossRef]
53. Liu, C.; Zhang, F.; Ge, X.; Zhang, X.; Chan, N.W.; Qi, Y. Measurement of Total Nitrogen Concentration in Surface Water Using Hyperspectral Band Observation Method. *Water* **2020**, *12*, 1842. [CrossRef]
54. Arango, J.G.; Nairn, R.W. Prediction of Optical and Non-Optical Water Quality Parameters in Oligotrophic and Eutrophic Aquatic Systems Using a Small Unmanned Aerial System. *Drones* **2019**, *4*, 1. [CrossRef]
55. Yuan, X.; Wang, S.; Fan, F.; Dong, Y.; Li, Y.; Lin, W.; Zhou, C. Spatiotemporal Dynamics and Anthropologically Dominated Drivers of Chlorophyll-a, TN and TP Concentrations in the Pearl River Estuary Based on Retrieval Algorithm and Random Forest Regression. *Environ. Res.* **2022**, *215*, 114380. [CrossRef] [PubMed]
56. Wang, X.; Gong, C.; Ji, T.; Hu, Y.; Li, L. Inland Water Quality Parameters Retrieval Based on the VIP-SPCA by Hyperspectral Remote Sensing. *J. Appl. Remote Sens.* **2021**, *15*, 042609. [CrossRef]
57. Vakili, T.; Amanollahi, J. Determination of Optically Inactive Water Quality Variables Using Landsat 8 Data: A Case Study in Geshlagh Reservoir Affected by Agricultural Land Use. *J. Clean. Prod.* **2020**, *247*, 119134. [CrossRef]
58. Soomets, T.; Toming, K.; Jefimova, J.; Jaanus, A.; Põllumäe, A.; Kutser, T. Deriving Nutrient Concentrations from Sentinel-3 OLCI Data in North-Eastern Baltic Sea. *Remote Sens.* **2022**, *14*, 1487. [CrossRef]
59. Guo, H.; Tian, S.; Jeanne Huang, J.; Zhu, X.; Wang, B.; Zhang, Z. Performance of Deep Learning in Mapping Water Quality of Lake Simcoe with Long-Term Landsat Archive. *ISPRS J. Photogramm. Remote Sens.* **2022**, *183*, 451–469. [CrossRef]
60. Isenstein, E.M.; Park, M.H. Assessment of Nutrient Distributions in Lake Champlain Using Satellite Remote Sensing. *J. Environ. Sci.* **2014**, *26*, 1831–1836. [CrossRef]
61. Sun, D.; Qiu, Z.; Li, Y.; Shi, K.; Gong, S. Detection of Total Phosphorus Concentrations of Turbid Inland Waters Using a Remote Sensing Method. *Water Air Soil. Pollut.* **2014**, *225*, 1953. [CrossRef]
62. Baban, S.M.J. Detecting Water Quality Parameters in the Norfolk Broads, U.K. Using Landsat Imagery. *Int. J. Remote Sens.* **1993**, *14*, 1247–1267. [CrossRef]
63. Li, L.; Chen, X.; Zhang, M.; Zhang, W.; Wang, D.; Wang, H. The Spatial Variations of Water Quality and Effects of Water Landscape in Baiyangdian Lake, North China. *Environ. Sci. Pollut. Res.* **2022**, *29*, 16716–16726. [CrossRef]
64. Gao, Y.; Gao, J.; Yin, H.; Liu, C.; Xia, T.; Wang, J.; Huang, Q. Remote Sensing Estimation of the Total Phosphorus Concentration in a Large Lake Using Band Combinations and Regional Multivariate Statistical Modeling Techniques. *J. Environ. Manag.* **2015**, *151*, 33–43. [CrossRef]
65. Gholizadeh, M.H.; Melesse, A.M.; Reddi, L. A Comprehensive Review on Water Quality Parameters Estimation Using Remote Sensing Techniques. *Sensors* **2016**, *16*, 1298. [CrossRef]
66. Mohseni, F.; Saba, F.; Mirmazloumi, S.M.; Amani, M.; Mokhtarzade, M.; Jamali, S.; Mahdavi, S. Ocean Water Quality Monitoring Using Remote Sensing Techniques: A Review. *Mar. Environ. Res.* **2022**, *180*, 105701. [CrossRef]
67. Morel, A.Y.; Gordon, H.R. Report of the Working Group on Water Color. *Bound. Layer. Meteorol.* **1980**, *18*, 343–355. [CrossRef]
68. Yang, H.; Kong, J.; Hu, H.; Du, Y.; Gao, M.; Chen, F. A Review of Remote Sensing for Water Quality Retrieval: Progress and Challenges. *Remote Sens.* **2022**, *14*, 1770. [CrossRef]
69. Gordon, H.R.; Morel, A.Y. *Remote Assessment of Ocean Color for Interpretation of Satellite Visible Imagery: A Review*; Springer: New York, NY, USA, 1983; Volume 4. [CrossRef]

70. Dekker, A.G.; Brando, V.E.; Anstee, J.M.; Pinnel, N.; Kutser, T.; Hoogenboom, E.J.; Peters, S.; Pasterkamp, R.; Vos, R.; Olbert, C.; et al. *Imaging Spectrometry: Basic Principles and Prospective Applications*; Springer: Berlin/Heidelberg, Germany, 2002; pp. 307–359. [CrossRef]
71. Zhang, B.; Li, J.; Shen, Q.; Chen, D. A Bio-Optical Model Based Method of Estimating Total Suspended Matter of Lake Taihu from near-Infrared Remote Sensing Reflectance. *Environ. Monit. Assess.* **2008**, *145*, 339–347. [CrossRef] [PubMed]
72. Chen, B.; Mu, X.; Chen, P.; Wang, B.; Choi, J.; Park, H.; Xu, S.; Wu, Y.; Yang, H. Machine Learning-Based Inversion of Water Quality Parameters in Typical Reach of the Urban River by UAV Multispectral Data. *Ecol. Indic.* **2021**, *133*, 108434. [CrossRef]
73. Ruescas, A.; Hieronymi, M.; Mateo-Garcia, G.; Koponen, S.; Kallio, K.; Camps-Valls, G. Machine Learning Regression Approaches for Colored Dissolved Organic Matter (CDOM) Retrieval with S2-MSI and S3-OLCI Simulated Data. *Remote Sens.* **2018**, *10*, 786. [CrossRef]
74. Tian, S.; Guo, H.; Xu, W.; Zhu, X.; Wang, B.; Zeng, Q.; Mai, Y.; Huang, J.J. Remote Sensing Retrieval of Inland Water Quality Parameters Using Sentinel-2 and Multiple Machine Learning Algorithms. *Environ. Sci. Pollut. Res.* **2022**, *30*, 18617–18630. [CrossRef]
75. Xiao, Y.; Guo, Y.; Yin, G.; Zhang, X.; Shi, Y.; Hao, F.; Fu, Y. UAV Multispectral Image-Based Urban River Water Quality Monitoring Using Stacked Ensemble Machine Learning Algorithms—A Case Study of the Zhanghe River, China. *Remote Sens.* **2022**, *14*, 3272. [CrossRef]
76. Zhang, F.; Wang, J.; Wang, X. Recognizing the Relationship between Spatial Patterns in Water Quality and Land-Use/Cover Types: A Case Study of the Jinghe Oasis in Xinjiang, China. *Water* **2018**, *10*, 646. [CrossRef]
77. Hafeez, S.; Wong, M.S.; Ho, H.C.; Nazeer, M.; Nichol, J.; Abbas, S.; Tang, D.; Lee, K.H.; Pun, L. Comparison of Machine Learning Algorithms for Retrieval of Water Quality Indicators in Case-Ii Waters: A Case Study of Hong Kong. *Remote Sens.* **2019**, *11*, 617. [CrossRef]
78. Chen, T.; Guestrin, C. XGBoost: A Scalable Tree Boosting System. In Proceedings of the 22nd ACM SIGKDD International Conference on Knowledge Discovery and Data Mining, San Francisco, CA, USA, 13–17 August 2016; Association for Computing Machinery: New York, NY, USA, 2016; pp. 785–794. [CrossRef]
79. Ogunleye, A.; Wang, Q.-G. XGBoost Model for Chronic Kidney Disease Diagnosis. *IEEE/ACM Trans. Comput. Biol. Bioinform.* **2020**, *17*, 2131–2140. [CrossRef]
80. Zamani Joharestani, M.; Cao, C.; Ni, X.; Bashir, B.; Talebiesfandarani, S. PM2.5 Prediction Based on Random Forest, XGBoost, and Deep Learning Using Multisource Remote Sensing Data. *Atmosphere* **2019**, *10*, 373. [CrossRef]
81. Zhang, D.; Qian, L.; Mao, B.; Huang, C.; Huang, B.; Si, Y. A Data-Driven Design for Fault Detection of Wind Turbines Using Random Forests and XGboost. *IEEE Access* **2018**, *6*, 21020–21031. [CrossRef]
82. Sheridan, R.P.; Wang, W.M.; Liaw, A.; Ma, J.; Gifford, E.M. Extreme Gradient Boosting as a Method for Quantitative Structure–Activity Relationships. *J. Chem. Inf. Model.* **2016**, *56*, 2353–2360. [CrossRef] [PubMed]
83. Chen, X.; Huang, L.; Xie, D.; Zhao, Q. EGBMMDA: Extreme Gradient Boosting Machine for MiRNA-Disease Association Prediction. *Cell Death Dis.* **2018**, *9*, 3. [CrossRef]
84. Fan, J.; Wang, X.; Wu, L.; Zhou, H.; Zhang, F.; Yu, X.; Lu, X.; Xiang, Y. Comparison of Support Vector Machine and Extreme Gradient Boosting for Predicting Daily Global Solar Radiation Using Temperature and Precipitation in Humid Subtropical Climates: A Case Study in China. *Energy Convers. Manag.* **2018**, *164*, 102–111. [CrossRef]
85. Bhagat, S.K.; Tiyasha, T.; Awadh, S.M.; Tung, T.M.; Jawad, A.H.; Yaseen, Z.M. Prediction of Sediment Heavy Metal at the Australian Bays Using Newly Developed Hybrid Artificial Intelligence Models. *Environ. Pollut.* **2021**, *268*, 115663. [CrossRef]
86. Chen, L.; Tan, C.H.; Kao, S.J.; Wang, T.S. Improvement of Remote Monitoring on Water Quality in a Subtropical Reservoir by Incorporating Grammatical Evolution with Parallel Genetic Algorithms into Satellite Imagery. *Water Res.* **2008**, *42*, 296–306. [CrossRef]
87. Ott, I.; Kõiv, T. *Estonian Small Lakes: Special Features and Changes*; Estonian Environment Information Centre: Tallinn, Estonia, 1999.
88. *EVS-EN ISO 11905-1:2003*; Water Quality—Determination of Nitrogen—Part 1: Method Using Oxidative Digestion with Peroxodisulfate. International Organization for Standardization: Geneva, Switzerland, 2003.
89. *EVS-EN ISO 15681-2:2018*; Water Quality—Determination of Orthophosphate and Total Phosphorus Contents by Flow Analysis—Part 2: Method by Continuous Flow Analysis. International Organization for Standardization: Geneva, Switzerland, 2018.
90. *EVS-EN ISO 6878:2004*; Water Quality—Determination of Phosphorus—Ammonium Molybdate Spectrometric Method. International Organization for Standardization: Geneva, Switzerland, 2004.
91. *ISO 10304-1:2007*; Water Quality—DETERMINATION of Dissolved Anions by Liquid Chromatography of Ions—Part 1: Determination of Bromide, Chloride, Fluoride, Nitrate, Nitrite, Phosphate and Sulfate. International Organization for Standardization: Geneva, Switzerland, 2007.
92. *ISO 7150-1:1984*; Water Quality—Determination of Ammonium—Part 1: Manual Spectrometric Method. International Organization for Standardization: Geneva, Switzerland, 1984.
93. *EVS-EN ISO 5815-1:2019*; Water Quality—Determination of Biochemical Oxygen Demand after n Days (BODn)—Part 1: Dilution and Seeding Method with Allylthiourea Addition. International Organization for Standardization: Geneva, Switzerland, 2019.
94. *EVS-ISO 15705:2004*; Water Quality—Determination of the Chemical Oxygen Demand Index (ST-COD)—Small-Scale Sealed-Tube Method. International Organization for Standardization: Geneva, Switzerland, 2004.

95. EVS-EN 15204:2006; Water Quality—Guidance Standard on the Enumeration of Phytoplankton Using Inverted Microscopy (Utermöhl Technique). International Organization for Standardization: Geneva, Switzerland, 1992.
96. EVS-EN ISO 10523:2012; Water Quality—Determination of pH. International Organization for Standardization: Geneva, Switzerland, 2012.
97. EVS-EN ISO 5814:2012; Water Quality—Determination of Dissolved Oxygen—Electrochemical Probe Method. International Organization for Standardization: Geneva, Switzerland, 2012.
98. Toming, K.; Kutser, T.; Tuvikene, L.; Viik, M.; Nõges, T. Dissolved Organic Carbon and Its Potential Predictors in Eutrophic Lakes. *Water Res.* **2016**, *102*, 32–40. [CrossRef] [PubMed]
99. Hutchinson, G.E. A Treatise on Limnology: Geography, Physics, and Chemistry. In *A Treatise on Limnology*; John Wiley and Sons: New York, NY, USA, 1957.
100. Brockmann, C.; Doerffer, R.; Marco, P.; Stelzer, K.; Embacher, S.; Ruescas, A. Evolution of the C2RCC Neural Network for Sentinel 2 and 3 for the Retrieval of Ocean. In Proceedings of the 'Living Planet Symposium 2016', (ESA SP-740, August 2016), Prague, Czech Republic, 9–13 May 2016; pp. 9–13.
101. Uudeberg, K.; Ansko, I.; Põru, G.; Ansper, A.; Reinart, A. Using Opticalwater Types to Monitor Changes in Optically Complex Inland and Coastalwaters. *Remote Sens.* **2019**, *11*, 2297. [CrossRef]
102. XGBoost Tutorials—Xgboost 1.0.0-SNAPSHOT Documentation. Available online: https://xgboost.readthedocs.io/en/stable/tutorials/index.html (accessed on 30 December 2022).
103. Pedregosa, F.; Varoquaux, G.; Gramfort, A.; Michel, V.; Thirion, B.; Grisel, O.; Blondel, M.; Müller, A.; Nothman, J.; Louppe, G.; et al. Scikit-Learn: Machine Learning in Python. *J. Mach. Learn. Res.* **2012**, *12*, 2825–2830.
104. Doxaran, D.; Ruddick, K.; McKee, D.; Gentili, B.; Tailliez, D.; Chami, M.; Babin, M. Spectral Variations of Light Scattering by Marine Particles in Coastal Waters, from Visible to near Infrared. *Limnol. Ocean.* **2009**, *54*, 1257–1271. [CrossRef]
105. Doxaran, D.; Froidefond, J.M.; Lavender, S.; Castaing, P. Spectral Signature of Highly Turbid Waters: Application with SPOT Data to Quantify Suspended Particulate Matter Concentrations. *Remote Sens. Environ.* **2002**, *81*, 149–161. [CrossRef]
106. Kutser, T. Quantitative Detection of Chlorophyll in Cyanobacterial Blooms by Satellite Remote Sensing. *Limnol. Ocean.* **2004**, *49*, 2179–2189. [CrossRef]
107. Smith, V.H. Eutrophication of Freshwater and Coastal Marine Ecosystems: A Global Problem. *Environ. Sci. Pollut. Res.* **2003**, *10*, 126–139. [CrossRef]
108. Xu, Z.; Xu, Y.J. Rapid Field Estimation of Biochemical Oxygen Demand in a Subtropical Eutrophic Urban Lake with Chlorophyll a Fluorescence. *Environ. Monit. Assess.* **2015**, *187*, 4171. [CrossRef]
109. Hébert, M.P.; Soued, C.; Fussmann, G.F.; Beisner, B.E. Dissolved Organic Matter Mediates the Effects of Warming and Inorganic Nutrients on a Lake Planktonic Food Web. *Limnol. Ocean.* **2022**, *68*, S23–S38. [CrossRef]
110. Erlandsson, M.; Cory, N.; Köhler, S.; Bishop, K. Direct and Indirect Effects of Increasing Dissolved Organic Carbon Levels on PH in Lakes Recovering from Acidification. *J. Geophys. Res. Biogeosci.* **2010**, *115*, 1–8. [CrossRef]
111. Grayson, R.B.; Finlayson, B.L.; Gippel, C.J.; Hart, B.T. The Potential of Field Turbidity Measurements for the Computation of Total Phosphorus and Suspended Solids Loads. *J. Environ. Manag.* **1996**, *47*, 257–267. [CrossRef]
112. Jones, A.S.; Stevens, D.K.; Horsburgh, J.S.; Mesner, N.O. Surrogate Measures for Providing High Frequency Estimates of Total Suspended Solids and Total Phosphorus Concentrations. *J. Am. Water Resour. Assoc.* **2011**, *47*, 239–253. [CrossRef]
113. Kusari, L. Turbidity as a Surrogate for the Determination of Total Phosphorus, Using Relationship Based on Sub-Sampling Techniques. *Ecol. Eng. Environ. Technol.* **2022**, *23*, 88–93. [CrossRef]
114. Lannergård, E.E.; Ledesma, J.L.J.; Fölster, J.; Futter, M.N. An Evaluation of High Frequency Turbidity as a Proxy for Riverine Total Phosphorus Concentrations. *Sci. Total Environ.* **2019**, *651*, 103–113. [CrossRef]
115. Viso-Vázquez, M.; Acuña-Alonso, C.; Rodríguez, J.L.; Álvarez, X. Remote Detection of Cyanobacterial Blooms and Chlorophyll-a Analysis in a Eutrophic Reservoir Using Sentinel-2. *Sustainability* **2021**, *13*, 8570. [CrossRef]
116. Buma, W.G.; Lee, S.-I. Evaluation of Sentinel-2 and Landsat 8 Images for Estimating Chlorophyll-a Concentrations in Lake Chad, Africa. *Remote Sens.* **2020**, *12*, 2437. [CrossRef]
117. Shang, Y.; Liu, G.; Wen, Z.; Jacinthe, P.A.; Song, K.; Zhang, B.; Lyu, L.; Li, S.; Wang, X.; Yu, X. Remote Estimates of CDOM Using Sentinel-2 Remote Sensing Data in Reservoirs with Different Trophic States across China. *J. Environ. Manag.* **2021**, *286*, 112275. [CrossRef]
118. Kutser, T. The Possibility of Using the Landsat Image Archive for Monitoring Long Time Trends in Coloured Dissolved Organic Matter Concentration in Lake Waters. *Remote Sens. Environ.* **2012**, *123*, 334–338. [CrossRef]
119. Cao, Z.; Ma, R.; Melack, J.M.; Duan, H.; Liu, M.; Kutser, T.; Xue, K.; Shen, M.; Qi, T.; Yuan, H. Landsat Observations of Chlorophyll-a Variations in Lake Taihu from 1984 to 2019. *Int. J. Appl. Earth Obs. Geoinf.* **2022**, *106*, 102642. [CrossRef]
120. Wei, L.; Wang, Z.; Huang, C.; Zhang, Y.; Wang, Z.; Xia, H.; Cao, L. Transparency Estimation of Narrow Rivers by UAV-Borne Hyperspectral Remote Sensing Imagery. *IEEE Access* **2020**, *8*, 168137–168153. [CrossRef]
121. Liu, C.; Duan, P.; Zhang, F.; Jim, C.Y.; Tan, M.L.; Chan, N.W. Feasibility of the Spatiotemporal Fusion Model in Monitoring Ebinur Lake's Suspended Particulate Matter under the Missing-Data Scenario. *Remote Sens.* **2021**, *13*, 3952. [CrossRef]
122. Wang, C.L.; Shi, K.Y.; Ming, X.; Cong, M.Q.; Liu, X.Y.; Guo, W.J. A Comparative Study of the COD Hyperspectral Inversion Models in Water Based on the Maching Learning. *Spectrosc. Spectr. Anal.* **2022**, *42*, 2353–2358. [CrossRef]

123. Zhang, Y.; Shi, K.; Sun, X.; Zhang, Y.; Li, N.; Wang, W.; Zhou, Y.; Zhi, W.; Liu, M.; Li, Y.; et al. Improving Remote Sensing Estimation of Secchi Disk Depth for Global Lakes and Reservoirs Using Machine Learning Methods. *GIScience Remote Sens.* **2022**, *59*, 1367–1383. [CrossRef]
124. Sommer, U.; Gliwicz, Z.M.; Lampert, W.; Duncan, A. The PEG-Model of Seasonal Succession of Planktonic Events in Fresh Waters. *Arch. Hydrobiol.* **1986**, *106*, 433–471. [CrossRef]
125. Welch, E.B. Should Nitrogen Be Reduced to Manage Eutrophication If It Is Growth Limiting? Evidence from Moses Lake. *Lake Reserv. Manag.* **2009**, *25*, 401–409. [CrossRef]
126. Schindler, D.W.; Fee, E.J. Diurnal Variation of Dissolved Inorganic Carbon and Its Use in Estimating Primary Production and CO_2 Invasion in Lake 227. *J. Fish. Res. Board Can.* **2011**, *30*, 1501–1510. [CrossRef]
127. Toming, K.; Tuvikene, L.; Vilbaste, S.; Agasild, H.; Viik, M.; Kisand, A.; Feldmann, T.; Martma, T.; Jones, R.I.; Nõges, T. Contributions of Autochthonous and Allochthonous Sources to Dissolved Organic Matter in a Large, Shallow, Eutrophic Lake with a Highly Calcareous Catchment. *Limnol. Ocean.* **2013**, *58*, 1259–1270. [CrossRef]
128. Brezonik, P.; Menken, K.D.; Bauer, M. Landsat-Based Remote Sensing of Lake Water Quality Characteristics, Including Chlorophyll and Colored Dissolved Organic Matter (CDOM). *Lake Reserv. Manag.* **2005**, *21*, 373–382. [CrossRef]
129. Tilzer, M.M. Secchi Disk—Chlorophyll Relationships in a Lake with Highly Variable Phytoplankton Biomass. *Hydrobiologia* **1988**, *162*, 163–171. [CrossRef]
130. Suursaar, Ü. Summer 2021 Marine Heat Wave in the Gulf of Finland from the Perspective of Climate Warming. *Est. J. Earth Sci.* **2022**, *71*, 1. [CrossRef]
131. Stefan, H.G.; Fang, X. Dissolved Oxygen Model for Regional Lake Analysis. *Ecol. Model.* **1994**, *71*, 37–68. [CrossRef]
132. Zhang, Y.; Wu, Z.; Liu, M.; He, J.; Shi, K.; Zhou, Y.; Wang, M.; Liu, X. Dissolved Oxygen Stratification and Response to Thermal Structure and Long-Term Climate Change in a Large and Deep Subtropical Reservoir (Lake Qiandaohu, China). *Water Res.* **2015**, *75*, 249–258. [CrossRef]
133. Krishnaraj, A.; Honnasiddaiah, R. Remote Sensing and Machine Learning Based Framework for the Assessment of Spatio-Temporal Water Quality in the Middle Ganga Basin. *Environ. Sci. Pollut. Res.* **2022**, *29*, 64939–64958. [CrossRef]

Disclaimer/Publisher's Note: The statements, opinions and data contained in all publications are solely those of the individual author(s) and contributor(s) and not of MDPI and/or the editor(s). MDPI and/or the editor(s) disclaim responsibility for any injury to people or property resulting from any ideas, methods, instructions or products referred to in the content.

Article

Using Imagery Collected by an Unmanned Aerial System to Monitor Cyanobacteria in New Hampshire, USA, Lakes

Christine L. Bunyon [1,*], Benjamin T. Fraser [1], Amanda McQuaid [2] and Russell G. Congalton [1]

[1] Department of Natural Resources and the Environment, University of New Hampshire, 56 College Road, Durham, NH 03824, USA; benjamin.fraser@unh.edu (B.T.F.); russ.congalton@unh.edu (R.G.C.)
[2] University of New Hampshire Cooperative Extension, 59 College Road, Durham, NH 03824, USA; amanda.mcquaid@unh.edu
* Correspondence: christine.bunyon@unh.edu

Abstract: With the increasing occurrence of cyanobacteria blooms, it is crucial to improve our ability to monitor impacted lakes accurately, efficiently, and safely. Cyanobacteria are naturally occurring in many waters globally. Some species can release neurotoxins which cause skin irritations, gastrointestinal illness, pet/livestock fatalities, and possibly additional complications after long-term exposure. Using a DJI M300 RTK Unmanned Aerial Vehicle equipped with a MicaSense 10-band dual camera system, six New Hampshire lakes were monitored from May to September 2022. Using the image spectral data coupled with in situ water quality data, a random forest classification algorithm was used to predict water quality categories. The analysis yielded very high overall classification accuracies for cyanobacteria cell (93%), chlorophyll-a (87%), and phycocyanin concentrations (92%). The 475 nm wavelength, normalized green-blue difference index—version 4 (NGBDI_4), and normalized green-red difference index—version 4 (NGRDI_4) indices were the most important features for these classifications. Logarithmic regressions illuminated relationships between single bands/indices with water quality data but did not perform as well as the classification algorithm approach. Ultimately, the UAS multispectral data collected in this study successfully classified cyanobacteria cell, chlorophyll-a, and phycocyanin concentrations in the studied NH lakes.

Keywords: cyanobacteria; unmanned aerial systems; water quality; multispectral imagery; machine learning classification

Citation: Bunyon, C.L.; Fraser, B.T.; McQuaid, A.; Congalton, R.G. Using Imagery Collected by an Unmanned Aerial System to Monitor Cyanobacteria in New Hampshire, USA, Lakes. *Remote Sens.* 2023, 15, 2839. https://doi.org/10.3390/rs15112839

Academic Editors: Flor Alvarez-Taboada, Miro Govedarica and Gordana Jakovljević

Received: 17 May 2023
Revised: 22 May 2023
Accepted: 24 May 2023
Published: 30 May 2023

Copyright: © 2023 by the authors. Licensee MDPI, Basel, Switzerland. This article is an open access article distributed under the terms and conditions of the Creative Commons Attribution (CC BY) license (https://creativecommons.org/licenses/by/4.0/).

1. Introduction

Globally, waterbodies are changing rapidly due to human development and changes in climate. These anthropogenic effects impact the structure of freshwater communities as well as the physical and chemical characteristics that drive many ecosystem responses [1]. Environmental monitoring is necessary to understand these occurrences and track changes over time to understand full ecosystem processes and inter-ecosystem interactions such as the effects of nutrient cycling within a changing climate [2].

As a result of changes such as increasing air temperature and altered nutrient balances, cyanobacteria blooms are occurring on many lakes and ponds in New Hampshire (USA) each summer. Cyanobacteria were one of the first organisms on Earth to produce oxygen and are naturally occurring in many of the world's waterbodies [3]. Although recently reclassified into the prokaryotic kingdom, Monera, cyanobacteria are classified as a bacterium despite their numerous algal characteristics [4]. Excess phosphorus entering the water column stimulates the growth and proliferation of cyanobacteria leading to eutrophic conditions while also triggering public health advisories, limiting recreational use, and reducing property values. Cyanobacteria harmful algal blooms (CHABs) are a subgroup of cyanobacteria blooms which release various forms of toxins that can cause skin irritations, nausea, vomiting, diarrhea, and fevers, as well as pet and livestock fatalities [5–7].

Existing and emerging studies have attempted to assess any possible connections with long term exposure and anthropogenic diseases [8,9]. Traditionally, scientists have studied cyanobacteria blooms in lakes and ponds with in situ field observations in addition to the analysis of water samples in laboratories. Monitoring this biological component of aquatic ecosystems is necessary to determine the internal processes at play and overall health of the local environment [10]. Understanding the occurrence, concentration, spatial patterns, and duration of CHABs will help communities and regulating agencies further understand CHABs from which to create effective management plans.

In the past decade, the integration of unmanned aerial systems (UAS), also known as drones, to study freshwater ecosystems has increased in scope and accuracy due to technological advances of lightweight UAS and the development of very high spatial and spectral resolution cameras. With the improved development of UAS including new and more effective sensors, longer flight periods, and improved processing software, scientists and researchers have begun using this tool to study aquatic systems. Spatial resolutions of UAS now include sub-meter pixels down to a few centimeters [11]. Multispectral sensors with high spectral resolution sense electromagnetic energy with narrow band widths [11,12]. UAS are more versatile than satellites with a minimum flying height of a few centimeters off the water's surface to 121 m (as permissible by Part 107 Federal Air Administration (FAA) regulations) while maintaining their high spatial resolutions [13,14]. Not to be confused with the imagery captured by satellites, the use of UAS in environmental studies is an emerging low cost and user-friendly application that provides the ability for rapid and frequent deployment of specific study sites, low altitude flights below the cloud deck, modification capabilities, and easy navigation of small lakes or stream networks which are difficult or impossible to assess with traditional methods or current satellite technology. These advances in UAS technology are well suited for small waterbodies and inland waters such as many of the lakes in NH.

The use of a multispectral sensor, which captures a spectral response in designated portions of the electromagnetic spectrum, enhances our ability to discriminate objects of interest both on land and water [15]. Multispectral sensors often capture imagery yielding one value in each of the blue, green, red, red edge, and NIR portions of the spectrum. This allows for increased accuracy in the detection, identification, and quantification of certain aquatic ecosystem components, particularly blue-green and green algae [16]. The MicaSense RedEdge-MX and RedEdge-MX Blue Dual Camera Imaging System was used for this study (Seattle, WA, USA). This dual camera system captures electromagnetic energy, in the form of reflectance, centered around the following 10 wavelengths: 444 (coastal blue), 475 (blue), 531 (green), 560 (green), 650 (red), 668 (red), 705 (red edge), 717 (red edge), 740 (red edge), and 842 (NIR) nm. In this study, reflectance values were extracted from the UAS-collected imagery and used to calculate derivative bands or indices to find a relationship with collected water quality data (the reference data).

Many studies have found the use of green, red, red edge, and NIR wavelengths are best for studying phytoplankton, chlorophyll-a, and submerged aquatic vegetation [11,17–19]. In addition, the blue portion of the spectrum has also been incorporated to study cyanobacteria [20,21]. Many others have used derivative bands made by mathematically combining multiple bands such as a normalized difference vegetation index (NDVI) and other indices to determine chlorophyll-a, algal, and/or cyanobacteria measurements [13,21–26]. This approach is rapidly evolving and less often applied to UAS applications than to satellite applications [27]. There is limited research within New England using remote sensing methods to study cyanobacteria in small lakes; a region where cyanobacteria blooms are becoming an ever increasing public and ecological issue.

Therefore, the goal of this study was to investigate an alternate method for quantifying the cell concentration of cyanobacteria in New Hampshire waterbodies using UAS multispectral data over the course of the growing season to identify areas within the waterbodies that exceed thresholds set by agencies and/or this study. To do this, each flight was paired with collected water samples. The water samples were analyzed for cyanobacteria cell concentration, chlorophyll-a, phycocyanin, and phycoerythrin to calibrate the relationship and model between the in situ sample data and the UAS imagery. These water quality parameters were selected based on the current NH State cyanobacteria monitoring procedures (cell concentration) of the New Hampshire Department of Environmental Protection (NHDES), and standard monitoring practices through pigment analyses for cyanobacteria (chlorophyll-a, phycocyanin, and phycoerythrin) [10,11,13,17–35]. The specific objectives of this study were:

1. To build a dataset of both UAS reflectance data and water quality data for cyanobacteria in NH lakes.
2. To target cyanobacteria blooms from multiple lakes in New Hampshire with different dominant species of cyanobacteria over the course of the bloom's life cycle.
3. To determine the best spectral relationship for classification between very high spatial resolution multispectral UAS imagery and cyanobacteria for the sampled lakes.

2. Materials and Methods

2.1. Site Selection and Descriptions

Candidate lakes in New Hampshire were identified for this study through a series of criteria using a scoring system developed for this analysis. This scoring system consisted of data on previous bloom duration, concentrations, and dominant cyanobacteria species, lake size, public accessibility, and distance from water quality and image analysis laboratories. The candidate lakes were then located on the FAA Sectional Aeronautical Chart and removed if in a restricted airspace. Stakeholders for the remaining lakes were contacted to determine their willingness to collaborate. Silver Lake (Hollis), Keyser Pond (Henniker), and French Pond (Henniker) were then selected as the three primary lakes to include in this study. These three lakes were sampled roughly every other week from the first week in May to the first week of September 2022. Greenwood Pond (Kingston), Showell Pond (Sandown), and Tucker Pond (Salisbury) were added to the study once a cyanobacteria bloom had begun on the respective waterbody to add to the dataset during August and September of 2022 (Figure 1).

The six selected lakes span a variety of lake trophic classifications including lakes designated as oligotrophic, mesotrophic, and eutrophic (Table 1). Identified based on ambient water quality by the State of New Hampshire, oligotrophic lakes are those with low nutrient concentrations and high water clarity. Eutrophic lakes contain high levels of nutrients and degraded water clarity Mesotrophic lakes contain higher levels of nutrients than oligotrophic lakes but not as high as eutrophic lakes, and moderate levels of water clarity degradation [36].

Table 1. Summary of New Hampshire lakes flown with the UAS and sampled for water quality measurements in 2022.

Lake	Town	Trophic State	Surface Area (ha)	Maximum Depth (m)	Advisories	Number of Days Under Advisory
French Pond	Henniker	Eutrophic	16	12	None	0
Greenwood Pond	Kingston	Mesotrophic	20	4	27 July–4 August	8
Keyser Pond	Henniker	Mesotrophic	7	5	6 July–9 August	34
Showell Pond	Sandown	Mesotrophic	8	3–4	2 August–27 September	56
Silver Lake	Hollis	Oligotrophic	16	7	21 June–28 July, 5 August–16 November	140
Tucker Pond	Salisbury	Mesotrophic	22	6	11 August–18 November	99

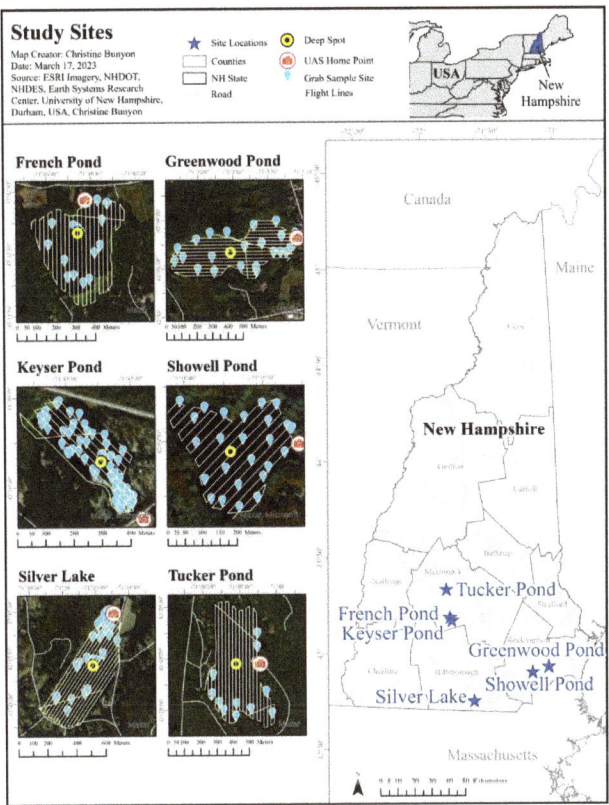

Figure 1. Study site locations within the state of New Hampshire.

2.1.1. French Pond

French Pond spans 16 hectares in Henniker, NH, is classified as a eutrophic lake, and has a maximum depth of 12 m (Table 1) [37]. There is a state-owned boat launch along the northern shore of the lake and one campground along the eastern shore. The rest of the shoreline is primarily forested and scattered with shoreline properties within a historically agricultural watershed. French Pond has had fewer cyanobacteria advisories than Silver Lake and Keyser Pond with just two from 2017 through 2021 which lasted 22 and 60 days, respectively. However, French Pond had many advisories from 2006 through 2017 (eight in total). Species of cyanobacteria present have included Aphanizomenon, Dolichospermum, Microcystis, and Woronichinia. French Pond did not experience any blooms of cyanobacteria in 2022 (Table 1).

2.1.2. Greenwood Pond

Greenwood Pond covers 20 hectares in Kingston, NH and has a maximum depth of 4 m (Table 1) [37]. The water was accessed from the town beach on the eastern shores of the lake. Classified as a mesotrophic lake, Greenwood Pond has experienced cyanobacteria blooms since 2004 which have become more frequent since 2017. There have been four separate NHDES advisories for CHABs from 2017 through 2021. Each has lasted between 4 and 34 days (average of 14 days). Species of cyanobacteria present have included Planktothrix, Oscillatoria, and Dolichospermum. In 2022, Greenwood Pond experienced a short bloom of cyanobacteria, with the advisory lasting only 8 days from the end of July into August (Table 1). The bloom was reported to be of scattered surface accumulations of Planktothrix.

2.1.3. Keyser Pond

Keyser Pond covers 7 hectares in Henniker, NH and has a maximum depth of 5 m (Table 1) [37]. Unlike Silver Lake, there is no state beach area, but a state operated boat launch is present along with a privately owned campground and cottage rentals which attract seasonal visitors. Keyser Pond is classified as a mesotrophic lake. Within the past five years, 2017 through 2021, Keyser Pond has had four advisories which have lasted between 22 and 112 days, with an average of 65 days. The first listed advisory was posted in 2007, but the second was not until 2015. Since then, cyanobacteria blooms at Keyser Pond have followed an increasing trend in duration. Species of cyanobacteria present have included Chrysosporum, Dolichospermum, Oscillatoria, Planktothrix, and Spirulina. In 2022, Keyser Pond experienced a full lake bloom primarily of Chrysosporum for 34 days from July into August (Table 1). This bloom drastically decreased the depth of secchi disk transparency measurements and consisted of some Planktothrix and Dolichospermum.

2.1.4. Showell Pond

Showell pond spans 8 hectares in Sandown, NH and has a maximum depth over 3 m (Table 1) [27] With permission, sampling was conducted from the lawn of a private residence along the eastern shores of the lake at the end of Showell Pond Lane. Classified as a mesotrophic lake, Showell Pond has recorded consistent blooms of cyanobacteria dating back to 2006 [38]. There were only two NHDES advisories from CHABs from 2017 through 2021. The advisories lasted 76 days in 2018 and 90 days in 2019 (an average of 83 days). Species of cyanobacteria present have included Dolichospermum, Coelosphaerium, Oscillatoria, and Aphanizomenon. In 2022, Showell Pond experienced a bloom similar to Keyser Pond. Lasting for 56 days, the dominant species were Chrysosporum, Planktothrix, and Spirulina, and turned the entire lake a greenish-brown color (Table 1).

2.1.5. Silver Lake

Silver Lake spans 16 hectares in Hollis, NH and has a maximum depth of 7 m (Table 1) [37]. The Silver Lake State Park beach area is located along the northern shores of the lake. The wind predominantly blows towards the State Park beach, bringing with it accumulations of substances on the surface of the lake. Classified as an oligotrophic lake, Silver Lake has experienced cyanobacteria blooms since 1991 [39]. Silver Lake has had a total of nine separate NHDES advisories for CHABs from 2017 through 2021. Each has lasted between 5 and 89 days (average of 37 days). Species of cyanobacteria present have included Microcystis and Dolichospermum. Woronichinia were also present in 2021 and 2022. In 2022, Silver Lake experienced two separate advisories, one from June into July, and the second from August into November. In total, these advisories were active for 140 days (Table 1). The 2022 blooms were dominated by species of Microcystis and Dolichospermum with some presence of Woronichinia. Surface scum appeared along the state park beach and swimming area.

2.1.6. Tucker Pond

Tucker Pond covers 22 hectares in Salisbury, NH and has a maximum depth of 6 m (Table 1). With permission, sampling was conducted from the dock of a private residence along the eastern shoreline on Sixth Road. Classified as a mesotrophic lake, Tucker Pond has had only three listed NHDES advisories from CHABs, all of which have occurred since 2019 [40]. These advisories lasted between 14 and 132 days (average of 68 days). Woronichinia is the dominant species present. In 2022, Tucker Pond experienced a cyanobacteria bloom lasting 99 days from August through November. Consisting of Worochinia and Microcystis, this bloom appeared as surface accumulations along the south and southwestern shorelines.

2.2. Workflow

Data analysis for this project followed two separate workflows which converge as seen in Figure 2. On each sampling day, UAS imagery was collected prior to the collection of water samples. UAS imagery was processed and spectral indices were developed and applied to the imagery. Water samples were analyzed for cyanobacteria speciation and cell count, phycocyanin and phycoerythrin concentrations, and chlorophyll-a concentration. The workflow then converges for the statistical analyses of classification and regressions to link the water quality data to the UAS imagery. The results of these analyses were evaluated for accuracy and adjusted as needed.

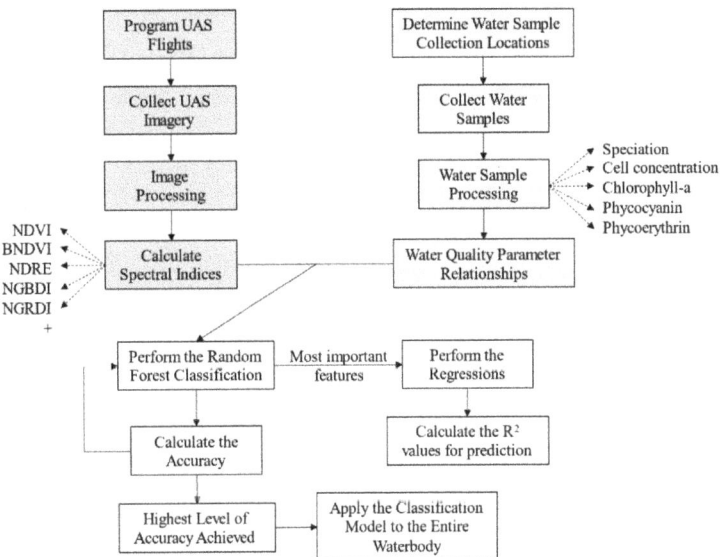

Figure 2. Flow chart of methodology. Gray boxes are part of the UAS methodology, blue boxes are part of the water quality methodology, and white boxes are part of the data analysis.

2.3. UAS Methodology

A FAA Part 107 licensed remote pilot in command operated the UAS with at least one visual observer present each time. The necessary permit was acquired to fly the UAS from Silver Lake State Park. A DJI Matrice 300 RTK (Nanshan, Shenzhen, China) was used as the primary aerial vehicle with the MicaSense RedEdge-MX and RedEdge-MX Blue Dual Camera Imaging System (Seattle, WA, USA) (Figure 3). This dual sensor consists of two cameras which function simultaneously to capture a total of 10 bands (i.e., wavelengths) of electromagnetic energy (Table 2). The UAS flight paths were preprogrammed using the DJI Pilot software on the enterprise smart controller for the Matrice 300 RTK. Because the sensors were not in communication with the aircraft, a smart device was connected to the Wi-Fi of the sensors to set the trigger speed. Initially, each flight was flown at 100 m above ground level, with 80% forward and side overlap of images along and between flight lines. Flight lines are flown parallel to each other over the entire area of study as shown in Figure 1. At a speed of 10 m/s, the sensors captured images approximately every 1.31 s. On and following 29 June, all flights were flown at 120 m above ground level with 80% forward and side overlap, and at a speed of 10 m/s. This adjustment was implemented to aid with post-processing difficulties in the imagery from flying over water. This processing was conducted using Agisoft Metashape (St. Petersburg, Russia). Each pixel covered roughly 9 cm^2 of ground area for flights flown 100 m above ground level, and 11 cm^2 of ground area for flights flown at 120 m above ground level. Sky conditions varied throughout the season for the flights and included overcast and bright days. Therefore, all images were corrected for solar illumination using the downwelling light sensor 2.0 at the time of capture to ensure all image dates were directly comparable. Wind speed below 8 m/s was required to reduce the risk of flying an unstable aircraft. Total flight times varied depending on the lake size but were between 12 and 27 min, all of which required only a single set of batteries per flight.

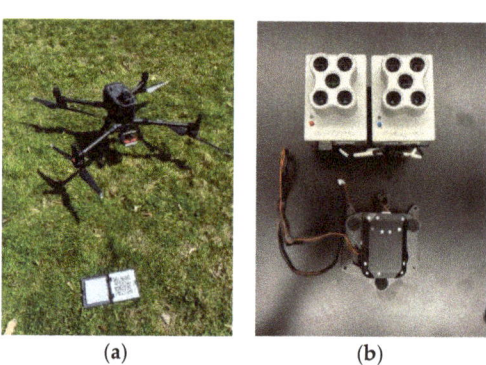

(a) (b)

Figure 3. DJI Matrice 300 RTK with calibration plate (**a**) and MicaSense RedEdge-MX Dual Camera Imaging System with downwelling light sensor 2.0 (**b**).

Table 2. Wavelengths (nm) captured by the MicaSense RedEdge-MX Dual Camera Imaging System with centers and band widths (nm) identified in parenthesis.

Coastal Blue	Blue	Green	Green	Red	Red	Red Edge	Red Edge	Red Edge	NIR
444	475	531	560	650	668	705	717	740	842
(28)	(32)	(14)	(27)	(16)	(14)	(10)	(12)	(18)	(57)

2.3.1. Image Processing

The objective of image processing was to extract average pixel values from each band captured by the sensor for a specified area surrounding each water sampling point. Three software packages were used: Agisoft Metashape, eCognition (Munich, Germany), and ArcGIS Pro (Redlands, CA, USA). Images were loaded into Agisoft Metashape to create an orthomosaic by stitching the individual images into a single scene (i.e., a mosaic). In Agisoft Metashape, all the images were calibrated using an image of the reflectance panel captured on the day of sampling to enable direct comparison between image dates. A batch processing workflow was then conducted to (1) align the images, (2) build a dense cloud, (3) build a digital elevation model, and (4) construct the orthomosaic. The final orthomosaic was given the WGS84 geographic and UTM 19N projected coordinate systems and exported as a tiff file. Meanwhile, the GPS point of each water quality sampling location was collected using the Fulcrum® (San Francisco, CA, USA) data collection mobile application and input into ArcGIS Pro 3.0 with the same coordinate systems. A 2 m^2 buffer was created around each point which was roughly equivalent to half the canoe's length squared (approximately 600 pixels). Once a day of sampling had both an orthomosaic tiff file and a sampling location buffer shapefile, eCognition was used to extract average pixel values per band from within the buffer area for each sampling location on the imagery. A ruleset was created for the vector-based segmentation and applied using the buffer areas at the pixel level. The vector-based segmentation overlays the buffered polygon data layer on the orthomosaic. It then identifies each pixel of the orthomosaic which falls within or touches each buffered area. The data from these pixels were then extracted. Attributes for each 2 m^2 sampling area included brightness, mean, and standard deviation for each of the ten bands. These attributes were then exported as a new shapefile. This new shapefile, containing only the 2 m² sampling areas and image attribute data, was then loaded back into ArcGIS Pro 3.0 to read and export the attribute data into Microsoft Excel. This process was repeated 21 times, once for each sampling day.

2.3.2. Calculating Derivative Bands

For aquatic studies of cyanobacteria, chlorophyll-a, and/or submerged aquatic vegetation, scientists have used the NDVI, normalized difference red edge index (NDRE), BNDVI, coastal blue normalized difference vegetation index (cBNDVI), normalized green blue difference index (NGBDI), normalized green red difference index (NGRDI) (aka NDGI), surface algal bloom index (SABI), florescence line height—blue (FLH Blue), SHI index (named after the author Kun Shi), and cyanobacteria index (CI) derivative bands (Table 3). The CI identifies the presence and concentration of chlorophyll-a (when centered around 681 nm) through the spectral reflectance of the sample (Equation (1)) [13,25]. When using alternative pigments to identify the CI, such as phycocyanin, the spectral shape is centered around 655 nm [25,26]. Due to slightly different bands captured in this study compared to others which used the CI, two versions of the CI were used, both of which were slightly different than in the previously referenced studies.

For this study, 78 versions of 10 derivative bands were created (Table 3, Appendix C). These derivative bands were selected based on those used in existing aquatic-UAS studies and algebraically calculated from the extracted band averages per water sample site using Microsoft Excel. A complete list of indices used can be found in Appendix C.

Table 3. Derivative bands used and/or created. See Appendix C for complete list of derivative bands. * See Equation (1).

Derivative Band	Description	General Equation	Source
NDVI	Normalized difference vegetation index	(NIR − Red)/(NIR + Red)	[21,22,24,41]
NDRE	Normalized difference red edge	(NIR − RedEdge)/(NIR + RedEdge)	[23,42]
BNDVI	Blue normalized difference vegetation index	(NIR − Blue)/(NIR + Blue)	[21]
cBNDVI	Coastal blue normalized difference vegetation index	(NIR − Coastal Blue)/(NIR + Coastal Blue)	[21]
NGBDI	Normalized green blue difference index	(Green − Blue)/(Green + Blue)	[43]
NGRDI aka NDGI	Normalized difference glacier index	(Green − Red)/(Green + Red)	[24]
SABI	Surface algal bloom index	(NIR − Red)/(Blue + Green)	[23,44]
FLH Blue	Fluorescence line height	Green − (Red + (Blue − Red))	[23,45]
SHI	The author's last name is Shi	$(e^{Red} - e^{NIR})/(e^{Red} + e^{NIR})$	[23,46]
CI *	Cyanobacteria Index	SS = $(\lambda - \lambda^-)/(\lambda^+ - \lambda^-)$	[25,26]

Equation (1): Formula for calculating the cyanobacteria index centered for phycocyanin. SS represents the spectral shape, λ represents 655 nm, λ^+ represents the adjacent bands longer than 655 (for example, 681 nm), and λ^- represents the adjacent bands shorter than 655 nm (for example, 620 nm). Cyanobacteria is present when the SS is greater than 0. Equation modified from Mishra et al. (2019) and Sharp et al. (2021) who both needed to compensate for atmospheric reflectance from satellite imagery [25,26].

$$SS = (\lambda - \lambda^-)/(\lambda^+ - \lambda^-) \quad (1)$$

2.4. Water Quality Sample Methodology

2.4.1. Water Sample Collection

Water sample collection immediately followed each UAS flight with as little delay as possible (beginning within minutes). Sampling sites within each waterbody were selected using a random stratified sampling approach. If bloom conditions upon arriving at a waterbody were likely present from a visual standpoint, or known according to the NHDES

Cyano Mapper, sampling locations were selected to target areas which appeared to have high concentrations, while spacing them out throughout the lake.

After arriving at a sampling site, the canoe was anchored to prevent drift. Per common lake water quality monitoring practices, a reading of surface water temperature and dissolved oxygen (percent and concentration) was collected using a YSI ProODO (Yellow Springs, OH, USA) which was routinely calibrated each sampling day. If the site was also the deep spot of the waterbody, a full temperature and dissolved oxygen profile was recorded. A water clarity measurement was then collected using a secchi disk and view scope off the shady side of the canoe. Notes on date, time, sky condition, and sample depth were also entered into an electronic data sheet on the Fulcrum® mobile application. These data were collected following standard practices but were determined not to be needed as part of the final data analysis in this study. The GPS location along with photos were collected at each site. A two-meter integrated core sample was collected of lake water at each site (if the site was >3 m deep and Secchi Disk Transparency (SDT) > 2 m deep) and mixed before pouring into the sample bottles for laboratory analyses. However, this case was not common. If the site was <3 m deep or SDT < 2 m, a subsurface grab was conducted with a mixing bucket which was then mixed and poured into the sample bottles.

Five of the six lakes included in this study experienced cyanobacteria blooms in 2022 according to the NHDES Harmful Algal Bloom Monitoring Program ranging from 8 to 140 days in total (Table 1). Silver Lake was the only one to experience two bloom advisories. In total, 7, 7, and 4 UAS flights occurred, with 45, 63, and 16 water samples collected from Silver Lake, Keyser Pond, and French Pond, respectively. One UAS flight occurred and 25, 26, and 12 water quality samples were collected at Greenwood Pond, Showell Pond, and Tucker Pond, respectively. Twenty-two water quality samples were not used for the water quality to UAS spectral data analysis due to poor reflectance data (Table 4).

Table 4. Dates of sampling in 2022 with the total number of samples collected per lake.

Lake	Sample Dates	Total UAS-Water Samples
Silver Lake	3 May, 20 May, 6 June, 15 June, 21 June, 29 June, 11 July, 10 August	43
Keyser Pond	12 May, 25 May, 15 June, 7 July, 20 July, 27 July, 16 August	63
French Pond	12 May, 25 May, 15 June, 7 July	13
Greenwood Pond	3 August	25
Showell Pond	25 August	26
Tucker Pond	2 September	9

2.4.2. Cyanobacteria Speciation and Cell Counts

A compound light microscope and a gridded Sedgewick–Rafter slide were used for the microscopy analysis of cyanobacteria speciation and cell counts. Samples were refrigerated and analyzed within 48 h of collection. The sample was inverted three times before 1 mL was extracted and pipetted on the slide. Results per sample included the total number of cells per genus, and the total number of cells per milliliter of sample.

2.4.3. Fluorometry

Analysis of phycocyanin and phycoerythrin was conducted per guidelines set by the UNH Center for Freshwater Biology using a FluoroQuik (Amiscience Corporation, Fremont, CA, USA) (Appendix A). Prior to reading samples, the FluoroQuik was blanked with deionized water, standards were measured, and pigment concentrations were recorded. Approximately 3 mg/L of sample was added to the cuvette and placed inside the FluoroQuik. Each sample was run in triplicate to calculate a sample mean for both phycocyanin and phycoerythrin relative concentrations in µg/L.

2.4.4. Chlorophyll-a Extraction

Analysis of chlorophyll-a concentration was conducted per guidelines set forth by the UNH Water Quality Analysis Laboratory using a hot ethanol extraction and spectrophotometric analysis. According to the laboratory standard operating procedure (SOP), "this method has the benefit of extraction without grinding, avoiding toxic methanol or acetone exposure" (Appendix B). After the hot ethanol bath preparation the day prior and settling overnight, the absorbance of each sample was measured at 665 nm and 750 nm before and after the addition of 0.25% HCl. Using these values along with the total volume of the sample that was able to be filtered, total chlorophyll-a concentration in µg/L was calculated.

2.5. Statistical Analysis

Field data entry was conducted using the Fulcrum® mobile application and then input into Microsoft Excel. Statistical analyses for water quality parameter simple linear regressions were performed using R (Indianapolis, IN, USA). This step was important to identify which water quality parameters had significant relationships to cell concentration, the parameter used by the NHDES for issuing cyanobacteria advisories. The water quality parameters with significant linear relationships in our dataset were used for the random forest classification algorithm to identify areas of the waterbody that are above or below thresholds set by agencies and/or this study.

Classification of the UAS imagery and indices for each water quality parameter was performed using the random forest classification algorithm in Python (Python Software Foundation, Wilmington, DE, USA). This algorithm uses a supervised machine learning process with two parts. First, the user inputs training areas of known data to teach the algorithm. Then, based on these training areas, the computer algorithm classifies the remaining data. The accuracy of the classification is then determined from the water samples set aside independent of the training data. The parameters within the random forest Python script yielded 500 "trees" and were repeated 20 times to produce an average overall classification accuracy.

Each viable water quality parameter, cell concentration, chlorophyll-a, and phycocyanin, were simplified (i.e., recoded) into classes. For recreational waters, the NHDES currently issues cyanobacteria advisories when cell concentrations exceed 70,000 cells/mL or if over 50% of the cells within an algal bloom are cyanobacteria. Cell concentration classes followed the State of New Hampshire 70,000 cells/mL threshold, with "Low" being samples less than the threshold, and "High" being samples equal to or greater than the threshold. Classes for chlorophyll-a were selected based on the NHDES designated chlorophyll-a concentrations for trophic classes and the World Health Organization (WHO) chlorophyll-a thresholds for potential exposure to cyanotoxins [36,47]. Mesotrophic and oligotrophic lakes are defined by having chlorophyll-a concentrations less than 11 µg/L (in addition to other factors), while eutrophic and nuisance statuses are applied to lakes with greater than 11 µg/L of chlorophyll-a [36]. Chlorophyll-a concentrations of 10 µg/L or less indicate low to not low risk of exposure, while concentrations at or above 10 µg/L indicate moderate to high risk of exposure to algal toxins [37]. Therefore, chlorophyll-a concentrations less than 10 µg/L were identified as "Low", and concentrations greater than or equal to 10 µg/L were identified as "High" for this study. Lastly, classes for phycocyanin were created following guidelines set in Almuhtaram et al., 2018. Because a significant correlation was found between phycocyanin and cell concentration, the equation of the line of best fit (y = 0.0005x + 19.822) was used with 70,000 input as the x value to determine the threshold for "High" and "Low" phycocyanin concentrations as 54.822 µg/L. Each water quality parameter was divided into only two classes to maintain the necessary 60 samples per class for accurate classification using an error matrix. An error matrix is the standard methodology for recording thematic accuracy in remote sensing [48].

For the random forest classification analysis, the reference data (water quality samples) and the UAS data were divided randomly into 50% for training the algorithm and 50% for validation or assessing the accuracy of the result. In other words, the algorithm is fed the entire dataset of paired water sample results (Highs or Lows for one water quality parameter at a time), with the UAS reflectance and indices (UAS data) per sample as the input to the model. The random forest classification algorithm then randomly subsets 50% of the data to train the model. It learns, based on the UAS data, the resulting water quality classification is either High or Low for each sample in the training subset. The remaining 50% of the dataset is then used for validation. The algorithm then takes the input UAS data and assigns water quality classifications based on what it learned with the training subset (to produce the output of the model). The accuracy of the model (i.e., properly assigning samples as either High or Low compared to the known water quality results) is determined using an error matrix [49].

Other variations of training/validation (45% and 55%) were also selected by adjusting the validation size in the python script from 0.5 to 0.45 then 0.55 but produced marginally less accurate results. The alternate validation sizes were tested per standard best practices when conducting the random forest classification algorithm to produce the highest possible accuracies [50]. Additionally, samples with poor reflectance data were initially left in but then removed. Poor reflectance samples were determined if a sample site's 2 m buffer contained pixels affected by orthomosaic holes, sun glint, emergent vegetation, or shoreline. These samples were identified and removed when the band standard deviation for pixels within the 2 m area was over 100 DN. Lastly, the random forest algorithm was run with all 78 UAS parameters included, with the 10% least important features removed, and with only the top 10% most important features included. The condition that produced the highest overall accuracies for each water quality parameter were when the sample set was divided into 50% training and 50% validation, with poor reflectance samples removed, and with only using the top 10% most important features. The random forest algorithm returned high overall accuracies with a smaller standard deviation for each water quality parameter. Accuracy results are presented as error matrices from which overall, user's, and producer's accuracies were calculated [49]. Simple linear and logarithmic regressions for the most important UAS bands and indices (found through the random forest algorithm) to each water quality parameter were conducted in Microsoft Excel. Determining which features were most important was based on the average feature importance score produced through the random forest classification and computing the average of the 20 iterations per water quality parameter. This analysis indicates which UAS features contribute most to the classification of a sample being "predicted" from those used to "train" the model. Simple regressions were calculated simply because this is the approach many similar studies apply [10,21–24,26,31,32], but produced less desirable results than from the random forest classification algorithm.

Lastly, to visually illustrate the random forest classification algorithm, the model was applied to every pixel of a waterbody to classify the water quality throughout the lake. UAS data from every pixel over a lake, one day at a time, were extracted (reflectance values per band) or calculated (indices) for the top 10% most important features identified from the random forest classification algorithm (a total of 8 features). The lake pixels were then classified as either "High" or "Low" for each of the three water quality parameters separately.

3. Results

3.1. Water Quality Parameter Relationships

Table 5 shows the correlations between the four water quality parameters. A significant linear relationship exists between many of the parameters but is not consistent across all lakes. Overall, there is an emerging trend between cell concentration and phycocyanin, cell concentration and chlorophyll-a, and phycocyanin and chlorophyll-a. Although significant results were found between cell concentration, chlorophyll-a, and phycocyanin, phycoerythrin did not follow suit except for Silver Lake (Table 5). Because there were only four water samples collected at Silver Lake exceeding the state threshold (cell concentration), these results were not deemed suitable to use phycoerythrin as a surrogate measurement for cell concentration.

Table 5. Simple linear regression outputs between water quality parameters (R^2 values). Bold, italicized, and blue values indicate significant results ($p < 0.01$). Cells = cell concentration (cells/mL), Chl-a = chlorophyll-a concentration (µg/L), PC = phycocyanin concentration (µg/L), PE = phycoerythrin (µg/L). Datapoints for cell concentrations over 1 million (n = 3) were removed for this analysis. For example, Cells/PC is the simple linear regression between cell concentrations and phycocyanin concentrations.

	Number of Samples	Cells/PC	Cells/PE	Cells/Chl-a	PC/PE	PC/Chl-a	PE/Chl-a
All Lakes	184	*0.76*	−0.0076	*0.94*	0.14	*0.69*	−0.023
French Pond	18	*0.98*	−0.26	0.29	−0.27	0.30	−0.079
Greenwood Pond	25	−0.16	−0.36	0.088	0.093	*0.72*	−0.041
Keyser Pond	61	*0.76*	−0.14	*0.78*	−0.094	*0.93*	−0.15
Showell Pond	25	−0.30	0.029	0.097	0.32	−0.29	−0.22
Silver Lake	43	*0.97*	*0.72*	*0.60*	*0.79*	*0.61*	0.36
Tucker Pond	12	*−0.72*	0.24	0.031	−0.37	0.14	−0.14

3.2. Random Forest Classification Algorithm

Building a relationship between data collected by the UAS and the water quality data was conducted using the random forest (RF) classification algorithm. The results for each water quality parameter are shown in Table 6. The average accuracies for the three water quality parameters were 92.9%, 87.4%, and 91.7% with standard deviations of 3% which shows the random forest classification algorithm produced both accurate and precise results to determine if samples were above or below state thresholds (properly classified within the High or Low classes)

Table 6. Overall classification results and standard deviations from the random forest (RF) classification algorithm for each water quality parameter. Results were generated using the top 10% most important features identified from the RF algorithm, with samples that had poor/obstructed reflectance values removed. Average overall accuracies were calculated from 20 repetitions.

	RF Average Overall Accuracy	RF Standard Deviation
Cell Concentration (cells/mL)	92.9%	3%
Chlorophyll-a Concentration (µg/L)	87.4%	3%
Phycocyanin Concentration (µg/L)	91.7%	3%

3.3. Simple Regressions

The R^2 value from a simple regression explains how much variation in the water quality parameter value can be explained by the UAS parameter. Higher R^2 values were generated from logarithmic regressions than linear and are shown in Table 7. The UAS parameter legend for index equations can be found in Appendix C. Table 7 shows the results from the simple logarithmic regressions for the top 10% of the most important features (UAS bands and indices) of the 78 features originally used for each classification to the selected water quality parameters.

Table 7. Simple logarithmic regression results for the top 10% most important features of the UAS parameters from the random forest classification algorithm for each water quality parameter. * Indicates $p < 0.01$, ** indicates $p < 0.001$. The scatter plots for the highest three R^2 values per water quality parameter are provided in Appendix D.

Water Quality Parameter	Regression Equation	R^2
Log Cell Concentration (cells/mL)	$= 6.5242 \times$ NGBDI_4 + 2.476	31% **
	$= 7.325 \times$ NGRDI_4 + 1.717	28% **
	$= -0.003 \times$ Blue_475 + 4.684	26% **
	$= -0.061 \times$ Green_Stdev_531 + 4.510	19% **
	$= -0.002 \times$ Green_531 + 4.487	18% **
	$= -0.042 \times$ Green_Stdev_560 + 4.454	16% **
	$= -0.034 \times$ Red_Stdev_650 + 4.242	12% **
	$= -0.004 \times$ CI_2 + 3.409	0%
Log Chlorophyll-a Concentration (µg/L)	$= -0.002 \times$ Blue_475 + 1.904	24% **
	$= 3.238 \times$ NGRDI_4 + 0.563	23% **
	$= -0.001 \times$ Green_531 + 1.901	22% **
	$= 3.146 \times$ NGRDI_3 + 0.713	14% **
	$= -0.001 \times$ FLHblue_2 + 1.314	4% *
	$= -0.598 \times$ CI_1 + 1.854	4% *
	$= -0.001 \times$ FLHblue_1 + 1.334	3%
	$= -0.000 \times$ CI_2 + 1.308	0%
Log Phycocyanin Concentration (µg/L)	$= 2.824 \times$ NGBDI_4 + 0.726	27% **
	$= -0.001 \times$ Blue_475 + 1.727	27% **
	$= 3.137 \times$ NGRDI_4 + 0.412	24% **
	$= -0.001 \times$ Green_531 + 1.687	22% *
	$= -0.028 \times$ Green_Stdev_531 + 1.642	19%
	$= -0.022 \times$ Green_Stdev_560 + 1.669	19%
	$= -0.018 \times$ Red_Stdev_650 + 1.575	16%
	$= -0.002 \times$ CI_2 + 1.131	0%

3.4. Application of Results to Keyser Pond

The most complete dataset portraying before, during, and after conditions of a cyanobacteria bloom in 2022 was for Keyser Pond. Here, 15 samples were collected from the 12 May 2022 through 15 June 2022 prior to the onset of the bloom and subsequent advisory. Once the cyanobacteria bloom had established, 36 samples were collected from 7 July 2022 through 27 July 2022. Twelve more samples were collected on 16 August 2022 after the bloom had subsided. The cyanobacteria bloom caused the water to turn a greenish brown color for the duration of the bloom. Figure 4 illustrates this trend through the water quality data over the course of the field season. Ideally, this pattern was desired for each lake for this study to capture UAS data from blooms with varying concentrations, but only occurred at Keyser Pond.

A visual application of the random forest classification algorithm applied to Keyser Pond before, during, and after the 2022 cyanobacteria advisory is provided in Figure 5 (15 June through 16 August). Each pixel is classified as either "High" (above the NHDES threshold for cyanobacteria, $\geq$70,000 cells/mL) or "Low" (below the NHDES threshold for cyanobacteria < 70,000 cells/mL). Technical difficulties were experienced with the UAS' internal GPS on 20 July which resulted in an incomplete orthomosaic as the flight was terminated prematurely for safety. Shadows from trees along the north-eastern shore also affected the model's results and can be seen on 20 and 27 July.

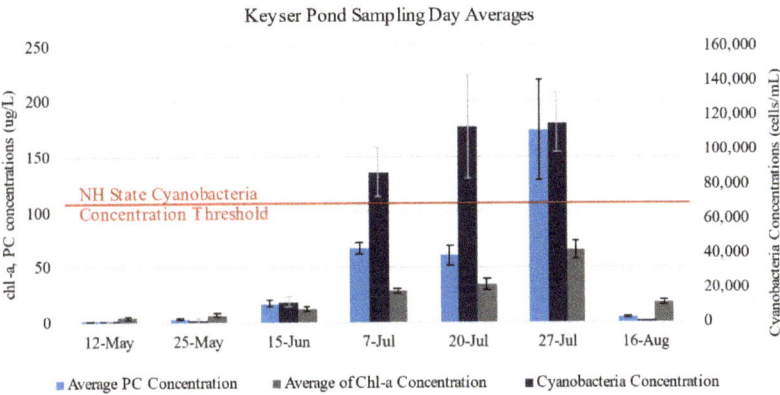

Figure 4. Sampling day averages for cyanobacteria concentration (cells/mL), chlorophyll-a (chl-a) concentration (μg/L), and phycocyanin (PC) concentration (μg/L) for Keyser Pond over the course of the sampling season. Samples collected from floating clumps detached from the benthic mat bloom were not included here (n = 2, cell concentrations were over 1 and 4 million cells/mL).

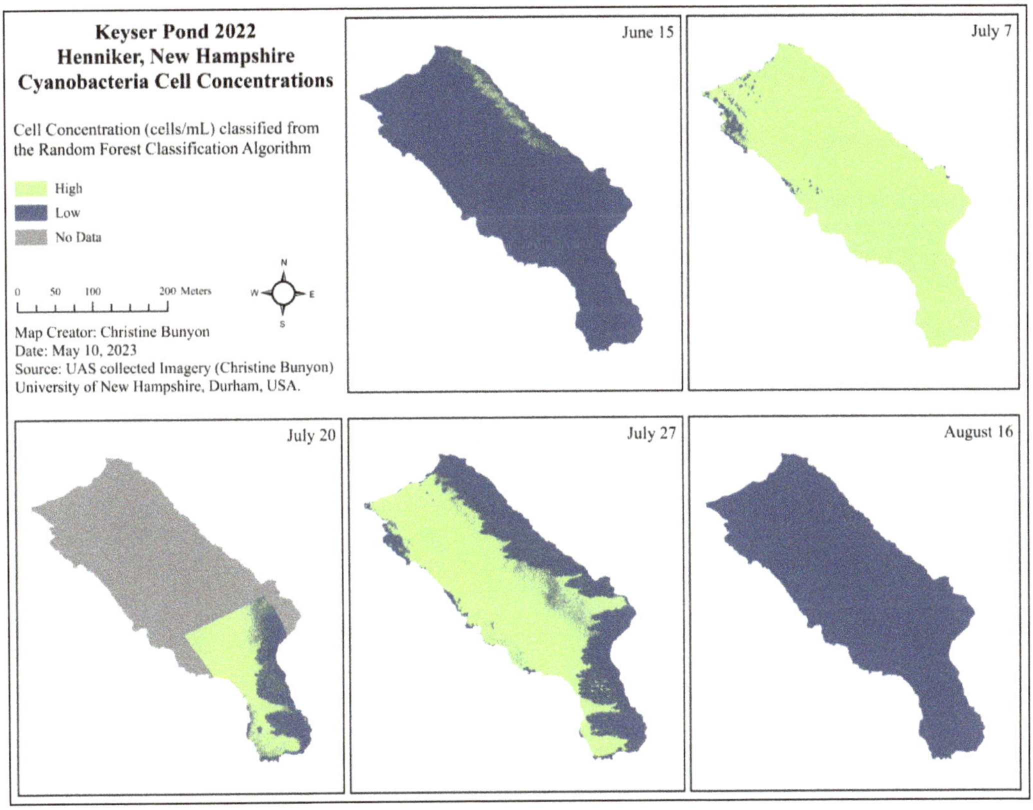

Figure 5. Cell concentrations (cells/mL) per pixel classified from the random forest classification algorithm as High or Low to represent areas of Keyser Pond exceeding the NHDES threshold for cyanobacteria (70,000 cells/mL) before (15 June), during (7 July, 20 July, and 27 July), and after (16 August) the 2022 NHDES cyanobacteria bloom advisory.

4. Discussion

Cyanobacteria blooms have been a growing concern for many lake stakeholders in New England, particularly in New Hampshire. Monitoring cyanobacteria blooms has become an increased need in many lake communities. Contrary to traditional water quality sampling, monitoring cyanobacteria blooms using a UAS allows the user to assess the entire waterbody, reduces sample analysis and processing times, and increases sampler safety. The use of a very high spatial resolution multispectral camera flown on a DJI Matrice 300 RTK was investigated to capture reflectance values centered around ten different wavelengths of light of lakes known to experience cyanobacteria blooms.

4.1. Explanation and Interpretation of Results

Through building paired datasets of both water quality and UAS spectral data, multivariate classification and regression analyses were conducted. Most importantly, discerning if a sample was above or below the New Hampshire state threshold for cyanobacteria cell concentration yielded an overall accuracy of 93%, a chlorophyll-a concentration above or below 10 µg/L had an overall accuracy of 87%, and a phycocyanin concentration above or below 54.8% was 92% accurate overall. Therefore, this process could help lake stakeholders make informed management decisions regarding closures of certain use areas of the waterbody throughout the bloom season. Looking at the random forest algorithm results, a potential explanation for the lower overall accuracy for chlorophyll-a could possibly be attributed to the method in which chlorophyll-a was extracted. During this laboratory procedure, water samples were filtered through a 47 mm filter with pore sizes of 0.7 µm (Appendix B). This was the only analysis to include a filtration step. Although unlikely, it is possible that some dissolved chlorophyll-a, less than 0.7 µm, was able to flow through the filter rather than be trapped by it, thus not being measured in the hot ethanol and fluorescence portion of the analysis. It is also possible that chlorophyll-a was captured on filters from organisms other than cyanobacteria, including green algae or plant cells as chlorophyll-a is not exclusive to cyanobacteria.

Multivariate regressions proved difficult with this dataset due to both structural multicollinearity and data multicollinearity in the spectral data. Simple regression was the preferred method for similar studies. Variation in cell concentrations, chlorophyll-a concentrations, and phycocyanin concentrations can be poorly explained by individual spectral features (Table 7). Simple regressions were calculated for the top ten percent of the most important features (determined from the average feature important scores from the random forest algorithm). As shown in Table 7, the reflectance data from the Blue 475 wavelength, NGBDI_4, and NGRDI_4 indices were the three most important features for classifying cell concentrations into "High" and "Low" categories based on the UAS or spectral data. The Blue 475 band is part of the NGBDI_4 equation, which also contains the green 560 band (Appendix C). The Green 560 band is also found in the NGRDI_4 equation along with the red 668 band. However, the Green 560 band alone was not found to be within the top 10% of the most important features. The NGRDI_4, Green 531, and FLHblue_2 features were the most important features for classifying chlorophyll-a concentrations into high and low categories based on the spectral data. The FLHblue_2 equation uses the Blue 444, Green 531, and Red 650, 668 bands. Lastly, the Blue 475, NGBDI_4, and CI_2 features were most important for classifying phycocyanin concentrations into high and low categories based on spectral data. The CI_2 contains data from the red 650 and 668 bands, in addition to the red edge at 705 nm. Four of the total seventy-eight features were found to be in the top 10% most important features for all three water quality parameters: Blue 475, NGRDI_4, CI_2, and Green_531 (Table 7).

Identifying which spectral features were most important for studying cyanobacteria concentrations with surrogate water quality parameters can guide emerging studies. Based on these findings, future studies should use sensors capable of capturing imagery from or near 444 nm, **475 nm**, 531 nm, **560 nm**, 650 nm, **668 nm**, and 705 nm; and especially, those in bold. The MicaSense RedEdge-MX Dual Camera Imaging System senses wavelengths comparable to the Landsat 8 and Sentinel 2 satellites [51,52]. The important similarities of the MicaSense sensor to the Sentinel 2 (S2) satellite include the 475 band (490 S2), 560 band (560 S2), and 668 (664 S2).

The collection and processing of the water quality samples took over 4.5 times longer than the collection and processing of the UAS data. The three most time-consuming components were determining cell and chlorophyll-a concentrations, and physically collecting each water quality sample via canoe. Other studies have evaluated the applicability and reliability of using phycocyanin as indicators for cyanobacteria rather than relying on the time intensive cell counting for cell concentration [10,29,30,53,54]. This study showed significant relationships between cell and phycocyanin concentrations at French Pond, Keyser Pond, Silver Lake, Tucker Pond, and for the entire dataset. The ability to use fluorometry to measure phycocyanin rather than the time intensive method of counting cells to determine cell concentrations or filtering and analyzing samples to measure chlorophyll-a concentrations would drastically improve the speed at which analyses could be made and results shared with communities. In the time it took to collect all the water samples alone, the entire UAS methodology could have been conducted and completed (Figure 6). This time comparison does not include tasks shared by both processes which include time traveled to each lake, communication with lake residents and stakeholders, or data analysis.

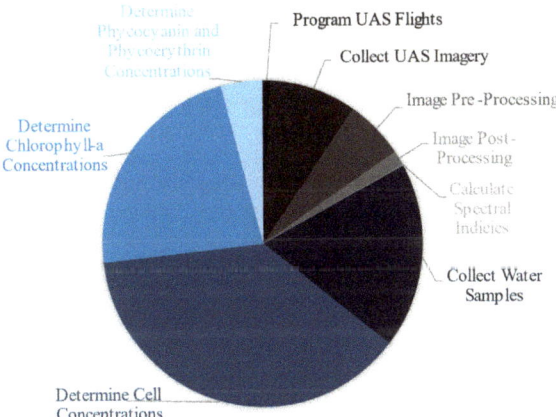

Figure 6. Approximate comparison of the amount of time each task took to complete. Blue sections represent those associated with the collection and processing of water quality parameters. Grayscale sections represent those associated with the collection and processing of UAS parameters. Traditional water quality tasks took roughly 310 h to complete while UAS tasks took roughly 65 h to complete.

4.2. Limitations

Five of the six lakes included in this study experienced cyanobacteria blooms in 2022 according to the NHDES Harmful Algal Bloom Monitoring Program (Table 1). However, samples showing bloom forming conditions were only collected at Keyser Pond, Showell Pond, and Silver Lake. There were no collected samples indicating bloom conditions from French Pond, Greenwood Pond, or Tucker Pond as follows:

1. French Pond did not have any cyanobacteria blooms during the 2022 field season; thus no "High" cell concentration samples were collected.
2. The cyanobacteria bloom present at Greenwood Pond in 2022 was very rapid. Once sampling was conducted, the cyanobacteria bloom had subsided.
3. At Tucker Pond, a pixilated surface bloom of *Worochinia* and *Microcystis* was present in small groupings along the southern and southwestern shores. Notes from lake residents indicated the bloom only appeared to span roughly 15 feet into the lake. On

the day of sampling, the concentrations of cyanobacteria were found to be below the state of New Hampshire's advisory threshold of 70,000 cells/mL.

4. On par with the *Microcystis* and *Worochinia* bloom in Tucker Pond, Silver Lake's bloom of primarily *Microcystis* and *Dolichospermum* proved difficult to capture. The ribbon of high cyanobacteria concentrations was isolated to the northern shores along the state park beach area, extending roughly 20 feet out into the lake at most. As a result, only a small fraction of the total samples collected throughout the lake surpassed the state threshold. During the peak of the first advisory on 6/29/22, collected samples ranged from 1150 to over 3.4 million cells/mL as the bloom was unevenly distributed throughout the lake.

Samples above the state threshold were collected at Keyser Pond, Showell Pond, and Silver Lake in 2022. Keyser Pond and Showell Pond contained very homogenous blooms of primarily *Chyrosoporium* with some *Planktothrix* in 2022 which turned the entire waterbodies a greenish-brown color. These blooms decreased water clarity measured with a secchi disk and view scope to less than 1 m. Cell concentrations ranged from 70,256 to 182,640 cells/mL at Keyser Pond, and from 320,400 to 650,250 cells/mL at Showell Pond for the samples collected during the advisories. Additionally, two samples were collected at Keyser Pond from clumps of *Planktothrix* that had broken off the benthic mat and floated to the surface after the advisory had lifted and ambient water cyanobacteria cell concentrations had fallen beneath the state threshold. These two samples, collected on 8/16/22, contained cell concentrations over 1 and 4 million cells/mL.

In addition to lake-specific analyses, this study identified the need for a more detailed analysis to be completed at a species-specific level. Different species of cyanobacteria alter lakes in varied ways. As seen in Keyser and Showell Ponds, blooms of *Chrysosporum* turned the entire waterbodies a greenish-brown color. This color alteration extended from the surface down into the water column. *Planktothrix* appeared in specks within the water column and as free-floating clumps that had detached from the benthic substrate. *Microcystis* was predominately found at Silver Lake in surface scum isolated to a single section of the waterbody. Often forming early in the morning and mixing with the water column as the wind and solar angle increased. This scum repeatedly came and dissipated quickly which caused the advisory to last for months and be illusive to the UAS.

Additional limitations arose in the image collection and processing phases of the UAS methodology. Due to the battery life of the UAS and not having a motorized boat, smaller lakes were targeted for this study. Lakes without islands or hidden coves were selected to maintain line of sight by the UAS pilot in command and to make canoeing to sites easier. Image processing in Agisoft Metashape proved difficult for waterbodies. Traditionally, tie points are used to properly align overlapping photos. However, the software struggles to identify tie points over a homogenous water's surface, thus creating holes (Figure 7). The solution to this problem was to fly the UAS higher to include more of the lake edge in more photos. Although not a perfect solution, this worked well enough for the purposes of this study. This limitation would be a hindering factor for wide lakes or those that are very large. Any in-lake features such as islands, floating docks, moored boats, etc. would help to build tie points over this homogenous surface. This challenge was also stated by many other scientists [17,24,31–33,55–57]. Due to this issue, ten water quality sampling points were not included in the UAS spectral data to water quality parameter analyses because they occurred in the reflectance data "holes." Another limitation to using UAS for environmental monitoring is caused by the weather. The DJI Matrice 300 RTK could only safely fly on days where the wind speed (including gusts) was less than 8 MPH or 3.6 m/s, and there was no chance of rain in the immediate forecast. The wind proved to be more difficult but was generally at its lowest earlier in the morning. However, this timing was beneficial since it occurred when the sun angle and glint were at their lowest even though some edges of the waterbodies were within shadows from shoreline vegetation on sunny days.

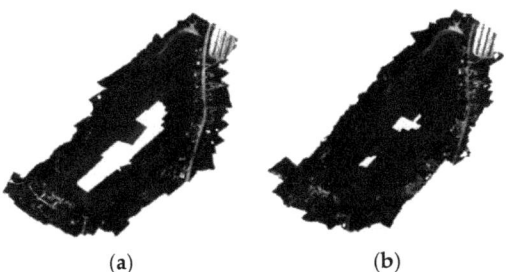

(a) (b)

Figure 7. Examples of black and white orthomosaic outputs for Silver Lake created from images flown at 100 m (**a**) and 120 m (**b**). More points in the point cloud were generated from the higher flying height which resulted in a more complete orthomosaic of Silver Lake.

4.3. Relation to Similar Studies

Contrary to other studies, this study involved multiple visits to various lakes with different dominant species of cyanobacteria from May to September in 2022. The revisitation allowed sampling to be conducted during various stages of the bloom cycle, ambient weather conditions, and seasonal changes in other water quality parameters including total suspended solids and emergent/submerged aquatic vegetation cover (not measured). It is difficult to draw usable conclusions from one flight over one lake on one day with only a handful of collected water samples for analysis without this replication.

However, many scientists have attempted to find correlations between chlorophyll-a concentrations and spectral indices collected by a UAS equipped sensor with less rigorous field studies. These studies include correlations to general "algae" [22,24,32], cyanobacteria [26], and a toxin associated with some species of cyanobacteria, microcystin [23]. A variety of sensors including a Parrot Sequoia multispectral sensor, a Canon ELPH 110HS, and a modified digital camera were used [21,24,32]. Two studies used the MicaSense RedEdge sensor [22,23]. A variety of indices were built for the chlorophyll-a regressions. R^2 values ranged from 0.004 to 0.88 depending on the index used. The most common index was a NDVI or modified blue NDVI (BNDVI). The NDVI_3 and BNDVI_3 regressions to chlorophyll-a in this study produced R^2 values of 0.50 and 0.66 respectively but were not of the most important for the random forest classification. These indices produced R^2 values of 0.15 and 0.16 [23], 0.51 [32], 0.70 [22], 0.77 to 0.87 [21] and 0.88 [24]. These regressions were also represented in various forms including linear, logarithmic, and polynomial.

The logarithmic R^2 values found in this study (Table 7) are comparable to those found in Sharp et al., 2021 [26]. However, the indices which showed the best correlations for the lakes studied in New Hampshire were not similar to those used in these referenced studies. The NGRDI did not produce a significant linear relationship with chlorophyll-a in Kim et al., 2021, though it produced one of the highest R^2 values for chlorophyll-a concentrations of the most important features for classification in this study [24]. The difference might be attributed to one being a linear and the other a logarithmic line of best fit, or due to different wavelengths of light used in the equations per the sensor's capabilities although they are both designed to be NGRDI = (green − red)/(green + red). García-Fernández et al., 2021 used the NGBDI to assess the quality of grape plants for wine production using a UAS equipped RGB sensor [43]. Although not an aquatic study, the NGBDI was used to assess alterations to growth due to water stress. This index proved to be very important for determining the presence of cyanobacteria associated parameters likely because it uses data from the blue and green portions of the electromagnetic spectrum (Table 7).

The use of phycocyanin concentration for assessing cyanobacteria blooms is growing in momentum [27]. This study serves as an additional source for verifying the cyanobacteria cell concentration to phycocyanin concentration relationship in addition to Almuhtaram et al., 2018 and Bertone et al., 2018 [53,54]. Few papers have discussed connecting phycocyanin concentration to UAS spectral features [26,34,35]. Sharp et al., 2021 studied a single cyanobacteria bloom in California, USA, over the summer of 2019 [26]. Sharp and colleagues included four visits to the lake for measurements of chlorophyll-a and phycocyanin paired with the overpass of the Sentinel-3a satellite. One visit corresponded with a small UAS (sUAS) mission over 12 sites in one portion of the lake when the dominant taxa were *Dolichospermum*, *Gleotrichia*, and *Microcystis*, but a CI was not recreated due to the limited wavelengths of the UAS sensor used. The sUAS was only used to map chlorophyll-a concentrations throughout the study area using a band ratio relationship from a previously published paper designed for a different waterbody. Pyo et al., 2018 studied the relationship between phycocyanin and chlorophyll-a to hyperspectral imagery using modeled simulations [35]. They produced R^2 values between 0.55 and 0.75 for their two and three band ratios when plotted against estimated phycocyanin, and between 0.25 and 0.56 for chlorophyll-a. J. M. Ahn et al., 2021 also used a UAS mounted hyperspectral sensor to form a correlation with phycocyanin concentrations (R^2 = 0.85) using a "generic algorithm" [34].

Using a multivariate classification algorithm approach rather than only simple regressions allowed the overall success of this study to drastically increase. Although less commonly conducted compared to simple regressions, models for remotely sensed data to water quality data using machine learning algorithms produce high accuracies across the board in many recently published studies. Surface sediment classification using an object-based classification method from UAS multispectral data in tidal flats produced an overall classification accuracy of 72.8% [58]. Scientists mapping percent cover of emergent vegetation in freshwater waterbodies of California (USA) used the random forest classification algorithm to discern overall accuracies of 82% [59]. In addition, researchers studying two lakes in China classified general water quality into three classes based on designated uses. Using a convolutional neural network with four convolutional layers, overall accuracies reached 92.5% within their study [60].

The argument can be made from a public safety standpoint for recreational waters, that knowing if cyanobacteria is classified as above or below regulatory thresholds is the primary goal. Only then would distinguishing between cell concentrations be useful, i.e., 25,000 cells/mL and 45,000 cells/mL. In other words, due to the high accuracy a classification approach produces, stakeholders can know if the waterbody is safe for the designated use. With the random forest algorithm method, this study found very high overall and user's accuracies from 87.4 to 92.9% for the three water quality parameters with UAS multispectral spectral data.

4.4. Recommendations for Future Research

The integration of using UASs to study and monitor cyanobacteria and harmful algal blooms is an emerging discipline [61]. Because of its infancy, there is lots of room for expansion and refinement. This study would be strengthened with a larger dataset, and one across multiple years. With a larger dataset, including more UAS reflectance data of cyanobacteria blooms with additional reference (water quality) data validation, one can then subdivide the dataset by lake, trophic class, or dominant cyanobacteria species and re-run all algorithms to create lake or species-specific trends. With a larger dataset, the number of classes used for classification could be increased to further refine assessments. It would also be interesting to build a dataset from lakes without homogenous blooms similar to Tucker Pond or Silver Lake. Once the dataset is large enough, images from a flight over the lake could then be processed to identify the status of the lake at a classified pixel level. If repeated, this could aid in determining where blooms begin on an individual lake, and where they reside. This information could be used to complement data gathered for remediation efforts such as alum treatments, physical removal, or aeration. Lastly, these findings could be applied to lakes large enough for studies incorporating imagery from satellites—particularly the Sentinel 2 satellite. This approach would only improve as satellite technology increases in spatial resolution.

5. Conclusions

The use of a 10-band multispectral sensor flown on a UAS to detect cyanobacteria blooms in NH waterbodies was found to be a viable approach to monitor the rising water quality issue of cyanobacteria blooms. Identifying cyanobacteria blooms through imagery allows the user to assess the entire waterbody, including coves, littoral areas, and open water areas which might be inaccessible by land or boat. The use of imagery also promotes sampler safety through decreased time spent at each waterbody and the elimination of the need to contact the water for sampling. Additionally, this study identified significant correlations between cyanobacteria cell concentration to chlorophyll-a concentration, and cyanobacteria cell concentration to phycocyanin concentrations. These relationships identified the validity of using secondary parameters to measure cyanobacteria concentration. In conjunction with the water quality data, the NGBDI_4, NGRDI_4, 475 nm, 560 nm, and 668 nm were found to be the most important indices and bands for identifying the presence and classification of cyanobacteria, chlorophyll-a, and phycocyanin through the UAS classification approach. These important features illuminate the ability for this methodology to be applied to data collected by the Sentinel 2 satellite for larger freshwater waterbodies. Lastly, the UAS approach took significantly less time to complete than the traditional water quality sampling and analysis approach, therefore opening the possibility for these results to be applied in larger area, state, or region-wide studies.

Author Contributions: Conceptualization, C.L.B.; methodology, C.L.B., B.T.F., A.M. and R.G.C.; software, B.T.F. and C.L.B.; validation, B.T.F. and A.M.; formal analysis, C.L.B.; resources, C.L.B., R.G.C. and A.M.; data curation, C.L.B. and B.T.F.; writing—original draft preparation, C.L.B.; writing—review and editing, C.L.B. and R.G.C.; visualization, C.L.B.; supervision, R.G.C.; project administration, R.G.C.; funding acquisition, R.G.C. All authors have read and agreed to the published version of the manuscript.

Funding: Partial funding was provided by the New Hampshire Agricultural Experiment Station. This is Scientific Contribution Number 2975. This work was supported by the USDA National Institute of Food and Agriculture McIntire-Stennis Project 1026105.

Acknowledgments: Thank you to the NH Lay Lakes Monitoring Program and the UNH WQAL for lending laboratory supplies. Thank you to the NHDES for providing historical cyanobacteria bloom data for New Hampshire, and the citizens at each studied lake. The Fulcrum® corporation provided a one-year free trial of the data collection app for this study. Much appreciation goes to FB Environmental for their support and field equipment.

Conflicts of Interest: The authors declare no conflict of interest. The funders had no role in the design of the study; in the collection, analyses, or interpretation of data; in the writing of the manuscript; or in the decision to publish the results.

Appendix A

Cyanobacteria Fluorometric Detection of Whole Lake Water—New Hampshire Lay Lakes Monitoring Program

For cyanomonitoring protocol, freeze all samples before reading, thaw quickly in a water bath, and read within 20 min of reaching target temperature (21–24 °C). It works well to thaw samples in small batches of 8–12 depending on the efficiency of reading. Be careful not to over warm the samples. The goal is to bring them up to temp but not over. If you over-warm samples, place them in a cool water bath to bring them back down to between 21 and 24 °C.

General tips: always place the cuvette in the fluorometer in the same orientation and ensure that there are no air bubbles or drips on the side of the cuvette.

Materials List

Kim Wipes, Waste bucket, DI Water Bottle, Infrared thermometer, bucket for thawing samples. Cyanofluor: Meter, 4-sided glass cuvette, calibration standard cuvette. Fluoroquick (model number FQ-PC-PE-RATIO-C, serial number DL072501): Methacrylate Plastic cuvette, charging cable.

FluoroQuik SOP

General Note: The FlouroQuik should be blanked immediately prior to analyzing lake water samples and both low and high standards should be "read" before proceeding to lake water samples. The following SOP is applicable to both dual channel instruments: the chlorophyll/phycocyanin model and the phycocyanin/phycoeurethrin model. The flouroQuik requires plastic cuvettes and the instrument measures pigments as micrograms per liter (µg/L)

1. Rinse a cuvette three times with DI water.
2. Fill the rinsed cuvette with DI water and place the cuvette in the FlouroQuik chamber.
3. Press "measure".
4. Press "blank".
5. Press "measure" and record both pigment concentrations (e.g., chlorophyll and phycocyanin or phycocyanin and phycoeurythrin).
6. Press "return".
7. Rinse the cuvette with low pigment standard.
8. Fill the cuvette with low pigment standard.
9. Place the cuvette in the FlouroQuik chamber.
10. Press "measure".
11. Press "sample".
12. Record both pigment concentrations.
13. Press "return".
14. Rinse the cuvette three times with DI water.
15. Rinse the cuvette with high pigment standard.
16. Fill the cuvette with high pigment standard.
17. Place the cuvette in the FlouroQuik chamber.
18. Press "measure".
19. Press "sample".
20. Record both pigment concentrations.
21. Press "return".
22. Rinse the cuvette three times with DI water.
23. Rinse the cuvette with a lake water sample.
24. Fill the cuvette with the lake water sample.
25. Place the cuvette in the FlouroQuik chamber.
26. Press "measure".
27. Press "sample".
28. Record both pigment concentrations.
29. Repeat steps 20 through 27 until all lake water samples have been analyzed.
30. Analyze a low pigment concentration and a DI blank as the last two samples and record the pigment concentrations.

Appendix B

UNH Water Quality Analysis Laboratory Standard Operating Procedure
Chlorophyll-a—Hot Ethanol Extraction and Spectrophotometric Determination
Introduction

This extraction is applied to samples on filters. This method has the benefit of extraction without grinding and avoiding toxic methanol or acetone exposure [62]. Samples are analyzed with spectrophotometric analysis at 665 and 750 nm using a 1 cm spectrophotometer cuvette (method in Standard Methods (10200 H) with different extinction coefficient for ethanol and conversion for chlorophyll per unit area).

Sample Preparation

1. Filter a known volume of culture onto a Whatman GF/F filter (47 mm). Swirl your culture before sampling to ensure homogeneous sampling. Keep vacuum level low (<10 in Hg) to prevent cell breakage and low filtration efficiency.
2. Rinse funnel walls with small amount of DI.
3. Remove the funnel. Fold the filter in quarters and place in aluminum foil. Label foil and freeze samples until analysis.

Hot Ethanol Extraction (Day 1)

1. Turn on the water bath 30–60 min before starting. Set point to 79 °C. Make sure the water is above the right inner port.
2. Keep samples in dark or low light at all times. If the sample is kept in the dark, only 1.3% of the chlorophyll degrades with the 5 min. hot extraction and 24-h storage.
3. Use test tubes with screw tops that have the tube numbers scribed on the side with a diamond pencil (ethanol extracts numbers written in sharpie).
4. Place the filter (Whatman GFF, 47 mm) or scraped material in the tube. Add 10 mL (pipette) of 95% ethanol. Make sure the filter is totally submerged in the ethanol.
5. Mark the location of the meniscus on the side of the tube and place the cap on loosely.
6. Heat the tube in a water bath at 79 °C for 5 min, then mix and cool for 24 h in the dark (at room temperature and can be sealed tightly).
7. Turn off the hot water bath.
8. After extraction, use 95% ethanol to bring up to mark on side of tube if ethanol has evaporated, then mix.
9. Clear sample by centrifugation, filtration, or settling. We normally use settling.

Spec Analysis (Day 2)

1. Analyze sample with spectrophotometric analysis at 665 and 750 nm using 1 cm cuvette (Standard Methods). The 7G on spec cuvette faces you.
2. Run the blank.
    a. Measure blank (fill the cuvette with 3 mL of ethanol only) every time you change from 665 nm to 750 nm. Record absorbance. Click set blank.
3. Run a sample.
    a. Take the test tube with the filter in it. Tighten the cap and then invert it to mix.
    b. Pipette 3 mL of sample into the cuvette.
    c. Read the sample at 665.
        i. If adsorption is over 1.5 absorbance units, dilute sample. Try 1:10 dilution first into cuvette: 300 µL sample and 2.7 mL of ethanol. This was only needed for one sample which came from a benthic mat of cyanobacteria that had broken off and floated to the surface.
    d. Record value.
    e. Set nm type 750, enter.
    f. Measure blank again.
    g. Measure the sample again but at 750.
    h. Record the value.
4. Add 0.1 mL of 0.25 N HCl into 3 mL of sample in spec cuvette of extractant after the first reading and let sit for 3 min to phaeophytinize all chl before reading (amount of acid is very important). Measure at 665 and 750 nm again with a blank in between, record absorbance.
5. Rinse 3x with DI and repeat to Step 3.

Calculations

Calculations are made as follows:

$$\text{Chlorophyll-a } (\mu g/L) = ((28.78((665_0 - 750_0) - (665_a - 750_a))v)/(A/l))1000 \quad (A1)$$

where subscript $_0$ = absorption at the designated wavelength before acid addition and subscript $_a$ = absorption at the designated wavelength after acid addition. v = volume of extractant used (in liters, 0.01 for this study), A = volume of original sample that was filtered in mL, and l = path length of cell (1000 for this study).

Appendix C

Table A1. Index equation versions. Refer to Table 3 for citations and descriptions. * Indicates this parameter is found in the top feature important scores in Table 7.

Index and General Equation	Specific Equation	ID
CI	(650 − 560)/(668 − 560)	CI_1 *
	(668 − 650)/(705 − 650)	CI_2 *
NDVI = (NIR − R)/(NIR + R)	(842 − 650)/(842 + 650)	NDVI_1
	(842 − 650)/(842 + 668)	NDVI_2
	(842 − 668)/(842 + 650)	NDVI_3
	(842 − 668)/(842 + 668)	NDVI_4
cBNDVI = (NIR − cB)/(NIR + cB)	(842 − 444)/(842 + 444)	CBNDVI
BNDVI = (NIR − B)/(NIR + B)	(842 − 475)/(842 + 475)	BNDVI_1
	(842 − 444)/(842 + 475)	BNDVI_2
	(842 − 475)/(842 + 444)	BNDVI_3
NDRE = (NIR − RE)/(NIR + RE)	(842 − 705)/(842 + 705)	NDRE_1
	(842 − 717)/(842 + 717)	NDRE_2
	(842 − 740)/(842 + 740)	NDRE_3
NGBDI = (G − B)/(G + B)	(531 − 444)/(531 + 444)	NGBDI_1
	(531 − 475)/(531 + 475)	NGBDI_2
	(560 − 444)/(560 + 444)	NGBDI_3
	(560 − 475)/(560 + 475)	NGBDI_4 *
NGRDI = (G − R)/(G + R)	(531 − 650)/(531 + 650)	NGRDI_1
	(531 − 668)/(531 + 668)	NGRDI_2
	(560 − 650)/(560 + 650)	NGRDI_3 *
	(560 − 668)/(560 + 668)	NGRDI_4 *
SABI = (NIR − R)/(B + G)	(842 − 650)/(444 + 531)	SABI_1
	(842 − 650)/(444 + 560)	SABI_2
	(842 − 650)/(475 + 531)	SABI_3
	(842 − 650)/(475 + 560)	SABI_4
	(842 − 668)/(444 + 531)	SABI_5
	(842 − 668)/(444 + 560)	SABI_6
	(842 − 668)/(475 + 531)	SABI_7
	(842 − 668)/(475 + 560)	SABI_8

Table A1. Cont.

Index and General Equation	Specific Equation	ID
KIVU = (B − R)/G	(444 − 650)/531	KIVU_1
	(444 − 650)/560	KIVU_2
	(444 − 668)/531	KIVU_3
	(444 − 668)/560	KIVU_4
	(475 − 650)/531	KIVU_5
	(475 − 650)/560	KIVU_6
	(475 − 668)/531	KIVU_7
	(475 − 668)/560	KIVU_8
FLH Blue = G − (R + (B − R))	531 − (650 + (444 − 650))	FLHblue_1 *
	531 − (650 + (444 − 668))	FLHblue_2 *
	531 − (650 + (475 − 650))	FLHblue_3
	531 − (650 + (475 − 668))	FLHblue_4
	531 − (668 + (444 − 650))	FLHblue_5
	531 − (668 + (444 − 668))	FLHblue_6
	531 − (668 + (475 − 650))	FLHblue_7
	531 − (668 + (475 − 668))	FLHblue_8
	560 − (650 + (444 − 650))	FLHblue_9
	560 − (650 + (444 − 668))	FLHblue_10
	560 − (650 + (475 − 650))	FLHblue_11
	560 − (650 + (475 − 668))	FLHblue_12
	560 − (668 + (444 − 650))	FLHblue_13
	560 − (668 + (444 − 668))	FLHblue_14
	560 − (668 + (475 − 650))	FLHblue_15
	560 − (668 + (475 − 668))	FLHblue_16
MODIS normalized spectral index [46] from [23] = $(e^{Red} - e^{NIR})/(e^{Red} + e^{NIR})$	(650 − 842)/(650 + 842)	MODIS_NSI_1
	(650 − 842)/(668 + 842)	MODIS_NSI_2
	(668 − 842)/(650 + 842)	MODIS_NSI_3
	(668 − 842)/(668 + 842)	MODIS_NSI_4

Appendix D

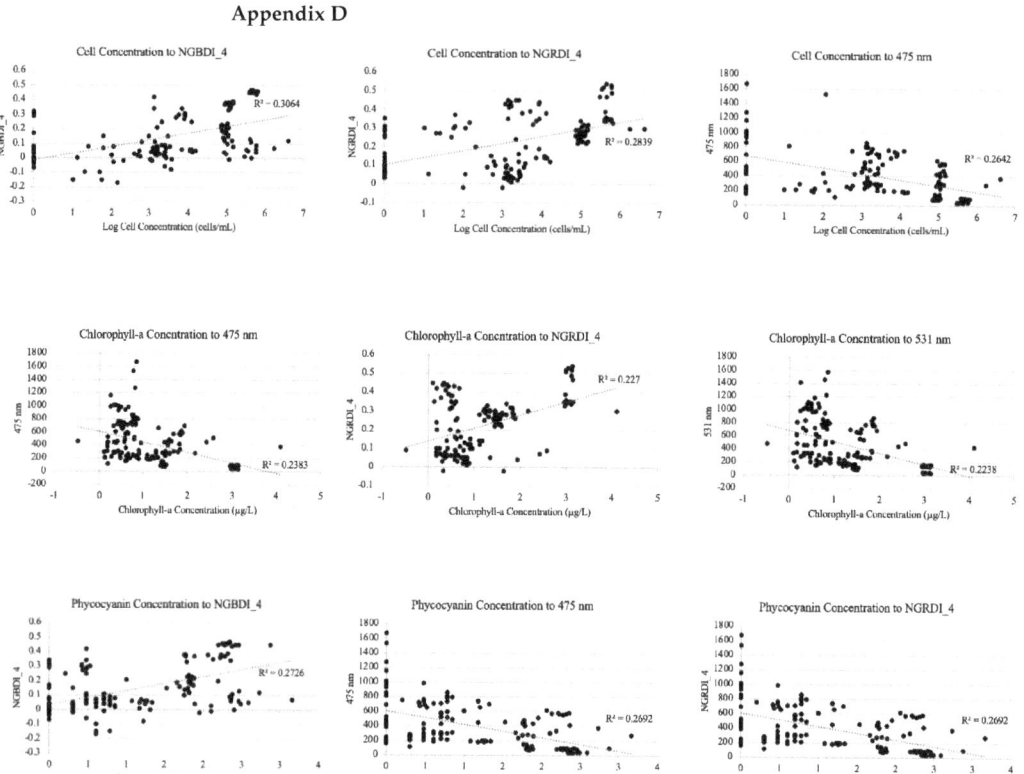

Figure A1. Scatter plots for the three highest R^2 values per water quality parameter from the simple regressions provided in Table 7.

References

1. USEPA. National Lakes Assessment: The Third Collaborative Survey of Lakes in the United States (EPA 841-R-22-002). U.S. Environmental Protection Agency, Office of Water and Office of Research Development 2022. Available online: https://nationallakesassessment.epa.gov/webreport (accessed on 18 March 2023).
2. Spyrakos, E.; O'Donnell, R.; Hunter, P.D.; Miller, C.; Scott, M.; Simis, S.G.H.; Neil, C.; Barbosa, C.C.F.; Binding, C.E.; Bradt, S.; et al. Optical types of inland and coastal waters. *Limnol. Oceanogr.* **2017**, *63*, 846–870. [CrossRef]
3. Cole, J.J.; Prairie, Y.T.; Caraco, N.F.; McDowell, W.H.; Tranvik, L.J.; Striegl, R.G.; Duarte, C.M.; Kortelainen, P.; Downing, J.A.; Middelburg, J.J.; et al. Plumbing the global carbon cycle: Integrating inland waters into the terrestrial carbon budget. *Ecosystems* **2007**, *10*, 172–185. [CrossRef]
4. Palinska, K.A.; Surosz, W. Taxonomy of cyanobacteria: A contribution to consensus approach. *Hydrobiologia* **2014**, *740*, 1–11. [CrossRef]
5. Carey, C.C.; Ewing, H.A.; Cottingham, K.L.; Weathers, K.C.; Thomas, R.Q.; Haney, J.F. Occurrence and toxicity of the cyanobacterium Gloeotrichia echinulata in low-nutrient lakes in the northeastern United States. *Aquat. Ecol.* **2012**, *46*, 395–409. [CrossRef]
6. Cole, J.J. The Carbon Cycle. In *Fundamentals of Ecosystem Science*; Elsevier: Amsterdam, The Netherlands, 2013; pp. 109–135. [CrossRef]
7. NHDES. *Cyanobacteria Advisory*; New Hampshire Department of Environmental Services: Concord, NH, USA, 2022.
8. Caller, T.A.; Doolin, J.W.; Haney, J.F.; Murby, A.J.; West, K.G.; Farrar, H.E.; Ball, A.; Harris, B.T.; Stommel, E.W. A cluster of amyotrophic lateral sclerosis in New Hampshire: A possible role for toxic cyanobacteria blooms. *Amyotroph. Lateral Scler.* **2009**, *10*, 101–108. [CrossRef]
9. Codd, G.A.; Testai, E.; Funari, E.; Svirčev, Z. Cyanobacteria, Cyanotoxins, and Human Health. In *Water Treatment for Purification from Cyanobacteria and Cyanotoxins*; Wiley Online Library: Hoboken, NJ, USA, 2020; Available online: https://onlinelibrary.wiley.com/doi/abs/10.1002/9781118928677.ch2 (accessed on 24 February 2023).
10. Rolim, S.B.A.; Veettil, B.K.; Vieiro, A.P.; Kessler, A.B.; Gonzatti, C. Remote sensing for mapping algal blooms in freshwater lakes: A review. *Environ. Sci. Pollut. Res.* **2023**, *30*, 19602–19616. [CrossRef]

11. Rhee, D.S.; Kim, Y.D.; Kang, B.; Kim, D. Applications of unmanned aerial vehicles in fluvial remote sensing: An overview of recent achievements. *KSCE J. Civ. Eng.* **2017**, *22*, 588–602. [CrossRef]
12. GISGeography. Spatial Resolution vs Spectral Resolution—GIS Geography. Available online: https://gisgeography.com/spatial-resolution-vs-spectral-resolution/ (accessed on 14 January 2023).
13. Becker, R.H.; Sayers, M.; Dehm, D.; Shuchman, R.; Quintero, K.; Bosse, K.; Sawtell, R. Unmanned aerial system based spectroradiometer for monitoring harmful algal blooms: A new paradigm in water quality monitoring. *J. Great Lakes Res.* **2019**, *45*, 444–453. [CrossRef]
14. Lyu, P.; Malang, Y.; Liu, H.H.; Lai, J.; Liu, J.; Jiang, B.; Qu, M.; Anderson, S.; Lefebvre, D.D.; Wang, Y. Autonomous cyanobacterial harmful algal blooms monitoring using multirotor UAS. *Int. J. Remote Sens.* **2017**, *38*, 2818–2843. [CrossRef]
15. Jensen, J.R. *Introductory Digital Image Processing: A Remote Sensing Perspective*, 4th ed.; Pearson Education Inc.: Saddle River, NJ, USA, 2018.
16. Lillesand, T.; Kiefer, R.W.; Chipman, J. *Remote Sensing and Image Interpretation*, 7th ed.; John Wiley & Sons: Hoboken, NJ, USA, 2015; Available online: https://www.wiley.com/en-us/Remote+Sensing+and+Image+Interpretation%2C+7th+Edition-p-9781118343289 (accessed on 3 December 2021).
17. Flynn, K.F.; Chapra, S.C. Remote Sensing of Submerged Aquatic Vegetation in a Shallow Non-Turbid River Using an Unmanned Aerial Vehicle. *Remote Sens.* **2014**, *6*, 12815–12836. [CrossRef]
18. Silva, T.S.F.; Costa, M.P.F.; Melack, J.M.; Novo, E.M.L.M. Remote sensing of aquatic vegetation: Theory and applications. *Environ. Monit. Assess.* **2007**, *140*, 131–145. [CrossRef] [PubMed]
19. Visser, F.; Wallis, C.; Sinnott, A.M. Optical remote sensing of submerged aquatic vegetation: Opportunities for shallow clearwater streams. *Limnologica* **2013**, *43*, 388–398. [CrossRef]
20. Su, T.-C.; Chou, H.-T. Application of Multispectral Sensors Carried on Unmanned Aerial Vehicle (UAV) to Trophic State Mapping of Small Reservoirs: A Case Study of Tain-Pu Reservoir in Kinmen, Taiwan. *Remote Sens.* **2015**, *7*, 10078–10097. [CrossRef]
21. Van der Merwe, D.; Price, K.P. Harmful Algal Bloom Characterization at Ultra-High Spatial and Temporal Resolution Using Small Unmanned Aircraft Systems. *Toxins* **2015**, *7*, 1065–1078. [CrossRef] [PubMed]
22. Choo, Y.; Kang, G.; Kim, D.; Lee, S. A study on the evaluation of water-bloom using image processing. *Environ. Sci. Pollut. Res.* **2018**, *25*, 36775–36780. [CrossRef]
23. Douglas Greene, S.B.; LeFevre, G.H.; Markfort, C.D. Improving the spatial and temporal monitoring of cyanotoxins in Iowa lakes using a multiscale and multi-modal monitoring approach. *Sci. Total. Environ.* **2020**, *760*, 143327. [CrossRef]
24. Kim, E.-J.; Nam, S.-H.; Koo, J.-W.; Hwang, T.-M. Hybrid Approach of Unmanned Aerial Vehicle and Unmanned Surface Vehicle for Assessment of Chlorophyll-a Imagery Using Spectral Indices in Stream, South Korea. *Water* **2021**, *13*, 1930. [CrossRef]
25. Mishra, S.; Stumpf, R.P.; Schaeffer, B.A.; Werdell, P.J.; Loftin, K.A.; Meredith, A. Measurement of Cyanobacterial Bloom Magnitude using Satellite Remote Sensing. *Sci. Rep.* **2019**, *9*, 1–17. [CrossRef]
26. Sharp, S.L.; Forrest, A.L.; Bouma-Gregson, K.; Jin, Y.; Cortés, A.; Schladow, S.G. Quantifying Scales of Spatial Variability of Cyanobacteria in a Large, Eutrophic Lake Using Multiplatform Remote Sensing Tools. *Front. Environ. Sci.* **2021**, *9*, 612934. [CrossRef]
27. Ogashawara, I. Determination of Phycocyanin from Space—A Bibliometric Analysis. *Remote Sens.* **2020**, *12*, 567. [CrossRef]
28. Ogashawara, I.; Mishra, D.R.; Mishra, S.; Curtarelli, M.P.; Stech, J.L. A Performance Review of Reflectance Based Algorithms for Predicting Phycocyanin Concentrations in Inland Waters. *Remote Sens.* **2013**, *5*, 4774–4798. [CrossRef]
29. Leland, N.J.; Haney, J.F. Alternative Methods for Analysis of Cyanobacterial Populations in Drinking Water Supplies: Fluorometric and Toxicological Applications Using Phycocyanin. *J. Water Resour. Prot.* **2018**, *10*, 740–761. [CrossRef]
30. Murby, A.L. *Assessing Spatial Distributions of Cyanobacteria and Microcystins in NH Lakes with Implications for Lake Monitoring*; University of New Hampshire: Durham, NH, USA, 2009.
31. Aguirre-Gómez, R.; Salmerón-García, O.; Gómez-Rodríguez, G.; Peralta-Higuera, A. Use of unmanned aerial vehicles and remote sensors in urban lakes studies in Mexico. *Int. J. Remote Sens.* **2016**, *38*, 2771–2779. [CrossRef]
32. Guimarães, T.T.; Veronez, M.R.; Koste, E.C.; Gonzaga, L.; Bordin, F.; Inocencio, L.C.; Larocca, A.P.C.; De Oliveira, M.Z.; Vitti, D.C.; Mauad, F.F. An Alternative Method of Spatial Autocorrelation for Chlorophyll Detection in Water Bodies Using Remote Sensing. *Sustainability* **2017**, *9*, 416. [CrossRef]
33. Qu, M.; Anderson, S.; Lyu, P.; Malang, Y.; Lai, J.; Liu, J.; Jiang, B.; Xie, F.; Liu, H.H.; Lefebvre, D.D.; et al. Effective aerial monitoring of cyanobacterial harmful algal blooms is dependent on understanding cellular migration. *Harmful Algae* **2019**, *87*, 101620. [CrossRef]
34. Ahn, J.M.; Kim, B.; Jong, J.; Nam, G.; Park, L.J.; Park, S.; Kang, T.; Lee, J.-K.; Kim, J. Predicting Cyanobacterial Blooms Using Hyperspectral Images in a Regulated River. *Sensors* **2021**, *21*, 530. [CrossRef]
35. Pyo, J.C.; Ligaray, M.; Kwon, Y.S.; Ahn, M.-H.; Kim, K.; Lee, H.; Kang, T.; Cho, S.B.; Park, Y.; Cho, K.H. High-Spatial Resolution Monitoring of *Phycocyanin* and *Chlorophyll-a* Using Airborne Hyperspectral Imagery. *Remote Sens.* **2018**, *10*, 1180. [CrossRef]
36. NHDES. Sources of Information and Explanation of Lake Trophic Data. New Hampshire Department of Environmental Services. 2019. Available online: https://www.des.nh.gov/sites/g/files/ehbemt341/files/documents/2020-01/laketrophic-explain-current.pdf (accessed on 24 February 2023).
37. NHFGD. (n.d.). Depth Maps of Selected NH Lakes and Ponds | Maps | New Hampshire Fish and Game Department. New Hampshire Fish and Game. Available online: https://www.wildlife.state.nh.us/maps/bathymetry.html (accessed on 24 February 2023).

38. Nelson, K.; Neils, D. New Hampshire Lake Trend Report: Status and Trends of Water Quality Indicators. NHDES. 2020. Available online: https://www4.des.state.nh.us/OneStopPub/TrophicSurveys/r-wd-20-08.pdf (accessed on 24 February 2023).
39. Nye, T.L. Microcystins in Water, Gastropods and Bivalves from Silver Lake, New Hampshire. Master's Thesis, University of New Hampshire, Durham, NH, USA, 1997.
40. Steiner, S.; Nelson, K. New Hampshire Volunteer Lake Assessment Program: 2014 Lakes Region Regional Report. NHDES. Available online: https://www.des.nh.gov/sites/g/files/ehbemt341/files/documents/2020-01/r-wd-16-08.pdf (accessed on 24 February 2023).
41. Mishra, S.; Mishra, D.R. Normalized difference chlorophyll index: A novel model for remote estimation of chlorophyll-a concentration in turbid productive waters. *Remote Sens. Environ.* **2012**, *117*, 394–406. [CrossRef]
42. Barnes, E.M.; Clarke, T.R.; Richards, S.E.; Colaizzi, P.D.; Haberland, J.; Kostrzewski, M.; Waller, P.; Choi, C.; Riley, E.; Thompson, T.; et al. Coincident Detection of Crop Water Stress, Nitrogen Status and Canopy Density Using Ground-Based Multispectral Data. 2000. Available online: https://www.researchgate.net/publication/43256762_Coincident_detection_of_crop_water_stress_nitrogen_status_and_canopy_density_using_ground_based_multispectral_data (accessed on 24 February 2023).
43. García-Fernández, M.; Sanz-Ablanedo, E.; Rodríguez-Pérez, J.R. High-Resolution Drone-Acquired RGB Imagery to Estimate Spatial Grape Quality Variability. *Agronomy* **2021**, *11*, 655. [CrossRef]
44. Alawadi, F. Detection of surface algal blooms using the newly developed algorithm surface algal bloom index (SABI). In Proceedings of the SPIE 7825, Remote Sensing of the Ocean, Sea Ice, and Large Water Regions, Toulouse, France, 20–23 September 2010. [CrossRef]
45. Kabbara, N.; Benkhelil, J.; Awad, M.; Barale, V. Monitoring water quality in the coastal area of Tripoli (Lebanon) using high-resolution satellite data. *ISPRS J. Photogramm. Remote Sens.* **2008**, *63*, 488–495. [CrossRef]
46. Shi, K.; Zhang, Y.; Xu, H.; Zhu, G.; Qin, B.; Huang, C.; Liu, X.; Zhou, Y.; Lv, H. Long-Term Satellite Observations of Microcystin Concentrations in Lake Taihu during Cyanobacterial Bloom Periods. *Environ. Sci. Technol.* **2015**, *49*, 6448–6456. [CrossRef] [PubMed]
47. USEPA. National Lakes Assessment: A Collaborative Survey of the Nation's Lakes (EPA 841-R-09-001). 2009. Available online: https://www.epa.gov/sites/default/files/2013-11/documents/nla_newlowres_fullrpt.pdf (accessed on 24 February 2023).
48. Congalton, R.G.; Green, K. *Assessing the Accuracy of Remotely Sensed Data Principles and Practices*, 3rd ed.; CRC Press: Boca Raton, FL, USA, 2019.
49. Story, M.; Congalton, R.G. Accuracy Assessment: A User's Perspective. *Photogramm. Eng. Remote Sens.* **1986**, *52*, 397–399.
50. Fraser, B.T.; Congalton, R.G. Monitoring Fine-Scale Forest Health Using Unmanned Aerial Systems (UAS) Multispectral Models. *Remote Sens.* **2021**, *13*, 4873. [CrossRef]
51. U.S. Geological Survey. (n.d.). What Are the Band Designations for the Landsat Satellites? Available online: https://www.usgs.gov/faqs/what-are-band-designations-landsat-satellites (accessed on 1 April 2023).
52. The European Space Agency. (n.d.). Spatial Resolution. Sentinel Online. Available online: https://sentinels.copernicus.eu/web/sentinel/user-guides/sentinel-2-msi/resolutions/spatial (accessed on 1 April 2023).
53. Almuhtaram, H.; Cui, Y.; Zamyadi, A.; Hofmann, R. Cyanotoxins and Cyanobacteria Cell Accumulations in Drinking Water Treatment Plants with a Low Risk of Bloom Formation at the Source. *Toxins* **2018**, *10*, 430. [CrossRef]
54. Bertone, E.; Burford, M.A.; Hamilton, D.P. Fluorescence probes for real-time remote cyanobacteria monitoring: A review of challenges and opportunities. *Water Res.* **2018**, *141*, 152–162. [CrossRef] [PubMed]
55. Guimarães, T.T.; Veronez, M.R.; Koste, E.C.; Souza, E.M.; Brum, D.; Gonzaga, L.; Mauad, F.F. Evaluation of Regression Analysis and Neural Networks to Predict Total Suspended Solids in Water Bodies from Unmanned Aerial Vehicle Images. *Sustainability* **2019**, *11*, 2580. [CrossRef]
56. Veronez, M.R.; Kupssinskü, L.S.; Guimarães, T.T.; Koste, E.C.; Da Silva, J.M.; De Souza, L.V.; Oliverio, W.F.M.; Jardim, R.S.; Koch, I.; De Souza, J.G.; et al. Proposal of a Method to Determine the Correlation between Total Suspended Solids and Dissolved Organic Matter in Water Bodies from Spectral Imaging and Artificial Neural Networks. *Sensors* **2018**, *18*, 159. [CrossRef]
57. Wu, D.; Li, R.; Zhang, F.; Liu, J. A review on drone-based harmful algae blooms monitoring. *Environ. Monit. Assess.* **2019**, *191*, 211. [CrossRef]
58. Kim, K.-L.; Kim, B.-J.; Lee, Y.-K.; Ryu, J.-H. Generation of a Large-Scale Surface Sediment Classification Map Using Unmanned Aerial Vehicle (UAV) Data: A Case Study at the Hwang-do Tidal Flat, Korea. *Remote Sens.* **2019**, *11*, 229. [CrossRef]
59. Kislik, C.; Genzoli, L.; Lyons, A.; Kelly, M. Application of UAV Imagery to Detect and Quantify Submerged Filamentous Algae and Rooted Macrophytes in a Non-Wadeable River. *Remote Sens.* **2020**, *12*, 3332. [CrossRef]
60. Pu, F.; Ding, C.; Chao, Z.; Yu, Y.; Xu, X. Water-Quality Classification of Inland Lakes Using Landsat8 Images by Convolutional Neural Networks. *Remote Sens.* **2019**, *11*, 1674. [CrossRef]
61. Fraser, B.T.; Bunyon, C.L.; Reny, S.; Lopez, I.S.; Congalton, R.G. Analysis of Unmanned Aerial System (UAS) Sensor Data for Natural Resource Applications: A Review. *Geographies* **2022**, *2*, 303–340. [CrossRef]
62. Sartory, D.P.; Grobbelaar, J.U. Extraction of chlorophyll a from freshwater phytoplankton for spectrophotometric analysis. *Hydrobiologia* **1984**, *114*, 177–187. [CrossRef]

Disclaimer/Publisher's Note: The statements, opinions and data contained in all publications are solely those of the individual author(s) and contributor(s) and not of MDPI and/or the editor(s). MDPI and/or the editor(s) disclaim responsibility for any injury to people or property resulting from any ideas, methods, instructions or products referred to in the content.

Article

Mapping Underwater Aquatic Vegetation Using Foundation Models With Air- and Space-Borne Images: The Case of Polyphytos Lake

Leonidas Alagialoglou [1,2], Ioannis Manakos [1,*], Sofia Papadopoulou [1], Rizos-Theodoros Chadoulis [1] and Afroditi Kita [1,2]

1 Information Technologies Institute, Centre for Research and Technology Hellas (CERTH), 57001 Thessaloniki, Greece; lalagial@mug.ee.auth.gr (L.A.)
2 Multimedia Understanding Group, Electrical and Computer Engineering Department, Aristotle University of Thessaloniki, 54124 Thessaloniki, Greece
* Correspondence: imanakos@iti.gr

Abstract: Mapping underwater aquatic vegetation (UVeg) is crucial for understanding the dynamics of freshwater ecosystems. The advancement of artificial intelligence (AI) techniques has shown great potential in improving the accuracy and efficiency of UVeg mapping using remote sensing data. This paper presents a comparative study of the performance of classical and modern AI tools, including logistic regression, random forest, and a visual-prompt-tuned foundational model, the Segment Anything model (SAM), for mapping UVeg by analyzing air- and space-borne images in the few-shot learning regime, i.e., using limited annotations. The findings demonstrate the effectiveness of the SAM foundation model in air-borne imagery (GSD = 3–6 cm) with an F1 score of 86.5% ± 4.1% when trained with as few as 40 positive/negative pairs of pixels, compared to 54.0% ± 9.2% using the random forest model and 42.8% ± 6.2% using logistic regression models. However, adapting SAM to space-borne images (WorldView-2 and Sentinel-2) remains challenging, and could not outperform classical pixel-wise random forest and logistic regression methods in our task. The findings presented provide valuable insights into the strengths and limitations of AI models for UVeg mapping, aiding researchers and practitioners in selecting the most suitable tools for their specific applications.

Keywords: few-shot learning; underwater aquatic vegetation; submerged vegetation; foundation model; machine learning; Sentinel-2; VHR; WorldView-2; UAV; Segment Anything model

1. Introduction

Aquatic vegetation holds immense significance within ecosystems, as it not only supports the food chain but also serves as the primary indicator of ecosystem quality [1]. Detailed information on the distribution, composition, and abundance of aquatic vegetation is widely utilized to assess the environmental quality of aquatic systems, thereby playing a crucial role in maintaining the proper functioning of lakes. In particular, submerged, or in general, underwater aquatic vegetation (UVeg), comprising plants that primarily grow underwater but may possess floating or emerged reproductive organs, plays a vital ecological and environmental role. These plants fulfill crucial functions, including providing habitat for various species, stabilizing sediments, regulating water flow, acting as a natural purifier, and participating in the biogeochemical cycling process [2].

Precise identification of UVeg distribution and growth duration can provide valuable information for effective lake management and future ecological restoration endeavors. As a result, numerous national and international water quality frameworks, including those employed by the European Union, integrate the assessment of submerged aquatic vegetation extent or health as key indicators in their evaluations. Remote sensing technology, particularly satellite data, has emerged as an effective tool for mapping UVeg.

In particular, multi-spectral data have been extensively employed for mapping the distribution of large-scale aquatic vegetation and evaluating its intra-annual and inter-annual variations [3–6].

However, accurately distinguishing between submerged aquatic vegetation and emergent or floating vegetation remains a complex task through satellite data. The transitional nature of aquatic vegetation, influenced by factors such as incomplete development, seasonality, water level fluctuations, and flooding events, poses significant challenges for accurate classification using remote sensing techniques. In light of these complexities, our research aims to overcome these limitations by focusing on monitoring all forms of vegetation occurring beneath the water surface. While our previous work [7] focused solely on identifying emergent and floating aquatic vegetation, our attention in this study lies on underwater aquatic vegetation, which encompasses all forms of vegetation occurring in submerged or partially submerged conditions.

To provide a comprehensive overview of the existing techniques, Rowan and Kalacska [2] conducted a review specifically tailored for non-specialists. Their paper discusses the challenges associated with UVeg mapping using remote sensing, such as water attenuation, spectral complexity, and spatial heterogeneity. Furthermore, they provide an overview of different remote sensing platforms, including aerial and space-borne sensors, commonly used for UVeg mapping and argue that understanding the capabilities and limitations of these platforms is crucial in selecting the appropriate tools for UVeg mapping. The authors also discuss the specific spectral characteristics of UVeg, as well as classification methods, and finally, they highlight the importance of validation and accuracy assessment in UVeg mapping studies. By incorporating insights from this review, our study aims to contribute to the existing knowledge and further enhance the accuracy and efficiency of UVeg mapping using remote sensing data.

The study of Villa et al. [8] introduces a rule-based approach for mapping macrophyte communities using multi-temporal aquatic vegetation indices. Their study emphasizes the importance of considering temporal variations in vegetation indices and proposes a classification scheme based on rules derived from these indices. The approach shows promising results in accurately mapping macrophyte communities, providing valuable insights for ecological assessments and environmental monitoring. The paper by Husson et al. [9] highlights the use of unmanned aircraft vehicles (UAVs) for mapping aquatic vegetation. They discuss the advantages of UAVs, such as high spatial resolution and cost-effectiveness. Their study demonstrates the accuracy of UAV-based vegetation mapping, including species distribution and habitat heterogeneity. UAV imagery provides detailed information for ecological research and conservation efforts. The paper also addresses challenges and suggests future directions for optimizing UAV-based methods in aquatic vegetation mapping. Heege et al. [10] presented the Modular Inversion Program (MIP), a processing tool that utilizes remote sensing data to map submerged vegetation in optically shallow waters. MIP incorporates modules for calculating the bottom reflectance and fractionating it into specific reflectance spectra, enabling mapping of different types of vegetation.

Machine learning (ML) approaches in remote sensing offer efficient and accurate methods for analyzing vast amounts of satellite data and extracting valuable insights about the Earth's surface and environment. However, previous studies on classifying wetland vegetation have often focused on single sites and lacked rigorous testing of the generalization capabilities. To fill this gap, Piaser et al. [11] compiled an extensive reference dataset of about 400,000 samples covering nine different sites and multiple seasons to represent temperate wetland vegetation communities at a continental scale. They compared the performance of eight ML classifiers, including support vector machine (SVM), random forest (RF), and XGBoost, using multi-temporal Sentinel-2 data as input features. According to their findings, the top choices for mapping macrophyte community types in temperate areas, as explored in this study, are SVM, RF, and XGBoost. Reducing the number of input features led to accuracy degradation, emphasizing the effectiveness of multi-temporal spectral indices for aquatic vegetation mapping.

The debate between classical ML techniques and deep learning (DL) revolves around computational resources and the available annotated datasets. Classical ML can achieve high discriminative performance with moderate processing speed, making it suitable for scenarios with limited computational resources [12]. In contrast, DL's undeniable success in computer vision tasks, particularly in remote sensing imagery [13,14], comes at the expense of requiring substantial computational resources. Additionally, DL models are data-hungry during training, posing challenges for the few-shot learning tasks commonly encountered in remote sensing applications. Despite this, techniques like pre-training on other datasets, data augmentation, and, most importantly, self-supervised learning (SSL) exist to mitigate this issue.

Based on SSL, foundation models came recently to the forefront of machine learning research, offering a unified, versatile approach that learns across various tasks and domains. As illustrated by Bommasani et al. [15], a key advantage of foundation models lies in their ability to perform with limited annotations, utilizing pre-existing knowledge to make sense of sparse or partially labeled data. The Segment Anything model (SAM) [16] epitomizes this advantage with its ability to effectively segment any class in an image, making it especially suitable for the analysis of complex and often poorly annotated environments.

In this study, we harness the capabilities of SAM in mapping and analyzing the underwater aquatic vegetation in Polyphytos Lake, Greece. Our approach combines a range of remote sensing data, including multi-spectral satellite images from WorldView-2 and Sentinel-2, UAV-acquired data, and expert annotations from marine biologists, in collaboration with local water service authorities.

Given the often-scarce annotations in aquatic ecosystem studies, the application of foundation models, such as SAM, offers a powerful tool to gain insights into aquatic vegetation, water quality, and potential pollution sources. The subsequent sections of this paper will detail our methodology, challenges, results, and their implications, demonstrating the significant potential of foundation models in data-scarce, complex environments like aquatic ecosystems.

2. Materials and Methods

2.1. Study Area

Our study took place at the Polyphytos reservoir, as shown in Figure 1 an artificial lake on the Aliakmon River, located in West Macedonia, Northern Greece, specifically in Kozani province. The reservoir's surface area is 75 km^2. The reservoir was formed in 1975 when a dam was built on the Aliakmon River close to the Polyphytos village. The longest dimension of the lake is 31 km and the widest is 2.5 km. It is the biggest of five reservoirs built along the river, with a drainage area of 5630 square kilometers, and it collects water from surface runoff and several torrents.

The reservoir is used to produce hydroelectric power and supply irrigation water, and since 2003, it has been the main source of drinking water for Thessaloniki, the second-largest city in Greece, with a population of 1.05 million people. Every day, around 145,000 cubic meters of surface water is taken from the Polyphytos Reservoir to Thessaloniki's Drinking Water Treatment Plant (TDWTP).

The Polyphytos region has a continental climate with cold winters and mild summers. The region's rainfall is not very high, but previous studies [17] have shown that rainfall does not drop much during summer. However, the months from June to September are seen as dry because of the relatively low average rainfall.

Over the years, Polyphytos Lake has transformed into a significant sanctuary for birds and a thriving environment for many fish species. Regarding vegetation, the vicinity of the reservoir boasts a considerable expanse of wetlands, marshlands, and muddy ecosystems. Additionally, a range of aquatic plant life resides within the Polyphytos Reservoir, e.g., as show in Figure 2, contributing to the area's rich ecological diversity.

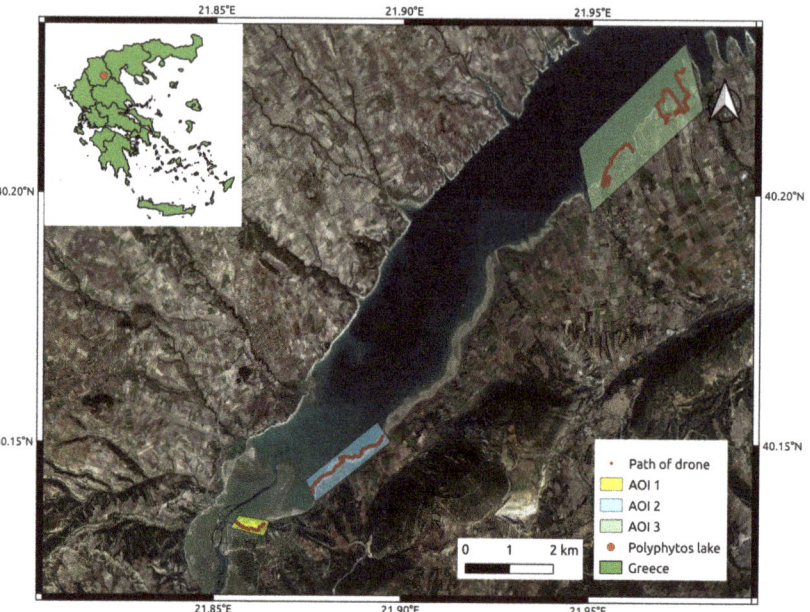

Figure 1. Three regions of interest within the Polyphytos Lake study area in Greece.

Figure 2. Aquatic vegetation (submerged and emergent vegetation) near the Kozani nautical club (field trip on 17 June 2022).

2.2. Data Sources

We obtained multi-spectral satellite images from two sources: WorldView-2 and Sentinel-2. The WorldView-2 images provided high-resolution data with a ground sampling distance (GSD) of 1.8 m, enabling detailed observation of the lake and its surrounding areas. The Sentinel-2 images complemented the WorldView-2 data by offering additional spectral information for our analysis, although with the lowest GSD of 10 m. In order to acquire more granular and comprehensive data, we executed a UAV survey over Polyphytos Lake. We deployed the DJI Mini 3 Pro UAV, maintaining a flight altitude between 50 and 70 m. The UAV came equipped with a high-resolution camera, enabling us to gather detailed and current data on the lake's attributes. A description of the data sources used in the study is given in Table 1.

Table 1. Summary of data sources, specifications, and sensing dates.

Data Source	Area	GSD	Dates
WorldView-2	AOI 1	1.8 m	31 August 2020
Sentinel-2	AOI 1	10–60 m	16, 21, 26 and 31 August 2020 5, 10 and 15 September 2020
DJI Mini 3 Pro UAV	AOI 1–3	3–6 cm	6 March 2023

2.3. Dataset Annotation

Through information exchange with local water service authorities and in situ visits by the authors, detailed annotations could be retrieved, specifically focusing on the UVeg present in Polyphytos Lake. The meticulous identification and labeling of underwater vegetation formations at various scales and depths using multiple uncertainty classes ensure the accuracy and reliability of these annotations. The availability of such comprehensive annotations allows us to assess the performance and effectiveness of our AI tools in accurately mapping and monitoring UVeg in Polyphytos Lake, providing valuable insights into the distribution, health, and ecological significance of underwater vegetation in the lake.

Manual annotation was performed separately for the WorldView-2 and UAV imagery, while the annotations of the Sentinel-2 data were extracted based on the WorldView-2 annotations. Due to the proximity of dates, we assume no modification in vegetation extent (UVeg extent). Therefore, only adaptation of the spatial resolution was performed by transforming the binary values of the pixels in the lower ground sampling distance (GSD) of WorldView-2 to percentage values of the higher-GSD pixels of Sentinel-2m, as shown in Figure 3.

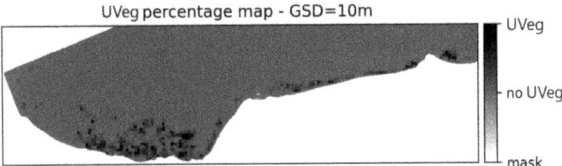

Figure 3. Adapted UVeg annotation matching Sentinel-2 GSD of 10 m. Each pixel represents the percentage of UVeg based on the binary values of WV-2 GSD of 1.8 m.

2.4. Comparison of ML Techniques

In this work, we compare two different AI methodologies for segmenting UVeg in Polyphytos Lake:

- Pixel-based Logistic Regression or Random Forest:

The first approach utilizes classical machine learning techniques such as logistic regression and random forest. In this method, we extract various spectral and textural features from the multi-spectral satellite images and UAV data. These features are then used to train pixel-based classification models, which can classify each pixel as either UVeg or non-UVeg. Logistic regression and random forest algorithms are employed for the classification task, leveraging their ability to learn complex relationships between the input features and the UVeg class labels. We recognize random forest, which is a bagging model, together with boosting models as powerful and widely-used ML techniques based on ensembling [11,12]. Additionally, we included logistic regression as a baseline ML method, as it represents traditional thresholding techniques commonly found in remote sensing studies when combining linear combinations of bands.

Apart from the multi-spectral bands, we utilized the QAA-RGB algorithm [18], a modified version of the quasi-analytical algorithm (QAA), to detect underwater vegetation in Polyphytos Lake using only the red, green, and blue bands. The algorithm was specifically designed for high-resolution satellite sensors, and it retrieves various parameters, including the total absorption, particle backscattering, diffuse attenuation coefficient, and Secchi disk depth, which have been used as additional features in our comparative analysis. By using remote sensing reflectance data from three specific bands (red, green, and blue), the algorithm ensures robustness and applicability across different water types. The implementation of QAA-RGB was carried out within the ACOLITE processor, which provides a comprehensive and accessible platform for the scientific community.

- Foundation Model for Semantic Segmentation with Prompt-tuning:

The second approach utilizes a foundation model called SAM (Segment Anything) [16]. SAM is a state-of-the-art deep learning model designed specifically for semantic segmentation tasks. It is pretrained on a large-scale dataset, enabling it to learn general patterns and features related to segmentation. However, what sets SAM apart is its prompt-tuning approach. During fine-tuning, SAM is provided with a small set of positive and negative UVeg pixels as prompts. These prompts guide the model to learn the specific characteristics and boundaries of UVeg in Polyphytos Lake. By adaptively adjusting the prompts, SAM refines its segmentation capabilities and improves its accuracy in detecting and delineating UVeg regions.

In our model evaluation, we employed three key metrics computed from the number of pixels as true positive (TP), true negative (TN), false positive (FP), and false negative (FN):

PA, the producer's accuracy (recall), quantifies the percentage of correctly classified pixels in relation to the ground truth, thus representing the model's ability to accurately identify and classify true positive instances:

$$PA = \frac{TP}{TP + FN}$$

UA, the user's accuracy (precision), measures the percentage of correctly classified pixels based on the model's predictions, reflecting the precision of the model in accurately identifying and classifying true positive instances:

$$UA = \frac{TP}{TP + FP}$$

Additionally, we computed the $F1$ score, a commonly used metric for evaluating such models. The $F1$ score can be interpreted as a weighted average of the precision (UA) and recall (PA), where an $F1$ score reaches its best value at 1 (perfect precision and recall) and worst at 0. It is defined as:

$$F1 = 2 * \frac{UA * PA}{UA + PA}$$

The $F1$ score tries to balance these two measures. A good $F1$ score indicates low false positives and low false negatives, which are especially important when false positives and false negatives have different costs, often the case in imbalanced datasets.

We established baselines for all three modalities—UAV RGB images, multi-spectral images from WorldView-2, and Sentinel-2 sensors—using logistic regression. To mitigate the effects of the imbalanced dataset in all three modalities, we employed resampling methods during the training phase. These involve artificially augmenting the dataset by repeating uniformly selected samples to ensure an equal representation of samples from different classes. This approach not only enhances the performance of logistic regression, but also provides an unbiased analysis for feature importance [19].

We further conducted a comparative analysis of three data sources using k-fold cross-validation. To account for the significant differences in dataset size among the modalities, we utilized different numbers of folds for each modality. This approach ensured that the training sets were sufficiently large for modalities with a smaller total number of pixels. To evaluate the performance of our models, we computed metrics based on the concatenated confusion matrices obtained from each fold. Instead of calculating the average values of metrics separately for each fold, this approach provides a more robust assessment. Specifically, for the Sentinel-2 modality, where the number of available pixels from the positive class is limited, averaging the metrics across folds can introduce bias into the estimate [20]. For the SAM method, resampling with replacement of a fixed number of pixel pairs was performed with 500 repetitions.

In addition, we carried out ablation studies on single-, double-, and triple-feature classifiers. The objective was to investigate the influence of feature selection on the predictive accuracy of our per-pixel classification model. By systematically excluding features from the model, we were able to quantify the contribution of each individual feature or combination of features. The evaluation of these ablation studies was based on the $F1$ metric. Through this ablation study, we obtained valuable insights into how different bands, or their combinations, affect the accuracy of the model in classifying UVeg pixels. This, consequently, directed our optimization of the band-selection process to apply the SAM, a foundation model that utilizes only three bands. A more sophisticated feature-importance analysis of WorldView-2 data was performed, focusing on pixel proximity to the shore. Specifically, apart from the analysis in the total WorldView-2 image, the analysis was also conducted on a manually selected subset of the image near the shore with a higher density of visually apparent UVeg regions, referred to as "shallow pixels". The areas of the lake farther from the shore did not exhibit visually apparent UVeg, likely due to the lake's depth.

Moreover, we conducted an extensive analysis of the two SAM variants, "huge" and "base", utilizing the ViT-B and ViT-H encoders developed by Meta AI Research and FAIR (https://github.com/facebookresearch/segment-anything, accessed on 10 July 2023). SAM has two encoder options: ViT-B (91M parameters) and ViT-H (636M parameters). The primary objective of this analysis is to gain insights into the performance disparities between the two variants under the few-shot learning task of segmenting UVeg.

In the context of the Sentinel-2 data source, we investigated the use of multi-class classification by comparing the performance of models with 2–4 classes instead of using a regression-based approach. Here, the number of classes refers to distinct categories or groups into which the satellite data can be classified. In a 2-class model, the data would be divided into two distinct categories, which might correspond to the "presence" or "absence" of a certain feature in the satellite imagery, for example. For the 3-class model, the data would be divided into three categories, possibly representing low, medium, and high levels of a certain feature. In the 4-class model, there would be four different categories, potentially providing an even finer granularity of the measured feature. Since the task was not binary classification but multi-class, we used the metric of balanced accuracy to evaluate the performance. Balanced accuracy is the average of the recall (the proportion of actual positives that are correctly identified) obtained for each class, which ensures that every class is equally weighted regardless of how often it appears in the data. This was particularly relevant because of the multi-class nature of our models. By comparing the 2-, 3-, and 4-class models, we were able to rigorously evaluate how different levels of class granularity impacted the accuracy of our Sentinel-2 data classifications.

Finally, to assess the transferability of the models in different areas of interest (AOIs) within the lake, a logistic regression model and a random forest model were trained on AOI1 near the Rymnio bridge and evaluated on AOI2 and AOI3 (described in Table 1).

The random forest model underwent hyperparameter tuning using a validation set from AOI1, while testing was conducted separately on the different lake AOIs [21].

3. Results

The primary findings from the comparative study on segmenting underwater aquatic vegetation data based on very limited annotations are illustrated in Figures 4–6. This study provides an exhaustive comparison of three machine learning techniques, namely a logistic regression model, a random forest model, and a foundational model referred to as the Segment Anything Model (SAM). The SAM model, which is based on the Vision Transformer architecture, is pretrained for the task of semantic segmentation and is specifically tailored for visual prompting. The comparative analysis is carried out across three distinct data sources: UAV, WorldView-2, and Sentinel-2. Baseline measures for each metric, represented as red dashed lines, are computed based on the training error of the logistic regression model.

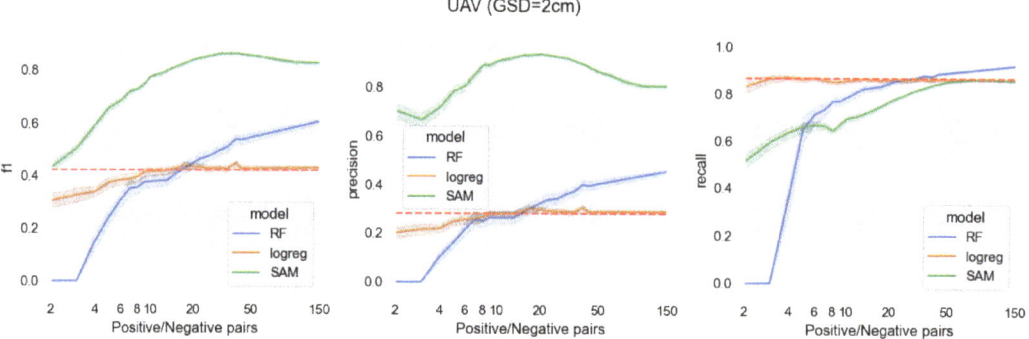

Figure 4. Comparison of machine learning techniques for segmenting underwater aquatic vegetation using UAV data with limited annotation. The SAM model yields an $F1$ score of 86.5% ± 4.1% when trained with as few as 40 positive/negative pairs of pixels, compared to 54.0% ± 9.2% using the random forest model and 42.8% ± 6.2% using logistic regression models.

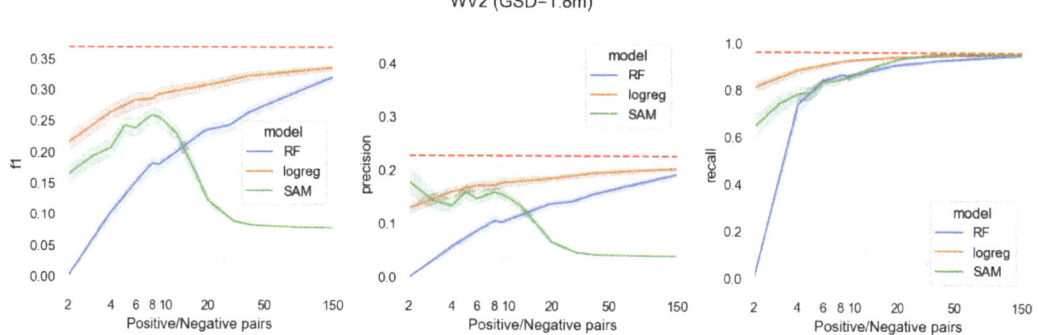

Figure 5. Comparison of machine learning techniques for segmenting underwater aquatic vegetation using WorldView-2 data with limited annotation.

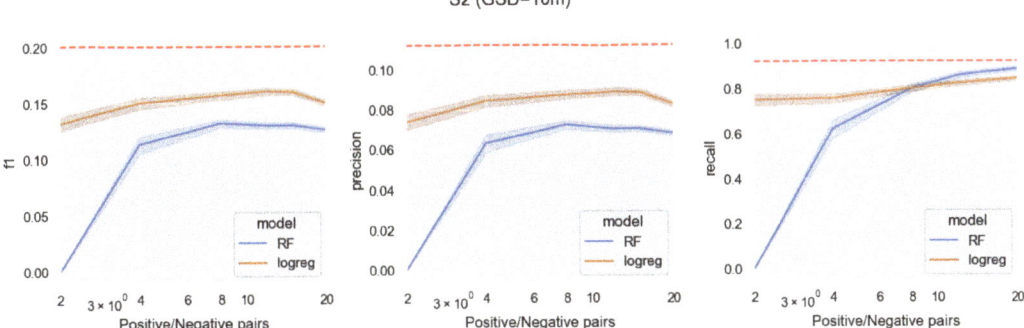

Figure 6. Comparison of machine learning techniques for segmenting underwater aquatic vegetation using Sentinel-2 data with limited annotation.

Figure 4 showcases a comparison of these methods over an area of 0.07 km^2, captured on a UAV mission. The GSD in this area varies from 3 to 6 cm, contingent on the drone's flight altitude.

Figure 5 depicts the comparison of the three machine learning techniques over a total area of approximately 1.4 km^2, captured using the WorldView-2 satellite. The pixel size in this area is 1.8 m. The data incorporate eight multi-spectral bands, one panchromatic band, and a synthetic band that estimates the Secchi disk depth based on the QAA-RGB algorithm.

Figure 6 demonstrates the comparison of the two machine learning techniques over an area of 1.4 km^2, as captured with the Sentinel-2 satellite. The pixel size in this region varies between 10 m and 60 m. The data utilized for this comparison include all bands from the Level-2A (L2A) products.

All evaluations are based on a bootstrap simulation, which involves the random sampling of positive/negative pairs with replacement. This simulation is conducted 500 times, providing a robust statistical analysis of the performance differences among the machine learning models.

Examples of the UVeg masks generated with the foundational model, SAM, can be seen in Figures 7 and 8. Figure 7 showcases masks created from a UAV mission scene, while Figure 8 presents masks derived from a WorldView-2 satellite scene.

The inter-modality comparison results are given in Table 2. For each method and modality, the performance from a sufficiently large training dataset size is demonstrated to facilitate the assessment of UVeg segmentation using the different data sources. Notably, the performance results for the Sentinel-2 data source using the foundational model SAM are not calculated due to its significantly poor performance, rendering any results meaningless or trivial.

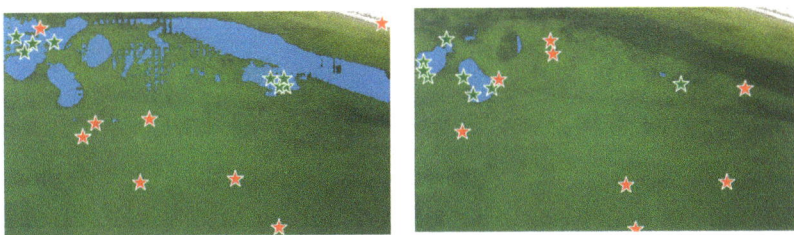

Figure 7. UVeg masks estimated with SAM with point-prompting in UAV data (RGB). In both examples 8 positive/negative prompt-point pairs are given. The estimated mask is shown with opacity on top of the RGB bands. Positive training points are shown in green and negative training points in red.

Figure 8. UVeg masks estimated with SAM with point-prompting in WV2 data (bands Green–RedEdge–NearInfrared1). On the **left**, a better UVeg mask is estimated based on 8 positive/negative pairs of points. On the **right**, there is an example of the artifacts using more (20) prompt-point pairs. The computed mask is shown with opacity on top of the selected WV2 bands. Positive training points are shown in green and negative training points in red.

Table 2. Comparison results of the different ML methods for the three data sources based on sufficiently large training datasets (different for each data source). Methods with highest $F1$ score are in bold.

Modality	ML Method	Size of Training Set	Dataset Size	$F1$	UA	PA
UAV	Log Regr	10-fold CV	~8M px	0.350	0.219	0.861
	RF	10-fold CV	~8M px	0.576	0.415	0.941
	SAM	20 px pairs	~8M px	**0.842** *	**0.957**	0.751
World View 2	Log Regr	20-fold CV	~400k px	0.340	0.207	0.956
	RF	20-fold CV	~400k px	**0.472**	**0.328**	**0.845**
	SAM	8 px pairs	~400k px	0.264	0.157	0.834
Sentinel-2	Log Regr	40-fold CV	~14k px	0.184	0.103	0.890
	RF	40-fold CV	~14k px	**0.331**	**0.231**	0.581

* The highest $F1$ score of 86.5% ± 4.0%, with corresponding UA of 89.6% ± 5.8% and PA of 83.9% ± 4.8%, is achieved for UAV images using 40 positive/negative pairs of pixels for prompting the SAM model.

Table 2 provides the comparative analysis of the three data sources using k-fold cross-validation. The table showcases the performance metrics obtained from the concatenated confusion matrices, which offer a robust evaluation of the models. Notably, different numbers of folds were utilized for each modality to address the variation in dataset sizes. The SAM method is assessed by resampling a fixed number of pixel pairs with replacement, and this process is repeated 500 times.

3.1. Feature-Importance Analysis

We further conducted a feature-importance analysis through an ablation study. By systematically removing specific bands and observing the resulting impact on model performance, we determined the significance of individual features in the context of single-feature, two-feature, and three-feature classifiers.

Figures 9–11 present the outcomes of the feature importance analysis conducted on the three distinct data sources. The analysis evaluates the performance of single-feature, two-feature, and three-feature classifiers. The horizontal axis represents the feature importance score ($F1$ score), while the vertical axis displays the various features and representative feature combinations considered. These figures offer valuable insights into the diverse significance of features and their influence on model performance across different classifier configurations. The red dashed line denotes the baseline $F1$ score, computed based on all the features from each data source.

Figure 9 demonstrates the comparison results for the RGB bands of the UAV imagery. Figure 10 displays the comparison results for the eight bands of the WorldView-2 imagery, along with a separate panchromatic channel and a synthetic channel estimating the Secchi disk depth, as calculated from the QAA-RGB algorithm [18]. Figure 11 exhibits the comparison results for the 12 bands of the Sentinel-2 L2A products. Finally, a closer investigation into the Secchi disk depth synthetic feature based on the RGB bands of the WorldView-2 imagery for separating UVeg pixels is shown in Figure 12.

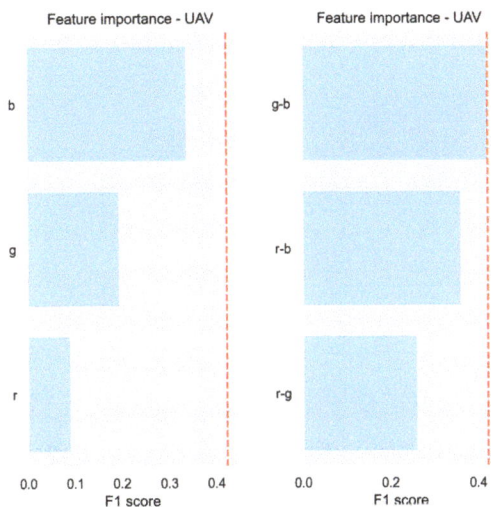

Figure 9. UAV ablation study: Comparison of feature importance in UAV RGB imagery based on single-feature, two-feature, and three-feature classifiers. UVeg segmentation baseline $F1$ score using logistic regression is shown in red dashed line.

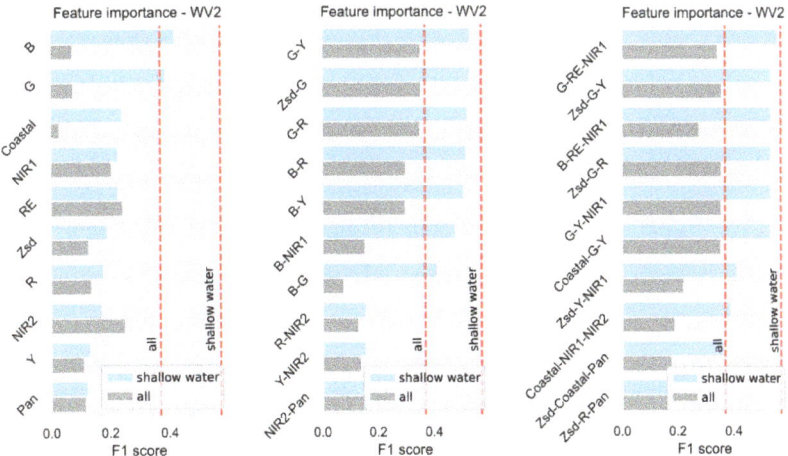

Figure 10. WorldView-2 ablation study: Comparison of band importance in WorldView-2 multi-spectral imagery based on single-feature, two-feature, and three-feature classifiers. A representative subset of band combinations (uniformly selected) is demonstrated. Apart from analyzing all image pixels, a separate study is presented based on shallow-water pixels only, close to the shore with a higher density of apparent UVeg. UVeg segmentation baseline $F1$ scores using logistic regression with all bands for both groups (all pixels/shallow water only) are shown in red dashed lines.

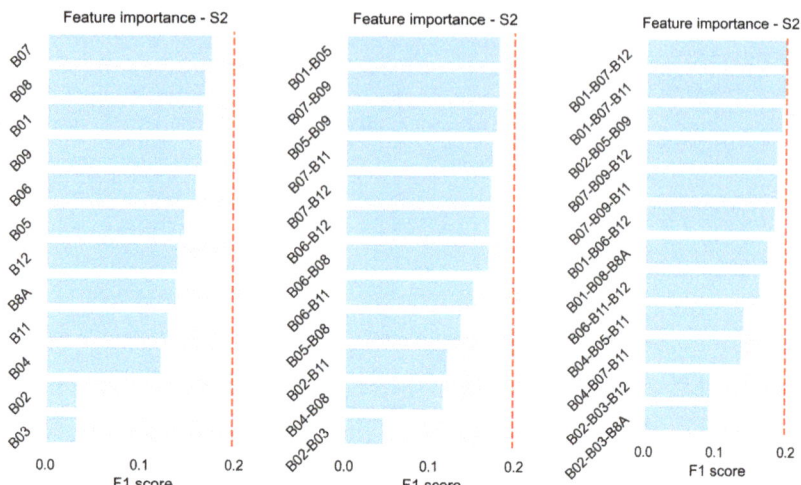

Figure 11. Sentinel-2 ablation study: Comparison of band importance in Sentinel-2 multi-spectral imagery based on single-feature, two-feature, and three-feature classifiers. A representative subset of band combinations is demonstrated from the available options for analysis. UVeg segmentation baseline $F1$ score using logistic regression with all bands is shown in red dashed line.

For reasons of practical interest, the feature importance analysis of WorldView-2 was also performed, apart from the total amount of pixels, on a subset of the image that exhibited a higher density of visually apparent UVeg regions and was close to the shore, which we thus consider "shallow pixels". In Figure 10, the feature importance analysis of the complete image is shown in a light blue color, similarly to the analyses of UAV and Sentinel-2 imagery, while the analysis of the "shallow pixels" only is presented in gray. The UVeg segmentation baseline $F1$ scores using logistic regression with all bands for both groups (all pixels/shallow water only) are shown in red dashed lines.

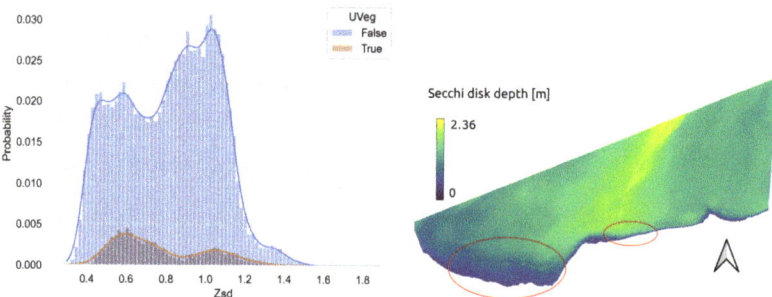

Figure 12. Histogram of Secchi disk depth values derived from the RGB bands of the WV2 image [18]. The right side displays an estimated Secchi disk depth map. UVeg regions are present within the red circles near the shoreline.

3.2. Segment Anything Model Variants

Figure 13 provides a comparative analysis of two variants of the Segment Anything Model (SAM)—the "huge" and "base" versions. The comparison is conducted under a "few annotations" regime, where the number of positive/negative pair annotations is limited. The X-axis represents the number of annotated pairs, while the Y-axis denotes the $F1$ score. The mean values of the $F1$ score are accompanied by the standard deviation, indicating the variability in the model's performance across multiple runs. This comparison is based on a bootstrap simulation conducted 500 times, providing a robust statistical analysis of the performance difference between the two SAM model variants.

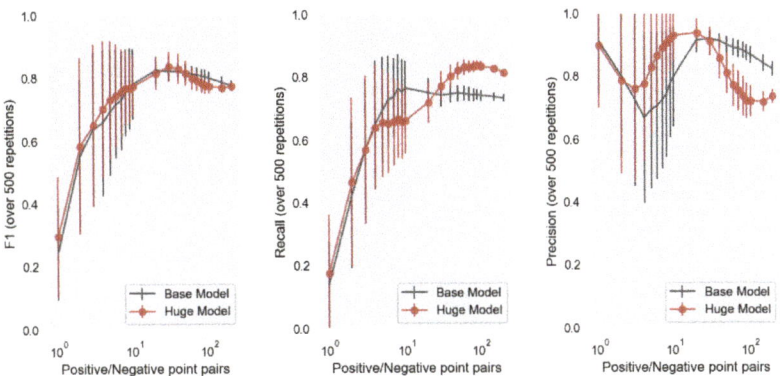

Figure 13. SAM performance with point-prompting in UAV data. The number of prompt-points on the horizontal axis represents pairs of randomly selected positive and negative points.

3.3. Different Quantization in Sentinel-2 Pixels (Two to Four Classes)

In the context of applying multi-class classification to the Sentinel-2 data source, we present two significant figures. Figure 14 illustrates the class distribution of the quantized annotation at a GSD of 10 m, showcasing the complexity and possible class imbalance in the dataset. Figure 15 further explores the impact of different class granularities (two to four classes) on the data representation at the same GSD. These figures collectively offer insights into the challenges and implications of multi-class classification tasks within the Sentinel-2 data source.

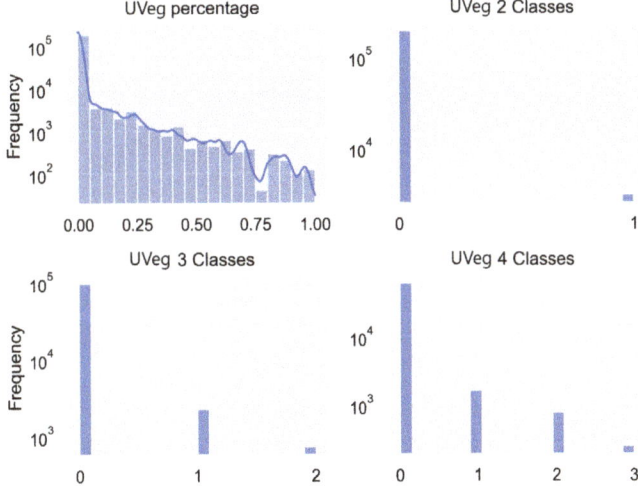

Figure 14. Descriptive statistics of the quantized annotation in GSD = 10 m.

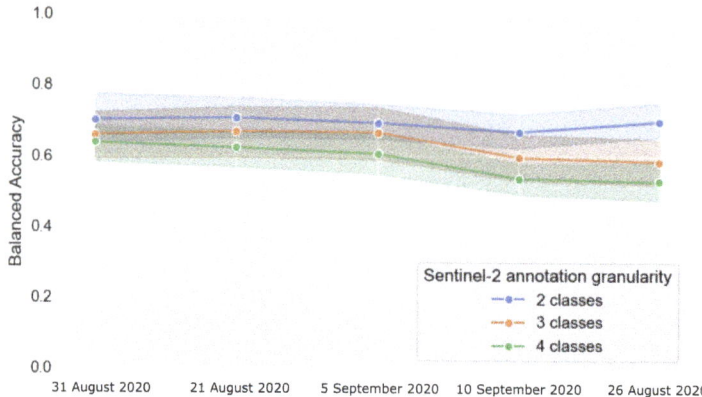

Figure 15. Impact of different class granularities on data representation in Sentinel-2: Investigation of 2–4-class models' performance at a ground sampling distance of 10 m for different sensing dates.

3.4. Transferring UAV Models in Different Lake Areas

Table 3 presents the results of model transferability across different lake locations. The logistic regression model and random forest model were trained on AOI1 and evaluated on AOI2 and AOI3. The random forest model underwent hyperparameter tuning using Bayesian optimization with a validation set from AOI1.

Table 3. Transferability of models in different lake locations using UAV data source. This table presents the results of evaluating the transferability of models across different locations within the lake. The logistic regression and random forest models were trained on AOI1 and tested on AOI2 and AOI3.

Data Source	Test Area	Test Area Size	ML Method	F1	UA	PA
UAV trained on AOI1	AOI 1 * (10-fold CV)	~8 M px	LogReg	0.350	0.219	0.861
			RF	0.576	0.415	0.941
	AOI 2	~8 M px	LogReg	0.312	0.228	0.493
			RF	0.291	0.291	0.292
	AOI 3	~17 M px	LogReg	0.384	0.256	0.764
			RF	0.342	0.279	0.442

* Baseline results from Table 2.

4. Discussion

The results in Figure 4 demonstrate the superiority of the pre-trained foundation model, SAM, in the few-shot learning regime, i.e., limited annotations of positive and negative pixel-pairs for segmenting UVeg from UAV imagery. The highest $F1$ score of 86.5% ± 4.0%, with a corresponding UA of 89.6% ± 5.8% and PA of 83.9% ± 4.8%, is achieved for UAV images using 40 positive/negative pairs of pixels for prompting the SAM model. The corresponding assessment metrics are much lower for the RF and logistic regression models, i.e., 54.0% ± 9.2% using RF models and 42.8% ± 6.2% using logistic regression models. The baseline $F1$ score for the UAV images is 42.3% (red dashed line), which is the best linear separator of the UVeg/no UVeg classes based on the three bands R, G, and B of the UAV images.

In general, the baselines marked with red dashed lines in Figures 4–6 serve as effective linear separators for all bands within each data source, considering the limited size of the available dataset. Consequently, we consider these baselines as valuable indicators of the information contributed by each modality in segmenting underwater aquatic vegetation.

A more comprehensive comparison of the three data sources based on different ML methods and sufficiently large training datasets (specific to each data source) is presented in Table 2. The methods with the highest $F1$ scores are highlighted in bold. Notably, the SAM method performs best for the highest-resolution UAV imagery, while the random forest pixel-wise method remains the state of the art for the WorldView-2 and Sentinel-2 data sources.

We believe that the inability to adapt SAM to lower-resolution remote sensing images can be attributed to the specific characteristics of the training data used for the foundation model. To support this argument, we attempted simple methods like upsampling and patch splitting for WorldView-2 and Sentinel-2 images to generate synthetic higher-resolution images, but without success. However, we firmly believe that future research efforts should focus on properly training and adapting foundational models for coarser-resolution remote imagery, such as Sentinel-2 and WorldView-2, given the available resources in terms of training data and computational power.

The choice of using RF as a comparison with the SAM foundation model was based on the well-established understanding that ensembling techniques tend to outperform more basic methods in machine learning. Random forest, being a bagging model, along with boosting models, has demonstrated superior performance compared to other ML approaches [11,12]. While deep learning has been successful in computer vision and remote sensing, we could not utilize such methods due to the limited annotated data for our task, making the foundation model the most suitable option. Additionally, we included logistic regression as a baseline ML method since it represents traditional thresholding techniques commonly used in remote sensing studies, where linear combinations of bands are designed.

In Figure 7, two masks were produced for the same scene captured during the UAV mission using three RGB bands. These masks were based on different random selections of eight prompt-input points, where the red stars denote negative class input points and the green stars indicate positive class input points. We observe the impact of the point-pair selection on the segmentation accuracy, with the segmentation mask on the left being more accurate than the one on the right, which can also be seen quantitatively in the model's variance in Figure 4, with eight point-pairs. The number of point-pairs for this demonstration was selected because with eight pairs of positive/negative points the SAM model results in generally accurate masks; however, in some cases the model fails and results in masks like the one on the right of Figure 7. Investigating the impact of the input-point selection strategy in an active learning regime (interactively), e.g., selecting the most prominent errors of the current predicted mask, is an ongoing focus of our research group with significant practical applications.

In Figure 8, two additional masks were produced for a scene recorded by the WorldView-2 satellite. The three most informative bands (Green–RedEdge–NearInfrared1) were selected for this operation, as per the feature importance analysis discussed in Section 2. The left panel shows a mask created using eight pairs of positive/negative input points, which yielded the highest $F1$ score according to the results presented in Figure 5. Conversely, the right panel exhibits a mask that contains notable artifacts. These artifacts were more prominent when using a greater number of positive/negative point pairs, resulting in a reduction in performance, as evident in the findings displayed in Figure 5.

The feature importance analysis of the three data sources, as depicted in Figures 9–11, was conducted through an ablation study. The analysis of the UAV bands using a single-feature classifier revealed that the blue band provides the most informative data, while the combination of green and blue bands, as a two-feature classifier, performed nearly as well as the baseline linear separation using all bands together. Regarding Sentinel-2 in Figure 11, the most informative bands for UVeg segmentation were found to be B07, B08, B01, and B09 when employing single-feature classifiers. Additionally, the combinations of B01-B07-B12 and B01-B07-B11 were demonstrated to encompass the complete information required for linearly separating pixels with UVeg presence.

In consideration of practical applications, due to the high cost of UAV imagery and the large GSD of the Sentinel-2 imagery, the WorldView-2 modality is considered a feasible choice for UVeg detection. Consequently, a more sophisticated feature importance analysis of WorldView-2 data was conducted that investigates the effect of pixels' proximity to the shore in feature importance. Specifically, apart from the total amount of pixels, a feature importance analysis in Figure 10 was conducted on a subset of the image that exhibited a higher density of visually apparent UVeg regions and is close to the shore, which we thus considered "shallow pixels". The areas of the lake further from the shore did not have visually apparent UVeg, probably because of the lake's depth. In "shallow waters", both the blue (B) and green bands (G) demonstrated high informativeness, whereas their significance diminished when considering the total amount of pixels due to the presence of deeper-water pixels. Despite B and G individually achieving the highest $F1$ scores in the single-feature classifier, the combination B-G did not result in further enhancement in the two-feature classifier. This can likely be attributed to the similarity in information content between both bands concerning UVeg segmentation, indicating that their combination does not yield better results. Moreover, the combination of green, red, and near-infrared1 bands encompassed almost the entire information content of all bands. Similar conclusions were drawn for the two- and three-feature classifiers, both for the "shallow water" subset and the complete image encompassing deeper waters. However, when examining the Secchi disk depth (Zsd) as a single-feature classifier, it exhibited poor discriminative power as a synthetic index computed by the QAA-RGB algorithm [18]. The lack of separability is further illustrated in Figure 12, where the histograms of the two classes are visually and quantitatively indistinguishable.

Figure 13 provides interesting insights into the performance of two SAM variants, "huge" and "base". The SAM model has two encoder options: ViT-B (91M parameters) and ViT-H (636M parameters). While ViT-H is expected to show significant improvement over ViT-B, we noticed a surprising change in the $F1$ score and precision for around 100 positive/negative pixel pairs. These findings are intriguing and will guide our future research.

Based on our analysis of the Sentinel-2 data source in Section 3.3, it appears that increasing the granularity of the class structure from binary to multi-class models, namely, two- to four-class models, inversely impacts the accuracy of the classifications. As evidenced in Figure 15, the performance, when measured in terms of balanced accuracy, diminishes as we progress from binary to multi-class classification. Furthermore, the class distribution depicted in Figure 14 underscores the significant data imbalance at a GSD of 10 m. This class imbalance might contribute to the decrease in model performance as the class granularity increases, as the models may struggle to learn from under-represented classes. Interestingly, this pattern holds consistently across different time periods, underscoring the robustness of these observations and contributing insights to the optimal approach to classifying complex, multi-dimensional datasets like those derived from Sentinel-2.

The results in Table 3 show comparable metrics for the different AOIs, thus clearly demonstrating the ability of the logistic regression models to be successfully transferred to different locations within the lake. The results based on the random forest pixel-wise classifier show a reduction in all metrics compared to the cross-validation baseline, which is attributed to the limited dataset size of the cross-validation study in AOI1. Although all AOIs were captured on the same date in a single UAV mission (as shown in Table 1), these findings provide valuable insights into the practical usage of such models. For example, during a UAV mission covering the entire lake, it would be feasible to segment all UVeg regions by training or fine-tuning a model on a smaller subarea and then transferring the trained model to the rest of the lake. No results are provided for the Segment Anything model due to insufficient data for fine-tuning; however, recent studies propose methods for adapting prompts with one shot [22].

Considering the successful transferability observed with the logistic regression model in Section 3.4, a potential direction for future research would be to explore adapting the Segment Anything model to new lake areas. Building upon the insights gained, incorporating the one-shot prompt adaptation methods proposed by Zhang et al. [22] may enable the transfer of the Segment Anything model's capabilities. This could facilitate the efficient segmentation of UVeg regions across larger areas of the lake, even on different dates, by leveraging a fine-tuned model from a smaller subarea.

5. Conclusions

In summary, this work demonstrates the effectiveness of the SAM foundation model for segmenting underwater vegetation in high-resolution UAV imagery in the few-shot learning regime. However, adapting SAM to lower-resolution images (WorldView-2 and Sentinel-2) remains challenging, and traditional pixel-wise methods remain the state of the art in our task. The specific characteristics of the foundation model training data are believed to be the reason for this inability to adapt SAM, despite attempts with techniques like patch splitting and upsampling.

The feature importance analysis and comparison of ML methods across the three data sources reveal important insights. The analysis of single-feature classifiers highlights the significance of specific bands in each data source and the limitations of synthetic indices like the Secchi disk depth. These findings provide valuable guidance for future research and practical applications in underwater vegetation segmentation.

Additionally, the study explores SAM variants and the impact of class granularity on Sentinel-2 classification. Logistic regression models demonstrate successful transferability across different areas within the lake, offering a practical approach to segmenting UVeg regions in larger areas using models trained on smaller subareas. Future research can focus on adapting the Segment Anything model to new lake areas using one-shot prompt-adaptation methods, facilitating efficient segmentation across larger areas and different dates.

Author Contributions: Conceptualization, L.A. and I.M.; Methodology, L.A. and I.M.; Software, L.A.; Validation: L.A., S.P., R.-T.C. and A.K.; Investigation, L.A., I.M., S.P. and R.-T.C.; Resources, L.A., I.M. and S.P.; Data curation: L.A. and S.P.; Formal analysis: L.A. and S.P.; Writing, L.A. and S.P.; Writing—review and editing, L.A., I.M., R.-T.C. and A.K.; Supervision, L.A. and I.M.; Project administration, L.A. and I.M.; Funding acquisition, I.M. All authors have read and agreed to the published version of the manuscript.

Funding: This research has received funding from the European Union's Horizon 2020 Research and Innovation Action programme under Grant Agreement 101004157—WQeMS.

Data Availability Statement: The data presented in this study are available on request from the corresponding authors. The data are not publicly available due to their use for ongoing research and intended publications on the topic by the authorship working teams.

Acknowledgments: The authors wish to acknowledge and thank the personnel of the Greek Biotope and Wetland Centre (Maria Toboulidou, Elpida Karadimou, and Vasiliki Tsiaousi) for their valuable insights about the behavior of submerged aquatic vegetation in lakes across Greece, and the personnel of the Thessaloniki Water Supply & Sewerage Company S.A. "EYATH S.A." (Matina Katsiapi, Catherine Christodoulou, and Ioannis Lioumbas) for sharing their experience about the submerged aquatic vegetation in the Polyphytos water reservoir and offering the opportunity to participate in field (boat) visits for validation and verification purposes.

Conflicts of Interest: The authors declare no conflicts of interest.

Abbreviations

The following abbreviations are used in this manuscript:

UVeg	Underwater Aquatic Vegetation
SAM	Segment Anything Model
UAV	Unmanned Aerial Vehicle
LogReg	Logistic Regression
RF	Random Forest
AI	Artificial Intelligence
TDWTP	Thessaloniki's Drinking Water Treatment Plant
QAA-RGB	Quasi-Analytical Algorithm—Red Green Blue
TP, TN, FP, FN	True Positive, True Negative, False Positive, False Negative
UA, PA	User's Accuracy, Producer's Accuracy
AOI	Area of Interest
ML	Machine Learning
DL	Deep Learning
SSL	Self-Supervised Learning

References

1. Haroon, A.M.; Abd Ellah, R.G. Variability response of aquatic macrophytes in inland lakes: A case study of Lake Nasser. *Egypt. J. Aquat. Res.* **2021**, *47*, 245–252. [CrossRef]
2. Rowan, G.S.; Kalacska, M. A review of remote sensing of submerged aquatic vegetation for non-specialists. *Remote Sens.* **2021**, *13*, 623. [CrossRef]
3. Luo, J.; Li, X.; Ma, R.; Li, F.; Duan, H.; Hu, W.; Qin, B.; Huang, W. Applying remote sensing techniques to monitoring seasonal and interannual changes of aquatic vegetation in Taihu Lake, China. *Ecol. Indic.* **2016**, *60*, 503–513. [CrossRef]
4. Liang, S.; Gong, Z.; Wang, Y.; Zhao, J.; Zhao, W. Accurate monitoring of submerged aquatic vegetation in a macrophytic lake using time-series Sentinel-2 images. *Remote Sens.* **2022**, *14*, 640. [CrossRef]
5. Chen, Q.; Yu, R.; Hao, Y.; Wu, L.; Zhang, W.; Zhang, Q.; Bu, X. A new method for mapping aquatic vegetation especially underwater vegetation in Lake Ulansuhai using GF-1 satellite data. *Remote Sens.* **2018**, *10*, 1279. [CrossRef]
6. Fritz, C.; Dörnhöfer, K.; Schneider, T.; Geist, J.; Oppelt, N. Mapping submerged aquatic vegetation using RapidEye satellite data: the example of Lake Kummerow (Germany). *Water* **2017**, *9*, 510. [CrossRef]
7. Manakos, I.; Katsikis, E.; Medinets, S.; Gazyetov, Y.; Alagialoglou, L.; Medinets, V. Identification of Emergent and Floating Aquatic Vegetation Using an Unsupervised Thresholding Approach: A Case Study of the Dniester Delta in Ukraine. 2023. Available online: http://eos.iti.gr/files/floating_paper.pdf (accessed on 12 June 2023).
8. Villa, P.; Bresciani, M.; Bolpagni, R.; Pinardi, M.; Giardino, C. A rule-based approach for mapping macrophyte communities using multi-temporal aquatic vegetation indices. *Remote Sens. Environ.* **2015**, *171*, 218–233. [CrossRef]
9. Husson, E.; Hagner, O.; Ecke, F. Unmanned aircraft systems help to map aquatic vegetation. *Appl. Veg. Sci.* **2014**, *17*, 567–577. [CrossRef]
10. Heege, T.; Bogner, A.; Pinnel, N. Mapping of submerged aquatic vegetation with a physically based process chain. In Proceedings of the Remote Sensing of the Ocean and Sea Ice 2003, Barcelona, Spain, 2004; Volume 5233, pp. 43–50.
11. Piaser, E.; Villa, P. Evaluating capabilities of machine learning algorithms for aquatic vegetation classification in temperate wetlands using multi-temporal Sentinel-2 data. *Int. J. Appl. Earth Obs. Geoinf.* **2023**, *117*, 103202. [CrossRef]
12. Thanh Noi, P.; Kappas, M. Comparison of random forest, k-nearest neighbor, and support vector machine classifiers for land cover classification using Sentinel-2 imagery. *Sensors* **2017**, *18*, 18. [CrossRef]
13. LeCun, Y.; Bengio, Y.; Hinton, G. Deep learning. *Nature* **2015**, *521*, 436–444. [CrossRef] [PubMed]
14. Alagialoglou, L.; Manakos, I.; Heurich, M.; Červenka, J.; Delopoulos, A. A learnable model with calibrated uncertainty quantification for estimating canopy height from spaceborne sequential imagery. *IEEE Trans. Geosci. Remote Sens.* **2022**, *60*, 1–13. [CrossRef]
15. Bommasani, R.; Hudson, D.A.; Adeli, E.; Altman, R.; Arora, S.; von Arx, S.; Bernstein, M.S.; Bohg, J.; Bosselut, A.; Brunskill, E.; et al. On the opportunities and risks of foundation models. *arXiv* **2021**, arXiv:2108.07258.
16. Kirillov, A.; Mintun, E.; Ravi, N.; Mao, H.; Rolland, C.; Gustafson, L.; Xiao, T.; Whitehead, S.; Berg, A.C.; Lo, W.Y.; et al. Segment anything. *arXiv* **2023**, arXiv:2304.02643.
17. Gikas, G.D.; Tsihrintzis, V.A.; Akratos, C.S.; Haralambidis, G. Water quality trends in Polyphytos reservoir, Aliakmon river, Greece. *Environ. Monit. Assess.* **2009**, *149*, 163–181. [CrossRef] [PubMed]
18. Pitarch, J.; Vanhellemont, Q. The QAA-RGB: A universal three-band absorption and backscattering retrieval algorithm for high resolution satellite sensors. Development and implementation in ACOLITE. *Remote Sens. Environ.* **2021**, *265*, 112667. [CrossRef]
19. King, G.; Zeng, L. Logistic regression in rare events data. *Political Anal.* **2001**, *9*, 137–163. [CrossRef]
20. Forman, G.; Scholz, M. Apples-to-apples in cross-validation studies: Pitfalls in classifier performance measurement. *ACM Sigkdd Explor. Newsl.* **2010**, *12*, 49–57. [CrossRef]

21. Bergstra, J.; Yamins, D.; Cox, D. Making a science of model search: Hyperparameter optimization in hundreds of dimensions for vision architectures. In Proceedings of the International Conference on Machine Learning, Atlanta, GA, USA, 2013; pp. 115–123.
22. Zhang, R.; Jiang, Z.; Guo, Z.; Yan, S.; Pan, J.; Dong, H.; Gao, P.; Li, H. Personalize segment anything model with one shot. *arXiv* **2023**, arXiv:2305.03048.

Disclaimer/Publisher's Note: The statements, opinions and data contained in all publications are solely those of the individual author(s) and contributor(s) and not of MDPI and/or the editor(s). MDPI and/or the editor(s) disclaim responsibility for any injury to people or property resulting from any ideas, methods, instructions or products referred to in the content.

Article

Flood Monitoring Using Sentinel-1 SAR for Agricultural Disaster Assessment in Poyang Lake Region

Hengkai Li [1], Zikun Xu [1], Yanbing Zhou [2,*], Xiaoxing He [1] and Minghua He [1]

[1] Jiangxi Province Education Department, School of Civil and Surveying & Mapping Engineering, Jiangxi University of Science and Technology, Ganzhou 341000, China; giskai@jxust.edu.cn (H.L.); 6120210132@mail.jxust.edu.cn (Z.X.); xxh@jxust.edu.cn (X.H.); 6720200506@mail.jxust.edu.cn (M.H.)

[2] Information Technology Research Center, Beijing Academy of Agriculture and Forestry Sciences, Beijing 100097, China

* Correspondence: zhouyb@nercita.org.cn

Abstract: An extensive number of farmlands in the Poyang Lake region of China have been submerged due to the impact of flood disasters, resulting in significant agricultural economic losses. Therefore, it is of great importance to conduct the long-term temporal monitoring of flood-induced water body changes using remote sensing technology. However, the scarcity of optical images and the complex, fragmented terrain are pressing issues in the current water body extraction efforts in southern hilly regions, particularly due to difficulties in distinguishing shadows from numerous mountain and water bodies. For this purpose, this study employs Sentinel-1 synthetic aperture radar (SAR) data, complemented by water indices and terrain features, to conduct research in the Poyang Lake area. The results indicate that the proposed multi-source data water extraction method based on microwave remote sensing data can quickly and accurately extract a large range of water bodies and realize long-time monitoring, thus proving a new technical means for the accurate extraction of floodwater bodies in the Poyang Lake region. Moreover, the comparison of several methods reveals that CAU-Net, which utilizes multi-band imagery as the input and incorporates a channel attention mechanism, demonstrated the best extraction performance, achieving an impressive overall accuracy of 98.71%. This represents a 0.12% improvement compared to the original U-Net model. Moreover, compared to the thresholding, decision tree, and random forest methods, CAU-Net exhibited a significant enhancement in extracting flood-induced water bodies, making it more suitable for floodwater extraction in the hilly Poyang Lake region. During this flood monitoring period, the water extent in the Poyang Lake area rapidly expanded and subsequently declined gradually. The peak water area reached 4080 km^2 at the height of the disaster. The severely affected areas were primarily concentrated in Yongxiu County, Poyang County, Xinjian District, and Yugan County.

Keywords: Sentinel-1; water extraction; flood disaster; decision tree; random forest; improved U-Net

Citation: Li, H.; Xu, Z.; Zhou, Y.; He, X.; He, M. Flood Monitoring Using Sentinel-1 SAR for Agricultural Disaster Assessment in Poyang Lake Region. *Remote Sens.* **2023**, *15*, 5247. https://doi.org/10.3390/rs15215247

Academic Editors: Soe Myint and Yoshio Inoue

Received: 24 August 2023
Revised: 28 October 2023
Accepted: 2 November 2023
Published: 5 November 2023

Copyright: © 2023 by the authors. Licensee MDPI, Basel, Switzerland. This article is an open access article distributed under the terms and conditions of the Creative Commons Attribution (CC BY) license (https://creativecommons.org/licenses/by/4.0/).

1. Introduction

Flood disasters are one of the major catastrophes in China, causing significant losses to the national agricultural economy each year, primarily by reducing the yields of food crops. Numerous crops thrive in water-rich environments and are commonly cultivated near rivers and lakes, and as a consequence, the widespread inundation of farmlands is a direct impact of floods on agricultural production. The flood season in southern China typically coincides with critical stages in the rice cultivation process, such as the heading and harvesting of early-season rice, the field management of mid-season rice, and the transplanting of late-season rice seedlings. This situation exerts adverse effects on rice production and can even lead to complete crop failure. According to the "2020 Annual Report on National Natural Disasters" issued by the Chinese Ministry of Emergency Management, the floods occurring in China during 2020 destroyed close to 3869 hectares of crops in July alone, causing direct economic losses of CNY 1097.4 billion [1]. Among them, the catastrophic floods caused by heavy rainfall in the Yangtze and Huai River basins were one of the top 10 major disasters in China in 2020 [2]. The accurate acquisition of temporal and spatial distribution information of floodwater can aid in dynamically monitoring floods, provide technical support for flood monitoring in the southern hilly areas of China, and act as a reference for the adjustment and optimization of agricultural production structures and food security in the future.

Satellite remote sensing technology is gradually replacing manual monitoring methods due to characteristics including coverage of large measurement areas, non-intrusive measurements, and low cost. In particular, optical remote sensing is widely used due to its rich data sources that can be applied to calculate numerous spectral indices for water bodies, including the normalized difference water index (NDWI) [3], super green water index [4], vegetation red-edge water index [5], etc. However, the cloudy and rainy conditions that frequently occur during the flood season in southern China adversely affect the performance of optical remote sensing sensors, making it difficult to obtain stable and usable optical images for flood monitoring [6]. As a result, the disaster assessment is often limited to comparing pre-disaster and post-disaster images, which may not effectively capture the entire process of prolonged and continuous floods in southern China.

The development of microwave remote sensing, particularly the release of free Sentinel-1 SAR data, has provided new data sources for flood monitoring. For example, Zeng et al. [7], Chen and Jiang [8], and Jia et al. [9] utilized microwave data to extract water body information using methods such as simple thresholding, change detection combined with thresholding, and the Sentinel-1 dual-polarized water index (SDWI). Additional research, both domestic and international, has proposed related methods including Otsu optimal threshold segmentation [10] and object-based approaches [11]. However, these methods primarily focus on enhancing water body characteristics while neglecting the influence of mountain shadows formed by the side-looking imaging of Sentinel-1 satellites. Mountain shadows and water bodies have similar backscattering coefficients, resulting in a similar dark tone in Sentinel-1 SAR images, making it challenging to distinguish between the two during the extraction of water bodies. In regions with frequent floods, such as the southern hilly areas of China, the terrain is undulating, and mountain shadows are prevalent. Thus, there is an urgent need to address the rapid and accurate extraction of flood-affected areas by accounting for the characteristic topography and water body attributes of these southern hilly regions.

In an attempt to acutely distinguish between shadows and water bodies in mountainous areas, Yang et al. [12] simulated radar images using terrain data and removed the shadows that were falsely identified as floodwater bodies, achieving the semi-automatic and accurate extraction of large-scale floodwater bodies. Therefore, this study focuses on removing mountain shadows based on terrain features. More specifically, decision tree nodes are introduced to rapidly assess the impact of terrain features on mountain shadows. Decision trees offer several advantages in binary classification, including fast calculation, simple principles, and accurate results, and thus they are widely used in water body extraction applications [13,14]. In recent years, with the continuous development of artificial intelligence algorithms, machine learning methods such as maximum likelihood, random forest, and support vector machines have been extensively applied in remote sensing research. Among them, the random forest method demonstrates high classification accuracy, a fast prediction speed, and the ability to handle multi-dimensional data [15–17]. Li et al. employed the random forest method based on multi-source data for land-use classification in the southern hilly mountains, effectively addressing the low classification accuracy caused by mountain shadows. Deep learning can fully explore the feature information in remote sensing images and has gradually become more popular in water body extraction applications [18–20]. Among the deep learning models, U-Net has proven to exhibit a high extraction accuracy and minimal spatial resolution losses [21,22], making it suitable for precise water body extraction. However, current research on deep learning-based water body extraction methods primarily focuses on optical remote sensing, while relatively few studies have been conducted on microwave remote sensing [23].

This study employs the decision tree, random forest, and improved U-Net algorithms for water body extraction using the flood disaster in the Poyang Lake area as a case study and Sentinel-1 SAR images from 30 September 2019 as the data source. A comparison of the shadow removal effect and accuracy of the water body extraction results for each method is performed to select the most suitable approach for floodwater extraction in the Poyang Lake region. The selected method is then used to analyze the spatiotemporal distribution of floodwater bodies in the Poyang Lake area from June to August 2020. This work provides valuable insights for the planning of agricultural infrastructure.

2. Study Area and Data Sources

2.1. Overview of the Study Area

Located in the northern part of Jiangxi Province, China, Poyang Lake (between 28°22′–29°45′N and 115°47′–116°45′E) is the largest freshwater lake in the country. Within Jiangxi, the total area of the county-level regions through which Poyang Lake flows is approximately 22,300 km^2, including 11 counties and cities such as Lianxi District, Hukou County, Lushan City, Poyang County, and Nanchang County (Figure 1). The surrounding area of Poyang Lake is characterized by complex land cover and significant topographical variations. The dominant landform type is hilly terrain, accounting for about 78% of the total area, followed by plains and hillocks (approximately 12.1% of the total), and water bodies (covering about 9.9%). Poyang Lake is located in a low-lying area and is influenced by the East Asian monsoon, with concentrated rainfall during the summer season. As a result, from July to September, the lake's water area rapidly expands during the flood season, and the limited drainage capacity, combined with its unique relationship with the Yangtze River, often leads to frequent flood disasters. Since 1949, there have been over 20 recorded major flood events in the area [24].

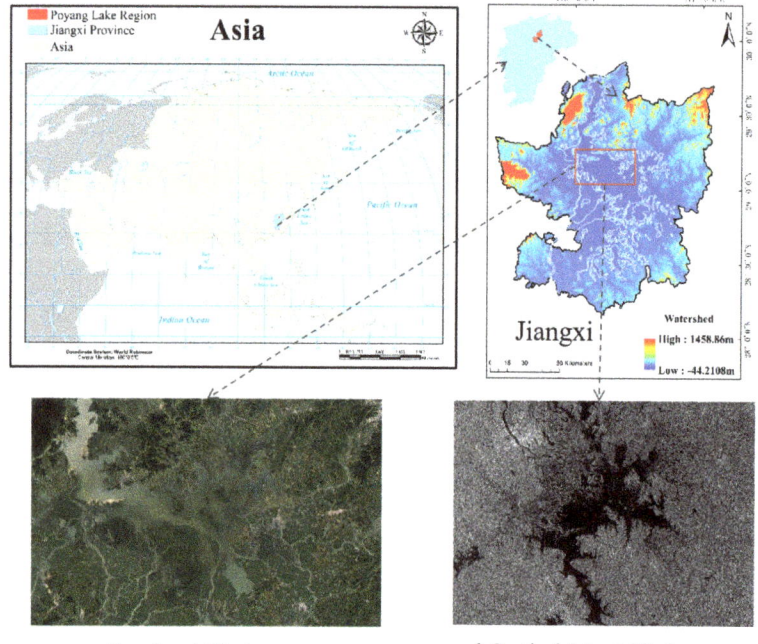

Figure 1. The location of Poyang Lake.

2.2. Data Source

Sentinel-1 SAR satellite imagery was downloaded from the European Space Agency's official website (http://scihub.copernicus.eu (accessed on 27 July 2023)), and corresponding precise orbit data were obtained from the website (https://s1qc.asf.alaska.edu/ (accessed on 27 July 2023)). Moreover, 30 m resolution SRTM-1 Digital Elevation Model (DEM) data were downloaded from the Geospatial Data Cloud Platform (http://www.gscloud.cn (accessed on 27 July 2023)). Supplementary data included vector maps of the administrative divisions of the counties in the study area, water level data, and Google Earth imagery.

Sentinel-1 SAR satellite imagery has a resolution of 10 m and comes in four imaging modes, with a maximum swath width of 400 km. These images are favored by many researchers due to their free availability and high resolution, and they have been widely applied in various fields. The VV (vertical-vertical) and VH (vertical-horizontal) polarized bands of Sentinel-1 imagery are typically used for water body extraction. Hence, we employed the Ground Range Detected Product (GRD) data from the Interferometric Wide Swath (IW) mode. Google Earth imagery was available only for 4 October 2019 in the study area, and thus a Sentinel-1B SAR image from 30 September 2019 was selected to construct the water body extraction method. Another Sentinel-1B SAR image from the flood period in 2020 was selected for flood disaster analysis in the study area. Detailed image information is presented in Table 1. The DEM dataset was used to remove misidentifications caused by mountain shadows, while the Google Earth high-resolution imagery and water level data were employed for the sample selection and flood disaster analysis, respectively.

Table 1. Sentinel-1 SAR image data information.

Data	Platform	Type	Polarization Mode
30 September 2019	Sentinel-1 B	GRD	VV, VH
20 June 2020	Sentinel-1 B	GRD	VV, VH
2 July 2020	Sentinel-1 B	GRD	VV, VH
14 July 2020	Sentinel-1 B	GRD	VV, VH
26 July 2020	Sentinel-1 B	GRD	VV, VH
7 August 2020	Sentinel-1 B	GRD	VV, VH
19 August 2020	Sentinel-1 B	GRD	VV, VH

2.3. Data Preprocessing

The data preprocessing steps included track correction, radiometric calibration, filtering, terrain correction, decibelization, mosaic creation, and clipping. Radiation calibration converts the intensity value of the image into the backscattering coefficient using the following conversion relationship:

$$\sigma^0 = \frac{A^2}{K}\theta \tag{1}$$

where σ^0 is the backscattering coefficient; A is the DN value of the original image; K is the absolute scaling factor; and θ is the angle of incidence.

The filtering process utilizes the Refined Lee filter, which effectively eliminates speckle noise while preserving the edge information of features [25]. The terrain correction combines SRTM-1 DEM data obtained through bilinear interpolation and corrects the geometric distortion caused by terrain using the distance Doppler algorithm. The conversion to decibels involves transforming the backscatter coefficients of the image into logarithmic form, which is more conducive to reflecting the differences in radar intensity.

3. Methods

3.1. Image Feature Extraction

(1) Radar image feature

The VV and VH backscatter coefficients are the main data features extracted from the Sentinel-1 SAR image data for water body extraction in this study. They provide different scattering characteristics between various objects, enabling the enhancement of floodwater identification by distinguishing the different scattering properties of water and non-water bodies in radar signals. The two backscatter coefficients are determined as follows:

$$\sigma_{VV}(\mathrm{db}) = 10 * \log_{10}(\sigma_{VV}) \tag{2}$$

$$\sigma_{VH}(\mathrm{db}) = 10 * \log_{10}(\sigma_{VH}) \tag{3}$$

where $\sigma_{VV}(\mathrm{db})$ and $\sigma_{VH}(\mathrm{db})$ are the backscatter coefficients, and σ_{VV} and σ_{VH} are the pixel values of the two polarized images.

(2) Sentinel-1 dual-polarized water index

Among the main water body extraction methods used for Sentinel-1 SAR images, threshold segmentation is simple, fast, and can rapidly provide valuable information for flood disaster assessments. However, the "double peaks" feature of a single band is not distinct, making it challenging to obtain accurate thresholds and consequently resulting in suboptimal water body extraction results. The SDWI, proposed by Jia et al. (2019), is inspired from the normalized difference vegetation index (NDVI) and NDWI, and is calculated as follows:

$$K_{\mathrm{SDWI}} = \ln(10 \times VV \times VH) \tag{4}$$

where K_{SDWI} is the SDWI, and VV and VH represent the VV and VH backscatter coefficients, respectively.

The SDWI multiplies the data from two polarized bands of the Sentinel-1 SAR satellite, enhancing the characteristics of water bodies while attenuating the features of soil and vegetation, thereby obtaining distinct "double peaks" that are effective for water body extraction. Figure 2 presents the pixel histogram of the preprocessed SAR image after SDWI calculation, revealing clear peaks and valleys. The lowest value of the valley, -7.4605, represents the threshold for the SDWI threshold segmentation method. In this study, the decision tree method uses this threshold as the root node, enabling the preliminary coarse extraction of water bodies in the study area.

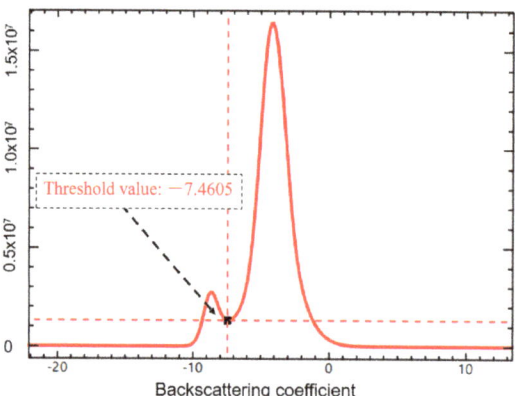

Figure 2. Pixel histogram of SDWI images in the study area.

(3) Topographic feature

The SDWI values for water bodies and mountain shadows are similar in the water body class, making it difficult to distinguish between them using just this index. To remove the mixed mountain shadows from the extracted water bodies, we incorporate terrain features such as elevation and slope into the decision tree and random forest decision tree nodes to suppress the false positives. By combining high-resolution Google Earth imagery from 4 October 2019, the coarse-extracted water bodies are visually examined, identifying the main areas of misclassification between water bodies and shadows. The elevation and slope information for these regions are then obtained to establish approximate threshold ranges to differentiate water bodies from shadows. Precise threshold values that effectively remove shadows are calculated using iterative analysis, with 300 m determined for elevation and 18 for slope. The elevation and slope information are derived from the SRTM-1 DEM data through terrain analysis processing.

3.2. Water Extraction Method

(1) Decision Tree

The decision tree (DT) model recursively partitions a set of training data into subsets with the same classification features by testing a single feature at the root node or multiple features at the leaf nodes [26]. This model is effective in solving binary classification problems. It quickly and intuitively captures the impact of each feature on the classification categories. Therefore, in this study, the DT method was initially applied to water body extraction to assess the influence of terrain features on mountain shadows. The proposed method considers the actual conditions of the study area, combining features such as the SDWI, elevation, and slope for water body extraction in the Poyang Lake area.

(2) Random Forest

The random forest (RF) algorithm is a classifier based on the Bagging ensemble learning theory [27]. This algorithm builds a series of decision trees by constructing different sample training sets and subsequently integrates all classification voting results obtained by majority voting decisions after K rounds of training. Finally, according to the principle of minority obedience to the majority, the category with the most votes is designated as the final output. The final classification decision is described as follows:

$$H(x) = arc\max_{Y} \sum_{i=1}^{K} I(h_i(x) = Y) \tag{5}$$

where $H(x)$ is the final classification result of random forest result; $h_i(x)$ denotes the classified results for a single decision tree; Y is the output variable; and $I()$ is the characteristic function.

This approach is independent of prior knowledge from interpreters and can thus handle high-dimensional and complex datasets, with extensive applications in land use classification and landslide hazard assessments, amongst other fields [28,29]. In this study, based on Sentinel-1 SAR imagery and DEM data, we selected three types of indicators for water body extraction in the random forest model, namely, radar feature variables, water index variables, and terrain feature variables.

(3) Improved U-Net

The U-Net network model, named after its U-shaped structure, is an improved end-to-end architecture based on the Fully Convolutional Network (FCN) framework [30]. This model can effectively fuse high-level semantic information and shallow features, leveraging context information and detail features to obtain more accurate feature maps [31]. However, the original U-Net model only uses three-channel imagery as the input and does not fully consider the terrain and landform characteristics within the study area. To address this limitation, we enhanced the model by modifying the image input to six channels, enabling the model to simultaneously extract radar features, water indices, and terrain characteristics. Moreover, to explore deep semantic information in the six-channel imagery, we replaced the original feature extraction network of the model with the deeper VGG16 convolutional neural network. We also incorporated a channel attention mechanism during the downsampling process of the convolutional network (Figure 3) to update the model's attention weights for different channels and further improve the segmentation performance. Finally, to better distinguish water body boundaries, we modified the model's loss function by introducing the Dice coefficient in addition to the Cross-Entropy Loss, creating the Dice Loss to assist the classifier and achieve better segmentation results. Based on these improvements, we obtained the enhanced U-Net, denoted as the Channel Attention U-Net (CAU-Net) semantic segmentation model for water body extraction in the Poyang Lake area. Figure 4 presents the structure of the optimized model.

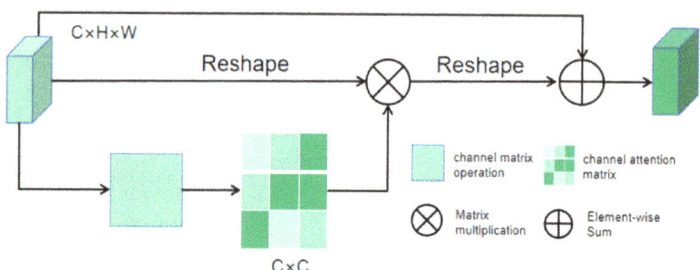

Figure 3. Channel attention mechanism.

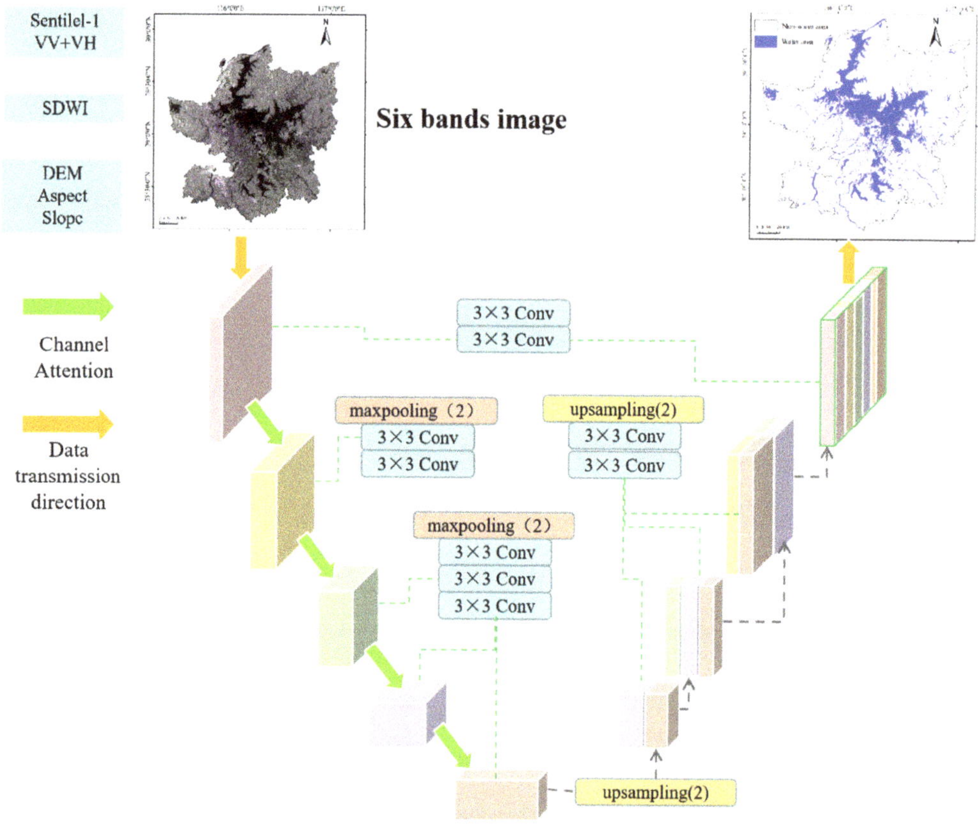

Figure 4. Model structure.

The CAU-Net model is implemented in the TensorFlow deep learning framework. To enhance the model training stability, improve generalization ability, and accelerate training speed, this study utilized the cosine annealing learning rate decay mechanism to adjust the learning rate during the model training process. The initial learning rate was set to 10-4, and it continuously decayed according to formula 6 during the training process, enabling the model to descend stably in the correct gradient direction. The model hyperparameters were adjusted using the Adaptive Moment Estimation (Adam) optimizer, aiming to improve the model's convergence.

$$\eta_t = \eta_{\min} + \frac{1}{2}(\eta_{\max} - \eta_{\min})(1 + \cos(\frac{T_{cur}}{T_{\max}}\pi)) \tag{6}$$

where $\eta_{\max}$ is the maximum learning rate; $\eta_{\min}$ is the minimum learning rate; T_{cur} is the current round; and $T_{\max}$ is half a cycle.

In order to increase the accuracy of the model water boundary segmentation, the Loss function used in the training process was constructed as Dice_Loss by introducing the Dice coefficient based on Cross Entropy Loss. Dice_Loss is expressed as follows:

$$Dice\_Loss = 1 - \frac{2\sum_{i=1}^{n} y_i a_i}{\sum_{i=1}^{n} y_i + \sum_{i=1}^{n} a_i} \tag{7}$$

where n represents the total number of test data; y represents the truth value; and a represents the predicted value.

During the model training process, the goodness-of-fit function of the model stabilized and converged when the number of iterations was close to 20. The training model obtained in the previous step was used for the extraction of water bodies in the Sentinel-1B SAR image of the study area.

3.3. Sample Selection

The number, distribution, and representativeness of training samples can significantly impact the accuracy of the water body extraction [32]. In this study, water bodies were treated as a binary classification problem, dividing the study area into two classes: water and non-water. Water bodies exhibit color differences in shallow and deep water areas, and thus a suitable number of samples were selected for each category while ensuring a diverse representation of non-water land cover types. For the decision tree and random forest methods, training samples were generated through visual interpretation and random sampling from Google Earth high-resolution imagery, resulting in a total of 1440 sample points that were split into training and validation sets at a ratio of 7:3.

For the CAU-Net method, a dataset must be constructed to train the model, considering the differences between water bodies and mountain shadows. The dataset was synthesized from six-band images including VV and VH radar features, SDWI data, elevation, slope, and aspect as the bands. The study area was covered by a large Sentinel-1 SAR image. In order to incorporate different water body types from various regions, six representative sub-regions were selected, including mountainous regions, flatlands (including urban areas), mountainous regions with rivers, flatlands with lakes, croplands with lakes, and flatlands with various types of water bodies (Figure 5). The images of these regions were batch-cropped to 256 × 256 pixels for model training and were manually labeled using the Labelme plugin to obtain the corresponding water body distribution labels. A total of 409 images were used to construct the water body distribution dataset, and were divided into training and validation sets at 4:1 ratio. During the training, data augmentation techniques, such as horizontal and vertical flipping, cropping, and scaling, were applied to enhance the model's generalization ability and prevent overfitting.

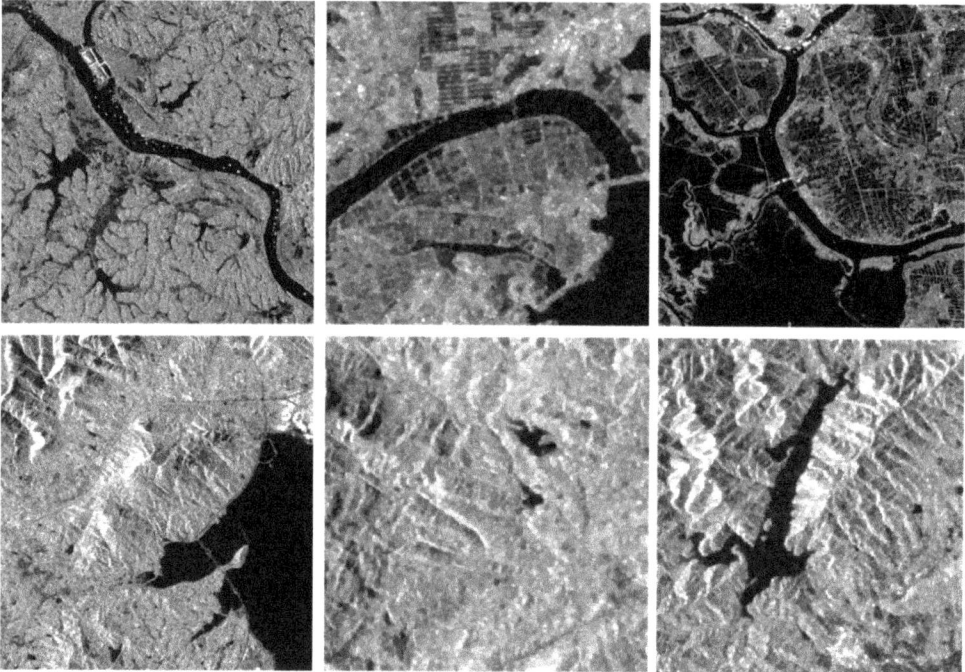

Figure 5. Typical area in the study area.

3.4. Accuracy Evaluation

In order to compare the extraction effects of different extraction methods on flood-affected water bodies, the accuracy was evaluated using two indexes, namely the overall accuracy (OA) and Kappa coefficient. Both indexes are calculated based on the confusion matrix of the extracted results as follows:

$$OA = \frac{\sum_{i=1}^{K} x_{ii}}{N} \tag{8}$$

$$\text{Kappa} = \frac{N\sum_{i=1}^{k} x_{ii} - \sum_{i=1}^{k} x_{i+}x_{+i}}{N^2 - \sum_{i=1}^{k} x_{i+}x_{+i}} \tag{9}$$

where N is the total number of samples; K is the total class number; x_{ii} is the number of samples assigned to the correct category; and x_{+i} and x_{i+} are the true number of Class i samples and the predicted number of Class i samples, respectively.

4. Results

In order to compare the three water extraction methods proposed in this study, a detailed comparison was conducted by qualitatively evaluating the effectiveness of the shadow removal based on the SDWI threshold method. Furthermore, real water samples were visually interpreted from Google Earth imagery and used to construct confusion matrices with the water extraction results obtained from the four methods. This facilitated a quantitative assessment of the water extraction accuracy. Through both qualitative and quantitative analyses, the most suitable water extraction method for the Poyang Lake region was ultimately determined.

4.1. Qualitative Comparison of Water Extraction Results

Figure 6 presents the water extraction results determined by fusing the pre-processed Sentinel images with DEM data and subsequently applying the SDWI threshold approach and the three methods proposed in this study. All four methods are observed to roughly outline the water bodies in the Poyang Lake area over a large scale.

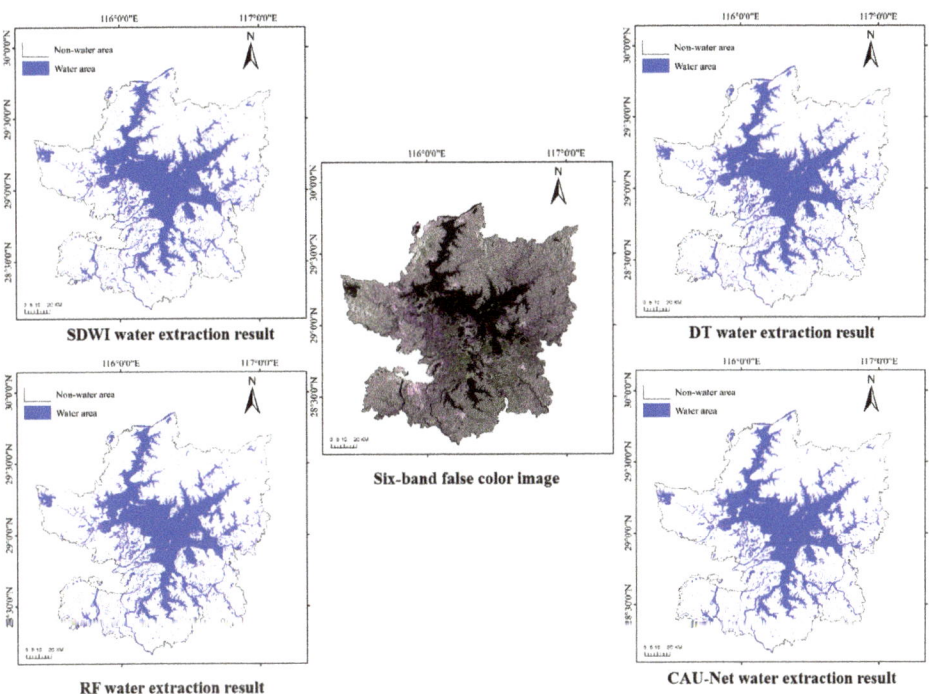

Figure 6. Results of water extraction by different methods.

In order to provide a more intuitive demonstration of the differences between the methods, we selected several typical water extraction results within the study area for a detailed comparative analysis. Figure 7 depicts the results. The water body extraction performance is observed to vary across the methods. The extraction of the SDWI method is fast and simple, yet it is influenced by various factors such as image noise and terrain, leading to suboptimal results with a significant amount of scattered misclassified water bodies. Following the incorporation of the terrain features, the decision tree and random forest methods exhibit improvements via the reduction in misclassified water bodies. However, their extraction of water body boundaries still remains relatively coarse. In comparison, the proposed CAU-Net method effectively mitigates the impact of image noise and terrain factors, greatly minimizing the misclassification of water bodies. The second row of Figure 7 reveals the presence of noise points generated due to water surface reflection. The SDWI, decision tree, and random forest methods are heavily affected by this noise, resulting in the misclassification of water bodies in the noisy regions as non-water bodies. In contrast, CAU-Net effectively suppresses the influence of this background noise. In particular, the analysis of neighboring pixels around the noise points using convolutional neural networks greatly reduces the misclassification of water bodies.

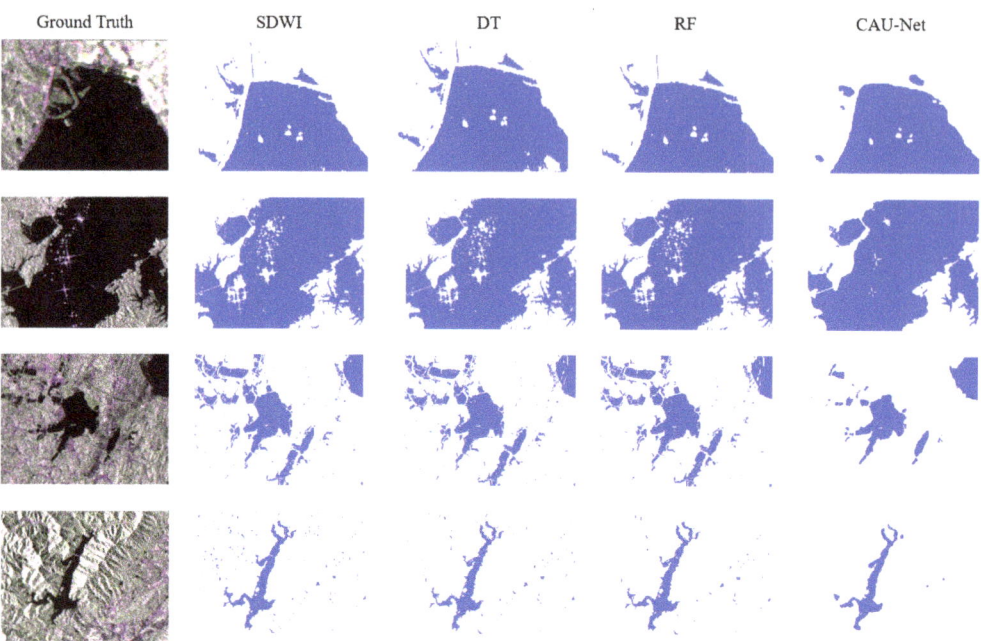

Figure 7. Water extraction results of different methods in typical areas.

The fourth row in Figure 7 depicts a typical area of high hills within the study region, vividly illustrating the impact of each method in suppressing mountain shadows. The SDWI method, which does not account for mountain shadow effects, is observed to greatly misclassify mountain shadows as water bodies in high hill terrain. The decision tree method, which is built upon SDWI threshold segmentation and incorporates terrain features, demonstrates a fast extraction speed with a certain level of shadow suppression in hilly areas. The random forest method has a strong applicability to high-dimensional datasets and effectively eliminates misclassified mountain shadows by incorporating the water index (SDWI) and terrain features as well as the original Sentinel polarization characteristics. When incorporating terrain features as training data for multi-band remote sensing images, the CAU-Net method extensively extracts feature information from the remote sensing images. The resulting water body extraction greatly suppresses the influence of mountain shadows, yielding accurate extraction results.

4.2. Quantitative Comparison of Water Extraction Results

In order to quantitatively compare the extraction accuracy of the various extraction methods, this study conducts a comprehensive analysis using two metrics, namely, the OA and Kappa coefficient. The CAU-Net model proposed in this study demonstrates a strong performance. Compared to the traditional methods of threshold segmentation, decision tree, and random forest in machine learning, CAU-Net significantly improves the accuracy of water body extraction. More specifically, it achieves an impressive OA of 98.71% and a Kappa coefficient of 0.97, both of which outperform the comparative methods. Furthermore, using the same six-band image as input to train the data, the OA and Kappa coefficient of CAU-Net increase by 0.12% and 0.02, respectively, compared to the U-Net model without the attention mechanism. This indicates that the method proposed in this study improves on the U-Net model for water body extraction.

Following this, to investigate the impact of mountain shadows on the accuracy of water body extraction, this study selected two typical areas: (i) a hilly region around Lushan

City, which has relatively high average altitude and significant terrain undulations; and (ii) a low hilly region at the border area between Poyang and Duchang counties, with a relatively low average altitude but still exhibits some terrain undulations. A total of 188 and 197 sample points were evenly selected for validation in the two respective areas. Table 2 reports the accuracy of different water body extraction methods in these two typical areas.

Table 2. The extraction accuracy of each method in different terrain.

Landform	Evaluation Index	SDWI	DT	RF	CAU-Net
High hill	OA	89.36%	95.87%	96.19%	96.45%
	Kappa	0.87	0.89	0.89	0.91
Low hill	OA	91.48%	94.69%	95.18%	95.11%
	Kappa	0.87	0.88	0.89	0.89

Compared to the SDWI threshold method, in the high hill area, all three experimental methods showed a significant improvement in accuracy. More specifically, the OA increased by 6.51%, 6.83%, and 7.09% respectively, while the Kappa coefficient increased by 2.43%, 2.57%, and 4.57%. Improvements in accuracy were also observed in the low hill area, despite the lower level of mountain shadows. The OA increased by 3.21%, 3.70%, and 3.63% respectively, and the Kappa coefficient increased by 1.04%, 2.19%, and 1.68%. Comparing the accuracy of the experimental approaches reveals that the decision tree, random forest, and CAU-Net methods are able to suppress shadows at varying extents, effectively enhancing the accuracy of water body extraction.

4.3. Analysis of Flood Disaster in Poyang Lake

The comparison of the water body extraction results using the three methods indicates that both the SDWI method and CAU-Net can achieve the desired accuracy while ensuring timeliness. Therefore, CAU-Net is chosen as the optimal water body extraction method. Based on CAU-Net, this study utilizes the deep learning model obtained earlier to predict the water body extent during the flood period from June to August 2020 using Sentinel-1B imagery captured every 12 days. Figure 8 presents the resulting maps of the water body during the six periods.

Due to the influence of heavy rainfall over several days, the water level in the Five Rivers of Jiangxi Province rose rapidly at the end of June. From 4 to 11 July, the water level in the Poyang Lake area increased by more than 0.4 m per day for 8 consecutive days, resulting in a total of 12 numbered flood events. According to Table 3, all five key river water level stations in the Poyang Lake area exceeded the warning level during this flood disaster and reached their highest levels around 12 July. Among them, the iconic water level station, Xingzi Station, reached a record high of 22.63 m, surpassing the 1998 flood level by 13 cm and exceeding the historical extreme value.

Table 3. Flood characteristic values of water level stations of key rivers in Poyang Lake in 2020.

	Gauging Station	Highest Water Level/m	Warning Water Level/m	Occurrence Time
1	Hukou	22.49	19.50	12 July 2020
2	Xingzi	22.63	19.00	12 July 2020
3	Yongxiu	23.63	20.00	11 July 2020
4	Duchang	22.42	19.00	11 July 2020
5	Poyang	22.75	19.50	12 July 2020

The total area of the study region is 24,279 km^2. Figure 9 presents the water body areas for each period from June to August 2020. The results indicate that the water body area in the study region was only 2639 km^2 on 20 June, reaching its maximum value of 4080 km^2 on 14 July and subsequently decreasing to 3596 km^2 on 19 August. Due to the existence of flood control embankments and low-lying areas, the change in the water body area lags behind the water level. This indicates that the maximum water body area obtained in this study is consistent with the time of the highest water level. The submerged water body area in the study area initially expanded rapidly and subsequently exhibited a slow recession during the entire flood period. At turning point 1 (2 July), the study area experienced continuous heavy rainfall, and the submerged water body area rapidly expanded, increasing by a total of 1441 km² during the rising period. At turning point 2, when the rainfall almost stopped and the floodwaters ceased to rise, the submerged water body slowly receded, decreasing by a total of 484 km² during the recession period. The rapid expansion of the floodwater in the study area placed significant pressure on the relevant departments of Jiangxi Province to respond promptly with flood control and disaster relief measures. Furthermore, the slow recession of the floodwaters posed considerable challenges for post-disaster rescue and recovery efforts.

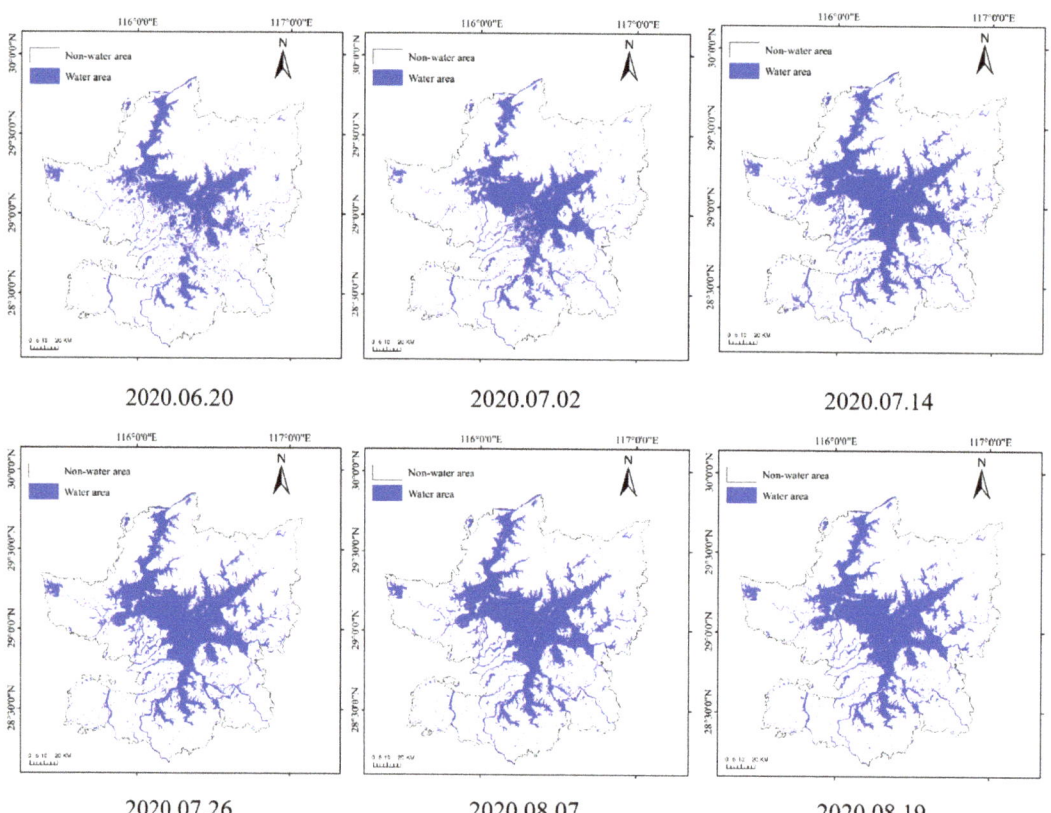

Figure 8. CAU-Net long-time series water extraction results.

This paper took 20 June, 14 July, and 19 August as the pre-flood, mid-flood, and post-flood times, respectively. Figure 10 presents the flood inundation maps determined by overlaying the water body extents during the (i) pre-flood and mid-flood periods; and (ii) the mid-flood and post-flood periods. The maps reveal the severely affected areas of the flood disaster to be concentrated around Poyang Lake, with significant inundation occurring in Yongxiu County, Poyang County, Xinjian District, and Yugan County.

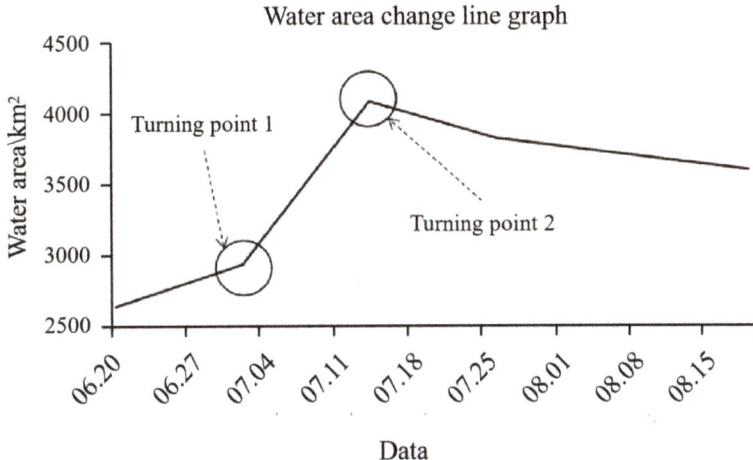

Figure 9. Water area change line chart.

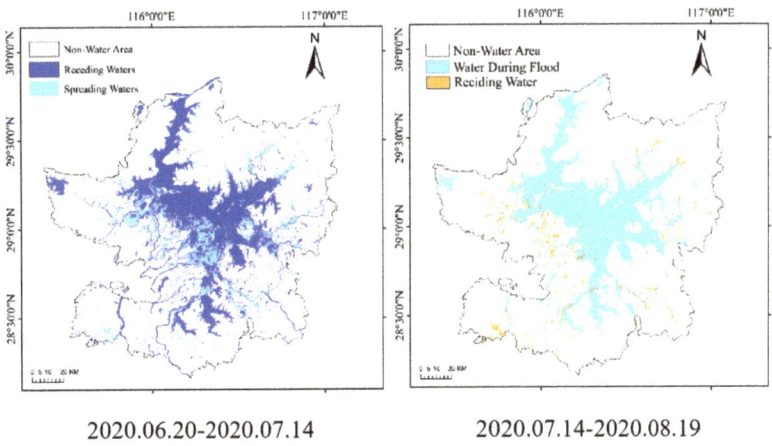

Figure 10. Change of flood inundation extent.

5. Discussion

In the southern regions of China, flood disasters occur frequently during the rainy season every year, causing the inevitable inundation of farmland around lakes and rivers, resulting in significant crop losses. The rapid and accurate acquisition of flood inundation extent and area is of great significance for quick disaster assessments and reducing crop losses. In this study, Sentinel-1 SAR images and SRTM-1 DEM data were employed to compare and analyze three models, namely decision tree, random forest, and CAU-Net. Based on the results, the CAU-Net method was selected to extract the water body extent during the 2020 Poyang Lake flood. The floodwater distribution areas for each period in the study area were subsequently obtained and the disaster situation was analyzed.

The extraction of water body information is critical to remote sensing-based flood monitoring. Optical remote sensing has evolved from simple visual interpretation to the construction of the NDWI, which can achieve relatively accurate water body extraction results, and different water body index layers can be generated under various conditions [33]. However, flood monitoring is distinct to simple water body extraction. During flood disasters, adverse weather conditions often prevail, making optical remote sensing ineffective for monitoring. Microwave remote sensing, on the other hand, with its ability to penetrate clouds and fog, has become a popular choice for flood monitoring [34]. The results of the three water body extraction methods meet the requirements for high accuracy in terms of the OA and Kappa coefficient. This demonstrates the feasibility of using SAR data for water body extraction, with CAU-Net achieving the highest accuracy.

Numerous shadows are cast by mountains in the study area. Due to their similar characteristics to water bodies in microwave remote sensing images, a considerable number of these mountain shadows are mistakenly identified as water bodies. To obtain a more accurate range of flood disasters, this study proposes three water body extraction methods based on SDWI and terrain features. The results indicate that all three extraction methods effectively suppress the influence of mountain shadows. Among them, by introducing the decision tree method based on SDWI threshold segmentation and conducting a series of experiments, we determined thresholds suitable for terrain features, thus effectively suppressing shadows within water bodies. However, it is worth noting that the segmentation thresholds and classification criteria for this method often rely on the interpreter's experience, resulting in a certain degree of subjectivity. On the other hand, the random forest method does not rely on the prior knowledge of the interpreter, yielding more reasonable extraction results. Our results indicate that the random forest method is more suitable for extracting floodwater bodies in small-scale hilly areas. In comparison, CAU-Net not only reduces the influence of human factors but also achieves high extraction accuracy with the best shadow removal effect on mountainous terrains. Although this method requires time for initial model training, it can be directly applied to multi-temporal flood range extraction in the later stages, making it more efficient. Therefore, the CAU-Net method is undoubtedly more applicable for water body extraction around Poyang Lake, with its extensive mountainous terrain.

The disaster analysis revealed the water area in the Poyang Lake region to exhibit a trend of "rapid expansion and slow recession" during this flood period. On 14 July 2020, the water area reached its peak at 4080 km^2. This flood disaster has caused severe losses, particularly in the heavily affected areas of Yongxiu County, Poyang County, Xinjian District, and Yugan County. The government should prioritize disaster reduction efforts in these regions. It is crucial to scientifically guide the post-disaster recovery of crop production, provide tailored technical support, and minimize disaster losses. In addition, the planning and construction of agricultural infrastructure should be enhanced in these areas. Additional emergency drainage facilities should also be present to prepare for potential rises in water levels or even flooding during future flood seasons, thereby minimizing crop losses.

6. Conclusions

(1) During the rainy season, optical imagery in the southern hilly regions is severely constrained by cloudy and rainy weather conditions. This study effectively addressed this issue by utilizing Sentinel-1 SAR imagery in conjunction with multi-source data. The results demonstrate the feasibility of employing SAR imagery in flood disaster monitoring in the Poyang Lake region, providing a key technological reference for future efforts in flood disaster management.

(2) The deep learning approach demonstrates notable advantages in land feature extraction tasks. With the aim of addressing the issue of interference from mountain shadows in the study area, we propose the CAU-Net method for water body extraction. This method achieves an overall accuracy of 98.71% and a Kappa coefficient of 0.97 in water body extraction within the study area, both of which are at the highest level among the various methods. In the highland areas with abundant mountain shadows, its extraction accuracy reaches 96.45%, representing a significant improvement of 7.09% compared to the SDWI method. CAU-Net effectively facilitates water body extraction in hilly regions. Moreover, it enables the water exaction of long-term image

sequences, thereby realizing the monitoring of flood disaster processes. CAU-Net provides a new technical means for flood monitoring in the Poyang Lake region.
(3) The analysis of long-term image sequences in the study area reveals that the flood area expanded rapidly and subsequently receded slowly. The severely affected areas are primarily located around lakes and rivers, or in relatively low-lying terrain, coinciding with the crop cultivation areas. By analyzing the water body extraction results before and after the flood, this study accurately quantified the flooded area, providing data support for disaster assessments and post-disaster reconstruction.

Author Contributions: Conceptualization, methodology, review and editing, H.L.; building method and model, writing—original draft preparation, Z.X.; validation, Y.Z.; data collection, preprocessing, and data set enhancement, X.H. and M.H. All authors have read and agreed to the published version of the manuscript.

Funding: This research was funded by the Open Fund of Key Laboratory of Mine Environmental Monitoring and Improving around Poyang Lake of Ministry of Natural Resources (No. MEMI-2021-2022-10), the Key Projects of Jiangxi Natural Science Foundation (No. 20232ACB203025) and Major Discipline Academic and Technical Leaders Training Program of Jiangxi Province (No. 20225BCJ23014).

Data Availability Statement: All data in this article can be obtained by reasonably contacting the corresponding author.

Conflicts of Interest: The authors declare no conflict of interest.

References

1. *The Ministry of Emergency Management Released the Basic Situation of National Natural Disasters in 2020*; China Disaster Reduction: Beijing, China, 2021; p. 60.
2. *Top Ten Natural Disasters in China in 2020*; China Disaster Reduction: Beijing, China, 2021; p. 60.
3. McFeeters, S.K. The use of the Normalized Difference Water Index (NDWI) in the delineation of open water features. *Int. J. Remote Sens.* **1996**, *17*, 1425–1432. [CrossRef]
4. Duan, J.W.; Zhong, J.S.; Jiang, L.; Zhong, M. Extraction Method of Ultra-Green Water Index for Flood Area After Rain Based on GF-2 Image. *Geogr. Geogr. Inf. Sci.* **2021**, *37*, 35–41.
5. Wu, Q.S.; Wang, M.X.; Shen, Q.; Yao, Y.; Li, J.; Zhang, F.; Zhou, Y. Small water body extraction method based on Sentinel-2 satellite multi-spectral remote sensing image. *Natl. Remote Sens. Bull.* **2022**, *26*, 781–794. [CrossRef]
6. Guo, X.; Zhao, Y.D. Floodinundation Monitoring in Ningxiang of Hunan Province Based on Sentinel-1A SAR. *Remote Sens. Technol. Appl.* **2018**, *33*, 646–656.
7. Zeng, L.F.; Li, L.; Wan, L.H. SAR-based Fast Flood Mapping Using Sentinel-1 Imagery. *Geomat. World* **2015**, *22*, 100–103, 107.
8. Chen, S.N.; Jiang, M. Application Research of Sentinel-1 SAR in Flood Range Extraction and Polarization Analysis. *J. Geo-Inf. Sci.* **2021**, *23*, 1063–1070.
9. Jia, S.C.; Xue, D.J.; Li, C.R. Study on New Method for Water Area Information Extraction based on Sentinel-1 data. *Yangtze River* **2019**, *50*, 213–217.
10. Qiu, J.; Cao, B.; Park, E.; Yang, X.; Zhang, W.; Tarolli, P. Flood Monitoring in Rural Areas of the Pearl River Basin (China) Using Sentinel-1 SAR. *Remote Sens.* **2021**, *13*, 1384. [CrossRef]
11. Tang, L.; Liu, W.; Yang, D.; Chen, L.; Su, Y.; Xu, X. Flooding Monitoring Application Based on the Object-oriented Method and Sentinel-1A SAR Data. *J. Geo-Inf. Sci.* **2018**, *20*, 377–384.
12. Yang, C.J.; Wei, Y.M.; Wang, S.Y. Extracting the Flood Extent from SAR imagery on Basis of DEM. *J. Nat. Disasters* **2002**, *11*, 121–125.
13. Li, F.; Sang, G.Q.; Sun, Y.; Cao, F.J. Research on Methods of Complex Water Body Information Extraction Based on GF-1 Satellite Remote Sensing Data. *J. Univ. Jinan (Sci. Technol.)* **2021**, *35*, 572–579.
14. Pal, M.; Mather, P.M. An assessment of the effectiveness of decision tree methods for land cover classification. *Remote Sens. Environ.* **2003**, *86*, 554–565. [CrossRef]
15. Li, H.K.; Wang, L.J.; Xiao, S.S. Random Forest Classification of Land Use in hilly and mountaineous Area of Southern China Using Multi-source Remote Sensing Data. *Trans. Chin. Soc. Agric. Eng.* **2021**, *37*, 244–251.
16. Zhang, W.C.; Liu, H.B.; Wu, W. Classification of Land Use in Low Mountain and Hilly Area Based on Random Forest and Sentinel-2 Satellite Data: A Case Study of Lishi Town, Jiangjin, Chongqing. *Resour. Environ. Yangtze Basin* **2019**, *28*, 1334–1343.
17. AKollert; Bremer, M.; Loew, M.; Rutzinger, M. Exploring the potential of land surface phenology and seasonal cloud free composites of one year of Sentinel-2 imagery for tree species mapping in a mountainous region. *Int. J. Appl. Earth Obs. Geoinf.* **2021**, *94*, 102208. [CrossRef]

18. Chen, Y.; Fan, R.; Yang, X.; Wang, J.; Latif, A. Extraction of Urban Water Bodies from High-Resolution Remote-Sensing Imagery Using Deep Learning. *Water* **2018**, *10*, 585. [CrossRef]
19. Song, S.; Liu, J.; Liu, Y.; Feng, G.; Han, H.; Yao, Y.; Du, M. Intelligent Object Recognition of Urban Water Bodies Based on Deep Learning for Multi-Source and Multi-Temporal High Spatial Resolution Remote Sensing Imagery. *Sensors* **2020**, *20*, 397. [CrossRef]
20. Zheng, T.H.; Wang, Q.T.; Li, J.G.; Zheng, F.; Zhang, Y.; Zhang, N. Automatic Water Extraction from GF-6 Image Based on Deep Learning. *Sci. Technol. Eng.* **2021**, *21*, 1459–1470.
21. Wang, B.; Chen, Z.L.; Wu, L.; Xie, P.; Fan, D.L.; Fu, B.L. Road extraction of high-resolution satellite remote sensing images in U-Net network with consideration of connectivity. *J. Remote Sens.* **2020**, *24*, 1488–1499. [CrossRef]
22. Wang, X.W.; Zhao, Q.Z.; Tian, W.Z. Influence of U-Net Model on the Accuracy of Shelter Forest Extraction with Different Spatial Resolutions. *Bull. Surv. Mapp.* **2021**, 39–43. [CrossRef]
23. Wang, J.M.; Wang, S.X.; Wang, F.T.; Zhou, Y.; Ji, J.; Xiong, Y.; Wang, Z.; Zhao, Q. Flood inundation region extraction method based on Sentinel-1 SAR data. *J. Catastrophol.* **2021**, *36*, 214–220.
24. Lei, S. Review and Thinking of Poyang Lake Flood in 2020. *Water Resour. Prot.* **2021**, *37*, 7–12.
25. Luan, Y.J.; Guo, J.Y.; Gao, Y.G.; Liu, X. Remote Sensing Monitoring of Flood and Disaster Analysis in Shouguang in 2018 from Sentinel-1B SAR Data. *J. Nat. Disasters* **2021**, *30*, 168–175. [CrossRef]
26. Zhang, D.Y.; Dai, Z.; Xu, X.G.; Yang, G.; Meng, Y.; Feng, H.; Hong, Q.; Jiang, F. Crop Classification of Modern Agricultural Park Based on Time-series Sentinel-2 Images. *Infrared Laser Eng.* **2021**, *50*, 262–272.
27. Breiman, L. Random forests. *Mach. Learn.* **2001**, *45*, 5–32. [CrossRef]
28. Zhao, X.; Tian, B.; Niu, Y.; Chen, C.; Zhou, Y. Classification of coastal salt marsh based on Sentinel-1 time series backscattering characteristics: The case of the Yangtze River delta. *J. Remote. Sens.* **2022**, *26*, 672–682. [CrossRef]
29. Yang, S.; Li, D.; Yan, L.; Huang, Y.; Wang, M. Landslide Susceptibility Assessment in High and Steep Bank Slopes Along Wujiang River Based on Random Forest Model. *Saf. Environ. Eng.* **2021**, *28*, 131–138. [CrossRef]
30. Ronneberger, O.; Fischer, P.; Brox, T. U-Net: Convolutional Networks for Biomedical Image Segmentation. *arXiv* **2015**, arXiv:1505.04597. Available online: http://arxiv.org/abs/1505.04597 (accessed on 27 July 2023).
31. Dong, Y.; Wang, G.; Amankwah, S.O.Y.; Wei, X.; Feng, A. Monitoring the summer flooding in the Poyang Lake area of China in 2020 based on Sentinel-1 data and multiple convolutional neural networks. *Int. J. Appl. Earth Obs. Geoinf.* **2021**, *102*, 102400. [CrossRef]
32. Ning, X.-G.; Chang, W.-T.; Wang, H.; Zhang, H.; Zhu, Q. Extraction of marsh wetland in Heilongjiang Basin based on GEE and multi-source remote sensing data. *Natl. Remote Sens. Bull.* **2022**, *26*, 386–396. [CrossRef]
33. Li, L.; Su, H.; Du, Q.; Wu, T. A novel surface water index using local background information for long term and large-scale Landsat images. *ISPRS J. Photogramm. Remote Sens.* **2021**, *172*, 59–78. [CrossRef]
34. Njoku, E.G.; Moghaddam, M.; Moller, D.; Molotch, N. Microwave Remote Sensing for Land Hydrology Research and Applications: Introduction to the Special Issue. *IEEE J. Sel. Top. Appl. Earth Obs. Remote Sens.* **2010**, *3*, 3–5. [CrossRef]

Disclaimer/Publisher's Note: The statements, opinions and data contained in all publications are solely those of the individual author(s) and contributor(s) and not of MDPI and/or the editor(s). MDPI and/or the editor(s) disclaim responsibility for any injury to people or property resulting from any ideas, methods, instructions or products referred to in the content.

Article

Future Land Use and Flood Risk Assessment in the Guanzhong Plain, China: Scenario Analysis and the Impact of Climate Change

Pingping Luo [1,2,3], Xiaohui Wang [1,2,3], Lei Zhang [1,2,3,4], Mohd Remy Rozainy Mohd Arif Zainol [5], Weili Duan [6], Maochuan Hu [7,*], Bin Guo [8], Yuzhu Zhang [9], Yihe Wang [10] and Daniel Nover [11]

1. Key Laboratory of Subsurface Hydrology and Ecological Effects in Arid Region, Ministry of Education, Chang'an University, Xi'an 710054, China; lpp@chd.edu.cn (P.L.); 2022229018@chd.edu.cn (X.W.); 2020129068@chd.edu.cn (L.Z.)
2. Xi'an Monitoring, Modelling and Early Warning of Watershed Spatial Hydrology International Science and Technology Cooperation Base, Chang'an University, Xi'an 710054, China
3. School of Water and Environment, Chang'an University, Xi'an 710054, China
4. Xi'an Xinsemi Material Technology Co., Ltd., Xi'an 710054, China
5. River Engineering and Urban Drainage Research Centre (REDAC), University Sains Malaysia, Nibong Tebal 14300, Penang, Malaysia; ceremy@usm.my
6. State Key Laboratory of Desert and Oasis Ecology, Key Laboratory of Ecological Safety and Sustainable Development in Arid Lands, Xinjiang Institute of Ecology and Geography, Chinese Academy of Sciences, Urumqi 830011, China; duanweili@ms.xjb.ac.cn
7. School of Civil Engineering, Sun Yat-sen University, Guangzhou 510275, China
8. College of Geomatics, Xi'an University of Science and Technology, Xi'an 710054, China; guobin12@xust.edu.cn
9. Shaanxi Key Laboratory of Earth Surface System and Environmental Carrying Capacity, College of Urban and Environmental Sciences, Northwest University, Xi'an 710127, China; xbdzyz05@nwu.edu.cn
10. Department of Civil and Environment Engineering, The Hong Kong Polytechnic University, Hong Kong SAR, China; 19083951d@connect.polyu.hk
11. School of Engineering, University of California, Merced, 5200 Lake R, Merced, CA 95343, USA; dnover@ucmerced.edu
* Correspondence: humch3@mail.sysu.edu.cn

Abstract: Continuously global warming and landscape change have aggravated the damage of flood disasters to ecological safety and sustainable development. If the risk of flood disasters under climate and land-use changes can be predicted and evaluated, it will be conducive to flood control, disaster reduction, and global sustainable development. This study uses bias correction and spatial downscaling (BCSD), patch-generating land-use simulation (PLUS) coupled with multi-objective optimization (MOP), and entropy weighting to construct a 1 km resolution flood risk assessment framework for the Guanzhong Plain under multiple future scenarios. The results of this study show that BCSD can process the 6th Climate Model Intercomparison Project (CMIP6) data well, with a correlation coefficient of up to 0.98, and that the Kappa coefficient is 0.85. Under the SSP126 scenario, the change in land use from cultivated land to forest land, urban land, and water bodies remained unchanged. In 2030, the proportion of high-risk and medium-risk flood disasters in Guanzhong Plain will be 41.5% and 43.5% respectively. From 2030 to 2040, the largest changes in risk areas were in medium- and high-risk areas. The medium-risk area decreased by 1256.448 km^2 (6.4%), and the high-risk area increased by 1197.552 km^2 (6.1%). The increase mainly came from the transition from the medium-risk area to the high-risk area. The most significant change in the risk area from 2040 to 2050 is the higher-risk area, which increased by 337 km^2 (5.7%), while the medium- and high-risk areas decreased by 726.384 km^2 (3.7%) and 667.488 km^2 (3.4%), respectively. Under the SSP245 scenario, land use changes from other land use to urban land use; the spatial distribution of the overall flood risk and the overall flood risk of the SSP126 and SSP245 scenarios are similar. The central and western regions of the Guanzhong Plain are prone to future floods, and the high-wind areas are mainly distributed along the Weihe River. In general, the flood risk in the Guanzhong Plain increases, and the research results have guiding significance for flood control in Guanzhong and global plain areas.

Citation: Luo, P.; Wang, X.; Zhang, L.; Mohd Arif Zainol, M.R.R.; Duan, W.; Hu, M.; Guo, B.; Zhang, Y.; Wang, Y.; Nover, D. Future Land Use and Flood Risk Assessment in the Guanzhong Plain, China: Scenario Analysis and the Impact of Climate Change. *Remote Sens.* 2023, 15, 5778. https://doi.org/10.3390/rs15245778

Academic Editor: Alberto Refice

Received: 7 October 2023
Revised: 23 November 2023
Accepted: 25 November 2023
Published: 18 December 2023

Copyright: © 2023 by the authors. Licensee MDPI, Basel, Switzerland. This article is an open access article distributed under the terms and conditions of the Creative Commons Attribution (CC BY) license (https://creativecommons.org/licenses/by/4.0/).

Keywords: CMIP6; BCSD; PLUS; MOP; flood risk assessment; multi-scenario simulation; climate change

1. Introduction

The dramatic changes in the global climate have led to an increase in the frequency of flood disasters. Meanwhile, anthropogenic activities have increased the proportion of impervious surfaces in the world and reduced the area of green space. In this case, it is causing serious economic and life losses on a global scale [1–5]. Especially in developing countries, the abuse of resources and environmental protection awareness is relatively low, making them more vulnerable to floods [6]. Recently, various parts of China have suffered from the effects of flooding [7]. For example, on 20 July 2021, Zhengzhou City, Henan Province, saw a "once-in-a-millennium" torrential rain, causing severe flash floods, landslides, river floods, and large-scale urban floods. The disaster caused 380 deaths and missing people in Zhengzhou City, with direct economic losses of CNY 40.9 billion, seriously affecting people's lives [8–10]. The frequent occurrence of floods is closely linked to climate change. The latest assessment report of the Intergovernmental Panel on Climate Change (IPCC) shows that human activities have led to increasing climate change and dramatic changes in the regional environment [11–13], with more frequent extreme weather events and climate change disrupting the smoothness in hydrological analysis, thus further increasing the intensity of regional flooding. Flood disasters and human activities have a direct impact on land use and land cover, and changes in land use and land cover can subtly change regional temperature, rainfall, vegetation, and other neglected climatic factors to a certain extent [14,15], making flood prevention more difficult. At present, China's research on the impact of climate change and land-use types on floods is still in its infancy, which poses a considerable challenge for future flood control and disaster reduction work and flood disaster risk management [16,17].

The research on global climate and land-use change has made great strides in recent years [14,18,19]. Climate models are indispensable for the prediction of climate change. The Coupled Model Intercomparison Project Phase 6 (CMIP6) global climate model (GCM) is now widely used in climate change research [20–22]. Chen [20] found that the CMIP6 model improved the modeling of extreme index trends in critical regions of the world, predicting a significant increase in extreme rainfall days and five consecutive days of maximum precipitation. It is crucial to predict areas prone to waterlogging on a fine scale. Studies showed that human activities change land-use conditions, which is an important reason for the occurrence of floods [23–27]. The probability of a waterlogging disaster is proportional to the proportion of the impervious surface and inversely proportional to the proportion of green space [28,29]. At present, the cellular automata (CA), future land-use simulation (FLUS), and PLUS models are widely used to simulate and predict dynamic changes in land use [30,31]. Lin et al. [31] used maximum entropy (MAXENT) and the FLUS model to predict future waterlogging-prone areas. Zhang [32] used the PLUS model to simulate future multi-scenario land-use types in the Yangtze River basin for 2035–2095, and the Kappa coefficient was 0.896. Most studies demonstrated that the PLUS model has a higher accuracy for the landscape pattern, location, and quantity simulation than the FLUS model [33,34]. Meanwhile, the PLUS model can be used to simulate regional ecological environment changes and to evaluate, design, and plan ecological management behaviors [35]. Compared with other models, the PLUS model can better reveal the internal relationship of land-use change. However, few studies have considered the impact of climate change and land use on flood disasters at the same time. This paper aims to fill this gap.

Another key issue is the selection and proportion of flood-disaster-causing factors [36,37]. In the current research, the methods of using multi-criteria analysis to evaluate flood disaster and vulnerability include the Technique for Order of Preference by Similarity to Ideal Solution (TOPSIS) and Simple Additive Weighting [38], hierarchical analysis (AHP) [39], the fuzzy analytic hierarchy process [40], the set pair analysis–variable fuzzy sets model [41], and entropy weighting [42]. The entropy weight method is mainly used in the study of environmental science, but it is a relatively new method for flood risk assessment. This method does not consider the decision maker's factors in the calculation process, calculating the weight by solving the mathematical model, so it produces more objective results [43,44]. In previous flood risk studies, higher-resolution data play an essential role in regional future flood risk evaluation. A coarse resolution product [39] was used to predict the runoff under four typical concentration paths (RCPs) using 21 general climate models (GCMs), and runoff estimates at 25 km resolution in Canada from 1961 to 2005 and from 2061 to 2100 were generated [45]; Rincón [45] used CMhyd to downscale seven GCMs in CMIP5, and the study based its calculations on station data, with the number of stations directly influencing the spatial resolution. In contrast, most of the existing multi-scenario flood risk assessments focus on RCPs; Li [46] constructed flood risk assessments for different scenarios (RCPs 2.6, 4.5, 6.0, and 8.5). However, less consideration is given to SSPs, where the main flood-inducing factors that should be considered are precipitation (SSPs-RCPs), land use (SSPs-RCPs), GDP, and population (SSPs-RCPs). To optimize the scenario change and the resolution of the flood assessment, this study builds on this to construct a high-resolution multi-scenario flood risk assessment framework.

The present work aims to construct a 1 km resolution future multi-scenario flood risk assessment framework in the context of climate change and urbanization, to conduct a multi-scenario flood risk assessment for the future Guanzhong Plain via coupling BCSD, PLUS, and the entropy weighting methods, to guide future flood prevention in the Guanzhong Plain, and to supply references for other plain areas globally.

2. General Situation of the Research Area

2.1. Research Area

The Guanzhong Plain is located in the Weihe River alluvial plain on the northern foot of the Qinling Mountains in Shaanxi Province. It is also known as the Weihe Plain. It is between 107.4°~111.49°E and 33.92°~36.05°N, with an average altitude of about 500 m (Figure 1a). There have been significant spatial and temporal differences in the occurrence of floods in the Guanzhong Plain over the last 400 years, compared to other regions [47]. In the first 200 years, the flood disasters in the Guanzhong Plain mainly occurred in Xi'an and Tongchuan, in the lower reaches of the Luo River. The occurrence of floods in the Guanzhong Plain over the last 200 years has had noticeable seasonal differences, with the extremes mainly occurring in the summer and autumn. In addition, the flat topography, loose soils, and sparse surface vegetation of the Guanzhong Plain are unique natural conditions that can lead to regional flooding.

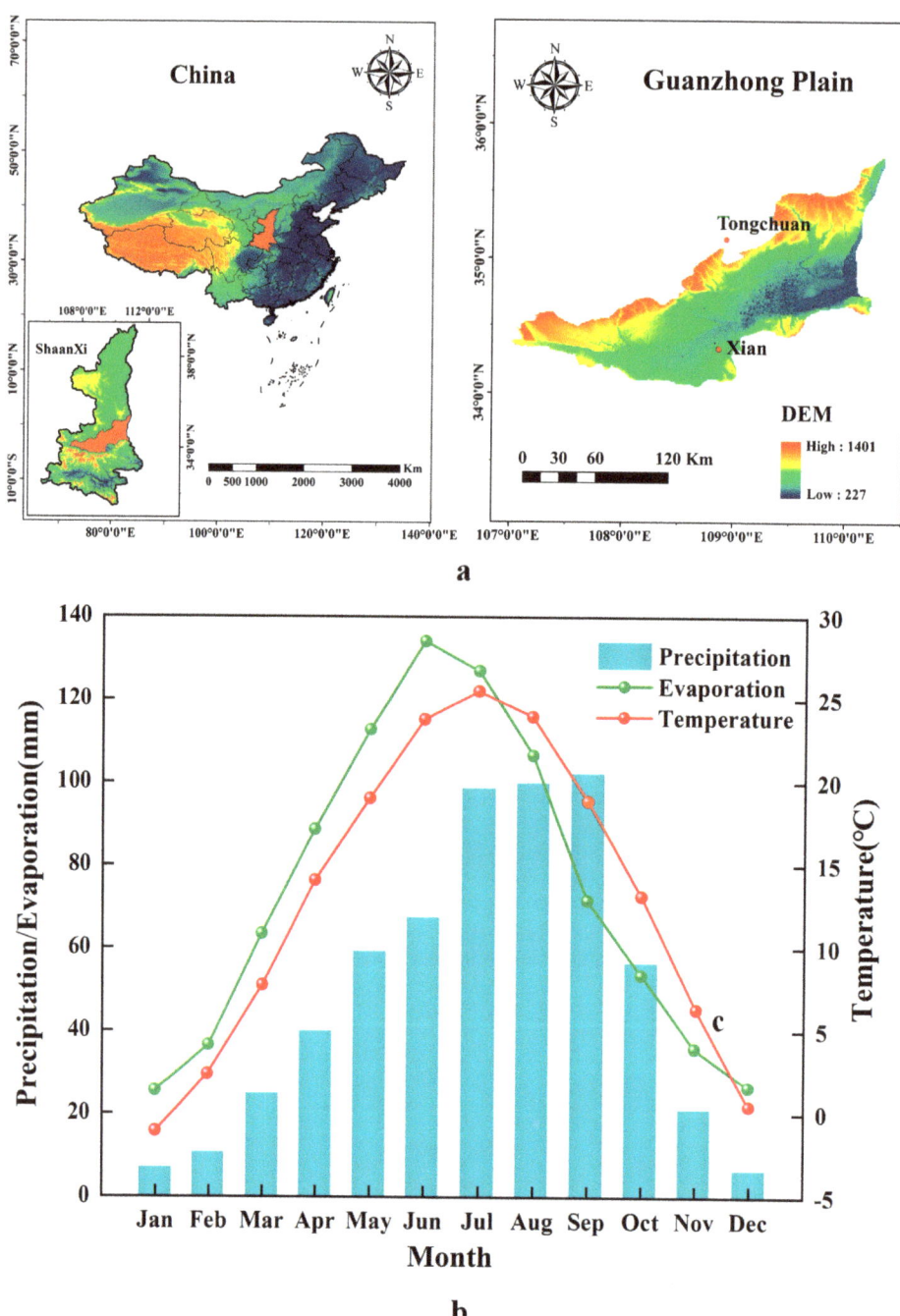

Figure 1. (**a**) Location map of the Guanzhong Plain; (**b**) monthly precipitation, evaporation, and temperature in Guanzhong Plain during the study year.

2.2. Data Sources

HRLT (1975–2014): Comprehensive statistical analysis methods such as machine learning, generalized additive models, and thin plate splines were used to interpolate daily grid data. They were based on the 0.5° × 0.5° grid dataset of the China Meteorological Administration, with elevation, aspect, slope, terrain humidity index, latitude, and longitude as the main covariates. The MAE, RMSE, Cor, R^2, and NSE were 1.30 mm, 4.78 mm, 0.84, 0.71, and 0.70. The resolution of the dataset was 1 km × 1 km [48].

CMIP6 data (1975–2050) were derived from the historical test data of cmip6 and the data of different shared social and economic paths (SSPs, including SSP126 and SSP245); this study predicts the daily precipitation in the Guanzhong Plain under different scenarios from 2030 to 2050.

The data on land use and driving factors used in this study are shown in Table 1.

Table 1. Driving factors and land-use data.

Type	Data	Time	Original Resolution	Resource
Socio-economic factors	Land use	2010 2020	1 km	www.globallandcover.com/, accessed on 3 January 2022
	POP	2010, 2020	0.5°	https://springernature.figshare.com/articles/dataset, accessed on 10 January 2022
	Gross domestic product (GDP)	2010, 2020		http://cstr.cn/31253.11.sciencedb.01683, accessed on 10 January 2022. CSTR:31253.11.sciencedb.01683.
	Grain sown area and output	2010, 2020		Statistical Yearbook of Shaanxi Province 2022
	Rural and urban population	2010, 2020		
	Grain purchase price	2010, 2020		
Natural environmental conditions	Digital elevation model (DEM)	2010	1 km	NASA SRTM1 v3.0
	Slope	2010	1 km	
Traffic location factors	Railway	2010		OpenStreetMap https://www.openstreetmap.org/, accessed on 10 January 2022
	Highway	2010		
	Expressway	2010		
	River	2010		

To ensure data consistency during the calculation, the drive factor data were uniformly resampled to 1 km × 1 km using ArcGIS.

3. Materials and Methods

3.1. BCSD

To obtain reliable datasets at a conventional resolution of 0.5°, GCMs at different resolutions need to be bias-corrected and downscaled. Based on the bias between the simulated and observed climate variables at each percentile, the simulated dataset's cumulative distribution function (CDF) is adjusted using the equidistant cumulative distribution function (EDCDF) method. The method can be expressed as follows:

$$x_{correct} = x + F_{oc}^{-1}(F_{ms}(x)) - F_{mc}^{-1}(F_{ms}(x)) \qquad (1)$$

where x is the climate variable, in which the precipitation is used in this paper; $F_{oc}^{-1}(F_{ms}(x)) - F_{mc}^{-1}(F_{ms}(x))$ is the deviation between the model output and the observation; F is the cumulative distribution function (CDF); F_{oc}^{-1} and F_{mc}^{-1} denotes the observation and the model output during the historical training period; and F_{ms} denotes the model output during the correction period.

3.2. MOP + PLUS

3.2.1. MOP

MOP [49] is an open and flexible method incorporating various ecological and macroeconomic policies. To construct a reasonable land-use structure, this study designs two scenarios according to different constraints and objective functions: (1) a sustainable development model that balances economic benefits and ecological values (SSP126); (2) natural development scenarios predicted by the Markov chain (SSP245).

The optimization objectives of MOP are listed in Table 2. The constraint conditions of these objective functions are shown in Table 3. Finally, the multi-objective optimization results are calculated using Lingo.

Table 2. Multi-objective optimization function for evaluation.

Function	Formula	Description
Function for estimating economic benefits.	$M_1 = max \sum_{i=1}^{6} eb_i x_i =$ $max\{5.89x_1 + 0.40x_2 + 24.37x_3 + 249.6x_4 + 0.001x_5 + 1.97x_6\}$	The coefficient eb_i is the economic benefits of each land-use type (unit: 10^4 CNY/ha), CNY = Chinese yuan.
Function for estimating ecological service value	$M_2 = max \sum_{i=1}^{6} esv_i x_i =$ $max\{0.68x_1 + 2.89x_2 + 0.22x_3 + 0.000142x_4 + 0.4x_6\}$	The coefficient esv_i is the ecological service values of each land-use type (unit: 10^4 CNY/ha).
MOP function under the SSP126 scenario	$SSP126 = max\left\{0.5\sum_{i=1}^{6} eb_i x_i + 0.5\sum_{i=1}^{6} esv_i x_i\right\}$	$x_1 \sim x_6$ represents the area of different land-use types (ha): cultivated land (x_1), woodland (x_2), grassland (x_3), urban land (x_4), bare land (x_5), and water (x_6).

Table 3. Multi-objective optimization constraints for evaluation.

Constraint	Description
$\sum_{i=1}^{6} x_i = 3552159.78$	The total land-use area remains unchanged.
$0.35 \sum_{i=1}^{3} x_i + 66.53 x_4 \leq P_i$	The population density of agricultural land and urban land are 0.35 and 66.53, respectively (person/ha). P_i is the total population by 2030, 2040, and 2050; P_i is, respectively, 30 million, 31.2 million, and 32.3 million.
$\frac{x_3 + x_5}{3552159.78} \geq 0.04$	To ensure the diversity of land use, the total grassland and bare land area in this study are less than 0.04.
$\sum_{i=1}^{3} x_i \geq 3080771$	Considering that the change in cultivated land should keep a dynamic balance, the total area of cultivated land should be greater than or equal to the current value.
$875920.6 \leq x_2 \leq w_i \times 120\%$	We set the woodland area to be between the woodland area in 2020 and $w_i \times 120\%$, and w_i is the predicted woodland area of the Markov chain in 2030, 2040, and 2050.
$0.038 \leq \frac{x_3}{3552159.78} \leq 0.043$	We set the grassland coverage in 2020 as the upper limit (0.043) and the grassland coverage in 2050 predicted by the Markov chain as the lower limit (0.038).
$u_i \times 80\% \leq x_4 \leq u_i \times 120\%$	u_i is what the Markov chain predicts as the urban land area in 2030, 2040, and 2050. We set $u_i \times 120\%$ as the upper limit (0.043) and $u_i \times 80\%$ as the lower limit (0.038).
$49539.33 \leq x_6 \leq v_i \times 120\%$	v_i is what the Markov chain predicts as the water area in 2030, 2040, and 2050. We set $v_i \times 120\%$ as the upper limit and the water area in 2020 as the lower limit.

3.2.2. PLUS

The PLUS model combines rule mining based on the land expansion analysis strategy with cellular automata based on multiple random patch seed types [34]. It allows the driver to be explored, and it is possible to obtain the reasonable probability of various kinds of LULC extensions using the RF classification.

(1) Land expansion strategy analysis (LEAS)

The transition rules obtained in LEAS have the characteristics of time, which can describe the nature of land-use change during a specific time interval.

$$P_{i,k}^d(x) = \frac{\sum_{n=1}^M I(h_n(x) = d)}{M} \quad (2)$$

where P is the final growth probability of the land-use type K in unit I, $I(\cdot)$ is the indicator function of the decision tree set, $h_n(x)$ is the prediction type of the nth decision tree of the vector x, and M is the total number of decision trees.

(2) CA

The CA model is a land-use simulation model driven by scenarios. Its main principle is divided into two parts: "top-down" (global land-use demand) and "bottom-up" (local land-use competition).

$$OP_{i,k}^{d=1,t} = P_{i,k}^{d=1} \times \Omega_{i,k}^t \times D_k^t \quad (3)$$

where $OP_{i,k}^{d=1,t}$ represents the change probability of the kth land-use type at the ith place of the data grid, D_k^t is the influence of k on the future land use in t time, and $\Omega_{i,k}^t$ represents the neighborhood effect at the ith position of the grid.

(3) Model validation

Based on previous studies and the principles of data availability, data consistency, data comprehensiveness, and data redundancy [50–54], this paper selects natural driving factors such as elevation, slope, and precipitation; accessibility driving factors such as river distance, road distance, and railway distance; and socio-economic driving factors such as GDP and population density. The land-use demand under the scenarios of SSP126 and SSP245 in 2030, 2040, and 2050, calculated by the Markov chain and MOP, is used to determine the land-use demand of the project. Based on the land-use pattern of the Guanzhong Plain in 2010 and 2020, the land-use patterns in 2030, 2040, and 2050 under the joint action of the above driving factors are simulated. By setting the same PLUS model parameters, this study simulates the land-use pattern in 2020 based on the land-use pattern in 2010 and compares it with the real land-use situation in 2020. The Kappa coefficient is 0.8507, which indicates that the prediction accuracy is higher, and the land-use pattern simulation results are reliable.

3.3. Construction of Flood Risk Assessment Model

This paper selects the flood risk evaluation index of the Guanzhong Plain from three aspects: disaster-causing factors, disaster-pregnant factors, and disaster-bearing factors. The disaster-causing factors are the average annual rainfall and Rx5day; the disaster-pregnant factors are the elevation, slope, distance from rivers, distance from roads, and land use, based on the land-use data for 2030, 2040, and 2050 under the two scenarios of SSP126 and SSP245 simulated by the PLUS model. Runoff coefficients (RC) were used to assign values to each of the six land uses: 0.60, 0.30, 0.35, 0.92, 0.70, and 1.00; and the disaster-bearing factors are the population density and GDP. All data were normalized to obtain the respective factor indicators. The flood risk assessment structure is shown in Figure 2.

For calculating the hazard, sensitivity, and vulnerability indicators, the entropy weighting method was chosen for each precipitation unit under different scenarios for 2030, 2040, and 2050.

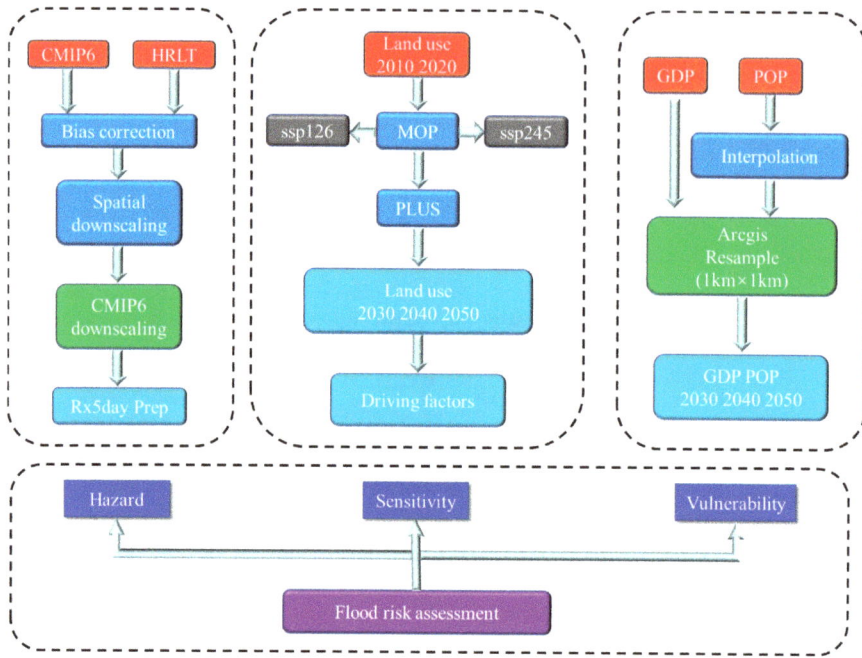

Figure 2. Flood risk assessment framework.

4. Results

4.1. Verification of Future Precipitation Accuracy

The GCMs data selected for this study are shown in Table 4. The research, first, compares the performance of observation data and model data during the historical period (1970–2014). From the deviation index between the root-mean-square error and the multi-year average value, the error of the multi-mode ensemble average is significantly smaller than that of the single mode. The precipitation of the multi-mode set is consistent with the observed monthly precipitation during the year (Figure 3). The Taylor chart shows that each model has a good simulation ability for precipitation in the Guanzhong Plain. Among them, the standard deviation of each mode is less than 1, and the correlation coefficient is more than 0.95.

Table 4. Basic information of 5 GCMs from CMIP6.

Model	Country	Original Resolution (°)	Resolution after Downscaling (°)
CanESM5	Canada	2.8 × 2.8	0.5 × 0.5
CNRM-ESM2-1	France	2.5 × 1.2676	0.5 × 0.5
GFDL-ESM4	U.S.A.	2.88 × 1.8	0.5 × 0.5
MIROC6	Japan	1.4063 × 1.4	0.5 × 0.5
MRI-ESM2-0	Germany	1.125 × 1.12	0.5 × 0.5

Moreover, the standard deviation is smaller than that of the single mode, and the correlation coefficient is higher than that of the single mode, reaching more than 0.98. As can be seen from Figure 3, the simulated monthly precipitation values before the model correction significantly deviated from the observed values. After the correction, the difference between the simulated and observed monthly precipitation values is controlled, with the maximum error within 5 mm (Figure 4). The constructed deviation correction model can correct the model deviation very well. In conclusion, the simulation effect of multi-mode ensemble averaging is better than that of single-mode. Still, the resolution and accuracy of the mode after ensemble averaging have not reached the accuracy required by this study, so deviation correction and downscaling are necessary.

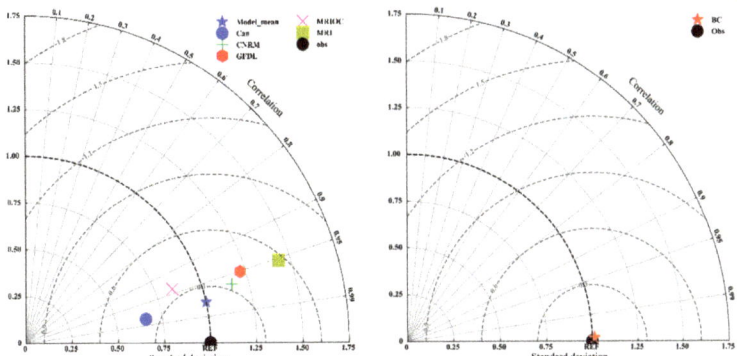

Figure 3. Taylor chart of monthly average precipitation based on climate model and meteorological observation data.

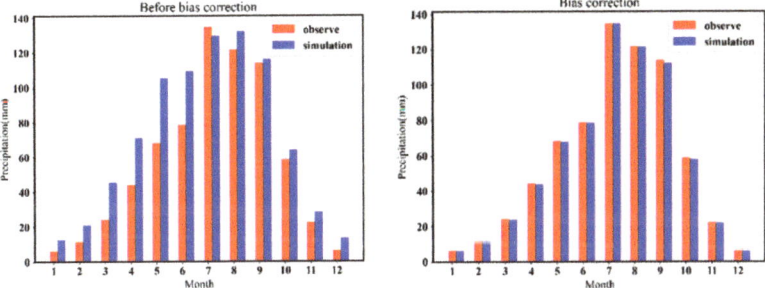

Figure 4. Comparison of monthly average precipitation between observation value and simulation value.

The corrected downscaling model is used to downscale the cmip6 data from 2030 to 2050 under the SSP126 and SSP245 scenarios, that is, to complete the future precipitation forecast in the Guanzhong Plain. Ultimately, this study uses the downscaled CMIP6 data to calculate the annual precipitation and Rx5day.

4.2. Future Land-Use Scenario Simulation Results

The spatial distribution of the drivers selected for this study is shown in Figure 5. Combining the drivers with the future land-use demand of the Guanzhong Plain under different scenarios obtained from MOP and Markov chain projections, the land-use pattern of the Guanzhong Plain can be simulated under multiple scenarios in 2030, 2040, and 2050 (Figure 6).

Figure 6 and Table 5 show the predicted results and the number of LULC types for the different scenarios. The area occupied by cultivated land is always higher, while urban land, water bodies, woodland, and grassland are lower, and bare land is always at the lowest level. In the SSP126 scenario, from 2030 to 2050, all land types show an increasing trend except for urban land, which decreases by 6.9% year on year. In contrast, urban land increases by 4.1% from 2030 to 2040 and by 2.6% from 2040 to 2050. Overall, it shows an upward trend and a slower growth rate. In contrast to the SSP126 scenario, urban land under the SSP245 scenario maintains a higher growth rate from 2030 to 2050, increasing by 18.4% year on year, with all other land types showing a decreasing trend.

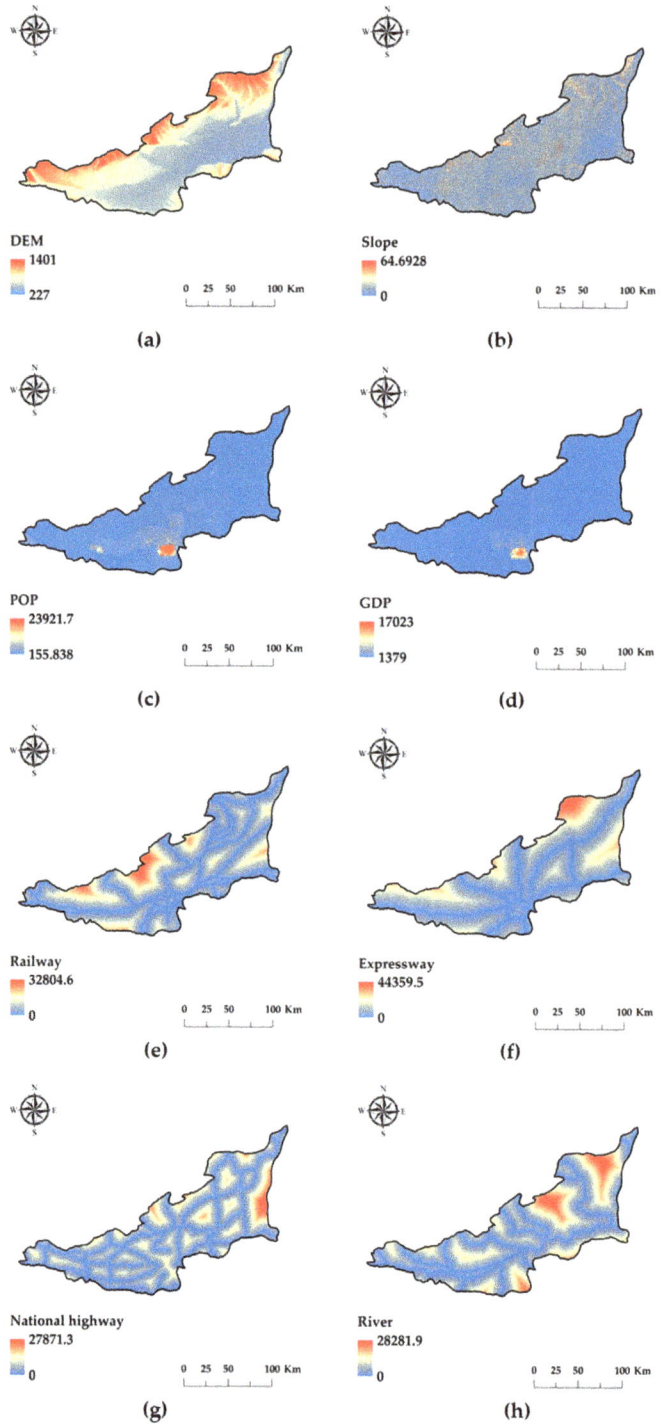

Figure 5. (**a**–**h**) Distribution of the drivers in the Guanzhong Plain.

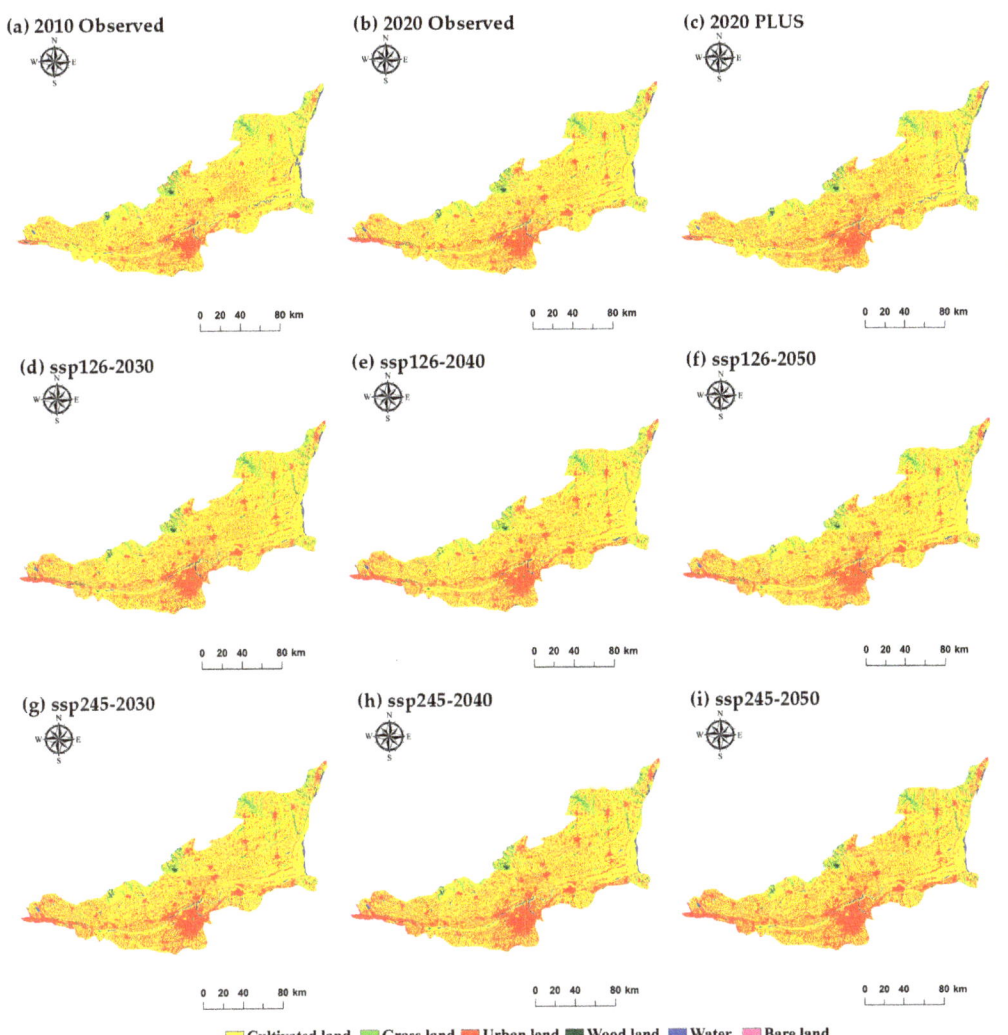

Figure 6. LULC simulation results and land class shares for different scenarios at different times.

Table 5. Land-use demands under different scenarios.

Type	SSP126				SSP245		
	2020	2030	2040	2050	2030	2040	2050
Cropland	22,879,843	22,628,622	22,396,611	22,240,356	22,398,817	22,005,502	21,685,365
Woodland	9,732,451	9,730,251	9,718,942	9,748,918	9,656,993	9,575,550	9,490,178
Grassland	1,618,498	1,697,143	1,657,674	1,660,798	1,569,406	1,529,747	1,497,225
Water	548,437	550,432	633,893	622,750	538,184	528,244	518,958
Urban land	4,660,253	4,831,098	5,033,004	5,167,280	5,276,346	5,801,081	6,248,796
Bare land	28,960	28,696	28,318	28,340	28,696	28,318	27,919

Figure 7 shows the simulated LULC changes for the SSP126 and SSP245 scenarios. In 2020–2030, the arable land in the SSP126 scenario is mainly converted to grassland and urban land. Between 2030 and 2040, 1.8% of the arable land converts to urban land, while 4.6% of the urban land converts to arable land (and vice versa, to a lesser extent), resulting in a lower rate of change for urban land between 2030 and 2040 and a similar shift in the previous period between 2040 and 2050, with a continued overall conversion of agricultural land to other land types and, significantly, urban land use. Under the SSP2-4.5 scenario, the main changes between cropland, urban land, and forest land occur between 2020 and 2030, with conversion rates from cropland to urban land and forest land of 3.8% and 1.1%, respectively. In addition, similar changes occur between 2030–2040 and 2040–2050, with arable land mainly being converted to urban land, resulting in a significant increase in the urban land area.

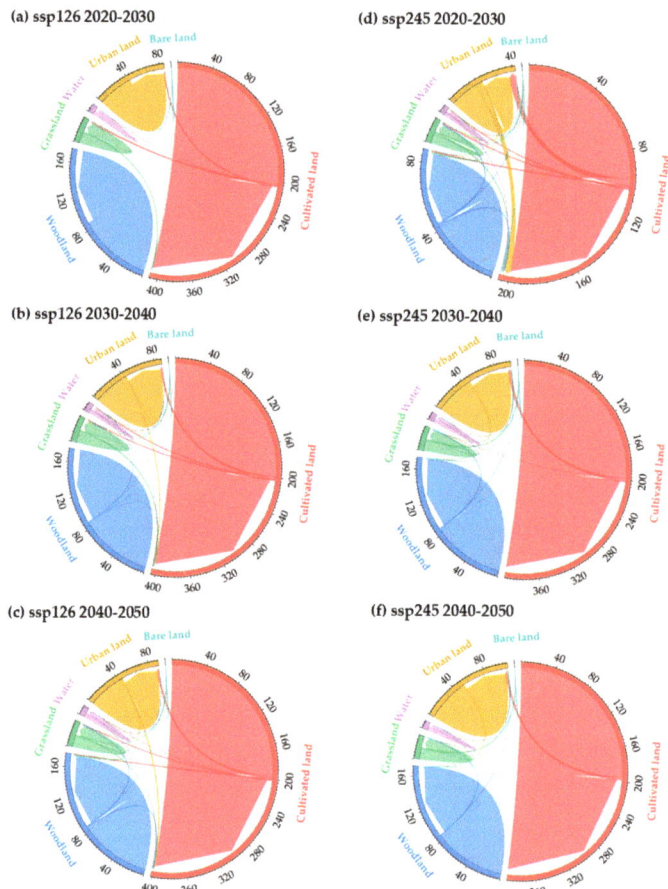

Figure 7. Variation in LULC types during different periods in the SSP126 and SSP245 scenarios.

4.3. Risk Assessment of Future Flood

4.3.1. Hazard Indicators

The Geographic Information System (GIS), as a visual technical means, is mainly used in flood disaster risk assessment [55]. Figure 8 shows the flood hazard maps under different scenarios during different periods, from which the spatial distribution characteristics of flood hazards in the Guanzhong Plain can be analyzed. Based on the GIS environment, the Jenks method creates a flood hazard map using the hazard index. The map shows the potential areas where flood events are more likely to occur. For scenario SSP126, the medium-to-higher-risk area gradually shifts from the northeast to the southwest of the Guanzhong Plain. There is a significant increase in the medium-to-higher-risk area. SSP245 is similar to the above, but the medium-to-higher-risk area is more significant. The rise in hazards in the southwest also contributes to a certain extent to the eventual concentration of the higher-risk areas for flooding in the southwestern part of the Guanzhong Plain. Combined with Figure 9, it can be seen that in the 25%–75% interval, more data exist for SSP245 than for SSP126. For Rx5day, the SSP245 scenario is mainly concentrated in the 80–90 mm range. The SSP126 scenario is primarily focused in the 70–100 mm range, with the former concentration associated with higher precipitation and more extreme values. In contrast, the annual rainfall also shows a similar distribution, which leads to the SSP245 scenario being more likely to produce higher precipitation in both scenarios relative to the SSP126 scenario, thus leading to flooding.

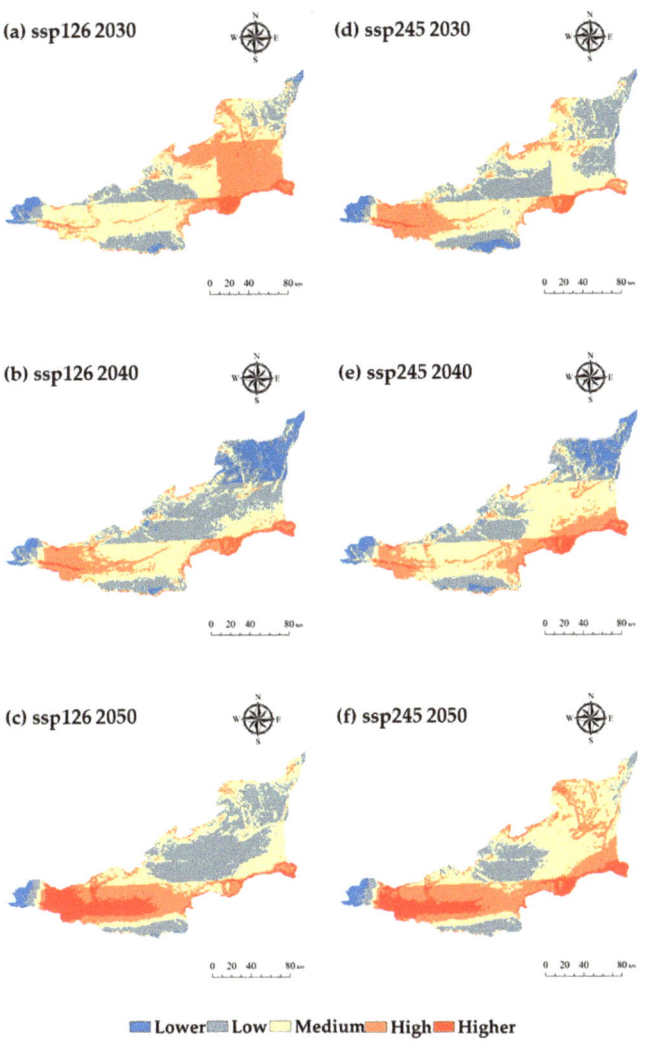

Figure 8. Spatial distribution of hazard indicators in the Guanzhong Plain between 2030 and 2050 under different development scenarios.

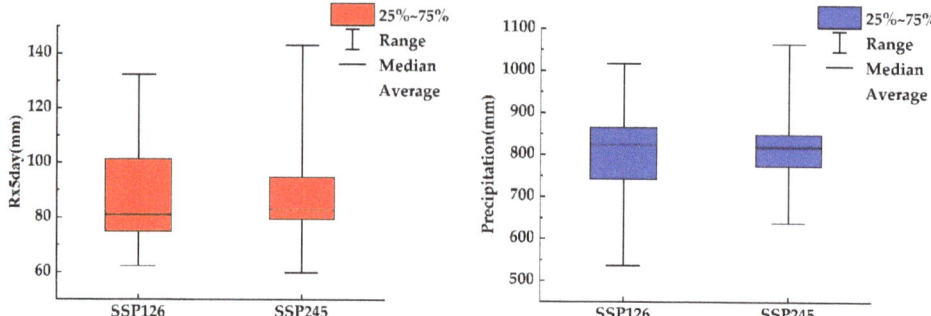

Figure 9. Distribution of Rx5day versus annual precipitation timing for the two scenarios during 2030–2050.

4.3.2. Sensitivity Indicators

The spatial distribution of the environmental sensitivity to flooding in the Guanzhong Plain between 2030 and 2050 is shown in Figure 10. The spatial distribution of the sensitivity to flood hazards in the Guanzhong Plain can be analyzed from this. To better analyze the changes, three typical areas of change are selected for analysis; when coupled with Figure 11, it can be seen that the green area mainly represents the variation in low-risk areas, which remains around 0.06 for all years, except for the SSP245 scenario, where it is 0.03 in 2030. The red areas mainly show the change from low-risk areas to medium- and high-risk areas, and the blue areas mainly show the transition from medium-risk areas to high- and higher-risk areas. As we set the distance from the river to remain constant, the changes in this part are mainly influenced by land use. Combined with Figure 6, it can be seen that there is a more obvious expansion of urban land in this area. Under the SSP245 scenario, the high- and higher-risk areas in 2050 account for more than 30%, with the higher-risk area reaching 38.9%, so the area's risk level is significantly higher.

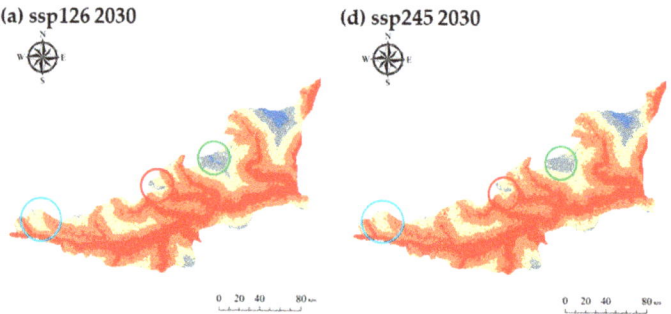

Figure 10. *Cont.*

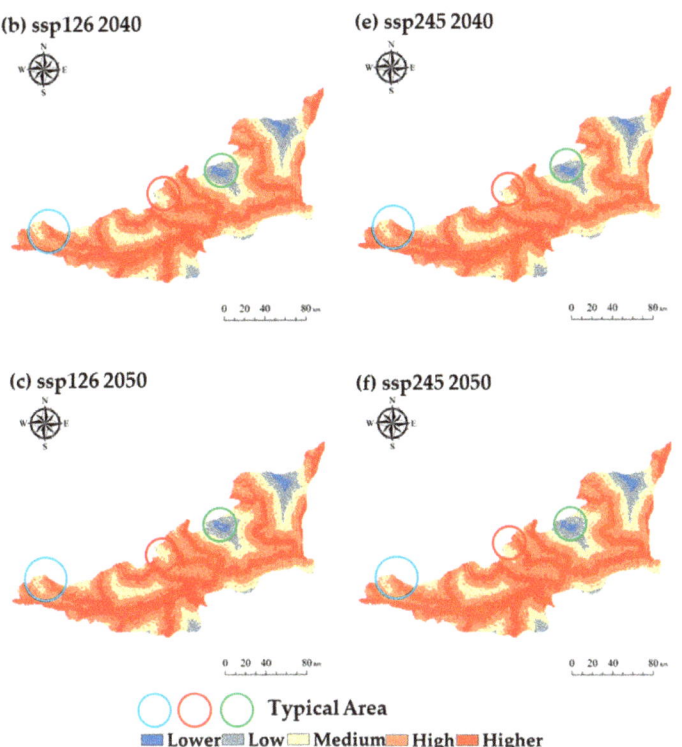

Figure 10. Spatial distribution of sensitivity indicators in the Guanzhong Plain between 2030 and 2050 under different development scenarios.

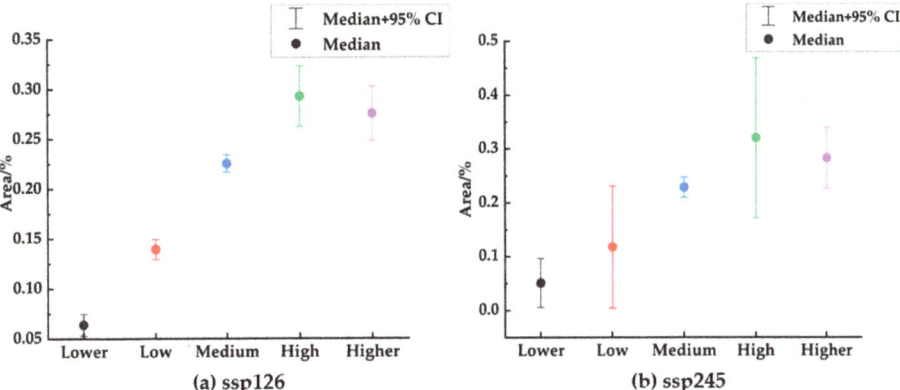

Figure 11. Map showing the percentage of area in different risk zones.

4.3.3. Vulnerability Indicators

This study primarily considers flood vulnerability regarding demographic and socioeconomic factors. On this basis, the Jenks methodology is used to classify the risk levels into five, which are lower, low, medium, high, and higher. Most of the medium–higher vulnerable areas are mainly located in urban land areas. Most areas have low vegetation cover but are densely populated and more economically developed, which has been shown to play a somewhat important role in increasing vulnerability. The areas of low vulnerability are mainly located in agricultural areas, and most are flat. As seen in Figure 12, there is little change in the vulnerability between the two scenarios, mainly in the form of a decrease in the lower-risk areas and an increase in the medium-to-higher-risk areas.

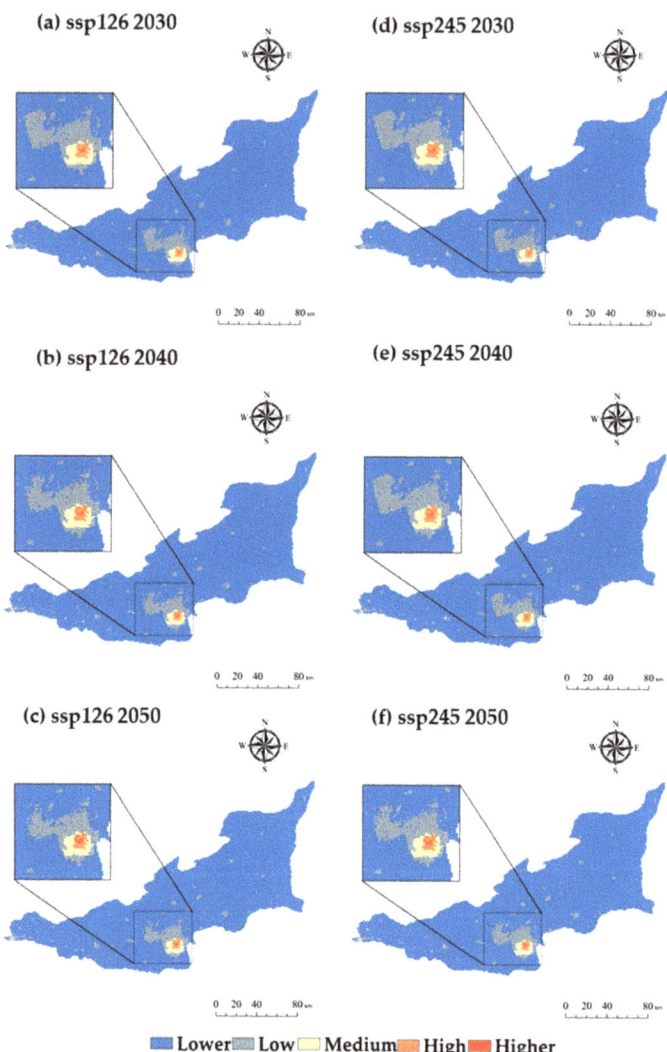

Figure 12. Spatial distribution of vulnerability indicators in the Guanzhong Plain between 2030 and 2050 under different development scenarios.

4.3.4. Future Multi-Scenario Flood Risk Assessment

The flood risk map for the Guanzhong Plain (Figure 13) was obtained by integrating the GIS environment-based hazard, sensitivity, and vulnerability maps described above. The equal spacing approach was used to classify the flood risk into five categories: lower, low, medium, high, and higher risk.

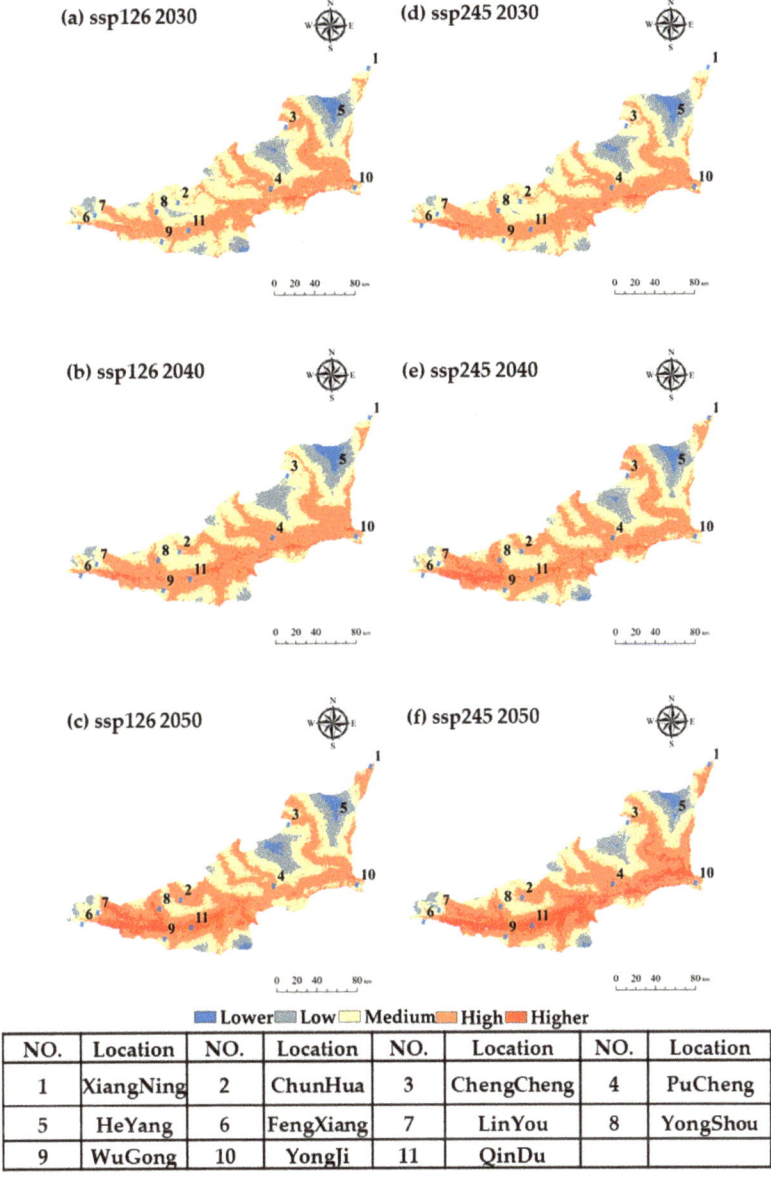

Figure 13. Spatial distribution of flood risk indices in the Guanzhong Plain between 2030 and 2050 under different development scenarios.

Combined with Figures 14 and 15, it can be seen that under the SSP126 scenario, the percentage of flood risk zone levels in the Guanzhong Plain in 2030 are 0.018, 0.123, 0.435, 0.415, and 0.009, where the high- and medium-risk zones occupy a large area and are mainly concentrated in the areas where rivers converge, with the high-risk zones located near the Weihe River (Pucheng, Wugong, Fengxiang, and Yongji). The largest changes in the risk area between 2030 and 2040 are in the medium- and high-risk areas, with the medium-risk area decreasing by 1256.448 km² (0.064) and the high-risk area increasing by

1197.552 km² (0.061); the increase mainly comes from the transition from the medium-risk area to the high-risk area. The spatial distribution of risk areas is similar, but the high-risk areas increase in Qindu and near the lower reaches of the Weihe River and the Ba River, and a comparison of Figures 5 and 7 shows that the increase in the high-risk areas is related to the rise in urban land use and precipitation. The most significant change in the risk area in the Guanzhong Plain between 2040 and 2050 is in the higher-risk area, which increases by 337 km² (0.057), while the medium- and high-risk areas decrease by 726.384 km² (0.037) and 667.488 km² (0.034), respectively, with a distribution similar to that of precipitation and urban land use in 2050. This distribution is identical to that of precipitation and urban land use in 2050. As shown in Figure 13, a large proportion of the area at risk overall is related to the distribution of DEM, the slope, and arable land, and the overall flat topography of the Guanzhong Plain and its well-developed rivers are more prone to flooding.

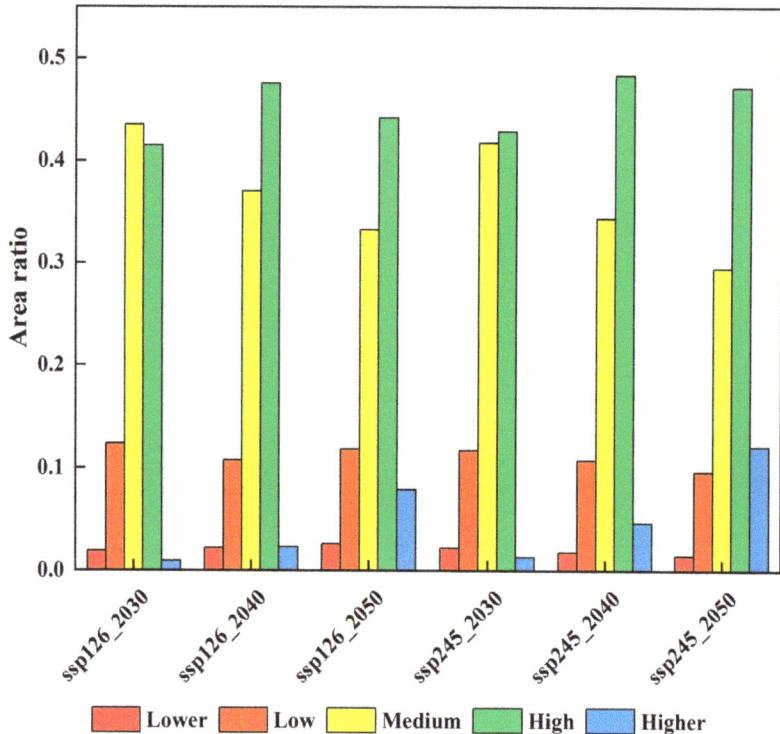

Figure 14. Map of the area at risk as a percentage.

In the SSP245 scenario, the overall risk distribution is similar to that in the SSP126 scenario, with an overall increase in the high-risk area in the central and western parts of the plain, with the percentage of flood-risk areas in the Guanzhong Plain in 2030 being 0.021, 0.117, 0.418, 0.429, and 0.012, respectively. Between 2030 and 2040, the medium- and high-risk areas continue to have the greatest change in the area, with the medium-risk area decreasing by 1433.136 km² (0.073) and the high-risk area increasing by 1099.392 km² (0.056), mainly due to changes in precipitation and an increase in urban land use; between 2040 and 2050, the increase in the area of the higher-risk area peaks at 1472.4 km². This is mainly in the vicinity of the Weihe River's mainstem. The urban land area has significantly changed, from 236.112 km² to 905.096 km² and, finally, to 2380.796 km².

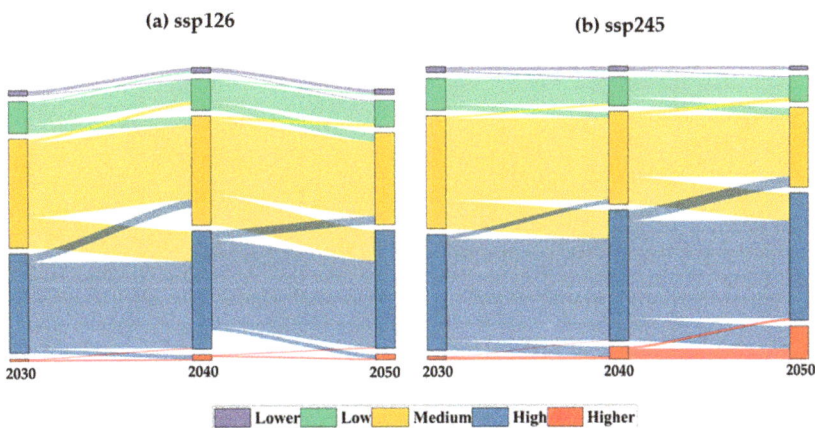

Figure 15. Change in risk transfer under different scenarios.

5. Discussion

5.1. CMIP6 Downscaling and Validation

Based on the CMIP6 data, we selected five GCMs' data that are suitable for the study area, and the selected data were revised for bias and downscaled by pooled averaging as well as BCSD methods, which showed that after ensemble averaging, the standard deviation of each mode is less than 0.5, the root-mean-square error is within 0.4, and the correlation coefficient is more than 0.95. For higher accuracy, the BCSD method was chosen to downscale the data after ensemble averaging, and it can be seen that BCSD can completely carry out downscaling and correction work. Zhu [56,57] used the model ensemble averaging method to validate the CMIP6 precipitation data for the Tibet Plateau and the Yangtze River Basin, and the results showed that the model ensemble averaging method can reduce model errors well, but further corrections are needed. Eum [58] ranked four downscaling methods, BCSD, the bias-correction/constructed analog, multivariate adaptive constructed analogs (MACA), and the bias-correction/climate imprint, based on performance metrics using the TOPSIS; the results showed that MACA and BCSD have considerable skills regarding the time series correlation criteria, while BCSD is superior to the other methods regarding the distribution and extreme value correlation criteria. This would suggest that the BCSD method chosen for this study has some advantages over other downscaling methods and is a tool that can be used well for downscaling.

5.2. MOP Coupling PLUS Multi-Scenario Simulation

This study uses the MOP and PLUS models for land-use multi-scenario prediction. The simulation accuracy can reach a Kappa of 0.85 and an overall accuracy of 0.92, which can better simulate the future land-type distribution of the Guanzhong Plain. The change in land use also shows different characteristics under different scenarios. In the SSP126 scenario, the conversion of agricultural land to forests, buildings, and water is constant [59]. In Europe, the area of forested land in a similar context has increased due to the introduction of policies and the designation of nature reserves [60]. "Forest conservation", "Reforestation and Revegetation", and other eco-civilizations promote environmental protection as well as sustainable development, which also leads to the continuous return of cultivated land to forest and grass [61]. This is in line with our results. In the SSP245 scenario, the future conversion of arable land to buildings and increased population density in the southeast will continue to affect climate change and lead to more extreme rainfall events [62].

5.3. Flood Risk Assessment

The entropy weight method is used in this article for flood risk assessment. The analysis shows that the higher risk areas for flooding in the Guanzhong Plain are mainly found in the central part of the Guanzhong Plain as well as in the northern part, which is in line with the findings of Dou's study [63]. In other regions, Liu [64] used the entropy weight method to assess flood risk in the Bangladesh–India–Myanmar region and found that the results were generally consistent with those obtained from the study when compared with historical flood hazards. The impact of different flood disaster risk factors on future flood disaster risk was quantitatively analyzed. The results of the quantitative calculation by the entropy weight method in this study show that when the flood risk is determined by spatial weight superposition, the weights of each factor in the two scenarios are similar, among which the distance from the river has the highest weight (16.8%), and the second is RMAX3 (16.3%). These results are deviated from those of previous studies [65–67]. Stefanos [65] pointed out that compared with natural factors, human factors are the main cause of flood disasters in most basins. Hammami [67] selected eight kinds of flood causes to evaluate the sensitivity of regional flood disasters. The results showed that the factor that had a significant impact on the occurrence of floods was elevation. Based on this study of flood disaster risk assessment, it is found that the most important flood-disaster-causing factors are different in multi-criteria systems in different regions. Therefore, the most appropriate flood control measures should be taken according to the evaluation results of different regions.

This paper combines the risk of flood disasters during historical periods with the accurate prediction of flood risks in future development scenarios, which is of great significance for future sustainable development. Previous studies have shown that this is an effective method to determine the future flood risk distribution through future land-use scenarios. Lin et al. [68] used the FLUS model to simulate future land-use scenarios in Guangzhou to assess the city's flood risk. Canters et al. [69] used the CA model to simulate land-use change on the Belgian coast and analyze its impact on flood risk. However, the commonly used land-use scenario simulation methods (FLUS, the Conversion of Land Use and its Effects at Small Region Extent model, etc.) have the disadvantages of an unclear model conversion mechanism and inconvenient operation. There are great deficiencies in excavating the law of land-use conversion and revealing dynamic changes in the landscape, and it is difficult to effectively identify the factors affecting the dynamic evolution of various land-use patches [60,70]. These problems limit the application of these models in land-use simulation and will inevitably affect the prediction accuracy of flood risk. At the same time, the assessment of flood risk is mostly based on history and the current situation [71,72] or climate change [73,74]. Few studies have linked the PLUS model to future urban land development planning and urban flood disaster risk evolution. In this study, the flood disaster risk maps under different development scenarios obtained by coupling PLUS, MOP, and the entropy weight method can provide a basis and reference for future urban planning and flood control in plain areas.

5.4. Flood Adaptation Strategies and Policies

In the 21st century, flood control in plain cities is a major challenge, and government departments need the guidance of risk analysis to determine flood control policies. In this study, the proposed framework can be used to explore future flood disaster risks. The results can provide support for land-use planning and provide a basis for decision-makers to decide how to set flood control measures and urban development directions, which is crucial for developing countries in the process of rapid urbanization. In the future, the Guanzhong Plain area must increase flood control planning, such as drainage systems, flood buffer zones, etc. Low-impact development and a sponge city can effectively reduce rainfall runoff, the amount of pollutants in rainwater, and return rainfall, which are sustainable flood control and disaster reduction measures [75,76]. Luo et al. [6] considered that the combination of gray (engineering measures) and green (natural measures) can effectively reduce the damage of floods to cities. Therefore, increasing the proportion of green space and green plants in Guanzhong and global plain urban areas, combining the natural conditions with urban flood control measures, and forming an integrated rainwater control system to reduce rainwater runoff are all suggested measures. At the same time, the government should incorporate the protection and restoration of natural systems into policies and regulations to promote urban flood control construction in plain areas.

For the urban areas that have been built, flexible and multi-spatial scale flood management strategies should be proposed. Among them, the most critical thing is to dynamically adjust the land-use function for future flood scenarios. For example, flood-prone agricultural areas can be changed to aquaculture models. In the planning of building types, the building structure should be innovated, the building specifications should be enhanced, and the flood control capacity should be improved. At the same time, the government should establish emergency strategies for flood risk management, plan evacuation routes in advance, improve rescue systems and assistance mechanisms, and ensure the safety of people's lives and property. According to the survey results of flood disasters in recent years, the disorder of social and economic development is the main reason for the increase in flood losses. The scientific land-use planning of the flood detention area can avoid large-scale development, thus greatly reducing flood losses [77].

6. Conclusions

In this study, after averaging the five GCMs by mode ensemble, the BCSD method was used for downscaling analysis. The results show that the standard deviation after ensemble averaging is less than 1, and the correlation coefficient exceeds 0.95. However, the resolution is still relatively low, and, to improve the resolution, the resolution and accuracy after the operation with the BCSD method are better than after ensemble averaging.

Under different scenarios, there is a wide range of future land-use changes. The SSP126 scenario, except for cultivated land, maintains an increasing trend, with woodland and grassland showing fluctuating growth trends and with cultivated land consistently shifting to woodland, urban land, and water bodies; the SSP245 scenario, except for urban land, maintains a decreasing trend, with cultivated land and other land types mainly shifting to urban land, leading to a large increase.

The results of the flood risk assessment using the entropy weighting method show that the overall spatial distribution of flood risk is similar between the SSP126 and SSP245 scenarios, with the central and western parts of the Guanzhong Plain being more susceptible to flooding in the future, mainly due to the regional increase in future precipitation and the expansion of urban land use. Under the SSP245 scenario, the higher-risk area increases to 2380.796 km^2 by 2050, and the higher-risk area for the whole region shows a gradual increase from east to west along the Wei River. This study can provide a guide for future flood hazard prevention in the Guanzhong Plain.

Author Contributions: All authors contributed to the work. P.L.: writing—original draft preparation and conceptualization. X.W.: writing—reviewing and editing. P.L. and X.W.: methodology. L.Z. and M.R.R.M.A.Z.: software. M.H. and W.D.: data curation. Y.Z.: visualization. B.G. and Y.W.: investigation and supervision. D.N.: article polishing. All authors have read and agreed to the published version of the manuscript.

Funding: This research was funded by the China Scholarship Council (grant nos.: Liujinmei [2022] no. 45; Liujinxuan [2022] no. 133; Liujinou [2023] no. 22), the International Education Research Program of Chang'an University (300108221102), the Project of Ningxia Natural Science Foundation (2022AAC03700; 2022BEG03059), the 2022 Guangdong University Youth Innovation Talent Program (2022KQNCX143), and the Yinshanbeilu Grassland Eco-hydrology National Observation and Research Station, China Institute of Water Resources and Hydropower Research, Beijing 100038, China, grant no. YSS2022004.

Data Availability Statement: No new data were created or analyzed in this study. Data sharing is not applicable to this article.

Conflicts of Interest: Lei Zhang was employed by Xi'an Xinsemi Material Technology Co., Ltd. The remaining authors declare that the research was conducted in the absence of any commercial or financial relationships that could be construed as a potential conflict of interest. The funders had no role in the design of the study; in the collection, analyses, or interpretation of data; in the writing of the manuscript; or in the decision to publish the results.

References

1. Manzoor, Z.; Ehsan, M.; Khan, M.B.; Manzoor, A.; Akhter, M.M.; Sohail, M.T.; Hussain, A.; Shafi, A.; Abu-Alam, T.; Abioui, M. Floods and flood management and its socio-economic impact on Pakistan: A review of the empirical literature. *Front. Environ. Sci.* **2022**, *10*, 2480. [CrossRef]
2. Merz, B.; Blöschl, G.; Vorogushyn, S.; Dottori, F.; Aerts, J.C.J.H.; Bates, P.; Bertola, M.; Kemter, M.; Kreibich, H.; Lall, U.; et al. Causes, impacts and patterns of disastrous river floods. *Nat. Rev. Earth Environ.* **2021**, *2*, 592–609. [CrossRef]
3. Tingsanchali, T. Urban flood disaster management. *Procedia Eng.* **2012**, *32*, 25–37. [CrossRef]
4. Wu, J.; Chen, X.; Lu, J. Assessment of long and short-term flood risk using the multi-criteria analysis model with the AHP-Entropy method in Poyang Lake basin. *Int. J. Disaster Risk Reduct.* **2022**, *75*, 102968. [CrossRef]
5. Dastagir, M.R. Modeling recent climate change induced extreme events in Bangladesh: A review. *Weather Clim. Extrem.* **2015**, *7*, 49–60. [CrossRef]
6. Luo, P.; Yan, P.; Wang, X.; Wu, Y.; Lyu, J.; He, B.; Duan, W.; Wang, S.; Zha, X. Historical and comparative overview of sponge campus construction and future challenges. *Sci. Total Environ.* **2023**, *907*, 167477. [CrossRef]
7. Luo, P.; Luo, M.; Li, F.; Qi, X.; Huo, A.; Wang, Z.; He, B.; Takara, K.; Nover, D.; Wang, Y. Urban flood numerical simulation: Research, methods and future perspectives. *Environ. Model. Softw.* **2022**, *156*, 105478. [CrossRef]
8. Zheng, Q.; Shen, S.-L.; Zhou, A.; Lyu, H.M. Inundation risk assessment based on G-DEMATEL-AHP and its application to Zhengzhou flooding disaster. *Sustain. Cities Soc.* **2022**, *86*, 104138. [CrossRef]
9. Guo, X.; Cheng, J.; Yin, C.; Li, Q.; Chen, R.; Fang, J. The extraordinary Zhengzhou flood of 7/20, 2021: How extreme weather and human response compounding to the disaster. *Cities* **2023**, *134*, 104168. [CrossRef]
10. Wang, X.; Luo, P.; Zheng, Y.; Duan, W.; Wang, S.; Zhu, W.; Zhang, Y.; Nover, D. Drought Disasters in China from 1991 to 2018: Analysis of Spatiotemporal Trends and Characteristics. *Remote Sens.* **2023**, *15*, 1708. [CrossRef]
11. IPCC. *Climate Change 2021: The Physical Science Basis. Contribution of Working Group I to the Sixth Assessment Report of the Intergovernmental Panel on Climate Change*; Technical Summary; Cambridge University Press: Cambridge, UK, 2021.
12. Wang, S.; Luo, P.; Xu, C.; Zhu, W.; Cao, Z.; Ly, S. Reconstruction of Historical Land Use and Urban Flood Simulation in Xi'an, Shannxi, China. *Remote Sens.* **2022**, *14*, 6067. [CrossRef]
13. Luo, P.; Zheng, Y.; Wang, Y.; Zhang, S.; Yu, W.; Zhu, X.; Huo, A.; Wang, Z.; He, B.; Nover, D. Comparative Assessment of Sponge City Constructing in Public Awareness, Xi'an, China. *Sustainability* **2022**, *14*, 11653. [CrossRef]
14. Guo, B.; Xie, T.; Zhang, W.; Wu, H.; Zhang, D.; Zhu, X.; Ma, X.; Wu, M.; Luo, P. Rasterizing CO_2 emission and characterizing their trends via an enhanced population-light index at multiple scales in China during 2013–2019. *Sci. Total Environ.* **2023**, *905*, 167309. [CrossRef]
15. Zhu, W.; Cao, Z.; Luo, P.; Tang, Z.; Zhang, Y.; Hu, M.; He, B. Urban Flood-Related Remote Sensing: Research Trends, Gaps and Opportunities. *Remote Sens.* **2022**, *14*, 5505. [CrossRef]
16. Luo, P.; Liu, L.; Wang, S.; Ren, B.; He, B.; Nover, D. Influence assessment of new Inner Tube Porous Brick with absorbent concrete on urban floods control. *Case Stud. Constr. Mater.* **2022**, *17*, e01236. [CrossRef]
17. Luo, P.; Mu, Y.; Wang, S.; Zhu, W.; Mishra, B.K.; Huo, A.; Zhou, M.; Lyu, J.; Hu, M.; Duan, W.; et al. Exploring sustainable solutions for the water environment in Chinese and Southeast Asian cities. *Ambio* **2021**, *51*, 1199–1218. [CrossRef]
18. Guo, B.; Wang, Z.; Pei, L.; Zhu, X.; Chen, Q.; Wu, H.; Zhang, W.; Zhang, D. Reconstructing MODIS aerosol optical depth and exploring dynamic and influential factors of AOD via random forest at the global scale. *Atmos. Environ.* **2023**, *315*, 120159. [CrossRef]
19. Torres, R.R.; Marengo, J.A. Climate change hotspots over South America: From CMIP3 to CMIP5 multi-model datasets. *Theor. Appl. Climatol.* **2014**, *117*, 579–587. [CrossRef]
20. Chen, H.; Sun, J.; Lin, W.; Xu, H. Comparison of CMIP6 and CMIP5 models in simulating climate extremes. *Sci. Bull.* **2020**, *65*, 1415–1418. [CrossRef] [PubMed]
21. Gusain, A.; Ghosh, S.; Karmakar, S. Added value of CMIP6 over CMIP5 models in simulating Indian summer monsoon rainfall. *Atmos. Res.* **2020**, *232*, 104680. [CrossRef]
22. Wang, Y.; Li, H.; Wang, H.; Chen, H.P. Evaluation of CMIP6 model simulations of extreme precipitation in China and comparison with CMIP5. *Acta Meteorol. Sin* **2021**, *79*, 369–386. [CrossRef]
23. Shi, M.; Wu, H.; Fan, X.; Jia, H.; Dong, T.; He, P.; Baqa, M.F.; Jiang, P. Trade-offs and synergies of multiple ecosystem services for different land use scenarios in the yili river valley, China. *Sustainability* **2021**, *13*, 1577. [CrossRef]
24. Zhai, H.; Lv, C.; Liu, W.; Yang, C.; Fan, D.; Wang, Z.; Guan, Q. Understanding spatio-temporal patterns of land use/land cover change under urbanization in Wuhan, China, 2000–2019. *Remote Sens.* **2021**, *13*, 3331. [CrossRef]
25. Li, C.; Yang, M.; Li, Z.; Wang, B. How will rwandan land use/land cover change under high population pressure and changing climate? *Appl. Sci.* **2021**, *11*, 5376. [CrossRef]

26. Haase, D. Integrating Ecosystem Services, Green Infrastructure and Nature-Based Solutions—New Perspectives in Sustainable Urban Land Management: Combining Knowledge About Urban Nature for Action. In *Sustainable Land Management in a European Context: A Co-Design Approach*; Springer International Publishing: New York, NY, USA, 2021; pp. 305–318.
27. Wu, J.; Sha, W.; Zhang, P.; Wang, Z. The spatial non-stationary effect of urban landscape pattern on urban waterlogging: A case study of Shenzhen City. *Sci. Rep.* **2020**, *10*, 7369. [CrossRef]
28. Liu, S.; Lin, M.; Li, C. Analysis of the Effects of the River Network Structure and Urbanization on Waterlogging in High-Density Urban Areas-A Case Study of the Pudong New Area in Shanghai. *Int. J. Environ. Res. Public Health* **2019**, *16*, 3306. [CrossRef]
29. Zhang, H.; Cheng, J.; Wu, Z.; Li, C.; Qin, J.; Liu, T. Effects of Impervious Surface on the Spatial Distribution of Urban Waterlogging Risk Spots at Multiple Scales in Guangzhou, South China. *Sustainability* **2018**, *10*, 1589. [CrossRef]
30. Janizadeh, S.; Pal, S.C.; Saha, A.; Chowdhuri, I.; Ahmadi, K.; Mirzaei, S.; Mosavi, A.H.; Tiefenbacher, J.P. Mapping the spatial and temporal variability of flood hazard affected by climate and land-use changes in the future. *J. Environ. Manag.* **2021**, *298*, 113551. [CrossRef]
31. Lin, J.; He, P.; Yang, L.; He, X.; Lu, S.; Liu, D. Predicting future urban waterlogging-prone areas by coupling the maximum entropy and FLUS model. *Sustain. Cities Soc.* **2022**, *80*, 103812. [CrossRef]
32. Zhang, S.; Yang, P.; Xia, J.; Wang, W.; Cai, W.; Chen, N.; Hu, S.; Luo, X.; Li, J.; Zhan, C. Land use/land cover prediction and analysis of the middle reaches of the Yangtze River under different scenarios. *Sci. Total Environ.* **2022**, *833*, 155238. [CrossRef]
33. Wang, J.; Zhang, J.; Xiong, N.; Liang, B.; Wang, Z.; Cressey, E.L. Spatial and Temporal Variation, Simulation and Prediction of Land Use in Ecological Conservation Area of Western Beijing. *Remote Sens.* **2022**, *14*, 1452. [CrossRef]
34. Liang, X.; Guan, Q.; Clarke, K.C.; Liu, S.; Wang, B.; Yao, Y. Understanding the drivers of sustainable land expansion using a patch-generating land use simulation (PLUS) model: A case study in Wuhan, China. *Comput. Environ. Urban Syst.* **2021**, *85*, 101569. [CrossRef]
35. Jiang, X.; Duan, H.; Liao, J.; Xue, X. Land use in the Gan-Lin-Gao region of middle reaches of Heihe River Basin based on a PLUS-SD coupling model. *Arid. Zone Res.* **2022**, *39*, 1246–1258. [CrossRef]
36. Tapia, C.; Abajo, B.; Feliu, E.; Mendizabal, M.; Martinez, J.A.; Fernández, J.G.; Laburu, T.; Lejarazu, A. Profiling urban vulnerabilities to climate change: An indicator-based vulnerability assessment for European cities. *Ecol. Indic.* **2017**, *78*, 142–155. [CrossRef]
37. Wang, Z.; Lai, C.; Chen, X.; Yang, B.; Zhao, S.; Bai, X. Flood hazard risk assessment model based on random forest. *J. Hydrol.* **2015**, *527*, 1130–1141. [CrossRef]
38. Meshram, S.G.; Alvandi, E.; Meshram, C.; Kahya, E.; Al-Quraishi, A.M. Application of SAW and TOPSIS in prioritizing watersheds. *Water Resour. Manag.* **2020**, *34*, 715–732. [CrossRef]
39. Roy, S.; Bose, A.; Chowdhury, I.R. Flood risk assessment using geospatial data and multi-criteria decision approach: A study from historically active flood-prone region of Himalayan foothill, India. *Arab. J. Geosci.* **2021**, *14*, 999. [CrossRef]
40. Wang, Y.; Li, Z.; Tang, Z.; Zeng, G. A GIS-based spatial multi-criteria approach for flood risk assessment in the Dongting Lake Region, Hunan, Central China. *Water Resour. Manag.* **2011**, *25*, 3465–3484. [CrossRef]
41. Zou, Q.; Zhou, J.; Zhou, C.; Song, L.; Guo, J. Comprehensive flood risk assessment based on set pair analysis-variable fuzzy sets model and fuzzy AHP. *Stoch. Environ. Res. Risk Assess.* **2013**, *27*, 525–546. [CrossRef]
42. Khosravi, K.; Pourghasemi, H.R.; Chapi, K.; Bahri, M. Flash flood susceptibility analysis and its mapping using different bivariate models in Iran: A comparison between Shannon's entropy, statistical index, and weighting factor models. *Environ. Monit. Assess.* **2016**, *188*, 656. [CrossRef]
43. Tien-Chin, W.; Hsien-Da, L. Developing a fuzzy TOPSIS approach based on subjective weights and objective weights. *Expert Syst. Appl.* **2009**, *36*, 8980–8985. [CrossRef]
44. Liu, T.; Deng, Y.; Chan, F. Evidential Supplier Selection Based on DEMATEL and Game Theory. *Int. J. Fuzzy Syst.* **2018**, *20*, 1321–1333. [CrossRef]
45. Rincón, D.; Velandia, J.F.; Tsanis, I.; Khan, U.T. Stochastic Flood Risk Assessment under Climate Change Scenarios for Toronto, Canada Using CAPRA. *Water* **2022**, *14*, 227. [CrossRef]
46. Li, L.; Yang, J.; Wu, J. Future flood risk assessment under the effects of land use and climate change in the tiaoxi basin. *Sensors* **2020**, *20*, 6079. [CrossRef] [PubMed]
47. Chen, X.-D.; Su, Y.; Fang, X.-Q. Social impacts of extreme drought event in Guanzhong area, Shaanxi Province, during 1928–1931. *Clim. Chang.* **2021**, *164*, 1928–1931. [CrossRef]
48. Qin, R.; Zhang, F. HRLT: A high-resolution (1 day, 1 km) and long-term (1961–2019) gridded dataset for temperature and precipitation across China. *Pangaea* **2022**, *14*, 4793–4810.
49. Gardiner, L.R.; Steuer, R.E. Unified interactive multiple objective programming: An open architecture for accommodating new procedures. *J. Oper. Res. Soc.* **1994**, *45*, 1456–1466. [CrossRef]
50. Long, Y.; Han, H.; Lai, S.; Mao, Q. Urban growth boundaries of the Beijing Metropolitan Area: Comparison of simulation and artwork. *Cities* **2013**, *31*, 337–348. [CrossRef]
51. Xu, L.; Liu, X.; Tong, D.; Liu, Z.; Yin, L.; Zheng, W. Forecasting Urban Land Use Change Based on Cellular Automata and the PLUS Model. *Land* **2022**, *11*, 652. [CrossRef]
52. Zhang, S.; Zhong, Q.; Cheng, D.; Xu, C.; Chang, Y.; Lin, Y.; Li, B. Landscape ecological risk projection based on the PLUS model under the localized shared socioeconomic pathways in the Fujian Delta region. *Ecol. Indic.* **2022**, *136*, 108642. [CrossRef]

53. Li, X.; Fu, J.; Jiang, D.; Lin, G.; Cao, C. Land use optimization in Ningbo City with a coupled GA and PLUS model. *J. Clean. Prod.* **2022**, *375*, 134004. [CrossRef]
54. Gao, L.; Tao, F.; Liu, R.; Wang, Z.; Leng, H.; Zhou, T. Multi-scenario simulation and ecological risk analysis of land use based on the PLUS model: A case study of Nanjing. *Sustain. Cities Soc.* **2022**, *85*, 104055. [CrossRef]
55. Chen, Y. Flood hazard zone mapping incorporating geographic information system (GIS) and multi-criteria analysis (MCA) techniques. *J. Hydrol.* **2022**, *612*, 128268. [CrossRef]
56. Zhu, H.; Jiang, Z.; Li, J.; Li, W.; Sun, C.; Li, L. Does CMIP6 Inspire More Confidence in Simulating Climate Extremes over China? *Adv. Atmos. Sci.* **2020**, *37*, 1119–1132. [CrossRef]
57. Babaousmail, H.; Hou, R.; Ayugi, B.; Sian, K.T.C.L.K.; Ojara, M.; Mumo, R.; Chehbouni, A.; Ongoma, V. Future changes in mean and extreme precipitation over the Mediterranean and Sahara regions using bias-corrected CMIP6 models. *Int. J. Climatol.* **2022**, *42*, 7280–7297. [CrossRef]
58. Eum, H.I.; Cannon, A.J.; Murdock, T.Q. Intercomparison of multiple statistical downscaling methods: Multi-criteria model selection for South Korea. *Stoch. Environ. Res. Risk Assess.* **2017**, *31*, 683–703. [CrossRef]
59. Nelson, E.; Mendoza, G.; Regetz, J.; Polasky, S.; Tallis, H.; Cameron, D.R.; Chan, K.M.A.; Daily, G.C.; Goldstein, J.; Kareiva, P.M.; et al. DSpace at UVM (CTL server badger.uvm.edu): Modeling multiple ecosystem services, biodiversity conservation, commodity production, and tradeoffs at landscape scales. *Front. Ecol. Environ.* **2009**, *7*, 4–11. [CrossRef]
60. Rounsevell, M.; Reginster, I.; Araújo, M.; Carter, T.; Dendoncker, N.; Ewert, F.; House, J.; Kankaanpää, S.; Leemans, R.; Metzger, M.; et al. A coherent set of future land use change scenarios for Europe. *Agric. Ecosyst. Environ.* **2006**, *114*, 57–68. [CrossRef]
61. Peng, L.; Wang, X.-X. What is the relationship between ecosystem services and urbanization? A case study of the mountainous areas in Southwest China. *J. Mt. Sci.* **2019**, *16*, 2867–2881. [CrossRef]
62. Pelletier, J.D.; Murray, A.B.; Pierce, J.L.; Bierman, P.R.; Breshears, D.D.; Crosby, B.T.; Ellis, M.; Foufoula-Georgiou, E.; Heimsath, A.M.; Houser, C.; et al. Forecasting the response of Earth's surface to future climatic and land use changes: A review of methods and research needs. *Earths Future* **2015**, *3*, 220–251. [CrossRef]
63. Dou, X. *Flood Risk Assessment Based on Flood Hazard Index Model: A Case Study of Guanzhong Area*; Northwest University: Washington, DC, USA, 2018.
64. Liu, Y.; Wang, S.; Wang, X.; Vijitpan, T. Flood risk assessment in Bangladesh, India and Myanmar based on the AHP weight method and entropy weight method. *Geogr. Res.* **2020**, *39*, 1892–1906. [CrossRef]
65. Stefanidis, S.; Stathis, D. Assessment of flood hazard based on natural and anthropogenic factors using analytic hierarchy process (AHP). *Nat. Hazards* **2013**, *68*, 569–585. [CrossRef]
66. Souissi, D.; Zouhri, L.; Hammami, S.; Msaddek, M.H.; Zghibi, A.; Dlala, M. GIS-based MCDM–AHP modeling for flood susceptibility mapping of arid areas, southeastern Tunisia. *Geocarto Int.* **2019**, *35*, 991–1017. [CrossRef]
67. Hammami, S.; Zouhri, L.; Souissi, D.; Souei, A.; Zghibi, A.; Marzougui, A.; Dlala, M. Application of the GIS based multi-criteria decision analysis and analytical hierarchy process (AHP) in the flood susceptibility mapping (Tunisia). *Arab. J. Geosci.* **2019**, *12*, 653. [CrossRef]
68. Lin, W.; Sun, Y.; Nijhuis, S.; Wang, Z. Scenario-based flood risk assessment for urbanizing deltas using future land-use simulation (FLUS): Guangzhou Metropolitan Area as a case study. *Sci. Total Environ.* **2020**, *739*, 139899. [CrossRef]
69. Canters, F.; Vanderhaegen, S.; Khan, A.Z.; Engelen, G.; Uljee, I. Land-use simulation as a supporting tool for flood risk assessment and coastal safety planning: The case of the Belgian coast. *Ocean. Coast. Manag.* **2014**, *101*, 102–113. [CrossRef]
70. Tian, L.; Tao, Y.; Fu, W.; Li, T.; Ren, F.; Li, M. Dynamic simulation of land use/cover change and assessment of forest ecosystem carbon storage under climate change scenarios in Guangdong Province, China. *Remote Sens.* **2022**, *14*, 2330. [CrossRef]
71. Sado-Inamura, Y.; Fukushi, K. Empirical analysis of flood risk perception using historical data in Tokyo. *Land Use Policy* **2019**, *82*, 13–29. [CrossRef]
72. Li, C.; Liu, M.; Hu, Y.; Wang, H.; Zhou, R.; Wu, W.; Wang, Y. Spatial distribution patterns and potential exposure risks of urban floods in Chinese megacities. *J. Hydrol.* **2022**, *610*, 127838. [CrossRef]
73. Toosi, A.S.; Doulabian, S.; Tousi, E.G.; Calbimonte, G.H.; Alaghmand, S. Large-scale flood hazard assessment under climate change: A case study. *Ecol. Eng.* **2020**, *147*, 105765. [CrossRef]
74. Hsiao, S.-C.; Chiang, W.-S.; Jang, J.-H.; Wu, H.-L.; Lu, W.-S.; Chen, W.-B.; Wu, Y.-T. Flood risk influenced by the compound effect of storm surge and rainfall under climate change for low-lying coastal areas. *Sci. Total Environ.* **2021**, *764*, 144439. [CrossRef]
75. Kourtis, I.M.; Tsihrintzis, V.A.; Baltas, E. A robust approach for comparing conventional and sustainable flood mitigation measures in urban basins. *J. Environ. Manag.* **2020**, *269*, 110822. [CrossRef]
76. Bhatt, A.; Bradford, A.; Abbassi, B.E. Cradle-to-grave life cycle assessment (LCA) of low-impact-development (LID) technologies in southern Ontario. *J. Environ. Manag.* **2019**, *231*, 98–109. [CrossRef]
77. Xia, J.; Chen, J. A new era of flood control strategies from the perspective of managing the 2020 Yangtze River flood. *Sci. China Earth Sci.* **2021**, *64*, 1–9. [CrossRef]

Disclaimer/Publisher's Note: The statements, opinions and data contained in all publications are solely those of the individual author(s) and contributor(s) and not of MDPI and/or the editor(s). MDPI and/or the editor(s) disclaim responsibility for any injury to people or property resulting from any ideas, methods, instructions or products referred to in the content.

MDPI
St. Alban-Anlage 66
4052 Basel
Switzerland
www.mdpi.com

Remote Sensing Editorial Office
E-mail: remotesensing@mdpi.com
www.mdpi.com/journal/remotesensing

Disclaimer/Publisher's Note: The statements, opinions and data contained in all publications are solely those of the individual author(s) and contributor(s) and not of MDPI and/or the editor(s). MDPI and/or the editor(s) disclaim responsibility for any injury to people or property resulting from any ideas, methods, instructions or products referred to in the content.

www.ingramcontent.com/pod-product-compliance
Lightning Source LLC
LaVergne TN
LVHW070149100526
838202LV00015B/1919